© 2000 Edition Axel Menges, Stuttgart/London
ISBN 3-932565-10-X

Printing and binding: Szegedi Kossuth Nyomda KFT,
Szeged

Editorial supervision: Nora Krehl-von Mühlendahl
Design: Axel Menges

Jacket photo: Leni Riefenstahl, *Olympia*, 1938.
(Photo: Filmmuseum Berlin.)

Contents

Foreword

by Volker Schlöndorff

Put simply, the German cinema grew from two sources: one is the silent film, as created by Friedrich Wilhelm Murnau, Fritz Lang and the early Ernst Lubitsch, among others. Their films were intended to entertain, but they also made great aesthetic claims for the new, seventh art. They were open to all the social trends of the day, to new political and technical ideas, and to movements in 20s century painting, literature and music. Any attempt to bring about a renaissance in German cinema draws on this brilliant period, which only lasted for about ten years. The New German Cinema in the sixties and seventies in particular tried to build a bridge to this glorious past. In the same way, all DEFA's efforts to make its mark on film history started with the realistic school of the twenties.

The other tradition of German film is pure entertainment of the kind offered by Ufa films. They have remained constant from the thirties to the present day in insulating themselves completely from aesthetic and social developments. Goebbels threw the whole might of the National Socialist apparatus behind this very particular kind of cinema so radically that its effects continued into the leaden Adenauer era, and even today the heirs of this genre are the German public's most popular entertainers.

How can a Minister of Propaganda have made such a mark on public taste for so long after his inglorious end – or was Goebbels himself only a precisely congruent expression of this petit-bourgeois attitude, hostile to any kind of artistic will or social criticism?

The Nazis and their helpers, led by the Minister of Propaganda, invented a Germany that draws on mystic origins and consists of a hotchpotch of Teutonic culture, fairy-tales and legends – leaving out all the historical facts. The National Socialist ideology's fatherland values are projected back into the past in time, and asserted in space far beyond the borders of Germany to the north and east. This was done so persistently that it is still all bubbling away in the depths of our collective unconscious.

Goebbels – whether alone or as a catalyst of the Zeitgeist – shaped the Germans' image of themselves and their country in the same way that Hollywood created an image of the limitless freedom of the individual, sustaining democratic values in the farthest outreaches of the Wild West or the narrow canyons of the big city streets, with the Colt, if necessary. We must accept that possibly Goebbels simply perceived and channelled these tendencies, that they existed anyway, and perhaps still do. This is how may writers link the Nazis' cult of the dead with German Romanticism's longing for death and the Reformation concept of "in the midst of life we are in death". The most cynical of remarks, like for example Göring's saying "soldiers are there to die", or references to Sparta and the Spartans taking pride in death when faced with hundreds of thousands of senselessly slaughtered soldiers at Stalingrad, were accepted by our people without open resistance. A similar death-wish-tainted brew is found at every end and turn in film melodramas intended to be "pure" entertainment.

If one is to believe Goebbels' diaries, he played the great Mephistopheles and had everything under control. Even before he became Minister of Propaganda he was probably the first modern election campaign manager. He couldn't yet exert any direct influence on the press, newsreels or the radio, but he realized that it is enough to offer a great spectacle if you want to appear in the news. This is now called "creating media-effective events". The media like to be able to pass on images of torchlight processions, a massively staged parade, a radiant woman's face, a child with a bunch of flowers, and such images can be more effective than any political programme. The image of a flawless German world is a programme in itself. In wartime it need only be swapped for an image of a heroic world, ultimately against the background of its end.

It becomes increasingly clear from diary entry to diary entry how omitting social realities and history, with all their contradictions, became the basis for both information and entertainment policy. Such entertainment, based in the art-world of the dream factory, was ideological in itself, but on top of that it was intended to sell specific political messages. This led to contradictions. The public got wind of what was intended and stayed away, as even Goebbels could not force them to come to see his films. He had to seduce them, just like a Hollywood producer. For this reason he analyses box-office returns in his diaries and tries to find ways to make what people want to see what they ought to see. He first has to realize: audiences are not crying out for politics. And so if he had only been bothered about box-office success he could have left it at undiluted entertainment. But he saw himself as a missionary of the National Socialist ideology, and in his eyes the cinema should be a pioneering champion of national culture.

Goebbels was there first and foremost to make propaganda. For example, if the people would not accept that "worthless life" should be exterminated, but he still wanted them to support the Nazis' "euthanasia programme", he tried to bring about a shift in opinion by calling upon argument and emotion. But the cinema audience distrusted things even more if they were particularly National Socialist in complexion. In *Ich klage an* (*I Accuse*) Goebbels finally had scenes reshot in which swastikas appeared (unavoidably in the courtroom). And so paradoxically the Minister of Propaganda abandoned what was probably the National Socialists' most distinctive symbol in most German films, but only because he told himself that this would be better publicity for his political aims. Audiences tended to be disinclined to accept pure politics if they were recognizable as such, and so he had to keep looking for ways and means to palm them off with his ideas. It was only rarely that ideology and public taste (also called popular sentiment) were one and the same thing, and then even a propaganda film like *Jud Süss* could become a box-office hit.

In fact Goebbels could be surer of popular acceptance than of support from artists. He had to recognize that art is not just a matter of ability, as he would have wished, but also of inspiration. And this cannot be forced, it depends on the truth behind the statement and the integrity of the artist. Certainly many Nazi artists believed in what they were doing, just as Eisenstein, Pudovkin, Renoir or Rossellini believed in Communism. But the ongoing fight for liberty, equality and fraternity is a driving force in all societies, and is correspondingly more inspiring than any false, cynical, destructive ideology. The values of Fascism are hollow and false, which is why its "artists" produce only applied art propaganda. It would be possible to measure the truth of a number of social orders against art in this spirit. Of course Goebbels never acquired this insight, he fished in the muddy waters of emotional associations – just as he also saw German artists as "creative draughtsmen", drawing on the dark, deep well-springs of German genius.

He is astonishingly frank about this in his diaries. His vanity is the greatest enemy of his attempts to falsify history. He simply cannot resist talking about his interventions and manipulations with all the pride of the successful achiever. And he speaks about his defeats just as tearfully. Like Hitler, he often despairs of the German people. Ultimately his belief in the feature film as a useful propaganda vehicle (he constantly cites *The Battleship Potemkin* as a successful example) was badly shaken, and he increasingly turned to newsreels. They claim to report objectively, but in fact they are pure fiction, for which the Propaganda Minister has prescribed every technique from backlighting to dramatic camera angles. As they are the only images of the period they are still used and analysed over and over again, and are in fact treated as objective records. Hitler destroyed Germany and large parts of the world. He left "only" ruins behind. But Goebbels' legacy continues to have its effect: through the newsreel pictures and the feature films, both the propaganda vehicles and also the ones that claim to be pure entertainment. And yet all of them continue to provide an image of our country, our society and our history that is distorted and does not mirror reality.

Consequently Goebbels is more fascinating today than Hitler – at least to media people. No one has ever had such exclusive power over all the media in existence at the time, and never has someone in a position of responsibility pursued his task with such passion (that of a frustrated artist). Today the media influence our lives to a much greater extent than was the case in the thirties, and so the present study of a man possessed in this way is of very great value indeed, especially as this possessed individual not only made radical use of his power over the media, but also kept a record about it daily – taking at least an hour to do it for over 20 years.

Something that is ironically very up-to-date for us Germans and Europeans is that Goebbels did not just set up generally valid rules for selling politics in the media, but also formulated permanent recipes for making pure entertainment. Ultimately he was pondering strategies about how to tackle the artistic, technical and commercial superiority of the American cinema: he loved *Gone with the Wind* even more than *The Battleship Potemkin*. He wanted German writers and directors to be able to cope with history in this melodramatic way. They were all perfectly happy to try, they made an honest attempt, and the Minister mentions them all by name in his diary entries, which makes the present study all the more explosive.

Goebbels was a past master of luring the stars he wanted and needed – whether they were actors or directors – with a whole variety of offers and methods. As Felix Moeller shows in detail, the sometimes simple, sometimes subtle preferential treatment extended from propaganda jobs, dream fees and tax advantages via the handing out of theatre directorships, orders and decorations to receptions with state or party bigwigs or the longed-for exemption from military service. And for many there was also insolently favoured luxury in the form of Aryanized villas and cars or constantly increasing fame as the pampered darlings of the people. Scarcely any of the artists were able to resist these temptations, which incidentally prevented only a very few from embarking on a new career in the fifties – despite or precisely because of their ostensibly apolitical views. Thus the concluding chapter on film artists is not only as disturbing as it is amusing, it also contains material for many more possible films …

The Legacy of Dr. G.

On 22 April 1945 the National Socialist Propaganda Minister Joseph Goebbels went with his wife Magda and their five children to the Reich Chancellery's underground Führer-Bunker, where he killed himself and his family one day after Hitler's suicide.

When soldiers of the Red Army were searching Goebbels' quarters in the bunker, they found a few loose pages containing his final diary entries – hidden under the screenplays for new film projects. The propagandist of the "Third Reich" – actually named by Hitler as his successor as Reich Chancellor – had kept his diary and made plans for films to the bitter end.

The diary entries record the rise of Dr. Paul Joseph Goebbels from unsuccessful journalist to be a politician whose complete power over the cinema, possible the most influential medium of the last century, still remains a striking phenomenon. There is no one like him under any other dictatorship. His only possible competitor is film fanatic Joseph Stalin, who is said to have seen some works hundreds of times, and who also sought directors and actors out personally. Many 20th century dictators, including Hitler and Mussolini, were definitely film fans. But a member of the ruling élite who was still looking through screen tests for casting supporting roles when the enemy armies had already crossed the borders – that was only to be found in Germany.

Today Hitler and Goebbels are called "master showmen" (Eric Rentschler): Rentschler maintains that without their theatrical abilities, without the dream machine that is film, the death and destruction meted out by the "Third Reich" would have been impossible.

Goebbels himself is no longer demonized and raised to the rank of supernatural propaganda genius as used to be the case in earlier years. But even if his skewed and one-sided image as the all-powerful Nazi "film dictator" is long out of date, he was in charge of the "greatest cultural business in the world", as he liked to call his ministry after it had secretly bought up radio stations, newspapers, film studios and cinemas all over Europe. Goebbels was at "the head of a gigantic apparatus for control and manipulation that is unique in history, with its boss as an amazingly personal presence" (Wolf Donner).

The films produced under Goebbels helped to shape public attitudes and mass taste well into the post-war period. Even today television broadcasts on private or public channels of light entertainment films made at the time attract considerable viewing figures, and criticism is regularly voiced if original material from newsreels is used in television documentaries about the Nazi era. Goebbels and his cameramen were far too good at their jobs "for the force of the images not to have retained its seductive power today".[1]

The portrait of Goebbels in the ZDF series *Hitlers Helfer* ("Hitler's Assistants") was watched at peak viewing times by over seven million viewers in February 1997. The banality of evil is still fascinating, and in Goebbels' case probably all the characteristics that have ever been ascribed to him are true – a cynical, crafty, brutal, intellectual, obsessive, hate-filled and inordinately vain man. But he did not just invent the Führer myth, and he was not only the "lying mouth of the Reich" or the rabble-rousing advocate of total war, but he personally advanced the cause of mass murder whenever he possibly could. It did not matter whether it was the deportation of Jews, shooting strikers in occupied areas or executing careless Ufa employees, Goebbels was always there to plead for the most brutal approach imaginable, even when other prominent Nazis did not want to go so far: "My standpoint is a radical one", he generalized at a conference after the Reich pogrom night.

Joseph Goebbels' diaries are a source of information on a completely new scale. Authentic, and handed down almost seamlessly, they are records from the inner circle of the Nazi power machine, and thus one of the most important documents of the period of Nazi rule. The Film Minister's diary offers a great deal of new material on film policy in the Third Reich, but at the same time it throws up serious problems in terms of source criticism. Even in the diary Goebbels remains a wily propagandist in many places, lying, falsifying, manipulating and smoothing. His entries do not add up to a real *journal intime*, they are not a "substitute confessional", and only in the rarest cases can they be called a "window" on Goebbels' and Hitler's secret thoughts. Ultimately there is a suggestion of "staging for posterity" (Bernd Sösemann). And so does it boil down to a mere stylized self-portrait of the "patron of the German cinema" as the head of a smoothly running propaganda machine?

At least these diaries, in which plans and intentions are discussed at length, it is remarkably easy to see that there is a yawning gap between claim and reality. In this way the results of Nazi film propaganda can be measured against Goebbels' actual aims, to the extent that these were not formulated rhetorically and unrealistically from the outset.

So sources have to be addressed critically if we are to get on to the track of the "minister of illusion", probe his motives and distinguish genuine information from whitewashing. Otherwise we would only be repeating the errors of film historians who have used quotations from Goebbels without thinking and merely as illustrative seasoning. What should emerge is no more and no less than a historiographical reconstruction of National Socialist film policy using all the sources and documents that are available beyond the diaries. Goebbels sets the direction, but it must be clear at all times what he is keeping quiet about, suppressing, manipulating.

"If a nationalist sees the film *Battleship Potemkin* today he is in danger of becoming a Communist, because the film is so well made",[2] said Goebbels in 1933. The director Billy Wilder, who left Germany after the Nazis came to power and went to the USA via France, shared the same opinion: "Anyone who has seen the *Battleship Potemkin* is a Communist, if only for a moment."[3]

Parallels with the present day and the up-to-date nature of some of Goebbels remarks are not surprising for long. Many of the problems that the European cinema has with its identity do not sound much different now than they did in Goebbels' day, even though the conditions are quite different. The Propaganda Minister appealed for "coming to terms with the American cinema" (22.7.1941) and also called upon "the countries of Europe to arm themselves for this competition". "When an American watches a German film he does not want to see a film that could just as well have been made in America, he wants to see something typically German", said Goebbels in 1933. In 1997 film critic Michael Althen wrote in the *Süddeutsche Zeitung*: "A person watching a French film is not looking for something generally European, but specifically French."

Goebbels complained about failed films by saying: "One wonders desperately: who was the script editor who read this entirely inadequate manuscript and passed it?" Surely similar thoughts come to us today. As we shall see, Goebbels was rarely satisfied in artistic terms with his productions that were successful at the box office. Present-day film critics complain in the same vein about German films that are successful commercially but less convincing artistically: "Do you want total cinema, do you possibly want something even more total and German than you could possibly imagine for yourselves?", asked Andreas Kilb in *Die Zeit* in 1997, with an eye on an industry that has regained its self-confidence and is turning over millions with popular "new German" films. The more successful German films and German film comedy are today, surely it is even more compelling to draw the comparison with the Ufa period, when similar concepts bore fruit?

But despite all apparent analogies, continuities, restrictions and continuing identity problems experienced by German and European films: popular Nazi cinema was not only commercially desirable, in contrast with today it was politically essential, for totalitarian reasons: among other things, it served the purpose of lengthening the war. We should not forget that, even if under the "Third Reich" – though certainly with a hermetically sealed market –, similarly to the present day or the fifties, there were certain suppression mechanisms that helped second-rate popular films to be successful.

Some of Goebbels' published writings have already been used in historical examinations of films. As early as 1969. Gerd Albrecht used a sociological evaluation of these diaries entries from 1942/43 to investigate the question of "which decisions in the field of film came directly from Goebbels, and which were the questions in this field to which he paid particular attention", and he discovered "a lack of fundamental guidelines" and a high degree of "ad hoc decisions".[4] Rainer Rother points out that the "diaries show a man who is obsessed with creating a popular cinema, a cinema without open intellectualism, political clumsiness and artistic ineptitude".[5] The director Arthur Maria Rabenalt, who made some propaganda films for Goebbels, feels that diary commentaries on film are "astonishingly general", indeed even "banal and clichéd, exhausting themselves in trivialities" and "superficial requirements",[6] but Klaus Kreimeier credits Goebbels' analyses of Hollywood's film successes with "an astonishing feel for the qualities of international show business".[7] Certainly Siegfried Zielinski expresses a fundamental doubt about whether diaries, even if they are written by an authoritative person, can come anywhere near reflecting the reality of economic and political production conditions and the artistic and aesthetic developments of the Nazi film.[8] Quite a few great film names of the "Third Reich", including Leni Riefenstahl and Heinz Rühmann, had to admit how accurately Goebbels had captured their closeness to the regime. Others, like Luis Trenker, picked out the passages that suited them from the diaries and used them to show that Goebbels had always been against them, as they had always asserted.

Of course there are a large number of questions that one would wish to ask about material of this kind, so it is necessary to limit the investigation to essential aspects.

First of all there is Goebbels' presentation of himself as a cinematically competent man who must have established his visual approach even before the "seizure of power".

When Goebbels proclaims very far-reaching artistic, personnel and institutional aims for the reorganization and "Gleichschaltung" (establishing conformity with National Socialism) of the film industry, then his success must be measured against his own ambitions.

It is often suggested that Goebbels had an aesthetic concept for cinema even at the time when the Nazis came to power. But the Film Minister's real creative requirements and production intentions only come to light if one follows Goebbels' influence on production from 1933 to 1945. This applies particularly of the thematic and psychological direction taken with respect to individual productions during the preparations for war, the blitzkrieg period and the propaganda aimed at boosting stamina. And: can any case be made for the existence of the much-invoked feature films that were "preparing for war" in 1938/39?

To what extent did calculation and ideology have a part to play in Goebbels' politics? This question also applies to his film policies: was he driven by ideological fixations like "anti-Bolshevism and anti-Semitism, or was he an unprincipled opportunist and "prototype of modern nihilism" (Carin Kessemeier), manoeuvring between party requirements, public taste, the necessities of propaganda and political conditions?

Another feature is that Goebbels' extensive commentaries on the development stages of important propaganda and feature films – from drafting the script to calculating possible effects on the "popular mood" – make great play of his being the (second) most important film censor as well as the most important producer. The background to some spectacular film bans is still unknown today. Could the high-handed Minister actually do precisely as he pleased as far as film censorship was concerned?

Goebbels devoted a great deal of his working time in the war to designing newsreels, which for a time were the National Socialists' most important "propaganda device". His technical and aesthetic method as well as the principles driving content and propaganda are interesting elements of his diary commentaries on the newsreels.

Most studies deal with Nazi feature films and threaten to swamp the non-fictional genre. Did Goebbels also neglect pseudo-documentary, cultural and compilation films?

Finally Goebbels' entries on artists' relationship with the Nazi regime are perfectly suited for comparison with many film-stars' attempts to clear their names after the war.

Only a few years ago it seemed that new writing on film history in the "Third Reich" left little further to be expected. So much was published for the Ufa anniversary in 1992[9] and the centenary of the film three years later. It was also to be feared that after the death of Karsten Witte, Wolf Donner and Peter Bucher a vacuum was created in the field of film analysis that is persuasive in terms of interpretation and academically sound. Then Hilmar Hoffmann, Georg Seeßlen, Eric Rentschler, Linda Schulte-Sasse and Klaus Kanzog triggered new discussions with surveys, innovative theses and monumental anthologies. Complaining voices, formerly justified, saying that there was a lack of serious academic literature in the field of National Socialist film history, have fallen silent.[10] Even the idea of great film-stars (Hans Albers, Hans Moser, Paula Wessely) coming to terms with their past has been the subject of remarkable studies.[11]

It is quite true that for a long time the field was dominated either by historical rumour-mongering, collections about the "greatest period of the German cinema" or largely cinematic-artistic examinations that were commendable, but cut out economic, political and technical conditions, or paid inadequate attention to them (David S. Hull, Pierre Cadars/Françis Courtade, Jerzy Toeplitz).[12]

Standard works and complete accounts include Erwin Leiser's *Deutschland erwache* (a first attempt to shed light on the link between the regime's foreign, war and film policy as well), Boguslaw Drewniak's collection of material,[13] Wolfgang Becker/Jürgen Spiker's work on economic and structural history,[14] Gerd Albrecht's sociological and statistical *Nationalsozialistische Filmpolitik*[15] with a copious selection of documents (it also assigns all the feature films produced from 1933 to 1945 to certain categories[16] of political function and propaganda content, with questionable results).[17] Albrecht's political analysis of films on the basis of a small number of Goebbels' entries (Lochner fragments) is less persuasive.

Klaus-Jürgen Maiwald and Kraft Wetzel/Peter Hagemann examine the background to Nazi film censorship on a broader material base[18] (now complemented by information on incomprehensible film bans from Goebbels' diary).

Klaus Kreimeier's outstanding Ufa monograph is bound to become a classic.[19] His portrait of this big studio in the Nazi state has a broad source base – production decision by firms, instructions from the Minister, reactions from the public – and thus provides a highly detailed view of German cinema history; but Goebbels' writings were not taken into consideration. And though it is true that Ufa was the largest production company to work for the Nazis, it was not the only one. Its programme only partially reflects film policy: in the heyday of the political film, during the so-called blitzkrieg of 1939 to 1941, the most important propaganda productions came from Tobis.

Most studies of Nazi cinema deal with propaganda films,[20] especially anti-Semitic productions and films promoting "euthanasia".[21] Klaus Kanzog provides a factual basis and analysis of films that were categorized as "valuable in terms of national policy". Finally Wolf Donner made a general survey including new interpretations of the best-known propaganda films.[22]

A posthumously published collection of essays by Karsten Witte again shows the whole breadth of discussion about ostensibly "apolitical" film entertainment in the "Third Reich".[23] One of Witte's central theses is that "aesthetic opposition" from some directors (including Helmut Käutner, Rolf Hansen, Peter Pewas) would have run counter to official propaganda aims. Ultimately Goebbels always put form before content. Witte mentions artistic devices forced into the service of Fascism in both political and entertainment films.[24] Hilmar Hoffmann also remarks on the subject of "Fascist artistic devices": "Taken as such, the artistic devices were not specifically Fascist, but when force was needed they were made into instruments of this tendency."[25] Which can mean only one thing: it is only in a climate of armament and warmongering that a revue film with disciplined girls on parade could be useful for the preparation of war. Line-ups like this seem quite harmless on afternoon television. Stephen Lowry – who shifted films like *Die goldene Stadt* ("The Golden City"), which were not ostentatiously propagandist, into the centre of the discussion – also takes this line with his distinction between films that were free of politics, but not of ideology.[26]

But it is beyond dispute that particularly in the early years of Nazi rule, when themes were being selected on a massive scale and reality was being faded out, not every production was or could be provided with subtly or openly presented messages. Later even the most escapist costume films may not have had any primary function, in other words one of propaganda, but they did have a secondary political one. This was to calm the public, to damp down critical thinking, to stabilize a certain "Haltung" ("attitude", which Goebbels expressly detached from the "Stimmung" ["mood"] of the population). The "war-worthiness" of armament workers, servicemen on leave from the front and soldiers' wives was to be guaranteed by continuous distractions.

But this answers by no means all the questions: we do not know what was considered normal, as traditional, as reactionary or as "Fascist", with within in the ideology of those people making the films or within the ideology of the public's response, precisely in the case of current schematic matters like the role of the sexes or values like loyalty, community or fatherland. What was happening in the heads of the scriptwriters and what in those of the spectators when the "servant" role of women was always stressed? Where did subliminal signalling of standards come into effect, where was it perceived neither consciously nor unconsciously? Film scholars like Witte argue and justify brilliantly, but incline to interpret things retrospectively into middle-class Ufa entertainment films that they have over-analysed. Distinguishing between conservative, traditional and typically National-Socialist values is not easy, even in the context of writing social history within the modernization debate.

Some of the multi-faceted and skilfully launched National-Socialist positions in film must also scarcely have been noticed. It is perfectly clear-cut in *Die goldene Stadt*, when a Slav drives blonde Anna (Kristina Söderbaum) to her death. But is it reasonable, when some early thirties' comedies caricature competitive middle-class thinking in commercial life, to conclude immediately that this is a condemnation of competition between the Weimar parties and thus a plea that they should be abolished and replaced by one sense of the public good and one party?[27] The same goes for an interpretation of the comedy *Die Nacht in Venedig* ("A Night in Venice"), which plays in the milieu of singers and night-clubs as something that stabilizes power and order.[28] Is it something typical of the Nazis or a universal dramatic device when in love comedies like *Abenteuer im Grandhotel* (1943, "Adventure in the Grand Hotel") the squabbling married couples come together again at the end? It is only typical of the Nazis if the authors had analysed and calculated so subtly quite consciously, and not for dramatic purposes. But it would be quite right to be doubtful about this. Some surviving minutes of script conferences[29] do not finally clear the matter up, but contain the desired, prescribed rough sketches.

Other refined analyses of light entertainment films deal with moral ideas and social guidelines that are conveyed throughout – for example the image of women or the way in which certain professional groups are presented –, concealed messages and characteristics that aid identification.[30] For example, there are many analyses of the revue-melodrama *Die große Liebe (The Great Love)*, but they show the limitations of an approach confined to individual box-office hits. The increasingly excerpt-like consideration of individual spectacular titles has now been complemented by a through examination of the production history of the last Ufa war-stamina *Das Leben geht weiter* ("Life Goes On"),[31] which remained incomplete. But it was not just a few elaborate major films that were crucial for changes of attitude and concrete consequences in terms of action for the public, but the sum total of certain ideological messages in the mass of small- and medium-scale "average films".[32] So far there is only an almost monumental record listing and evaluating all the feature films, documentaries and shorts shown in Germany for the year 1929.[33]

The relationship between film policy and everyday policy is still scantily treated. When people say today that feature films under the National Socialists were "less suitable for propaganda with reference to everyday policy because of the long planning and production process", for which reason only "basic attitudes and values" like large numbers of children and national feelings could be promoted,[34] that is a retrospective insight. Surely Goebbels had to reach this conclusion, paying for the process with much bad planning? This dependence is usually examined only peripherally outside the more recent analyses of individual films, and quite often runs out of steam in references to the halt called to "anti-Bolshevik" films after the conclusion of the German-Russian non-aggression pact.

One direction taken in recent research has particular implications for the future: this is the question of the value of the (feature) film as a historical source. National Socialist history films in particular always say more about the time at which they were made than the epoch presented. The analytical components, in other words the conditions under which the film was made, the intended effect and required response,[35] are essential for research into film history. However, the actual amount of insight acquired in the sense meant by Peter Bucher and Günther Moltmann – "portraying a milieu", conveying "historical atmosphere", complementing other sources about the actual course of events at the time – is interesting only for certain types of question.[36] And anyway there are disagreements about problems of method and source-criticism; they are approached differently according to the research discipline.[37]

There is astonishingly little independent investigation of the non-fictional genre of the documentary film, which has hitherto been treated along with feature film.[38] While the party rally films *Sieg des Glaubens* ("Victory of Faith") and *Triumph des Willens* (*Triumph of the Will*), and also Leni Riefenstahl's Olympic film have always attracted a great deal of attention,[39] the cultural and educational films[40] – a category that expanded greatly after 1933 as an obligatory component of every cinema show – have only been shown appropriate interest recently.

There are as yet no monographs about the newsreels as the National Socialists' most effective propaganda device for a time, or about the propaganda companies (PK groups) who provided pictorial material during the war. Individual essays providing a general survey[41] provide important starting-points, but are no substitute for a full treatment, as they do not reflect the changing significance of newsreels over the years from say 1938 to 1944. As well as this there are some film editions with accompanying publications that deal only with individual newsreel films.[42]

A final word on the most important additional sources with reference to Goebbels' film policy. The minutes of his daily conferences with his principal colleagues are extremely valuable. They include instructions on the use and planning of feature and documentary films and newsreels in Germany and in the occupied territories.[43]

Goebbels' numerous speeches on film are forceful to an extent, despite the propaganda element; some of them were made to specialist audiences at the time, and have been published only after years of delay.[44]

Goebbels' diaries are well complemented by the Propaganda Ministry's press releases[45] or notes on the cultural and political press conferences. These as well as the magazine service (ZD) show which films the propaganda ministry wanted to attract the most attention and which the press would be better advised to ignore. Highly detailed campaigns were controlled in this way for important political films like for example *Ohm Krüger*, *Jud Süss* or *Die Entlassung* (*The Dismissal*). Such campaigns were often complicated in their argument, and provided lines to be followed by reviews in the appropriate organs.[46]

The mood reports by the SS security service (SD-Berichte)[47] also turn out to be a valuable source, but one that needs careful interpretation. The reactions from the public that they record are objective only to a certain extent, as the reports from informers planted all over the Reich were presented in selected form and tend towards a popular and orthodox point of view. Thus for example there are regular reports that the public was asking for "realistic farming films" and rejecting urbane light entertainment.[48] The limited force of such mood reactions and other responses from the general public is sometimes obvious. Thus it seems risky to draw conclusions about levels of anti-Semitism among the German population at the beginning of the war from the success of the "disguised" anti-Semitic feature film *Jud Süss* and the failure of the pseudo-documentary "Hetzfilm" ("smear film") *Der ewige Jude* (*The Eternal Jew*).[49] But because the SD was an authority dependent on Goebbels, interesting indications can be found of the interplay between "popular mood" and film policy or newsreel design. Because the SD reports were distributed among the NS leadership, with possible consequences for Goebbels' position within the regime, he had to take criticism of his working field very seriously.

In the field of picture sources, most of the important films of the Nazi period from the stock of the GDR film archive (formerly the Reich film archive) have survived. The only serious gaps are in pre-war newsreels[50] and productions by various state and NSDAP departments. In the Bundesfilmarchiv in Berlin,[51] in contrast with the different copies – suitable for TV transmission – formerly circulating in the West, there are not only feature films in the version prepared at the time for the première, but also numerous foreign films that were shown in the propaganda ministry as examples of "enemy productions".

The rest of the propaganda ministry's documents are stored in the Bundesarchiv in Koblenz and Potsdam. The film department was particularly badly affected by damage.[52] The are some other interesting estates in the Potsdam Bundesarchiv (including Karl Ritter's among others; there are some film items hidden among the Deutsche Bank's documents).[53]

The material from the film companies, nationalized from 1937, that came into the Bundesarchiv Koblenz as "Ufa in Liquidation" is to be evaluated as a key source on film policy in the "Third Reich". The minutes of the meetings of their various boards of directors, supervisory boards and other committees deal with commercial matters, and also provide valuable glimpses of directives from the Propaganda Ministry, production dispositions, editorial suggestions for individual films, casting and so on. The documents can be used to reconstruct the production history of many important films very vividly.

In contrast, the minutes of the "Dramaturgenbesprechungen" – the script conferences – dealt with desirable and undesirable political subjects, and recorded the requirements in terms of subject and content imposed by the "Reichsfilmdramaturg" ("Reich film script officer") in the Propaganda Ministry on screenplays and film projects.[54]

Over 3000 personal files on "Filmschaffende" ("film people"; creative people in the film industry)[55] deposited by the "Reichsfachschaft Film" ("Reich film department") in the "Reichsfilmkammer" ("Reich film chamber") or the "Reichskulturkammer" ("Reich chamber of culture"), now handed over to the Bundesarchiv, give information on political "reliability", employment and attitude in the war, but also show mutual denunciations by actors, directors, producers and ministry officials.

The records of the "Reichspropagandaleitung" ("Reich propaganda directorate") are also a surprisingly rich source of material, partly identical with the reconstructed material from the NSDAP-Party chancellery,[56] as the NSDAP film functionaries, keenly, bureaucratically and keeping good records, even though not very successfully, wanted to influence film policy and censorship.

To the extent that Hitler, the "Reichkanzlei" ("Reich chancellery") or his adjutancy were concerned with film questions, the various sources provide insight into expressions of taste, censorship wishes and curious interventions by the dictator, for example his commission to build gigantic film studios near his favourite Austrian town of Linz.[57]

Joseph Goebbels' diaries. An introduction

Published diaries continue to be popular. This is shown by the recent highly successful publication of the diaries of the Romance scholar Victor Klemperer, Thomas Mann's last notes or the large number of other, personal writings by diplomats, journalists, politicians and writers.[58] Diaries as a means of passing things down that presumably suggests intimate insights and has a potential for revelation, cannot only contain information that is important historically and politically.

For many of these authors, writing a diary was a literary and stylistic device. Alongside the literary enjoyment of this genre, which is often indisputable, the most important sign of quality in terms of historical importance is that both private and political matters must be analysed and described beside each other, or one after the other, "by a well-informed and self-critical contemporary in 'non-literary sincerity'", and not with a view to publication.[59] Private diaries by people involved in the events of the day are always political to some extent, and it is precisely when dealing with politics that one "single quality is crucial in terms of method", namely the "fearlessness of the revelations."[60] The starting-point for any categorization or interpretation is the author's intention – whether explicitly announced or discernible without any doubt –, the function that he allots to his entries (and thus also the circumstances in which they were written). One more reason to take a critical look at the diaries, dictated material and diary-like notes made by the NS Minister of Propaganda.

From June 1924 at the latest, and from then on to the last days of April 1945,[61] Joseph Goebbels made almost daily entries and notes in his diary, interrupted only by illness, personal crises or extraordinary political circumstances.[62] The former Propaganda Minister filled at least 16, probably over 20 hand-written notebooks with a total of 6000 pages up to 8 July 1941; after this date about 35,000 sheets have survived in dictated, typewritten form (top and carbon copy).

The exciting story of how the Goebbels diaries survived is not to be dealt with here, especially as many questions about the changing places where the material was stored, and about various owners, countries and archives have still not been fully cleared up.[63]

The majority of the material was taken to the USSR as spoils of war, smaller fragments were found in the seventies, for example, on the site of the former Reichskanzlei. One reason why the material got into a complete muddle was because some of it was removed by the Soviet Union and the GDR who were accumulating incriminating documents involving highly placed Nazis for various trials or possible blackmail. Microfilm copies made in the Soviet Union were channelled into West Germany by various detours. The Munich Institut für Zeitgeschichte (IfZ) published all the available hand-written notes available to that date in 1987, despite the largely poor condition of the copies.

In spring 1992, after the fall of the Soviet Union, access was gained to a special archive in Moscow and the glass-slide microfiches that had always been assumed to be there. Goebbels himself gave orders for them to be made, and the process was supervised by Richard Otte, the Propaganda Minister's stenographer, late in 1944. The fiches contain almost all the hand- and typewritten entries.[64] As well as this, all the original hand-written diary volumes – with the exception of those found destroyed in Berlin – and the first draft of the daily dictation from 1941 to 1945 are said to be in Moscow.[65] Original Goebbels diaries and copies are to be found in Stanford University, USA, in the Moscow foreign ministry and in the special archives of the Russian Federation, in the National Archives, Washington, in the Bundesarchiv Potsdam and Koblenz and the Munich Institut für Zeitgeschichte (IfZ).

The Munich K. G. Saur Verlag published 15 volumes containing all Goebbels' dictated diaries, with very few gaps in the material. The hand-written diaries, now more easily legible because of the glass plates, are also republished in a completed and improved edition in several volumes.

Texts, publications

Some special features have to be taken into account when analysing Goebbels' diaries. From 1924 to 1941, Goebbels – as far as can be made out until now – made his hand-written notes in volumes of different sizes, approximating to standard A5 paper.[66] The length of the entries varies from half a page to six pages. Goebbels' handwriting – by no means in Sütterlin style[67] – is relatively uniform, but also cramped and individual, and subject to enormous changes in the

1. Goebbels' office in the Propaganda Ministry: daily dictation.

course of the years.[68] Evenly written lines at times of relaxation, especially in the travel diary, contrast with rudimentary words, often obviously written at tremendous speed in phases of great pressure and lack of time. At last nine letters are almost indistinguishable, so that any deciphering, especially using poor copies hitherto, is something of a nerve-shredding test of patience.[69] Sometimes Goebbels kept several diaries in parallel: in his various residences, in the Propaganda Ministry and one "for holidays and travel".[70]

Goebbels usually composed his notes – in the present tense – in the morning, but for the previous day. Thus the date of every entry relates to the day before ("Yesterday:"). In places he broke off and left gaps, and then filled them in retrospectively, hours or days later.

However, several days combined in one entry are just as much an exception as long interruptions as a result of extraordinary political or private circumstances.[71] Goebbels made many careless and spelling mistakes, and coins some strange words.[72] But there are none of the crossings-out, additions or corrections that are so typical of diaries.[73]

Goebbels switched to dictation not least because of the considerable shortage of time shortly before and after the attack on the Soviet Union on 22 June 1941. The entries become consistently longer in this period, and are preceded by remarks ("In a tearing hurry. Therefore just notes.", 20.6.1941)[74] showing how time-consuming it must have been for Goebbels to write the entries by hand.[75]

Goebbels is said to have dictated his thoughts in the morning, before the ministerial conference held at 11 a.m., again for the previous day. He spoke rapidly and freely but used a few handwritten notes as basis for the dictations to his stenographers Otte and Jacobs,[76] who typed up the material; high-quality paper was covered on one side with the over-large "Führer type", so that one page of the notes occupies only about 35 per cent of a normal A4 page. This puts the relatively large volume of the dictated notes in perspective: they averaged 30 pages, and in special cases went up to 119 (20.8.1942) or even 144 (23.9.1943) pages.

These service reports, official in places, prepared and kept in the ministry, always followed the same pattern in the war years: Goebbels' actual report was preceded by a report on the military situation, headed "Militärische Lage". Then the midday and evening situation was discussed again in the text itself. There are detailed statements and commentaries in the course of the entry on the international press, reports and narrative from colleagues on the internal political situation in other states and summaries of various reports on mood, directives and discussions. There is usually a concluding remark in the form of a résumé of the general situation, linked with hopes for improvement that sound like short prayers; this replaces the fateful rhetorical questions, fits of Weltschmerz and details about when he went to sleep, and how well he slept, in the hand-written sections.

In contrast with his speeches, Goebbels' diary style is typified by a large number of rapturoussly and impassioned sentences, but also by limp and lame[77] formulations, only in note form and sometimes showing a degree of grammatical uncertainty, and also by a restricted vocabulary, further reduced after he starts to dictate, and also officious and peppered with clichés, though given the rapid dictation it is fairly fluent. Goebbels had difficulty in dealing with Anglicisms and Germanizations, but sometimes indulges in dry, cynical humour. For example, in an entry on 13.6.1941 on mass arrests of Anthroposophists, clairvoyants and occultists he makes the comment: "Strangely not a single one of the clairvoyants foresaw that they were going to be arrested. A bad sign for the profession." Even as minister he sometimes use slangy and vulgar formulations. He wanted to "beat down" and "stink out" opponents to the war, and he compared the German U-Boot sinking figures with a "slurp from the bottle". "Daft democrats"[78] were to be found in hostile countries, and he agreed with the formula "monarchy = shit".[79] He called other NS leaders things like "dirty swine", "skunk" or "bug".[80]

Doubts about whether the material is genuine, of the kind raised after experience with numerous falsifications,[81] even in document editions by distinguished historians, and especially also the forged Hitler "diaries",[82] scarcely occur any more, at least not on a level that can be taken seriously. It was known in his lifetime that Goebbels kept a diary, and by the war years at the latest colleagues could follow the process in the ministry. Forensic examinations and questioning gave no cause to question the authenticity of the material received.[83] Textual criticism would also make it possible to identify possible manipulations.

For decades the Swiss banker, former National Socialist and Goebbels admirer François Genoud claimed the right to the entire literary estate of Joseph Goebbels and other representatives of the Nazi regime, which he had ostensibly acquired as a result of the unclear legal position in the fifties.[84] However, it has been known for a long time that Goebbels sold his diaries in his own lifetime to the Eher-Verlag, which was owned by the party, and all the publisher's property passed to the state of Bavaria after the war.[85] Genoud acquired undeniable influence on National Socialist research through compulsory forewords and interventions about the content and design of published speeches and writings by Goebbels and other National Socialists.[86] Genoud committed suicide in Pully near Lausanne on 12. December 1996, at the age of 81.

The four volumes of material by Goebbels that appeared in the Munich K.G. Saur Verlag in 1987 contain all the copies available so far of his hand-written notes from 1924 to 1941. Transcription mistakes and a large number of gaps caused by deciphering problems were inevitable because of the bad originals. The edition can be used, but in all cases of doubt it is worth looking at the copies of the manuscripts. Otherwise it can happen that Goebbels is writing about Lilian Harvey, only for her to be deciphered as Brigitte Horney.[87] On pages 456 to 459 is a generally useful set of corrections and adjustments to errors and gaps, which had hitherto been designated "definitely illegible".[88]

A "popular edition" of the complete diaries from 1924 to 1945 was published by Ralf Georg Reuth in the Munich R. Piper Verlag in 1992.[89] Reuth's publication contains extracts (about 20 per cent of the whole) from the entries that were already available in German archives and – although in minute quantities – some new additions from Moscow, especially passages dating from 1933/34 and 1938/39. We owe these novelties to the disputed British historian (and denier of Auschwitz) David Irving, whose "kind support" is noted under the entries in question. He did manage some spectacularly mistaken readings, however: for example Goebbels – according to Irving – noted on 24.8.1939 that the "Führer" now believed in a "regeneration (Mauserung) of Bolshevism", but the correct reading is "transformation, change (Wandelung)".[90] Irving himself has published a German and an Italian edition of Goebbels' diaries for 1938.

Value as a source

For Goebbels the diary form was a literary stylistic device even before he started to make regular notes. *Michael Vormann. Ein Menschenschicksal in Tagebuchblättern* ("A Human Fate in Pages from a Diary") is the title of an early attempt at writing;[91] He called a long confession to his friend Else Janke "Aus meinem Tagebuch" ("From my Diary").[92]

The climax of these exercises in literary style is the publication in 1934 of *Vom Kaiserhof zur Reichskanzlei* ("From the Kaiserhof [hotel] to the Reichskanzlei"), for which Goebbels

2. Diary entry for 7 November 1935.

used his notes as a basis for a National Socialist propaganda description of the last 16 months before the seizure of power.

The Propaganda Minister definitely had an eye on posterity in his diaries. A striking sign of this is the change he made between January and March 1934 from calling Hitler "Chef" ("boss") or "Hitler" to the stereotypical "Führer".[93] In the notes themselves he makes the following portentous statement on 22.10.1936: "I am selling Amann my diaries. To be published 20 years after my death. 250,000 marks down then 100,000 marks per year. That is very generous. Magda and I are very pleased. Amann has made a sound capital investment."

There is no doubt that Goebbels intended to publish his diaries,[94] and so launched the efforts that have already been mentioned to secure and duplicate the material shortly before the end of the war.

All this is grounds for a few critical reminiscences about the material as a source. As early as 1962 Helmut Heiber correctly reached the conclusion that the entries do not contain "ultimate revelations", but were intended as "raw material for the future historian and pensioner Joseph Goebbels", that they reflect "events from the viewpoint of the superior statesman, presented for posterity".[95]

In fact large parts of the diaries give the impression of a basic scheme of self-representation, self-reflection and "fixing a message for posterity".[96] But light and shadow are very close together. Many "revelations" or insights into National Socialist power techniques are provided by Goebbels as mere routine. As he has the possibility of making cuts later, Goebbels could ex-

19

press himself on the same subject within a few lines in terms that were critical and reasonable at first, and then unmistakably in the form of propaganda. The borders between conscious manipulation, genuine conviction and subjective honesty seem fluid at times. A system cleverly devised by a rational faker is not to be found behind every half sentence. Often they are merely reports on his everyday work.

Beyond this, Goebbels had different standards – compared with today – when dealing with explosive topics. Thus he is just as open about the persecution, shooting and gassing of Jews as he is about the murder of the mentally ill, because he did not see this an incriminating in any way, but as an achievement worth recording, promising understanding, agreement if not fame when considered by future generations.[97]

But in contrast with this he takes over the propaganda lie about the "Polish attack on the Gleiwitz transmitter" – on the night of 31 August 1939 – for his entry on the first day of the Second World War, although only a few sentences earlier he writes about Hitler's "order to attack at about 5 a.m." and about special orders for the SS. Also: even after the non-aggression pact between Berlin and Moscow has been concluded, he says: "In the afternoon he (Hitler) gave me a detailed survey of the situation: Poland's situation is desperate. We shall attack it at the next possible opportunity. The Polish state must be smashed, just like the Czech state". (24.8.1939)

In recent years the propaganda dimension, the "staging for posterity", in Goebbels' diaries had been proved in detail, and warnings have been given against "historical stylizations that are consistently heeded",[98] serving in the first place to "prepare the bequest" to the reader. At least care should be taken not to continue the mistake of using the diaries uncritically. Goebbels' writings are "not a 'journal intime', written in subjective sincerity"; they were prepared by the "chief propagandist of National Socialism", with an eye on "future generations".[99]

Otherwise, when Goebbels is quite obviously reporting without any reservations, a crucial feature is always what material was available to him at the time. As far as international political events were concerned, all he had available were reports that can be called insider knowledge, but were still accessible to a wider circle. Goebbels – anyway in a leading position in the National Socialist State – often seems to have only superficial knowledge. Thus for example he speculates about Stalin's shooting of the Russian general staff around Marshall Tuchachevsky in June 1937 and obviously suspects nothing about Heydrich's attempts at disinformation, when even "lower circles" of the capital's élite often knew just as much, if not more, and more precisely, as can be seen from the diary of the Berlin journalist Bella Fromm.[100]

Historically significant dates

Of course it is essential to examine how Goebbels dealt with the most important dates in Nazi history within his "basic scheme" of truths, half-truths, propaganda stylization, distortions, selections and embellishments. The passages that have become known so far on the Reichstag fire of February/March 1933[101] immediately triggered a controversy along the old battle lines about the pros and cons of whether the Nazis were responsible for it.[102] According to Goebbels the Nazi leadership was surprised by the fire, but immediately saw an opportunity to get rid of the opposition. This confirms the findings of the vast majority of historical research.[103] But it is not acceptable to conclude from this that the fact that the Dutchman van der Lubbe was the sole culprit is now finally "scientifically proven".[104] A passage dated 9.4.1942, in which Goebbels records a conversation with Hitler about possible "authors" of the Reichstag fire, and has his "Führer" accuse the former chairman of the parliamentary Communist Party, Ernst Torgler, is of equally little value as evidence. In the spirit of conspiracy theories of the kind typical of dictators and faithfully following the official propaganda line at the time, Otto Strasser and the English secret service are simultaneously identified as being behind the assassination attempt in the Bürgerbräukeller in November 1939, which can also be traced back to a single culprit.[105] The version involving "men behind the scenes" is always preferred.

Similarly, it is not possible to use Goebbels' retrospective evaluation of the 1938 November pogrom – as an expression of the people's spontaneous anti-Semitism and not as a result of campaign run by the Party – as proof that this is the case.[106]

In the passages on the "Reichskristallnacht" Goebbels paints a striking picture of Hitler pulling the strings in the background, thus contradicting later impressions of a Propaganda Minister rushing ahead against the dictator's will.[107] In an entry on 10.11.1938 Goebbels speaks al-

3. Goebbels addressing the nation on New Year's Eve 1939.

ternately of "popular anger" ("The whole populace is in turmoil"), which should be allowed to take its course, and then of deliberately instructed SA "storm troops", doing "fearful work". Goebbels presents himself as Hitler's executor, whose views about the Jews and the pogroms he describes as "very radical and aggressive".

Goebbels' varying response to Hitler's war policies and their feared effect on the popular mood in summer/autumn 1938 is interesting, right up to his clear relief about having avoided conflict with the Western powers in the entry on 29.9.1938.[108] The entries contain partial flashes of reason, reveal uncertainty and admissions that are absent, or present only in rhetorical form ("What may the future bring, war or peace?", 24.8.1939) a year later during the political, diplomatic and military build-up before and after the "non-aggression pact" with the Soviet Union was concluded.

Goebbels' copious descriptions of the resistance campaigns of 20 July 1944 and the crucial counter-measures that he organized reveal no new insights.[109]

Slight scepticism can be discerned about Hitler's prediction of the failure of the Allied Normandy landings on 7 June 1944.[110]

Goebbels on Hitler, the Holocaust and the attack on Moscow

One of Goebbels' favourite stylistic tricks is to express his own views, criticisms or aims indirectly: as an opinion of Hitler's, of someone else he is talking to, or even as the people's wish. So Goebbels' desire, which was first of all constantly rejected by Hitler, to be given greater powers to wage "Total War", sounds like a wish coming from the people: "It is regretted that the Führer has too much on his plate, and people wish that he should pass on a series of powers to a hard man, and point to me in particular in this context." (5.2.1943)

If Goebbels admits that people are in an unfortunate mood, for example after Rudolf Hess's flight to Britain (14.5.1941), at the beginning of the evacuation of children from towns (1.10. 1940) or in precarious military situations, he usually blames them not on his own propaganda, but on the Wehrmacht High Command's (OKW) news policy, Göring's unrealistic promises or over-hasty announcements of victory by his rival, the Reich government press chief Otto Dietrich.

In war propaganda, Goebbels emphasizes the superiority of German methods, stereotypically claims that it is "highly effective" in hostile states and neutral countries,[111] reports on rifts in foreign governments and the catastrophic plight and morale of the people there. He even stylizes German propaganda to the extent of using the SD reports to turn proven mistakes like the so-called victory propaganda in occupied Poland in July 1941 into success, quite contrary to the truth.[112]

Critical assessment of propaganda by opponents in the war remains the exception, for example when Goebbels happens to praise a speech by Churchill (22.8.1940), or assesses Hermann Rauschnigg's book *Gespräche mit Hitler* ("Conversations with Hitler"), published in 1939, as "enormously dangerous".[113] Goebbels always emphasizes the contribution made by his journalistic activities to enhancing the internal mood, the forward-looking function of his speeches and essays: "My 'Reich' articles are currently the people's daily bread, as it were." (7.10.1944) Negative messages in the Security Service (SD) report on propaganda work are often simply omitted by Goebbels, who criticizes the authors as "defeatist" or identifies "grousing voices" who are not prepared to join unreservedly in the chorus of praise for his "Total War" speech.[114]

A large number of entries of a private nature represent a field in their own right in Goebbels' diaries. They cover marital rows and crises, illness and so on, showing a degree of intimacy from time to time, as for example in the entry for 3.1.1934: "Magda receives guests in her négl</br>ligé. There is a terrible row about this." Or in the entry for 31.3.1943: "I am having a lot of trouble with my eczema at the moment. I have been plagued by this malady for about two years now, and I cannot find a doctor who can get rid of it for me." There are similar passages about cigarette smoking (6.6.1944), Magda Goebbels' illnesses, gastro-intestinal problems, financial problems, tax debts, matters concerning real estate.[115] Incidentally, Goebbels does not mention the role of Hitler's mistress Eva Braun until June 1943, and then in a very roundabout way.

His long-standing affair with the Czech actress Lida Baarova is treated far from frankly, and appears only in coded references.[116] The same is true of the many insertions in summer 1939, when his wife Magda's relationship with his Staatssekretär ("permanent secretary") Hanke became known, with a whole mass of self-pity and self-justification that is typical of the diary.[117]

The picture that Goebbels presents of Hitler is one-dimensional, a "continuation of the journalistic promotion of a Führer myth".[118] In fact Hitler appears as a central fixed point for the diaries as a whole, who is "under the protection of the Almighty" and will not die "until his mission is fulfilled" (9.11.1939), who is as kind "as a father" in private (16.8.1938), but with strong nerves and steady qualities in political crises, in brief a statesman of genius and an "expert in all fields". Even in the moments of greatest crisis Hitler appears "reliable" and "unshakeable": "The Führer is showing us the right way", he writes on 27.8.1939, a few days before the outbreak of war,[119] and on 12.10.1939 Goebbels writes: "We will always win with the Führer, he combines all the virtues of the great soldier: courage, intelligence, prudence, flexibility, a sense of sacrifice and a total contempt of comfort and convenience. To fight under him can only be an honour." More, seemingly almost grotesque hymns appear to the end – like the one for Hitler's 55th birthday on 20.4.1944: "I want the Führer to live for at least another 30 years. If this wish were to come true, he would raise the Reich to the status of a world power, and make it the ruler of Europe." Thanks to the asserted consensus with Hitler, Goebbels can permit himself polemics against other leading state and Party bosses, especially Ribbentrop[120], Göring[121], Bormann[122], Lammers[123], Keitel[124] or Himmler[125].

Goebbels notes differences with Hitler extremely rarely. They usually refer to questions of detail or secondary matters. These extend from the seating-plan for the state and Party leadership at the Olympic Games (15.8.1936), an opposite judgement of the puppet government of German-occupied Norway under Quisling (18.4.1940), differences of opinion about art (9.3.1940), about the closure of the *Frankfurter Zeitung* (10.5.1943) or propaganda influence on the population of the occupied Soviet Republics (9.3.1943).

Goebbels does not become markedly more critical of Hitler until the war is nearly over. Here he carefully sketches a picture of a Hitler who is overworked and often not in the best of health, influenced by incompetent advisers, and then offers himself as right-hand man and effective representative of the "internal political leadership" (27.2.1943, 22.6.1944).[126] Goebbels' doubts about Hitler's leadership are always balanced by passages of demonstrative propaganda – including ambiguous statements about Hitler's military prognoses: "It is impressive to see the Führer believing so fervently in his mission." (7.6.1944) But he was very quick to express his anger when Hitler repeatedly rejected or even completely ignored suggestions and memos about home and foreign policy: "If things go on like this, the Russians will very soon be on our East Prussian border. I keep desperately asking myself in despair what the Führer is doing about it." (9.7.1944)

It almost seems as though intermediate notes of this kind were silenced by the events of 20 July, which again make Hitler appear as the "greatest genius in history" (23.7.1944), but

4. Goebbels the minister: diary as a propaganda bequest?
5. Hitler critic Goebbels: the strong hand is missing.

they start to sound again, more strongly than ever, in the last months of the war. Thus on 2.9. 1944 Goebbels complains that Hitler is working with divisions "that practically do not exist any more, or at least only partially", and even announces on 9.4.1945: "If I were the Führer, then I would know what is to be done now … In Germany people can do exactly as they like. The strong hand is missing." Writing about reports about the final military operations, which were directed by General Rundstedt, rather than Hitler, Goebbels remarked on 10.1.1945: "Nothing is heard about the Führer anywhere. In either a positive or a negative sense." Admittedly here too there is no lack of contradictory statements, which is evidence of the split nature of Goebbels' thinking. For example: "We could continue the war only with difficulty without the Führer, but with the Führer there is justifiable hope of a German victory." (11.10.1944)

Another, highly revealing complex in the diary entries is provided by the "Jewish Question". Despite Nazi terminology and language control it is actually clear from the outset that the intention is to annihilate them. Even in the thirties we find an abundance of declarations of intent[127] and personally initiated persecution campaigns in Berlin[128] that are further intensified immediately after the beginning of the war: the Jews must be "rendered harmless" (7.10.1939), which is a "clinical" and "surgical" task (2./3.11.1939).[129] On 19.3.1941 he writes that in Posen there had been "liquidations of all kinds, above all of Jewish rubbish. And that also has to be." The massacres in Kiev and Dniepropetrovsk, which extended over several days in 1941 ("Jews shot on a gigantic scale", 19.10.1941) are mentioned, and so are discussions with Heydrich about setting up "camps" in the East (also the "polar sea camps"; 29.9.1941 and 18.11.1941) or the November executions in Riga, which took place with considerable assistance from indigenous groups – Goebbels expressly emphasizes this: "They were shot down in their thousands and are still being executed by firing squads in their hundreds … The Jews are the lice on civilized humanity. They have to be eliminated in some way …" (2.11.1941) But Goebbels is not, as has become clear in the meantime, revealing a "Geheime Reichssache" ("secret Reich matter") here, and no more information than was in the hands of middle ranks in the Wehrmacht, the administration and the SS.

In the early stages of the mass deportations – the first trainloads of European Jews were arriving in Auschwitz and Belzec – Goebbels, in one of his diary entries that has attracted the most attention, expressly refers to the clearing of the Lublin ghetto, which was accompanied by rampant execution excesses, and the gassing at the destinations:

"From the General Government (German Occupied Poland) the Jews are now being pushed away to the East starting with Lublin. A process is being used here that is fairly barbaric, and not to be described more closely, and there is not very much left of the Jews themselves. On the whole it is probably true to say that 60% of them will have to be liquidated, while only 40% can be set to work. ... Here too the Führer is the stalwart champion of and spokesman for a radical solution that is required by the state of things and therefore seems unavoidable. Now that we are at war, thank God, we have a whole series of options available that would be denied us in peacetime. We must use them. The ghettos that are emptied and the General Government will now be filled with Jews expelled from the Reich, and after a certain period the process will start afresh."[130]

Goebbels, who helped to pursue National Socialist mass murder ("our historic mission, which cannot be held up by the war, but only accelerated by it", 13.5.1943), talks about the Jews over the years in terms of incredible, open brutality. He comments on the executions after the assassination attempt on Heydrich, the events in Lublin, the Warsaw ghetto uprising, the treatment of the Hungarian Jews,[131] and ends up with a horrifying piece of self-affirmation: he says that they had not "tackled" the Church and the old élites, especially the military leadership as "hard" as, say, Stalin, but: "We only carried out such radical policies in terms of the Jewish question. This policy was correct, and now we are benefiting from it. The Jews can do us no more harm. Nevertheless, before the Jewish question was tackled it was stressed over and over again that there is not answer to the Jewish question. One can see that it is possible, if one only wants to." (4.3.1944)

His much-published passage on the tactical withdrawal in the face of the so-called Rosen-straße protest in Berlin in March 1943 is also of some historical significance. At the time, Jewish partners in mixed marriages had to be released by the SS after protests from their wives.[132]

It is consistently astonishing that even the most intimate-sounding passages from the dairy follow anti-Semitic Nazi propaganda and public statements, for example, when Goebbels states on 18.8.1941:

"We also talk about the Jewish problem. The Führer is convinced that his earlier prophecy in the Reichstag that if the Jews once again succeeded in provoking a world war, it would end with the annihilation of the Jews, is being confirmed. It is proving to be true during these weeks and months with an certainty that seems almost uncanny. The Jews are having to pay the bill in the East; in Germany they have paid in part, and they will have to pay even more in future."

And it is a fact: this passage appears quite openly, with only superficial changes, in an essay by Goebbels in his weekly newspaper *Das Reich* on 16 November 1941.[133]

Hitler's "prophecy" in his Reichstag speech on 30 January 1939 is generally the fixed point for Goebbels' commentaries on the murder of the Jews in the war years. It also crops up in Goebbels' description of Berlin Reichs- and Gauleiter conference on 12 December 1941, which is incidentally also seen as the forum in which Hitler have his long sought-for "Führerbefehl" ("Führer's order") for the final solution:[134] "With reference to the Jewish question the Führer has decided to clear things up. He has prophesied to the Jews that if they were once again to bring about a world war, they would be exterminated in the course of it. This was not an empty phrase. The world war is here, the annihilation of the Jews must be its necessary consequence." (13.12.1941)

Finally, the treatment of the preparations for the Russian campaign in spring 1941 is still worth looking at. Goebbels – according to the diary – found out about this on 28.3.1941 at the latest, and immediately noted: "... only a very few people know about it." But the Propaganda Minister confirms Hitler's intentions to attack, which had been cherished since July 1940,[135] only retrospectively, on 22.6.1941. Previously he had contented himself with repeating Hitler's unchanged "Anti-Bolshevism" (9.8.1940) and general expressions of distrust relating to the So-viet Union.[136] Numerous contradictory and ambivalent quotations show that Goebbels must have been ambivalent about the non-aggression pact of August 1939 and partnership with "Bolshevism".[137] The diary entries also give absolutely no sense of a concrete subjective feel-ing of threat by a Russian invasion on the part of the German leadership in spring 1941.[138] The fact that Goebbels' preventive war statements are intended as a justification is all too transpar-ent.[139] Other things that become clear are Stalin's assumed knowledge of the German invasion plans,[140] the astonishingly concrete build-up of rumours in the German population[141] and the underestimation of the Red Army.

Obviously the impact of Goebbels' diaries is quite different according to the subject matter. We shall find out whether film policy deserves a place in the first rank of themes that Goebbels addressed only with a view to an intended effect. So should Goebbels' attention have slipped to the extent that he did not weigh up all his expressions – the investigation can only benefit from this.[142]

"An extraordinarily effective piece of avant-garde work": the ruler as connoisseur?

Goebbels thoughts on film and cinema are a fixed component of his diary for almost the whole period they cover. He comments on his first cinema experiences in September 1924, and ends up in March 1945 by remarking: "It is amazing that the German people still feel like going to the cinema at all."

Over the 20 years or more in between we see the full range of devices available to a diary-writer: sometimes he just writes a single sentence on the subject, sometimes a page, and sometimes, on rainy Sundays, almost half the whole entry (for example on 6.11.1939). And then the Film Minister had all or part of up to five films (on 15.8.1938, for example) shown in his private cinema at home on Schwanenwerder. But these are not just his opinions about specific films, Goebbels simply touched on everything involving the medium, whether it was of a technical, aesthetic or organizational nature: meetings with prominent figures from the film world, questions about organization and casting, drawing-board approaches to film planning, reports on the commercial situation, aspects of colour film development, newsreel design.

Even before Goebbels started to dictate his diary in July 1941 a certain scheme had started to develop – like the pattern of the day – for the presentation of his film activities: an "official" section – discussions in the Ministry, instructions or acknowledgements of reports in the first section of the daily entries – are juxtaposed with descriptions of semi-private examinations of films in the evening or screenings seen with some film people at the end of the particular entry.

This procedure produced a remarkable degree of continuity. From 1935 onwards he has ideas about film almost every day – interruptions of any length occur only as a result of travel, awkward tensions in his private life or dramatic political events – like the preparations for the invasion of Poland and the Soviet Union in summer 1939 and June 1941 respectively. The film commentaries reach their climax in 1937, before the entries are dominated by foreign policy crises and war propaganda. Here he also deals with trivialities, like little problems affecting prominent film people, or casting questions, which Goebbels preferred not to mention anymore.

As the war situation became increasingly critical, Goebbels unmistakably neglected the world of film, though the trend is not constantly downward. His entries in July/August 1943 are more extensive and diverse in terms of content than those for the previous months. The same applies to February/March 1944 in relation to November/December 1943. (The film entries do not break off finally until January 1945, and then fairly abruptly.)

6. First sound film *The Singing Fool*: face the future.

It was not unusual for him to add – in a transparently stylized manner – remarks to film entries in the final years of the war to the effect that "in view of the German people's struggle for survival", these problems interest him "only peripherally". He was obviously concerned to justify, for himself and for posterity, the fact that he was censoring light film comedies at this fateful hour – if posterity was intended to find out about the Minister's film consumption at all: he cut almost all the film passages from his entries for 1932/33, which he published as a propaganda book.

Early insights

Recently in particular greater attention has been paid to cinema experiences recorded in diaries. These include some that are written particularly succinctly, like those of Franz Kafka[143] or Victor Klemperer,[144] to name two complete opposites to Goebbels. It was by no means unusual for intellectual filmgoers in the twenties and thirties to write little film reviews in their diaries, even if they saw the cinema mainly as an amusing pastime. Not a few of these observations are often cleverer and more elegant than those written by the self-appointed National Socialist film expert.

It is certainly scarcely possible to identify Goebbels' great passion for film from the first passages from 1924. His amateurish judgements are highly emotional, usually extreme and seldom the result of cool analysis. He uses particular vocabulary for recurrent subjective views and emotional outbursts, claiming to be either "enthusiastic" and "moved", or rejecting films out of hand as "repugnant". Thus his comments on cinema visits to see classic films like *Die Nibelungen* (*The Nibelungs*, 11.4.1925,) and *Wege zur Kraft und Schönheit* ("Ways to Strength and Beauty", 9.6.1925) are dominated by personal impressions ("pure joy", "beautiful and enchanting").

Despite all his muddled standards of quality one thing is more than clear: this is a propagandist in spe, making political judgements, and always with one eye on the public's reactions – "it makes the red children clap", he says about one Soviet film (28.10.1928) – and someone who was quick to sense the possibilities of the new medium.

At first he is deeply entrapped in kitschy, banal and nationalistic terminology (he writes on Fritz Lang's *The Nibelungs*: "A pinnacle of German achievement. I am once more deeply moved by this grandiose depiction of German power, greatness and beauty. How old this film already is – and yet how modern! Everyone in the Phoebus-Palast full of a deep and secret horror. This was the epitome of German fate", 4.11.1929). He emphasizes his preference for "heroic, military and world-war-stamina[145] films and is "moved" by the *Flötenkonzert von Sanssouci* (*The Flute Concert of Sanssouci*, 29.12.1930) from the reactionary series of films about Frederick the Great.

But he also voices doubts about the effectiveness of nationalist German films in the twenties: thus a "Blücher film *Waterloo* with (Otto) Gebühr" was "definitely vigorous, but essentially characterless" (5.1.1929), above all in comparison with foreign productions: "*Kampf um Paris*! *Die Kommune von 1871* ("Battle for Paris! The Commune of 1871"). If you compare this knowing approach with what Hugenberg is doing with his film, then you can see what the middle-class citizen is worth and why he must lose." (15.8.1929)

Faced with such deficiencies, it was not difficult for Goebbels – despite all his slogans against "Jewish kitsch" from the "Hebrews" in Hollywood[146] – to recognize immediately the high technical standard and professional qualities of the American cinema:

"… saw the first sound film. American. *Singing Fool*. I was surprised how far the technique of the sound film has already advanced. There is a future here, and we are wrong to reject it all as American bungling. Convinced! Won over! The content was dreadful New York sentimental kitsch. But nevertheless: we must face the fact that this is the thing of the future, and see the possibilities that are to come." (2.12.1929)

The Berlin National Socialist Gauleiter Joseph Goebbels, who was already a born-again anti-Bolshevik, must have been even more fascinated by the revolutionary work of Sergei Eisenstein. The Russian cinema provided him with fundamental, impactful impressions of film as an effective means of influencing mass opinion, whose importance for his later development cannot be overestimated:

"In the evening we saw *Potemkin*. I have to say that this film is fabulously made. With quite magnificent crowd scenes. Technical and landscape details of succinct power. And the hard-hitting slogans are formulated so skilfully that it is impossible to contradict them. That it what is actually dangerous about this film." (30.6.1928)

Goebbels did not take long to grasp the possibilities of conveying political messages visually. He puts the political and ideological success of the precisely targeted and easily remembered "hard-hitting slogans" in *The Battleship Potemkin* down to the radical and realistic style, the expenditure, the innovations in terms of technique and montage. He was so impressed by the directorial achievement that he publicly praised the film about the mass uprising in Odessa several times after coming to power, and demanded a "National Socialist *Potemkin* – quite incomprehensibly, for many people".[147] And Goebbels retained his sense of impact on an audience even in the case of less highly esteemed Russian films:[148]

"*Kampf um die Erde*. Soviet film by Eisenstein. Well made, but greatly exaggerated, and thus embarrassing. … But nevertheless the film is dangerous and we should learn from this." (16.2.1930)

The functional separation of propaganda form and ideological message, which Hitler could obviously not understand in the case of *The Battleship Potemkin*,[149] and Goebbels' comments on other Russian films also adopt aesthetic and political suggestion for his own manipulative interests ("it is all outstandingly well done"). Ultimately "the Russians are pretty good at it, and we must learn from them". On the German-Russian adaptation of Leo Tolstoy's drama *The Living Corpse* he writes: "Everything is there, completely without any sense of sham, Pudovkin is a great artist. Even bad ideas can awaken great talents." (26.2.1929)

The triumph of form over content – Goebbels had to wrest this insight from his admiration for "Jewish" American and "Bolshevik" Russian films. He was aware that this power over the masses should not be left to their ideological opponents. It was all too clear that the public was susceptible to this brilliantly staged "Bolshevik" propaganda. The people, he noted after a cinema visit on 10.12.1928, "long for spiritual bread".

Goebbels did not manage to put the insights he had acquired about the effectiveness of film into practice as part of National Socialist film work before 1933,[150] but as Minister of Propaganda he was able to draw on them and so did not have to start from scratch. His instinct for film propaganda and his inner drive to gain control over this medium whatever happened were awakened by his cinema-going in the twenties.

The Propaganda Minister as a cinema enthusiast?

The attempt to use the diaries to find out how Joseph Goebbels, who after all had a doctorate in the history of literature, understood art and culture is a somewhat disappointing enterprise. The entries hardly reflect a serious analysis by the capital-dwelling, intellectual National Socialist on artistic and cultural question or controversies.

Goebbels – as a quite conventional devotee of the fine arts – agreed with Göring on the cultural and political course set at first, that of preferring middle-class high culture and the achievements of the German artistic elite to a Fascist but dilettante loyalty to the party line. In the Nazi "Kulturkampf" of 1933 to 1935 Goebbels was opposed to Rosenberg's populist-orthodox course for reasons of power politics and patronized painters and sculptors who were considered "art Bolsheviks".[151] He later went back on this attitude, in just the same way as his early sympathies for Expressionism disappeared. In the early days of the Nazi dictatorship he may have had vague ideas of a kind of Fascist avant-garde, using futurist or surrealist artistic devices – as in Mussolini's Italy – to glorify their own ideology.

Anyway there are indications in the early diaries that he was definitely touched by works of Nolde, Barlach and Slevogt. But evaluations of this kind disappear later, and thus the most he asks himself in the case of Nolde is: "Bolshevik or painter"? (2.7.1933)

The texts known so far give little evidence of Berlin's bubbling cultural life, nothing about Dix, Beckmann, Picasso or Kandinsky, nothing about productions by Piscator – whom he obviously liked (20.10.1930) –, Kortner or Reinhardt. Pure Nazi stage pamphlets after the seizure of power he once called "A dramatized Rosenberg programme … . One almost goes to sleep over it." (31.10.1937) But he also rejects everything that is too far out of the ordinary, if it is actually still allowed – like the "philosophical dances" by Mary Wigman or Gret Palucca[152] of Dresden: "Dance must be lively and show beautiful women's bodies." (27.6.1937)

Compulsory reading for the unrecognized poet Joseph Goebbels were classics, from Dostojevsky to Thomas Mann, although he makes very few strong comments about them. Goebbels also sometimes tries to separate the work from the person of the artist: "Buddenbrooks" is of course "fabulous" (23.2.1930), but not its author, who was an "senile windbag" (22.3.1941) for Goebbels, even before his anti-Nazi appeals from exile. He liked G. B. Shaw as early as 1930, but he finds the "brilliant scoffer" even better when he started to criticize his own British government. Richard Strauss remained a genius for Goebbels even after some political clumsiness.

Goebbels was well aware of the faults of Nazi art, as his repeated derogatory comments on official art prizes show, but he had only limited powers as a cultural politician: he must have thought that he had scarcely any chance of pushing through his own line against Hitler and Göring, who were obsessed with art. And so he increasingly followed the "Führer's" line, with whom he used to philosophize about the quality of operatic performances and conductors like Karajan, Furtwängler or Knappertsbusch, and following the National Socialist geniuses cult he revered the artistic titans Wagner, Bruckner and Nietzsche. He defended Hindemith against attacks by radical party activists.

Although Goebbels may originally have seen art as an individually moving element, and not just from the point of view of using it as a mere instrument,[153] but his biographer Helmut Heiber feels that Goebbels did not have an inward relationship with art and culture. He says he saw culture "largely as a function of propaganda"[154] and simply pursued the goal of "building up an extensive culture business that attempted to cover up all hollowness and triviality with the slogan 'art to the people' and the statistical intoxication of growing attendance figures.."[155]

But Goebbels' great expertise in relation to film is scarcely doubted. Françis Courtade and Pierre Cadars emphasize Goebbels' maxim that "the propaganda purpose of a film" must "always remain bound to its aesthetic and technical qualities.".[156] Even though there are voices that declare him to be a dilettante, the dominant image is that of a connoisseur with "secure aesthetic judgement",[157] indeed of a genius.[158]

Such judgements are mainly based on popular literature, opinions passed from person to person, anecdotes and film speeches from 1933 to 1941. However, Goebbels' speeches and writings are largely free of any theoretical basis. There is a lack of any clear definition of film art, if one ignores some remarks on the perception of film as "sensual art".[159] The assertion that Goebbels was familiar with all essential contemporary writing on film by Bela Balazs or Siegfried Kracauer,[160] is not confirmed, at least in the diary entries.[161]

There are few constant statements and theses about film politics in the diaries, speeches and essays from 1933 to 1944. One of Goebbels' essential programmatic aims was to establish film as a genuine, independent art form, and to confirm it as the "people's art", with the same rank as the other traditional cultural fields of theatre, music and painting.[162] To this end the "primacy of the stage and literature" over film has to be broken. Goebbels repeatedly spoke of this state of tension between stage and film. Here too the model of America plays a part, though the enviously agrees that the American film never had to free itself from the stage.

Clichés continue to dominate when he fulminates against "kitsch" and "literature", "pale aestheticism" and an "anaemic l'art pour l'art point of view"[163] or attacks the "vulgar flatness of mass amusement" and the "most stupid society kitsch".[164]

Even in the entries before 1933 there is almost inflationary use of clichés of Nazi cultural rhetoric like "kitsch" and "Kintopp" (popular word for cinema) to induce contempt of light films made in the Weimar Republic, especially for films by Jewish actors and directors: "Film Kampf der Tertia, dreadful Jewish kitsch!" (31.1.1929)

Goebbels favoured material that was "close to the people" using historical models that are taken over "from the inherent laws of a theatre drama or a piece of epic material to operate within the inherent laws of film".[165] There should be a treatise on film art, the minister suggested, that would be as significant as Lessing's Hamburgische Dramaturgie was for the theatre.[166]

Goebbels disapproved of the film's dual character as art and commerce; the responsibility of the individual artistic personality should be strengthened in order to work against this antagonism between "profitability bigwigs and artists". Only in this way could the film shake off its disreputable image in the eyes of educated citizens as an unserious seasonal business with an insecure economic basis and dependent on short-lived tastes, he said on the occasion of the international film congress in Berlin in 1937.[167] But a financially healthy, solid and serious film could be produced only if it was in the hands of the state.[168] Only then could it develop into real art.

In his very first speech as the new Minister of Film and Propaganda in the Kaiserhof hotel in Berlin Goebbels presented himself "as a man who has never distanced himself from the German film" and as a "passionate lover of film art":[169] "I can further add in my favour that I have seen most films made at home and abroad. Therefore I have a certain fund of knowledge and experience, so that I am in a position to give a judgement on things that is in any case of substance."[170] Here Goebbels also mentioned some film titles a models for future German film production: The Battleship Potemkin, and also Fritz Lang's The Nibelungs, the American Greta Garbo melodrama Anna Karenina (the 1928 silent film) and Luis Trenker's Der Rebell (The Rebel).[171]

Goebbels' ideas are revealed much more strongly in film commentaries and analyses than in fundamental and public utterances. Certainly in his own reports he constantly follows the line of showing himself in the right light as a film connoisseur. It was more important than clearing out mere propagandists aiming at mass effect to present himself as an omnipotent expert with a precise eye for the design and details of cinematic works of art.

Even in the very first surviving film entry so far – on the silent Swedish classic Gösta Berling – Goebbels claims to have found "discretion in facial expressions" (24.9.1924) in Swedish acting as compared with German acting.

His tendency to divide films into individual performances meant that his vocabulary also became more refined. He can identify good camera-work and bad acting, knows how to distinguish a bad screenplay from good direction, and thinks about milieu, "handling actors", "atmosphere" and "scenic management".[172] He takes over concepts from contemporary film terminology like "Volksfilm" ("popular film"), "problem film", "dialogue film", calls foreign anti-Nazi productions "Hetzfilme" ("smear films"). "Propaganda film" is usually used for documentary productions, "tendentious film" a German political film. The latter are either reproached, like *Menschen ohne Vaterland* ("People without a Fatherland"), for being without "contours, line, tendentiousness" (8.2.1937) or they are praised, like *Ritt in die Freiheit* ("Ride into Freedom"), for being "very decent" in "plot, direction, conviction" (19.10.1936). Other political criteria are expressed in concepts like "attitude", "heroic", "manly", "skilful", "psychological" or "dangerous".

Comedies on the other hand are called "amusing", "side-splitting", "funny", and "pacey". Melodramas can be "delightful', "moving", "useful" or "inept", "unfocused", "embarrassing", "rubbish", "lousy", "stiff", "lifeless", "sterile", "flat", "dragged out", "mind- and witless" or simply "trash".

After he started to dictate, Goebbels' choice of words became less varied, and stereotypes like "extraordinarily successful" and "effective", "excellent" or "completely corrupted" and "failure" tend to dominate. He seldom provides a complete analysis. On *Fronttheater* ("Front Theatre") he wrote on 14.8.1942: "The characters are badly drawn, the conflict dragged in by the ears and the plot evolves very superficially and conventionally." And on *Paracelsus*: "Too Baroque, too contrived, more theatre than film. The artificial, medieval style gets on one's nerves, and Werner Krauß's exaggerated way of acting is also not for everyone." (28.2.1943)

Goebbels' intention to provide convincing film analyses is frequently countered by very spontaneous judgements and uncertainties in terms of taste: "Saw *M* by Fritz Lang. Fabulous. Against humanist stupidity. For the death penalty. Well made", he notes surprisingly on 21.5. 1931, completely contradicting contemporary film criticism with this interpretation of the classical masterpiece. Probably he simply did notice the nuances, thus, for example, when in the joint hunt by police and the underworld for a mentally deficient child murderer the differences between the two are deliberately blurred. When the ringleader of the criminals, in his passionately caricature of a plea finally demands the death penalty for the murderer, Goebbels obviously saw nothing more in this than an indictment of Berlin criminality in the thirties.[173]

The positive reaction to *M* is juxtaposed with the expected rejection – even though it has been described as his favourite film[174] – of *Der blaue Engel* (*The Blue Angel*), with Marlene Dietrich, based on the novel by Heinrich Mann. He simply calls the film "dreadful", like the novel before it.[175] (4.4.1930)

After 1933 it is probably scarcely possible to separate Goebbels' expressed taste in films from state film policy. He was now personally involved in too many important films until 1945 to be able to allow himself an objective opinion. Other factors also have to be considered, from Goebbels' opportunism to Hitler's influence on his minister's film judgements, which could sometimes lead to grotesque contradictions. On 8.11.1936 Goebbels sees Willi Forst's *Burgtheater* (*Burg Theatre*) as "a good film", but he revises this opinion discovering that his "Führer" rejected it. Now, on 12.11.1936, the film is suddenly a "dreadful abortion".

At the most, the productions dating from the transitional years 1933/35 permit some conclusions about Goebbels' taste in film, although here his judgements are often influenced by functional and legitimizing motives in the sense of the reshaping of the film landscape that he is aiming for. He was characteristically displeased by any production that moved even slightly away from the conventional style or had avant-garde tendencies: thus the documentary film *Das Stahltier* ("The Iron Horse"), the mystical and gloomy *Fährmann Maria* ("Ferry Boat Woman Maria"), much praised by film literature ("an experiment, but not a good one. Contrived. Literature!", 21.12.1935), the elaborately fantastic film about the future *Gold* ("fabulous from the technical point of view", "personal scenes strongly kitschy", 2.4.1934), the jazz film *Heut kommt's drauf an* ("Today is the Day") with Hans Albers ("dreadful trash", 14.7.1933)[176] and Reinhold Schünzel's satirical *Amphytrion* (*Amphytrion – Happiness Comes from the Clouds*) ("a conglomeration of contradictory stylistic elements". 13.7.1935).[177] Goebbels' reputation as a connoisseur is strengthened by praise for what was probably the best German screwball comedy, *Glückskinder* (*Lucky Kids*), with Willy Fritsch and Lilian Harvey (ostensibly Ufa's answer to Frank Capra's comedy *It Happened One Night*, which was also very successful in Berlin), where he expressly praises the witty dialogue and Curt Goetz's "song texts celebrating idleness".[178] (17.9.1936) *Lucky kids* is one of the films that we can identify as being highly rated by Goebbels, but at the same time was attacked by the Nazi press – in this case by the *Schwarzes Korps*.[179] He also assesses the gag-packed comedy *Allotria*, directed at an American tempo by Willy Forst very professionally: "very snappy and with a great deal of pace. But with exaggerated effects, and therefore not entirely satisfying." (10.6.1936)

Goebbels tended to be automatically critical of some genres: he was not keen on detective films, revues, or films of peasant life. But there is scarcely a field that he rejects out of hand. He threatens to ban the "eternal sing-song in light entertainment films" and "filmed operettas" (31.7.1937) and notes on Marika Rökk's *Gasparone*: "A typical operetta film, but quite uncinematic, unstylish and intolerable. I can't watch that any more."[180] (17.12.1937) But he was enthusiastic about the well-known revue films *Eine Nacht im Mai* (*A Night in May*) ("an amusing and well-made dance film", 12.7.1938) and *Wir tanzen um die Welt* ("We're Dancing Around the World") ("a very good, rousing light entertainment film", 10.12.1929). He is critical of films in the milieu of Viennese operetta – with the exception of Willi Forst's international success *Maskerade* (*Masquerade in Vienna*), which had its première in Venice ("very well done", 22.8.1934).[181] His comment on *Es leuchten die Sterne* ("The Stars are Shining") is typical: "not art, but good entertainment." (11.3.1938)

And so we cannot expect Goebbels to provide any clues that might be useful in interpreting German revue films as military analogies – Nazi-specific "costumed marching in step" or "the Propaganda Ministry reviews the army",[182] in which civilian troops are on parade.

Goebbels also tends to be inconsistent about regional and peasant films. As a city-dweller, he was fundamentally reserved about the blood and soil mythology of Rosenberg and Darré. But harmless comedies like the "very funny peasant comedy" (4.7.1933) *Krach um Jolanthe* ("Trouble with Jolanthe") were entirely to his taste – unless they were too "vulgar" *Das Bad auf der Tenne* ("The Bath on the Threshing Floor"; 14.2.1943). During the war he was particularly concerned that these productions should not be too "stolid", but they had to make a light and amusing impression, like *Kohlhiesels Töchter* ("Kohlhiesels Daughters", 7.3.1942). He said that *Der Flachsacker* ("The Flax Acre") showed "for the first time that it is possible to represent the peasant milieu in a way that had some artistic status". (15.3.1942) He prefers regional novels set in the Bavarian mountains and Ganghofer films to Weiß Ferdl's farces. But the "melancholy, gloomy tome" *Im Schatten des Berges* ("Shadow of the Mountain", 11.12.1940) is again in complete contrast with the mountain drama *Die Geierwally* ("Vulture Wally"), which is praised in the diaries and in public.[183]

Goebbels picks out the court drama *Der Fall Deruga* ("The Deruga Case", 6.7.1938) and the Sherlock Holmes adventure *Der Hund von Baskerville* (*The Hound of the Baskervilles*, 10.12.1936) as perfect examples of the detective film. But *Autobus S* ("filthy criminal milieu", 2.8.

1937), *Schuß im Rampenlicht* ("A Shot by the Footlights") and *Kriminalkommissar Eyck* ("Police Inspector Eyck") are "the old criminal rubbish". (18.12.1939)

Given the number of unsophisticated remarks he makes about German cinema production, it would be easy to assume that Goebbels understanding of film had been much overestimated. But thanks to the fact that he dealt with film so much over the years, Goebbels did develop, and his eye for craftsmanship became sharper. He accurately identifies the miserable way the acting was handled by Herbert Selpin and Werner Klingler in *Titanic* (1943) on 17.12.1942. But he did not fail to notice great film art. He saw Helmut Käutner's outstanding melodrama *Romanze in Moll* (*Romance in a Minor Key*) as an "extraordinarily effective piece of avant-garde work (10.1.1943), and Käutner's atmospherically dense masterpiece *Unter den Brücken* (*Under the Bridges*) as an "excellent work of art, appealing above all in its clever psychological direction and its modern psychology. Käutner represents the avant-garde among our German film directors". (28.12.1944)

Foreign films as models

Often Goebbels comments on foreign film styles and films, largely of American, French, Russian and Italian origin, are more revealing than his remarks on German productions, which are largely artistically unrewarding, with a few exceptions. Goebbels decided personally whether and which foreign films could be shown until the beginning of the war – or until 1941 in the case of American films. Although the French cinema helped to shape European film style in the thirties, with works by Marcel Carné, Jean Renoir, Julien Duvivier and Jacques Feyder, Goebbels does not seem to have paid any particular attention to French films. He was obviously quite unable to make anything of the internationally successful poetic realism movement, if he was anyway in a position to understand it. Even though he notes that Jacques Feyder is "one of the greatest living directors" on 18.5.1938, he fails to point out that Feyder is the only well-known European director who was still prepared to come to Germany in 1938, to make *Fahrendes Volk*, this was the German version, which Goebbels praised highly, of his French circus film *Gens du voyage* ("Travellers").[184]

10. Jean Gabin in *Pepé le Moko* (1936): "typically degenerate product".
11. Goebbels model *Gone with the Wind* (1939): "You have to see it more than once".

Goebbels' comments on Julien Duvivier's work are significant. *Un Carnet de bal* (*Life Dances On*) is called "degenerate art of the most staggering kind. ... Immensely disappointing. No sign of any attitude or purpose" (18.11.1937); *Pepé le Moko* is also "a typically degenerate product. Morbid and decadent. It is increasingly easy to understand why France was bound to fall." (9.1.1941) Quite obviously Goebbels was not in a position to see fatalistic and melancholy films about social outsiders without reference to the realities of politics and propaganda. The only time he seems to feel some sense of esteem is for *La fin du jour* (*The End of a Day*), also by Duvivier: "Very skilful portrayal of people and of the milieu. But as always with the French, it is full of profound pessimism and crippling resignation." (27.9.1939) By consciously introducing these completely non-cinematic criteria, along with his political criticism, Goebbels lined himself up precisely with the right-wing, middle-class French press, who denounced these "pessimistic" films as subversive (including *Quai des brumes*/*Port of Shadows*).[185]

Goebbels was able to place the French anti-Nazi films that fell into German hands after the fall of France into familiar categories: he called the unusual feature-documentary *Hitler – Mes crimes* ("Hitler – My Crimes"), which called Nazism to account very skilfully, "subtle, effective and dangerous".[186] (26.6.1940). Later in the war Goebbels apparently saw only French productions made by Continental Films in Paris – which was under German control – and produced feature films like *Caprice, Annette et la dame blonde* ("Annette and the Blond Lady"), *Les Inconnues dans la maison* (*Strangers in the House*) in France from 1940 to 1944.

Goebbels was undoubtedly most taken by American films. Melodramas like Greta Garbo's *Grand Hotel, Anna Karenina* or *Maria Walevska* (15.2.1933, 26.12.1937) regularly "moved" him personally to a high degree. "That is the way the world feels now", he said on 8.6.1933, to explain the success of Hollywood films. He quite openly confirms the superiority of American musicals from the Broadway Melody series – it was even suitable "to be studied" (18.3.1936, 29.10.1937) –, romantic comedies like *It Happened One Night* ("a witty, sparking film from which one can learn a great deal", 18.10.1935), of classic adventure films like *Mutinity on the Bounty*. (6.9.1936) "How easily the Americans bring off something like that", he noted on the subject of professional American entertainment: "One can only admire it."[187] (4.4.1937) Goebbels never mentions issues raised by what he saw as "alien", "niggerized" jazz and swing music in this context, which placed him in harmony with most of the controlled press, which was otherwise quite positive in its attitude to American films until shortly after the outbreak of war.[188]

Goebbels was most impressed, for political reasons, by the films aiming at social reform made in the early Roosevelt New Deal era. They criticized American society and emphasized the contrasts between the honest, upright middle-classes and the corrupt nouveau-riche during the economic crisis. Goebbels wrote about Frank Capra's *Mr. Deeds Goes to Town* on 27.5. 1939: "Very high American standard with Cooper. Magnificently done, wonderfully tendentious, excellently acted. I am most enthusiastic." Perhaps Goebbels could not always grasp the internal American background to the stories. Thus he praises the "good acting of people" in

Our Daily Bread, but otherwise he simply calls this work, which was even attacked as Communist by the reactionary American press, "nice". (18.6.1936) It was way beyond his imagination that films could mercilessly criticize circumstances in their own country. He wrote of John Ford's Steinbeck film *The Grapes of Wrath*, which shows the exploitation of the rural population, and which he saw in the last few months of the war, that "we could not make a more anti-American film ourselves". (22.11.1944)

For Goebbels, *Gone with the Wind*, that classical drama of the southern states, stood very high in the rank order of the American cinema. He repeatedly had it screened for visitors and film people: "You have to see it more than once. We should take it as an example."[189] (30.7. 1940) The same was true of the Disney cartoon *Snow White* (12.2.1940), which he used as a model when promoting German cartoon film production, and of the children's films with Shirley Temple. (27.5.1939) He can even get something out of Hollywood's anti-Nazi productions – indeed he actually uses them for self-aggrandizement. Thus he says that *Confessions of a Nazi Spy* may be "an American sham, with some skill, I play a principal part in it, and not a particularly unpleasant one at that." But otherwise he thinks the film is "not dangerous": "It makes our enemies afraid, rather then filling them with rage or hatred."[190] (30.9.1939) Goebbels feared a different effect from Alfred Hitchcock's *Foreign Correspondent*: "It is a first class example of a shoddy contrivance, effectively got up as a piece of criminalistic trouble-making, which will certainly make a certain impression on the general public in enemy countries."[191] (22.1.1942) Overall – despite some propaganda inserts about "Jewish-dominated and primitive US culture" – it is possible to see all this as a mixture of envy and admiration:[192]

"We saw the American colour film *Swaney river* together in the evening ... . The situation today is that the Americans know how to use their relatively small cultural reserves by using modernized presentation to create something that is also useful at the present time. ... The Americans have only a few negro songs, but they present them in such an up-to-date way that they conquer large sections of the modern world with them, where the people then feel very personally involved. We have far greater cultural resources, but we have neither the art nor the strength to modernize them." (3.5.1942)

Goebbels therefore does not miss the chance of conjuring up a global competition with the American film and even admits that as soon as US competition returns to the European markets from which it has now been driven by German occupation, "we would have our work cut out with it, and could even lose under certain circumstances". (1.11.1942)

Goebbels also admired Soviet cinema in the Stalin era to a certain extent. His love-hate affair with Russia and his distinction between despicable Jewish influence and model Russian nationalist and socialist ideas[193] reflects a considerable split. He pursues his twenties insights by treating Russian film productions – with a very few exceptions ("Bolshevik artistic mischief", 7.6.1936) – from a strongly political rather than an artistic point of view, including Dzigan's *We are from Kronstadt*, 1936, "a Bolshevik propaganda film ... totally devoid of talent, full of improbabilities, cramped and contrived." (20.2.1936)

However, given the hostile stance against "Bolshevism" there were few opportunities to gain insights into Soviet film production, as scarcely any films got to Germany. And very little changed after the conclusion of the non-aggression pact between Germany and the Soviet Union – because Hitler forbade cultural exchange.[194] Goebbels reports on some newsreels and documentary films, but obviously made very contradictory judgements on them. "I tell him (Hitler) about my impressions of Russian films. He shares them completely. He too has only contempt for Moscow." (16.8.1940) But then a few lines further on he says: "A film of the red sports Olympics in Moscow. It is good. It shows a lively Russia full of joie de vivre. The other face of Bolshevism. A great organizational achievement. Bolshevism will always remain a mystery to us." After the invasion of the Soviet Union he then regularly arranged screenings of so-called booty films, mainly propaganda pieces about great figures of Russian history, some of which were personally commissioned by Stalin. Here Goebbels always makes an effort to discover the propaganda intentions. In Pudovkin's *General Suvorov* he sees an attempt "to recreate the link between present-day Russia and its old and heroic history", and he states that: "Some passages in the film are childlike and naïve, as if they had been made by a twelve-year-old; other passages again have an astonishing vital force. There is a whole series of possibilities to be found within the Russians.."[195] (25.3.1942) He also sees this motif in the historical film *Peter the Great* by Vladimir Petrov, dating from 1937, which aims, in his view, "to use Russian history in the service of the Bolshevik state view". (12.4.1942) But he admits that this was handled "not unskilfully", and is achieved "to an extent with powerful artistic resources".

Goebbels particularly admired the Soviet documentary war propaganda films. He writes on 24.3.1942 that the "Bolsheviks had hit the nail on the head in propaganda terms" with *Retreat at Klin*. However, the minister does seem to be making an impression that he is consciously exaggerating Russian propaganda for his own purposes. The "first-class piece of agit-prop sham" *A Day in the Soviet Union* may be "easy to refute", but will "make some impact (in the) neutral and hostile countries". And to propagate his political programme he adds: "Incidentally, this film has once again made it clear to me that we have to be extraordinarily careful with Bolshevism. … If we do not use all our strength, it could overrun us one day. So our motto should be more strongly than ever: total war is the order of the day."[196] (4.3.1943)

Here Goebbels no longer follows the method he used especially for English war propaganda films, which was to present the enemy's films as ridiculous and ineffective. He thought the Soviet documentaries were so effective that he tried to keep even the highest Nazis away from them and to shut all the films away in the Reich Film Archive, which he controlled. He wrote to the head of the Reich Chancellery to justify this in March 1943:

"From my own experience I know that Soviet war films in particular are put together in a way that is extraordinarily effective in terms of propaganda, and that their brutal method of presentation makes a very powerful impression on German spectators. … For my own part I always watch these films alone and use a carefully selected projectionist."[197]

Goebbels seems to have accepted Italian propaganda films, which were mainly highly emotional, bold and simple, because of their political effectivenes, but not from an artistic and aesthetic point of view. At least this is the conclusion suggested by his comments on *Mario* ("well and effectively made", 24.3.1937), *Luciano serra pilota* ("well made nationalist film on the Abyssinian war. But not good artistically", 7.11.1939) and *Scipione l'Africano* (*Scipio the African*). For Goebbels' taste Italian cinematography was still far too caught up in the aesthetics of the past. Rumour had it in Italy that the Propaganda Minister has said that a German director would have been shot for a film like *La corona di ferro* (*The Iron Crown*) by the Italian star director Alessandro Blasetti. Jerzy Toeplitz explains this by saying that Goebbels, unlike the Italian public, had recognized the film's pacifist and idealistic message.[198] Goebbels' comment may show considerable lack of respect, but his criticism does not seem to be politically motivated: he says that the film represents "a grandiose mass of cinematic impossibilities that cannot be discussed at all". "Aestheticizing" and "literary film experiments" of this kind are "not possible here", he asserts on 2.9.1941, writing about Blasetti's fantasy history of the Middle Ages. He was all the more outraged when *The Iron Crown* won the "coppa Mussolini" for the best film at the Venice Biennale. (15.9.1941) It is almost impossible to detect an objective judgement of Italian films anywhere in Goebbels' utterance during the war. His point of view is too strongly restricted by rivalry and competition in his thinking, by arrogance and the rhetoric of superiority.[199] His ally's productions were the only ones in Europe that could still compete with German films.

Passages on Jewish films become exclusively dedicated to anti-Semitic propaganda. Here it ought to be unimportant whether Goebbels was actually capable of assessing films by Jewish directors and actors.[200] It is not the films that are in the foreground, but the Jewish protagonists: "how the Jew Harry Bauer sees Beethoven. Made with clumsy, brashly impertinent devices." (5.8.1937) Goebbels often and aggressively repeats that all Jewish film must be effectively anti-Semitic per se. (15.9.1936) He reviles *Judel spielt Fidel* ("Judel Plays the Fiddle") in just the same way (13.2.1938) – he found watching it a physical torment – as the documentary shots used in the anti-Semitic film *Der ewige Jude* (*The Eternal Jew*):

"And then shots for the ghetto film. Never shown before. Portrayals that are so cruel and brutal in their details that one's blood runs cold. One shudders back from all this rawness. This Jewish race must be annihilated."[201] (17.10.1939)

During the war the distinction between writing a film commentary and propagating mass murder is completely removed:

"In the evening I watch the Polish-Yiddish film *The Dybbuk* in a small group. This film is intended as Jewish propaganda. It seems so anti-Semitic that one can only be amazed how little the Jews know about themselves and how unclear they are about what is repellent to a non-Jewish person and what not. When watching this film it is suddenly clear once more that the Jewish race is the most dangerous to populate the globe, and that one may not permit oneself an mercy or indulgence when dealing with them. This rabble must be eradicated root and branch; otherwise it is not possible to bring peace to the world."[202] (18.2.1942)

"We are now masters of the German film": seizing the film industry

Goebbels and the emergence of a state concern

The industry's economic situation after 1933

The world economic crisis had placed the German film industry in a precarious financial position in the late twenties. Lack of capital and a dramatic drop in audience figures meant that of an original ten large film companies only three survived: the Universum Film AG (Ufa), the mixed Tobis studio and Terra.[203] These three dominated film production and distribution in 1933, but were faced with large deficits. It was only with difficulty that production losses could be balanced against profits in the picture house and distribution sectors.

Even before the National Socialists seized power, far-reaching economic and structural reforms were discussed inside the film industry, aiming at state co-ordinated and centralized direction for the film business, and also state subsidies. The newly created Ministry of Propaganda took up these ideas, although it met with resistance from anti-monopolistic Nazi groups and cinema owners, who preferred middle-sized firms. Other sections of the film industry feared tendencies towards a planned economy.

The first step towards the proposed joint approach by the state and the film industry was the foundation of the "Filmkreditbank GmbH" (FKB) ("Reich film bank"), on 1 June 1933, which made state credits available to the film industry at attractive interest rates. The FKB board included representatives of various major banks, the Propaganda Ministry and the big film studios. Nominally the intention was that the private financial structure of the film studios should remain fundamentally untouched, but anyone who wanted to claim the credits, which could cover up to two thirds of production costs, had to allow the film projects to be examined by various state authorities. At first this was the "Reichsfilmkammer" ("Reich film chamber"), then from 1934 the "Reichsfilmdramaturg" ("Reich film script officer") in the Propaganda Ministry. By 1935 70 per cent of feature films were already receiving outside funding. Although it was originally intended to support the hard-pressed small and medium film producers, ultimately it was overwhelmingly the big studios that benefited from the credits.[204]

By 1935 the critical position of the big studios had been stabilized for the time being by additional measures, for example import restrictions on competing foreign films ("Kontingentgesetz"), the reduction of entertainment tax, easy ways of writing off and a tax-effective grading system. In the 1935/36 season they screwed their market share for feature films up to over 80 per cent (87 of a total of 108 films), and in the distribution business it was no less than 70 per cent.[205] But even in 1936, new negative factors were coming into play, despite increased audience figures. Politically motivated boycotts led to a rapid fall in foreign sales, the loss of experts who had emigrated or been forbidden to work – technicians, directors and actors – could not be compensated for without difficulty, and excessive fees for top stars were a burden on the budget. As well as this, stricter preliminary censorship extended shooting time, increased production costs and thus reduced profits. Average production costs for a feature film rose from 250,000 RM in 1933 to 425,000 RM in 1936 and to 537,000 RM in 1937.[206] This development now threatened the large companies, which were still relatively strong financially, like Ufa and Tobis, whose deficit reached over 12 million Reichsmarks in 1936.[207] Terra and Bavaria in Munich were facing bankruptcy by early 1937.[208]

As it seemed scarcely possible to get the big studios that continued to be run privately back on their feet despite all the funding programmes and subsidies, the Propaganda Ministry was in favour of a state takeover of this industry, which was so important for state propaganda purposes. The ministry promised itself considerable cost reductions from uniform control and central direction: co-ordinated production, sensible use of studios and agreed filing should at least mean a definite end to the ruinous competitive struggle. The regime was in any case planning to tighten its economic policies, and so economic targets as part of the four-year plan were joined by the Propaganda Minister's calculations in terms of power: he felt he had too little influence on areas like management staff, organization and material planning.

Mayor Max Winkler, Goebbels' close friend and head of the "Cautio-Treuhandgesellschaft mbH" (Cautio Trust), and later "Reichsbevollmächtigter für die deutsche Filmwirtschaft" ("Reich film finance plenipotentiary") advanced to become a key figure in all transactions relating to film finance. Winkler had a doctorate of law, and had worked for various governments since 1920 as a Reich Trustee. After 1933, he used the Cautio to help Max Amann, who was all-powerful in National Socialist press and publishing matters, in the "Gleichschaltung of the press in the economic sense",[209] and brought numerous newspaper publishing houses at home and abroad under the Nazi government's control.[210] Even in 1936 he managed to exploit a diverse company structure to bring the Tobis film company into majority state ownership, via indirect shareholdings and secret purchases of some subsidiary companies ("Intertobis"), but this made no difference at first to the big studio's desperate financial situation.[211]

This very complex development of the film industry up to 1936 is covered in Goebbels' diary entries only in a very fragmented form, and so cannot be followed fully. Even so, it is clear that he started to be involved in questions of film finance immediately after taking office, with the support of his Staatssekretär Walther Funk. Thus he writes on 7.5.1933: "Discussion with (managing director Ludwig) Klitzsch of Ufa. We agree. Set up a new film bank. Production begins immediately."[212] We also discover that the "problem of a new large film studio with majority state ownership" (12.6.1936) must have been discussed in the ministry as early as summer 1936. Goebbels mentions the secret purchase of Tobis on 5.11.1936, which Funk was obviously pushing forward again. As with the politicization of the cinema in late 1936 (see next chapter), here too the link with the new, more aggressive phase of the four-year plan is obvious. On 10.12.1936 plans for direct nationalization had reached a concrete stage: "Our plans to buy up the entire German film industry are also making vigorous progress. Soon it will belong to us. But then the real work will begin." The associated "plan for central organization of the entire German film industry"[213] does not appear in the files until 14.12.1936.[214] But Winkler himself is not mentioned by Goebbels until 9.3.1937, immediately before the "Reich takeover" of Ufa, which had been in majority ownership by Alfred Hugenberg's Scherl-Verlag in 1927.

The Ufa takeover: a power struggle?

There is not a single gap in the Propaganda Minister's diaries in the weeks that contained an event that had far-reaching consequences for the German film industry. The background to this remained controversial for a long time. It was the nationalization of the largest German film company, the Universum Film AG (Ufa), which had a long and important tradition, in spring 1937.

Goebbels' was critical of film standards, and he was keen to get rid of the man – Ufa chief of production Ernst Hugo Correll – who was crucial to policy in terms of content and film production.[215] This makes it quite clear how things stood in late 1936: the minister was not at all content with the scope for action he had had so far. His circle was overwhelmingly of the opinion that it would not in fact be possible "to achieve financial and also political control, and the associated organizational and personnel changes, if Ufa's capital were to remain in private hands ".[216] The company's board still included "the formerly German-Nationalist clique put together by Hugenberg, consisting of bank directors, industrialists, estate owners, domain tenants and retired naval officers"[217] – thus a mixture that was quite particularly offensive to the Propaganda Minister. And then in February 1937 there was an escalation in the quarrel about establishing and manning so-called "Kunstausschüsse" ("artistic committees"), which Goebbels felt should take over the board of directors' right to make autonomous decisions about film-making. Here his model was Tobis, which had been gradually brought under state control by January 1937, and had an "artistic board". The Ufa management, however, did not agree with his aim of separating artistic decisions about making a film from the idea of profitability. Hence his polemic against "artistic parliamentarianism" (14.1.1937), "excessive organization" and "irregularities" continued: "Distribution and management have far too much to say for themselves." (4.1.1937)

Ufa's financial situation was desperate in early 1937. Despite enormous registered capital of 35 million RM, of which about 51 per cent was in the hands of the Scherl-Verlag (Hugenberg Group) and about 27 per cent in the hands of a consortium led by the Deutsche Bank, Ufa had a production deficit of almost 10 Million RM. This could no longer be absorbed by other sections like distribution or companies that ran cinemas.

Purchase negotiations between Winkler and Klitzsch, who was also chairman of the Scherl-Verlag, started in February 1937 minutely accompanied by Goebbels in his diary entries. In parallel with this, the Propaganda Minister had to persuade the Finance Ministry to agree to millions of marks for the takeover. But Goebbels was optimistic about this: "We are also making progress on the question of buying Ufa. Then we will have a gigantic film studio in our possession." (22.1.1937) He tried to realize his concept of "Kunstausschüsse" ("artistic committees")

even while negotiations with the Scherl management were still proceeding. This meant that Hugenberg's resistance played into his hands, as it gave him a chance to put on pressure to strengthen the negotiating position:

"Hugenberg writes me a long letter about the Ufa business. Kunstausschüsse rejected, at least for the time being. He wants to be available to do this job himself. Enough to make me laugh myself silly. Now I shall keep Ufa on tenterhooks. (The director of the "Filmoberprüfstelle" ["Supreme censorship office"] Ernst) Seeger is to subject them to censorship. We'll see who can hold on the longest. Hugenberg's lot are bad tacticians. This letter will cost them at least 3 million marks." (5.3.1937)

As with all major projects, here too Goebbels did not forget to secure Hitler's support: "He does not approve of Ufa either. It reminds him of Harzburg, where the German Nationalists were so disloyal as well. They have not changed at all. I will get the better of them about films as well", he notes on 8.3.1937, thus additionally formalizing the clash as a political struggle.

The following day he writes, apparently in the context of what Goebbels sees to be excessive financial demands and more conditions laid down by the Ufa management:

"Winkler brings me up to date on Ufa. Klitsch and Hugenberg really want to do us down. But I am not as stupid as I used to be. I instruct the press to make a major attack on Ufa. This will start today, with the reviews of the film *Menschen ohne Vaterland* ("People without a Fatherland").Ufa will be surprised. I shall now go my own way, obstinately and stubbornly, until Ufa is ours. Funk and Winkler are entirely on my side. Winkler is also a genuine business genius. Keep him warm."

The very next day he is delighted with the bad reviews that he has ordered[218] and Hitler's agreement with "my moves against Ufa". It is quite possible that Goebbels' reprisals had the desired effect: under point 1 of the Ufa board minutes for 11 March is the remark that the board " took indignant note of the review of the film *Menschen ohne Vaterland* published in the midday paper (Verlag Ullstein), and decided to institute professional tribunal proceedings against the serious accusations it contains."[219] The *Völkischer Beobachter* and the *Berliner Tageblatt* also launched massive attacks on Ufa.[220] The note "Klitsch has gone mad. Wants a fight. He can have one. I'm not afraid of him. So let's go" (12.3.1927) also suggests resistance from Ufa's majority shareholders to Winkler's conditions. This is followed by a real report from the front by Goebbels, in which the "Hugenbergers" must either "capitulate", or are "resigned and worn down" or "shot to pieces": "A sale is now just a question of time. My bombardment has worked. Klitsch totally blown to pieces." (13.3.1937)

On the day after the crucial discussion between Goebbels and Reich Finance Minister Schwerin von Krosigk[221] – 34 million Reichsmarks were finally approved for the purchase of Ufa – he writes: "Our offer has now been precisely finalized. Hugenberg has until Friday to think. He will probably accept. Then I can start work. Funk is really pulling his weight." (18.3. 1937). Then Goebbels was able to proclaim victory on 20 March:

"Ufa finally bought. Hugenberg held out to the last minute. But it was no use. Winkler has delivered his masterpiece. I am very grateful to him and Funk. All the partners worn down. This means that I have an instrument in my hands with which I can work."

The purchase price for Scherl's shares was 21.25 million RM, the nominal value of the shares, which was no longer realistic. The Deutsche Bank holding was taken over at a rate of only 67 per cent. At first Winkler gained only a tiny majority of votes from the share transfer from the Hugenberg group on 18 March, negotiated for the Reich by the Cautio Trust, but by March 1939 he was able to increase it to 99 per cent by buying up other diversified holdings.[222]

So what new insight can we acquire about the background to the transaction from Goebbels' presentation of it? There can scarcely be any doubt that Hugenberg really was interested in selling his film interests. The German Nationalist politician was well aware of Ufa's precarious financial position. Given the pressure and threats from the National Socialists against a privately run Ufa, he could scarcely see any further chances of profit for himself. Indeed, the "long-standing majority shareholder had to see selling his Ufa package as opportune, because in this way he avoided an otherwise inevitable conflict with the Ministry of Propaganda, and was thus able to pursue his financial interests in the rearmament process that had just started without loss."[223] The generous purchase price, which was tax free, was another factor. Hugenberg's demands for compensation because of ostensible compulsory purchase were rejected by the reparations committee after the war because of his function in advancing the Nazis' seizure of power and the high honours awarded to him and Klitzsch in 1943, on the 25th anniversary of the company's foundation. Klitzsch, who retained the chairmanship of Ufa AG even after the restructuring in 1942, explained in June 1949, in support of Hugenberg's claims about the circumstances in early 1937:

"The climax was reached with the Propaganda Minister's personal demand that Ufa's long-standing production chief, Hugo Correll, who was not Pg. (party member), should be dismissed. The same applies to the whole board. Both demands were rejected. This meant open war. … In this situation I went to Dr. Goebbels to face up to him. It was clear in a very few minutes that the assumption was true. Dr. Goebbels wanted to take over Ufa. The negotiations, which started under heavy pressure, then also quickly achieved the end desired by Dr. Goebbels. The purchase price agreed in this process did not correspond with the internal value of the business."[224]

But on more precise analysis, even Goebbels' martial description and extremely stylized "fight" rhetoric does not indicate a fundamental refusal to sell, but reflects the tough way in which the Scherl-Verlag conducted negotiations for a optimum conditions and the highest possible purchase price.[225] Passages like "Hugenberg held out to the last minute" are more indicative of the wily businessman's hard negotiating tactics than compulsory purchase by blackmail. This attitude was in Goebbels' interest when presenting himself: the tougher the resistance, the greater his own victory. Of course Goebbels would like to have brought Ufa to its knees himself. But despite all the exaggerated emphasis on his own involvement and his press "bombardment" he still confirms that Winkler and Funk played key roles. And yet there is no room for overall evaluations: it is not possible to show that there was smooth "readiness to co-operate". Nor is it true to say that "there were apparently no objections to the sale from the leading committees within the big studio."[226] Because the material written by Goebbels, the only contemporary source about the course of negotiations, did not completely exclude the possibility that Hugenberg and Klitzsch were even prepared for a time to allow the sale to collapse. They certainly do not suggest an apologetic rehabilitation of Hugenberg either.[227]

The rest of the purchase manoeuvres ran a less dramatic course. Contrary to the original plan – "we want to buy (Terra) first. And then it will be Ufa's turn" (23.1.1937) – the distribution and production firm Terra was not re-established as Terra while Terra Filmkunst GmbH until the middle of the year, after a restructuring and incorporation of parts of the big Tobis studio that were in deficit in June 1937.[228]

Goebbels had already gained some influence over Tobis, the second-largest German film company ("I shall take Tobis very much under my wing", 6.2.1937), even before the purchase by Cautio, which was not completed until 1939. Winkler first allowed the run-down Bavarian film company Bavaria to go bankrupt. "Bavaria must go bankrupt, and then we shall take it over", was Goebbels' summing-up of the trust's plans on 17.4.1937. Winkler had not intended to re-establish the Munich production site as an independent company, but then had to yield to pressure from the Munich Gauleiter Adolf Wagner, who could quote Hitler's express wish that Munich, the city of art, must also have extensive film production facilities. After some attempts at intervention by Bavarian state and party offices (including one by the Bavarian Finance Minister Siebert, 30.7.1937), who wished to bring Bavaria under their own control, the company was refounded as Bavaria Filmkunst GmbH in February 1938.[229]

After the Austrian "Anschluß" in March 1938, Winkler started to build up independent film production in the "Ostmark", using Austrian offshoots of the big Tobis studio that had already

been secretly bought up, including the Tobis Sascha AG with its extensive distribution company. Then Wienfilm GmbH was founded in December, intended to produce about 15 feature films per year.[230] The firms, now directly owned by the state, had to be supported with budget funds or state credits. Subsequently Goebbels announced on 26.6.1937 that the Film Credit Bank, established to support the weakened private film companies, would be abolished as it was now superfluous to needs. The nationalization process was largely kept from the public before 1941.[231]

The film industry's economic situation was slow to improve after nationalization – a source of concern for Goebbels.(10.10.1937) Production costs remained high, because the restructuring measures and organizational reforms caused a lot of slack periods and losses through friction at first. Tobis in particular found it impossible to get rid of its deficits in the early stages. Winkler's further aim, mentioned by Goebbels even during the takeover transactions in 1937 (17.4.1937, 14.10.1937), was therefore to set up a state holding company and syndicate for the film companies owned by the Reich. Bringing the individual elements even closer together was intended to make it easier to rationalize increasingly, to finance expensive research into film and sound techniques, to co-ordinate the studios, to reach agreement about film personnel, especially the casting of actors, to promote exports and to balance losses against the different profit levels.

The independent production firms that still existed did largely undertake commissions for the large companies, but Goebbels felt that they were undesirable profiteers from the film boom that started after the outbreak of war, and also competed with the state firms when engaging stars and directors. It was impossible to reconcile their existence with his desire for overall control of production.[232] Several entries even in the thirties indicate that Goebbels and Winkler intended to cut out these private firms. Finally Goebbels proclaimed on 9.5.1941: "We have now decided to buy up the private producers completely. They are no longer a stimulus, and they are simply raking in money on the basis of our work success. They must all be gone by 1 September." The ground was withdrawn from most of the independent companies with the aid of a order by the Reichsfilmkammer dated 6 June 1941, providing for re-licensing all existing film companies. They were then taken over and brought together by Cautio, and re-established as another state firm, called Berlin-Film GmbH, on 2 September 1941.[233]

Max Winkler, who was appointed Reichsbevollmächtigter für die deutsche Filmwirtschaft after the nationalization process was concluded, was intended to make sure that capitalist production forms were maintained in the state business in future. He had immense powers in terms of economic and personnel questions, and his reports formed the basis of statements about the film industry in the Propaganda Minister's notes. Goebbels occasional distrust of Winkler's policy, which was directed at economic soundness and profit, and of the primacy of financial considerations in the production sector, did not surface until 1942.

Further concentration by 1942

After the beginning of the war, numerous diary entries record Goebbels' great relief that the cinema boom did not collapse completely, as some people feared, but went through another major upsurge ("The financial success of our films is absolutely amazing. We are making real war profits", 21.10.1939). Goebbels constantly uses this to justify the costly nationalization process: "The most recent film statistics show straight profits of 35 million since the beginning of the war. And Crosigk didn't want to buy." (22.3.1940)[234]

About seven cinema visits per inhabitant per year in the 1937/38 season contrasted with over 13 in 1940, and attendance figures rose from just under 400 million to 80 million. The profits from this remained largely in Germany: the proportion of foreign films sank from 78 in 1937 (approx. 40 per cent) to a mere 18 in the first year of the war, 1940 (approx. 17 per cent).

For example, the Tobis deficit, still 1.35 million RM in 1937/38, was turned into a profit of 5.4 million in 1940/41, despite high transfers to reserves.[235] The film industry's gross box-office receipts from the outbreak of war to mid 1940 were about 70 million RM. The number of venues also rose, as a result of new buildings, modernization and increased numbers of seats in the cinemas, while Hitler's annexation policy opened up new markets: firstly German ones like Austria and the Sudetenland, then later other European countries, where local film production was restricted after occupation. American competition, which was sometimes overpowering, was eliminated in favour of German film exports.

But at the same time the war economy demanded considerable savings in terms of personnel and materials. Winkler's and Goebbels' first attempts at "large-scale centralization of the economic power of the cinema" (25. 7. 1939) and this for the formation of a "film syndicate" failed in 1939 because of objections from the Finance Ministry, which was concerned about tax income and its powers in the film industry.[236] The principle behind Winkler's organization: a holding company working independently of the Reich budget, bringing together all previous film production, and putting an end to the vertical structure of Ufa (productions, sales, cinemas) fitted in with Goebbels' repeatedly announced division of art (film production) and business (distribution, export, profitability). He had complained frequently enough even after the outbreak of war that German film production still carried "strong characteristics of an industry". (21.8. 1941) These last remains of a "seasonal and industrial business" had to be eliminated so that film could develop into "real and pure art". (25. 9. 1941)

There are isolated hints that fundamental film production problems remained unsolved despite increasing profits: excessively high production costs and long production periods, and also the extravagant use of negative film. In fact Goebbels instructions to produce lavish political films or extensive political corrections involving changes and retakes were partly responsible for this. In 1941, about 15 times as much scarce raw material were used to shoot a film about 2500 metres long.[237] Annual production sank to 67 films in 1941, and was thus a long way from the 100 that had originally been fixed. Goebbels said of a clearly concerned "detailed account" by Winkler on 8. 8. 1941: "We are producing too few films and have become too expensive. We must therefore maintain our high quality standard but reduce our cost estimates." But it needed several interventions by Winkler[238] for structural changes to be made while Ufi (see below) was being set up in terms of the very expensive interventions caused by post-production censorship from the "Reichsfilmintendanz" ("Reich film supervision"), requirements dated 28 February 1941.

Goebbels mentions what is so far the only document about preliminary work on the foundation of Ufi on 12. 6. 1941 ("We shall shortly be setting up the holding company for all German film"), a memorandum from Winkler in June 1941 entitled "Thoughts about the organization of a holding company for state film-making".[239] It is very probable that this had been planned to happen earlier than January 1942.[240] Winkler's plans must have been close to completion in November at the latest, and this at least adds an additional detail to earlier studies.[241]

Winkler did not achieve his aim until the end of 1941: Ufa was divided into three. The holding company and major state holding for the whole field of film was the Ufa-Film GmbH, founded with effect from 10 January 1942 – the name had to be retained at Hitler's express wish despite other ideas from Winkler and Goebbels.[242] The Ufa-Film GmbH included the pure film production companies Ufa Filmkunst GmbH, Tobis Filmkunst GmbH, Terra Filmkunst GmbH, Bavaria Filmkunst GmbH, Berlin Film GmbH, Wien Film GmbH and Prag Film AG, which emerged from former Czech production companies in November 1941. Alongside these was the main big studio Universum Film AG, now relieved of its film production function, with a unified cinema-house company and a neutral, central distribution and sales company (DFV) and the Deutsche Wochenschau GmbH (newsreels). So the old Ufa AG ran all sections except film production, which meant that Ufi was divided into a purely production and a financial sector. Goebbels' Staatssekretär Leopold Gutterer chaired the Ufi board, which contained representatives of the NSDAP, the film industry, the Reichsfilmkammer and the Propaganda and Finance Ministries. Instructions to management came from the Reich official responsible for the German film industry, who also filled key positions with close friends, financial experts and lawyers from the Cautio Trust.

Goebbels announced to his film people that this gigantic new trust had been set up in his last film speech on 28 February 1942, together with a "Leistungssteigerungserlaß" ("improvement performance decree") that came into force on the same day. Its first provisions foresaw dramatic rationalization at all production levels (studio co-ordination, multiple use of sets and costumes, reduction to two rehearsals only per shot and so on).[243]

On the day after the publication of the 28. 2. 1942 reorganization the diary contains only a very rough summary of the speech to the film people. But there are indications that some of his audience were not a little surprised and also disturbed by the setting up of the big studio and the rationalization measures. Clearly representatives of the Bavaria and Wien production companies saw a threat to the remnants of their independence from Berlin – a factor in terms of distance alone.

Another important requirement in Goebbels' mind for the holding company was to "neutralize" the gigantic Ufa screening facilities – they had well over 100 cinemas (13 / 16. 7. 1941).

The aim was that these should no longer be supplied exclusively by one firm and thus be forced to take its productions blindly and en bloc. Additionally, a new cinema-house company was funded to the tune of 120 million RM for the purchase of cinemas at home and abroad.[244]

Goebbels proudly announced on 22.1.1943 and 3.6.1943 that the annual overall production target for all the Ufi production companies set in February 1942 of 110 films had been met fully. At a first glance this seems to be an easily refuted falsification given that there were only 57 German films were passed for showing in 1942, but ultimately it is only a slight exaggeration. In fact the first Ufi production year (June 1942 to May 1943), to which the numerous films that had already been produced but had been held back by censorship also counted, passed extremely successfully.[245] In 1944 there were still eight films from the 1942/43 production year that had not been passed. Admittedly this success tempted Goebbels to make some entirely unrealistic plans: "I set the target for the next production year as 120 films, despite the very grave difficulties imposed by the war."[246] (22.1.1943) It would have been impossible to get anywhere near this figure, as production slumped considerably in the second half of 1943.[247] Goebbels rightly stated: "Film costs have been reduced from 1.5 million to something over one million. And so one can see that the war film production target that I named can be met." But what he did not say was that the reduced production costs per film were more than eaten up by increased fixed costs outside mere production. This meant that there was no real saving and the 1942 rationalization targets, which had been fixed very high, could not be met. Finally, the calendar year 1944 saw an annual production (!) of only about 60 films, because of inadequate production capacity, lack of staff and specialist workers as a result of "combing out campaigns" as well as a shortage of unexposed film. And Goebbels' plan to have German-language films produced by the French company Continental Films in Paris, which Ufi owned, had also come to nothing.[248] A lack of adequate copies meant that the production guideline for 1945 was only 46 films, because, as Goebbels admits on 11.11.1944, "we still have a hundred films in reserve from this year's programme." Total contrary to his announcement, the German film industry was not coming to terms with the "war-related difficulties" of "Total War".

It was not possible to implement Goebbels' intention that the profits from the film business should "also immediately benefit film itself or at least cultural life".[249] (8.8.1941) Despite his praise for Winkler's skills in protecting some of the surplus from high war taxation,[250] it proved possible to retain only 18 million RM after tax from profits given as 155 million RM in 1942/43 and 175 million RM in 1943/44.[251] On 22.1.1943 he then also concedes: "Our financial profits are enormous; but they do not really make their full effect because we have to bear an enormous tax burden. But that is the way of the world in wartime."[252]

In this context, Goebbels constantly repeats his view that for national-political and financial reasons the film industry has to be "exclusively in the hands of the state"[253] (12.6.1941): "Despite the war, the film industry is flourishing in an extraordinary fashion. How fortunate it was that I took film over for the Reich a few years ago! It would be dreadful if the high surpluses that the film industry now generates were to benefit private enterprise." (22.1.1942) Winkler on the other hand did not exclude the idea of reprivatization after the war. But Goebbels insists categorically that suggestions "that the German film industry could be reprivatized some time or other" are "naïve thoughts: for as long as National Socialism is in charge and I am in my place there can never be any suggestion of it."[254] (21.5.1942) Goebbels supported Winkler's resistance to increasing municipal control at first, but rapidly changed his mind when Hitler spoke out in favour of "local communities owning cinemas" under the influence of Bormann and the Party Chancellery.[255] (24.7.1943)

Arbitrariness rules

Personal presence at every level

The nationalization process starts in autumn 1936, and Goebbels' writings begin to provide evidence of his wide-ranging interventions in film production and the commercial policy of the film companies. Hitherto the boards of the various businesses had made the decisions exclusively, but now the Propaganda Minister took over.

Very few direct interventions are recorded for the period before spring 1937.[256] Usually it was a matter of discussions with Ufa general director Klitzsch, who kept his firm's dealings with the new rulers in his own hands from the outset,[257] for example when faced with Goebbels' demand that the Ufa production chief Ernst H. Correll should be replaced, or questions about film production. Wide-ranging processes like "Aryanization" of the film industry and the emigration of numerous film artists, technicians and directors were largely complete in 1933/35. The Ufa board dealt with the dismissal of Jewish employees and also decided on specific cases just a day after Goebbels' first film speech in the Kaiserhof hotel on 28 March 1933 and the subsequent discussions between National Socialists and representatives of the film industry[258] which affected Erik Charell, Otto Wallburg, Wilhelm Thiele and Ludwig Berger among others. Peter Lorre, Conrad Veidt, Elisabeth Bergner and Fritz Kortner had already gone into exile. Many firms tried to get Goebbels to make an exception for some especially important artists, as is also said to have happened in the case of the legendary Ufa producer Erich Pommer.[259] Goebbels notes only isolated direct interventions from artists.[260]

Until nationalization the Reichsfilmkammer had managed to seize some powers for itself and to regulate film industry questions by decree. Thus Goebbels was occasionally passed over by Reichsfilmkammer president Oswald Lehnich, who sympathized with the industry.[261]

On 23.3.1937, a few days after the successful acquisition of the Ufa majority shareholding by the Cautio trust, Goebbels made the following announcement: "I shall now involve myself very closely in all questions affecting production and casting. I will gradually get on top of things."[262] This was put into practice on the Ufa board meeting on the following day, and a comprehensive list was announced of everything that had to be submitted to the ministry, for information or seeking permission – from film planning to engaging artists.[263]

Something of the "permanent pressure exerted by the minister and his officials on the big studios' artistic and commercial decisions"[264] was felt immediately. The phrases in the minutes and notes on documents are the same: "desired in a higher place", "as desired by Reichsminister Dr. Goebbels", "at the (express) wish of the Prop. Min.", "on behalf of the Prop. Min.", "received opinion from the Propaganda Ministry", "suggested by the Propaganda Min.". Even apparently minor points on the agenda were affected, for example Ufa's wish to engage the actor and director Willi Forst: "Herr (Reichsfilmdramaturg) v. Demandowsky, as Herr Correll tells us, has declared that he does not agree to Ufa's engagement of Forst, as Forst is a Tobis artist. The board takes note of this."[265] The following note is made on Zarah Leander's film *Es war eine rauschende Ballnacht* (*It Was a Gay Ballnight*): "Herr Leichtenstern tells us that the minister has decided that his film can be premièred any day from 15.8. onwards."[266] The company's documents contain several lists of "General Instructions" from the script officer or the director of the film department, indicating which performer or composer would be "undesirable", who was favoured and to be "used" immediately, that doubling was forbidden and to casting suggestions must be included when submitting a screenplay.[267]

This kind of detailed intervention in all spheres continues through the entries from 1937 to 1944. Goebbels draws up complete cast lists, prepares "secret lists" of performers who are worth promoting (9./10./23.6.1937), decides to ban directors from making films (Richard Schneider-Edenkoben on 25.9.1937, Hans H. Zerlett on 16.3.1940),[268] issues guidelines for salary increases (30.11.1937, 2.7.1938, 7.2.1940) and for the "engagement of film extras" (5.11. 1938), exempts film specialists from war service (5.11.1940) and personally engages foreign actors ("We must extend the types we use as well, because we will have to supply a lot more nations with films after the war", 13.6.1941). Admittedly intentions formulated in the diary were not always put into practice.[269]

The full breadth of Goebbels' obsessive interventions can only be indicated in the form of highlights: as well as working on treatments and screenplays he emphatically promoted every technical development – from colour films to cartoons –, he bought up cinemas abroad and had new studios built in Vienna, Munich and Linz, he decided which films could be shown abroad, he decided on launch times, prizes, certificates – a list that could be continued at will.

Goebbels managed to cut out producers and directors almost completely when it came to casting ("Harlan shows me tests for his new film. I decide on Dahlke and Liebeneiner", 3.4. 1937).[270] While Goebbels came very close to forbidding the engagement of Zarah Leander, who was later a great box-office draw,[271] he foisted the obviously entirely incompetent Spanish diva Imperio Argentina on to the company because Hitler had given orders that the actress "should be acquired for the German cinema".[272] The resulting production, *Andalusische Nächte* ("Andalusian Nights"), was a resounding failure and remained her only film in Germany.[273] During the war and after the Reichsfilmintendanz had been set up the interventions did not become any less frequent, but actually occurred more regularly.[274] Goebbels used his "casting supremacy" without any apparent consideration for the prevailing political circumstances and other strains. Only a few days after the assassination attempt on 20 July 1944, which could have meant the end of Hitler and Goebbels, we again find him casting even the tiniest supporting roles.[275]

Nationalization also gave the Propaganda Ministry access to foreign subsidiaries of the film companies, in many of which there were still a lot of Jewish employees – some displaced by the seizure of power in Germany, but some who had been born there. They were affected by the "Reichskulturkammer's" "Jew elimination campaigns" in spring 1937, but Goebbels also had his eye on them: "We must eliminate Jews in Tobis and Ufa abroad. (Staatssekretär) Funk is too lax in these matters."[276] (9.5.1937) But he met with some difficulty over this. "Eliminating Jews" in foreign subsidiaries of the film companies was in fact "more difficult" that eliminating "those within the Reichskulturkammer, because of the international effects", noted Goebbels on 9.6.1937. He then clearly tried to run foreign sales of German films via the NSDAP's foreign organization, rather than through the company branches, so that he could shut some of the Ufa and Tobis branches if he didn't manage to force out the Jewish employees. (11./30.9.1937) In December 1937 he is still recording "great difficulties" in "Aryanizing German film exports" (9.12.1937), justifying the lack of desired success by the fact that it was a "very complicated area". (9.2.1938)

The minister was also strictly and personally in charge of promoting so-called new blood, i.e. the training of actors and directors. Goebbels retained the right to decide about every training contract and every first film, and he regularly checked screen tests until shortly before the end of the war.[277] He appointed Reichsfilmdramaturgie employee Frank Maraun to be director of the training school in February 1942,[278] always corrected his monthly reports meticulously and high-handedly laid down training guidelines. Maraun was informed by Goebbels' office when the minister had reached his decisions about screen tests:

"The minister decides as follows: voice thin, already fairly old for a beginner, face too broad, waist too fat. Acting potential cannot yet be predicted. Receives a training contract."[279]

Goebbels evidently already recognized Wolfgang Staudte's talent on an occasion like this ("The minister decides as follows: Staudte is capable of making a full-length film")[280] and indeed picked out Hildegard Knef as well: "She is nice. But she has to have an operation on her nose. Approved for six months. Then make a new text and submit it with this one."[281] These "recruitment questions" often trigger Goebbels' harshest criticism about the use of actors and the film companies' personnel policies. The Propaganda Minister had to realize that despite vigorous advances[282] – for him the "recruitment question was a crucial problem affecting our entire film policy" (16.5.1942) – his maxims were repeatedly ignored by the production chiefs.[283] Maraun noted, on the occasion of an outburst of anger by Goebbels in June 1943:

"The minister was also strictly opposed to a young director … being given a young actress. He said experience had taught him he was always right about this. … He was now simply giving an order and was not prepared to argue further about such fundamental matters."[284]

The Reichsfilmdramaturgie: control without a guiding plan

The Reichsministerium für Volksaufklärung und Propaganda ("Reich Ministry for Public Enlightment and Propaganda") was established on 13 March 1933. Shortly afterwards, on 14 July 1933, the Reichsfilmkammer (RFK) came into being. The RFK was intended to be an organization for everyone – entrepreneurs and employees – working in films, implementing National Socialist ideology. Unlike the managing ministry, its function was administrative. Goebbels was also concerned that films and culture should not be swallowed up by the Kampfbund für die deutsche Kultur, which was run by his opponent Alfred Rosenberg.[285] Anyone who was not accepted by the Filmkammer or the Reichskulturkammer (RKK), founded on 22 September 1933 – as an umbrella organization for the individual arts sections – was not granted a work permit. Thousands of artists emigrated abroad; film boycotts, demonstrations of "popular rage", particularly against films by Jewish directors and actors, were the order of the day.

The new Ministry of Propaganda took over the film department from the Reich Ministry of the Interior, along with many other powers. The department was small in terms of staff, with first three then later five main sections. Goebbels' intention was that it should not be an administrative but a planning and management department, creating an institutional link between the Propaganda Ministry and the individual film companies, so that the German cinema could be "centrally directed and assimilated into the leadership's political planning".[286] An official brochure written by Goebbels' adviser Georg Wilhelm Müller stated that the film department "had

14. Hildegard Knef, discovered by Goebbels in 1941: has to have an operation on her nose.

the task of directing, supervising and guiding German film-making, financially, technically and artistically".[287]

The Reichsfilmdramaturgie's responsibilities as one of the main sections of the film department lay mainly in the preliminary censorship of proposed feature films.[288] The Reichsdramaturgie evolved from the script office of the Reichsfilmkammer. The new department derived its powers of determining and controlling the subject and content of feature films from §2 of the cinema act of 19 February 1934.[289] The costs that could be caused by a ban or compulsory revision of a film had previously even led some of the film industry to demand financial risk reduction.[290] The film companies had to submit their feature film proposals in the form of an outline or short summary to the Reichsfilmdramaturg, in order to gain permission to write a screenplay and finally to shoot the film. The script officer could then use this information on subject and title to call in screenplays, reject them or classify them as "worth promoting".[291]

Ufa complained in October 1934 that the script office's activities so far has led to "delays" and a "standstill".[292] And by November 1935 great confusion had also arisen because of contradictory instructions from the Reichsfilmkammer about whether it was voluntary or compulsory to submit scripts. For example, the fact that subjects had to be submitted meant that the film companies – who did not have to put forward a manuscript that was ready to be shot – showered the script office, which was understaffed and incompetent in the early stages, with enormous numbers of film treatments that no one intended to realize. They simply hoped that some of them would be classified as "worth promoting", but clearly also intended to sabotage the pre-censorship system, which was thought to be going too far.[293] The submissions of title and content were still required until they were stopped by decree on 24 November 1935.[294] But although his activities were now defined as advisory, the Reichsfilmdramaturg could still intervene in a film project or pronounce bans on his own initiative at any time. And finally, in autumn 1939 the film department also required a personal declaration from all production chiefs about the seriousness of a particular film project.

According to Goebbels' notes, the Reichsfilmdramaturgie had been unable to discharge its duties in the field of production control and above all pre-censorship efficiently in the early stages. After complaints by Ufa about persistent interventions that increased their costs, he recognised as early as 13.10.1935: "Our junior departments are not working well. Too bureaucratic. I shall intervene. Too many bans." The film companies were obviously resisting the wide-ranging intervention in production – right up to constant presence at shooting sessions –,[295] which Goebbels also mentioned to the Reich Cabinet as a reason for the first change to the "Reichslichtspielgesetz" ("Reich cinema act").[296] A few days before the obligation to submit treatments was abolished he wrote: "We are cramping the cinema's style far too much. More freedom. Get rid of the army of examiners and experts in particular." (21.11.1935)

After the outbreak of war there was a new change in the way in which pre-censorship was handled. On 23.11.1939, Max Winkler sent the production chiefs a decree signed a few days earlier by Goebbels and justified by the requirements of the war. This again provided for compulsory pre-censorship of every film project, based on the submission of a roughly twelve page treatment:

"A treatment is to be submitted to my film department for fundamental approval before work starts on the screenplay and practical preliminary work for all feature films. … The screenplay produced on the basis of the approved screenplay must be submitted again at the latest four weeks before shooting begins."[297]

This had very little practical effect in the first few months, as the Propaganda Minster had been increasingly examining film material and screenplays since 1936 anyway.[298] The Reichsfilmdramaturgie staff were now to be attached to particular fixed projects and film types, rather than to individual companies.[299] But the companies were afraid that the film producers would lose their power, and stressed that it was "impossible to control the whole of the Reich's film output from one office", which was why the "institution of the Reichsfilmdramaturgie" could "only inhibit production".[300] Goebbels confirms these predicted difficulties: "Film pre-censorship is not working yet. The companies submit so late that rejection always causes expense. I shall put an energetic stop to it." (25.4.1940) And yet in comparison with 1934/35 the new regulation was applied more rigidly and expertly during the war, and gradually led to a tried-and-tested system of reinsurance and anticipatory obedience. In Goebbels' writings the Reichsfilmdramaturgs are appearing pale and essentially out of their depth. The first appointments turned out to be spectacularly mistaken as they – like many film department employees – were more interested in furthering their own ambitions as film directors, of Party documentaries, for example, rather than supervising film production.[301] The minister had not forbidden this firmly enough from the outset.[302] There is even talk of abolishing the Reichsfilmdramaturgie on 18.5.1938. It is to be replaced by a pool from the film companies' own script departments, a "central script department".[303] With the outbreak of war and stricter control of film production he wanted to "extend our script department", not least to push political material forward in the way he wished, as the production chiefs and script editors in the film companies "are insecure in their critical abilities" (26.3.1940): "We are now appointing 5 new script editors for feature film production. They will then work under my personal supervision."[304] (27.3.1940)

There is an unmistakable tendency to shrug off personal responsibility for film failures, but some entries do suggest actual deficiencies in selecting material and in communication between the script editors and Goebbels.[305] The script department's position was also weakened by the fact that the powerful production chiefs often turned directly to Goebbels. Thus Reichsdramaturg von Reichsmeister reprimanded the Bavaria production chief, Schweikart, for intervening in the "Philine" project: "Did you have to write to the Reichsminister directly?"[306]

Goebbels formulated his ideal notion of being able to plan a film project as if on the drawing-board through the Reichsfilmdramaturgie at the Reichsfilmkammer war conference in February 1941:

"It is the Reichsfilmdramaturgie's job to prevent emerging potential errors in good time, so that correction work is not started when the film is already finished, but when it is started. In this way the big censorship job at the end of a film is reduced to a minimum, but the state's involvement in the film is maximized at the moment when work on the film is about to start in the studio."[307]

At first no one was allowed to deviate from this state control: in May 1941 a message from Winkler was passed around the film companies saying that Goebbels had given each firm the right to make five films per year without prior permission, but this was retracted only a few days later.[308]

The Reichsfilmintendanz was set up in February 1942, and this took the control procedure another step further: everything had to be approved, from a two- to three-page summary via a treatment to the screenplay with casting suggestions, by the Intendant or the "Reichsfilminten-dant's chief script officer".[309] But the script officer had to restrict himself to preparing suggestions in the form of ministerial drafts, and had no authority to make production decisions.

But in practice many people – including Goebbels himself – did not keep to this basic principle of the Reichsfilmintendanz, formulated as early as 1941, according to which there would be only a "minimum" of interference[310] after permission to proceed (direction, casting, costs etc.) and the start of shooting. The minister muses over a possible way out on 23.7.1943:

"I can see that I am going to have to make a few things easier in terms of film management. The present approach, which means that material has to be submitted in draft as well as in screenplay form, and also the fact that every cast list has to be approved by the Reichsfilm-dramaturgie has not turned out to be manageable. (Ufa-Film-GmbH production chief Wolf-gang) Liebeneiner has written to me about it in detail. I see from his letter that the present rules restrict film production very severely in terms of initiatives and enthusiasm about work. I am therefore giving instructions that film subject matter should be submitted only in the form of a short summary, which will then be approved and the production chief will retain the right to develop the screenplay properly and to cast the film. I will involve myself personally in work on the screenplay and casting only in the case of important individual projects. But this will occur only in exceptional cases."

Goebbels had threatened to dismantle the Reichsdramaturgie on previous occasions, as it had passed inadequate manuscripts. (25.2.1943) But even if this self-limitation had been intended to be taken seriously[311] – in fact Goebbels did work hard to strengthen the role of the production chiefs – there was still plenty of scope for interference by him or the script department. Goebbels scarcely took any notice at all of the many judgements on film material made by the last script officer, Kurt Frowein.

The experiment with the "Kunstausschüsse" ("artistic committees")

Precisely because he had never been satisfied by the script department, Goebbels undertook an experiment that is worthy of mention because it is almost unique in 1937. His intention was to get the matter in hand and to give the principle of higher art a boost.

Various diary entries by Goebbels and also surviving records for the directors of the film companies' production departments reflect the Propaganda Minister's increased demands for more political and propaganda films in late 1936. Here the minister's main target was Ernst H. Correll, who had been the Ufa production chief since 1928. Correll stood for a film style that did not appeal to Goebbels, and as a recognized authority and expert he also resisted a change of direction in film policy. Correll's long-running quarrel with the ambitious Reichs-filmdramaturg Willi Krause, who blamed Correll for the failure of his artistic ambitions as a director, led in autumn 1936 to intrigues by Krause and other National Socialists in the ministry against the Ufa production chief.[312] Goebbels tried to exploit the opportunity and to get rid of the "self-confident production chief with superior expertise",[313] even though, as he admitted himself, there was no competent successor available ("Out, out! But who to put in his place? Big question", 3.12.1936). On 14 December 1936 the Ufa board's working committee under Ludwig Klitzsch rejected the demand for Correll's dismissal by "influential quarters".[314]

After the failure of this attempt to adjust production management by the largest of the film companies Goebbels, who was beginning to sense Hitler's impatience,[315] had to look for other ways of influencing the choice of film material. The Reichsfilmdramaturgie could help only to a limited extent here: it decided whether to reject or allow a project to proceed, but it had neither the staff nor the powers to intervene creatively in the search for material. The board of directors still made all the decisions about choice, implementation or withdrawal of (approved) material. Even when Goebbels prescribed political lines and themes, there was no one inside the company to make sure that they were implemented with commitment. Goebbels' ideologically inspired principles were a further factor: businessmen were not allowed to make artistic decisions and commercial and artistic film production questions had also to be dealt with by separate staff.

The Propaganda Minister's attempts in early 1937 to smuggle a few artists on to the Ufa and Tobis boards or at least to place them in an advisory capacity to management are to be seen against this background.[316] The Ufa management, who saw Goebbels' request merely as a device in the argument about nationalization, resisted the idea ("artistic advisers rejected", 5.3. 1937), but the Propaganda Minster felt himself that Tobis, which was already substantially under state influence, showed "much more understanding" for the idea of "increasing artistic influence". (24.2.1937)

At the international film congress held in Berlin in February 1937, Goebbels criticized very fiercely the previous system by which "commercial people" and "film entrepreneurs" sought out material, and announced for the first time in public his "opinion that there is a place for artists on the board committees of our major film companies that make decisions about artistic questions in the German cinema".[317] (24.2.1937)

Goebbels hoped that introducing artistic committees, who were to be invested with some of the powers of both the Reichsfilmdramaturgie and the production chiefs, and decide about subjects, choice of screenplay and casting, would lead to what he considered to be better films. The members of these so-called Kunstausschüsse – mainly actors, directors, screenplay authors – also became part of their company's board. The other half of the board was made up of the commercial committee, also newly created, of the firm in question, which was to be responsible for business questions only. Two weeks after Goebbels' final discussion with Funk and Winkler about "film reorganization" (17.4.1937) the setting up of the arts committees was announced.[318] Director Carl Froelich and actors Mathias Wieman and Paul Hartmann represented the artists at Ufa, and the Tobis committee included Emil Jannings and Veit Harlan. The new system put individual art committee members in charge of certain films in co-operation with the director and the production chief, whose freedom to make decisions was greatly reduced – and this was aimed at Correll. This meant that the film artists also worked as producers – but without being responsible for the financial consequences, which was why Winkler and the Finance Ministry accepted the new institution only with considerable scepticism.

Given the fact that the division of powers was less than lucid,[319] this inevitably led to conflict with between the committee and Klitzsch, the chief of the company.[320] Froelich, the chairman of the committee, who wanted to involve himself in the current production programme immediately in May 1937, tried to set himself up as the top production chief, according to the board- and committee minutes, after having had to abandon hope of succeeding Correll after the "shift of power" at Ufa.[321]

Goebbels' regular diary comments on the work of the committees cast considerable light on quarrels of this kind and on the new system's general impracticability. Goebbels, who had the minutes sent to him after each committee meeting, started to find fault as early as 2 and 3.6. 1937: "The Kunstausschüsse are doing nothing at all or are working too slowly" or: "The Kunstausschüsse chatter instead of working." Hans Weidemann, who was also the deputy head of the film department, did not want to restrict himself to choosing material as a member of the Ufa artistic committee, but "interferes in production. Quarrels with Klitsch. I shall call him off". (23.6.1937) On 27.8.1937 Goebbels contentedly noted harmony and progress in the Ufa and Tobis committee work ("Corell agrees as well"), but he must have realized shortly afterwards that his attempts to change the direction of film production was threatening to fail. He repeatedly quotes announcements and reports of committee meetings that show a high level of ineffectiveness, with the exception of Terra. (23.10.1937) Goebbels suggests that the artists are merely trying to feather their own nests ("Jannings is just after good parts for himself").[322] (14.10. 1937) The individuals who like him could have driven the committee work and had the right sort of minds to produce innovative suggestions for films apparently were not at all keen to involve themselves in laborious, carefully planned and continuous work on the material, and were also unreliable ("Jannings comes too rarely and is too self-willed", 28.1.1938). Max Winkler

had explained the failure of the Kunstausschüsse in a similar way in February 1939: the "desire
to declare individual artists responsible for the companies' films did not work because there are
not enough suitable personalities, the more so because some of the possible gentlemen refused
to take part."[323]

But the foibles of the prima-donna like committee members were not the major problem.
The committees' activities were plagued by excessively irregular meetings, lack of agreement
and co-ordination ("They have to work more actively. And more systematically", 19.11.1937),[324]
by too many incomplete screenplays and ideas for films, and with quarrels about who was responsible for what between directors, production managers, production chiefs and the Reichsfilmdramaturgie.[325] And on top of all this, the Kunstausschüsse experiment took place during a
transitional period that was difficult anyway, with the nationalization process under way and
company organization being restructured:

"I am unhappy about the situation at Tobis. Nobody is responsible there. One mishap after
another. They all quote the ministry. And I know nothing. … The Kunstausschüsse haven't
achieved much either. Artists are completely unsuitable for practical work, organization in particular." (14.10.1937)

It is not possible to establish exactly which films emerged from the work of the committees,
but after six months Goebbels felt that his actual aim had not been achieved: "Ultimately our
films are very bad." (6.11.1937)

Goebbels' suggestion that his speeches to the committees about "mistakes and deficiencies"
in film planning could bring about a change there is easily seen through as wishful thinking
("Art committees now working better. My speech has worked wonders").[326] (10.12.1937). Even
illustrious names like Leni Riefenstahl and Heinz Rühmann, whom he took on as additional
members of the Tobis committee, did not bring about any real improvement. In May 1938 it
seemed to Goebbels that the committees had finally become accepted – he was apparently even
considering abolishing the Reichsfilmdramaturgie (18.5.1938) –, but in December 1938 he tersely announced that they had been disbanded, linking this with another proposal that came to
nothing: "I shall soon abolish the Kunstausschüsse in the film companies and replace them with
strong artistic directors." (11.12.1938) This must have happened towards the end of 1938, as
Winkler stated in February 1939 that "the Kunstausschüsse were to be totally abandoned".[327]
At the 1941 Filmkammer conference Goebbels did not refer directly to this failed experiment,
but distanced himself from his arrangements in 1937 as a deliberately transitional solution, and
a first breakthrough for artistic influence on production.[328]

The Kustausschüsse experiment, carried out against the "Führer principle", remained an episode in feature film planning that was apparently without a guiding concept. The chaotic organization of film planning in 1937/38 was bound to have consequences for film policy and the propaganda impact of the films made in the last years of peace, as will be seen. Goebbels was short of capable colleagues and reliable artists who were faithful to the Party as production chiefs.[329] If they had existed, the committees would probably never have been created in the first place.

Goebbels' "reform" and staffing policies: major aims, changing helpers

Film officials in the thirties

Goebbels addressed the abilities of people who held office and worked for his controlling instruments in the film world even more closely than their institutional and organizational development. This applied equally to the film department, the Reichsfilmdramaturgie and the Reichsfilmkammer.

At least there was continuity at the head of the Propaganda Ministry's film department in the first few years after the seizure of power: Goebbels had taken over ministry section head Ernst Seeger, an experienced administrative lawyer, who had been director of the "Filmoberprüfstelle" ("supreme censorship office") since 1924. He was not a Party member, but had proved his conservative and nationalist credentials by several censorship decisions, some of them spectacular.[330] He was more competent in terms of film finance, organization and quotas than in artistic matters, and he was head of the department from April 1933 until his sudden death in August 1937. Goebbels wanted to complement Seeger as the administrative head of the film department with deputies who were young, completely inexperienced in the field of film but fresh, revolutionary Party propagandists, some of them journalists who worked on various Party newspapers.[331] Only Arnold Raether, Seeger's first deputy, had professional experience in the film industry, as former head of the film section in the Reichspropagandaleitung, (RPL) and Ufa management employee. Following the practice of accumulating offices that was also practised in the film department, Raether also held the post of vice-president of the Reichsfilmkammer and head of the film section of the Reichspropagandaleitung. Raether became the butt of Goebbels' criticism after only a few months in the ministry. (6.7.1933) He was dismissed from his offices in the Reichsfilmkammer and the Propaganda Ministry in October 1935 – for reasons that are hitherto "largely unexplained".[332] "Raether has behaved corruptly. I shall sack him immediately. Order and decency must prevail", is the reason provided by Goebbels in his diary entry on 13.10.1935. But he could not just simply throw the long-standing Party member out. After an interlude as a member of the Tobis board Raether moved to the Cautiotrust office of Max Winkler, the Reichsbeauftragter for the German film industry.[333]

Raether was replaced as deputy director of the film department and vice-president of the Reichsfilmkammer by Hans Weidemann,[334] director of the main film department in the Reichspropagandaleitung. This Party propagandist, who also had ambitions as a painter, also performed various functions in Party institutions and organizations. In the Propaganda Ministry he devoted himself largely to newsreel work and his own work as a documentary film-maker. Goebbels seems to have been critical of Weidemann's artistic abilities at first, but was then rather more benevolent about them. In any case he supported him when Ufa had Weidemann's involvement in the propaganda film *Verräter* ("Traitors") examined. Questions put to Ritter, the director and Riedel, the script editor had embarrassingly revealed that "artistic director" Weidemann had in fact scarcely had a hand in making the film at all.[335] But Goebbels saw *Verräter* as Weidemann's own work, and on top of that thought it "brilliantly made". (30.7.1936). He said that it was all part of his struggle with Ufa: "Now Weidemann is being attacked by Ufa in the same old way. Funk has allowed himself to be influenced as well. But I will not give in." (16.10.1936)

But Goebbels came to doubt Weidemann's suitability for his actual work in the film department increasingly, and he may also have been getting fed up with Weidemann's continuing squabbles with Klitzsch and Correll – after the nationalization of Ufa. To Goebbels' taste, Weidemann spent far too much time "discovering stars". In March 1937 Weidemann submitted a wide-ranging plan for reorganizing the film industry. It suggested that the Führer principle should be followed strictly, and a kind of general directorate created, independent of the min-

16. Third annual conference of the Reichsfilm-kammer in 1937: RFK vice-president Hans Wei-demann, RFK president Oswald Lehnich, per-manent secretary Walther Funk, Goebbels (from l. to r.).

istry, with powers of decision in all artistic and financial matters.[336] But Goebbels' adviser Hanke did not pass the report on correctly, with the result that the minister jumped to incorrect conclusions: "Weidemann is offering himself as head of Ufa. That would just suit him."[337] (1.4.1937) And: "Weidemann has now been called to order as well. He will be careful." (2.4. 1937)

But then when the personnel department confirmed that in the first six months of 1937 Wei-demann had appeared in the ministry on only 64 of 145 working days,[338] Goebbels took this as grounds for firing his associate: "Weidemann cannot be kept in the ministry any longer either. He has no staying power." (26.6.1937) Hans Weidemann left the film department in July 1937, officially because of undue pressure of work and at his own request, but retained his responsi-bility for newsreels and documentary films for the time being.[339] Weidemann does not seem to have succeeded in his later role as Ufa production chief either. There is a note in the Ufa min-utes for January 1942 to the effect that after a clear overspend on the production costs for the propaganda film *Anschlag auf Baku* (*Attack on Baku*) (production chief: Weidemann) "Dr. Goebbels has ordered that Herr Weidemann should be excluded from involvement in German film-making for the time being."[340]

Seeger's post was not filled at first after his death in 1937. The new director of the Filmober-prüfstelle, Wolfgang Fischer, became acting head of the film department. The entries for this period reveal a certain sense of helplessness on Goebbels' part: he was unable to find suitable staff for a film department that was becoming increasingly disorganized and chaotic. He was clearly unable to drum up able applicants from within the Party. Goebbels noted "final" ap-pointments on several occasions, only for them to be rejected shortly afterwards.[341] This sug-gests that it was not a deliberate vacancy,[342] but an unusually difficult staffing problem. The new head of the department, Ernst von Leichtenstern, did not take office until January 1938.

Goebbels did not fare much better with the Reichsfilmdramaturgie. The first Reichsfilmdra-maturg, playwright and songwriter Willi Krause, formerly a journalist on the Party paper *Der Angriff*, joined the ministry in February 1934[343] with no film experience, but soon found a taste for the cinema. Like Hans Weidemann he was soon directing himself – under the pseudonym Peter Hagen –, making the anti-Communist *Friesennot* ("Frisians in Peril", 1935), for example. Goebbels was impressed by Krause's direction at first (9./11.11.1935) – saying he was definitely "industrious, talented and imaginative" –, but to have another associate working on films could only be detrimental to the ministry's control activities, and so Goebbels asked him to choose between script selection work and direction.[344] (13.10.1935) As Krause obviously wanted to stay in the film business, he resigned with effect from 1 June 1936.[345] Later he shamelessly foisted himself upon Ufa as a "political adviser", author and director, emphasizing his connections with the ministry.[346] But Goebbels was beginning to find Krause's work increasingly distasteful. He even mentioned possible professional debarment for Krause in March 1940.[347]

Hans-Jürgen Nierentz succeeded Krause as Reichsfilmdramaturg in mid 1936. He was also a journalist on the *Angriff* and the author of numerous screenplays and radio plays.[348] The "young poet of the National Socialist movement"[349] was another newcomer in the ranks of the "National Socialist fighters" who came to the film department from the Party's propaganda machine. Goebbels shuffled him off to run the Berlin "Paul Nipkow" television station after just under a year at the ministry. This was quite obviously another mistake by the minister in terms of personnel, as Goebbels is accusing Nierentz of being "inactive" after only a few months (9.12.1936), and he notes on 13.4.1937: "High time we had a new Reichsfilmdramaturg. Nierentz is a dead loss."

The Filmkammer had just as many people in new jobs as the ministry. The lawyer and industrial adviser Fritz Scheuermann became its first president after it was set up in June 1933. But Scheuermann, who had helped Goebbels to set up the "Filmkreditbank" ("Reich film bank"), had lost his job again as early as 18 October 1935 – ostensibly because of denunciations suggesting that he was half-Jewish and had attracted attention to himself by making anti-Nazi statements.[350] He was praised at first for his work as chairman of the Filmkreditbank board (21./27.5.1933), but Goebbels announced his dismissal in July 1935.[351] It is not possible to establish whether it was the "racial" denunciation that was the crucial factor for Goebbels or whether additional accusations of corruption played a part.[352]

Oswald Lehnich was the second president of the Reichsfilmkammer (took office on 18.10.1935), and remarks about him show that things went in much the same way. The "good and solid impression" and initial satisfaction ("Lenich is doing a good job", 23.1.1936)[353] are soon followed by constant criticism of the way in which the convinced National Socialist and economics professor is doing his job.[354] Goebbels rejects his settlement of actors' fees (8.9.1936) and criticizes him as a "film capitalist".[355] He says that Lehnich has been merely "clumsy" and "slack" in representing German interests at the Venice Film Festival. In October 1937 he wants to "push (him) out" completely. But there was obviously no successor in sight (19.10.1937), so that Lehnich was not dismissed until 30 June 1939 "at his own request".[356]

Ineffective staffing policy and personnel management and the creative ambitions of incompetent "Party artists" make it easy to understand some critical passages from autumn 1936, in which Goebbels confirms major faults in building up a film planning and production control system, for which he was admittedly himself to blame:

"And then I give the film officials, in particular Lenich, Weidemann and Nierentz, a piece of my mind. They are working as if they were private individuals, but, but still use their title. That will not do. They should be leading, not making films. Herr Weidemann discovers stars, and does no work. Their endless streams of orders are strangling the …" (18.12.1936).[357]

Goebbels wrote on 3.2.1937 that while the theatre programmes for the season were "perfectly exemplary", (but) "things are not right for films. Our people are not establishing their authority here." Statements like this were more than just a tactical justification for the planned takeover of power in the film companies, especially as the situation he is complaining about persisted in subsequent months: "Krause has written me a completely muddled letter as well. These boys just dream up theories, without doing anything practical. I must look around for some other, more reliable men." (1.4.1937) It was not until Ewald von Demandowsky started to run the Reichsfilmdramaturgie and Fritz Hippler rose to be head of the film department that the phase of hasty staffing decisions, employees of dubious competence and a control apparatus that was only half capable of functioning came to an end.

The Propaganda Ministry film department under Hippler 1939 to 1943

The person in charge of the film department was a key figure for Goebbels in wartime as well, hence the diaries tell us a great deal about the department's structural development, management practice and film policy initiatives.

Goebbels writings from 1939 to 1943 also shed light on the emergence of one of the most ambivalent figures working in the Propaganda Ministry: Dr. Fritz Hippler, who later became well known as the director of the anti-Semitic film *The Eternal Jew*. Born in 1909, he joined the NSDAP as early as 1927 and rose rapidly through the Party ranks, entering the Propaganda Ministry in August 1936. He started there by assisting Hans Weidemann with newsreel-making, until he was appointed to succeed him as director of the "Deutsche Wochenschauzentrale" ("German newsreel office") in January 1939. After Ernst von Leichtenstern moved to Ufa, Goebbels also appointed Hippler head of the film department in August 1939, and in February he additionally took over the newly created post of Reichsfilmintendant. Hippler's unusually long period in office gave the film department the continuity it needed, and was thus certainly necessary for the highly political and "most successful" period in National Socialist film policy.

Apparently Goebbels at first only wanted to make Hippler the successor of Reichsfilmdramaturg Demandowsky – and this too only on a temporary basis – as he was not yet confident of Hippler's "mature judgement" (9.6.1939) – Hippler was only 29. In the difficult weeks before and after the outbreak of war Hippler is already clearly an indispensable colleague, who not only continued to direct newsreel production, but did film work of his own: in August the propaganda film *Der Westwall* ("The West Wall"), which was about the "Siegfried Line" and compiled from newsreel material, was made under his direction, and in October 1939 he started to prepare the pseudo-documentary (smear) film *The Eternal Jew*.

Goebbels portrays Hippler, who had a doctorate in political science, as intelligent but also arrogant, "too young and also a little too saucy", and utterly obstinate.[358] Hippler's essay "Betrachtungen zum Filmschaffen" (Observations on Film-Making) is still quoted today as a basic text on Nazi filmcraft, even though he uses an orthodox film rhetoric that did not always agree with his actual programme policies.[359] Hippler also perfected the system of the closest possible agreement between the companies and the ministry in film planning, by sorting out the individual film treatments in numerous discussions with the production chiefs.[360]

Goebbels regularly blamed occasional "disorganization" in the film department on Hippler's illnesses or weak phases.[361] He was appointed Reichsfilmintendant in February 1942, but remained head of the ministry film department. He moved his office, which also included the Reichsfilmdramaturgie, to the headquarters of Ufa-Film GmbH on the Ufa studio site in Babelsberg, Potsdam. The responsibilities of the "ministerial section head, who was extraordinarily reliable in film management",[362] derived from the Reichsfilmintendant statute:

"The post of Reichsfilmintendant will be established as part of the Ufa management. The Reichsfilmintendant is responsible for general production planning, for directing the overall artistic and intellectual approach of the programme, and finally for supervising the use of artistic personnel and for training new recruits."[363]

Although Goebbels often continued to deal directly with company managing directors and leading film people, Hippler effectively became the minister's deputy for dealing with the pro-

17. The 1935 Film Ball in Berlin: Goebbels, RFK President Dr. Fritz Scheuermann, Staatssekretär Walther Funk: Filmkammer failures.
18. Film department director Hippler: too brash.

53

duction chiefs, particularly in artistic matters, and remained indispensable to Goebbels even after moving out of the ministry:

"In the evening I work on the newsreel and then I have to discuss a whole series of new film questions with Hippler. … Hippler has already worked himself in at 'Ufa-Film GmbH' and is running a tight ship". (11.3.1942)

Repeated illnesses and differences with Winkler seem to have weakened Hippler's position in 1942.[364] Goebbels threatens to remove "organizing film in the ministry", and the film department, from his brief completely. He said that Hippler was better suited "to questions of film themes and scripting, and intellectual matters" (9.9.1942, similarly 15.9.). Finally, Hippler's decline in the first six months of 1943 caused Goebbels anger, regret and helplessness. The minister clearly heard negative things about Hippler from various sides, and immediately justified his dismissal. Obviously Max Winkler had an interest in Hippler's removal as Reichsfilmintendant.[365] SS-Obersturmbannführer Hippler's meteoric rise to be head of a ministry section had started to meet with resistance as early as 1942.[366]

The hitherto unknown background to Hippler's recall in June 1943 is largely explained by Goebbels' diary entries. Hippler himself insists that the was dismissed from the ministry and sent to the front in March because he had become too friendly with some Czech Filmschaffende and because of a scandal about the screenplay by the banned author Erich Kästner for the prestigious *Münchhausen* (*The Adventures of Baron Munchhausen*) film project. But Goebbels mentions incompetence, "mishaps", alcoholism and family problems.. Finally Hippler was moved and after others of Goebbels ideas' came to nothing, he was responsible for the science section in the propaganda department of the ministry until at least 1943.[367] Officially Hippler's replacement was explained as part of a major personnel reshuffle on 1 July.[368] Goebbels made Peter Gast, from permanent secretary Leopold Gutterer's office, acting director of the film department. Goebbels' personal assistant Kurt Frowein had been already working as head of the Reichsfilmdramaturgie and successor to Carl-Dieter von Reichsmeister since March. Frowein had been a war reporter until 1940, and had made a name for himself during the western campaign with particularly offensive descriptions of black French soldiers as bloodthirsty "beasts" and "bush niggers".[369] The post of Reichsfilmintendant remained vacant, although at first Goebbels apparently had the inexplicable idea of entrusting the post to Hans Nieland, the mayor of Dresden,[370] while Winkler – after a transitional period – preferred the director Wolfgang Liebeneiner, who had just taken on the job of Ufa production chief. (27.5.1943)

Hans Hinkel versus Max Winkler

Goebbels tried unsuccessfully to find a convincing successor to fill the vacuum in the film department and the Reichsfilmintendanz caused by Hippler's dismissal, but then did not address it directly at first. The Propaganda Minister did not allow himself to be beset by doubt about the "removal of Hippler",[371] but blames him for the bad "standard of films at present" in late 1943: "At the moment we are dealing with Hippler's legacy. He was not such a good Filmintendant as I first thought." (24.12.1943) Of course Goebbels is also indicating considerable difficulties with wartime film production here. Even at the end of the Hippler era, film planning and censorship were both progressing extremely slowly.[372] The film companies were producing largely routine light entertainment that was politically desirable but very weak in terms of quality. In fact this trend could only continue, as after the departure of Hippler, and Reichsmeister, who had anyway been in office for three years, employees came into the department who were strangers to the subject and utterly naïve. As well as the low "level of films" and the decreasing production figures, the continuous destruction of cinemas in air raids was also a problem. Discipline among the film people left something to be desired as well: some film celebrities refused to shoot in Berlin because of the danger from bombs, and others were making black market deals.

As well as this, the film department remained effectively leaderless. After Peter Gast had proved himself "unsuitable" (23.1.1944), Karl Fries, responsible for foreign questions, became head of department for a few weeks in February 1944, and was then replaced by the Hanover Gau propaganda officer Kurt Parbel, already the sixth "Leiter Film" in five years. The film department's unsystematic approach after Parbel's appointment led to protests to Winkler from an Ufi company, Deutscher Film-Verleih (DFV).[373] At the same time Chefdramaturg Frowein – the head of scripts – announced that his department had come almost to a standstill with its manuscript checking due to lack of material and the fact that the post of Reichsfilmintendant had not been filled.[374]

As it was becoming increasingly difficult to examine material carefully in advance of production, and as Goebbels had in fact also promised the production chiefs that he would hold back on preliminary censorship, the Propaganda Minister and Frowein took to intervening in production again. Their reaction to films "that defied description" (20.2.1944) was to instigate greater activity in the post-production process, and to order reshoots. This led to numerous postponements, changes and delayed premières.[375] In March 1944 Winkler spoke to the Ufi management, making it abundantly clear that he intended to repudiate the constant interventions in the film-making process:

"It was said that apart from the considerable effects of the war in the air, which are making themselves felt increasingly, the state of affairs that existed before the performance improvement decree of 28.4.42 was issued threatens to return, as a result of the way in which material is developed and treated, and through interventions in productions activities. The generous assent given by the minister to the approach of requiring permission only for the material, and regularly leaving the rest of the planning process to the production staff, is not working out as well in practical terms as was intended when assent was given. He (Winkler) says that he himself, as the "Reichsbeauftragter" for film industry, sees a duty to draw the minister's attention to the great dangers threatening film-making at present. It is urgently necessary to emphasize the responsibility for this development."[376]

Clearly Goebbels wanted to counter such a tendency – however carefully expressed – to undermine the state's right to intervene in cost problems by strengthening the political side in the film sector over and above the commercial side. A few days after Winkler's observations, the minister unmistakably distances himself from and shows lack of trust in his Reichsbeauftragter, in a remarkable passage:

"It seems particularly important to fill the post of Reichsfilmintendant again, so that I can establish a counterweight to Winkler and the men behind him. I intend possibly to remove Hinkel from the office of general secretary of the Reichkulturkammer and to bestow the post of Reichsfilmintendant upon him. I need a man in the position of Reichsfilmintendant who is energetic and forceful. Frowein is good as Reichsfilmdramaturg, but he is not sufficiently on top of the technical and organizational questions, and he is still too young to be fully accepted here" (22.3.1944).[377]

Goebbels' reference to the "Hintermänner" – the men behind Winkler – is as surprising as it is interesting: surely Winkler himself was at the very top of the film hierarchy, and ultimately, who could oppose the almighty minister? As Klitzsch had been largely rendered powerless by now, Goebbels is probably referring to the purely commercially oriented management of the firms, or Winkler's close associates – lawyers, bankers and distribution specialists from the Ufi board like Friedrich Merten, Fritz Kaelber, Karl Julius Fritzsche and Heinz Zimmermann, or the directors of various major banks from the Ufa supervisory board: Johannes Kiehl (Deutsche Bank), Hans Pilder (Dresdner Bank) and Joseph Schilling (Commerzbank).

As announced, Goebbels appointed SS-Gruppenführer and general secretary to the Reichs-kulturkammer (RKK) Hans Hinkel to the post of Reichsfilmintendant in April 1944. Hinkel, who was power-conscious, and had been particularly radical in the "elimination of Jews" from the RKK,[378] tried at first to retain his post as director of the RKK and also demanded the rank of a permanent secretary so that he could be independent of Leopold Gutterer. (31.3.1944) Finally he gave up both the RKK post and the task of supervising the radio light entertainment programme, which had been transferred to him in autumn 1941, and made do with being vice-president of the Reichsfilmkammer. Hinkel took over direction of the film department from Parbel and moved his office back into the Propaganda Ministry, while the Filmintendanz personnel stayed in Babelsberg.[379]

Goebbels expected Hinkel to be rigorous in carrying out rationalization measures and also organizational and personnel reforms to benefit political film management in the ministry. The film department and the Reichsfilmintendanz were to be reactivated with new targets in terms of the film business and power politics.

Goebbels installed his permanent secretary Gutterer, whom he had recently criticized severely (17.3.1944), as chairman of the Ufi board (previously chairman of the supervisory board), "with a tremendous salary" (18.4.1944). The obvious intention here was to get him out of the ministry, where he was replaced by the more dynamic Werner Naumann. Goebbels, deliberately egged on by Hinkel, soon began to observe that Gutterer was failing in his new position: he wrote that he would "possibly go through a fiasco here as well". (16.6.1944) The minister welcomed the fact that Hinkel now stripped Gutterer of all his powers. Anyone who "lived like an idle drone", writes Goebbels, should not find this surprising.[380] (31.8.1944).

Hinkel's bid for power was bound to lead to a clash with Winkler's purely commercial policies; these were not under threat, as Winkler had no opponents in this field. In late July 1944 the new Reichsfilmintendant issued a series of drastic rationalization measures – without informing the Reichsbevollmächtigter or Gutterer – "in the spirit of the more total view of the war" (including further reduction of production costs and of the annual production requirement, overall staffing cuts of up to 50 per cent, abolition of small production sections and the companies' press departments).[381] Hinkel intended to use the special powers to control the normal course of the film business as well. To this end he intended to allow the production chief of each company, who had hitherto been restricted to policies concerning material, "to decide on all questions that are fundamentally linked with film production and its aims, or that influence this production directly". The production chief was to "receive his instructions (directly) from the Reichsfilmbeauftragter or from someone directly commissioned by him to handle the matter in question".[382] The company heads, whom Hinkel saw as allies, were to be deprived of their powers and to function merely as "business managers", with the "usual role of representing their firms in public". Ultimately Hinkel intended, as he wrote to his close friend Hans H. Zerlett, to undertake "the most brutal simplification imaginable of the whole process of production and organization, which was to have been done 10 years ago",[383] i.e. to remove the privately financed film industry from Ufi and place it under the sole supervision of the ministry.

This would mean that the complicated chain of command from Goebbels via Winkler to the boards and supervisory boards would disappear and there would be a direct command structure in all spheres. Winkler must have been particularly provoked by the fact that Hinkel, on his own authority and without bringing in the Cautio and the Ufi board of directors – although with Goebbels' approval – appointed the Nazi film functionary Heinz Tackmann to be the chief executive of Ufa-Filmkunst. After several complaints to Goebbels about Hinkel's power-seeking and general approach, Winkler finally asked the minister in September 1944 to decide whether privately financed management of the film industry by Cautio was to be replaced by direct political management. He warned insistently against a change of direction: "Taking financial management into your ministry would run counter to the arrangements that you have made so far."[384] But Goebbels shrank from taking precisely this step:

"Differences had arisen between Winkler and Hinkel about the management of film finances. I do not want to take these out of Winkler's hand despite Hinkel's efforts in that direction. Winkler is a solid businessman who guarantees to me that film finances will be managed from a commercial point of view, which one cannot yet assume on the part of Hinkel. But otherwise Hinkel has raised film production to a very high level." (27.9.1944)

The two adversaries then tried for several weeks to agree about the future distribution of powers. The result was that on 13 November 1944 an "organization plan for the German film business" was announced, providing for a separation of "film policy" (ministry film depart-

21. RFK war conference, February 1941. (Front row from l. to r.): Fritz Hippler, Carl Froelich, Goebbels, Leopold Gutterer, Berlin City President Ludwig Steg, Heinrich George, RFK vice-president Karl Melzer, Emil Jannings.

ment), "film art" (Reichsfilmintendant) and "film finance" (Reichsbevollmächtigter),[385] but essentially this confirmed Winkler's responsibilities and thus the ruling that had been made as early as February 1942. Hinkel was now responsible only to Goebbels in matters of production planning, and did not have to pass on certain instructions via the Cautio, as Hippler did, but Winkler retained control of staffing policy and "continued to control the business of the holding company. … His sphere of influence had not been reduced. Civil-law business practice remained the basis of the mediate film industry: thus Hinkel's attempt to remove Winkler from his leading position had failed; he had simply managed to make him wobble for a time."[386] Although – as Hinkel had intended – the position of the production chief was strengthened. For questions outside the production sector the organization plan provided for "an agreement with the chief executives", but in an instruction dated 1 October 1944 Goebbels granted them "management primacy" in the companies.[387]

Apart from the interesting insights we gain into the power struggle over management of the film industry, one thing in particular is remarkable: Goebbels takes the side of Max Winkler and his "commercial point of view". This marks an end to all the intentions – a constant part of the rhetoric since 1933 – for fundamentally changing the capitalistic structure of the film industry – and thus removing the source of persistent discontent. It also meant an end of removing "Hintermänner" (men behind other people) and "film capitalists", overhauling the film industry's personnel from a National Socialist point of view" (21.4.1944) and having the whole sphere of film managed directly by the ministry, without considering economic factors. Film's successful balance, with a turnover that was still 460 million RM in the first six months of 1941, was quite clearly an argument for Winkler's system to date. But when Hinkel even advanced as far as becoming chairman of the Ufa supervisory board in March 1945, most cinemas were already in ruins.

Personnel policy as a revolutionary element

"Far-sighted personnel policy", Goebbels noted on 30.7.1937, "is the most important thing in all fields." And he regularly repeated in the years leading up to the end of the war: "Personnel policy is at the heart of every piece of work. Success comes from people and not from things." (16.10.1941) The minister followed Nazi ideology very closely by being obsessed with people and their responsibility for certain fields. Goebbels tended to personalize structural deficiencies to great extent, and one of his favoured ways of solving problems was to change the individuals performing the function. Fluctuation among his employees and in his sphere of influence was correspondingly high.

The "personnel field" is the most important feature of the "reform programme" for the film sector that he presented over the years. On 12.10.1941 he states:

"In terms of material the film has so far followed our authoritarian lead, but in the personnel field it has remained liberal to a certain extent. This must stop. I can only reform the film as I wish if it is changed from top to toe."

The film, he writes as early as 21.8.1941, still has "the characteristics of an industry, and it will take some time until I have got it to shed the last vestiges of a past time".[388] His statement on 16.4.1942 sounds even more insistent:

"In the evening I have a very serious discussion with Hippler about personnel policy in film, which in many cases incurs severe displeasure. The film still carries the decadent signs of the system era to large extent. There has actually been the least possible cultural reform in this sphere. We have approached film a little too hesitantly, and have let the film capitalists prevent us from making the necessary interventions. We must catch up as quickly as possible on what we failed to do last year. The most important reform, here as elsewhere, will be needed in the personnel field, as it is people who shape things and not things that shape people."[389]

These constant attacks on a film industry that was still "middle-class" are the clearest admission of his own failure. He certainly also tried to use his own rhetoric to counter the impression of complete lack of progress or resignation in the face of film management's inertia.

Goebbels had the impression that the wrong people were being given a chance at all levels: in the studios, on the boards and especially in the fields of casting and recruitment policy. (21.8. and 12.10.1941) He said that this almost industrial consumption led to "idle periods" and cost "enormous sums of money".

Personnel was the concrete level on which Goebbels could justify his ideological polemics about the contradictions between commercial interests and artistic freedom, between mass production and individual works of art, between the "characteristics of an industry" including mechanical casting policy and desires for an artistic élite. He gleaned not a little of this from speeches and articles by Wolfgang Liebeneiner, a highly esteemed director who was also talented in the field of theory.[390]

Thus the minister's access to the "decision-makers" had to be at the highest level of production.

The film élite in the Nazi state: failures, artists, capitalists

One group of people in the film industry was particularly important under National Socialism: the "artistic managers" and commercial operators who were completely responsible for any film artistically and financially. Goebbels had to gather a particularly competent and loyal band of followers around him here.

As we have already seen, he was inclined to criticize his own film staff, and that makes it possible here too to identify some weaknesses in the Nazi film production machinery.

Immediately after nationalization in 1937 Goebbels' euphoric and power-crazed comments are full of references to "cleaning out" and "tidying up" at all management levels within the big film studios. (20.3.1937, 6./17.4.1937) But he did find that there were limits to his intention to "get rid of" all the "German-nationalist Party blokes" and "Hugenbergs". He tersely announced the appointment of Hugenberg's former deputy Emil Georg von Stauss, an influential banker, to be chairman of the admittedly very different Ufa board (17.4.1937),[391] which now also included Carl Froelich, Hans Weidemann and Karl Ritter, along with Paul Hartmann, added at Göring's request. (28.3.1937)

The function of the production chief seemed much more important to Goebbels, as he worked with the script experts and screenplay authors on selecting the programme before it reached the Reichsfilmdramaturg. This is vividly confirmed by the surviving minutes of Bavaria production chief Schweikart's discussions with his script department.[392] This is the only way in which it is possible to understand the replacement of Correll at Ufa, which was pursued with such determination – while Goebbels found the Ufa general director Klitzsch so professional that for a time he apparently considered making him boss of Tobis as well. (14.10.1937) Correll finally resigned in February 1939, after Ufa, with Winkler's approval, had agreed to a generous settlement in the form of a contract to produce six films. Goebbels, who suspected secret agreements between Max Winkler and Ufa, managed to have the deal cancelled.[393]

Goebbels wanted production chief Fritz Mainz "out of the way" at Tobis Filmkunst: "He is a philistine and a proletarian as well. He must be replaced by a Nazi." (27.4.1937) After an elaborate search (8.5.1937, 10.6.1937), Mainz was then replaced not by a party man, but by the director Hans H. Zerlett, a close friend of Hans Hinkel. But Zerlett obviously had difficulty in establishing himself as an artist within the firm,[394] and gave up again in late 1937. Goebbels then reduced the demands he made on a politically immaculate production chief: "We must put a new production chief into Tobis. I definitely am going to take someone from the Party now. The questions to be dealt with here are largely of an organizational nature." (31.7.1938)

In February 1939 the Minister announced a great "reorganization of German cinema" staff at Tobis, Ufa, Terra, Bavaria and Wien-Film, which he said would be final: "I don't want to change anything else now. I shall announce it on Wednesday." (12.2.1939) But the actual choice looked quite different. Reichsfilmdramaturg Ewald von Demandowsky took over Tobis, Terra producer Alfred Greven, whom Goebbels had intended to put in the Terra post, was to direct Ufa production. The Minister had wanted Emil Jannings for Ufa, but he dropped out at the last minute. Directors Hans Schweikart and Karl Hartl took over Bavaria and the newly founded Wien-Film respectively. Only the new Terra boss Peter Paul Brauer could be considered a died-in-the-wool Party activist.[395]

A few months later the picture had completely changed again: Greven had been able to hold his own for only a short time at Ufa, and had been replaced – ostensibly "because of his pro-gramme policy",[396] Goebbels speaks of "intolerable conditions" (27.5.1939 – in May by Minis-terialrat Ernst von Leichtenstern, till then director of the film department in the Propaganda Ministry.[397] But then the inexperienced Party man Leichtenstern, former head of the culture de-partment of the RPL in Munich and ex marine officer also fell victim to Goebbels' negative judgement on several Ufa films in the first half of 1940. Goebbels wanted to be rid of him as early as January 1940 (24.1.1940), but obviously changed his mind when no replacement was in sight: "Leichtenstern's failure at Ufa is in fact not as catastrophic as I had feared." (7.3.1940) It was not until the production chief had provoked serious resistance within the firm that was unpleasant for the Minister ("Ufa does not want to do as it's told", 7.5.1940; "trouble at Ufa again. Leichtenstern/Ritter", 9.8.1940) that Goebbels returned to his original intention.[398] (13.8.1940). Otto Heinz Jahn was put in temporary charge of Ufa productions in October.[399] Party man Brauer also had to hand Terra over to former Ufa script manager Alf Teichs in No-vember 1940. (14.11.1940) Hans Schweikart asked to return to direction as early as June 1939, but Goebbels wouldn't agree as there was no successor.[400] (25.6.1939) Although the Minister expressed his own doubts about Schweikart's suitability in the following year (20.11.1940), the director, who was also much admired by Hitler, was not replaced by his deputy Helmut Schrei-ber until May 1942.[401]

As the production chiefs had such an important role to play it seems appropriate to look at some of them who were closest to Goebbels, particularly during the war years. People like Ewald von Demandowsky and Wolfgang Liebeneiner actually carried out film policy – and were at the same time the reason why Goebbels ideals about the film industry were never real-ized.

Along with Fritz Hippler, Ewald von Demandowsky,[402] editor of the *Völkischer Beobachter* until 1937, then Reichsfilmdramaturg until 1939, crops up most frequently as the most impor-tant colleague and regular visitor to Goebbels' countless discussions in the most intimate circle. As the first Party man in the post of a production chief he directed Tobis Filmkunst from Febru-ary 1939 to 1945. At first Demandowsky was not able to deliver what the Minister had expected from him in terms of political dynamism and acquiescence. In fact he seems to have adapted rapidly to his new surroundings: "Asked Demandowski to keep in closer touch with us and not to do too much in literature. He is slipping too deep into pure film stuff and is thus gradually losing his roots." (13.10.1939) Thus the production chief even wanted to abandon the super-expensive anti-British propaganda film *Ohm Krüger* that Goebbels had demanded. (5.3.1940) Such weaknesses and other "mishaps" in film planning even brought Goebbels, in June 1940, to threatening Demandowsky with being called up into the Wehrmacht. But from mid 1940 Tobis developed and came to be the film studio with the highest proportion of political and "nation-al" material and war films.

This fact seems to have protected Demandowsky from dismissal, despite Goebbels' criticism of the "unserious" conditions at Tobis: "Demandowsky is not a solid and systematic worker. I keep him only because so far he has had the greatest practical success, despite everything. The main thing is that good films should come along, and with him this is undoubtedly the case."[403] (3.4.1942) Ultimately Goebbels seems more concerned to be able to present a more than half-way successful politically reliable person in the companies. Goebbels remarked on Demandow-sky's five years of work for Tobis, apparently repaid with a "large sum of money in recognition": "He is the actual Nazi among our production chiefs" (28.2.1944), an assertion that he finds confirmed shortly afterwards by a showing of *Die Degenhardts*, a film that takes up "the subject of the war in the air": "Demandowsky is the only production chief who can approach political material, and usually masters it." (5.3.1944) Goebbels says nothing about the bitter quarrel, which went as far as mutual denunciation, between Demandowsky and the Tobis company managing director Karl Julius Fritzsche in autumn 1944.[404]

Demandowsky may not always have been Goebbels' closest film confidant, but ultimately it was the connection that lasted longest. Hildegard Knef, who was Demandowsky's partner for a time, even said that the production chief venerated Goebbels and that had a "pupil-teacher relationship" with him.[405]

In Goebbels' eyes Otto Heinz Jahn, the third Ufa production chief after Correll's dismissal, after Alfred Greven and Ernst von Leichtenstern, also failed. His position was not made permanent until early 1942, and Goebbels complained on 13.5.1942 that he had transformed Ufa into a "mediocre middle-class company" when writing about the slow pace of production in the Ufa studios.[406] But it was not just the companies' regular performance reports based on completely unrealistic quota figures, it was the quality of some Ufa films as well that must have moved Goebbels to the insight that he had to undertake "a staff change at production management level at Ufa, and definitely as quickly as possible. ... Ufa is well on the way to losing its world-class reputation." (1.6.1942) Only a few days before Hippler had threatened those responsible that the poor figures would be "recorded in the minutes and shown to Reich Minister Dr. Goebbels, who would doubtless very quickly carry out wide-ranging staff changes in the production firms that very often came out in last place".[407]

Although Goebbels saw that replacements were needed,[408] Jahn and the other production chiefs remained in post. It is not until 28.2.1943 that we read again: "The most recent film productions were not particularly good; I must try to get this sorted out again. Staff changes in the whole film field are inevitably going to be needed." But he adds: "But who do you put in if you haven't got anyone!" In order to prevent "his" films from making a very negative impression he cites the "Führer" – despite the obvious contradiction to his criticism: "The Führer is full of admiration for Ufa's work. He has heard nothing but praise of our film work." (9.3.1943)

There was a major reshuffle in spring 1943, after mature consideration and a large number of names being mentioned and then rejected. First of all Ludwig Klitzsch, still director of Ufa AG, which included all the old sections of the big studio except film production, was replaced by Fritz Kaelber in March, and made chairman of the company's supervisory board, which met only once a year. Klitzsch wrote to Hugenberg about his dismissal, saying that Winkler's two years of efforts "to exclude me" had been successful, but that "as far as the new arrangements were concerned (he had) a feeling that the intention at first was to make the new situation easier for me by treating me kindly."[409]

The change was rather more momentous for the production chiefs. Despite his allegedly very poor performance at Ufa, Goebbels mentions Jahn as a possible choice for Terra or Prag-Film. Wolfgang Liebeneiner finally became Ufa production chief in April 1943, with Heinrich Jonen as managing director, whose work as production chief of Berlin-Film Goebbels had repeatedly praised as "very pleasing". (8.12.1942, 19.1.1943) Liebeneiner was a high-profile director of well-known propaganda films like *I Accuse* and *The Dismissal*, and so this meant that once more an artist was placed in a key position for film production – though he also discharged a number of state functions.[410] But the recruiting of artists and directors was to continue: according to the entry for 27.5.1943, Goebbels and Winkler were planning to make Liebeneiner Reichsfilmintendant and offer his director-colleague Veit Harlan the post of director of production for Ufa. (27.5.1943) Heinz Rühmann was under consideration as Terra production chief at the same time,[411] and from March 1944 comedy director Emmerich W. Emo was heading production for Prag-Film,[412] a post for which Goebbels had at first selected Zarah Leander's preferred director Rolf Hansen. (20.7.1943) Together with the production chiefs who were already in office, Karl Hartl (Wien-Film) and Alf Teichs (Terra-Filmkunst), who were also former directors, there was considerable recourse to directors to occupy the key film programme policy posts. "Political" candidates from the Party machine or the ministry were discussed briefly (Hippler and Frowein for the Terra job), but after Leichtenstern's failure at Ufa none of them made it. Goebbels must finally have come to trust the grouping he ended up with, as he writes on 29.7.1943:[413]

"I talk over the question of treating film production more flexibly with Frowein. I can no longer concern myself so much with film production details. So the production chiefs must take more

22. Actor and director Wolfgang Liebeneiner (1938): "young, fanatical, ambitious, industrious".
23. Hugenberg and Klitzsch receive high honours from Goebbels on the occasion of Ufa's 25th anniversary on 4 March 1943.

responsibility, but will also have to be given greater powers. The Reichsfilmdramaturgie should essentially concern itself only with the film projects that are important to the state."

Although this intention, which was also reinforced in subsequent remarks,[414] came into effect only partially and was followed somewhat arbitrarily by Goebbels, the production chiefs became an exclusive circle, with separate working meetings, high salaries, privileges and regular discussions with the Minister, at which Goebbels issued his "guidelines" to them.[415]

Goebbels felt that Liebeneiner represented the correct mixture of "young, modern, ambitious, industrious and fanatical" (11.6.1937) and he was showered with honorary titles like "Staatsschauspieler" ("state actor") and "Professor". Now Goebbels expected a move away from mass production and a breakthrough to films with greater artistic input. "Liebeneiner and Jonen thus have the job of doing justice to the name of Ufa and again producing high-calibre films. The company has been seriously discredited by developments over the last two years." (17.4.1943) Goebbels dedicated a great deal of time and energy to the "Ufa reform work". He was soon able to report on "outstanding plans, all aimed at systematizing our new film work" (6.5.1943) and new ideas of Liebeneiner's for bringing on fresh directors: "A great deal can be expected of him in the future." (17.5.1943) Goebbels shifts the blame for the films that still continue to be merely average on to Liebeneiner's predecessor Jahn.[416]

And so the Propaganda Minister must have found it all the more painful when he saw the first signs that Liebeneiner did not have any ideas for resisting Ufa's faceless mass entertainment either. Critical notes can clearly be discerned after a long discussion with the production chiefs:

"But Liebeneiner must involve himself more closely in the films that he plans. Such bad films produced under his management, even though this is only formally the case, bring discredit on Ufa, but on him as well. I am giving Liebeneiner absolute authority to assert himself against the refractory directors; I hope that he will do so. He gets too involved in general talk and has already earned the nickname 'Promise Me Nothing' at Ufa."[417] (3.2.1944)

Towards the middle of the year reports from Ufa and other companies started to accumulate that suggested no hope of improvement in the quality and number of films, which caused Goebbels some "worry". He felt that Liebeneiner too had "in no respect met expectations". (10.4.1944) But Goebbels obviously lacked the will to confront this critical situation with anything other than the usual solutions: "I will now have to make a large number of staffing changes so that I can at least prevent our film companies from coming up with excessively dilettante productions in future." (19.5.1944) Finally it was company managing director Jonen, but not Liebeneiner, who was also rated highly by Hitler, [418] who was dismissed, although in the Ufi management chairman Kaelber and Tobis director Fritzsche made Liebeneiner responsible for the faltering Ufa production programme. [419] But Hinkel obviously tried to exploit Liebeneiner's weakness – he offered "him a 'lift up' as far as questions of direction and casting were concerned" – by suggesting the faithful Party functionary Heinz Tackmann to Goebbels as Jonen's successor: Tackmann would "complement Liebeneiner outstandingly and be the first National Socialist film boss in the whole area of film".[420]

Hitler had spoken to his Propaganda Minister on 10 November 1936 about some recent bad films, and Goebbels tried to justify himself: "We just don't have the people, the NS artists. But they will gradually emerge." But the Party managers with artistic competence that Goebbels was so desperately looking for did not exist.

Goebbels' relationship with the film world's commercial and administrative experts remained contradictory. The diary entries largely confirm the "exemplary loyalty of top management",[421] and the frequent staff changes can certainly "in no case" be explained "by opposition in principle to the NS regime",[422] but latent resistance is definitely present. There is still a trace of distrust and antagonism between Goebbels and the company managements, even disregarding any empty rhetoric. It seems unlikely that the staff fluctuations and disputes were simply part of standard behaviour within a private-capitalist production system. A close look at the Minister's staff planning and emergencies is much more redolent in places of makeshift solutions, half-measures and helplessness. Even his plan to "delegate a few reliable people from my inner working group to film so that they can sort things out there" (16.7.1942) did not come off.

Ultimately the Propaganda Minister had no alternative to the "failures" from the Party, to the capitalist experts and unreliable artists. The Ufi management had a "clear excess of commercial experts",[423] including as it did in 1944 Ufa AG director Fritz Kaelber, Tobis company managing director Karl Julius Fritzsche, distribution expert Heinz Zimmermann and ex-banker and Winkler confidant Friedrich Merten. All this – along with the strictly private financial arrangements imposed by Winkler's Cautio – was at best tolerated by Goebbels. But it was all too clear that the system was efficient. And so Goebbels refused to support the one concrete attempt at reform by SS Gruppenführer Hinkel.

But there are other unmistakable signs in Goebbels' writing, alongside the critical remarks about his relationship with the nationalist "film capitalists" and old élites: outwardly in the form of high honours and public praise awarded to Klitzsch and Hugenberg, and through scattered references in the notes. Goebbels even expresses "gratitude and recognition" to Klitzsch for "large-scale reorganization of the German film business" on 17.9.1941. And there are some emphatically positive words about a "long but interesting speech", larded with anti-Semitic slogans, by the former Ufa manager at the 25th anniversary of the foundation of Ufa, alongside remarks about past "Jewish-American domination of the German cinema". Then when Hugenberg was honoured with the "Adlerschild" ("eagle medal") and also generally treated "in an exceptionally friendly and courteous fashion" (5.3.1943), reconciliation with the former Harzburg Front allies and opponents in the Ufa dispute is complete: "The Führer is pleased that Hugenberg was so touched." (9.3.1943)

"The non-political days are over now, for film as well": 1933 to 1939 – the hard road to the new film

The transitional films, 1933/1934

The early stages of National Socialist film policy are only partially documented in the Goebbels entries for 1933/34 that have been made public so far, although it is scarcely likely that any major planning approaches are hidden in the gaps. In fact the fresh start in German film after the seizure of power progressed haltingly. Radio and press were given priority in the "Gleichschaltung" that was being attempted. And it was also necessary for effective control instruments to be created before any actual material could be produced. Any innovation in the creative-artistic and technical field was additionally hampered by considerable production difficulties arising from dismissals and the exodus of important actors, directors, screenplay writers, technicians and producers.

Making feature films is a slow process. It was not possible to implant an imposed production ideology and a new aesthetic for German film production over night, especially as the Nazis did not devise an approach to film before the seizure of power. In other cultural fields various Nazi leaders with ambitions about arts policy quarrelled violently, for example about questions relating to Expressionist, naturalistic or "decadent" art.[424] But in the case of film no one seemed to know what to do, expect in disputes about films to the greater glory of the Party.

It is not possible to deduce clear guidelines for a future production ideology from the new Propaganda Minster's speeches about film in 1933/34. Goebbels spoke to the film people in the Kaiserhof hotel on 28 March 1933 – one speech among many in a very few weeks. Writers, publishers, radio people and press representatives also wanted to hear something concrete. But at first the main thing was to make a clean break with the past:

"We will not even entertain the idea of tolerating a re-appearance in some disguised or open form by ideas that are being eradicated root and branch in the new Germany. Thus one break into film production is complete."[425]

Goebbels used three films that he considered exemplary – *Anna Karenina*, *The Nibelungs* and *The Battleship Potemkin* – to identify four essential guidelines: a political slant and art have to work as one, as in *The Battleship Potemkin*: "This shows that a work of art can definitely have a political slant, and also that even the worst form of political slant can be promoted if it is done with the resources of an outstanding work of art."[426] Stage plays can also be "moving" if they are translated using the correct filmic resources; to this end film has to be recognized as a work of art in its own right. Even material from the distant past, according to Goebbels, could be modern and even make a powerful impact on "champions of the National Socialist cause" (*The Nibelungs*). But he adds that it is not just convictions that make a film, but technical skills and quality (*The Rebel*).

Goebbels held "shallow and shapeless" films responsible for the crisis in film, recommended "nationalist contours" and "popular material". And if the public did not want this, then the "regeneration of public taste" had to be tackled. But he went on to say that this "public taste is not the kind of thing that goes on in the head of a Jewish director. It is not possible to form an impression of the German people in a vacuum."[427] Of course one should not "pursue conviction from dawn till dusk", but "totally idiotic social kitsch"[428] has to go as well, which in its turn is not intended to mean that "our SA men have to march across the screen or the stage. They are intended to march in the streets."[429] Goebbels criticism of unduly zealous Party films ran like this: "People 'who don't know better' believe that they have to use the National Socialist symbols to prove the quality of their convictions",[430] and he rejected "aping outward symbols" and attempts "to turn the Party programme into a dialogue".

Another less than constructive warning from the Minister was that foreign films were being taken as models to too great an extent: German films should no "not ape any old foreign film, blindly and mindlessly".[431] Barely a year later, on 9 February 1934, Goebbels was already talking about success and boasting about having "confidence of the artistic world". In terms of planning material, he once again offered nothing but a negative distinction: "… and we also don't want National Socialism to be represented by the choice of material, but by the way in which the material is handled creatively."[432]

The 1933/34 cinema programme, consisting largely of "naïve, apolitical farces and melodramas",[433] shows almost direct continuity with the last years of the Weimar Republic.[434] It was dominated by the "milieu of operetta and high society, carefree artists and travelling idlers".[435]

These were all films that were artistically relatively unrewarding, which Goebbels wanted to be things of the past. The most successful films were the mistaken-identity comedy *Viktor und Viktoria*, the Jan Kiepura film *Ein Lied für Dich* ("A Song for You") and *Masquerade in Vienna* by Willi Forst.[436] The number of essentially political films dating from this period is higher than generally assumed, on closer analysis, but this is not because film policy changed, but the result of compliant opportunism and national continuity in parts of the film industry. This applies to the melodramatic U-Boot film *Morgenrot* (*Dawn*), which was completed even before 1933,[437] and to *Grenzfeuer* ("Frontier Fire"), *Flüchtlinge* (*Fugitives*, with Hans Albers)[438] or the anglophile *Ein Mann will nach Deutschland* ("A German Wants to Go Home"), and not least to *Du sollst nicht begehren* (*Blut und Scholle*/"Blood and Soil"), a populist mixture of problem film and farming drama.[439] The Nazi press received many of these films enthusiastically, but they were not yet products of the Propaganda Ministry's suggestions or influence. They were made by small production firms, who leaped on to the bandwagon of the increasing need for National Socialist themes in film.[440] But some of these hasty productions were pretty inept, *Du sollst nicht begehren* (*Blut und Scholle*), for example, and led to conflicts between "Reichsnährstand" ("National body of agriculture") and Ufa, but also within the NSDAP.[441] National Socialist directorial skills were at first directed mainly towards countless rituals, celebrations, parades and cults of the dead. Only a few documentary films were made in 1933/34 under Party supervision or influence.[442] Ufa reacted to the new power structure even before Goebbels' speech in March 1933: additional "national" material found its way into the production programme in 1933/34. Here Ufa anticipated later demands by Goebbels with themes like "anti-Bolshevism", the "Führer principle" and colonial ideas.[443]

But in the main the transitional period was one of wait and see, characterized "one the one hand by anachronistic films, and on the other by anticipatory ones".[444] Basic trends were taken up, but the industry was afraid to commit itself too far politically in case it occurred heavy losses in the event of a sudden collapse of Nazi rule, unexpected as this would have been.

Goebbels entries before January 1933 already show that he had practical film experience drawn from active work on Party propaganda and campaign films from 1928 onwards.[445] In autumn 1930 – Goebbels held the Party office of "Reichspropagandaleiter" ("Reich propaganda director") – the first Party film office was set up in the "Gau Berlin" under his direction,[446] and some amateurish shorts like *Mit der Berliner SA nach Nürnberg* ("Berlin SA Goes to Nuremberg") had been made there. The film propagandist was then held up by inadequate "technical resources" (5.4.1929), but the ambition was still there: "If only we had money. I would write an N.S. film that was quite something."[447] (16.2.1930) This culminated in a note made after being shown Luis Trenker's *The Rebel*, which was the prototype for a whole series of "liberation films"[448]: "Fantastic scenes. Here you see what can be made of film and what we will make of it ourselves some time."[449] (19.1.1933) Nothing is being said about "conflicting ideas within the

24. Model film *Der Rebell* (1933) by Luis Trenker: fantastic scenes.
25. *SA Man Brand* (1933) by Franz Seitz: not as bad as feared.

Party"[450] about film propaganda as a means of agitation or for conveying nationalistic ideas of culture and popular education.

At first Goebbels notes mainly distinctions and negative examples in his diary, and these are as unrevealing as his public statements. It is therefore hardly surprising that he didn't like the typical light entertainment films of the period, or those about musicians and artists, like *Ein Lied geht um die Welt* (*My Song Goes Around the World*) ("embarrassing", 10.5.1933). He also found the marine detective story *Der Stern von Valencia* ("The Star of Valencia") bad ("rubbish", 6.7.1933) – probably because of the slightly frivolous milieu, later also called "grubby". Goebbels also thought that the very successful Hans Albers film with jazz interludes *Heut kommt's drauf an* ("Today is the Day"), directed by Kurt Gerron, was "terrible rubbish". (14.7. 1933) And he found Erich Engels' thriller *Der Fall Roberts* ("The Roberts Case") equally "terrible".

Goebbels praises the pre-Fascist film *Dawn* as "very good within limits", but with the reservation that the "homefront scenes are too cosy. The people do not talk like that."[451] (5.2.1933) He rejects the first of a series of films about the Prussian Wars of Liberation against Napoleon, *Schwarzer Jäger Johanna* ("Johanna of the Black Volunteer Corps") ("badly made", 24.9. 1934). The only light entertainment film that Goebbels thought was any good is Willi Forst's *Masquerade in Vienna*. (24.9.1934) This did not offer any real prospects, as both the intellectual director and the plot, which is typical of the transitional period – a social scandal in turn-of-the-century Vienna – are unlikely models.

Comments of this kind still do not give any hint of the guidelines that light entertainment and national films should follow in future. Goebbels' notes on the much-discussed Party films *Hitlerjunge Quex* (*Hitler Youth Quex*), *SA-Mann Brand* (*SA Man Brand*) and *Hans Westmar, einer von vielen* ("Hans Westmar, One of Many") are not much more help. As "typical examples of commercial kitsch",[452] these films are more an expression of compliance by Ufa (*Hitler Youth Quex*) and Bavaria (*SA Man Brand*) than the result of instructions or stimulus from Goebbels.

The first of these films, *SA Man Brand*, was launched at a great gala première in the presence of Hitler on 14 June 1933. Goebbels had apparently seen the film only the day before. At first he found it "not as bad as I feared. some sections quite intolerable. But good otherwise. The characters above all. Can run like this." (14.6.1933) Probably he had expected that the first attempt to portray the "movement" in a feature film would produce an entirely inadequate result.[453] But after the première he wrote: "*SA Man Brand* in the Ufa-Palast in the evening. Big gala performance. Hitler there too. There is too much talking in the film. Make heavy cuts. Some of it quite good." (15.6.1933) Goebbels revised his opinion, probably influenced by a lukewarm reception from the première audience – or even from Hitler himself. The Nazi press was also confused: *Der Angriff* panned it two days later – in complete contrast with a positive review in the *Völkischer Beobachter*.[454] Cuts were made after the première, but they did not stop the film from failing or prevent clashes within the NSPAD about how to present Party organization on film.[455]

Film historians consider *Hitler Youth Quex* to be one of the most skilful of the Party films because it discreetly and convincingly portrays a working-class boy finding his way to the Hitler Youth. It is also "very well made from the formal and technical point of view",[456] in the style of the realistic Communist Party films of the twenties and early thirties. It was shown repeatedly in subsequent years, at special screenings in the country, in places without cinemas and at young people's gatherings.[457] The première on 19 September 1933 was very successful, and after it Goebbels claimed to have been involved in the emergence of the Ufa production,[458] but a note made on 6.7.1933 about discussions with Ufa production chief Correll while the film was still being made suggests that his participation can only have been minimal. The project was very much an initiative by the great film company to catch up with their rivals Bavaria and *SA Man Brand*.[459]

Goebbels also mentions a feature film about Party legend Horst Wessel for the first time on 6.7.1933. This was made by the "Volksdeutsche Filmgesellschaft", which was founded specifically for the purpose. After the bad experience and internal Party squabbles caused by *SA Man Brand*, the phrase used here was "official Party consultation". In fact Goebbels withdrew *Horst Wessel* before the première, which was planned for 9 October 1933, and only gave permission for the launch[460] under the new title *Hans Westmar, einer von vielen* after some modifications.[461] Goebbels justified all this on grounds of artistic inadequacy – but the true motives lay in internal antagonism between the Party organizations, and the Nazi leadership's new aims: instead of highlighting the SA, which some people still saw as a gang of thugs, there was increasing stress on integration, so that "citizens and workers who were 'still standing apart'" were not distanced any further.[462]

Goebbels consequently dismissed these films from the early stages of development, which he viewed as failures, as the work of profiteers with no feeling for art. The Minister spoke at the opening of the Reichskulturkammer conference on 19 November 1933 and also to the producers on 9 February 1934. The latter meeting also involved the party sections, whom the film companies were swamping with unacceptable proposals. He made it absolutely clear to all concerned that films of this kind were no longer desirable. He had already denied any personal responsibility when explaining why *Horst Wessel* was banned: "The National Socialist Government has never asked for SA films to be made."[463]

Thus the film producers' anticipatory obedience turned out to be extremely helpful in terms of organization, and when purging film people on grounds of racial ideology. But the content of the films left a great deal to be desired. Neither the traditional nationalist production of 1933/34 nor the insignificant number of controversial Party films became models for future production.

Goebbels makes himself out to be active and interventionist, especially in the reorganization of the film industry, in the diary fragments from May 1933. When looking for material, the Propaganda Minister seems at first to have adopted the method of planning certain projects with film people who seemed to him to be ready to co-operate, artistically convincing and competent, Luis Trenker (20.5.1933) and Leni Riefenstahl (17.5.1933), for example. Here we find entries like: "p. m. Leni Riefenstahl: she tells me about her plans. I suggest a Hitler film to her. She is very enthusiastic about it." (17.5.1933) This and numerous other meetings noted by Goebbels (12/20.6.1933) contradict later portraits of the "Third Reich's" legendary director. Leni Riefenstahl also accompanied Goebbels to a number of social functions and on a visit to the Ufa studios in Babelsberg to see work on *Blut und Scholle*.[464] Finally he writes on 14.6.1933: "Riefenstahl has spoken to Hitler. She's starting her film now." This date is probably too early for the planning stages of the first Party rally film *Sieg des Glaubens* ("Victory of Faith"). Riefenstahl has also always asserted that Goebbels was not involved in this project at all, and that the commission came directly from Hitler in late August 1933, and in fact that Goebbels did his utmost to prevent her. Probably there was a definite intention to make a documentary film, which the term "Hitler film" suggests. But it is not clear whether a project that Goebbels repeatedly calls "our big film" is the same as the Riefenstahl project.[465] (15.6.1933) When all the gaps in the Goebbels' diaries are closed, it will be possible to see how much the Minister actually influenced the "unique phenomenon in film art"[466] that is the second Party rally film *Triumph of the Will*.

The same applies to March 1933 and Goebbels' now almost legendary offer to the director Fritz Lang to take on some sort of overall control role of German cinema.[467] Fritz Lang asserted in various modified versions that the Propaganda Minister made a suggestion of this nature to him a few days after the "Kaiserhof hotel" speech on 28 March, whereupon he left Germany for ever on the same day.[468] It seems entirely plausible that Goebbels had a conversation with Lang, as he had previously with Riefenstahl and Trenker. And it is possible that he also made the great director similar offers of co-operation and suggested that he should make several films. But the idea of setting up a film controller's post and transferring real power to a producer or director never cropped up at this time, regardless of the person of Fritz Lang. It is perfectly true that Goebbels thought very highly of Lang's films, and that he put *The Nibelungs* forward as a model for German film production. He had also pronounced after seeing *M* in the cinema: "Lang will be our director one day." (21.5.1931) But Lang was a half-Jew, and thus not able to make his allegiance to the Nazis. It is scarcely possible that Goebbels could have intended to appoint him to an outstanding position, especially as his film *Das Testament des Dr. Mabuse* (*The Testament of Dr. Mabuse*) was officially banned on 29 March 1933.[469]

Imprecise guidelines

The transitional period ended in 1935, when the Reichslichtspielgesetz was passed and updated. The Reichsfilmdramaturg's office was now able to function to some extent. The unpredictable censorship system and the lack of positive guidelines from the Propaganda Ministry created a need for streamlined film production early in 1935. The severe financial crisis within the film business forced the producers to "assert their basis for debt repayment" and to "increase production of popular genres like comedies or musicals".[470] Continuity from the Weimar period was assured by choosing unassuming and artistically unrewarding popular subjects for films (employees dreaming of being artists, and of consumer goods, happiness and promotion),[471] and by glorifying order, bravery, the military, authority and obedience – a striking example is the seamless continuation of the series of films about Frederick the Great started in 1922. Bold innovations in political and "Volksfilme" ("popular fims") alike only increased the risk of bans or expensive demands for editing or retakes. After the war only four of 34 films made by Ufa in 1935/36 were banned as National Socialist propaganda by the US military authorities.[472] Numerous political films were made by small and private production companies thinking that propaganda presented opportunities for them.[473] These should not be overlooked by concentrating exclusively on Ufa, Bavaria, Tobis etc., even though they had restricted audiences because distribution facilities were too limited. Many of these productions that had not been examined in advance adopted confused political and ideological approaches that made it impossible to use them.

Goebbels refers in 1935/36 to an increasing number of model films, though these were certainly not influenced by the Propaganda Ministry. These included, in the field of Volksfim without serious political intent, the Austrian Erich Engel production *Nur ein Komödiant* ("Only an Actor", 17.8.1935), which promoted the idea of freedom in a small authoritarian state in the 18th century, and the Ibsen film *Stützen der Gesellschaft* ("Pillars of the Community", 6.12. 1935), a typical melodrama based on dual standards of middle-class morality and hypocritical conventions. But Goebbels' personal favourite was the Carl Froelich film *Traumulus* (*The Dreamer*) with Emil Jannings, which won the national film prize: "A huge success. A brilliant caricature of pre-war Germany. Wonderful! … I then watch *The Dreamer* again with him (Hitler). He is spellbound. Jannings very good indeed." (11.1.1936) Ambiguous, petit-bourgeois morality, intellectual narrowness and petrified structures, the contrast between youth and age, the "repressive atmosphere of a remote small town" with its "provincial milieu and the bar-room mentality of its notables"[474] – all these were among Hitler's and Goebbels' pet topics. Both men were bound to recognize the conditions of their childhood and youth here. Such subjects were ideally suited for contrasting the old days with the new regime. The tone was similar in official comments on *The Dreamer*:[475] The fug of the pre-war period is blown away by the "fresh wind" of classless National Socialism. Many film in subsequent years followed this scheme, and Goebbels liked almost all of them.[476]

Goebbels obviously thought that the Ufa film *Inkognito* by the Nazi director Schneider-Edenkoben was outstanding among the comedies; it was one of the many average stories of mistaken identity aiming to provide sophisticated entertainment:[477] "*Inkognito*, a delightful German film comedy with a lot of laughs in it." (6.7.1936) The same applied to the comedy *Lucky Kids*, which has already been mentioned ("Brilliant dialogue. Thrown together. Written by Curt Götz. But bravura stuff. Acted very well too. A real pleasure", 17.9.1936), in which Goebbels recognized the brilliance of the well-known screenplay author Curt Goetz, and to the bachelor comedy *Männer vor der Ehe* ("Men Before Marriage"), "a very jolly and amusing comedy". (26.8.1936) Heinz Rühmann's *Wenn wir alle Engel wären* ("If We All Were Angels") was intended to show that a little in subordination was sometimes permitted even under National Socialism – for Goebbels "the best comedy for a long time. Laughed till I cried. Rühmann excels himself. I am delighted." (14.10.1936)

But as soon as films no longer addressed the "male erotic desires"[478] and conventional paths and sexual roles were abandoned, Goebbels reacted negatively: consequently Reinhold Schünzel's *Das Mädchen Irene* ("The Girl Irene"), "a middle-aged woman's difficult struggle for sexual fulfilment" is a "very bad, forced, revolting business" (17.10.1936) for him.[479] For Goebbels, films like *Ein Lied klagt an* ("The Accusing Song") ("dreadful trash", 6.9.1936),[480] the carnival film *Drei tolle Tage* ("Three Great Days") ("mindless", 26.8.1936), the film about singers *Paul und Pauline* ("rubbish", 16.3.1936) and the operetta adaptation *Im Weißen Rössl* ("Hotel Weisses Rössl"), ("stupid kitsch", "intolerable", 6.12.1935) represented the shallow, kitschy products that he felt should be resisted. But Goebbels thought that coarse, completely indecent jokes about miraculous sources of increased potency were intelligent and witty: "(Hans) Deppe's *Tal des Lebens* ("Valley of Life") piquant and sparkling. Führer must see it too." (29.11.1935)

So Goebbels could not have meant solidly traditional, carefully made, not over-demanding but professional popular Ufa films when he attacked "utterly stupid social nonsense" and asked producers to break with the past. He was far too fond of the products of this genre. There were already adequate products in the popular sector, even if there were not enough of them. And so it was a matter of stopping productions like *Das Mädchen Irene*, pushing out shallow films and above all adding as many "contemporary films" as possible to the list of popular works.

But the diary entries comment only fleetingly on Goebbels' involvement in production in 1935 and 1936. Once again there are discussions with film performers above various – mainly non-political – projects,[481] though nothing concrete came of these. He often just indicates "my support" generally in passing (for example for *Pygmalion*, 31.8.1935). Often failures in terms of political ambition like *Das Mädchen Johanna* ("The Girl Johanna") about Joan of Arc can be identified indirectly. At first it is still "my great success", but then shortly afterwards he writes: "too noisy, too contrived. Unfortunately not quite what I wanted". (19.4.1936) Goebbels describes the demands made by *Victoria* and *Pan* in surprising detail. Both were film versions of stories by his favourite writer Knut Hamsun.[482] He pays considerably less attention to political projects. Only in the case of *Friesennot* ("Frisians in Peril"), the first clearly anti-Soviet film directed by Reichsfilmdramaturg Willi Krause, are there signs of a successful revision (9.11.1935): "*Friesennot*, now finally edited. Indescribably exciting. A masterpiece by Krause."[483] (13.11. 1936)

Apparently Goebbels was able to correct the Luis Trenker production *Der Kaiser von Kalifornien* (*The Emperor of California*) easily enough in the cutting-room (17.6.1936),[484] and only one studio visit is noted for *Fridericus*. There is no detailed consideration of the political direction taken by individual films, with the exception of *Friesennot* and the spy film *Verräter* (*Traitors*), ("rather long-winded at first, but then an enchanting furioso", 30.7.1936, see below), a film commissioned by the Ministry.

Political dynamics and "anti-Bolshevism" 1936

At the International Film Congress in Berlin in 1935 Goebbels demanded that films should increasingly "adapt to the spirit of the time",[485] but he again avoided revealing his ideas about material. The political thrust of film production in 1935/36 seems nebulous and imprecise at times, swinging from being anti-British (*Das Mädchen Johanna*, *Verräter*) and pro-British and anti-French (*Der höhere Befehl*/"The Higher Order").[486] At the same time, numerous German-French and German-Polish co-productions were made, which excluded resistance to the country of the co-producer in question.[487] There is no evidence of Anglo-German understanding as result of the naval agreement of June 1935 affecting film policy,[488] but there are next to no anti-British films, or the English simply appeared[489] as "reluctant enemies".[490]

There is no sense that Goebbels is trying to condemn all conventional patriotic films. He approved of many of these productions: "*Henker, Frauen und Soldaten* ("Hangmen, Women and Soldiers"), an exciting and enchanting film with Albers. *Auf höheren Befehl*, a nationalist and enchanting film of the Napoleonic period, with Diehl, Dagover and Finkenzeller. All first class. The German cinema is clearly improving."[491] (11.12.1935) Comments on *Standschütze Bruggler* ("Home Guardsman Bruggler") also sound very positive – although he did not fail to notice the problems caused by the anti-Italian elements[492] – and also on *Ritt in die Freiheit* ("Ride into Freedom"):"Well made. Decent in terms of plot, direction, approach and acting. I am pleased to have supported it." (19.10.1936) He made cuts in the first version ("at last, long anticipated") of *Fridericus*: "It has some very fine, enchanting points, but weaknesses too. Gebühr outstanding. The great king, the only king!" (4.11.1936) But Goebbels felt that contemporary political projects like *Stärker als Paragraphen* ("Stronger than Regulations") were not successful: "a shoddy German effort with N. S. elements. Dreadful trash." (23.8.1936)

The Nuremberg NSDAP-rally in September 1936, which was completely given over to "anti-Bolshevism", also showed a new way forward for film propaganda. There was now a possibility of going beyond previous nationalist films and putting genuine National Socialist ideology on the screen. Goebbels had talked of a "new anti-Bolshevik film plan" before. (19.1.1936) But after

26. "Anti-Bolshevik" film *Weiße Sklaven* (1936): close to the limit.

the première of *Friesennot* in November 1935, the only anti-Communist project to that date, there was a pause in the planning process in 1935/36. Only *Weiße Sklaven* ("White Slaves"), made under Karl Anton's direction in 1936, addresses the cruelty of the "Bolsheviki" during the Russian Revolution in Sevastapol. Goebbels was able to reverse a ban on the film by Hitler in October 1936 ("realistically based on Bolshevism. Close to the limit. A break at the end", 14.10. 1936) by producing a heavily modified new version.[493] Though it seems to have been very popular with the public,[494] this was not yet the Nazi settling of accounts with Communism that Hitler and Goebbels had in mind.

While revising *Weiße Sklaven* in October and November 1936, Goebbels put more energy into film planning. On 22.10.1936 he wrote that his "Führer" also wanted "more National Socialism in films and press", whereupon Goebbels immediately responded, "so I shall launch a move towards anti-Bolshevik films." The new thrust is expressed even more clearly on 27.10.1936: "Speech to film producers and directors: more up-to-date material. The non-political days have gone now, for the film as well. We now have to take time by the forelock. That is the only chance we have. … I shall now confirm this in private meetings with Krause, Nierentz, Köhn and Weidemann."

And so now the new political directions taken in the "turning-point year" 1936 were starting to affect films as well. Hitler's and Goebbels' intentions are clear in the context of the four-year plan announced in September. This heralded an aggressive phase of National Socialist preparations for war,[495] and two years of military service were announced in August ("The Führer has made another great decision in his loneliness", 25.8.1936) and increased anti-Communist propaganda (see below). At the same time Goebbels started – and this is reinforced by the ban on art and film criticism in November 1936 – to abandon his resistance to Rosenberg's racial and nationalist ideas of culture, after a cultural conflict lasting for several years, and now "completed the ideological radicalization that Rosenberg had always required".[496] The question now arose of how these new intentions should be implemented. Certainly Hitler was unhappy, as he could not come to terms with Goebbels' suggestions of a lack of creative potential,[497] and this put further pressure on the Propaganda Minister, who continued to brood over "great new film plans" (13.11.1936) and the "question of the new political film".[498] (14.11.1936)

After the anti-Comintern pact of 25 November 1936 and the propaganda following the Party rally there should have been concrete "anti-Bolshevik" film plans. Even shortly before Goebbels developed his new dynamic there were two relevant projects in preparation in autumn 1936, following "Ufa's concept of regularly including material with anti-revolutionary or anti-Communist tendencies in the production programme".[499] The two films were *Starke Herzen* ("Strong Hearts") and the adventure film *Menschen ohne Vaterland* from the series of volunteer corps films.[500] Shooting had already finished on *Weiße Sklaven*. Goebbels' demands for political and anti-Communist material had already been discussed on the production side. Ufa production chief Correll referred at a board meeting on 9 December 1936 to Goebbels' insistence that "films should be made showing the conflict between white and red".[501] But he was not referring to direct instructions here, but to Goebbels' speech on 27 November 1936 at the opening of the Reichskulturkammer's 4th annual conference.[502] But, surprisingly, no anti-Soviet films were then taken on until 1939, with the exception of *Menschen ohne Vaterland* and *Starke Herzen*, which were already planned before "launching a move" in the direction of "anti-Bolshevism".[503]

Why did the Propaganda Ministry's pronouncements not make any impact? Ultimately a number of National Socialist organizations were demanding political films, which Goebbels tried to meet[504] with targeted press reports about "anti-Bolshevik" films planned for the 1937/38 season – none of which was later realized.[505]

Hitler and Goebbels were quite obviously aiming to deal with Communism in a much more radical way cinematically than German film companies could deliver in 1936. *Weiße Sklaven* escaped Hitler's ban only by subsequent editing, *Starke Herzen* was refused approval entirely,[506] and *Menschen ohne Vaterland*, which Goebbels found particularly ineffective (8.2.1937), was severely attacked by the press under instruction from the Propaganda Ministry in March 1937, in order to put pressure on the Ufa management during the nationalization negotiations.[507] Goebbels' comments on *Starke Herzen*, which range from "supposed to be anti-Bolshevik" via "utterly middle-class and simplistic, without sharp lines or contrasts" (24.6.1937) to "too middle-class. How the *Stahlhelm* sees Bolshevism. Typical of Ufa" (22.9.1937), are symptomatic of Goebbels' and Hitler's rejection of anti-Communist film production that is too lax and not National Socialist enough, conceived by "middle-class businessmen". The heroes of these films – barons, cavalry captains and other aristocrats – were figures that the nationalist Ufa bosses could identify with, but Hitler and Goebbels could not.

The fact is that "anti-Bolshevik" film production started in 1936 but never got off the ground. The new film planning dynamic was influenced by the new aims of National Socialist foreign and propaganda policy (singing the praises of the anti-Comintern pact and the Spanish Civil War) and the "ready for war in four years" strategy. But translating this into effective anti-Communist film propaganda remained a mere intention.

Higher profiles in 1937

First successes

The year 1937 was characterized by clashes about production power and material selection between the film companies and the Propaganda Ministry. Thus many of Goebbels' damning criticisms were not so much directed at individual films as intended to justify his attacks on certain big studios and film-makers.[508] Positive tirades of hatred are to be found about director Reinhold Schünzel's film *Land der Liebe* ("Land of Love") in the diary, not least because he was half-Jewish, and Goebbels wanted to get rid of him.[509] Nevertheless: precisely because of the (critical) judgements and the (considered) consequences, the Minister became ever more concrete in the demands he made to film producers in terms of content.

It is difficult to establish the extent to which the new political dynamic of late 1936 applied only to "anti-Bolshevik" films, and which of the other six films with a nationalist political slant (*Fridericus, Ritt in die Freiheit* / "Ride into Freedom". *Togger, Der Etappenhase* / "The Base Wallah", *Der Herrscher* / "The Ruler" and *Condottieri*) that appeared in the first quarter of 1937 may have been influenced by it. But Goebbels was not impressed when it came down to detail. *Fridericus* ("also not ideal, but it will do. The film is a mess overall. There is nothing more to be done about this", 23.1.1937) came off particularly badly, and so did the military comedy with soldierly notes *Der Etappenhase*: "a long, teased-out, war comedy, almost all dialogue, mainly bad, no intelligence, no wit, no flair. Unpleasant." (24.2.1937) But the biggest disappointment for Goebbels must have been Luis Trenker's *Condottieri*, which he was doubtful about at first (12.3.1937), and then condemned it after Hitler rejected it: "not heroic, a film about campaigning Ca-

27. Luis Trenker in *Condottieri*: much too Catholic.

tholicism." (18.3.1937) Goebbels notes that the "Führer" had been particularly displeased with the "tendency towards Catholicism" (31.3.1937), and concludes: "Trenker is too Catholic. He is messing the whole thing up for us." (14.3.1937) But the action-packed film *Ritt in die Freiheit*, already censored by Goebbels in 1936, comes off rather better. Goebbels is not sure about *Togger*, an agit-prop press film that is unique of its kind, full of Nazi slogans, anti-Semitic allusions and SA parades, finding defects in the direction ("somewhat stiff") and acting ("slightly inhibited"): "Could have been better, but also quite effective as it is." [510](12.2.1937)

It was not until Veit Harlan's film *Der Herrscher* ("The Ruler") was completed that Goebbels was able to chalk up an unqualified success. As he confirms himself, this very free adaptation of a play by Gerhart Hauptmann is the first successful National Socialist production: "*Der Herrscher*: a wonderful achievement. Modern and National Socialist. Just the kind of film I like. Brilliant casting and direction." (12.3.1937) Goebbels particularly stresses the "milieu presentation" on 15.3., thus underlining his weakness for anti-middle-class rhetoric. The press praised *Der Herrscher*, which achieved the highest possible classifications and won the national film prize in 1937, as a "first-rate work of political art".[511] Emil Jannings appears as a responsible entrepreneur running an enormous steelworks, which he finally leaves to the state rather than his money-grubbing family. The inefficient directors of the company are supposed to justify the "Führer principle" in commercial life. Although it is full of Nazi terminology like "community of people", "allegiance" and "self-sufficiency", the film is dominated by the family drama and the constant, gratingly loud clashes about the director's relationship with his young wife, and so it is less obviously a propaganda work than *Togger*, for example.[512] The effect of Jannings' factory director Klausen as a Hitler substitute is somewhat diminished by obsession with his private problems.[513] *Der Herrscher*'s long-held reputation in film history as an exceptional phenomenon in terms of quality and a breakthrough for Nazi feature films has suffered somewhat recently.[514]

Goebbels did not have to bother about the fact that the "socialist" economic policies promoted in the film triggered a public row about the problems of nationalization.[515] The community of people rhetoric obviously chimed precisely with the political mood and propaganda requirements of these months.[516] (16.1.1937) Thus Goebbels identified a speech by Hitler to car-workers as "markedly socialist" on 21.12.: "I have not heard the Führer sound like this for a long time."[517] Whether *Der Herrscher* was created in response to this mood identified in January 1937 is still doubtful. Harlan asserts that the Nazi commercial slogans had been added in by Goebbels' Staatssekretär Funk,[518] but unlike all other major political material involving Emil Jannings it is not possible to discern any sign of participation by Goebbels in making *Der Herrscher*. There are none of the usual large number of entries about Jannings' suggestions for material and the progress of the film production.[519]

In the same year as the success of *Der Herrscher* another attempt to address new political film subjects through the medium of documentary turned out to be a failure. On 30.9.1936 Goebbels recorded that he was very impressed by some of the clashes in the Spanish Civil War, especially the legendary siege of the Alcazar in Toledo, held by the Falangists, which was ended by Republican forces on 28 September: "A modern heroic epic! This is the right material for our times. And the film composes products of the imagination that do not exist in life." (30.9.1936) Shortly after this Goebbels asked Ufa to make a film about the siege of Alcazar, but met with resistance there. C.W. Köhn, who was responsible for party matters at Ufa, reported that "Ufa has expressed reservations about whether it seems the right moment to make an epic film in view of the fact that the ruins are still smoking."[520] The project was finally shelved. Hitler personally rejected a film compiled in autumn 1936, obviously from Spanish documentary material, about "Spain and its Revolution" (4.12.1936), which Goebbels asked Weidemann to revise to make it even "more precise and impactful".[521] And so after the Party films and the anti-Communist projects, the third innovative initiative, the Spanish Civil War as a subject for film propaganda, also came to nothing.

In spring 1937 Ufa produced *Starke Herzen*, and also *Patrioten* ("Patriots"), another nationalist project directed by Karl Ritter. This production particularly attracted Goebbels' attention. He had given Ufa detailed requests about the writing of the screenplay even at the preliminary stages, for example that the leading man was to be an air force lieutenant. Goebbels also made sure that his mistress Lida Baarova, who was playing the female lead, should have the actor Mathias Wieman as her leading man in the film – and not Baarova' actual partner and leading man Gustav Fröhlich.[522] He also says that the material should again be "nationalistically slanted", so that it is "quite focused and clear", on 13.1.1937. It took several revisions of the screenplay, test shots and further corrections (17./20.1., 14.2.) to produce the desired result: "quite clear and nationalistic in tendency." (24.4.1937) But on the other hand it is not clear whether Goebbels kept such a keen eye on the film because his mistress was in it, or as a result of keen political interest.

Shortly before and after the Reich-owned Cautio Trust acquired a majority shareholding in Ufa, there are an increasing number of passages in which Goebbels records his rigid control of the production programmes. In the first week of March 1937, in which the International Film Congress was also meeting in Berlin, there is not a single daily entry without a reference to film policy. Surprisingly enough, these are dominated by positive assessments of most film projects, even though one would have expected Goebbels to emphasize the need for corrections to justify the imminent purchase. On 20.2. he calls the Ufa plans "well thought through", and the same applies to Tobis. (6.3.1937) Only after the transaction does he write: "The Ufa and Tobis programmes still need a lot of work doing on them." (24.3.1937) But the Ufa bosses attempted to implement the production plan that they had already compiled in the face of the new pressure, which was probably motivated by a need for action rather than political content: the board agreed that "nothing is to be changed about this programme as it has been submitted to the Minister" as "otherwise there will be delays, which would inevitably be associated with considerable financial losses given the very complicated distribution system."[523] Goebbels says nothing about these objections. so that despite his announcement on 24.3.1937 there seem to have been no far-reaching changes. Further pressure came from Party offices, who felt encouraged by the journalistic campaign against Ufa's "middle-class" productions during the takeover negotiations. Thus Goebbels received more requests that Party films should be made: "(SA Chief of Staff Viktor) Lutze wants to make SA films as well. But I shall prevent this. Otherwise everyone will be sticking their noses into my business again." (3.3.1937)

Goebbels also seems to have set his sights high in terms of programmes in spring 1937. He announced that his speech at the film congress would "develop an entirely new programme. Then we shall be on the way up again." (2.3.1937) But his statements remained as vague as they had been on previous occasions. A note after a conversation with Hitler about film policy ("We talked about film problems for a long time. We must capture life in them more. No pale theories. Life! Life!" 8.2.1937) already reflects the essence of the film speech. Goebbels did not stint on praise for himself, and even asserted that he had fully implemented his "clearly outlined annual programme" in the last twelve months, and that he had given the cinema "a new face".[524] He also pointed out several times that art had a duty to "capture life, that art to a certain extent represents life in an enhanced form"[525] and "any material must be taken from life".[526] In doing this he was once again taking up the traditional line of criticism that had been done to death even under the Weimar Republic and by the Nazi press.

28. Première of *Der Herrscher*: Veit Harlan keeps an eye on Marianne Hoppe, Goebbels and Emil Jannings.

Goebbels hinted at the possibility of filming historical material, where the artist would be relatively free in handling facts, ultimately he was not a historian.[527] But National Socialism could not yet be seen as history. "For the time being a certain amount of reserve" should be shown in terms of the National Socialist movement as a "historical phenomenon: because National Socialism is still so new and so young that we cannot distance ourselves from it sufficiently to be able to present it maturely. We must first achieve this historical distance."[528] Goebbels did not want to see propaganda and tendentious material presented too vividly. The aim was precisely not to create art "that can only prove its National Socialist character through displaying National Socialist emblems and symbols, but art that expresses its approach by being National Socialist in character and by drawing National Socialist problems together." Only when propaganda "is manifest through plot, through the sequence of events, through processes, and by contrasting people with each other can it be effective in every respect."[529] Goebbels stressed. And conversely: "The moment propaganda becomes self-conscious, it is ineffective." Goebbels was carried away to the extent of asserting that if you want to seen German films, "you want to see National Socialist films",[530] and demanded more skilfully contrived screenplays, with dialogue that

73

was "hard, masculine and realistic", devised by "psychologists", "people who are not only artists, but also know the human mind, and who can work out in advance how this or that conflict will effect the broad mass of the public."[531]

Goebbels worked on various material with a whole range of political themes up to the end of 1937, but overall the projects seem piecemeal, rather than the result of setting clear targets. *Mein Sohn, der Herr Minister* ("My Son the Minister") is an anti-French, anti-Communist version of a French comedy by André Birabeau, and Goebbels found it "intelligent mockery of parliamentarianism" and thus "politically very attractive". (16.1.1937) He thought that is was "successful overall" though also "not light enough as an idea. Too forced".[532] (18.6.1937) After the papal encyclical *With Burning Sorrow* of March 1937, which was critical of the Nazis, and the reprisals against the clergy that followed it, it seemed a good idea to extend anti-ecclesiastical propaganda on film. But a film scenario about Lola Montez which was ready for filming in June ("acutely anti-clerical. Bravo!", 20.6.1937) was constantly revised (18./23.11.1937), but possibly not shot because the actress Imperio Argentina, acquired from Spain, turned out to be a catastrophic mistake. Then at the end of the year Nazi propaganda switched back again, and an anti-clerical film possibly no longer seemed opportune.[533]

Goebbels particularly liked colonial themes, another focal point for propaganda in 1937/38. But the world war film about the far eastern front, *Aufruhr in Damaskus* (*Tumult in Damascus*),[534] did not reach the cinemas until February 1939. The planned propaganda portrait of colonial politician Carl Peters, which Goebbels found "extraordinarily topical", because "naturally everything (could be) done with it" (20.10.1937), was immediately killed off by yet more new guidelines: "The Führer rings up again in the evening: he wants to hold the press polemic on the colonial question back a bit. Otherwise the business will be trivialized to an extent. He is quite right."[535] (5.11.1937) Before this could be implemented in film the general propaganda line had changed. The idea was not taken up again until 1940, as an anti-British gesture.

The propaganda films[536] in which Goebbels was obviously not involved were largely awarded poor marks. These include *Alarm in Peking* (20.6.1937, 26.6.1937). *Signal in der Nacht* ("Night Signal", 25.9.1937), the "Kraft durch Freude" film *Petermann ist dagegen* ("Petermann Is Against It", 17.11.1937) and the Ibsen film *Ein Volksfeind* ("An Enemy of the People", 8.10. 1937), which was sold as inspiring "courage and readiness for sacrifice for the greater good".[537] The only film which Goebbels comments upon is *Die Warschauer Zitadelle* ("The Warsaw Citadel", 10.8.1937).[538]

The first so-called military war educational films were produced in 1937, under the direction of Karl Ritter, the most fervent of the National Socialist adherents in the film industry. He had himself served as a front-line officer, and preferred the radical and patriotic approach of the World War atmosphere, equating the Weimar Republic with the "Semitic" parliamentary reign of the "November criminals", which offered no home to the officers who had been "betrayed". Many films were produced on Ritter's initiative that were later counted among the most presentable products of National Socialist film propaganda. His qualities as a master of "open racism" and "barracks humour"[539] became all the more important from 1937 onwards, as there were no comparable "political" film people.[540] Luis Trenker, in whom Hitler and Goebbels had invested so much hope, disappointed them with the "Catholic" *Condottieri* in 1937, and had fallen even further into disfavour by the end of the year.[541] After *Der Herrscher* and *Mein Sohn, der Herr Minister*, Veit Harlan put his energies into melodramas and comedies until late 1939, and Emil Jannings annoyed Goebbels with his film version of Heinrich von Kleist's play *Der zerbrochene Krug* (*The Broken Jug*), and largely pursued his own projects. Hans Weidemann failed in Goebbels' eyes with his propaganda documentaries. (14.8.1937, 23. 11.1937)

A love story had been in the foreground rather than propaganda in Ritter's film *Patrioten*, which has already been mentioned. Goebbels stresses the successful première in September 1937 several times because of Lida Baarova (for example 24.11.1937). *Unternehmen Michael* ("Operation Michael") and *Urlaub auf Ehrenwort* (*Furlough on Word of Honor*) followed in the same year. Ritter contrived that Ufa replaced the anticipated "anti-Bolshevik" material of *Staatsfeind Nr. 1* ("Public Enemy No. 1") with *Furlough on Word of Honor* in the 1937/38 production programme.[542] Goebbels, who had obviously not initiated the military films, was probably pleased with the idea, but remained sceptical about the screenplay (13./14.5.1937) and constantly monitored the rest of the film's progress. (2./6.8.1937) The final version was ready by the end of the year, after six month's shooting. The stylized approach, showing dutiful solders in a rackety, red Berlin corresponded precisely with Goebbels' intention to do down the 1918 revolution and the

29. Emil Jannings in *The Broken Jug*: embarrassing analogies.

hour of the Weimar Republic's birth: "Wonderfully done by Ritter. Accurate milieu portrayal. Berlin 1918. Critical themes handled very delicately. Will certainly be a big success. Ritter is one of the few people who can make political films."[543] (1.12.1937)

But the *Unternehmen Michael* project, shot from May in the Babelsberg studios, met with reservations on Goebbels' part: "Watched Ritter's new film *Unternehmen Michael*. Good idea, direction not so good. Too much studio. And the officers argue too much. Wieman too sloppy as a hero at the front. I don't like that aspect of it. … I must have some things about the film changed. Above all in the handling of the dialogue." (23.7.1937) The proposed changes, intended to tighten up the film, probably contributed to the fact that the soldiers' exaggerated death-wish even caused the War Ministry to object to the film after the première in September.[544]

Thus the systematic presentation of images of the enemy and glorification of contempt for death and blind obedience at the front and at home did mean that Ritter's films were an important propaganda element. But the exaggerated approach and the brutality of the presentation did give rise to doubts about whether the "Ritter films" which were so rapturously received by the Nazi press could actually do a convincing job in terms of education for war, rather than simply confirm the existing attitudes of sections of the population that were anyway inclined towards National Socialism.

Distasteful film entertainment

The lack of political films was only one of Goebbels' reasons for nationalizing the film industry. He felt that it was just as important to get rid of "shallow entertainment at the pictures". The quality of lighter German films was much criticized in 1937. A reporter from the exiled SPD presented this somewhat exaggerated view of their attractivity: "There is not a great deal to be said about the new German light films, film farces and film operettas. Certainly such productions operate at a modest level in most countries, but they are particularly boring and humourless in the Third Reich. When these films try to be jolly or amusing they seem mainly nervous, contrived or silly. … In the more recent film operettas one can see the increasingly routine technical approach of substitute directors and young performers; they try to give themselves a boost by imitating Hollywood. But they do not have the resources, the manpower or the elegance of Hollywood productions."[545]

There was no lack of complaints from the film industry about inadequate material and poor scripts on the fringes of the International Film Congress in Berlin in March 1937. The personnel that had emigrated or been removed had not been replaced, and there was no systematic training for young personnel. There were ten more competent and more experienced directors who the film companies trusted to implement a project successfully. Some stars were losing their appeal (Jan Kiepura, Lilian Harvey), and it was too soon for other big names to have established themselves (Marika Rökk, Zarah Leander).

For Goebbels, every increase in power in the sphere of film production inevitably meant increased responsibility for developing film programmes. He was very pleased to accept this when things went well. If they didn't, sole blame was apportioned to the film companies. He very rarely admitted that there could be no guarantee of success for the films that he particularly promoted and monitored, not even for his favourite project *Pan*, pampered in 1936 but not premiered until 1937: "A bad film. Drawn out to epic proportions. There is no dialogue, but no plot either. Is it possible to film Hamsun at all?" (23.4.1937) The same applies to the production *Revolutionshochzeit* ("Revolution Wedding"), which he also promoted (planning 3.4., 16.4.1937, negative judgement 14.6.1937). In spring 1937, Goebbels was in a state of great euphoria, and felt a sense of a new start simply because he was in control of film production. (23./26./31.3. 1937) He had to make his new powers of intervention work first of all in questions of organization, commerce, finance and staffing. Planning the correct material ("read film scripts deep into the night", 6.5.1937) was often time-consuming and haphazard.

It was now no longer enough to realize ministerial ideas and projects with the assistance of a few high-calibre film people. Goebbels discussed several ideas for films with Emil Jannings on 6.5.1937. Two of these were never even started, and he cancelled one of them himself.[546] Finally – if one follows reports from the post-war period[547] – because of the comparison the audience drew between the Propaganda Minister and the lying, club-footed village judge Adam in *The Broken Jug* was an embarrassment for Goebbels even at the première, and he tried to cover this up by transparent retouching in the diary.[548]

Goebbels must have realized by summer 1937 at the latest that nothing fundamental had changed in Volksfilm production. Despite acclaimed productions like *Versprich mir nichts* ("Promise me Nothing") by Liebeneiner (21.7.1937) or *Der Mann, der Sherlock Holmes war* ("The Man Who Was Sherlock Holmes") with Hans Albers (3.7.1937), Goebbels saw films like Gustaf Gründgens' *Capriolen* ("Caprioles") (14.7.1937) and the musical comedies *Austernlilli* ("Oysterlilli") and *Karussell* ("Carousel") and *Husaren heraus* ("Go Hussars") (all 15.7.1937) as within the hated tradition of Ufa light entertainment, which was rarely intelligent and more likely to be kitschy. More annoyance was caused when the largest German film company refused to engage the Spanish diva Imperio Argentina, whom Goebbels had selected for the roles of Carmen and Lola Montez (31.7.1937). All this led to a new outpouring of action rhetoric: "The Führer has had enough now as well. I am bringing in new forces. Young talents to the front. Get rid of the old reactionaries. Fresh air and a more humane atmosphere. No false stagey Romanticism." (3.8.1937) Spurred on and further legitimized by Hitler ("The Führer was acutely displeased with the bad films") Goebbels wants "to impose order" even more strongly "now that I have the cinema in my hands."[549] (3.8.1937)

Then, in a note about a long meeting with the "3 production chiefs of the film companies and artistic boards", Goebbels protests "about recent rubbishy films, without standards or wit", and points out that there will be far-reaching consequences, as otherwise his "prestige" would be affected by the bad films. (12.8.1937) What is ultimately needed is "films set in Germany".

By the end of 1937, Goebbels' assessment of Volksfilm production had become even more negative. His frustration is underlined by many outbursts (for example about Jürgen von Alten's adventure film *Heimweh* ("Nostalgia") or about another operetta adaptation called *Die Landstreicher* ("Vagabonds", 24.8.1937), to the extent that he planned individual campaigns against certain film subjects. For example, he says on 2.10.1937 that the Polish film tenor Jan Kiepura, star of many film musicals and leading actor in the film about singers *Zauber der Bohème* ("Bohemian Magic"), should be slowly "phased out". The expensive two-part film *Der Tiger von Eschnapur / Das indische Grabmal* (*The Tiger of Eshnapur / The Indian Tomb*), one of the greatest box-office successes of the thirties and the "main work in the German large-scale exotic adventure film genre",[550] was also subject to the most severe disapproval: "A dreadfully heavy effort by Eichberg. Cost a ridiculous amount and is shocking trash."[551] (11.11.1937)

In addition to the "failure of film production" (25.11.1937) and artistic deficiencies, objective financial problems were increasingly cropping up by late 1937: "The cinema is in a very poor financial situation. We absolutely must do something." (24.11.1937) Attacks against firm managements had proved just as fruitless as the usurpation of even more power. Despite some outstanding individual successes in the field of political films and the discovery of two of the most important supporters of National Socialist films in future years, in the spheres of melodrama and propaganda, Veit Harlan and Zarah Leander,[552] the improvements announced in the spring had failed to materialize.

Preparing for war

Propaganda and politics 1938/39

In his speech to leading military figures on 5 November 1937, known as the Hoßbach minutes, Hitler confirmed his intention to "attack", accepting that this would represent a hostile stance vis-à-vis the Western powers. One requirement for this new aggressive phase of German politics was that within a few months moderate representatives of the "old élite", including Finance Minister Schacht, the Commander in Chief of the Army Fritsch and Foreign Minister Neurath, had been replaced by unconditionally loyal National Socialists like Funk, Keitel and Ribbentrop. Hitler became increasingly threatening in speeches at the Nuremberg Rally in September 1937 and in the Reichstag on 20 February 1938. In March 1938 – the huge scale of the armament policy was already in danger of overheating the German economy – German troops occupied Austria in what was still a bloodless "flower campaign".

If film policy in the pre-war years 1938/39 is seen from the point of view of "psychological mobilization", a careful distinction has to be made between the propaganda aims of the Nazi leadership at any given time, Goebbels' (verbal) intentions, directives to the film production companies and the film programmes that were actually shown. Historians often point out the "complicated and contradictory double role"[553] played by Nazi propaganda in the pre-war period, which had to sell assurances of peace and at the same time promote intellectual militarization and enhance military will.

Although this psychological mobilization was skilfully graduated and achieved without a radical swing, the regime was unable to arouse enthusiasm for war to the same extent as in 1914.[554]

It is questionable whether the "image that the German people was indoctrinated with military and heroic ideals in a way that was variously secured institutionally and pursued continuously"[555] applies to all fields of propaganda to the same extent, and in particular to feature film propaganda.

It is of course not possible to deduce from Goebbels' diary entries whether the 1938/39 cinema programme was adequately suited to meet the psychological requirements for war. But they can suggest the extent to which there was an intention to produce intensified film propaganda.

Jerzy Toeplitz and Rainer Rother suggest film policy that deliberately concentrates on "preparing for war".[556] There is a big difference between intentions when making a film and the corresponding response from the public, but that is not all. Any attempt to establish conclusively what proportion of propaganda feature films must have in order to be designated as "preparing for war" is bound to meet with considerable methodological difficulties. Does it need obvious images of the enemy, like shifty French ministers, English spies or even the heroism and glorification of death of Karl Ritter's radical and military films? Is it enough to establish "invisible" tendencies in the fine drawing by constant representation of general national and patriotic virtues and values? Or is it even adequate to invoke the community and the Nazis' achievement in building it up? As we know very little about "the mechanisms of contemporary effect" (Friedrich P. Kahlenberg) on the public as there is a dearth of recorded audience reactions from the prewar period, then there is a great deal to be said for setting the criteria as broadly as possible. Finally the number and presentation of feature films identified as "preparing for war" should be considered in the context of the full range of films on offer in 1938/39.

First of all we must recall the principal lines taken by Nazi propaganda in the course of 1938/39.[557] To accompany the "unparalleled armament" (Hitler in his Reichstag speech on 20 February 1938), German military strength was constantly invoked, with alternate threats and assurances of peace, even before the Wehrmacht marched on Austria. While preparations were being made for "a solution to the Czech problem" ("Case Green"), and especially after the partial Prague mobilization in late May 1938 and Hitler's instruction to "smash" Czechoslovakia (30.5.1938), the Sudeten German minority there and "bringing (them) home" became the focal point for press and radio. This propaganda campaign reached a climax in August while the British special emissary Runciman was attempting to mediate in Prague during August. In September as well – Hitler had fixed the attack for 25 September 1938 – not a day passed without some reference to alleged Czech "atrocities". After the "Munich agreement" of 30 September 1938, which provided for secession of the Sudeten territories to Germany, to which Hitler agreed only because the German population had become acutely afraid of war and the Western powers were visibly taking military counter-measures, there was a temporary change in the propaganda line: Hitler had announced the end of the previous "peace propaganda" and what he called "grandiose playing down of ourselves" in a secret speech on 10 November 1938, and demanded that the people should now be psychologically attuned to military strength and conflict.[558] (He had instructed the Wehrmacht to "smash the remainder of Czechoslovakia" as many as three weeks before.) But this certainly did not indicate the start of a shrill war campaign: in fact "public propaganda was shifted to trust, security, national solidarity and general confidence after the débâcle of the Sudeten crisis".[559] The key feature was that an omnipresent "intensification of Wehrmacht propaganda was to reinforce the German people's confidence in its own strength, i.e. in the resources of its military might".[560] In terms of foreign policy anti-English polemic was intensified (Hitler's Reichstag speech on 30 January 1939), and the American President Roosevelt increasing became a target for the controlled German press.

It was not until spring 1939 (occupation of the rest of Czechoslovakia in March), after Poland had been selected as the next target for invasion ("Case White" at the commanders' in chief meeting on 23.5.1939) and despite the risk of a clash with England and France, that the propaganda was "tailored directly for war preparations":[561] after warnings about the encirclement of Germany (essays by Goebbels in the *Völkischer Beobachter* in May/June 1939) under the direction of British "plutocrats", the acquisition of "Lebensraum" was formulated as the war aim. In may, a smear campaign following the pattern of Sudeten crisis against alleged Polish "atrocities" and warmongering and for the separation of Danzig was gradually expanded. In early August the

Propaganda Ministry issued the guideline that reports of Polish "terror" and attacks on "German nationals abroad" should be placed on the front page wherever possible.

Goebbels' film planning in 1938

Goebbels was still speaking very harshly about the state of film production even in late 1937. But even early in the next year he seemed inclined to make a more positive assessment. (11.1. 1938, 4.2.1938) The great success of the carefully planned Karl Ritter film *Furlough on Word of Honor* both when Hitler saw it (1.1.1938) and at the première (20.1.1938) came at just the right moment for him. He also praised the tendentious adventure film *Mit versiegelter Order* ("Sealed Order") very highly (10.1.1938), and Veit Harlan's melodrama *Jugend* ("Youth") is greeted most emphatically. (31.12.1937, 2.1.1938)

Then the fact that he felt that a few films were successful and a short-term increase in box-office returns led Goebbels to a rapid revaluation: "Our film industry is starting to perk up again. A few big hits have saved our skins. Some wonderful plans are about to be realized. I thoroughly enjoy doing this work."[562] (4.2.1938)

This optimism was not shared in some National Socialist party circles. Some of the party press organs criticized the lack of productions and themes that were unmistakably National Socialist.[563] The Hitler Youth magazine *Wille und Macht*, for example, wrote as follows in a surprisingly rebellious article: "Because the last thing we could do is to reproach the film world with showering the unsuspecting cinemagoer with an undue amount of tendentious films. You have to look a long way in the film programmes before finding a film made with clearly emerging political intentions. Even the most suspicious cinemagoer could not assert that German feature films are trying to influence their political and general view of the world against their will. With the exception of part of the newsreel the cinema is a non-political oasis in a politicized Germany. And even someone who tries to be very clever by suggesting that there are no particularly tendentious films but that tendencies are delineated in the details of the film's approach would find scarcely any examples to support such an argument. The more one goes to the cinema, the more clearly one feels that in the majority of cases the world that is presented there has nothing at all to do with our National Socialist present. Certainly we have seen some good films, and a great deal of technical progress has been made. But our new feelings of life have penetrated only into a very small number of films."[564]

Although Goebbels immediately imposed all sorts of sanctions on the magazine and threw out the editor, a "snotty-nosed fool" (20.2.1938), his notes sound agitated enough to show how much the criticism had made its mark. On the same note, the Reichsfilmkammer's magazine *Der deutsche Film* felt a lack of "stronger links with real life, of the kind that Reichsminister Dr. Goebbels has always demanded".[565]

Goebbels' attempts at justification sounded different from year to year. In April 1938 the Minister declared that there had not been more unambiguously political films because of organizational problems and difficulties in controlling the film industry.[566] But on closer examination the reproaches seem almost unjust: in the first six months of 1938 in particular a number of privately produced films were showing that had responded to Goebbels repeated and less than original call for "real life" and "topical problems". A whole series of Zeitfilme ("films of the time"), which were almost all set in the "Third Reich", but at least after 1918, were to be found on the cinema programme. Scarcely any attention is paid to them today, not least because they were not very widely distributed at the time.[567] These were mainly modest productions addressing primarily social and public issues of National Socialism – though they were often extremely diffuse politically. As they present no images of external enemies or military virtues they are certainly not in the top category of films "educating for war". But they promoted the Nazi state's progress and socio-economic successes by pouring scorn on the imperial and republican past.

Examples of this are two films that ran in the cinemas from September 1938 and were highly praised by Goebbels: *Du und ich* ("You and I") ("splendid and moving", 1.11.1938) and *Am seidenen Faden* ("On a Silk Thread"), both with industrial settings.[568] The tried-and-tested form of Nazi social criticism of the ossified middle-class of the years up to 1914 in *Heimat* (*Homeland*, with Zarah Leander and Heinrich George) unleashed storms of rapture from Goebbels: "Brilliant captures the feel of the pre-war period ... The mask is torn of a false and insincere morality of honour." (22.5.1938) He also found the patriotic melodrama *Dreiklang* ("Triad"), which is still inconsistent politically, "decent in approach and outstanding in atmosphere". (19.5.1938)

30. Leni Riefenstahl's Olympics film *Festival of Beauty*: beneficial to the regime.

The indirectly invoked pride in "modern" and "better" conditions under National Socialism may – along with other current connotations – have helped to strengthen defence readiness to an extent. But to completely uncertain effect: all records suggest that a considerable fear of war was rife in the German population in summer and autumn 1938.

Besides this, these films are by no means products of the line of "confidence propaganda" taken after the Munich agreement,[569] they simple follow the demand expressed by Goebbels from 1937 that films should show "human conflicts" and "real life".

At the same time these social, "lifelike" themes in films also involved risks, which Hitler at least recognized: "The Führer has expressed a wish that he would like to see fewer professional and more human problems in films. And he is quite right. I shall set course appropriately", noted Goebbels on 21.6.1938, this indicating his intention to correct the content of "everyday and contemporary films". This was aimed at films that presented unemployment and a generally miserable existence for employees, as well as men overburdened with work and neglected women. The Nazi press had already criticized themes like this in *Einmal werde ich dir gefallen* ("Some Day You Will Like Me").[570] *Der nackte Spatz* ("The Naked Sparrow"), with a background of tram workers (Goebbels on 5.4.1938: "a direct scandal"), deals with the "professional problems" alluded to by Hitler. These were probably felt to be undesirable on the screen, as blue- and white-collar workers were under excessive pressure from performance-related work and piecework and extended working hours. In December 1938 Hitler personally banned the unduly realistic film about a white-collar worker *Das Leben kann so schön sein* ("Life Can Be So Beautiful"), involving an insurance salesman plagued by the housing shortage and poor pay. But this title and some others as well (*Frau Syvelin*, *Kleiner Mann ganz groß*/"Little Big Man"), and especially the film about workers *Mann für Mann* ("Man by Man"), which was also important later, show that subjects that could easily be misinterpreted were not going to go away. In any case it is starting to become clear that films dealing with current social and political problems are more likely to be counter-productive in an overburdened population.

But if the "everyday films" are counted as political films of 1938 despite controversies of this kind, then there were more than just ten obviously political ones.[571] But only seven of a total of 106 films made in that year can be definitely allotted to the "preparing for war" category (compared with nine of 114 in 1937).[572] It is striking here that three were released in January and three in December – long before and long after the Sudeten crisis of September 1938, even though the odd screening went on into the summer. These seven "war education films" obviously met Goebbels' expectations; he assesses four of them positively (*Ziel in den Wolken*/"Target in the Clouds", *Mit versiegelter Order*, *Der Katzensteg*/"Catwalk", *Furlough on Word of Honor*),[573] and finds only one of them dubious: an early version of *Pour le Mérite*, the most spiteful and aggressive settling of accounts with the Weimar Republic. (1.11.1938)

If Goebbels was satisfied with this work, he probably saw no need for notching up the propaganda levels again. Goebbels even felt that the action-packed film *Kautschuk* (première: 2.11. 1938), launched in early November, and a "hymn to British colonial imperialism",[574] was "magnificently political and artistic". (1.11.1938) *Kautschuk* was withdrawn a few days after the outbreak of war, along with some other films, because "it glorifies a historical act by an English-man". [575] *Kautschuk*, with its "official friend-foe scheme of contradictory positions"[576] – neither expressly consciously pro-British nor a slip that is disapproved of – also symbolizes Hitler's complete lack of firm foreign policy vis-à-vis Great Britain.

Leni Riefenstahl's two Olympic films, both released in 1938, are difficult to fit into the normal film planning pattern. Their public launch was unlike anything ever seen before, and peaked in the première for Hitler's birthday on 20 April 1938. The dictator had also personally ensured that the two parts, *Fest der Völker* (*Festival of the Nations*) and *Fest der Schönheit* (*Festival of Beauty*) should be released simultaneously. Goebbels was of course delighted with the photography and montage in this exceptional documentary. (24./26.11.1938) This "sporting spectacle as a kind of civilian party rally",[577] like the Olympics themselves, brought considerable prestige to the regime, whose representatives also appeared in it in large numbers. It was seen as an outstanding individual aesthetic achievement in 1938, but the Fascist representation of the Aryan competitive spirit will not have failed to make an effect on the audience.

Goebbels certainly shifted his position in terms of film production, and his changing assessments can scarcely be seen as crucial to changes in film policy. That would be to overestimate his influence. But: who, other than Goebbels, could have given important impetus to massive film propaganda creating the right mood for war? The film companies and producers did submit nationalist film material of their own accord, but how were they to know whether this fitted in with changing policies in terms of timing, specially requested subject matter and precise images of the enemy? Especially as this phase in particular was dominated by juggling with the staff in the Ministry and the film companies, which considerably hindered smooth progress. Reichsfilmdramaturg Ewald von Demandowsky moved from the Ministry early in 1939 to the post of Tobis production head. His very young successor Fritz Hippler was only a temporary appointment at first. Then Ernst von Leichtenstern, head of the film department and acting head of production at Ufa from spring 1939 on, was a dilettante with no sense of personal initiative, for which reason Goebbels immediately dismissed him from the Ufa job. Great film-maker like Emil Jannings or Veit Harlan were usually most concerned to get their own projects of the ground. They could not be expected to come up with concrete political themes following the regime's requirements.

It is also permissible to doubt whether Goebbels ever intended to construct a film policy intended to "prepare for war". His activities could have been held back by his lack of certainty about the foreign policy situation.[578] In summer 1938 Goebbels was not completely convinced about Hitler's war plans – to the extent that he was aware of them – and obviously not fully involved in a number of decision-making processes.[579] At the beginning of the second half of 1938 only Hitler's basic intentions in terms of foreign policy and military intentions were clearly discernible (3./17.6.,1.17.7., 21.8.1938): "The Führer is moving vigorously against Czechoslovakia. We must renew our incitement and pressure. Don't let them off the hook. Something will be the last straw." (3.6.1938) Goebbels' scepticism, which can often be perceived only in his mood, probably derives mainly from his assessment of the popular mood as far as readiness for war is concerned. There were rumours even in government circles that the Propaganda Minister tended to be reluctant to go to war.[580] The fact that at the same time Goebbels had technical preparations made for the planned attack and staged a systematic press campaign through his departmental head Alfred Ingemar Berndt, and was thus engaged in "war-related work" in the Propaganda Ministry (13./21.8.1938), is no contradiction. The campaign in the topical media, unlike long-term film propaganda, could easily be fine-tuned at any time. Some entries about tactical restraint in incitement propaganda because of possible panic and fear of war[581] are not consistent with the image of a clearly calculating minister, but convey uncertainty. This is the politics of improvisation and confusion. Future alliances and opponents were not yet fixed. And it was precisely in this situation that Goebbels should have given clear and energetic guidelines to the film companies, thus introducing film production that would "prepare for war". This is the only way in which it would have been possible to fill the cinema programmes with political productions in good time for the start of 1939. But the political initiative was clearly stifled by his inconsistent attitude to Great Britain, for which there is evidence in his attempt to settle on a direction by consulting Hitler and scepticism towards Ribbentrop's clearly anti-English approach:[582] Goebbels did not commission a single anti-British project in 1937/38.[583] And so far there is also not a single passage that shows that the otherwise very impatient Hitler might have recognizably tried to force his Propaganda Minister to sharpen up his film policies.

Anything that we could identify as "preparing for war" in Goebbels' case tends to sound rather half-hearted. The tried-and-tested director Karl Ritter, whose radical and patriotic "war edu-

31. Goebbels' mistress Lida Baarova: minister in crisis.

cation films" should have been the order of the day, was not used at all at first. Goebbels went as far as saying that he "warned Ritter against his new light-hearted film *Capriccio*" because he felt Ritter should "make only major political and national films" (14.1.1938), but the director of *Furlough on Word of Honor* and *Unternehmen Michael* went for the light-hearted genre, with the exception of preparing for *Pour le Mérite*: the "nonsense musical" (Karsten Witte) *Capriccio* came out in August 1938, followed in April 1939 by *Die Hochzeitsreise* ("The Honeymoon Trip"), a 19th century romance. Goebbels accordingly condemned the two films as "dreadful rubbish" (on *Capriccio*, 1.5.1938) and "dreadfully long-winded, literary nonsense, scarcely tolerable" (on *Die Hochzeitsreise*, 23.3.1939).[584]

A cinematic "preparation for war" without Ritter? When Goebbels had said: "Ritter is one of the few people who can make political films." (1.12.1937) Then when Ritter finally turned to political material again in the last three months before the outbreak of war, Goebbels had changed his mind. He was now beset with not inconsiderable doubts about the effectiveness of Ritter's one-dimensional, simplistic propaganda. It was not until the war had started that this led to his being forbidden to direct, but even on 30.7.1939 Goebbels wrote: "I think that Ritter has been ridiculously overestimated. He handles nationalist material in a very unscrupulous way."

At the same time it was inconsistent to accommodate "refined psychological insights" in individual projects aimed at military education, if this was not happening on a larger scale. Thus from July to September 1938 Goebbels was planning a large-scale Emil Jannings film, *Der weite Weg* ("The Long Way"), with a screenplay by Hans Fallada. He expectantly describes the project as the "first major political film" (10.7.1938), a statement that devalues other films in production at the same time. But the project was held up by difficulties in presenting the period after 1914. Goebbels criticized Jannings' and Fallada's draft as "too pessimistic" (13.7.1938) and "demoralizing" (13.7.1938): "The film is intended to present the virtues of war as well as its vices." (13.7.1938) Despite the fact that the Minister was highly committed personally, first banning the screenplay and then editing it himself, according to the diary a complete script was still not available in late September. (28.9.1938) An equally long-standing project for a colonial film by Luis Trenker called *Leuchtendes Land* ("Shining Country") also displeased Goebbels, and so did a draft for a winter relief fund propaganda film. (31.5.1938) The Minister did not seem to be in a hurry, just issued bans or commissioned revised versions.

Goebbels' private situation in autumn 1938 did not leave much room for careful thought about film propaganda projects either. He was in the midst of what was so far the most difficult personal and political crisis of his period of office. At first Goebbels' attention was still drawn to the consequences of the Reich Pogrom Night, especially how to proceed with anti-Semitic propaganda. His marital crisis then became more acute because of the Baarova affair; his wife Magda appealed to Hitler in order to get rid of her husband's mistress. It seemed possible that the Propaganda Minister might resign. Goebbels responded with health problems, maudlin sentiment, complaints and announcements that he did not feel like doing anything, rather than long-term calculations in terms of film policy. He did very little checking of films: "Seen parts of films, but without peace and quiet." (28.9.1938) When he watches an unsatisfactory film and then announces that he wants to "take more trouble over things again", there are no discernible consequences. Questions about films, he writes on 9.12.1938, "do not interest me all that much at the moment". But a proper degree of stylized loud regrets and self-pity cannot cover up his real inactivity. Goebbels let things slide: "Watched a few films. But without real interest. I simply don't feel like it any more." (30.12.1938) There is not a single important thought about film policy before the end of the year. Two films were banned without Goebbels' involvement in November/December (*Preußische Liebesgeschichte* / "Prussian Love Story" and *Das Leben kann so schön sein*). He remorsefully admits the organized protest about the Baarova film *Der Spieler* ("The Gambler"), whose première "might have been worse" (29.10.1938), but which had to be banned a few days later. He even broke off his diary entries for two weeks – for the first and only time. Shortly before this he had to record criticism of the newsreels from Hitler. (17.12.1938)

A lack of film propaganda in the year the war broke out?

In spring 1939 – according to film historian Jerzy Toeplitz when summing up National Socialist film policy six years after they came to power – Goebbels was scarcely able to conceal the "list of failures" at the Reichsfilmkammer conference any more by blaming them on organizational problems.[585] And indeed the Minister's statements about his "extraordinary efforts to put the cinema at the service of the people"[586] did not lay down any concrete direction. A few weeks before the departing Reichsfilmdramaturg Ewald von Demandowsky had expressed gentle self-criticism, but at the same time warned of "current and topical problems".[587] His remark, which is actually correct, that "comedy can be ideological" too must have seemed like an excuse at the time. The absence of "political works of cinematic art" was not addressed more rigorously because of the tame "observations on art" that had replaced traditional film criticism and prevented bad reviews in the daily press. Even the editors of the *Völkischer Beobachter*, the Party newspaper, made an effort – and curiously so do contemporary analyses – to find political messages in humdrum comedies. Even films like Willi Forst's ambiguous comedy *Bel Ami*, which is sometimes interpreted as critical of the regime, were then received positively.[588] But there was still criticism of a lack of ideology and philosophical outlook in favour of presenting a private and "individualistic" striving for happiness by the film's protagonists from the Reichsfilmkammer's magazine *Der deutsche Film*.

In the early days of 1939 Goebbels did record the consequences of his continuing inactivity in the field of film because of his marital crisis and fear that he would lose his job: "Things are stagnating in the cinema. I must put on a bit of pressure again. But all that is still to come." (22.1. 1939) There was one "press film" project (31.1.1939) that did emerge at this time, probably from sheer desire to act. Goebbels praises this as a wonderful idea: "I am still working on a new idea for a press film late in the evening. *Die siebte Großmacht* ("The Seventh Great Power"). I think it will be quite something!" (31.1.1939), and it crops up several times in the course of the year, but never got beyond the planning stage.[589]

Only the "life-like" topical films developed into an omnipresent component of the cinema programme. *Drei wunderschöne Tage* ("Three Magnificent Days"), an unsophisticated leisure film, is packed with moving human fates and "Kraft durch Freude" ("Strength through Joy") propaganda.[590] *Mann für Mann* deals with another focal point in the propaganda directed at social themes. It is about workers involved in the autobahn building programme. But here solidarity among the workers is only one part of keeping the community together. The individual worker, and this is the message, progresses only through hard work and achievement, and ultimately is looking only for higher wages and private, middle-class happiness.[591] Although Goebbels found the first version "politically good and artistically a success" (9.2.1939), several retakes were demanded for propaganda purposes.[592] In May the Propaganda Ministry insisted that human failure should not be seen to have caused the disaster scenes at the end of the film, but that there should be an "earth tremor as the reason for the caisson accident".[593]

Die Stimme aus dem Äther ("The Voice from the Ether") deals with radio as a life-enhancing medium that educates the people and endows things with meaning. This is a Zeitfilm initiated by Goebbels as early as October 1936 and decked out with numerous Nazi symbols (there is a picture of Goebbels in the station director's office)[594]. In the problem film *Fräulein* ("very good ideologically", 26.5.1939) the "lifelike" quality lay in the allocation of gender roles. But there were limits to topicality. Faced with the courtroom drama *Im Namen des Volkes* ("In the Name of the People"), based on a 1938 court case, Goebbels found fault with the "official character" (24.1. 1939) of the film and after making short-term changes uses it as a basis for fundamental statements: "Demandowski's films criticized by me. We must avoid being didactic whenever themes are intended to educate. A little too much in this respect destroys the whole effect." (25.1.1939)

There are also next to no signs that Goebbels took Hitler's foreign policy as a reason for changing his film policy in 1939 either. No co-ordination with the dictator's instructions in April that 1 September is the earliest possible date for the beginning of the war can be discerned. The strongest impression is of a Propaganda Minister who is himself saturated, and damping down expectations. Goebbels notes on 23.3.1939: "The Führer is developing his future foreign policy. He wants to let things calm down a little now, so that he can regain confidence. And then the colonial question will come up. Just one thing after another." Perhaps Goebbels is not being completely open about his thoughts here, or possibly Hitler did not put him properly in the picture. In any case, the people's "bubbling joy" over Lithuania'a renunciation of the Memel territory prompts Goebbels to issue a warning that there is now a danger that the petit bourgeoisie will believe things will always be like this. There are all sorts of fantastic ideas about the next lot of German foreign policy plans in the air. I will inveigh against this some time." On the other hand he records Hitler's intentions for "solving the Danzig question": "He wants to try putting a bit of pressure on Poland and hopes she will respond." (25.3.1939)

It is questionable that a "long debate" with Hitler on the same day "about film production as such, which is still greatly in need of reform" identified deficiencies in terms of content, or that they discussed following the daily propaganda slogans more closely. Rather than allotting urgent tasks to Goebbels, the dictator gave express permission for the Propaganda Minister to travel to Hungary, Greece and Turkey for several weeks.[595] It is interesting that the next day, certainly also as a reaction to the meeting with Hitler, there is a striking passage about a conversation with Leichtenstern, the head of the film department: "Talked over the situation and role of the film again with Leichtenstern. We want to film more topical material. Get on top of contemporary problems. This needs rapid initiatives." (26.3.1939) But in fact Goebbels, in the course of several meetings with the Ufa, Terra and Tobis production heads (22./23.3.1939), had finally approved the film companies' production plans for the autumn. Given the long planning periods involved, this would have been the last opportunity to influence the cinema programme for the coming months. Another "discussion with our 3 film company production chiefs" (20.3.1939) must therefore have been about training questions and looking after actors.

Another disturbing factor in film planning was the Ufa management crisis, which had been smouldering for weeks. In May 1939 Goebbels fell victim to a strange plot by his rival, secretary Karl Hanke, who tried to force Ufa production chief Alfred Greven out of the office (see entries for 24–28 May 1939). Differences with Greven of opinion about material and planning really did not exist[596] and there is still absolutely no indication that Goebbels wanted to force Ufa to make propaganda films. There is also no background to Greven's statement of 9 May 1939 about the company's 1939/40 production programme. He said "that some changes were still possible with respect to the new guidelines that the Herr Minister has recently issued to the production chiefs".[597] These "new guidelines" do not have to have been political: on 26.6. Goebbels mentioned another address to the production heads ("I explain my programme again. Against silly ideas or intellectualism. For full-blooded material. I hope that it will work out now"). This suggests that it was a continuation of the "real life" directives issued in March and May.

If one considers the situation reports, available only for Ufa and dated 9 May 1939 and 8 June 1939, about the 1939/40 production programme, there are five projects that are clearly political:[598] *Das scharlachrote Korps* ("The Scarlet Corps"), *Sprung über den Schatten/Attacke* (*The Leopard Changes its Spots*), *Bayer 205*, *Legion Condor*, *Offiziersehe* ("Officers Marriage").[599] *Kadetten* ("Cadets"), directed by Karl Ritter and *Maria Ilona*, *Das Lied der Wüste* (*The Desert Song*) and *Alarm auf Station III* ("Alert on Station III") were already being shot in May/June. Of these five plans for political films by Ufa none was actually realized or completed. For example, the following was said about *Offiziersehe* on 8 June 1939:" … the question of whether this film can be made is discussed. The material on which it is based, the marriage of Lieutenant Colin, deals with a German officer's love for a Frenchwoman. The board considered it expedient to refrain from filming this material, following the suggestion of Herr Min.rat Leichtenstern, as the evaluation of the film is to a large extent dependent on the political situation at the time."[600] This reference by Leichtenstern to the uncertain development of the political situation makes it clear how uncertain the planning of film productions was. *The Leopard Changes its Spots* was delayed "because Herr Staatssekretär Hanke sees the material differently".[601] This plan was finally shelved at the latest after the war began. *Bayer 205* was abandoned in subsequent weeks and not realized until 1942, under the title *Germanin*, *Legion Condor* (see below) was not taken any further after the non-aggression pact of 22 August 1939 because of its anti-Soviet tendencies.

Ufa also gave up *Das scharlachrote Korps*[602] in the autumn, after very little preparation work, ostensibly because it was to be set in Canada.[603] *Maria Ilona*, a drama of "duty before personal love" set in the Hungarian revolt against the Habsburg monarchy in 1848, was refused a certificate after shooting finished in July/August 1939 – allegedly because of tension before the outbreak of war.[604] *Alarm auf Station III* and the elaborate, cautiously anti-English Zarah Leander melodrama *The Desert Song* did not appear until November 1939, after the war broke out. The director Carl Froelich tried to get filming started immediately in June on *Maria, Königin von Schottland* ("Mary Queen of Scots"), an idea that had been in circulation for some time, and was anti-English per se, but to no avail. Work on it did not start until 1940.[605] And the Tobis programme for 1939/40, introduced in late July had plans for 46 films – nine of them were already complete and twelve more were already in the studio – but none of these showed any features redolent of propaganda.[606] As well as this, it is justifiable to assume for 1939 as well as 1938 that Goebbels hoped for an accommodation with Poland at least until the early summer,[607] and thus directed short-term press and radio propaganda, which could be stopped at any time, towards war, but not long-term film propaganda.

Another distraction for the Propaganda Minister came in the form of the fallout from Goebbels' marital crisis in June/July 1939. His permanent secretary Karl Hanke's relationship with

Magda Goebbels had trickled out, which was another embarrassing matter for the Propaganda Minister. Goebbels took a longer summer holiday than he usually did in July: visits to festivals in Vienna, Bayreuth and Venice kept him away from Berlin for weeks. He was unable to involve himself to any great extent in current projects and examining films. With the exception of the "press film", whose treatment must still have been a long way from Goebbels' own ideas in August 1939 ("Strange how little feel our people have for modern material", he said of the new draft on 1.8.1939), there is scarcely any sign of closer imagination or detailed planning.[608] Goebbels maintained a remarkable journalistic silence in July/August as well.[609] A clear example of this passive approach is his comment on the diplomatic comedy *Kitty und die Weltkonferenz* (*Kitty and the World Conference*) by Helmut Käutner, a lightly politically accentuated film version of a stage play about an international conference that had run in Berlin in 1938. Goebbels praised it on the day of the German-Soviet non-aggression pact: "A very nice and amusing film with the very talented Hannelore Schroth." (23.8.1939) It almost seems as though he failed to notice the problems raised by this "topical" and "contemporary" film and the pleasant impression given by the British and French politicians. Far from being held back for safety's sake it was premiered in Stuttgart on 25 August. It was not banned until 17 October 1939, two weeks after the Berlin première. It seems that the way the English ministers were portrayed had displeased Foreign Minister Ribbentrop.[610] The *Völkischer Beobachter* wrote with a clearly critical undertone that Käutner could have "put a political satire together: but he chose not to, and concentrated on the harmlessness of girlish grace".[611] A fat exclamation mark and the film title heavily underlined on a list of films drawn up shortly afterwards by Max Winkler headed "losses as a result of war" – the costs were to be borne by the Ministry of Finance – make it clear that even at a later stage Goebbels did not really understand that he had missed the point when assessing this film.[612]

Rather like the films offered in 1938, the 1939 cinema programme does not seem to have made Goebbels feel that there was not enough propaganda. So dissatisfaction is not a motive for greater effort. Four political films in the "military" category opened from January to the end of August: *Tumult in Damaskus*, *Drei Unteroffiziere* ("Three NCOs"), *Grenzfeuer* ("Frontier Fire") and *Flucht ins Dunkel* ("Escape into Darkness"). *Der Gouverneur* ("The Governor") is a special case: the main character, Willy Birgel, is introduced in the cinema advertisements as a "soldier who only knows his duty", but his struggle is directed against the "corruption of parliamentarianism". *Ziel in den Wolken* ("Target in the Clouds"), *Dreizehn Mann und eine Kanone* ("Thirteen Men and a Cannon") and *Pour le Mérite* were still present in the cinemas from 1938. They were joined by the documentary *Im Kampf gegen den Weltfeind – deutsche Freiwillige in Spanien* ("At War with the Enemy of the World – German Volunteers in Spain"). Goebbels does not mention every one of the films. There is nothing on the title *Dreizehn Mann und eine Kanone*, and no comment on the love-versus-duty film *Drei Unteroffiziere*[613] – but on the whole his reaction is positive. In *Tumult in Damaskus* "milieu, slant and attitude" were simply magnificent, Goebbels enthused on 14.2.1939, topped only by *Der Gouverneur*, which was also "delightful in attitude and slant and sometimes distressing to the point of tears". (16.4.1939) *Grenzfeuer*, "a very nice and exciting film" (27.5.1939) and *Flucht ins Dunkel* ("Escape Into Darkness") ("has come out well in direction, acting and slant", 2.7.1939) are to Goebbels' taste. Ritter's documentary about Spain is "somewhat long-winded at first, but then very good", Goebbels decides on 14.6.1939.

Hitler was rather more critical about the political productions of 1939, according to his adjutants' records. He only liked *Grenzfeuer* ("well acted")[614] because of Attila Hörbiger's performance, and in *Drei Unteroffiziere* as well only the "characters and filming (were) good", but the "plot not exciting enough".[615] But on *Der Gouverneur* there is only the terse comment "nothing special",[616] while *Im Kampf gegen den Weltfeind – deutsche Freiwillige in Spanien* was judged "good".[617] Compared with the "very good" for *Stimme aus dem Äther* [618] for example, the dictator's judgements – incidentally he did not see any of the films until after the première, which made interventions difficult – do not sound exactly fulsome. But a note on *Frau am Steuer* ("Woman at the Helm") shows that things could get a lot more negative: Hitler found this comedy about an unemployed house-husband "very bad", indeed "repulsive", at a time that demanded maximum manliness.[619] Later, in December, Hitler had some hard things to say to his Propaganda Minister about inadequate ideological films in the course of the year.

And so film policy that "prepared for war" was not made on the plane of film content. Something that has blurred the issue so far is over-interpretation of the film industry's vigorous technical preparation for the "state of emergency". For instance, a few months before the war started Ufa was taking precautions against air raids at its gigantic studio complex in Babelsberg, Pots-

32. Willy Fritsch as a man at the stove in *Frau am Steuer* (1939): rejected by the Führer.

dam, and to secure operations if personnel were called up. The first planning of this kind even dates from the time of the Sudeten crisis. Goebbels wrote on 30.8.1939 about a "discussion with Winkler, Hippler and Demandowski about the present state of the film": "The whole business is coming to a halt. We must make a series of appeals, or it's all going to fall apart." It was not until this moment that Ufa was informed about the imminent outbreak of war.[620] Even before this discussion the company had urgently requested that measures should be taken "promptly" to secure the "continuation of German film production in case of war".[621] This included protection against call-up (which is what Goebbels means by "appeals"), securing fuel and material supplies, preferential treatment for film transport etc.

These long-standing, careful preparations should not be confused with intentions to complete films: the making of a smuggling film like *Alarm auf Station III* can scarcely be seen as proof that Babelsberg had "not been unprepared" because the film "must have been planned well in advance".[622] When film historians (Rother, Kreimeier, Toeplitz) talk about "systematic preparation" by a "supremely well informed" film industry, they are erroneously equating technical and organizational preparations for the event of a war with plans for propaganda films.

The question of defective policy and mobilization in terms of film planning and films actually made also and particularly applies to the sphere of the anti-Communist film. After the German-Soviet non-aggression pact of 23 August 1939, all the anti-Soviet films produced up to 1939 were forbidden,[623] and all the current anti-Bolshevik film projects were stopped as well.[624] And so if there had been a war, as many people thought there would be, against the Soviet Union, the ideological opponent that had been resisted for years, would there have been a "military "film programme devised for this end already in place? It is clear that the producers were taken completely by surprise by the change of direction. In the end the planning and showing of "anti-Bolshevik" films continued even after the press was instructed to stop "any polemic against the Soviet Union and Bolshevism immediately".[625] The documentary propaganda film *Im Kampf gegen den Weltfeind* was actually launched with a great deal of to-do as late as July.

The halt called to "anti-Bolshevik" film production first affected the Karl Ritter film *Kadetten* ("Cadets"), about the invasion of Berlin by Russian troops in 1760 and – by the same director – *Legion Condor*, a paean of praise to the Luftwaffe's intervention in the Spanish Civil War. *Kadetten* was ready for the censor in August, but *Legion Condor* had only just started shooting. The Ufa board discussed the two Ritter films on the same day that the non-aggression pact was signed.[626] It was decided that *Kadetten* should be withdrawn immediately, or rather that the planned première at the Nuremberg National Socialist Party Rally on 5 September 1939 should be cancelled. The following extremely cautious statement was made about *Legion Condor*: "We should draw Herr Prof. Ritter's attention to the censorship difficulties that could occur for the said film project in the light of the newly created world-political situation given that Russian characters are shown in an unsympathetic light. Here we should point out that the censorship difficulties that arose with *Kadetten* are possibly also linked with the changed world political situation. Herr Prof. Ritter should be caused to submit the screenplay of for the film 'Legion Condor' to Herr Minister Dr. Goebbels so that he can decide personally whether the film project can be completed on the basis of the existing screenplay."

Goebbels then states with regret on 9.9.1939: "Ritter's *Legion Condor*, 2 acts. Turned out very well. But unfortunately cannot be used at the moment because of its strongly anti-Bolshevik tendency. I shall have everything put back for a time."[627] He had already said that *Kadetten* was "unsuccessful overall" and "too artificial" on 30.7.1939.

Max Winkler's above-mentioned list, corrected by Goebbels in the closing days of October 1939, includes all the "film losses" by the big companies "as a result of political tension before the war and as a result of the war itself".[628] *Legion Condor* and *Kadetten* together lost 1.5 mill. Reichsmarks, and two other titles are listed that were allegedly discontinued "because of an anti-Bolshevik tendency". Goebbels wrote on this subject: "Our film losses caused by the political change are enormous. Above all because the anti-Bolshevik films have been dropped. The Finance Ministry will have to intervene here, as an act of God is involved." (29.10.1939) But closer examination shows that in this case – and Winkler tried this with numerous other titles as well – ancient "non-sellers", i.e. screenplays that already existed were presented as current losses, so that these could be reclaimed from the Finance Ministry. Thus *Staatsfeind Nr. 1* and the Wien film *Summa cum laude* showed only 6,000 and 13,515 Reichsmarks of preliminary costs respectively. This would suggest that the most that existed was a draft script. These projects were announced in the press as coming "anti-Bolshevik" film events as early as 1936/37. Nothing suggests that anyone was thinking of making them in summer 1939. Further to this, Winkler's list contains other titles of abandoned film projects with no clear political agenda: *Radetzkymarsch* ("Radetzky March", "cancelled, as not up-to-date",film set in 1914/ 18), *Reiterattacke* ("Cavalry Charge"), the Tobis film *Der letzte Appell* ("The Final Appeal", allegedly for technical reasons) and the Terra film *Der Kommandant* ("The Commandant", allegedly because the outdoor scenes could not possibly be shot). Hans Weidemann's *Kameradschaft* project also had to be broken off. Of this it says in the Ufa minutes "that work on the film *Kameradschaft* (previous working title *Helden des Alltags*), produced by Herr Weidemann, had to be broken off because of changed circumstances. Current political conditions mean that the content of the film has to be seen as out of date."[629]

In any event, these film plans are not a large-scale "anti-Bolshevik" film programme, nor do they suggest particular efforts in anticipation of a war. They are at best part of the regular political propaganda film planning process. The costs are largely set too high because Winkler and Goebbels hoped to get higher refunds in this way. But in the case of *Der Kommandant* and *Reiterattacke* the preliminary costs are very low, suggesting that the productions were at a very early stage, or even fictitious planning.

This suggests that even if the war had started under totally different circumstances, in other words against the Soviet Union, film production would have been only marginally better prepared. They would have had to rely mainly on older political productions and repeat them when the war broke out.

Films available and film impact in the year the war started

"Ufa did not have a 'war education film' on its ideological books in the year the war broke out",[630] according to the assessment in Klaus Kreimeier's monograph on Germany's largest big film studio. There were only three clearly political productions to balance the 19 Volksfilme: *Drei Unteroffiziere*, a "failed hymn of praise to doing one's military duty", the contradictory workers' film *Mann für Mann* and *Der Stammbaum des Dr. Pistorius* ("The Family Tree of Dr. Pistorius"), a particularly dull Volksgemeinschaft film ("national community film").

But what do all these figures and film analyses say if we do not look at the way in which all these political propaganda and Volksfilme were actually presented on the spot in the cinemas? Ultimately psychological preparation for war could have been achieved with the aid of repetition, extended runs or elaborate advertising campaigns for the few political films there were.

A systematic examination of cinema programmes in the Reich capital Berlin from January 1939, as advertised twice weekly on the cinema pages of the *Völkischer Beobachter*, sheds some light on this question. The programme pages are broken down into the 17 Ufa première theatres in Berlin (Ufa-Palast am Zoo, Gloria, Capitol etc.) and the other cinemas – over 130 of them – in all the city districts. There is one major reservation: Berlin was certainly never representative of the rest of the Reich, neither of other large cities nor middle-sized or small towns, and not for the provinces, with a maximum of one cinema per town. Even the structure of the audience, which was metropolitan and demanding, with a lot of alternative amusements available, is not comparable elsewhere. Thus the following observations make no claim for general validity. But at least the Reich capital was a trend-setter: bans, repeat campaigns, film cancellations, withdrawal of undesirable films, successes and failures, changes from propaganda to Volksfilme and vice versa – all this came into effect here quicker than anywhere else. Immediate delivery of large numbers of copies and swift implementation of instructions from the highest authority were guaranteed by the short distances between the authorities and the people who ran the cinemas.

The majority of film premières took place in the Berlin première cinemas; only a very few were reserved for other cities. The distribution system was geared to exploiting films as quickly and massively as possible, to make room for titles that were pushing up behind. Thus many productions ran only relatively briefly in the individual cinemas and were extended only if they were very successful. The première cinema system meant that expensive, prestigious major films were often only to be seen in selected première cinemas in the first weeks after the launch; there was often only one copy, or very few. It was only after this that they got to the regular cinemas, in a maximum number of copies, and were able to reach a mass audience. This system applied to a few major cities at least. But in the rest of the Reich a politically important film was often launched in the largest possible number of cinemas at the same time.

Thus the actual date of the première does not actually reveal anything about when mass exploitation took place. It was the successful popular and propaganda films in particular that stayed in a few cinemas for a long time – not infrequently only at the Ufa-Palast am Zoo – where they enjoyed a great deal of attention from the press, but could reach only a relatively restricted number of spectators.[631] But for a major launch, for a time up to 50 per cent of all the cinemas were occupied by a single film and up to two thirds by three or four films, even though this was usually for a maximum of a week to ten days. Theoretically this method offered a good basis for using the cinema in war preparation.

Attendance at certain films had been deliberately promoted since 1933 by the National Socialist Party, which sent whole sections off to the cinema.[632] In provincial areas without cinemas the Party has so-called Gau film offices, which tried to provide the local people with films; ideally works of propaganda, through mobile "sound film vans". In the year the war broke out – and later as well – a third of the population still had no access to film showings in normal cinemas. The Party's efforts in the pre-war period are difficult to present in figures, as we have little but the NS's own version. Allegedly over 1.5 million viewers were "taken care of" as early as 1937.[633] The showings were arranged so that the often bucolic spectators, saw a newsreel, then a short cultural or documentary film and finally a propaganda feature film. In 1939 activities of this kind must have been backed up by special events and performances for the Party youth.[634] Curt Belling, the organizer of the Party's mobile film scheme, writing in April in an essay called "Sound film vans travel nation-wide" stressed the "Party propaganda mission" of the film screenings, with political supporting films accompanied by a speaker.[635]

The overall staging of this "ritualized mode of presentation" was also perfected in urban cinemas throughout the period, and the "special context in which the films were viewed used to reinforce the propaganda message".[636]

It remains questionable whether this National Socialist Party film effort was ultimately effective as "preparation for war" and managed to make up for the lack of current productions, at least in the country, by one-sided screenings of old political films. The high proportion of racial and ideological "documentary films" suggests a different set of intentions.

The mobile film performances[637] (restricted to the rural population,[638] which was secondary in terms of propaganda significance) – in contrast with increased efforts after the war started – cannot ultimately have been adequate. Young people's "film education" was carried out very systematically[639] as part of the Sunday young people's film hours and Jugendfilmstunde ("Hitler Youth Film Ceremonies"), but here too it remains difficult to assess how crucial shaping the opinions of this target group was for the success of psychological war preparation.

Back to our examination of the films offered by the Berlin cinemas. The propaganda film *Pour le Mérite* was launched in the penultimate week of December 1938 and was still running at the Ufa Palast am Zoo on 1 January, but it was making only sporadic appearances by the end of the month. *Kautschuk* and *Du und ich* ("You and I") were the only other political productions to be seen, and they were spread fairly thinly, as cinemas were dominated by the comedy *Napoleon ist an allem schuld* ("It's All Napoleon's Fault"). In February *Im Namen des Volkes* was the only openly political film, while Hans Albers' *Sergeant Berry* was occupying most screens. In March *Dreizehn Mann und eine Kanone*, *Ziel in den Wolken* and *Tumult in Damaskus* were alternating as the most widely distributed political films, but they were certainly well behind Zarah Leander's *Der Blaufuchs* (*The Fox Fur Coat*).

The *Völkischer Beobachter*'s cinema programme shows major appearances by the Harlan melodrama *Das unsterbliche Herz* ("The Immortal Heart") for the invasion of remnant Czechoslovakia on 14/15 March 1939; brief revivals include an obviously counter-productive documentary about the First World War, *Trommelfeuer an der Westfront* ("Barrage at the Western Front"),[640] and also *Musketier Maier III* ("Musketeer Maier III") and the US war film *Seekadetten* ("Cadets at Sea"). The week after the invasion (17–20 March 1939) saw a striking surge for *Dreizehn Mann und eine Kanone*, which was now trailed as the "powerful war film and thriller" (seven cinemas, instead of two in the previous week). Small suburban cinemas in particular tried to involve themselves in the supposedly patriotic mood. But *Dreizehn Mann und eine Kanone* disappeared almost completely in the last two weeks in March, and the majority of cinemas were showing the melodrama *Der Schritt vom Wege* ("Step off the Path"). There was only one political film running in the 17 large Ufa cinemas: *Tumult in Damaskus*. In April military films started to be revived to encourage "'military fitness' in the 'national comrades'".[641] The première of *Drei Unteroffiziere* in the Ufa-Palast am Zoo was accompanied by military documentaries like *Minen in Sperrlücke X215* ("Mines at Barrage X215"); the film played there for only eleven days because there was a poor audience response, while *Der Gouverneur* occupied the première cinemas from its first showing on 25 April until 14 June. Two "tendential films" dating from 1938 were still around (*Ziel in den Wolken* and *Tumult in Damaskus*), thus increasing the proportion of propaganda material for a time, along with the "Special newsreel for the Führer's birthday", which was to be seen in almost every third cinema, but they remained well behind the Volksfilme. And so early in May, when the *Völkischer Beobachter* stepped up its smear campaign against Poland, *Drei Unteroffiziere*, *Ziel in den Wolken* and *Tumult in Damaskus* were to be seen only sporadically. For almost the whole month *Der Gouverneur* was the propaganda title running in the 17 première cinemas. It was not joined by *Die Stimme aus dem Äther* until the last week in May. Comparison with the cinema programme in Vienna shows that *Ziel in den Wolken*, *Drei Unteroffiziere* and *Tumult in Damaskus* were playing in 15 of 65 cinemas (*Völkischer Beobachter* for 15.5.1939) there in the same period, thus beating Berlin, where the screens were completely dominated by films like *Prinzessin Sissi*, *Die Hochzeitsreise* ("The Honeymoon Trip"), *Hotel Sacher* and *Liebe streng verboten* (*Love Strictly Forbidden*), while documentary films like *Unsere Artillerie* ("Our Artillery") were on hardly anywhere.

The situation was not much different in June: *Ziel in den Wolken* and *Tumult in Damaskus* were the only films that unambiguously "promoted war". They were not joined by the documentaries *Helden in Spanien* ("Heroes in Spain") and *Deutsche Freiwillige in Spanien* ("German Volunteers in Spain") until the middle of the month, sometimes as the supporting programme, sometimes as the main film. *Der Gouverneur* enjoyed mass screenings only for just under two weeks.

Finally, July showed propaganda performances that were unambiguous but brief. *Der Gouverneur*, *Grenzfeuer* and the Karl Ritter film *Im Kampf gegen den Weltfeind* occupied over 50 per cent of cinemas for a time. Only *Im Kampf gegen den Weltfeind* ("At War with the enemy of the World") was shown in 51 cinemas for a time, including eight première houses. But by the end of the month showing of this documentary had sunk to almost zero, to be replaced by Volksfilme and thrillers (*Frau am Steuer*, *Steputat & Co.*, *Morgen werde ich verhaftet*/"I'll be Arrested Tomorrow").

In the first half of August *Der Polizeifunk meldet* ("Police Radio Reports"), *Robert und Bertram* and *Mann für Mann* represented the political repertory, with none of them from the "military" category. In accordance with the official order dated 10 August 1939,[642] the documentary film *Der Westwall* ("The West Wall") was often screened in support, but obviously not in all cinemas, which was the aim.

Between 29 and 31 August 1939, it is significant that political programmes were shown in only 14 of a total of 130 cinemas. They included *Mann für Mann*, *Grenzfeuer* and *Der Gouverneur* in first place. But the rest of the cinemas were dominated by films like *Die Geliebte* ("The Mistress"), *Fräulein*, *Hallo Janine* ("Hello Janine") and *Die Frau ohne Vergangenheit* ("Woman without a Past"). The 17 Ufa première theatres were showing nothing but Volksfilme and melodramas: *Die Geliebte* seven times, *Heimatland* ("Homeland") twice and *It Was a Gay Ballnight* and *Junggesellen* ("Bachelors"). The change in the first ten days of the war in September is also revealing: there were no repeats, and there was no discernibly political film running in the 17 première cinemas except *Mann für Mann*. *Robert und Bertram* and *Der Polizeifunk meldet* were shown only sporadically. *Mann für Mann* was the only one being shown on a large scale after war broke out. There were no changes throughout September. On the contrary: the proportion of propaganda fell below five per cent for the first time.[643] The only omnipresent element was announcements of the first war newsreels from the eastern front.

This listing actually contains nothing to suggest that the film programmes in early 1939 really were suitable for "creating the necessary psychological requirements for the German aggression strategy".[644] A very small number of films that were somewhat questionable as far as their political effect was concerned would have had to cover the whole range of film "preparation for war", alongside a very few extremely short-lived documentaries (other than the newsreels). Only the Volksfilme actually preferred by the public were shown on a large scale for several weeks, treatment accorded to propaganda films for only a few days. The laws of the market could not be suspended artificially. If unspectacular political films had lingered unduly, this would have damaged overall audience ratings. Also, the authorities could certainly prescribe supporting films, but it was considerably more difficult to force repeats of feature films on owners of middle-sized cinema groups, who were profit-oriented and anyway stubborn. *Im Kampf gegen den Weltfeind*, a documentary propaganda film officially commissioned by Hitler, was unsuccessful with the public despite a mass launch, and was completely withdrawn from circulation after the non-aggression pact in late August.[645] Thus the concentrated propaganda campaign in June (launch of the newsreel about the return of "Legion Condor" and two films on the Spanish Civil War) had been the peak of "preparation for war" in summer 1939.

An ultimately complete picture of the effect of the 1939 film programme could really only be provided with the addition of cinemagoers' reactions. But audience reactions are known only for the war period.

The audience figures look only a little better. A film that turns out to be a crass error at the cinema box office is hardly like to have a high indoctrination potential. But even a financial success does nor necessarily mean an actual effect or concrete consequences in terms of people's actions. This was shown in a very complex way in 1941 by the example of the film *I Accuse*, which was very successful as far as numbers were concerned.[646] And anyway, audience ratings are truly reflected only in the total number of cinema tickets sold, and thus a film's turnover – and even this is true only to a limited extent, as prices were always reduced for important political films – and not, as frequently happens, by the financial bottom line, in other words the profit. Excessively expensive propaganda films like *Ohm Krüger* made practically no profits because they cost so much to make; only the considerable turnover shows the very large audience figures.

Audience figures to 1939 are extremely unsatisfactory. For example, in 1938 the figures seem to have fluctuated very greatly from month to month. The film industry provides a list of reasons: "poor weather for going to the cinema" in July/August, "political unrest" in September/October (Czechoslovakia), "Jewish events" in November and a "lack of good films" in December.[647] In summer 1939 the downward trend in cinema attendance,[648] triggered by international tensions, mobilization and the outbreak of war, was reinforced by an extraordinary heat-wave, which reached its climax in the period between 18 August and 9 September. "Only the production costs and the estimated box-office income for the German home market (are) known" for the films that could be seen to be "preparing for war".[649] These estimates show good figures for *Unternehmen Michael*, *Patrioten*, *Furlough on Word of Honor* and *Pour le mérite*.[650] Figures for audiences, film copies and detailed regional information in the daily press and film magazines like *Der Film* or *Film-Kurier* are not always reliable, as they were also used for advertising and were intended to provoke curiosity.[651]

And so unfavourable conditions for making the desired impact have to be considered alongside the clearly inadequate number of "war education films". Even in the context of additional propaganda efforts made in 1939 these films – aesthetically and psychologically inferior to the war-time productions – seem to have contributed little to the country's "readiness for war".[652]

After the invasion of Poland and the war that this unleashed the Propaganda Minister wrote even more in his diary each day and tried to redefine his role. He carefully crafts his image as the most important man after Hitler at the head of a nation at war. But despite all this: failures to make sufficient propaganda preparation in the previous months, even if this is disputed by Goebbels, were now being inevitably revealed. What could the Minister do to make up for lost time? Apart from efforts, now urgently needed, to adjust the propaganda machine and the reporting media to the new requirements, the territory available for a through reorientation of feature film propaganda remained uncharted.

On 28 August 1939, the date originally set for the invasion, Goebbels informed the production heads via Max Winkler that he wanted "to change the film programmes when things get serious". He continues, still vaguely: "This programme change is mainly intended to work in favour of apparently suitable material that is not unduly expensive; only in the last resort should it entail reducing the actual number of films available." Ufa decided on the basis of this that only five of their total of 91 film projects, including the films that had appeared since 1 July 1939, were "unsuitable for the war period in terms of material" (including *Fremde Rosen*/ "Strange Roses", *Der ferne Ruf*/ "The Cry from Afar", *Jagd ohne Gnade* / "Hunt without Mercy", *Die scharlachrote Brigade*/ "The Scarlet Brigade") and that another 26 "feature films that were suitable in terms of theme and scope" were to be made for the 1939/40 season, and 60 more for the 1940/41 season.[653]

Goebbels first addressed shifting the thematic direction of films three weeks after the war broke out. The Ufa minutes for 20 September 1939 note "the wishes of Reichsminister Dr. Goebbels" for the 1939/40 production programme: "The Minister wants to see anti-English material, and if possible one film based on the age of Frederick the Great. No films markedly dealing with operetta are to be made. ... He has further agreed to a Rothschild theme that has been passed on to him."[654] As far as the films that were already under examination were concerned, it was decided "that in consideration of current political conditions it is often necessary to alter some films that have already been completed to some extent, especially to cut some passages that are no longer tolerable under the present conditions".[655] This led to bans on productions that were "pro-English" (see *Kautschuk*, for example) or "anti-Bolshevik".

Goebbels tried to make his wishes more concrete at several meetings in the course of the next few weeks, with Tobis production head Demandowsky, for example. "I suggest a Bismarck film to him. But not Bismarck's resignation, but Bismarck at the outbreak of war in 1866. This is the best way to show this genius's lonely greatness and for that reason it is also the most topical today." (22.9.1939) This also confirms that Goebbels was behind the Tobis film *Bismarck*, directed by Wolfgang Liebeneiner, which was released in 1940.[656]

His less than original choice of German leaders and anti-English material for the thematic focus for future productions shows that Goebbels saw the lowest possible level of risk in the period since the outbreak of war, which was marked by improvisation. Other attempts to explain the programme tend to seem indecisive, however ("Received the production chiefs of the five film companies in the afternoon. Explained the new course to be taken by German films to them briefly. More material that is closer to the times and the people. I hope it will work out now" (1.10.1939), and show that the "lifelike" line that had reached another successful climax with *Mutterliebe* ("Motherly Love") was to be continued. To this extent it is not possible to talk about a fundamentally "new course". But saying that he hopes it will "work out now" Goebbels is giving very low marks to film production so far. The fact that Goebbels did not marshal all his film forces for the time being is shown – similarly to 1938 – by the films planned for Karl Ritter. Instead of committedly allotting his preferred subjects to the tried-and-tested propaganda director, Goebbels notes: "He wants to stage a Munich folk piece. That is perhaps all right." (6.10.1939)

As well as developing new film material, Goebbels started to reflect more subtly about the relationship between entertaining films and films that were overtly political. On the one hand he wanted to take the opportunity, given the constraint of more economical productions and savings, to reduce the annual production of films and thus limit the mass produced goods in the popular sphere: "In this way the film will probably stop being in such a ridiculous hurry and be able to work more artistically." (20.10.1939) On the other hand, the audience's need for diversion has to be taken into account. The displacement mechanisms that had kicked in at the same time – which the American Berlin correspondent William S. Shirer also observed[657] – meant that people were looking for more amusement and full cinemas. Goebbels admits to being pleasantly surprised (20.10.1939) by the resulting "financial successes" at the cinema box office, which the nationalized film industry urgently needed.

Some strikingly positive remarks on mediocre Volksfilme in the early months of the war[658] are to be found and they should be seen against this background. Of course Goebbels also presents himself as the people's friend and kindly pilot of the state, generously creating well-deserved distractions for a hard-working people that is hungry for entertainment: "A very nice Volksfilm that will certainly make its way because it is so light-hearted, particularly at these difficult times", he writes on 22.12.1939 on *Sommer, Sonne, Erika* ("Summer, Sun and Erika").[659] *Rheinische Brautfahrt* ("Bridal Trip through the Rhineland") is also "a good Volksfilm" according to Goebbels, and "wonderfully suitable for today" as: "We need good, entertaining fare. The people demand it." At the same time Goebbels made it clear that he would continue to insist on artistic principles, and personally had not taste for the lighter subjects ("all this material is so far away from one today, so far away", 23.9.1939). Fundamentally, Goebbels had not abandoned his ideological rejection of trivial, mass-produced light entertainment material, but he was starting to make a distinction between essential needs and the actual artistic aim. This shows the beginning of a dichotomy that was to become even more marked in the ensuing years before the end of the war.

The political films available in autumn 1939 were meagre in number, but Goebbels was not impressed by the tentatively "military" films *Alarm auf Station III* (29.10.1939) and *The Desert Song* (12.10.1939), nor by *Gewehr über* ("Shoulder Arms") ("a bad Wehrmacht propaganda film. Came close to a ban", 16.11.1939).[660] Goebbels notes that the Volksgemeinschaft film *Der Stammbaum des Dr. Pistorius* is a "modern film slanted in the right direction", but unfortunately "not quite as definite and convincing as I had hoped. There is a lack of plot and wit" – incidentally a remark that would be generally applicable to Nazi conviction films.

Faced with such weak productions, *Robert Koch* and *Mutterliebe* came out at precisely the right time, as new variations on the subtle political film. *Robert Koch* was awarded the highest possible classifications and won the top prize at the Venice Film Festival, and celebrates the great medical man and "fighter against death". Here some typical stock Nazi themes are further perfected: the stuffily conservative middle-class milieu of the old reactionaries, a man's all-conquering faith in his mission, martial terminology and systematic denunciation of the Kaiser Reich's parlamentary system.[661] In Goebbels' words a "triumph for Germany".[662] As the security services also confirmed, this anyway extraordinary public success received a tremendous boost from the National Socialist Party's film work,[663] and thus became a "positive experience for almost all the people".[664]

But the French film historians Courtade and Cadars are wrong when they suggest that *Robert Koch* is "preparing for war". The film was premiered at the Venice Film Festival three weeks before the war, but this was its only screening before it was launched in Germany in late 1939. It did not have its major exposure in Berlin until November.

Gustav Ucicky's *Mutterliebe*, a "moving work of art, a noble and honourable approach, well acted and not remotely exaggerated" (19.10.1939), was ideally suited to be the first contribution to the series of "wife and mother" films. These were intended to show the "Volksgenossinnen" (the "female national comrades") their role as serving, waiting wives and mothers at the beginning of the war, and to present self-sacrifice in favour of husband and children as the greatest good. An enormous propaganda campaign was mounted for this film. Goebbels appeared among mothers of outstanding merit in a newsreel report on the Berlin première.[665]

Both films were effective "war accompaniments" – the rest of the "everyday films" that came out from September to December 1939 were far inferior. But the classical war propaganda themes were still missing: increased readiness to fight and enthusiasm about the war, trust in the country's own military superiority, clear outward images of the enemy. This purpose was served by newsreels, and by documentary films, "a very valuable propaganda device for us at the moment". (19.11.1939) Goebbels was working almost exclusively on the *Feldzug in Polen* (*Campaign in Poland*) compilation film in December.

In the feature film sector Goebbels' remarks almost give the impression that the success of *Mutterliebe* and *Robert Koch*, some Volksfilme that he praised (10./11.12.1939), melodramas and adventure films, along with the material that had already been planned, was enough for him in winter 1939. On 11.12.1939 he writes: "It can generally be said that our films have got better."

Somewhat to his surprise, Hitler did not share this satisfaction, so that Goebbels had to note on 12.12.1939: "The Führer is being very critical about films, and particularly about newsreels. I do not think this is quite justified. He behaves like this in front of all his officers and aides. But he has the right to do so, he is a genius." Generally Goebbels preferred to pass over incidents like this, especially if they happened in public. What is typical is that he shifts the whole thing in to the realm of the metaphysical by referring to the Hitler's almost divine and inviolable higher authority. The Führer is in the right even when he is wrong. Goebbels' old adversary Alfred Rosenberg also relished recording the incident: "Goebbels was also there during the meal. The Führer repeated what he had said in his absence 3 days ago in his presence, extremely caustically: the newsreels was shallow and put together without any sense of a more profound interest. Enormous things are happening in G.(ermany) in terms of popular mobilization, but film takes no notice of this. He cuts his footage to size without giving the nation what it wants through consistently interesting management. … established, that we have had a N.(ational) S.(ocialist) revolution. There is no sense of this kind of subject matter at all. Dr. G.(oebbels): But we do have good nationalist films (Ritter). Führer: Yes, a few generally patriotic ones, but nothing N. S. Many things had been criticized, but our films hadn't dared to attack the Jewish Bolsheviks. The complaints were general, they were right, there was nothing to be said about it. It went on like this for about 20 minutes, and G.(oebbels) couldn't find a word to say in his own defence. He cursed this lunch-hour – and in my presence too – more than almost any other hour."[666]

For Goebbels the whole thing was actually quite serious. His authority over the imminent war propaganda was at stake. He had already lost the foreign propaganda brief to Foreign Minister Ribbentrop in September, which was a particularly heavy set-back for him.

It is nevertheless not certain to what extent Hitler's criticism of the available films is to be taken seriously.[667] Hitler had made constant demands across the board for films that showed more National Socialist conviction. But he had probably not seen a single feature film since the war began; his reprimand could only have been prompted by informers and gossips. In fact Rosenberg expressly mentions the lunch-time rounds at which Hitler liked to deliver wide-ranging monologues on a number of subjects. Hitler criticized Karl Ritter's "generally patriotic" films, even though he liked many of these 1937/38 productions. But there is no doubt that three months after the beginning of the war Hitler was disturbed by the fact that there was no sign of a contribution by feature films to justifying the attack and mobilizing the nation to be ready for war before and after 1 September.

Certainly Goebbels authority in the film sphere was too well established to have been under threat from reproaches like these. But his position within the regime was essentially based on his relationship with Hitler. If he was to be able to continue to put his various interests into practice he had to show some propaganda success in films. This meant that a more sharply focused political profile was inevitable.

Once the course had been changed to a higher proportion of political films and "war education" films, Goebbels admitted more or less clearly that Hitler was right to have complained about the lack of stress on military will and patriotism in autumn and winter 1939. The weekly paper *Das Reich*, which Goebbels edited, spoke of the "colourless, unreal world of the film" at the beginning of the war and castigated the "almost eerie distance from real life in September 1939, when the film was shockingly distanced from the heartbeat of those days".[668] The Propaganda Minister himself made similar remarks in his speech at the annual meeting of the Reichsfilmkammer in February 1941, but with some reservations: "It was only because the film did not do justice to the times that it was felt to be anachronistic in September, October and November 1939."[669]

In any case, Hitler's criticism meant that forward planning was needed and policy directions had to be set for the coming campaigns and military developments. Anyway Goebbels had already announced a sharper approach: "Press conference. We must put our propaganda on to more of a battle footing. Otherwise the people will not take the war seriously enough. … And generally speaking I shall sharpen up all German propaganda after Christmas."[670] (21.12.1939)

Goebbels drew his conclusions in subsequent weeks. After a visit to Hitler on 29.12.1939 he noted with reference to "a series of instructions" about new films: "Here too we have to apply greater pressure." At the same time it was clear to Goebbels that Hitler preferred an unambiguously open approach and would not be satisfied with nuances built into Volksfilme or "military" revue films like *Wir tanzen um die Welt* ("We're Dancing Around the World"). What was wanted was openly political films.

"The war will provide us with subjects": Film policy from 1940 to 1945

The Blitzkrieg period

New guidelines

At the turn of the year 1939/40 the film companies' script departments were already examining a large quantity of military and "topical" material, and then sending treatments into the Propaganda Ministry. Goebbels seems to have anticipated that fighting would also start in the west in the early years of 1940, though it is again unclear how precisely he was aware of Hitler's plans. (15./16.1.1940) The war had very definitely made its entrance into the new production programmes that the companies submitted to him at the beginning of the year. Goebbels states emphatically in January 1940 that he had received "a whole series of excellent nationalist and political material" (19.1.1940), even though the Ufa selection was "not particularly outstanding" (24.1.1940) and the Wien Film programme "not topical and up to date enough. (31.1.1940) But time was pressing, and shooting had to start as soon as possible. The new Ufa production chief Leichtenstern, who had been appointed by Goebbels, reported to the board a few days later "that he had presented the new production programme to the Herr Reichsminister, and that only 4 of 55 items had been rejected".[671]

Many classic Nazi propaganda films, some of which did not reach the cinemas until the end of 1941 and later, were conceived in the first few months of 1940. Goebbels mentioned the idea of the anti-Polish Hetzfilm *Heimkehr* (*Homecoming*, première: October 1941) as early as 4.2. 1940. More plans followed: on 13.2.1940 Karl Ritter's war film *Über alles in der Welt* ("Above All in the World", première: March 1941), on 6.3.1940 the political Volksfilm *Wunschkonzert* (*Request Concert*, première: December 1940), and on 17.3.1940 the Karl Lueger biography *Wien 1910* (première: August 1943). On 27.3. Goebbels mentioned the *Bismarck* project (première: December 1940), and on 5.4. the Frederick the Great film *Der große König* (*The Great King*, première: March 1942,) was assigned to director Veit Harlan.

But by no means all the material met the requirements. The Propaganda Minister was certainly delighted that numerous authors and writers had responded to his demands and worked out ideas for political films: "(The president of the Reichsfilmkammer Hans) Johst brings me film drafts by distinguished German writers. Almost all anti-English." (28.2.1940) Although he sounds somewhat deflated two weeks later: "Scarcely anything I can use among them. I reject almost everything." (13.3.1940)

Goebbels took the expansion of the war in early April as a result of the invasion of Norway and Denmark and prospect of an imminent offensive in the west as a reason for taking measures that he had previously avoided in relation to films. Thus he reacted unusually rapidly to isolated critical voices in the audience about "shallow" films and marital comedies like *Ein Mann muß so sein* ("The Way a Man Has to Be") and *Eine Nacht im Mai* (*A Night in May*): "I am discontinuing the purely problem films, above all films about marriage. More manly, heroic films."[672] (23.4. 1940) The Security Service even reported that some cinemagoers would feel that "behaviour constituting a marital offence" was glossed over in films from the world of the "social élite".[673] It is unlikely that Goebbels was fully in agreement with this view, and anyway there were scarcely any depressing everyday "human conflicts" around in spring 1940. Goebbels calls one latecomer from this repertoire, *Mädchen im Vorzimmer* ("Girls in the Outer Office"), about professional life in a publishing house, "a harmless matter". (22.4.1940) The Nazi innovation known as "life-like films", which Goebbels quite unambiguously called "problem films", really did turn out to be counter-productive in the war.

Goebbels promoted political films more emphatically then ever: "New material discussed. Less shallow material. We can't go on like that." (25.4.1940) And he did not restrict himself to rhetorical formulae here, as the following note about a Tobis supervisory board meeting shows: "Minister wants political films (*Bismarck*, *Ohm Krüger*, *Friedrich Schiller*), even at the risk of making losses. Programme 50:50 political and Volksfilme. There are plenty of screenplays in reserve."[674]

This requirement apparently applied only to Tobis, for which company Goebbels' requirements meant a hitherto unparalleled upheaval and an extraordinary financial burden because of high production costs and an uncertain effect on the box office.[675] But other concerns were to be involved as well: Ufa had "two war pieces" among other things foisted upon it by the Ministry for 1940/41,[676] though it is very doubtful that the Ufa board followed this recommendation. The company's "war pieces" for 1940/41 (*Über alles in der Welt, U-Boote westwärts*/"U Boats Westwards") were already projected at this time or were in the studio by May.[677]

The production firms stonewalled quite a lot at first. The Bavaria production chief, Helmut Schreiber, claimed to be amazed by Goebbels' requirement he "knew nothing about the Minister's sudden instruction that light-hearted material was to be completely eliminated". And anyway, they already had "a large quantity of nationalist and political material in preparation" and could not meet this request for technical reasons: the "studios had already been allocated and their was a lack of casting availability", which were factors that spoke against it. Schreiber tried to justify the "light-hearted" films by saying that "much of the material (would be) complete when peace is made and will certainly be seen as very welcome then".[678]

It is thus interesting that Goebbels intended to go well beyond the propaganda film programme that actually was realized in 1940/41. The latent resistance by many production companies to an undue proportion of political films at the expense of more popular material, for fear of cutting profits, must have made the Minister uneasy. Ultimately there were no political films in the cinemas for the whole of the first half of 1940. Goebbels noted that he was "very worried" abut feature film production on 5.6.1940: "Our production chiefs are working as if they are living in Cloudcuckooland. Far away from life and the war."[679]

But the war had "activated the cinema's world of subjects", as Ufa production chief Leichtenstern put it in the Filmkammer magazine *Der deutsche Film*.[680] He said that a lot of material was no longer desirable and filmable, anything set abroad, for example, but the war was providing substitutes. Elsewhere in the magazine it said that the "new world affirmation of life and of the reality of life (was) no longer based on love and jealousy, but on the key ideas of the day: struggle, comradeship, technology and leadership".

Efforts directed at a clear increase in the number of political films also continued after the end of the western offensive and the cease-fire with France on 22 June 1940. The guideline still applied that "lifelike material (was to be) filmed, portraying real people" (7.2.1941),[681] but that a rather more subtle approach should be taken. Many film proposals were much "too unpsychological". (7.2.1941)

It was now considered lifelike to link private fates with war events, as in *Request Concert* and *Auf Wiedersehen, Franziska* ("Goodbye, Franziska"): farewell scenes and images of women waiting for their menfolk accumulated on screen. At the same time a heightened sense of the pain of parting and anxiety was to be brought to marriages broken by the war. Speaking about fine psychological delineation, Goebbels said at the Reichsfilmkammer meeting in February 1941 that it was "very advisable to disguise this educational element, not to let it become visible, to work on the principle that we should not notice the intention, so that one's mood is not spoiled. And so actually the great art lies in educating without appearing to educate. An educational task is completed without the subject of the education even noticing that it is being educated, and that is the actual role of propaganda as well."[682]

Thanks to reports on morale from the Security Service and the Reichspropagandaämter, ("Reich Propaganda Agencies") Goebbels was only too well aware how carefully audiences followed the portrayal and actions of the protagonists, even in average films, picked up social messages and guidelines and saw through attempts to influence them if they were laid on too thickly.[683] He followed the suitability of certain subjects very closely: "I do not want to see so many conflicts about illegitimate children in films. The legitimate child must at least remain the norm." (18.4.1941) It is not always entirely clear whether Goebbels is acting on his own initiative or as a reaction to reports views of the public's opinion. In fact in this case he had not seen a film addressing problems of this kind for weeks. It is possible that his response was triggered by the Terra film *Unser kleiner Junge* ("Our Little Boy", première 13. February 1941), which he had already censored on 13.1.1941; his criticism: "very bad and totally untrue-to-life. A relapse into old times". Here the story of a working woman and her illegitimate child once more illustrates the conflict of aims between undesirable representation of everyday life and avoiding moral conflicts in films. Probably Goebbels was faced with further, entirely undesirable plans with similar subject matter. The film companies were required "not to touch upon the problem of illegitimate children in films for the time being"[684] by Filmdramaturg von Reichmeister.

Goebbels never lost sight of the fact that the public needed entertaining escapist material, even at the height of national feeling in spring 1940 – and even a year later. He knew that "light-hearted material is most in demand at the moment."[685] He was already defending the need for entertaining films even in wartime against attacks from some of the National Socialist Party at a working meeting of the Reichsfilmkammer committee in April 1940.[686] But it was only after a large number of successes with political films and shortly before the propaganda avalanche in spring 1941 that Goebbels, aware that "so many impeccable major national films"[687] had already been shown was able to put in a plea that was as convincing as it was skilful at the Reichsfilm-kammer's war conference: "Entertainment can also sometimes have the task helping to equip a people for their life struggle, of providing them with the necessary edification, entertainment and relaxation."[688] But he did make it clear that: "This does not make the film a mere entertainment device, it is an educational device" and has to be a "force for state morality".[689] The main principles of the popular escapist film – "relaxation, edification, entertainment" – became more important, especially after the second winter of the war.

The propaganda offensive is delayed

Months passed before the propaganda productions started in early 1940 could be seen. But Goebbels wanted to improve film availability immediately. This meant that projection facilities and the range of films and newsreels had to be increased. At first the Propaganda Minister had trouble, and even had to appeal to Hitler, in resisting demands that theatres and cinemas should be temporarily closed because of coal shortages.[690] (11.1.1940) He repeatedly reminded the National Socialist Party regional film offices that they should make more mobile projection facilities, the so-called film vans, available for "cultural provision" in rural areas. (24.1.1940) Another 400 such vans were to be acquired at the film companies' expense, because Goebbels was not satisfied with their efforts so far.[691]

The possibility of resorting to older nationalist films was greatly restricted by an instruction from the Reichsfilmkammer in February 1940, saying that "films based on the World War may no longer be brought out".[692] This ban seemed understandable, as Germany had lost the last war against the same opponents. This affected Karl Ritter's militaristic productions like *Furlough on Word of Honor*, *Unternehmen Michael* and *Pour le mérite*, and also the 1933 U-Boot film *Dawn*. This last had been immediately revived by Ufa in November 1939, with some success.[693] But Goebbels obviously did not think that the film was all that effective in its present form: "*Dawn*, an old U-Boot film. Two much patriotic hot air. But it can still be sorted out." (7.1.1940)

The war newsreels moved into the centre of public interest with the start of the western offensive with the invasion of Belgium and Holland on 10 May 1940. This caused new problems. Goebbels obviously found the discrepancy between the sensational newsreel and the subsequent popular main programme unacceptable – not a single propaganda film was shown in the Berlin cinemas from 31 May to 11 June 1940: "I shall have these shallow films withdrawn and replaced with good repeats. Our people can stand literary drivel less than ever today", he writes on 2.6.1940, and just two days later: "Comedy films are being gradually withdrawn. They clash with the newsreel too badly."[694] (4.6.1940) And indeed the premières originally fixed for Berlin for the second week in June and described as "too silly" (11.6.1940) by Goebbels were replaced by "a series of decent nationalist films", including *Togger*, *Dawn*, *Mann für Mann*, *Der Herrscher* and *Der höhere Befehl*. These repeats remained on the programme for the whole of June, but they still made up only a small proportion of the whole range showing. There was a complete lack of more recent productions: there was not a single première from 2 to 16 July 1940.

The nationalist revivals seemed to fit in with what Goebbels describes as a "magnificent mood" (22.5.1940) after the beginning of the western offensive: "Everything is quite magnificent for us in Germany. The people are filled with absolute and unlimited confidence in victory." (21.5.1940) Even entirely unsuspicious observers, like the American Berlin correspondent William S. Shirer, shared this impression.[695]

Documentary films glorifying the war like *Campaign in Poland* and *Feuertaufe* (*Baptism of Fire*), partly compiled from newsreels, could be brought into play much more quickly than new cinema films. But they met with varying degrees of success. The Security Service, after an initial, rather more complex response, said that the "effect on people's mood" made by Fritz Hippler's minute battle report[696] *Campaign in Poland*, which attracted large audiences, was said to be "extraordinarily favourable", "especially in view of a possible intensification of the war situation".[697] But *Baptism of Fire* seemed rather to suggest that the martial documentary war films and images of total destruction did little to make people more enthusiastic about the war. Even the fanatical Security Service registered agreement, but also "depressed, fearful spirits caused by the horrors of war", which overtook female cinemagoers in particular when faced with this brutally realistic mode of presentation.[698] Goebbels comments after the première of *Baptism of Fire* also confirm precisely this impression: "The film makes a magnificent effect, but its exaggerated realism is somewhat wearing. This affected the mood at the end accordingly." (6.4.1940) The makers also chose, as a stylistic device, to dominate the sound-track with a constant, deliberately exaggerated background of howling engines, noisy machine-gun salvoes and remorselessly blaring soldiers' songs, which must also have been a little wearing.

The third film in this documentary trilogy, Svend Noldan's *Sieg im Westen* ("Victory in the West"), did not satisfy Goebbels either. He felt that the film "still (had) a number of faults" but found the material so strong "that it is ultimately convincing" (1.2.1941), which still sounds quite mild. But at the ministers' meeting Goebbels said that *Sieg im Westen* "showed considerable faults, which cannot be covered up by a powerful propaganda evaluation" and pointed out "historical and political errors in the direction of this film".[699]

When the "publication ban on Volksfilme" was raised in late June 1940[700] – according to the Security Services people had welcomed the withdrawal of "shallow" films[701] –, there was still a lack of recent propaganda feature films. It is remarkable that the "western campaign" was not supported by a single "military education" film, with the exception of repeats.[702]

While Hippler explained this by citing the technical turn-around in film production after the beginning of the war,[703] Goebbels later said vaguely at the Filmkammer meeting in February 1941 that "the breakthrough to the great nationalist film" had already "been risked in September/October 1939". But indirectly he also admitted the deficit in spring 1940: "I didn't call a meeting of the Reichsfilmkammer in 1940 because I was convinced that although there were new films on the way, they were not yet there, and there could be a danger that all I would do would be to develop a programme without being able to put forward any concrete evidence of it."[704]

With the exception of *Die Rothschilds* and *Request Concert*, even Ufa did not bring out any recognizably political films in 1940, but instead twelve Volksfilme "without any 'nationalist and political' theme".[705] Consequently Goebbels again had to put up with Security Service notes reporting the rejection of these "society films", from a "chairman of the board" milieu.[706]

Some everyday films like *Mädchen im Vorzimmer*, Luis Trenker's *Der Feuerteufel* ("The Arsonist") ("patriotic rubbish", 16.2.1940) or the pro-Russian melodrama *Der Postmeister* (*The Postmaster*) did not improve the political balance sheet by early autumn 1940. *Feinde* ("Enemies"), an anti-Polish film justifying the start of the war ("not quite mastered", 14.7.1940) and the Hitler Youth film *Kopf hoch Johannes* ("Chin Up, Johannes", 12.8.1940)[707] did not represent a breakthrough for Goebbels either. But *Das Herz der Königin* (*The Heart of a Queen*) with Zarah Leander helped least of all: "Was intended to be anti-English and anti-church, and has ended up pro both." (21.8.1940) People in general, according to the Security Service in October, were still "expressing the wish that feature film programmes should adapt to current events as well".[708] They felt a lack above all of "relevant political and satirical films (for example Jewish warmongers, lying British lords etc.) and films with relevant ideological and social themes (problems for prisoners of war, evacuation, the effect of the home front in wars etc.)". Political films that people were aware of from preliminary press announcements were "already eagerly awaited".[709]

Goebbels had to take note of this, but he was already looking at the coming premières: "But look at the films we're bringing out now. Each better than the one before."[710] (4.10.1940) He took credit for this personally: "My purge has worked wonders." (4.10.1940) He continues to sing his own praises throughout the autumn (and also on 15.11.1940), with bitter admissions about Volksfilm production striking the only gloomy note: "Some of the most recent films were bad. But we have to bring films out, otherwise there will be a general shortage." (10.12.1940) And so Goebbels was also able to give instructions in later October 1940 that the repeats were to be taken off in the smaller Berlin cinemas as they were only blocking new premières. But the programmes show that with the exception of three anti-Semitic films the long desired propaganda offensive in the cinema did not start until December 1940, with major films like *Bismarck* and *Request Concert*.

Goebbels comments on no less than 21 explicitly political films from July 1940 to the outbreak of war with the Soviet Union in June 1941. But he slightly undermines the effect of this impressive number himself by striking some critical notes. The Propaganda Minster very much approved of *Trenck der Pandur* ("Trenck, Officer of the Pandurs"), *Das Fräulein von Barnhelm* (*Lady from Barnhelm*), *Request Concert*, *Achtung Feind hört mit* ("Beware! The Enemy is Listening"), *Alcazar* (an Italian production), *Bismarck*, *Friedrich Schiller*, *Kampfgeschwader Lützow* ("Battle Squadron Lützow") and *Ohm Krüger*. He assesses the following as fundamentally satisfactory, but with a noticeable touch of slight scepticism: *Feinde*, *Über alles in der Welt*, *Stukas*, *Mein Leben für Irland* ("My Life for Ireland"), … *Reitet für Deutschland* (*Riding for Ger-*

many) and *U-Boote westwärts*. And he more or less clearly rejects: *Kopf hoch, Johannes, The Heart of a Queen*, *Blutbrüderschaft, Jungens, Spähtrupp Hallgarten* ("Hallgarten Patrol") and *Carl Peters*.[711] These productions dominated German cinemas from late 1940 to summer 1941.

For the first time since the beginning of the war the military operations from April 1941 were accompanied by a gigantic film propaganda campaign. Goebbels was particularly insistent that the anti-British Boer film *Ohm Krüger* should open throughout the provinces before easter 1941, to reach the widest possible audience.[712] The picture was absolutely clear in Berlin as well: from 9 to 12 May 1941, for example, there were only two films running in 76 of Berlin's 168 cinemas, *Ohm Krüger* and the simplistic war film *Über alles in der Welt*. The 17 première cinemas showed *Ohm Krüger* seven times, *Jungens, U-Boote westwärts* and the "sacrifice film" *Auf Wiedersehen, Franziska* once each.

Things could not have been more different from the situation on 1 September 1939: on 22 June 1941, the day German troops invaded the Soviet Union, 111 Berlin cinemas were showing *Carl Peters, Spähtrupp Hallgarten, Auf Wiedersehen, Franziska* and *U-Boote westwärts*. This was followed by large-scale screenings in the others.. Goebbels also planned a mass launch of the Italian war film *Alcazar*, which he esteemed very highly, about a Fascist fortress garrison in the Spanish Civil War. This was prevented only because the Italians refused to make a few cuts. But even so, Goebbels had every cause for content in the months form April to June 1941. Something that was not the case in September 1939 and May 1940 had now been successfully achieved: the feature films matched military events.

Focal points for political films in 1940/1941

Anti-Semitic film propaganda and the legends of the directors

One question is of course bound to arise when dealing with the question of anti-Semitic film production in the "Third Reich" today: can there possibly be anything new to say about it? There can scarcely be an area of Nazi film propaganda that has been better researched. And yet Goebbels' diaries can provide details about questions that have so far remained open. For example, until now we have not known exactly when and how the anti-Semitic films were initiated. Was Goebbels personally responsible for them or did Hitler give the crucial instructions?

According to the judgement in the trial of the *Jud Süss* director Veit Harlan in 1950, Goebbels commissioned the three firms to make one anti-Semitic feature film each,[713] allegedly even on Hitler's insistence.[714] Other investigations see Hitler's Reichstag speech on 30 January 1939 as the source, in which the dictator threatened to produce anti-Semitic films as a response to American anti-Nazi films.[715] Or were they "in fact not premiered until 1940, but already prepared at the time of his speech"?[716] According to this, the fact that the cinematic smear campaign did not begin sooner could be ascribed to Goebbels' scepticism about "Party themes", the lack of screenplays and Hitler's caution in terms of foreign policy.[717]

In Goebbels' diary is film not mentioned as a suitable propaganda device in connection with the intensified anti-Semitic smear campaign in summer 1938[718] or with the November pogroms. And not even when Goebbels talks about starting a "major anti-Semitic campaign" in the press and on the radio on 17./18.11.1938, after a conversation with Hitler about the Jewish policy. There is also nothing to suggest that Hitler insisted on anti-Semitic films.

Goebbels and Hitler obviously had difficulties with the form that anti-Semitic propaganda should take. Goebbels at least rejected crude anti-Semitic Party film polemics in the thirties. For example, a short documentary film denouncing the Jewish film actors of the Weimar period was shown in Munich in 1937 as part of the exhibition on *The Eternal Jew*. Goebbels opinion: "A bad propaganda film about Jews in films. Made despite my ban. I shall not pass it. Too pushy." (5.11. 1937) And yet the film was shown at Party events in 1938 and 1939.[719] And Goebbels only indirectly mentions the Swedish film *Peterson und Bendel*, which was anyway classified as "valuable in terms of national policy" and used from 1935 to 1938 as an "anti-Semitic stopgap".[720] Neither Hitler nor Goebbels did like the anti-Semitic vagabond farce *Robert und Bertram* (première 7 July 1939).[721]

Goebbels' diary deals with the following anti-Semitic films: *Robert und Bertram, Leinen aus Irland* ("Linen from Ireland"). *The Eternal Jew, Jud Süss* and *Die Rothschilds*. The brief note on 16.9.1939 about *Leinen aus Irland*, which was shown in 1939 ("Checked anti-Semitic film *Leinen aus Irland*. Has turned out very well."), could suggest that Goebbels was not personally involved in planning and making this anti-Semitic work. It seems that the production was prepared by Wien-Film, which was only loosely directed by the Propaganda Ministry at first, just a few months after the "Anschluss" of Austria in 1938.[722]

At a first glance there seems to be a plausible link between Hitler's criticism of Goebbels' film policy in December 1939, which has already been mentioned – according to Rosenberg, the dictator had expressly complained that German films "hadn't dared to attack the Jewish Bolsheviks". But it is very quickly clear that this cannot be the reason for the start of anti-Semitic film production. We have earlier planning dates for all three of the 1940 anti-Semitic films.

First of all, in September 1939 Ufa passed the Propaganda Minister a proposal – we do not know whether he had asked for it – for a "Rothschild film" for the production year 1939/40. According to the board minutes, Goebbels agreed to this project.[723] The first entries about planning for the notorious "documentary" smear film *The Eternal Jew* followed in October 1939: "Talked to Hippler about a ghetto film that I am having shot in Poland. This has to turn out as the kind of sharpest anti-Semitic propaganda we have in mind." (5.10.39) Similarly on the next day: "Talked to Hippler and Taubert about a ghetto film. The material for it is being shot in Poland now. It is going to be a first-class propaganda film. I'm providing the outline. It must be finished in 3 to 4 weeks."

This entry shows, as has long been assumed, that the director Fritz Hippler is a bare-faced liar. Hippler had previously always asserted that he was only supposed to shoot material for "archive purposes" in the Warsaw ghetto, which gave Goebbels the idea of an anti-Semitic film later. As recently as 1991, unaware of these diary passages written on 5.10.1939, Hippler wrote about his trip for "archive purposes": "Nothing had yet been said about making a film; he (Goebbels) did not even mention this job in his diary; he does not seem to have had the idea for a film until he saw the first sample films."[724]

Goebbels also justifies the film: "The Jewish problem will be the most difficult one to solve. Jews are not human beings. Predators equipped with cold intellect that have to be rendered harmless." (7.10.1939) After Hippler's return from Poland on 16 October Goebbels immediately informed Hitler about "my preliminary work on the Jewish film, which interested him very much", and also has the film material shown immediately: "And then shots for the ghetto film. Still never been there. Things shown that are so cruel and brutal in detail that your blood runs cold. Such brutishness makes you recoil with horror. This Jewish race must be annihilated." (17.10.1939) From then on Hitler constantly interfered in the making of the film and constantly demanded changes – which he had never done in such detail for any other film. Even at the height of the military operations in the west in May/June 1940 he still found time for corrections.[725] This meant that completion was delayed until summer 1940. It was not until 3.9.1940 that Goebbels could say: "Hippler has done a good job." All Goebbels' timetable plans – on 6.10.1939 ("It must be finished in 3 to 4 weeks") and on 28.11.1939 ("Now it's right") – suggest that the Propaganda Minister wanted to bring the film out early, possibly even in 1939. Goebbels again thought it was ready in January 1940: "Final version of Jewish film. I think its ready now. Anyway we've got as much as we can out of it."[726] (9.1.1940)

This suggests that the late date for the première, 28 November 1940, was not chosen deliberately, but emerged as a result of Hitler's interventions. "*The Eternal Jew* is now finished at last. It can come out without any qualms now. We've been working on it long enough as well." (11.10.1940) And so the sequence of premières of the anti-Semitic production in summer and autumn 1940 now seems not to have been the result of calculated planning.[727] It was only the delays that made *The Eternal Jew* collide with *Die Rothschilds* and *Jud Süss*. This and the brutal scenes – they were only toned down in a version for the afternoon programme – certainly contributed to its lack of success.[728] But Goebbels says not a word about this, even though there is no other title before 1941 that he mentions more frequently and worked on more intensively.[729]

Goebbels' notes contradict the director's justifications in the case of *Jud Süss* as well.[730] This is not particularly surprising, as no one believed Veit Harlan anyway when he said that he was forced to make the film and that he would have been shot if he had not carried out the commission.[731] On 9.11.1939 Goebbels praises "the manuscript of the film *Jud Süss*" for "having turned out excellently". "The first really anti-Semitic film."[732] And a few days later he writes: "Talked to Harlan and Möller about the Jud Süss film. Harlan, who is to direct, has a lot of new ideas. He's revising the screenplay again."[733] There were obviously no differences between Harlan and Goebbels, except that Harlan set a far higher budget than the Propaganda Minister. (1.5.1940) Later notes about Harlan's refractoriness over *The Great King* show that Goebbels would not have kept quiet if there had been any.

33. *The Eternal Jew* (1940) by Fritz Hippler: "This Jewish race must be annihilated."

Goebbels followed the project with great enthusiasm at every stage and constantly examined trial shots and rushes.[734] He writes as early as 30.12.1939: "The Jud Süss film is coming on." And he is jubilant about the final version: "A huge success, a work of genius. Exactly the kind of anti-Semitic film we wanted." (18.8.1940) This time he doesn't keep quiet about audience reactions. Both the box-office take[735] and the reported reactions from cinemagoers seem to have exceeded his expectations. Of course Goebbels sees the political element as most important, though film historians feel that the work was successful because it was "received (as) erotic, melodramatic entertainment".[736] Finally the Minister summed up like this: "… Reports about the response to Jud Süss abroad. Quite magnificent. It caused demonstrations in the streets in Hungary. This film really is a new programme. Proof that films too can work and arouse enthusiasm that is entirely in line with our views." (8.3.1941)[737]

The anti-Semitic production *Die Rothschilds*, by Erich Waschneck, will be dealt with later in another context. Just a few points: Here Goebbels was very taken at first by the screenplay (13.3.1940) and the first rushes (26.4.1940), but later shows scepticism about the effect the film will have.[738] Differences with "Führer" deputy Rudolf Hess and others led to the film being banned from performance for three months in the first instance as early as September, after its première on 17 July 1940, even though it had already taken 1.3 mill. Reichsmarks at the box office.[739]

Propagating "euthanasia"

The subject of "euthanasia" and ending "life that was unworthy of life", as propagated in *I Accuse*, the best-known Nazi film after *Jud Süss*, have proved just as interesting to film historians. Numerous studies are available,[740] but none of them has so far been able to use Goebbels' notes. He writes briefly but revealingly about *I Accuse*: only five remarks are available so far.[741] The film is about a doctor's wife with incurable multiple sclerosis, who asks first a doctor friend and then her husband to "release" her by administering a fatal dose. The subsequent murder trial provides a forum for rehearsing all the arguments for "death on request" and for defusing skilfully placed artificial objections.[742]

The project was under the overall control of the "Führer's office", whose director, Philipp Bouhler, was "one of the men principally responsible for mass murder" by "euthanasia" and one of Goebbels' few personal friends with the Nazi élite.[743] Planning for the film had been under way since June 1940. Goebbels first mentions "liquidation procedures for lunatics"[744] at the same time, and in September at the latest the Tobis production chief and director Wolfgang Liebeneiner in particular were brought in to work on the screenplay.[745] The Propaganda Ministry does not seem to have been as heavily involved at the early stages as it was with *Jud Süss*, a comparable project. The following note does not appear until 14.2.1941: "Talked to Liebeneiner about some new film material on euthanasia. A very difficult and tricky subject, but an urgent one as well. I give Liebeneiner some guidelines." Incidentally, Liebeneiner was still asserting in 1983 that he never exchanged a word with Goebbels about *I Accuse*, and that the Propaganda Minister had not shown the slightest interest in the film.[746] Goebbels may have become involved in the project at this point because of a conversation about mass murders that had taken place shortly before: "Talked to Bouhler about the question of the silent liquidation of the mentally ill. 80,000 have gone, 60,000 have still to go. This is a difficult job, but a necessary one. And it has to be done." (31.1.1941) And yet it seems "very questionable whether this influence by Goebbels essentially went beyond the usual final checks and and the question of certification and the deployment of the film".[747] In fact Geobbels' note of 21.6.1941, which also stresses Hippler's responsibility and that of Tobis production boss von Demandowsky, clearly refers to the Minster's copy or first version of the film: "New Liebeneiner film *I Accuse*. For euthanasia. A proper discussion film. Wonderfully made and very National Socialist. It will trigger the most heated debates. And that is what it is for. Hippler and Demandowsky are very proud of their achievement." (26.6.1941)

Goebbels' aims are clear: moral taboos and resistance from the Christian churches are to be broken down for cinemagoers by discussions that are started quite harmlessly. *I Accuse* served as a kind of reaction test, making it possible for the regime "to soften people's inclination to reject euthanasia without showing itself in its true colours".[748] But the film had to be revised. After the invasion of the Soviet Union and a much-quoted sermon preached on 3.9.1941[749] by Clemens August Graf von Galen, the Bishop of Münster, who came out strongly against annihilation, it was "downgraded (to) suggestive hints"[750] by extensive toning down. Both the people's response

to the sermon and also advances in the east, which were halting at first clearly made Goebbels feel that his intended propaganda for euthanasia was no longer appropriate:

"I must ask the Führer to look at the question of whether he actually wants a public debate about the euthanasia problem at the moment. We could probably link such a debate with the new Liebeneiner film *Ich klage an*. I am against this, at least at the present time. A debate like this would only make feelings run high again. This would be extraordinarily unimportant during a critical period of the war." (15.8.1941)

After speaking to Hitler again, there is only vague talk of his agreeing to defer "all home subjects" that "could distract from the aim of victory". Thus the "heated discussions" that Goebbels still welcomed in June were no longer desirable because of the state of the war and the church's protests. Consequently the press were instructed to refrain from discussing *I Accuse* from then on and "in no case to bring up the problem of euthanasia in this regard".[751] Hitler ordered a tactical reduction of "euthanasia" on 24 August 1941. This did not mean the end of the murder campaigns.[752]

But the Nazi propaganda withdrawal did not go as far as completely abandoning the launch of the film. Goebbels probably decided that the careful indirect approach and above all the final scene, which left all interpretations open,[753] took away the danger. It was precisely because *I Accuse* "no longer seemed to have much to do with the murder of the mentally ill, as obvious connections had been cut, the main problem had been shifted towards death on request and because of the requirement that euthanasia should be correctly treated in legal terms, that it could be shown at all a few weeks after the uproar about the Galen sermon".[754] There is no comment by Goebbels on the effect this film, which was seen by about 18 million people, had on its audiences, even though he had himself precisely informed about audience reactions.[755] "The film did more to convince national comrades than many speeches could have done", said a very sophisticated report by the Gauleiter of Hanover to the Party Office in January 1942.[756] But the film cannot have significantly softened Christian resistance to annihilation.[757]

The fact that Goebbels remained interested in the idea of film propaganda for the murder of the mentally ill is shown by his hitherto unknown involvement in "scientific film documentaries" in 1942.[758] But the Propaganda Minister had at first to take the people's fragile state of mind into account, and so he introduced his retreat in a veiled fashion on 22.8.1941: "Whether it was right at all to bring up the question of euthanasia on such a large scale as happened in the last few months is a question that can be left open for the moment. In any case we can all be pleased when the campaign associated with it is at and end. It was necessary. ... But nevertheless I represent the point of view that open conflict should be avoided where possible. We do not have sufficient time or nerve now to implement it with ultimate consistency."

34. Mathias Wieman and Heidemarie Hatheyer in the "euthanasia" film *I Accuse*: "80,000 have gone, 60,000 have still to go."
35. Emil Jannings as *Ohm Krüger* (1941): like a man possessed.

Anti-British films

In September 1939 Goebbels has asked for anti-English material to be prepared. This request introduced the essential thrust for film propaganda in subsequent years: there were far more films with an open or concealed anti-British slant that anti-Semitic or "anti-Bolshevik" productions. Before Goebbels could study the above-mentioned, unsuitable anti-English "film drafts by major German authors" (28.2.1940), he heard about the actor Emil Jannings' idea for a film about a subject that was very popular in the Nazi period. This was the "wars of liberation" waged by the South African Boers against Britain as a colonial power around the turn of the century: "Jannings is developing new film material for me. A very good *Ohm Krüger* about the Boer War." (29.11.1939) The production history of this famous anti-British film is very vividly presented in the diary entries. And here too someone involved in Nazi films is unmasked by Goebbels: Jannings made a statutory declaration after the war that he was "opposed to all tendentious and political films, especially *Ohm Krüger*, which I refused to play and did everything to prevent it from being made".[759] But Goebbels repeatedly praises Jannings for his active and full support of the project, and writes after a "conversation with Jannings": "He is working on his Boer film like a man possessed. I am seeing the rushes. They suggest it's going to be a great success." (17.12.1940)[760] When the film was finished, Goebbels wrote: "Jannings excels himself. An anti-England film you wouldn't dream was possible." (2.4.1941)

The brutality of the presentation in *Ohm Krüger* which is also thanks to the experienced propaganda director Hans Steinhoff, was well calculated; but if we are to believe the Security Service's observations, Goebbels' idea that the film had to be cruel "if it was to have an effect on the people" (5.4.1941) was true only to an extent.[761] They do point out that the "mass scenes in which the Boer women are shot are seen as a particularly impressive climax everywhere. Here the film went to the limits of the tolerable in terms of realistic presentation",[762] but apparently "some scenes were (also) felt to be 'laid on too thick' or 'too repulsive', like for example the distribution of guns and prayer-books by English missionaries. There is a danger that exaggeration of this kind for propaganda purposes could weaken the credibility of historical film plots."[763]

But there can be no doubt about the extraordinary success and propaganda effectiveness of *Ohm Krüger* ("Enthusiasm for war against England is being fundamentally stepped up and deepened").[764] Even after running for a few weeks it was producing top attendance figures and turnover, thanks to an elaborate advertising campaign and wide distribution, and took approx. 6 mill. Reichsmarks at the box office by late May 1941 – more than any other comparable propaganda film over a considerably longer period.[765] But it did not bring in any profit for the production firm Tobis, because of the enormous production costs and the expensive advertising campaign. Another negative factor was the time-span of over eighteen months from planning to the première: *Ohm Krüger*, along with *The Great King* (1942), *Kolberg* (1945) and *The Dismissal* (1942), the feature film subjected to the most detailed control by Goebbels,[766] was actually needed much earlier as anti-British propaganda.

Only one topical anti-British production reached in cinemas in the whole of the first six months of 1940: *Der Fuchs von Glenavron* ("The Fox of Glenavron"), directed by Goebbels' brother-in-law Max ("Axel") W. Kimmich, glorified the Irish struggle for independence against British occupation. After a great deal of reworking, Goebbels stressed the film's usefulness for day-to-day propaganda, which did not occur very frequently in the case of feature films, on 17.4.1940: "*Fuchs von Glenavron*, a film about the Irish struggle for freedom by Axel Kimmich. It is wonderful now, and will come in very useful for our propaganda."

After the defeat of France and the Compiègne armistice of 22 June 1940 Goebbels stepped up his smear campaign, dressed up as anti-capitalism, against "plutocratic rule" in England. He said that now was the time "to start up the anti-English propaganda machine again",[767] not least to orchestrate German intentions to land in the British Isles effectively. The people were "quite clearly in favour of defeating England completely". (25.6.1940)

Goebbels was particularly decisive about conflict with England, and even refers to Hitler's procrastination from time to time. Despite being disappointed by the British Government's reaction to his "generous offer" to make peace on 19 July, Goebbels says that the dictator "didn't really (want) to get on with it yet".[768] But Goebbels seems impatient and decisive: "I am putting our home propaganda increasingly on a war footing. Otherwise the mood is going to deflate gradually. Our report of major successes against the English navy are now being announced with great fanfares again." (30.7.1940) But it is not true that feature film propaganda did not get "coarser", as Erwin Leiser suggests, until "Hitler's hopes of a separate peace with England

(were) not fulfilled".[769] There was absolutely no film propaganda of this kind before July to be compared with a "coarser" version later. And besides, most of the anti-British productions were already in the studio by July, including *Ohm Krüger*, *Über alles in der Welt*, *U-Boote westwärts*.

Axel Kimmich made another "rebel" film about the Irish struggle for liberation after *Der Fuchs von Glenavron*, it was *Mein Leben für Irland* ("My Life for Ireland"). But Goebbels had become more sceptical in the meantime. It was not just that the "thickly applied pro-Irish approach"[770] was not always enthusiastically received in Party circles. The Security Service's reports also repeatedly indicated that the "rebel" films had undesirable side-effects in occupied territories like Poland, for example, Czechoslovakia and some border regions. Films like Luis Trenker's *Feuerteufel* and *Maria Ilona* were tending to fire up resistance against the German occupation regime there: "People keep pointing out that the plots of these films can immediately be reinterpreted by Poles and Czechs and applied to their own struggle for freedom against Germany." This comment appears in a report dated as early as May 1940.[771] There were obvious parallels between British occupation, which was being denounced, and the brutal German approach. Thus Goebbels took *Mein Leben für Irland*, which he did not seem to have thought much of anyway, as a reason for declaring the subject closed: "And so we've had enough of these Irish films now. The theme is not quite convincing."[772] (10.12.1940)

War and home front films

It is generally felt today that the cinema programme of the Blitzkrieg period 1940/41 was dominated by war or "war education" films, all of which glorified the German armed forces, from the army via the air force to the U-Boot fleet. As nearly all these productions (*Über alles in der Welt*, *U-Boot westwärts*, *Stukas*, *Spähtrupp Hallgarten*, *Kampfgeschwader Lützow* and *Sechs Tage Heimaturlaub*/"Six Day Furlough") were planned or begun at about the same time,[773] and they were all premiered between late February and late June 1941. There was scarcely a cinemagoer who could escape this total war film offensive. The ceaseless hymn to soldierly virtue, to bombers, tanks and warships, was supposed to show the superiority of the Wehrmacht and the irresistible triumphant progress of the German war machine.[774]

To keep things in proportion, the war films always have one particular type of weapon in the foreground: the Luftwaffe pilots in the French campaign in *Stukas*, the infantry in the German invasion of Norway in *Spähtrupp Hallgarten*; only *Über alles in der Welt*, in which the French soldiers are mainly North Africans,[775] offers a panorama of all fronts and fighting forces.

The civilian Goebbels, who preferred indirect propaganda, did feel that the exaggerated brutality of the war films was necessary, but that it had not been executed to the best possible effect in the films.[776] He is particularly effusive when declaring what is actually the weakest film in this series, *Kampfgeschwader Lützow*, to be "very well made, clear, realistic, with wonderful angles and shots. A true film of war and the people" (1.3.1941);[777] and he is sympathetic to *Stukas* – although it is ultimately "too loud" as a "typical Ritter production" – because of the "wonderful aerial shots". (2.6.1941) But Goebbels' doubts start to show when faced with Karl Ritter's *Über alles in der Welt*, which was already complete as a conception shortly before the height of the war euphoria in April/May 1941. Goebbels seems to have found the first version of this cinematic war-cry far too heavy-handed: "Extremely naïve and primitive, but will probably be popular with audiences. Ritter makes nationalist points with a lack of inhibition that would make others blush." (10.10.1940) Goebbels pronounces in his entry for 3.1.1941 that this is a "patriotic hotchpotch that still needs changing". He was still criticizing the episodic film's lack of a coherent plot months later: he said that Ritter had to be sure that he did not let his next films "fall apart like reportage" (28.8.1941), "so that ultimately they become documentaries rather than feature films".

Goebbels found the "heroic but over-long" *U-Boote westwärts* to be "without any real momentum and with little atmosphere". (11.3.1941) It was only after certain improvements that he was partially convinced by the inspired shots at sea and a successful première. He does not accept responsibility for the film: "the navy's business". (10.5.1941) Goebbels was also annoyed that he had been able to intervene in the making of all these war films only to a limited extent. For example, *Spähtrupp Hallgarten* was not made by a state company controlled by the Propaganda Ministry, but by a private firm supervised by the OKH ("Army Supreme Command"). His judgement was consequently particularly disparaging: "pretty much a failure." (8.3.1941) The latecomers in the war film series in autumn 1941 did not fare much better, for example *Sechs*

36. *Der Fuchs von Glenavron* (1940): a double-edged message from the "Irish films".

Tage Heimaturlaub, a film about men on leave from the front: "A so-called propaganda film from a private production company, *Sechs Tage Heimaturlaub*, turns out to be an anti-propaganda film. National Socialism is laid on so thick here that it becomes positively embarrassing." (8.9.1941)

In addition, an attempt was made for the first time since 1933 to give a Party organization the key role in a film plot. In the Hitler Youth films *Kopf hoch Johannes* and *Jungens* ("Boys"), young people who are mostly "rebellious and anti-social at first"[778] find their way into society through life in camp and strict training. Of course young people had to be made fitter for war, but Goebbels fails to provide a reason for ever allowing Party films to be made again. They seem timely at most as a concession to local Party offices: although *Kopf hoch Johannes* was a "shoddy effort that we can scarcely show" (21.1.1941), it was premiered on 11 March 1941. And likewise "no masterpiece": the similarly constructed *Jungens*. (2.3.1941)

We have only very unsatisfactory evidence of the audience reaction to the "Blitzkrieg films". The "estimate of the financial results for the films that appeared from 1 July 1940 to 31 May 1941",[779] compiled by the film companies, shows very poor figures for *Kopf hoch Johannes*, and good results for *Kampfgeschwader Lützow* and *Über alles in der Welt*. But despite heavy publicity from March until late May, *Über alles in der Welt* brought in less than the Willy Birgel film … *Riding for Germany*, which was not launched until April. Ultimately all these films can be said to have been successful to some extent,[780] with *Kampfgeschwader Lützow* and *U-Boote west-wärts* (relating turnover to run) coming out better than *Über alles in der Welt*, which this would suggest was not "popular with audiences" – contrary to Goebbels' expectations.

Despite all the scepticism about the military films, for Goebbels they were part of the contribution to film propaganda expected by the public and the Party. There is a great deal to suggest that Goebbels even wanted to offer more of them, and was looking for more material that would "make the soldiery into heroes". (25.7.1940) But he never kept up with his own intentions, or the intentions of military personnel who were interested in projects of this kind. Most plans remained at the script stage: these included a "Schlieffen film" with Rudolf Forster (10.9.1940), a film about the general staff by Emil Jannings (12.5.1941), and a project about the occupation of Norway that Goebbels always called the "Narvik film" (25.7., 18.9.1940), which was obviously pursued for longer than the others.[781] (1.9.1941) Goebbels put a stop to a "Scharnhorst" project (15.4.1941)[782] as early as May 1941. (4.5.1941) A "new war film about the army", called *Der Weg nach Abbéville*, probably planned to keep things in proportion after the Luftwaffe films, also came to a halt. (8.3.1941)

Developing more "soldierly" film material made sense in terms of the military situation in spring 1941. After several postponements German and allied troops crossed the Russian border along a length of over 2000 kilometres on the night of 21 June 1941. Here Goebbels' diary confirms the Nazi leadership's assessment, confirmed by other sources as well, that the Wehrmacht was going to have a rapid victory over the Soviet divisions: "The Führer estimates that the campaign will last 4 weeks, I think it will be less. Bolshevism will collapse like a house of cards.." (16. 6. 1941)

But even by late summer Goebbels' confidence had given way to prognoses that veered to and fro increasingly hectically. Optimistic and pessimistic assessments of the war situation and the popular mood give way to each other daily. Goebbels' prophecies about the course of the campaign ("won already", 19. 7. 1941, similarly on 24. 7.) turn out to be miscalculations; he seems increasingly uncertain and nervous. During the battle of Smolensk, which unexpectedly held up the German advance in late July 1941,[783] Goebbels' entries sound extremely sceptical, and in part dramatic (24./29./30. 7): now he is already saying that Germany is having to fight for "bare existence". (25. 7.) Goebbels is following the news here, which changes by the hour, and is no longer able to undertake any fundamental analysis. If positive reports come from sections of the front then the Propaganda Minister sees the whole situation in a better light again. Then in mid August 1941 he hopes that "the eastern campaign will be brought to a conclusion that is satisfactory for our needs and for further military operations, before the onset of winter, which will probably be in mid October". (19. 8. 1941)

Shortly after this he starts to criticize the Supreme Command's "over-optimistic" pronouncements and considers various precautionary measures for maintaining morale (8. 8.), in the sphere of care for the troops, for example. (5. 9. 1941) Chief Reich press officer Otto Dietrich's over-hasty announcement of victory on 9 October 1941 went "too far" for Goebbels, even though Hitler had expressed himself similarly in the speech opening the Winter Help appeal on 3 October.[784] Goebbels felt that it could cause a "psychological setback".[785] But when the weather was favourable: "I think that we have won the war against the Soviet Union and that there is no question of a further serious threat from the east." He doubts only "whether we should completely adjust all our propaganda in this very far-reaching direction". (10. 10. 1941)

Goebbels was preoccupied with the mood of the population throughout the autumn, but can only record that it keeps moving up and down. Sometimes the people are "too optimistic" (12. 10. 1941), and "ultimate victory is already taken for granted by some", then there is "fear of the coming winter" again.[786] (4. 11. 1941) This is followed by another upsurge, which is again replaced by uncertainty at the end of the month. It is not until early November that "signs of public depression" can be observed.[787] The German troops' offensive had definitely failed. Goebbels makes the contradictory remark: "The Bolsheviks are even more brutal than we are." (7. 2. 1941)

The Propaganda Minister tried to put the premature reports of victory straight in his article "Wann oder Wie" in the weekly magazine *Das Reich*. On 21 December he broadcast his remarkably dramatic "appeal for a collection of winter things for the soldiers at the front",[788] which was deliberately "intended to work as shock therapy".[789] As a precaution, Goebbels discharges himself of any responsibility for the fact that things had gone wrong. The fault lay with Otto Dietrich's "optimistic propaganda, i.e. that propaganda that went against my wishes by insisting that the eastern campaign was already decided", which of course had a "disastrous effect". (22. 12. 1941)

Goebbels had to make up his mind about future film planning in precisely this military, psychological and political context. Once again a distinction had to be made between the topical media, the press, the radio and the weekly war newsreels, which were dependent on news and information policy, and long-term film planning. Were martial military films like *Über alles in der Welt* still appropriate in the light of the way the war was progressing and the people's nervous mood?

Goebbels set priorities in terms of the political and military developments in the second half of 1941. At first, in the first weeks after the invasion, while rapid advances were being made, it was still possible to discern a seamless continuation of the film propaganda course. He talks about "new political film material" (13. 7. 1941) in July and August: "I am discussing a series of major nationalist film subjects, intended to go into the studios as soon as possible, with the experts responsible." (27. 7. 1941) To fit in with the "great campaign against Bolshevism",[790] Goebbels once more gave the go-ahead for the interrupted production and screening of "anti-Bolshevik" films, in August 1939.[791] As in spring 1940, during the offensive against France, he again complained vigorously about shallow films that are markedly inferior to the battle newsreels (5. 8. 1941) because they make the "difference between appearance and reality" too clear.

Then there are some comments on films that are already starting to suggest concern and re-thinking. He wants to have the Ufa Film *Annelie* revised "because it contains some scenes that are shot very pessimistically. We cannot use films like this for the coming autumn and winter." (21.7.1941) The music film *Leichte Muse* ("Light Entertainment") is "extraordinarily welcome" to Goebbels for a simple reason: "as entertainment for the coming winter".

"We must take care in the winter that lies before us to put all our energies into keeping the people in a good mood. There must not be any sense of a pessimistic, gloomy or desperate mood in the coming winter. Here radio and films are our best aids." (6.9.1941)

He expects the same thing from *Das andere Ich* ("The Other Me"), a "very funny, up-to-date film that we will definitely be able to use in the coming winter". (11.9.1941) Goebbels wanted to apply this to the other mass media: he ordered a careful "lightening" (25.8.1941) of the weekly war newsreels, which were exciting, but too monotonously concerned with victory and battle scenes,[792] and a large-scale light entertainment programme was to be introduced for the radio.[793] He said that he would not let himself be "put off" by resistance to the new approach to radio music programmes: "The crucial thing now is what the people want. Good sprits also help to win the war", he pronounces on 17.11.1941. Goebbels was now helped by the fact that there was never any lack of entertaining films. He sets himself up as a champion of this good mood and even defends Heinz Rühmann's jokes at the expense of the National Socialist Party in *Der Gasmann*, ("Gas-man") which went too far for some people: "We have a number of Gauleiters who have absolutely no sense of humour. They think that spirits will suffer from harmless jokes that might sometimes even refer to Party or state institutions. Of course this in not the case." (28.9.1941)

October 1941 saw an end for the time being to the mass deployment of political films that had started in the spring, and the cinema programmes were again dominated by light entertainment. In November the proportion of propaganda once more rose to almost 50 per cent again. All the propaganda films that were ready for screening opened as planned, including the disgraceful anti-Polish smear film *Heimkehr* (*Homecoming*),[794] which for Goebbels was an "educational memo for the whole German people".[795] He said that he was proud to be able to show "such a magnificent political and artistic success". (24.10.1941) The racist smears and justification of the invasion of Poland fitted in with the official confidence in victory and propaganda line, while the "sub-human" Poles were like the captured "Asiatic" Red Army soldiers shown in the newsreels.

Goebbels' rethink in favour of light entertainment films was not completely restricted to programming declarations. For example, he announced that the new autumn production programme was to "contain a whole series of light-hearted and entertaining material" (25.9.1941), but at the same time warns that care needs to be taken with the change of orientation. He did not have a consistent and convincing strategy at this stage; there was too much uncertainty about how things would go in 1942: "It is extraordinarily difficult now to place the right feature films in terms of material. The situation is subject to such major changes at the moment that one scarcely knows what one should actually bring out, whether we want political, or military or music films, or simply light entertainment." (30.12.1941) Some political film projects that had been elaborately planned were actually not taken any further. Instead, Goebbels puts educational melodramas alongside light entertainment films, for example *Annelie*, "a typical film for women which we can well use at this time. We must continue along the path it has started out on." (22.11.1941)

Goebbels did not make any public statement about the farewell he had introduced to the typical Blitzkrieg political films. His speech at a Hitler Youth film congress on 12 October 1941, which had a heavy propaganda bias because of the Party audience, had nothing to add to the previous speech in February 1941. The Minister had nothing at all to say this time about the entertainment function of the film, and contented himself with pointing out that films were "one of the most important factors in brightening up the few hours left to the individual German today, as well as his work, for revitalizing his spiritual forces".[796] The aim of films is art, and propaganda only a by-product, said Goebbels in his masterly cover-up: "We do not want to make propaganda with our films, we want to create art with them, art that serves in its highest sense to educate the people. If this art is propaganda at the same time, because its goodness cannot be exceeded, in other words if it puts us and our views forward, that is not one of our unspoken intentions, but can doubtless be counted as a desirable addition to our artistic successes."[797] Goebbels seemed to feel that only the title *Komödianten* (*Travelling Players*) was worth mentioning in this speech. But he nevertheless hinted, in his remark that the German film was "about to throw off the last degenerate manifestations of a past inartistic development", that he felt that the new direction taken by film policy was by no means at an end.[798]

Between evasion and business interests: melodrama and light entertainment in the war-time film

The new models

The great crisis on the eastern front, the retreat, which was officially played down as "re-aligning the front", and the people's poor state of heart made the situation even more acute as 1941 gave way to 1942: "The war against the Soviet Union is a war that is taking us into uncertainly", wrote Goebbels on 6.1.1942, and later points out that the people are even gently criticizing the "Führer" himself for the first time. (16.1.1942)

As external conditions had taken a turn for the worse, and no end to the war was in sight, the film policy measures that had already been adumbrated in autumn 1941 had to be speeded up and the concept of distracting entertainment translated into effective films.

Goebbels was concentrating hard on his intention to bring about a clear increase in the proportion of light entertainment in the cinema, theatre and radio even in the early weeks of 1942. The proportion of films "of a lighter and more entertaining character, which the people have a rightful claim to in this difficult wartime period", was to be increased.[799] (13.2.1942) And if necessary also in the teeth of all the deep-seated resistance from "ideologues who believe that the U-Boot man, when he comes out of the engine-room oily and dirty, most likes to turn to the *Mythos des 20. Jahrhunderts* ", as Goebbels said in a side-swipe at the well-known book by his long-standing enemy Alfred Rosenberg. There are enough "National Socialist fanatics", above all those "who would be best pleased if any hint at all of happiness and peace were cut out".[800]

The film companies must have been made aware of Goebbels' guidelines in January 1942 at the latest, which we can see from a report by the Bavaria production chief in early February 1942: "In accordance with the most recent ministerial instructions, artistic and popular light entertainment films will now be mainly fostered … alongside politically significant films."[801] Furthermore, individual propaganda projects had had "the Minister's permission approval at the last minute".[802] Goebbels thought he could identify the first successes as early as 17.2.1942: "Tobis is now gradually starting to follow the lines I have laid down and makes light entertainment films for mass audiences. These are vitally necessary at the moment. Good spirits are a war commodity."

In the "Leistungssteigerungserlaß" ("performance improvement act") for German film-making dated 28 February 1942, which contained technical production reforms, rationalization measures and new command chains and organizational structures, the new approach became an official guideline.[803] In his last film speech, which was made on the same day, Goebbels explained the new measures in great detail, not without first underlining the German film industry's wartime achievements,[804] with its one billion visitors per year. For the first time Goebbels brought the greater European dimension and the supply of German films to the European market into play, and made it unmistakably clear, with the aid of skilful references to past achievements, that major, expensive propaganda films had had their day, "that a number of films have been made on my initiative that were essentially intended to be representative films, films about national politics; films that have cost three, four, five and almost six million and that were made for a particular purpose. I was not afraid to invest so much money because I believed that the aim I intended to achieve in terms of national politics would justify the resources invested."[805]

For a film like *Ohm Krüger*, which was "of great significance in terms of both domestic and foreign policy", one could "could happily put six million marks on the table". This was "the visiting card that we have to present", the Propaganda Minister added. But now cheaper films were needed, as "now, in wartime, we cannot compete with major, monumental American films".[806] Goebbels stressed that the cheapest films had often been the most successful ones. Arguing very carefully, he tried to present the move away from monumental political films as inevitable to the Party audience as well: "I do not want to get away with large-scale films as such. I simply want to put the point that not every firm is compelled to produce one huge film after another and one heroic epic after another. That is not what's wanted. I shall myself initiate major films about national politics that need to be made. … But it is necessary to make 80% of good light entertainment films of guaranteed quality to set alongside this 20% of large-scale films. This too is valuable in terms of national poltics."[807]

Goebbels concealed his drastic intention of ending the radical propaganda film phase behind renewed publicity for the meaning and purpose of film entertainment.[808] It must already have been clear at this point that even the 20 per cent of political films – however hard it may be to draw the line – was a figure that was far too high and probably not really aspired to.

The "large-scale films" had simply become too expensive. Goebbels had already come to the conclusion he described in his speech a few weeks before, when Max Winkler laid out "the increase in production costs for a normal film" to him: "Films that are important in terms of national politics are produced in such large quantities today, and they cost so much in personnel and material that they are scarcely affordable. What we are missing are good, reasonably priced light entertainment films. I shall find myself compelled to take up the cudgels on their behalf." (9.1.1942)

Jerzy Toeplitz points out the dwindling proportion of "expressly political" films in the last three years of Nazi rule: it sank from about 30 per cent in 1941 to 25 per cent in 1942 (16 films) – of which the majority were shown before the turning point in 1941 –, seven per cent in 1943 (six films) and six per cent in 1944 (4 films). Only a single political production appeared in 1945. Even if some titles could be disputed and others added, the statement about the ratio in each case remains accurate.[809]

Goebbels also made the change to cheap light entertainment films in his film commentaries, which show new model films and favourites; they were sometimes more markedly political, sometimes escapist, but always "of guaranteed quality". He clearly thought the "excellent" and reasonably priced home front film *Zwei in einer großen Stadt* ("Two in a Big City") was exemplary, "proof that we can also make art with less expenditure". (13.1.1942) In this skilful, cheerfully insincere film, a mixture of leave from the front and comedy of mistaken identity, the women at home worry about their husbands at the front, who then turn up on leave and report briskly and optimistically how they "bring down Tommies".[810] The Gauleiter of Berlin was also pleased that this studio film using young actors contained a number of scenes that made good publicity for Berlin. (25.1.1942) He had in fact only just asked for films, using the motto "Berlin instead of Paris or New York", "that are set in Berlin without relating to Berlin directly, ... to show the city with its people and architectural beauties. This is propaganda whose motivating force and origin one does not recognize, and that will be all the more effective for precisely that reason." (28.10.1941)

The Zarah Leander revue-melodrama *Die große Liebe* (*The Great Love*) follows a similar pattern; this is a film from the Nazi period that has been much analysed recently.[811] This "melodramatic contribution to psychological warfare" (Karsten Witte), directed by Rolf Hansen and premiered in June 1942, is set in the period from March to July 1941, and ends with the German advance on the Soviet Union. Legendary National Socialist hits like "Davon geht die Welt nicht unter" ("That won't be the end of the world") and "Es wird einmal ein Wunder geschehn" ("Some time there'll be a miracle") round off one of the most perfect dramatic achievements of the war years. Goebbels praised it as well, saying that the film tried "to integrate a private event into the great events of the war, and does it quite skilfully", and that it will "doubtless be a great success with the public", even without "any claims to great artistic worth". (14.5.1942) The scene in which Zarah Leander – representing many of her fellow-citizens – overcomes her prejudices against her "unpleasant" fellow air-raid shelter users and in fact learns to enjoy an idyllic sense of Volksgemeinschaft there is certainly one of the most subtle in National Socialist film history. The constant presentation of farewells, renunciation, self-denial and fidelity was intended to reassure men at the front and at the same time remind women of their duty to be faithful given the many married couples separated by the war. One demand is promoted for both, that of "doing without a private life for the long term as well".[812] Willingness to fight and make sacrifices for the fatherland were no longer in the foreground. The message was that people should fight "in the hope that being involved in the war would open up the pathway to private existence that the war had closed".[813] *The Great Love* had been seen by about 12 million people by 1944.[814] Almost 400,000 saw it at the Ufa-Palast alone in the first few weeks.

Alongside more "educational" exceptional phenomena like *The Great Love*, started in autumn 1941, the light repertoire of musical comedies, costume comedies and operettas set in a court, artistic or manufacturing milieu was dominant. Goebbels was strikingly positive a few days before the première about the Johann Strauss operetta film *Die Nacht in Venedig*,[815] which he had greeted as welcome entertainment for the "broad masses" as early as 27.2.1942: "This film is exemplary entertainment. We really can use productions like this in the present situa-tion." (31.3.1942) The opulently mounted Wien-Film production *Wiener Blut* (*Vienna Blood*) from the "harmless dream-world of the waltz",[816] also based on a Johann Strauss operetta and with stars like Willy Fritsch, Theo Lingen and Hans Moser, even made him "green with envy" and led to complaints that there were no such films "with zip and elegance" to promote the Reich capital Berlin. (3.4.1942) And finally *Kleine Residenz* ("Small Residence Town"), which drew on the small state, theatre and court milieu, was for Goebbels an "exemplary achievement of the kind of good light entertainment film for the war that I have been asking for and promoting for some time".[817] (2.5.1942)

Goebbels expressly welcomes marital comedies that are now seen as a formal and aesthetic caesura and breakthrough to the more elevated "society film": for example, *Meine Frau Theresa* ("My Wife Theresa"), because it fits in completely "with my present wishes and requirements for German film production in approach and execution. It is cheap, entertaining, witty and brilliantly directed". (16.9.1942) Something that could be discerned only indistinctly in 1939 and 1940 becomes a system for Goebbels in this phase: light films are fundamentally necessary, and they are also art when they comply with certain guidelines and criteria; "zippily made, with a lot of wit, not too expensive, … readily comprehensible at home and abroad" (9.10.1942) – this is the common denominator to which Goebbels reduces his ideal (in this case Helmut Käutner's comedy *Wir machen Musik* ("We're Making Music"). Society and marital comedies should be easily digestible and timeless, and the main thing is that they were "lighter in character and more tasteful in format" (14.9.1942, on *Ein Zug fährt ab* / "A Train Leaves").

Goebbels' comments show that he liked to see a hint of politics in costume drama as well. He notes with satisfaction that in *Die heimliche Gräfin* (*The Secret Countess*), set at the time of the Austro-Hungarian Empire, provides good entertainment to the disparagement of the Austrian monarchy and also sends up and pokes fun at Habsburg Vienna, while following all the rules of art". (13.8.1942)

As long as "dramatic conflicts" were "movingly" portrayed by excellent actors and not too generally gloomy, Goebbels found them more than welcome as a means of distraction as well, for example *Der große Schatten* ("The Great Shadow") with Heinrich George and Heidemarie Hatheyer and an "exciting and captivating plot". (13.8.1942) In the case of the serious films, Goebbels places "education" alongside the need for entertainment. Thus the deliberately tragic end to the famous Veit Harlan melodrama *Die goldene Stadt* can be traced back to Goebbels. Kristina Söderbaum as a blonde landowner's daughter who had become involved with a Czech had to commit suicide at the end of the film, on the instructions of the Propaganda Minister. "We have to insist that the conflict be played through to the end, even if there is no happy ending", says Goebbels, dressing up his ideologically motivated order as a purely artistic and dramatic one[818] (15.5.1942) And of course Goebbels justifies himself: "The film is moving with the ending that I wanted. It is bound to be seen as a masterpiece of German film art." (24.7.1942)

There are two more film genres that were very popular with the film companies because they went down well with the public and could usually be got past the Propaganda Minister without difficulty. These are also particularly interesting in the context of the reorientation of the German film in 1942: so-called country films and biographical films. The great success of *Das unsterbliche Herz* (about Peter Henlein) and *Robert Koch, der Bekämpfer des Todes* ("Robert Koch, the Enemy of Death") had inspired more films about "great Germans" and leading figures in art, science, politics and the military. All these "charismatic artist-leaders"[819] embodied genius, stubbornness, strength of purpose and uncompromising faith in their own mission. "This use and development of the Führer myth"[820] deliberately did not make parallels with Hitler, so that the public could draw – much more effective – conclusions of their own.

By spring 1942 numerous biographical films were already showing in the cinemas or were at the planning stage: *Friedrich Schiller*, *Friedemann Bach*, *The Great King*, *Bismarck*, *The Dismissal*, *Ohm Krüger*, *Carl Peters*, *Wen die Götter lieben* (*Whom the Gods Love*, about Mozart), *Andreas Schlüter*, *Diesel*, *Geheimakte WB I* (*Secret Paper WB 1*, about Wilhelm Bauer, the inventor of the U-Boot), *Rembrandt* and *Paracelcus*. Some of these films can be included only with reservations; the Bismarck films (*Bismarck*, *The Dismissal*), the Frederick the Great series and *Ohm Krüger* occupy a special place. The "heyday of films about creative people"[821] from the world of music, painting, architecture and science led to a tightly defined individual genre – which incidentally was the most striking National Socialist innovation, along with everyday films dating from the thirties. In contrast with earlier political films, the past was not painted in gloomy colours. Glorious chapters of German history were picked out and "complex and contradictory events and developments" were condensed how outstanding personalities successfully affected German culture and science, and the arts of statesmanship and war".[822]

Given the rising number of these films even by mid 1941, Goebbels feared that the subject could be done to death: "In the film sphere I am making sure that not too many biographical films go into production. Ultimately we must produce a likeness of life, and not just of a few great men." (22.7.1941) But production continued undiminished, contrary to his announcement.[823] Eight such productions appeared in 1942 alone. It was not until August 1942 – triggered by the film about Rudolf Diesel, the pioneer of mechanical engineering, which was technically realistic rather than heroic – Goebbels once more remarks that film producers confused "art with instruction" and had made the biographical films too long-winded and wordy. For this reason we "must now generally get rid of these personality films and come back to themes about the matter in hand. The personality films were a makeshift device at the beginning of the war to get German film production back on to the right route. And now we are back on the right route we can focus on films about real issues again." (16.8.1942).

Shortly before he had liked the emotional films *Andreas Schlüter* (2.8.1942) and *Secret Paper WB 1*, however. And yet his statement does seem to have meant something this time, as permission to shoot had been withdrawn from almost all the biographical film material by 1942/1943. Thus for example Ufa was told: "As this is a film about Edvard Grieg, the material was set aside as it is biographical, following the Reichsfilmintendant's instruction in principle."[824] Proposals for films about Richard Wagner (Tobis), Clara Schumann (Ufa), Theodor Körner (Tobis) and Otto Lilienthal (Berlin-Film) were treated similarly.[825] Of the production plans submitted by Bavaria in 1942, which anticipated up to 50 per cent of biographical films for the serious sector,[826] only *Paracelsus* (28.2.1943)[827] and *Wien 1910* (about mayor Karl Lueger) were made. This abandonment of biographical films also shows a clear turning away from political material.

The so-called country film, which was extremely popular with large sections of the public, extended from comedies in south German dialect about boys climbing through their sweethearts' windows, full of clumsy jokes and pugnacious lads in lederhosen (for instance *Hochzeitsnacht/* "Wedding-night", 1941) to essentially stolid rural melodramas, of which *Die Geierwally* ("Vulture Wally") is probably still one of the most interesting examples artistically. The desire for "realistic" country films was also regularly reinforced by the Security Service's reporters. So long as the films were entertaining, Goebbels seems to have settled for some artistic deficiencies from autumn 1941. On 23.2.1942 he writes about the Joe Stöckl film *Der verkaufte Großvater* ("The Sold Grandfather"): "It is less than overwhelming in its artistic effect, but still a film that will please the people." Otherwise the Minister tried to work out any problems that might arise in terms of effects on the public mood: "I have the impression that we have been producing too many country films recently. The intention is very good, but the effect will not be on correct proportion with the effort and expense. In any case we must not find ourselves with nothing new to show but heavy, serious films about country life next autumn, when the people will be wanting something light-hearted and relaxing." (15.5.1942)

And indeed there was an accumulation of country film premières in the first six months of 1942. *Der Strom* ("The River"), a film about the rural north German dike communities, which Goebbels had pronounced "a masterpiece" on 22.12.1941, but "somewhat too gloomy and melancholy", was followed by *Anuschka*, a poor light entertainment film in Goebbels' view (21.3.1941), *Die Erbin vom Rosenhof* ("The Rosenhof Heiress"), *Violanta* and *Hochzeit auf dem Bärenhof* ("Wedding at Bärenhof"). This rapid succession of rural films, some of them steeped in conflict, made the Minister worried about there being too many films that would depress people' spirits. Shortly after this, some proposals for rural films were rejected by the Reichsfilmintendant, partially because "material that is too tied to the land" was "not desirable at the moment". But this instruction from Goebbels does not seem to have held for very long: there really were no premières of films of this kind in autumn 1942, but the genre was back again with "heavy and serious" dramas in the following year. Despite the fact that the war was going very much worse, and the downward shift in mood after Stalingrad, Goebbels now judged these films positively from purely artistic points of view.[828]

Goebbels and the chic film world

Dominance by light entertainment in the cinema was seen as desirable. But it also caused problems when the war started to go increasingly badly. The cinema's light, escapist and entirely unrealistic approach had always been scorned by some of the National Socialist Party. After the dramatic "heroic battle for Stalingrad", critical voices of this kind started to be raised more loudly. Goebbels seems to have been aware of the increasing contradictions as well: "In the cultural sphere, there is vigorous criticism of a number of light entertainment films that no longer quite fit in with the way things are. But how can one tune into a period that is 12 months later in the case of light films that were made a year ago. The problem posed by light entertainment in the cinema is becoming increasingly critical. I do not think that there is any way at all in which it can be solved to satisfy everyone."[829] (26.2.1943)

As Klaus Kreimeier accurately remarks, "Goebbels' inner turmoil" about smart diverting films "was symptomatic of one of the regime's central dilemmas."[830] On the one hand, National Socialist propaganda was preaching readiness to fight and make sacrifices in the dramatic and fateful battle for the life of the whole people, or its end. On the other hand, elegant society films were urgently needed to distract a nation that threatened to sink into resignation. Nothing can make this dilemma clearer than the Berlin cinema programmes before and after the 6th Army capitulated at Stalingrad. There is no sign of even the slightest effort in the weeks before or after 2 February 1943 to underline the "hour of fate" and to invoke a sense of holding out by using nationalist films.

In February 1943, cinemagoers in the capital could choose between love comedies, farces and thrillers, and nothing else. For example, from 2 to 12 February 1943 *Liebeskomödie* ("Love Comedy"), *Geliebte Welt* ("Beloved World"), *Liebe kann lügen* ("Love Can Lie"), *Dr. Crippen an Bord* ("Dr. Crippen on Board") and *Hab mich lieb* ("Love me") were running. On 12 February 1943 there was just one of over 100 cinemas that was showing *The Great King*. On 18 February 1943, the day of Goebbels' famous appeal for "total war", the situation did not look any different: *Zwei glückliche Menschen* ("Two Happy People"), *Hab mich lieb* and *Die große Nummer* ("The Great Number") were providing the lion's share of the cinema programmes. No nationalist films were repeated in subsequent weeks either, which is particularly surprising given the attempt at mass mobilization after Goebbels' speech. There is an impression that the unduly flat comedies and farces were giving way to more serious melodramas, but (older) propaganda films like *Feinde*, *Der Gouverneur* and *Gewehr über* were limited to about half a dozen venues. This imbalance is remarkable, even though the demand for weary old propaganda movies would probably not have been very high.

The gulf between the film world and the real world was still disturbing, and had led as early as 1942 to deliberately launched announcements about the alleged abandoning of light entertainment films.[831] These were issued from the Reichspropagandaleitung in particular, and often aimed only at a Party audience. Despite this, Goebbels did not allow any doubts to arise about the light entertainment course he intended to follow: "The people now only want light entertainment films or films dealing with large human themes, even if they are tragic or dramatic", he proclaimed programmatically on 23.3.1943. Goebbels' comments in the early months of 1943 seem extremely pointed. He writes on 16.2.1943 that "the entertaining character" of *Der kleine*

Grenzverkehr ("Small Scale Frontier Traffic") made it "excellently suited to the present time". Goebbels even said on 14. 3. 1943 that even the cheap rustic comedy *Das Ferienkind* ("The Holiday Child") fitted in with "current taste and the demands that are being made on our film production at the moment". He makes similar comments about the harmless love comedies *Geliebter Schatz* ("Beloved Darling", 15. 4. 1943) and *Die Gattin* ("The Wife","witty and amusing", 21. 5. 1943). Goebbels even welcomes frivolity and adultery in films: "It has turned out to be very amusing and shows the right sort of thing for the present moment. We can help the public to relax even at the most difficult of times with films like this", remarks the Propaganda Minister on 22. 2. 1943, when examining the marital comedy *Ich vertraue Dir meine Frau an* ("I Trust You With My Wife"), which was violently attacked by the Party offices.

Goebbels also managed to present himself as a paragon of virtue, in direct contradiction to this. He obviously could not completely ignore objections to unduly loose morals in films. And so he wanted to acknowledge his critics by looking for "clean" subjects, as a curious entry shows:

"I had been lodging protests for a long time about the fact that German feature films are so concerned with marital crises and divorce. The production chiefs will not listen to my arguments. And so for this reason I have had statistics prepared about the ration of divorces in Berlin and the rest of the Reich. This has revealed that there are six times more divorces in Berlin than the Reich average; this proves that my objections were right." (29. 6. 1943)

As early as November 1942 the Party office had pointed out very firmly that it feared the possible deleterious effect of "so-called society films, in which city-dwellers do nothing but laze around in good clothes, have nice homes, the best possible food and drink and one aim only in life, that of dealing with their amorous affairs".[832]

Efforts were also made to cut back on films set in a medical or artistic milieu. In July 1942, the production chiefs were instructed "that medical material should not be submitted for the time being. In the same way, material set in the world of painters was to be avoided".[833] Even this demand made little or no impact. Goebbels complains about *Du gehörst zu mir* ("You Belong to Me") on 15. 1. 1943: "My warnings about medical films turn about to have been justified again here. The film is extremely bad, and this milieu in particular is entirely intolerable at the moment and seems unduly assertive." Shortly afterwards Hippler again appealed to the film companies, saying that it was "not acceptable to set every second film in an artistic, medical, circus or boardroom milieu. There are many more rewarding themes that films have not yet investigated, to mention only radio, the press and the family." Hippler made the production chiefs responsible for "directing authors and script editors towards creating new milieus and different professional categories in films".[834] But what conclusions were the producers to draw when Goebbels simultaneously (13. 1. 1943) pronounced the Emil Jannings film *Altes Herz wird wieder jung* ("Old Heart Is Young Again"), which is set in the world of upper middle-class manufactures, to be a "masterly achievement".[835] Especially as the illegitimate child theme, which had always been rejected, cropped up again, despite a few modern insertions (Nazi salute, neat girls doing community service).

The "artistic and medical professions are being so over-presented that the public are gradually getting fed up with this approach", Goebbels explains,[836] then shortly afterwards comes up with a completely contradictory assessment of a film: "a plot set in the Munich art milieu … directed by Erich Engel (was) extraordinarily successful."[837] (11. 7. 1943) This contradiction also applies to positive comments on Hans Schweikart's artist film *Ich brauche Dich* ("I Need You", 19. 4. 1944) or other films about doctors and artists dating from 1944. Goebbels seems half-hearted here: he was less concerned with slant or milieu than with the overall impression, working to the motto "form before content".

Undoubtedly attempts were made to use "national and family" material instead of films about doctors and artists. The Propaganda Ministry regularly pointed the production chiefs towards themes of this kind, at numerous meetings.[838] But the film companies' writers had difficulty in doing just that: "developing the family material that I have long been asking for". (17. 4. 1943) And this remained the case even when Goebbels provided detailed guideline intended to place "family films" – and they should not be "too problematical" and conflict-filled – in an "upper middle-class" and "tidy human and landscape setting".[839]

When explaining the National Socialist cinema's irreconcilable split between appearance and reality, we must also not overlook the German film industry's attempts to expand into Greater Europe. The director Arthur M. Rabenalt feels that the "great formal and structural change in light entertainment film during the war" that could be discerned from 1942 inwards, moving in the direction of "chic and the last work in tasteful elegance, hyper-modernity in the exquisite style of American penthouses or French millionaires' apartments in the 16th arrondissement"[840] could be explained only against this background. Rabenalt also describes his own film *Meine Frau Theresa* ("My Wife Theresa") as a "triumphal breakthrough" for the genre; for Goebbels saw it at least as a model. (16.4.1942) He felt that upper middle-class Euro-entertainment film in a timeless atmosphere, also called "gracious living" films by Rabenalt, would have the best chance of standing up to export competition in the European and world markets after Germany's victory.[841] Had Goebbels not already praised *Wir machen Musik* ("We're making Music"), because it was "readily comprehensible at home and abroad?" (9.10.1942)

Hippler had told the film companies as early as 1942 that the Nazi salute could not be used on large scale in German films as it could damage their commercial chances in Europe.[842] The criterion also reappears frequently in subsequent years – particularly when faced with German films' decreasing ability to pay for themselves because so many cinemas had been destroyed. The German film industry's decision-makers summed it up like this in February 1942: "As we have already stated, our efforts will not meet with success until we produce films that are suitable for export, in other words films that are mainly aimed at the light entertainment market, with gripping plots, music, costumes and design."[843] Finally, Max Winkler pointed out at a film managers' meeting on 14 January 1944 that even at the material selection stage the "film's ability to succeed abroad" should be considered. Political films are not in demand here, as the regular lists of German films that are successful abroad confirm.[844]

Goebbels also expressly emphasized the fact that some films were produced for the foreign market, at the same time scenting welcome foreign propaganda: "Wien-Film is presenting a new film: *Der weiße Traum* ("White Dream"), which was specially made for export purposes. It is very ostentatious in its costumes and design, and will certainly attract attention abroad, above all given that we are still in a position to bring out films like this at the beginning of the fifth year of the war."[845] (29.8.1943) Goebbels also anticipates that *Zirkus Renz* ("Circus Renz") will "certainly (be) a great success for us abroad". (3.9.1943). Goebbels always had his eye firmly on the "world market after the war". He indulges himself for pages on end with visions of a German film hegemony in Europe and all over the world, with only the Americans remaining as competitors: "It is my ambition to build up the German film as a dominant world force." (16.12.1941)

Fundamentally there was no alternative to the light entertainment policy, although it was accompanied by an increasing number of undesirable aesthetic phenomena that Goebbels could not ignore. Psychology and commercial interests were on the side of lighter material. But Goebbels had to live with the contradiction that he had actually put forward quite different artistic claims. He increasingly feared that the light entertainment strategy would again lead right back to the comedies of earlier years, which were quite without substance, and always controversial. This also explains which the Film Minister did not think very highly of a large number of productions for which he was responsible in the last three years of the war.

Goebbels identified one particular genre of "inartistic", rudderless films with no export value. For example, *Der Seniorchef* ("Senior Boss") had "no clear sense of plot, and above all absolutely no aim or slant. Films of this kind simply should not be made any more in our day". (19.8.1942) Here he is paradoxically almost discharging himself from responsibility for film production and falling back into the old role of the spectator. And so Goebbels also shows behaviour typical of governments that have been in office for a long time with a bad balance sheet: denouncing serious irregularities, rhetorically demanding a change of course, looking for others who can be blamed, all to distract attention from one's own failures. In the first place this was all about the threadbare artistic claims that Goebbels had been holding up for years, in the light of which he had to justify himself.

Goebbels seems to use this method of distancing himself from a film output that has decidedly modest artistic qualities. The revue and film with a jealousy theme *Liebespremiere* ("Love Premiere") is "very bad", says Goebbels angrily (1.4.1943), and so is the Theo Lingen comedy *Johann.* (18.4.1943) The film *Musik in Salzburg*, which is set in an opera and concert milieu (24.12.1943) induces him to state: "I must complain much more heatedly about the present level achieved by films, which is subject to criticism from all sides." (2.4.1943) *Junge Herzen* ("Young Hearts"), a film about musicians, is just a "dilettante piece of work" according to Goebbels on 5.12.1943. But then the innocuous "everyday" latecomer *Ein schöner Tag* ("A Beautiful Day") is welcomed as a "fine national film for wartime": "Here at least we have topical subjects treated in a very attractive way." (13.11.1943)

This recession into the rhetoric of the early years continues in 1944, with nasty reviews by Goebbels of the Marika Rökk revue film *Die Frau meiner Träume* ("The Woman of My Dreams"),

38. Revue film *Der weiße Traum* (1943, "White Dream"): made for export.

for example, which he finds "vulgar and too heavy-handed". (16.1.1944) And now everything has to be done "at least to prevent our film companies from coming up with excessively dilettante productions in future", Goebbels demands on 19.5.1944.[846]

Positive comments on *Die Zaubergeige* ("The Magic Violin", "a young artist's life seen from an appealing point of view", 26.2.1943) and the medical film *Der gebieterische Ruf* ("The Imperious Call", "a work of art of the first order", 11.5.1944) show how much Goebbels vacillated in terms of his basic judgement on milieu.

Certainly Goebbels' dissatisfaction with almost half of all the films produced is also partly due to his own personnel policy failures and stalled attempts at reform. He had underestimated the inertia, the laziness and the lack of inspiration, in brief the whole momentum inherent in the eternal repetition of successful patterns when it came to material for films as well. Though certainly Goebbels did not restrict himself to threatening, but acted according to his convictions in many cases in 1944: never before had so many films been banned for lack of quality, becoming victims of "taste censorship". Banning as a warning: this returned things to where they were in 1935, when Goebbels, just appointed, was tackling there fact that an undue number of "shallow" films were being produced.

His analyses here are as convincing as they are contradictory. When he criticizes anti-Modernism in the craftmen's drama *Aufruhr der Herzen* ("Hearts in Uproar", 24.4.1944), when he condemns "film production's flight into the time before the World War" with its "middle-class conflicts" and "plush ideals",[847] he is already starting to sound abstruse: "In films I am now making a radical move against the tendency to run away from the difficult conflicts we are faced with today and take refuge in middle-class convention. I have recently been shown a whole series of films that were definitely operating in a plush milieu, and that addresses problems that no longer mean anything at all to us as modern people. The Ibsen atmosphere is of no interest to people today, and possibly even repellent …"[848] Goebbels was additionally disturbed by the fact that some melodramas were coming perilously close to "filmed theatre", which had been heavily resisted. The change was accelerated by the increasingly catastrophic state of the war: he had praised a film version of Ibsen's *A Doll's House* as recently as late 1943.

But the contradiction becomes clearer still when Goebbels questions another pillar of his film policy: the annual production figures, which every effort went into sustaining despite the war: "We have been shown so many bad films recently that I am getting rather anxious about it. It is probably mainly because we have put more emphasis on the number than the quality of films in the last two years. This must change as quickly as possible." (7.5.1944)

Veit Harlan's films were always glowing exceptions from the charge of conveyor belt production for Goebbels. But in 1943/44 this was only to an extent true of the colour melodramas *Im-*

mensee and *Opfergang* (*The Great Sacrifice*), which were made in parallel, both with Harlan's wife Kristina Söderbaum in the leading role. He still welcomes the utterly alienated version of Theodor Storm's novelle *Immensee*, anticipating that it will be a huge success with the public, as a "lyrical love-epic, extremely warm-hearted", but goes on to say: "Unfortunately Harlan again pushes his wife into the foreground far too much again in this film. But here too I will put everything in order with the scissors."[849] (12. 6. 1943)

The significance of this film for the regime's stamina propaganda should not be underestimated. Kristina Söderbaum claims to have received heaps of military postal service letters from soldiers at the front who saw her performance as a blonde German girl who is true even unto death as an assurance that their wives were faithfully waiting for them at home.

In the case of *The Great Sacrifice* Goebbels was obviously bothered – despite the desired transfiguration by death and emotion about faithfulness – by the heavy-handed scenes of emotion and pain, and by the music, which was interspersed with "mysterious choirs". He went on to say that "the dialogue is constructed somewhat too sentimentally and superficially. I must give Harlan a good talking-to. At the moment he is taking a line that does not seem to bode much success." (24. 7. 1943)

Propaganda films 1942 to 1945

Limited themes and final successes

Given that the field was dominated by light entertainment and indirect propaganda (in the form of subcutaneous messages), there was not much room left for open film propaganda. In any case, the psychological, military and political context became increasingly difficult from 1942 onwards for films with an unambiguously political background, which could officially make up 20 percent of production at the most.

The drastic cut-back in political films on a colossal scale in favour of profitable "nationally palliative" light entertainment and refined political material was caused mainly by lack of resources for costumes and design that would make an impact on audiences. Goebbels did not seem particularly depressed by this. After the last major project before *Kolberg*, Emil Jannings' *The Dismissal*, he said: "We cannot accommodate monumental films at the moment, merely in terms of material, because they swallow up to much raw material and labour. I do not even see this as unfortunate; if we are forced to make cheaper films, then we can increasingly direct the main thrust of our work at penetrating the material intellectually and psychologically." (2. 7. 1942) But it was precisely this correct material that was the problem. When Goebbels tried to cut back on the important genre of biographical films it became all the harder to find suitable subjects.

Then in the case of topical and "relevant" topics there was an increasing danger of being caught out by the changing political and military situation. Military productions in the style of *Stukas* or *Über alles in der Welt* were bound to be less effective because of the halting advance or partial retreat on the eastern front; something simiilar had applied to the newsreels since early 1942. The war film *Der 5. Juni* ("Fifth of June"), about the fate of an infantry unit in the 1940 western offensive (Goebbels: "powerful instruction", 15. 8. 1942) was never shown in public, and neither was Karl Ritter's *Besatzung Dora* ("Crew of the Dora"). The latter, a film about airmen and home leave planned in spring 1942 (shooting started in August) contained too many scenes from the Russian and North African fronts, where German troops were already in retreat by autumn 1942. Goebbels seems to have recognized that the subject of future colonization in the east and "talk about a farm in Russia"[850] were no longer appropriate.[851] Occasional improvements in the war prospects, e. g. during the euphoria of May/June 1942, no longer affected the turn away from military films.

The film companies' production summaries in 1943 – one example is the Ufa project *Charkow*, which had been given the go-ahead by the Reichsfilmintendant on 23 May 1942, increasingly include the additional note: "Further work on the material was temporarily suspended because of the military situation."[852] Complications also arouse because the Supreme Command of the Wehrmacht (OKW) was apparently increasingly inclined to intervene in war film projects as the war situation became more precarious. Numerous projects came to nothing because of conditions laid down and objections raised by the military. Carl Froelich's *Potsdam* project, with dealt with an officer in love in the period before and after 1933 – Froelich even intended to use extracts from Hitler's speeches – was mentioned by Goebbels as early as 1941: "I am just inventing a story intended to provide a framework for the film." (23.9.1941) There is a record of official approval for the material on 20 July 1943.[853] Planning extended over two years, until Goebbels finally stated that the project had "been treated with hostility by some OKW sections": "The OKW's point of view is too rigid and dogmatic here." (18.9.1943) In 1945 a committee of civilian and military experts was still complaining about the "military scenes" in the film *Regimentmusik* (which was never shown); they "were seen as particularly offensive to the modern, newsreel-trained eye".[854]

Other political subjects did not fare any better. The controversial introduction of compulsory work for women was to be supported by an Ufa feature film "about the female community service", produced by Karl Ritter and with a screenplay by Luise Rinser, called "Schule der Mädchen". But after the "Reich Labour Service" ("RAD") had "objected to essential parts of the screenplay", the project was shelved[855] – despite Goebbels' express support, though with reservations: "All the previous films about Party organizations have failed. This is mainly because they were poorly cast and had mediocre direction. I will pass this film project only on condition that one of our top directors is in charge." (29.4.1942) Other propaganda films were criticized and delayed from within the Party. Thus, for example, Goebbels had to defend the film *Wien 1910*, about Vienna's mayor Karl Lueger, against attacks from the Vienna Gauleiter's office. They felt that the Austrian Nazi forerunner Georg von Schönerer, a rival of Lueger's, was not sufficiently acknowledged in the film.[856] At the same time, Goebbels was aware that Hitler had been a particular admirer of the Viennese mayor ever since his youth.[857]

But more subtle political material was restricted as well. Suggestions for a film about "medical services" and "military hospitals",[858] which Goebbels had sent several reminders about, were first of all sent back for revision on a number of occasions, then finally rejected in 1944. Neither the intended action during the Polish campaign nor "the military hospital as a setting from private anxieties about love" seemed opportune "at a time when thousands of Germans knew that their nearest and dearest were wounded in military hospitals".[859] Apologists for the non-political National Socialist film will see their views confirmed in the case of *Am Vorabend* ("Last Evening"), which shows the fate of a family before the outbreak of war,[860] as Goebbels himself toned down some political references: "This is a very delicate film with a markedly poetic atmosphere. Unfortunately Menzel has related the events in the film to the outbreak of the war, which can work only to the film's disadvantage. I shall try to cut this link out of the film. What will be left will be a particularly beautiful and poetic film." (6.7.1943)

In fact the Propaganda Minister did have extensive cuts made to connections with September 1939, which he apparently found unsuitable at this stage of the war and also artistically disadvantageous, this meant that in August 1944 his Reichsfilmdramaturg Kurt Frowein was able to present him with the "Menzel film *Am Vorabend*, which has been changed to make it timeless and private" under its new title *Ein Blick zurück* ("A Look Back"). [861] This delayed the première until December 1944.

German screenings of Herbert Selpin's famous anti-British film *Titanic* were probably prevented by the disaster scenes on board the giant ship as it sunk – probably too explicit in view of the increasingly violent air raids in 1943 – as well as the risky allegorical potential. Goebbels also objected strongly to images of this kind in other films and projects: Harry Piel's *Panik* ("Panic"), in which wild animals escape from the zoo after an air raid, was banned completely, and a film project that Goebbels had been promoting since early in 1942 (11.2.1942) about camaraderie among miners (*Der innere Ruf*/ "The Inner Call") was delayed for so long that it had still not been completed, after revision on several occasions under the title *Die Schenke zur ewigen Liebe* ("The Eternal Love Inn"), by the end of the war.[862] The reason: in the case of this "film about working life with an ethically affirmative slant" (Frowein) he at first had "some reservations about passing a film that played in part in a 'disaster milieu'".[863]

It may be surprising, despite repeated demands on the part of the Reichspropagandaleitung and the Party Chancellery[864] during the "anti-Bolshevik" propaganda campaign, which had intensified again after Stalingrad and especially after the discovery of the corpses in Katyn, that no relevant feature film was commissioned in 1943. Goebbels offers no direct justification for this omission. The last two anti-communist films, Karl Ritter's major project *GPU* and Hans Weidemann's *Anschlag auf Baku* (*Attack on Baku*) – which was changed several times within two years –, were launched in 1942.[865] Goebbels had called *Attack on Baku* "very disagreeable" as early as December 1941, and referred to the director as "muddleheaded". Goebbels reacted similarly to *GPU*, denouncing it as a "shoddy, dilettante effort". It is a particularly unpleasant piece of propaganda in which the Soviet secret service officials are all Asiatic torturers, suggesting a threat that is more racial than ideological.[866] He says that Ritter is a failure: "He treats political and military themes merely superficially, and so they do not actually succeed any more in these realistic times." (3.7.1942) *GPU* was not given a classification either, which was more or less equivalent to an open rejection for a political film.

Goebbels seized the opportunity to push Ritter out: with the exception of *Besatzung Dora*, which was banned (and *Sommernacht*/"Summer Night", which was pure light entertainment), the director, who was always in debt in his private life, was given no more direction work until the end of the war, which meant that he had to restrict himself to working as a production chief.[867]

Goebbels was probably keen not to add to the list of unsuccessful propaganda productions. Some references suggest that anti-Communist "subhuman" propaganda, which would inevitably have been a key feature of any feature film of this kind, had anyway been undermined by the Germans' changed image of the Russians force labour: there were hundreds of thousands Russians force working in Germany by this time.[868]

Goebbels dismissed most of the propaganda films up to 1944: this included Arthur M. Rabenalt's *Fronttheater* ("Front Theatre"),[869] which was about troop care during the 1941 spring offensives, the anti-British colonial film *Germanin*, on which work had already started in 1941,[870] and which Goebbels took as an opportunity to "divert" the director (his brother-in-law Max W. "Axel" Kimmich) "towards non-political themes" (27.1.1943), and *Paracelsus*, which was set in the Middle Ages ("artificial" and "too Baroque", 28.2.1943). Goebbels calls the last biographical film *Der unendliche Weg* ("The Endless Way"), about the Württemberg politician Friedrich List, "boring and official" (23.3.1843) and also "a shoddy piece of patriotic work". (24.6.1943) Goebbels was also not convinced by the return to the Prussian milieu of duty and obedience in *Die Affäre Roedern* ("The Roedern Affair"), saying that the film was "well meant in the line it took, but unfortunately turned out very badly in artistic terms". (7.5.1944) Of the 1943 to 1945 political film programme, only the spy and Gestapo propaganda film *Die goldene Spinne* ("The Golden Spider"), "which distinguishes itself by achieving a happy synthesis of tension and instruction" (11.11.1943) and the Tobis film *Die Degenhardts* end up with favourable comments.[871]

Die Degenhardts is the story of a Lübeck family, and is an interesting new release for 1944: "The war in the air is included as a subject here for the first time, and it is done in a very tactful and psychologically ingenious way. Demandowsky is the only production chief who will touch political material and usually brings it off", writes Goebbels with delight on 5.3.1944. The Allies' air raid on Lübeck is skilfully shown as the destruction of centuries-old German cultural heri-

tage. Heinrich George explains in a voice cracking with emotion what used to be here before the ruins. This meant that Goebbels stopped resisting the presentation of images of destruction. In October 1942 he would still not permit "beautiful old Lübeck to be juxtaposed with Lübeck in ruins, as it is today", as the film images would be too shocking for the audience. (11.10.1943) But throughout the war the Propaganda Ministry never found a convincing strategy for dealing with news and images of ruins and destruction.

Die Degenhardts avoids mistakes that Goebbels discerned in other political films that were unduly crude. His model – which also stood for the *Degenhardts* film – was the prize-winning American production *Mrs. Miniver* (1942):[872] "It portrays the fate of a family in this war with a propaganda slant that is tremendously subtle and effective. Here you can see everything that I have been demanding and requiring of the German film industry for months, indeed for years. The Americans are past masters of turning trivial events into artistic ones. This film describes an English family and its fate, which cannot fail to attract sympathy. There is not a bad word said about the Germans; nevertheless the anti-German slant is perfectly in place. I am going to screen this film for the German production chiefs, to show them how it's done. (8.7.1943) Goebbels was possibly aware of Winston Churchill's public pronouncement that a film like *Mrs. Miniver* is worth more than six divisions.

Die Degenhardts was not one of a "series of films about about stamina",[873] but because the tricky material was handled so well it could have triggered *Das Leben geht weiter*, the most important project after *Kolberg* in the last year of the war: "I want it to show a Berlin air raid night in a block of flats in the Hansaviertel. It will involve the whole building, with all its individual

39. Director Karl Ritter: untimely propaganda.
40. A model film for Goebbels: *Mrs. Miniver* (1942); a perfect example of discreetly slanted material.

floors and families." (30.3.1944) Once again the damage was to be deliberately incorporated, and large numbers of shots of bomb damage in cities were to be taken to this end. In September 1944 this film under the direction of Wolfgang Liebeneiner, which had been commissioned directly by the Propaganda Ministry, was costed at over 2.2 million Reichsmarks as "part of the mental war effort" (Hinkel).[874] Goebbels pursued the realization of his idea with particular interest ("I think that this could be made into an effective film about night bombing in Berlin", 13.7. 1944).[875] But a screenplay modified by Liebeneiner in accordance with Goebbels' wishes was not available until October 1944, so that only two thirds of the film had been shot by the end of the war.[876]

Goebbels made another exception to his policy, valid since 1942, of not making any more films on Party themes by approving another film about the Hitler Youth. At first, given the failed films of 1940–42 (*Jakko*, *Jungens*, *Kopf hoch, Johannes*, *Hände hoch* / "Hands Up"), there was talk about "major reservations against a youth feature film that is not carefully prepared": "We already have four failed youth films to chalk up; I think that that is enough." (29.6.1943) Even though Goebbels' original measures, "less intention" and fewer Nazi organizations, were kept to only partially,[877] he seems pleased that the Hitler Youth are deployed in the arms business in Alfred Weidenmann's *Junge Adler* ("Young Eagles", 9.5.1944). But he takes a deliberately naïve approach about whether the film, which opened on 24 May, stood any chance of being a success: "It is astonishing that I feel I should remark in passing that the new Hitler Youth film *Junge Adler* has failed with audiences. This is probably because the public do not want to see political films at the moment. They do not go to the cinema to be educated or taught, but to be entertained and diverted." (10.6.1944) No new insights, but another justification for the lack of political films.

In May 1944 a newcomer to film was entrusted with the job of Reichsfilmintendant: he was the radical SS Gruppenführer Hans Hinkel. The motives for this were certainly concerned with organization and film finances in the first place. But even so, Hinkel's appointment – at a time when Goebbels' dissatisfaction with film production had peaked – also impinged on programming,[878] especially as Kurt Frowein, the dogmatic Reichsfilmdramaturg, was trying to find film material following National Socialist categories.[879]

Goebbels obviously intended to make serious changes to film production in terms of both quality and subject matter by the middle of the year. Too many films were "simply not fit to show", which had led to a "very displeasing backlog", despite the lack of films, he complained on 1.6.1944, in the context of productions that had been set aside. But the new will to change emphases lacked consistent execution in detail. Despite this, Goebbels expressly stresses[880] that new efforts would have to be made in the political sector. When he received a report "that the Americans were now putting even more political films on the market than before", and that they were "slanderous Hetzfilme against Germany" that also "made the desired impact as they were very well made", it was essential "to make political films, even if they are not out-and-out Hetzfilme, at least on a larger scale than before". (24.10.1944) There is no evidence of concrete plans arising from such statements, which would anyway have meant departing from the sales policy that is constantly reaffirmed in 1944 as well. It is not longer possible to find out whether film projects with title like *Flakstelle 77* ("Flak-position 77") or *Vorpostenboot 04* ("Boat on Outpost 04"), which are to be found in Propaganda Ministry documents for productions in 1945, were actually intended seriously.[881] But obviously the screenplay writers made heavy weather of even the most tentative anti-American slant. For example, in January 1945 Frowein rejected a film suggested by a close friend of Hinkel, the author and director Hans H. Zerlett, because the "side-swipes at the USA" would not have the "corrosive effective" that "would be necessary today".[882]

As it would have taken months to give film production a stronger political slant – if this was ever actually intended – a new campaign of repeating "national" films was launched to accompany the ever more fanatical slogans about holding out and "ultimate victory" and the establishment of the "Volkssturm", the territorial army created from October 1944 onwards. The Berlin Reichspropagandaleitung thus instructed the press as follows: "Repeat films of military and nationalist content will be featured … in our cinemas, appropriately to the gravity and significance of our times." They were "to support this campaign with suitable articles".[883] Hinkel commissioned the Deutsche Filmverleih (DFV) to "screen" these films "quickly", and provided Goebbels with a list of appropriate titles.[884] A week later he was able to point out a large number of political films in the *Völkischer Beobachter*'s cinema listings. As far as the public's response was concerned, the Filmintendant felt that the performances were "uniformly quite well attended in comparison with the films that had been premiered recently", with *Annelie*, *Der Fuchs von Gle-*

navron and *Der Katzensteg* ("Catwalk") showing the best audience figures.[885] The film companies' sum came out differently. The Ufa board stated "that the repeat screenings of politically significant films, as instructed, (had) led in part to considerably reduced cinema audience ratings".[886]

The Propaganda Minister compensates in detail in the course of 1944 for the decline of the political film by raising a subject that he finds particularly rewarding: the fact that cinema attendances had held up despite the intensified air raids. Goebbels usually received the cinema attendance figures for the previous month on about the 20th of each month; his comments are like triumphant announcements. On 23.3. he says: "Cinema box office income has risen again this month despite the air raids. Films will simply never be defeated." Despite the fact that a lot of cinemas were out of commission, Goebbels points out on 25.4. that "big box office successes" had been recorded. People were looking for "entertaining and edifying films", especially in the areas that were hardest hit by air raids: "Now that Berlin is not being attacked so heavily people are visibly heaving sighs of relief and turning to the more attractive aspects of life again." On 7.5.1944 he is pleased to record that the Berlin cinemas are showing "90 and 100 percent attendance figures again"; and likewise on 23.5.: "The new film statistics show good results for last month as well. Film attendances are going up rather than down, despite enormous strains."

Similar pronouncements in the autumn about the "most recent film statistics": "Despite the enormous strain placed on the German people by the air raids in particular film attendance have not gone down even in the cities that have been most severely damaged by the terror from the air." (24.10.1944) He does admit in December that "film attendances (have) gone down heavily in recent weeks" in some areas, but that in others they had gone up, so that "the lower box office figures do not make too great an impact" and that overall "film attendances (were) continuing to increase, despite the bombing terror and the critical state of the war". (21.2.1944)

These statistic confirmed Goebbels' faith in the possible effects that film could have. Otherwise it would not have been possible to justify the money spent on films like *Kolberg*. Goebbels transferred the figures he quotes in his diary largely correctly from the statistics submitted to him. After the high point in mid May the absolute visitor figures went down in the second half of the year for the first time since the beginning of the war,[887] but they rose again markedly early in 1944 and then went down continuously from about August 1944 until the end of the war.[888] Compared year on year, 1943, with 1.11 billion sold tickets, was not significantly in terms of attendance that 1944, with 1.1 billion.[889] Also the number of cinema visits per year and head remained constant at 14. Goebbels' delight with capacity attendances as a success as such was rather more problematical – the figures were bound to be higher because so many venues had been destroyed. Even in December 1943 there were 751 cinemas that could no longer be used, and by 31 October 1944 the number of cinemas out of commission had risen to 1279.[890] Winkler did insist that film production profits be used in a campaign to convert theatres of all kinds into cinemas; this was resisted by local authorities, however, who did not want to lose their theatres and also demanded some say about film programming.[891] And the impressive attendance figures also do not say anything about the way the audience composition had changed. It was scarcely possible for films to reach important target groups like armaments workers, for example, any more because of lack of leisure and constantly changing shifts – a conclusion with which the Security Service agreed.[892]

The number of new films was shrinking from year to year, and the attempt to counter this by showing more older titles that were already familiar and this less of a draw posed another problem. The proportion of non-current productions in the film programme was already about 24 per cent by 1942, rose to 25 per cent in the following year and reached over 40 per cent in November 1944.[893] Of course the "second-hand goods" had very little indoctrination potential left, and thus the high attendance figures were mainly a financial success, and a political one only to the extent that they contributed to the desired general diversion of the public.

Goebbels wanted to prevent the few new "politically significant" from being swamped by the flood of repeats, and so he tried to reorganize the way in which the number of copies was fixed. Thus *Die Degenhardts*, which he thought was an effective film, opened in the Reich territory in July 1944 with a total of 151 copies, a figure that was objectively inadequate, and yet relatively high in relation to other film launches. When the film department complained as well that the DFV's autonomous fixing of the number of copies meant that "the good films with a healthy slant desired by the state film management ... were pushed more into the background",[894] Goebbels criticized the fact that "the necessary number of copies (was) fixed for each film according to the taste of the censor in question, without consulting the Ministry offices". (2.4.1944) He also uses this to justify the lack of success of important (political) films and some inaccurate predictions: "For this reason a whole series of films that I would have hoped would be very successful did not achieve this success because a sufficient number of copies was not available. This will now be changed, as I shall lay down how many copies should be available and the cinemas in which it will run at the time the film receives its classification."

Three films in the diary: *The Great King* (1942), *The Dismissal* (1942), *Kolberg* (1945)

The three most lavish films of the National Socialist period, *Der große König*, *The Dismissal* and *Kolberg* were also the most important films in Goebbels' career. He devotes pages to describing their progress from idea to première, often with meticulous precision. Rarely has production history been so vivid, as we see it here, as Goebbels guides, controls, plans, and organizes screenplays down to the last detail, despite being stretched to the limit by the war. Nowhere else does Goebbels present himself so firmly as producer and supreme artistic director. In no other case did he so overestimate the feature film as a medium or so miscalculate production times. The story of these monumental films also illustrates the phases of wartime film policy once more: while *The Dismissal* and *The Great King* were started at the height of military success in spring 1940 and 1941 respectively, *Kolberg* is a product of the will to hold on that was demanded after Stalingrad.[895]

Shortly after the war started in September 1939 the Propaganda Minister asked the film companies for "Fridericus material" – for a film about Frederick the Great. He intention was to link up with the series of films on Frederick II, which had proved their worth, but he also wanted to portray the Prussian king in an entirely different way. This led to differences with the proposed director, Veit Harlan, who was chosen in April 1940 (5.4.1940) – even before shooting started on *Jud Süss*: "Harlan wants to work on new Fridericus material now. But I want to see Frederick as he was after Kunersdorf, and not Gebühr's summerhouse Frederick." (26.4.1940)[896] Goebbels and Hitler had both read Frederick the Great's writings several times, and both quoted them at critical moments of the war. Goebbels, who was not slow to use analogies with the Prussian king in his speeches either, ultimately wanted a film about Frederick that fitted in with his image and ideas of the king precisely. Goebbels also seems to have preferred a film that was more powerfully military and propaganda-orientated, with the Prussian army's major defeat at Kunersdorf in 1759 as the starting-point of the plot. This would make it easier to stage the "miracle of the House of Brandenburg" and the end of the Seven Years War in 1962 with the victories at Schweidnitz and Freiberg all the more effectively. Only the situation at that time, at the height of Hitler's military successes, can make it possible to explain that he project was attempted at all, despite the critical points of the historical model – Russian troops in Berlin, war on two fronts. After a few changes had been made, he declares the Harlan screenplay "magnificent except for a few details. This is going to be some film." (22.8.1940)

The idea for *The Dismissal* dates from June 1941. After the huge success of Wolfgang Liebeneiner's *Bismarck* with audiences in late 1940, it made sense to continue with the character, especially as the film ended with the victory over France and the foundation of the Reich in 1871, and left scope for a sequel. As had already happened with *Ohm Krüger*, the actor Emil Jannings figures as the source of the political material: "Jannings tells me about his new material for a film; *Die Entscheidung* ("The Decision"), Bismarck from 1885 to his dismissal. Good stuff, which I will support to the hilt." (15.6.1941) Jannings, who also wanted to play the lead, was going back to an idea that first came up in the thirties, in other words long before the first *Bismarck* film. Tobis production chief von Demandowsky, explaining the situation to Paul Hartmann, who had played the title role in *Bismarck* but was ditched for the sequel, said that the new project was based on a screenplay dating from before the war triggered by Jannings' performance as Bismarck for the Staatstheater; he went on to say that Goebbels had had reservations about filming it at the time because of the figure of Kaiser Wilhelm II, and so put the project back until the former monarch had died.[897] This version is confirmed by Goebbels' entry on 11.4.1936.[898]

It is clear that differences of opinion arose between Jannings and Goebbels as ideas for the screenplay developed in 1941. Apparently the actor wanted to make the material into a two-part film from the outset. At first Goebbels states delightedly that "the preliminary work on this has already gone a long way and that Jannings has got down to all this preparation with real enthusiasm, so that we probably will be dealing with another major work of cinematic art". (3.8.1941) But he definitely took a stand against two films, indeed he even suggested that he was only going to film three days of the Reich Chancellor's life (21.9.1941), as Jannings' "gigantic mountain

41. Heinrich George as Nettelbeck, Kristina Söderbaum as Maria in *Kolberg*: "Made a Nettelbeck film into a Söderbaum film."

of a script" ran counter to the "commission I had given".[899] Then a few days later he was already dealing with the detail of the manuscript, "now cut down to a single film": "The difficult question that remains is whether Wilhelm II should appear personally." (21.11.1941)

Goebbels produced a final through revision of the screenplay in the last fortnight of November, and fixed the political details in a discussion with Jannings and Liebeneiner, the director. This meant "two delicate questions" in particular: "Bismarck's attitude to the social question, and to the problem of Russia". Goebbels found answers to both. He made Bismarck appear rather more socialist than he did in Jannings' draft: the former Chancellor was not allowed to talk like Hugenberg or seem "hostile to the workers". He corrected Bismarck's pro-Russian treaty policy because the historical truth unfortunately "absolutely (did not fit) in with the current political landscape": "The film mustn't seem to be arguing against our present war with the Soviet Union." (1.12.1941)

The idea of a film glorifying the Pomeranian town of Kolberg's resistance to Napoleon's troops in 1806/07 had been in the air in the production companies' script departments even before 1943. Sometime in the weeks after the defeat at Stalingrad, but in late April at the latest, Goebbels must have decided to commission this project, which was practically predestined propaganda to urge resistance and stamina. He wrote about the first plans on 7.5.1943: "Harlan is to use this film as an example of manly courage and a community's powers of resistance, even in desperate conditions. This film will teach a wonderful lesson, especially in air raid areas. It is to be built entirely on historical fact. Harlan, who resisted the film at first because he wanted to make the film on Beethoven, is now full of enthusiasm. He has written a brilliant treatment in a week and wants to start shooting in late July. He is promising me a Christmas première. It will probably come in very handy."

And so Goebbels official contract to Veit Harlan on 1 June 1943[900] did not coincide with the actual start of the monumental project. On 25.5.1943 Goebbels reported that his Staatssekretär Naumann had arranged for "military contingents" to be available for shooting – essential given the planned crowd and battle scenes –, and repeated his time-scale: "I am promising my self a very great deal from this Harlan film. It fits perfectly into the political and military landscape that will probably be in place when the film comes out."

He must have been additionally motivated by reports of "widespread severe depression" among the public: "Something has to happen to put a stop to the increasing collapse of morale and attitude."[901] (28.5.1943) But Goebbels seemed disappointed with Harlan's screenplay: "Unfortunately Harlan, as is so often the case with him, has made a Nettelbeck film into a Söderbaum film. The girl Maria is central to the entire plot, rather than Nettelbeck, and of course Sö-

derbaum, his wife, has been chosen for the part. Here again it will be difficult to wean Harlan away from his first manuscript suggestions. Nevertheless that will have to happen, as I anticipate a great deal for our stance at home from the Kolberg film, in which so many resources are being invested. It must become *The Great King* film for winter 1943/44. Who knows what situation we'll be in then. We must have films at our disposal that foster and praise hard resistance." (5.6. 1943) Goebbels wanted to be sure that the figure of Nettelbeck, the leader of the Kolberg civic guard, was placed firmly in the foreground, as he seemed to identify with him: Nettelbeck worked on mobilizing the "fighting people", in contrast with the hesitant military under town commander Gneisenau. It may be surprising here that the mighty Goebbels has to talk the "Third Reich's" most successful director into things, and cannot simply give him instructions. Harlan himself talks of nothing but compulsion and orders. Numerous passages about the conception of the film are in evidence over the next few weeks. Goebbels criticizes the missing dimension in Harlan's screenplay: "It needs to be more nationalistic; he has made it too patriotic." (14.6.1943) He also maintained that the film was threatening to be "too long", like the Frederick the Great film. He finds the "rewritten manuscript" submitted to him on 14.7.1943 "better than the first draft", but two days later he is complaining again: "Harlan gets too bogged down in the terror scenes and neglects the more intimate effects. He must let up on his monumental plans a bit and make the film more in the style of 'Mrs. Miniver'."[902] This seems illogical, as the American film made its propaganda effect entirely from casual, discreet scenes, which ran counter to the basic concept of Kolberg. But the most interesting thing here is Goebbels' deadline planning: if it was meant seriously at all, given the scale of the project it must have been clear that it was entirely unrealistic as early as mid 1943. Up to that time – and the war was going much better as well – films on a similar scale like *Ohm Krüger* or *The Great King* had taken at least eighteen months from planning to première.

After about ten months' work shooting and editing *The Great King*, Goebbels' first comment on Harlan's film on Frederick was strikingly negative: "A total failure. Absolutely no demonic element. The opposite of what I wanted and expected. Frederick the Great as an urban bumpkin. I am very disappointed." (1.6.1941) Harlan had asked Otto Gebühr, who was playing the title role, to speak in an ordinary Berlin accent, which Goebbels found extremely "overbearing and tasteless", because it ran counter to the "great king's demonic quality".[903] (6.8.1941) The film would probably have had its première in autumn 1941 if Goebbels had not found the version politically inadequate. But Harlan apparently proved "resistant" to the Minister's requirements for changes at first. Goebbels responded by threatening to find "a completely new director" (6.6. 1941) to complete the film. In another confrontation Goebbels once more reproached Harlan with his most recent film and only total "failure" (Goebbels on 23.3.1940), *Pedro soll hängen*

42. Gustav Fröhlich, Otto Gebühr and Otto Wernicke in *The Great King* (1942): educational for the nation as a whole.

43. Expectations disappointed: Emil Jannings as Bismarck and Werner Hinz as Wilhelm II in *The Dismissal* (1942).

("Hang Pedro!"), and summed up: "Unfortunately he will not admit, and probably does not even agree, that his film *The Great King* is a failure. And so I don't know whether he will be able to reshape it fundamentally." (23.7.1941) Goebbels was obviously not satisfied with the first changes. (6.8.1941) The extensive retakes went until early in 1942, as the image of Russia had to be changed as well because of the invasion of the Soviet Union.[904] One historical fact, still innocuous in 1941 – Russian auxiliary troops contributed to Frederick's victory over the Austrians – now needed some correction.

The political mood was entirely different after the failed advance on Moscow. The film as modified at Goebbels' request, with its demonstrative "understanding of the people, suffering from the war and despairing of the war"[905], now suddenly met the propaganda requirements – though probably not because it had been precisely "tailored to the public mood":[906] The figure of the miller's daughter, played by Kristina Söderbaum, skilfully articulates the people's reservations and their criticism of the war. This is also a condemnation of the king, the Hitler substitute, but such ideas are equally skilfully rebutted by allusions to Frederick's higher insights and devotion to duty. Goebbels was able to feel that his views were reinforced, as his "wishes and expectations" about the project, which he had "held from the outset" (2.3.1943) had turned out to be absolutely prophetic – even though he could not have foreseen these changes.

From this point onwards Goebbels is unable to find a single word of real criticism; the film becomes a vehicle of "Total War", and is the object of both rabble-rousing rhetoric and overpowering praise. Now that the film presents "what I wanted it to", wrote Goebbels on 25.1.1942, it will send "a wave of edification through the whole nation": "It shows the king in all his greatness and loneliness and offers surprising parallels with the present." But Goebbels did miscalculate in his intention to show the film in "as many cinemas as possible" on the anniversary of the seizure of power on 30 January, as changes had still to be made "in various minor ways": "The Austrian scenes in particular have turned out to be too critical and too aggressive. We cannot afford this at the moment, as the film is supposed to be exemplary and to show the way for the whole of Germany, and not just for the Prussians." (28.1.1942) But the film had achieved its essential intentions: "We can use this film for political purposes as well. It is a fine aid in the fight for the soul of our people and in the process of permanently stiffening German powers of resistance, which we need to happen." (19.2.1942) Goebbels also used Harlan's production as a tool in his clashes with the Wehrmacht leadership, who had complained to Hitler about the portrayal of the Prussian generals.[907]

When Goebbels spoke about "so many amazing parallels with the present"[908] and this also with Hitler at the ministers' meeting, he pointed out to the press that "the historical events portrayed in the film really are historical and that the great king's pronouncements came from his own lips". (3.3.1942) Furthermore, "all comparisons of Frederick with the Führer" were to be avoided; the public were to make them for themselves.[909]

Of course the film is not "really historical", as is to be expected from an educational and propaganda device.[910] The opening credits referred specifically to the fact that planning started in spring 1940, so that the audience would not find the very striking analogies too heavy-handed.[911] Goebbels seems to have been unsure only about the effect of the early scenes, which showed unusually explicit images of death, destruction, suffering and despondency after the defeat at Kunserdorf: the press was told that the "pessimistic tone that dominates much of the dialogue in the early parts of the film" was "by no means to be identified with the German people's attitude in the present war".[912]

After the great gala première attended by war invalids, armament workers and holders of the "Ritterkreuz" {"Knight's Cross") in the Ufa-Palast am Zoo on 3 March passages about the "sensational success" of the film, which also received the highest classification, "Film of the Nation", came thick and fast: "It works just as I anticipated it would. There is no doubt that it will be a major educational force for the German people, especially in the present situation." (4.3.1942) With an eye to his efforts to "totalize" the war, Goebbels adds: "The film comes at just the right time to justify conducting the war more rigorously in this way as well." And he states with innocent delight, as though there had been absolutely no precise press directives: "The press are writing about it in the warmest possible tone." (5.3.1942) Thanks to a massive advertising campaign, Goebbels is able to report a "storm at the box-offices" and can also afford to appear tactically sophisticated: "I had secretly feared that this film might be too difficult, to serious and too logical to be really popular. But this seems not to be the case." (8.3.1942) *The Great King* was Goebbels' biggest film policy success after *Jud Süss* and *Ohm Krüger.* All he now needed for the desired "educational effect" ("the film is not too hard") were correspondingly high audience figures. He consequently presents detailed information: after 3 1/2 weeks the film had been seen by 120,000 people in Berlin alone, and thus put "all previous film successes in the shade". (31.3. 1942) On 22.4. he calculates that 5.5 million Reichsmarks in box office receipts are enough to count as "a battle won over people's souls" (1.6.1942) and "reinforcement of resistance on the home front". (14.4.1942) But by late 1944 the film had recorded total receipts of only 6 million Reichsmarks, which is relatively high for a political film, but still makes it last, in 21st place, on a list of the most successful productions since 1941.[913] However, there must have been a considerable number of non-commercial screenings for the armed services and the Party to be added to this.

Goebbels only hints at the reservations met by the film in Austria, which were probably due to the Prussian subject matter in general and the anti-Habsburg scenes, even though they had been toned down. He had contributed to this himself by leaving Empress Maria Theresia's entirely fictitious attempt to poison Frederick in the film, which drew protests from Austria. But the Gauleiter of Berlin managed to twist this lack of sympathetic response at the same time by fanning the flames of Hitler's old hatred of Vienna, as Goebbels was constantly locked in a dispute with the Viennese Party leadership: "It is typical, incidentally – as I have also reported to the Führer – that the film *The Great King* has been enormously successful in all the cities in the Reich, with one exception: Vienna". (30.5.1942) Goebbels says nothing about the fact that *The Great King* was an indifferent success in almost all the Austrian cities, and not just Vienna. Almost all the comparable films (political ones like *Jud Süss* or light entertainment like *Operette*) came off better in the ratio of days screened to audience ratings. The audience figures, which really were particularly low in Vienna, were very little higher in Innsbruck, Klagenfurt or Salzburg. Even in Hitler's favourite city of Linz *The Great King* had smaller audiences than *Jud Süss* or *Ohm Krüger*, for example, had achieved in 1940/41, when the cinema was generally less successful.[914] All in all this was not a good basis for Goebbels' aim, formulated on 28.1., that the film should not be seen as hostile to Austria, but had to be "exemplary and show the way for the whole of Germany". Goebbels explained the Harlan production's unanimous rejection at the Venice Biennale by citing the "Venetian plutocracy" in the audience.[915] (31.8.1942) But despite this the German-Italian axis ensured that the Prussia film won the Coppa Mussolini for the best foreign film.

The Security Service was manifestly of a different mind about the effect of the Veit Harlan film, and in no way confirmed Goebbels' eulogies. Half of the report is an account of critical points and reservations. Fundamentally the "extraordinary and lasting effect" is not disputed, and there is even mention of "enthusiastic approval" at all levels of the population. Thus "the new image of Frederick made an enormously attractive and captivating impression on the broad mass of the people in particular", which meant that the Propaganda Minister must have achieved his aim of not "vulgarizing" Frederick's image, but of bringing him down "from his pedestal". (6.8.1941) On the other hand large sections of the public apparently found some scenes of flight and destruction too explicit, which meant that female cinemagoers in particular had rejected it as "too great a strain on the nerves". There was in any case no sympathetic response in Austria to the "emphasis on Prussian qualities" and "that particularist view of things". While the analogies with Hitler obviously worked, the Security Service's informers maintained that the parallels between Prussia's position then and Germany's now were drawn 'too coarsely'" and "laid on too thick" – despite all the film's merits in "steeling the people's stamina and will for victory".[916]

Unlike *The Great King*, the Bismarck film *The Dismissal* lacked useful connections with current propaganda aims. The plot repeated set-pieces that had often been used: the cult of the dead celebrated right at the beginning, shifty Jewish parliamentarians, intriguers in the imperial entourage and bureaucracy, the glorification of Bismarck as a superior helmsman of the state. Goebbels seems to have had his own doubts after seeing the first rushes about this "entirely superfluous new edition of propaganda that is no longer in keeping",[917] which seems to exude a sense of resignation given Bismarck's enforced departure. Even the scenes featuring Wilhelm II, played by Werner Hinz, prompted Goebbels to note: "The scenes are very discreetly and tastefully made and by no means caricatures; but I still doubt whether it is right to present a film like this to the public now. Though the sections I have seen are still too short for me to be able to form a final opinion." (3.2.1942) Goebbels analyses the situation even more critically on 15.3.: "Major difficulties (are) to be expected", and he adds that his Staatssekretär Naumann was "very sceptical about continuing shooting" after examining the manuscript again. But then Goebbels was convinced by the completed film and the superior quality of the work. He is definitely euphoric in tone, but he does not suppress persisting reservations: "German film art has

rarely had a success like the one we have here. The early years of Wilhelm II's reign are observed with a mercilessly critical eye, and its effects summed up in a cinematic show with the quality of genius. Even so, I don't know whether this film can be shown at the moment." The film could "perhaps give offence in some circles. I must show it to several other categories of people to get a sense of how it affects them." (28.6.1942)

When the Party Chancellery and other opponents like Alfred Rosenberg started to criticize the film, Goebbels put all his undispelled reservations on one side. Now he speaks only of a "brilliant performance of the first water". Goebbels organized – as announced – a screening for selected state and Party luminaries. A survey subsequently carried out among the participants showed some negative voices about the Kaiser's appearance and the presentation of Germany's role in the years prior to the First World War, and praise for the good actors.[918] The Party Office summed up the scepticism that ultimately predominated in the formulation that the film was lacking in "a positive view".[919] But Goebbels chose to ignore the reservations. Instead he quoted a reaction that he found convenient from the Gauleiters, who had allegedly rejected all doubts and come out "on a massive scale" for the film's "immediate release". (7.8.1942) But despite Goebbels' questionable assertion that Hitler had "heard only good things" about the film, the dictator, called upon to arbitrate once more, certainly had his own initial doubts: "He does not want to make a final decision about whether it can be shown at present. He has therefore given orders that I should release the film on trial in some town or other and wait for a public reaction, then talk to him about it again."[920] (21.8.1942) Goebbels thereupon described the test screening in Stettin on 15 September as an "enormous success" (16.9.1942): "I shall pass these opinions on to the Führer. I hope that the Führer will now say that he is able to agree that the film should be released." Hitler did not give his permission until 14 September 1942, which meant that *The Dismissal* could be launched in Berlin's Ufa-Palast am Zoo on 6 October, despite renewed protest from Rosenberg.[921]

The excessively long, laborious and extremely complicated press directive[822] with its many instructions and restrictions illustrates the problems *The Dismissal* raised in terms of historical presentation, which was factually unconvincing and inappropriate to National Socialism. The film attracted large audiences at first, in October – Goebbels hoped that it would do better than *Die große Liebe* – but then interest rapidly diminished. Overall this film, which was re-released after the war as *Schicksalswende*, must have had box-office receipts of about 5 million Reichsmarks.[923] Goebbels was informed about the essentially muted public reaction by the Reichspropagandaämter. Although his assessment is entirely honest, he has an escape route ready in terms of the obvious failure: "I am receiving news from various cities that the film *The Dismissal* is not being as successful in certain circles as one had actually hoped. It is a typical men's film and is generally rejected in the world of women because it does not show any real women's conflicts. And also a certain degree of prior political and historical knowledge is needed if the questions addressed here are to be understood at all. But nevertheless the film's success makes it a cut above all normal light entertainment films. But if the ultimate test is applied, the film does not seem to have fulfilled the expectations placed in it at first." (13.12.1942)

According to the Reichsfilmintendant's production summary shooting on *Kolberg* started in late October 1943 and should have finished on 13 May 1944.[924] Goebbels' original plan to show *Kolberg* in "winter 1943/44" proved impossible because of the gigantic numbers involved, which Harlan put at 187,000 soldier-extras, 6,000 horses and 10,000 uniforms. Equally impossible to fulfil was his instruction on 4 July 1943 that the project should not cost more than 4 million Reichsmarks.[925] Even the preliminary work and requisitioning of the necessary material caused Ufa considerable difficulties.

The Propaganda Minister monitored progress on the shooting at least every two months, using the first "rushes from Harlan's colour film *Kolberg*, which is in production. These rushes are outstandingly successful. If the film comes out as these rushes suggest it will then I promise myself a huge, impressive success for German film production." (6.2.1944) But miscalculations about the time needed continued: "Professor Harlan, to whom I am awarding a good sum of money, reports to me about his work on the film *Kolberg*. He thinks he will have finished in two to three months. The rushes I have seen so far suggest it will be a first-class film. Harlan in one of our most outstanding film directors, who can be confidently entrusted with a major job." (21.4.1944)

In June as well all the increasingly impatient Goebbels could do was examine and report on "new samples" and hope "that Harlan will make this a masterpiece of German cinema". (12.6.1944) When shooting was completed in late November, Goebbels was certainly not "very dissatisfied with the result", as was later asserted.[926] On the contrary: "It is a true masterpiece of the director's art. Harlan has also positioned it so skilfully in political terms that one could almost suspect that it hadn't been commissioned until about three weeks ago ...". Goebbels felt that very little needed changing, simply where "Harlan at various points falls into his old error of mystical choral singing and exaggerated performances". (1.12.1944) Goebbels even lets Hitler speak for him, which can be seen as a special distinction for this major project: "I tell him about the new *Kolberg* film, describe a few scenes from it, which move the Führer almost to tears. He asks me to bring the film out as quickly as possible, calling it a battle won in the political conduct of war, on the basis of what I have told him." (3.12.1944) After that there were a few test screenings in the Ministry, including one for 150 leading Nazi officers and officers of the Berlin Regiment of Guards (9.12.1944),[927] until Goebbels again mentions necessary cuts on 12.12.1944, "which will be very easy to carry out". But Harlan obviously had ideas of his own about changing the film: "Harlan has made the film worse instead of better", says Goebbels on 23.12.1944. Completion was further held up by "major cuts" that were needed in their turn. This did not involve additional tinkering with history (Kolberg is rescued in the film, in reality it was conquered by the French), nor adding further Sportpalast-style stamina slogans from the lips of Nettelbeck. Unduly realistic "scenes of despair and destruction" were removed, as they would lead to "large sections of the public refusing to do so much as see the film in the present situation" (Goebbels on 23.12.), but the Minister was also bothered about the "monstrous battles and town scenes",[928] about Harlan's "mystic choir" in the prologue, the "final prayer" and the music-of-the-spheres effect that he had also disliked in *Immensee* and *The Great Sacrifice*. The final editing conference took place on 22 December 1944. The differences with Harlan were less that the director contended:[929] Hinkel also noted that Harlan "agreed with all the suggestions the Minister made".[930]

The final version was ready on 5 January 1945 – too late to meet Frowein's intention, expressed in October, that the film "would have to open in all the major cities in the Reich, so that it could have the effect in breadth that we desire as quickly as possible".[931]

The relevant passages say little about what Goebbels really expected from the film. Is it really true, as Harlan put it, that Goebbels and Hitler were obsessed with the idea "that a film like this would be more use to them than winning a battle in Russia"? Delivery of copies to all the larger towns and cities, with preference given to the threatened eastern districts (Breslau, Danzig), was painfully slow. Remarks like the one about a "battle won over people's souls" are clear signs of self-deception and an inability to see reality in the fanaticized atmosphere of the imminent end. At the very least they show that Goebbels was not prepared to admit that the film, which was premiered in the Tauentzien-Palast in Berlin (the Ufa-Palast am Zoo had already been destroyed) and in the encircled Atlantic fortress of La Rochelle on the 13th anniversary of the seizure of power on 30 January 1945, had been a propaganda disaster. And so it seems almost like an eerie confusion of film and reality when Goebbels remarks on 19.3.1945: "We have had to abandon Kolberg now. It was no longer possible to hold the town, which has defended itself with such extraordinary heroism. I will make sure that the withdrawal is not recorded in the OKW report. That would be no good to us, given the severe psychological consequences for the Kolberg film."

"Führer thinks it's better not to show it": Goebbels and film censorship

Film censorship after 1933

Under the "Third Reich" the state was practically a film producer in its own right, supported by a highly organized production system and compliant staff. Films were initiated or passed by the Propaganda Ministry, and supervised through to the final stages in the cutting room. Under these conditions, film bans were on a par with "industrial accidents": the "consequence of actually unforeseeable, i.e. completely incalculable circumstances" and absolute arbitrariness.[932] This gave rise to "a pattern of impenetrable censorship criteria",[933] which meant that the background to film bans was often mysterious. Goebbels' diary entries help to explain some of these decisions, as a direct source from the Propaganda Ministry, where decisions were made about the majority of film cuts and bans, without everything being recorded in official documents.

Film censorship underwent a fundamental change after the film industry was nationalized, and above all after Ufi was founded in 1942. Preliminary censorship, in other words project planning and screenplay control, became part of the production process. Post-censorship (cuts, retakes and other changes to films that had already been shot) were part of production to a large extent. Where can actual censorship be said to lie under circumstances like these? Goebbels himself justified this intensive "involvement on the part of the state" by saying that "the major task of censorship after completion of a film is kept to a minimum from the outset".[934] Censorship took place only in terms of the fundamental decision about approval. When Goebbels controlled all phases of film production, work in the cutting room leading to the copy-ready version was actually not censorship. Goebbels does not operate as a censor, but as a final court of appeal working politically and artistically, as an all-powerful producer with an automatic right to decide on the final cut.

He appears as censor only when there is no perceptible sign that the Minister was involved in the production process, as in the case of most light entertainment films, and then tries to assert his ideas about politics, morals and taste. Incidentally, censorship as a whole was not just about revising films or spectacular bans. However much self-adulation Goebbels indulged in, the sphere of censorship in particular makes it clear that the Propaganda Minister was subject to unpleasant constraints within the complex power structure of the "Third Reich", even on his rightful ground.

Institutionalized film censorship in the years after 1933 shows considerable continuity in terms of both personnel and standards. The censorship laws remained unchanged for over a year after the seizure of power: numerous films made under the Weimar Republic were now banned by the authorities on the basis of the same legal norms on which they had been approved.[935] The censorship officials, including Heinrich Zimmermann, director of the Filmprüfstelle from December 1929 (until he was transferred to the Propaganda Ministry film department in 1939) and Arnold Bacmeister, (1939–1945, also responsible for censorship matters in the Propaganda Ministry), were loyal to the new regime, too. Ernst Seeger, the head of the Ministry section, continued to act as director of the Filmoberprüfstelle. This reliable administration expert was already responsible for film matters in the Reich Ministry of the Interior, and had also been head of the Propaganda Ministry film department since April 1933. Seeger, who had been responsible for the famous ban of *All Quiet on the Western Front* (*Im Westen nichts Neues*), the film of the novel by Erich Maria Remarque, guaranteed the smooth running of the censorship apparatus and drafted key sections of the new "Reichslichtspielgesetz" ("Reich cinema act") of 16 February 1934,[936] which provided the basis for preliminary and post-censorship. It extended to the previous grounds for a ban[937] in §7 (adding "endangering public order and safety" and "infringement of National Socialist, moral and artistic sensibility"), and removed some old one – including the "general philosophical tendency", which had anyway been rendered more or less ineffective by the screening of the first National Socialist films like *Hitler Youth Quex* in 1933. The completely arbitrary regulation "infringement of National Socialist sensibility" was aimed in the first place against "racially" unwelcome films (involving Jewish performers, directors, composers etc.), and the "artistic" criterion was directed against so-called "Kintopp" (tasteless films, 'weepies') and "shallow, kitschy films". In addition to the new reasons for bans, editing requirements (§9) and screening conditions (§10) were made more rigorous and the imposition of foreign film quotas made part of censorship law for the first time. The definition of "German" films now required "racially pure" participants as a "provisional Aryan paragraph" in the film censorship legislation.[938]

Numerous bans of older films were followed in 1934 by spectacular bans on two more recent productions. Goebbels banned the comedies *Ein Kind, ein Hund, ein Vagabund* ("A Child, a Dog and a Vagabond", Arthur M. Rabenalt) and *Die Liebe siegt* ("Love Wins", Georg Zoch) in November 1934, not "because they ran counter to state political interests or to the National Socialist philosophy, but because they were shoddy pieces of work, inartistic, shallow and tasteless".[939] Even though the official censorship process was only a façade as early as 1934, Goebbels created sole and total film approval rights for himself, in legal form, by altering §23a of the Reichslichtspielgesetz of 28 June 1935: "Acting independently of the procedures of the Filmprüfstelle and the Filmoberprüfstelle, the Reichsministerium für Volksaufklärung und Propaganda is empowered … to ban a film if he deems it necessary for urgent reasons pertaining to the public good."[940]

After this "Enabling Act of Film censorship",[941] which actually represented nothing more than formal sanctioning of something that was already practised, the Propaganda Minister could now ban films even in the purely theoretical case that they had been approved in a contradictory procedure by the Filmoberprüfstelle. This was quickly followed by a general ban on all films approved before 30 January 1933.[942] No reasons for the Filmprüfstelle's decisions from 1933 to 1945 are recorded.

The Minister as censor

Goebbels' perception of himself as the nation's number two film expert did not start to change until 1935: he went from being an apparently uninvolved observer, a passive consumer, making incisive but inconsequential judgements, to being the responsible censor. When all was said and done, the conditions were not right for effective post-censorship for a long time: Goebbels saw 29 of the 41 film titles mentioned in his diary in 1935 shortly before, or sometimes even after their première.[943] Thus Goebbels was not able to change the final versions, which would have taken about two weeks for editing or a month for retakes. His only option if he disapproved completely was a ban with subsequent revision and where appropriate subsequent approval, as has happened to Zoch's and Rabenalt's films in 1934. But expensive measures of this kind could only further weaken the film companies, which were already ailing financially, when in fact Goebbels wanted to restore them to profitability.

And so the Propaganda Minister saw most of the films released in 1935 and 1936 (here the proportion is 38 of 64 films, which he was shown a few days before or after the first public screening) too late to be able to undertake effective post-censorship.[944] The film censorship system was not yet working anything like smoothly enough for the film companies to submit copies of every film at the right time, and Goebbels also came into the censorship procedure at a later stage than in subsequent years.

From mid December 1936 Goebbels always writes "film censorship in the evening:" or "films censored". Now there are several weeks between the daily film examinations and the première. this led to frequent orders for cuts and changes; from summer 1937 – Ufa and Tobis had already been nationalized by then – there were scarcely any films that Goebbels did not see until after the date of the première.[945] But completed feature films were still not checked and approved on a regular basis, and in contrast with newsreel control, not according to any fixed scheme. Goebbels certainly did not censor every domestic or foreign film personally, even though he may have tried to do so for a time: "One now has to check every film oneself, as it is so important for them to be psychologically right as well." (4.2.1940) And contrary announcements in the later war years indicating a desire to withdraw from film censorship[946] – which was presumably of secondary importance – did not hold good for long either. It is quite obvious that Goebbels sometimes had problems within the Ministry in keeping a grip on the frequent bans imposed by his subordinates in all fields.[947] Certainly there are cases in which he withdrew bans imposed by colleagues.[948]

It is impossible to establish the number of films censored by Goebbels personally, as he does not mention every film he examined in the diary. From 1937 to 1942/43 he must have censored approximately two thirds of the feature film output himself, then after that less than half. He had only a fraction of these shown to him again once or more often after revision. A conclusion was drawn from the Goebbels diaries published at an early stage (1942/43) that films he viewed negatively were premiered later than those that found favour. This is a false impression if the whole range of films is considered. Besides, there is an obvious explanation for this observation, which was true only in isolated cases: premières had to be postponed when criticism led to revision.[949]

No edited material or lists of cuts exist for the vast majority of films mentioned by Goebbels, nor any other material that could lead to conclusions about subsequent changes.[950] Thus it is not clear whether revisions announced by Goebbels were actually carried out.

45. Leny Marenbach in *Frau nach Maß*: too obscene.
46. *Bel Ami*, a film that "criticized the regime", with Willi Forst and Olga Tschechowa (1939): perhaps a little too cheeky.

His threats of bans and damning criticism are particularly interesting, as even "dreadful", "repulsive", "completely unsuccessful" or "crappy" films are usually untouched by censorship.[951] Otherwise half the annual production would have had to be revised. The nationalization of the most important film companies of course gave Goebbels more opportunities to "sort things out with the scissors". Goebbels' attack on Reinhold Schünzel's *Das Mädchen Irene* ("a very bad, excessively forced, disgusting business", 17.10.1936) may have come to nothing in 1936, but in the following year he had the same director's *Land der Liebe* ("Land of Love") ("A typical Jewish sham. Quite intolerable. It cannot go out like this", 28.4.1937) completely re-edited.[952]

But Goebbels also sometimes liked films and yet still intervened for political or "moral" reasons. This did not make him a prude within the National Socialist spectrum. He also made a public stand against "holier-than-thou petit bourgeois".[953] He agreed with Hitler: "stubbornly opposed to political jokes in artistic life, but all the more generous from an erotic point of view". (30.1.1939) Nevertheless he slipped into the role of the supreme guardian of morality. Thus he finds the version submitted to him of *Frau nach Maß* ("The Tailored Lady") "somewhat too obscene" and announces: "I shall have the offensive section cut."[954] (11.2.1940)

He also introduced political and racial censorship criteria for the foreign film quotas. A year after the accession to power he felt that the Howard Hawks/Jack Conway film *Viva Villa!* ("well made") could "not be screened here, still too dangerous". (18.4.1934) He intends to refuse the leading lady permission to screen a US dance film with Sonja Henie: "Her film features a whole lot of Jews."[955] (9.9.1937) He says that the German spy film *Hotel Sacher*, set immediately before the First World War, is "wonderfully well made" and yet feels that extensive changes are necessary: "But it is not yet politically watertight. I'm having it edited again, and some scenes reshot."[956] (27.1.1939)

Two other examples refer to remarkable films that were later interpreted as "critical of the regime": *Tanz auf dem Vulkan* ("Dancing on the Volcano"), directed by Hans Steinhoff, and Willi Forst's *Bel Ami*: "A cheeky film, perhaps a little too cheeky, but wonderfully well made. The approach is a bit frivolous at times, but then better at the end. Perhaps a few more cuts and then release." (5.2.1939)

Forst shows the social rise of an unscrupulous former officer with the aid of corrupt politicians and journalists who are open to bribery against the background of the Belle Époque in Paris.[957] Goebbels apparently found that the erotically liberal scenes (an "enormous number of beautiful women") and the scenes that could be interpreted as current political references went too far. Finally it is unlikely that the skirt-chasing minister in the film appealed to him very much, given his own image. Further measures seem to have been prevented only by the anticipated – and actual – "huge financial success".[958]

Tanz auf dem Vulkan was later categorized as "critical of the regime" because of some songs sung by Gustaf Gründgens calling for rebellion and liberation from repression and dictatorship at the time of the French revolution of 1830.[959] Goebbels found fault: "a typical Gründgens. A bit too much brain-work. Still needs heavy editing". (18.11.1938) Despite "brain-work", for Goebbels the opposite of light fare and the expression of demanding, ambiguous and unconventional dialogue and sensitive, subtle "intellectual" humour: the première took place twelve days later.

New information about unexplained bans

At least 28 productions made during the National Socialist period remained "films without a première".[960] It is still not clear why some of these films were banned. In most cases the bans were not spectacular and very sudden, however. What tended to happen was that the films concerned were repeatedly returned by the Propaganda Ministry with requests for changed that could not all be met, or "put back" for months and not accepted for censorship, which was something like a silent liquidation. Now how much explanation and genuine information can we expect from Goebbels about this area of National Socialist film history, which always attracts a good deal of lay interest?

Some indirect information refers to Fritz Lang's famous thriller *Das Testament des Dr. Mabuse* (*The Testament of Dr. Mabuse*). This was the last film the director made in Germany, and it was banned on 29 March 1933, one day after Goebbels' first film speech. It seems that the Filmprüfstelle and leading Nazis decided at the last minute before the launch, which had been announced, that the film, which was about terrorist activities by a gang of criminals and the vision of "mob rule", could contain too many undesirable allusions to the Nazis' seizure of power. Seen from another point of view, closer analysis shows that the film does not relate to the Nazis' behaviour, which does not necessarily mean that the presentation of criminality and indeed the danger of glorifying and also the style of the film might actually have caused the ban.[961] Different sources again suggest that Goebbels only disliked the end of the film, as the criminal is not punished, but simply takes refuge in madness.[962] But the film's topical references could not have been clearer and the political context could not have been more unfavourable: these days saw the start of the enforced boycott of Jewish businesses together with SA terror in Germany.

The Minister's notes for this period are still not available. But Goebbels said in a speech to the Reichsfilmkammer on 4 March 1938 that he had "seen a film a few days ago that had been shot in late 1932 and completed early in 1933. This film was banned for political reasons at the time". Goebbels did not mention a title, but it sounded very much like *The Testament of Dr. Mabuse*. And Goebbels had in fact seen the film "again" only two days before: "But it seems quite old-fashioned today. Almost impossible to look at it any more." (3.3.1938) He makes no direct reference to the reasons for a ban at the time. He will certainly not have been pleased that all Lang's big-time criminals (Dr. Baum, Dr. Mabuse) have doctorates like him. But Goebbels is in no doubt about the link with reality. The film was explosive and could not be shown in the political conditions of its day, but it is harmless today: this does not suggest fundamental rejection and a ban based on formal criteria, but a ban that was motivated very much by contemporary events.

A ban that is still "puzzling" today was placed on the semi-documentary Reichsbahn film *Das Stahltier*. Goebbels did not see this film until two months after the official ban. It is assumed to have been based on the "experimental, avant-garde stylistic devices",[963] on rivalry within the Reichsbahn directorate, and on being "damaging to German esteem" because it acknowledged English and French railway pioneers[964] to far too large an extent. His negative judgement (9.10.1935) is also confirmed by director Leni Riefenstahl, who was present at the screening and claims to have argued for its release.[965] According to her the Propaganda Minister found the film "too modern and too abstract" and declared that the decision about its not being passed was the Reichsbahn's affair, and no one else's.[966]

Goebbels provides all the crucial information in the case of *Starke Herzen* ("Strong Hearts"), whose production history has been researched in a exemplary fashion using all the available sources.[967] The project was one consequence of his increased demands for "anti-Bolshevik" feature films from 1935/36. Though he was unmistakably sceptical about the draft ("Studied Ufa film treatment *Starke Herzen*. Not up to much. More or less middle-class", 9.2.1937) Goebbels agreed that it should be made: costings and cast list were already in place on 16 February 1937.[968] Shooting finished in mid June 1937, but the film was surprisingly "rejected for censorship on the instructions of the Propaganda Ministry" and so far "sources have failed to provide the actual reasons for its non-acceptance".[969] Goebbels writes: "Ufa film *Starke Herzen*. Supposed to be anti-Bolshevik. Has the same faults as *Weiße Sklaven* ('White Slaves'). Entirely middle-class and simplistic, without strong lines or contrasts. A dreadful mish-mash. Told Demandowsky to re-work it completely. That will cost a lot of time and money." (24.6.1937) He seems to have been displeased by the imprecise settling of account with Communism, rather than the image of the military.[970] The film was supposed to have been screened again in the Ministry after revision in October 1937.[971] But Goebbels in fact writes about "*Starke Herzen* again, after revision" on 22.9.1937: "But still not good. Too middle-class. How the *Stahlhelm* sees Bolshevism. Typical Ufa." As the Propaganda Minister continued to reject the film, Ufa had to withdraw it from censorship again on 7 December[972] and finally wrote it off as a dead loss in 1938. It is fair to assume that Goebbels wanted to punish Ufa for their inadequate propaganda by refusing to pass the film, and to push them into taking a more radical propaganda line. And he also couldn't afford to show a film that was not convincing "anti-Bolshevik" propaganda from a National Socialist point of view. Hitler had already rejected the anti-Soviet productions *Weiße Sklaven* and *Helden in Spanien* for similar reasons. *Starke Herzen* was not even shown after the invasion of the Soviet Union, despite the lack of anti-Russian films; it had to wait until 1952, in the German Federal Republic.

Hitler is said to have banned Carl Junghans' realistic agricultural drama *Altes Herz geht auf die Reise* ("Old Heart Goes Wayfaring") personally between late October and mid December 1938 because it ran counter to the Nazi image of farmers. Goebbels called the film "boring and incomprehensible" on 6.12.1939. Ufa then decided not to bring it out, as "it is impossible to change the film in accordance with the Prop. Min.'s requirements".[973]

Der 5. Juni, an Ufa production by Fritz Kirchhoff about the fate of an infantry unit during the invasion of France, was held back for a few months after it was completed in May 1942 and then banned completely[974] – allegedly because of the changed war situation in late 1942,[975] Germany's political links with Vichy France[976] and the presentation of the military.[977] Goebbels found the film, "which claims to be a feature, though it is more like a documentary", "boring and vacuous", and an "accumulation of instructive material". (15.8.1942) He makes no direct link with the state of the war in 1942. But neither the way in which it was made nor the military content of this war film fitted in with film policy guidelines for 1942. The Propaganda Minister also disapproved of any Wehrmacht activities in the field of film. The OKW had involved itself very heavily in the making of the film and had expensive post-production shots taken; thus this ban should possibly also be seen as part of Goebbels' long-term quarrel with the Wehrmacht leadership.

Karl Ritter's film *Besatzung Dora*, which has already been mentioned, was quite clearly a victim of the war situation. Goebbels had nothing against this propaganda picture, which he said was "very appealing", but he felt that it was more suitable "for the second than the fourth year of the war. And so I am somewhat sceptical when assessing the new Ritter production's chances of success." (29.3.1943) Too many sections of the film with scenes about fronts that could no longer be held would have had to be removed, which is why it was finally banned in November 1943. In any case there is no basis for Karl Ritter's claim that Goebbels did not like the film.[978]

Die heimlichen Bräute ("The Secret Brides") is a comedy of mistaken identities. Goebbels said that it was being "criticized from all sides" on 19.5.1944, and announced drastic measures to "prevent (such) unduly dilettante productions by our film companies in future". The title first crops up in the list of productions that have been held up in August 1944, and the Ufa-Film GmbH was informed of the ban, which is still incomprehensible today, on 5 December 1944.[979] This could have been the "drastic measure", if Goebbels wanted to make a warning point to Berlin-Film, a company that was already in his bad books because of a failed film, and to all the other producers, to cut down the large number of "dilettante" films.

Ostensibly Goebbels and his Filmintendant Hippler were guided by the insight that pessimistic and "gloomy" films would make the nation apathetic and resigned, and consequently make it weaker in wartime.[980] And it would indeed seem that some of Goebbels' comments on pre-war French poetic realist films are to be understood in this way, and considerations of this kind could have come into play when assessing German dramas like the film *Der Strom*, which is about the rural community living among the dikes of northern Germany.

Certainly some ambitious films like *Nora* or Käutner's *Romance in a Minor Key*, which Goebbels admired, can be interpreted similarly without such elements of suspicion. The Minister is at his clearest when writing about the Terra film *Zwischen Nacht und Morgen* ("Between Night and Morning"), which dates from 1943: "The film is dreadful; three quarters of the action is in hospitals and operating theatres. I am always warning the production chiefs that they should not use this kind of setting. this proves again how right I was and am to issue this warning." (2.11.1943) The fact that the film was not premiered by 1945, despite revisions,[981] could be less about refusal to follow Goebbels' guide-lines than anxiety about a deleterious effect on morale because of the film's problematical content.

If the intention was to prevent "heavy", "enervating" and "depressing" films to protect public morale, this could have affected the Wien-Film production *Am Ende der Welt* (*At the Edge of the World*) as well. Goebbels had criticized Wien-Film in October and November 1943, even before the point assumed to be the moment of the first rejection by the Propaganda Ministry.[982] He attacked the company and its team responsible for the stolid drama about woodcutters ("maggoty milieu"), Gustav Ucicky (direction) and Gerhard Menzel (screenplay): "They have not made a single film of any distinction in the last year. All they have done is worked through a series of extraordinarily dubious film projects that are more suited to the realms of psychiatry than film art." (21.11.1943) The censors did not accept the film after retakes either. Goebbels' reference to "psychiatry" could have been aimed at the portrayal of a relationship between an older man and a young woman, which was probably disturbing to the average audience. The Propaganda Minister could well have had reservations about interpersonal conflicts of this kind, which lay outside the usual scheme of "love and faithfulness". But perhaps there was something else that was even more important. Nazi propaganda had always resisted the contrast between town and country, which is very much to the fore in this film, and had already been responsible for all sorts of prejudices and criticism among film audiences.[983] But the Minister did make his own contribution to the simplistic contrasts in *At the Edge of the World* by demanding that a negative urban banking character had to be a Jew.[984]

One of the best-known film bans of the Nazi period must be the film version of John Knittel's novel *Via Mala*, directed by Josef von Baky. Goebbels had rejected the material, which had been accepted at first in May 1941, at the turn of the year 1941/42, saying that it was "too gloomy",[985] but then apparently agreed that the film should be produced after all in February 1942.[986] Shooting did not start until July 1943, as Goebbels had become dubious again; the final version was screened in the Propaganda Ministry on 8 April 1944. Two days later Goebbels remarked that the film has "turned out to be extremely gloomy and pessimistic despite my warnings. I don't think that we can present it to the public in its present form in today's conditions." Goebbels wanted to rescue the film, but even extensive retakes did not change his critical view.[987]

The Ufa production *Träumerei* ("Dreaming") shows that being detrimental to morale was not on its own sufficient to trigger a ban. Goebbels told Ufa production chief Wolfgang Liebeneiner that both it and *Via Mala* were too "gloomy and pessimistic", but *Träumerei* was in the cinemas two weeks later. But in the case of *Via Mala* it is not clear why the project was taken up at all, given constantly declining morale.

Finally, Rabenalt's *Regimentmusik* ("Regimental Music") was not premiered during the "Third Reich", because it fitted precisely into Goebbels' category of antiquated middle-class conflicts, something he found particularly displeasing in 1944: "It is set in Wilhelminian Germany and its whole approach to problems is so alien and repellent at the moment that I can scarcely allow it to be shown." (19.11.1944) It was also useless as a contribution to military and national resistance because of a few military scenes that seemed rather outmoded.[988]

Goebbels' disputed supremacy as censor

Hitler as the highest authority

Hitler's taste in films is usually touched upon only briefly in most discussions of film. A lot of this material is imprecise or even inapplicable. Like Goebbels he was a regular and enthusiastic cinemagoer. After the seizure of power, the film world had to be convinced that the new regime offered its "heartfelt commitment". Goebbels explained that "on many evenings recently (he had) sat with the Reich Chancellor in the cinema, after the nerve-racking struggles of the day, and found relaxation".[989] Even in the Berlin and Munich of the "period of struggle", the Capitol in Berlin, the Gloria or the Ufa-Palast am Zoo, or the Luitpold-Lichtspiele in Munich, were among his preferred cinemas. He hardly missed an important picture, from *The Nibelungs* to *Der Rebell*. Trenker's film of the "national uprising" in South Tyrol chimed in with Hitler's mood pretty well in 1933. With the Chancellorship in his grasp, he saw the Tyrolean struggle for freedom twice in succession – "most enthusiastic" according to Goebbels. (19.1.1933) After the seizure of power Hitler no longer had to rely on public cinemas for his film ration. He even kept away from the numerous gala première's at the Ufa-Palast (he made exceptions for state visits, the Riefenstahl films and Party films like *Hitler Youth Quex* or *SA Man Brand*).

After dinner, or even after coming back from a concert or the opera (31.3.1934), Hitler would order projector and screen to be set up. He did not have his own projection room until he moved in the new Reich Chancellery. And he was often a welcome guest at film evenings chez Goebbels or in the Kameradschaft der deutschen Künstler (KddK), a German N. S. artists' association.

Joachim C. Fest writes about the dictator's taste in films in his biography of Hitler: "Hitler was particularly fond of social comedies with feeble jokes and sentimental endings. Heinz Rühmann's *Quax der Bruchpilot* ("Quax, the Crash-Happy Pilot") or his *Feuerzangenbowle* (*Punch Bowl*), Weiß Ferdl's street-porter comedy *Die beiden Seehunde* ("The Two Seals"), Willi Forst's revues, but also numerous foreign productions that could not all be shown in the public cinemas were among his preferred repertory, and were shown up to ten times and even more frequently."[990] Assessments of this kind are based less on actual documentation than on superficial memories taken down from the orbit of the "Führer's" headquarters. Hitler probably never saw the two Rühmann films, for example, and he loathed the Viennese setting of films by the wilful Austrian director Willi Forst.[991]

Hitler was shown a large number of German and foreign films in the period from 1935 to 1939 in particular. His adjutants' office documents contain Hitler's remarks and reactions, which have been quoted dozens of times. They range from "excellent", "very good", "good", "well acted", via "mediocre" to "very bad", "disagreeable", "repulsive" and even "utter rubbish".

Hitler very much liked stolid melodramas like *Verwehte Spuren* ("Lost Traces") ("liked it very much", 2.6.1938) by Veit Harlan, not only in the form of typical National Socialist anti-middle-class pre-world war films like Carl Froelich's *The Dreamer* of 1936 ("He is quite carried away", 1.11.1936).

Hitler was interested in acting, but also in "genuine depiction of a milieu", and he several times expressly noted "bad direction".[992] But his main concern was an exciting plot – otherwise Hitler soon got tired and had the screening stopped. He was fond of thrillers for this reason: *The Hound of the Baskervilles*, a German Sherlock Holmes adventure, and the courtroom drama *Der Fall Deruga*, with Willy Birgel, were among the dictator's favourites.

Dialogue films, filmed classical dramas and novellas like Storm's *Der Schimmelreiter* (*Rider of the White Horse*) and Heinrich von Kleist's *The Broken Jug* were in the Berghof film archive, as well as the obligatory propaganda productions. Froelich, Harlan, Liebeneiner and of course Ritter were some of Hitler's favourite directors, as was to be expected.

But often Hitler just looked to light entertainment films to take his mind off things; this happened at the height of the Sudeten crisis: "Saw a nice, funny old film to take our mind off things. The Führer doesn't like watching serious films now. That is understandable." (18.9.1938) As far as can be seen from the surviving material, Goebbels never indicated when he didn't share Hitler's film preferences, and only marginal differences are recorded in the diaries: "Führer also enthusiastic about the Fröhlich film *Wenn wir alle Engel wären*. I feel differently in some other cases. But these are matters of taste." (21.10.1939)

Hitler was also interested in foreign films, mainly from France and the USA. Favourites included comedies like *Smith With*, Westerns and Lubitsch comedies were at the bottom of the list,[993] along with Charlie Chaplin's or Buster Keaton's comedies. But he was amused by "a number of nice ideas and witty jokes"[994] in Hal Roach's *Blockheads* (1938), with Laurel and Hardy. Hitler was particularly fond of Walt Disney's cartoons. Numerous early Micky Mouse adventures called *Cheese Pirates* and *The Great Dog Race* were to be found in the Berghof archives as early as 1937. Goebbels gave him another 18 titles for Christmas.[995] The cartoon fairy-tale *Snow white and the seven dwarfs* had to be shipped from the USA via a circuitous route.[996]

There is room for doubt about whether Hitler always saw foreign-language productions in the original French, English and Italian, and actually understood them despite lack of knowledge of the languages.[997] The film companies made detailed summaries available, and sometimes provided dubbed versions, or prints with intermediate titles added. For example, Goebbels remarks about a pleasant evening threesome with Jenny Jugo: "The Führer really jovial. We watch the naval film again, which the Führer likes very much, and a French one that we don't understand at all." (11.1.1937)

And there is one occasion when Goebbels relates that Hitler read a screenplay and made a suggestion about direction. Significantly, this was at a time when the dictator was no longer watching films. Hitler pounced on a Lola Montez project that Goebbels had already "called off": "The Führer read the manuscript and thought it was quite inadequate. He was particularly displeased that Hörbiger had been cast. ... The Führer would like a film about Louis I to be made; but Louis I should not be shown as a fool or merely as a ladies' man."[998] (30.5.1942)

But these interventions came to nothing, along with other "requests" from the "Führer", for example not to dub foreign films in Germany any more (Goebbels: "not practicable"), to add a sound-track to Fritz Lang's *Nibelungs* or better to shoot the whole thing again,[999] to ban smoking in all feature films or to start filming the 500 year history of German emperors.[1000] Despite his great indirect influence on film policy Hitler does not really sound like a film expert; he understood the medium far less well than Goebbels.

But Hitler's interventions in the field of censorship indisputably had effects. However powerfully Goebbels presents himself as master of film censorship, and he does this at great length in the diary in particular, here too one figure towered over the rest: Adolf Hitler. Of course the "Führer" was not bound by any of the usual censorship procedures.[1001] When the grass-roots of the Party started to disrupt cinema performances after the Nazis came to power, the National Socialist hooligans were checked by reference to Hitler's supreme authority as supreme film censor: "Demonstrations against films that have been passed have also taken place in cases in which the Führer and Reich Chancellor had personally and expressly decided that there were special reasons for not banning public performances", ran one public proclamation.[1002] If Hitler wanted to ban a film absolutely, that was enough for Goebbels. But Hitler's interventions in the field of film censorship also make it clear how diffuse the decision-making process could sometimes be.

The dictator frequently demanded immediate action against films that had been vigorously rejected or even had their showing broken off at private screenings.[1003] These protests generally came to nothing, because according to Hitler's office the dictator – similarly to Goebbels up to

1935 – usually did not see films before their première even in 1939. When Hitler stopped seeing feature films at all after the outbreak of war,[1004] various individuals from his Berghof and Führer headquarters entourages tried to influence film censorship in his name.[1005] Martin Bormann and Eva Braun were particularly active in this respect. Hitler's mistress, long hushed up by Goebbels in his diaries, had very definite opinions of her own as well. She also showed the Propaganda Minister her private and now famous colour film collection, made with her own hands (14.3. 1944).

The selection of films consumed by Hitler at the Berghof or in the Reich Chancellery cinema was largely beyond Goebbels' control. The Propaganda Ministry regularly compiled lists of films available for screening that Hitler could choose from, but his office also deliberately requested other films. In rare cases some production and distribution companies avoided the censorship authorities and sent copies directly to the Reich Chancellery or the Berghof "to be examined if wished".[1006] In the case of the medical film *Die ewige Maske* (*The Eternal Mask*) the Propaganda Ministry and the official censorship office are said to have been played off against each other. Hitler was shown the film after it had been banned, and he passed it for release.[1007]

It is also said that *Das Leben kann so schön sein*, a film about everyday life and problems, and *Altes Herz geht auf die Reise* were seen before the première by Hitler in December 1938, who then banned them because of their unvarnished portrayal of social reality in the "Third Reich". This was while Goebbels was going through his weak phase.[1008] This obviously came as a complete surprise to Goebbels. He was particularly embarrassed by the fact that he was not even familiar with the films. For this reason the Propaganda Ministry once more told Ufa that completed films should "as far as possible be given first to Dr. Goebbels for examination, and only then to the Führer"[1009] which is what happened as a rule.[1010]

The case of the 1936 anti-Soviet film *Weiße Sklaven* provides a vivid example of how censorship worked at the highest level: according to a note made by Goebbels on 14.10.1936, Hitler rejected the final version of the film as submitted to him. The Propaganda Minister then first tried to have the ban lifted[1011] and after that had the manuscript rewritten or contributed some scenes himself (26.10., 11.11.1936): "The film is quite usable now, indeed quite moving in parts. ... The film has the right slant as well." (9.12.1936) On 16.12. the new version was with Hitler, and a few days later Goebbels noted that the film had been released with a new final scene containing day-to-day, anti-Bolshevik Nazi slogans.[1012] Goebbels' remarks on 15.10. also show that films could be banned even before 1939 by Hitler's entourage in his name, without the "Führer" having seen the picture himself.

Hitler also disapproved of a much-revised documentary "film about Spain and its revolution" (4.12.1936): "Führer thinks it's better not to show it. Still not clear enough, and imprecise. Text too emotional. Therefore ban." (12.1.1937) Goebbels announces that this has been carried out the next day: "Spanish film banned".[1013] Another attempt to exploit the Spanish Civil War through a documentary films also came to grief because of Hitler. Although Goebbels' first called this German-Spanish co-production *España Eroica* (*Helden in Spanien*) a "horrible exhibition of the Civil War" that was "not suitable for us" (7.8.1938),[1014] he finally agreed that it should be shown. But after an appraisal on 22 December 1938 Hitler had cinema screenings of the film unceremoniously halted.[1015] Efforts by the Propaganda Ministry in February 1939 to have the film released by pointing out how badly the Bavaria film company would suffer financially were ultimately unsuccessful. After being briefly re-released the film was banned again. Hitler reacted sensitively to the important question of Spain: it was better to have a complete ban than a politically imperfect presentation.

Hitler's omnipotence came up against boundaries when he had to consider his allies politically. For example, the 1939 Italian-Spanish co-production *L'assedio dell'Alcazar* (*Alcazar*), which dealt with Spanish nationalist forces fighting to defend themselves in the encircled fortress of Toledo was intended to reinforce German film propaganda. Goebbels, "carried away" by the "deeply moving heroic epic" (24.8.1940), reports on a number of screenings for select groups (22.9.1940), but soon realizes: "We must cut the religious sections from the *Alcazar* film. Otherwise things will get awkward." (20.12.1940) The background to this is an eight-minute scene with a heavily Catholic slant about a service for which there is historical evidence, from which the besieged Franco troops drew new strength for the fight.[1016] The Church as a source of moral strength: this was entirely unacceptable to the Nazi's strongly anti-clerical ecclesiastical policies and propaganda. But the Germans' Italian allies flatly refused to cut the offending scenes: "*Alcazar* is now being launched in Berlin in a big way. But the Duce is ferociously determined to keep the church scenes in. I am sceptical about this and will ask the Führer again." (15.6.1941) Goebbels' authority to cut this war film, which was most welcome and would no doubt have been a highly effective accompaniment to the invasion of the Soviet Union was not sufficient in this case. As Mussolini, himself a film-lover, was also personally involved, the decision fell to Hitler, who hesitated ("He wants to think again about whether we cannot release *Alcazar* uncut", 16.6. 1941), but finally decided not to give in to the Italians.[1017] He obviously felt that the ecclesiastical question was more important, even though the alliance with Italy was now more important than ever because of the war with the Soviet Union that had just started. Goebbels too had repeatedly pointed out that they could "not afford to annoy the Italians" (1.10.1941) and that they had to be "very carefully and generously handled at the moment". (16.9.1941) But the Nazi leadership were forced to play down the conflict with the Church and especially the sermon against euthanasia by Bishop Clemens Graf von Galen[1018] and thus risk the Italians' wrath. Thus a seemingly routine piece of censorship could conceal conflicts on a considerable scale.

Interventions in film censorship were not restricted to friendly nations. Apparently the Chinese government also tried to prevent the film *Alarm in Peking* from being shown because of the negative image it presented of China during the so-called Boxer Rebellion of 1900: "The Chinese have mobilized all their ministers." (26.6.1937) But Goebbels quotes an uncompromising Hitler: "Führer refuses to ban the film *Alarm in Peking*. Where will it end if we let the countries concerned certify certain films. Anyway he rather let's the China business go." (30.6.1937) Despite what was clearly increased pressure on the part of the Chinese,[88] Goebbels notes on 13.7.1937: "*Alarm in Peking* still not banned. Führer will not be deterred by threats of any kind."[1020]

Hitler was also appealed to as the supreme authority in matters of censorship by rival groups within the Nazi leadership to an astonishing extent, and claimed as witness for individual opinions. However, Goebbels interprets some of these incidents rather questionably. His version of the clash about the performance of *The Great King*, the film about Frederick II, has often been taken too much at face value.[1021] According to Goebbels, some of the OKW had protested that Frederick's generals were portrayed as too defeatist,[1022] and had tried to have passages edited or to prevent the film from being shown at all, but that Hitler refused to do this.[1023] (20.3.1943)

But Goebbels is all too obviously linking the film with the "total war measures" that he has promoting in both the civil and military fields. Goebbels wants to take Hitler's decision to show the film as a sign "that the Führer is in favour of the harder approach to waging war, and is determined to have this introduced on as large a scale as possible". (20.3.1942) Goebbels also presents his victory over the military gentlemen at great length, so that is appropriate to express serious doubts about the truth of this episode, especially as there are no other sources for it.

Goebbels' version of the difference of opinion about the film comedy *Capriolen*, starring Gustaf Gründgens, casts further light on conditions within the regime. Goebbels' comments on *Capriolen* are negative, as they were on most films by this director, actor and theatre manager, whom Goebbels eyed with considerable mistrust: "typical Gründgens. Cold, intellectual, overpointed and icy wit. Really embarrassing in places". (14.7.1937) In addition to this the roles of the sexes were blurred, which Hitler particularly hated. His obviously equally critical judgement (17.7.) encouraged Goebbels. he would now "keep a sharper eye on Gründgens". Goebbels seems to have denounced Gründgens to Hitler on a number of occasions to create the right atmosphere for having the film banned.[1024] Goebbels does not want to "give in about this" (28.7. 1937)[1025] to Hermann Göring, who comes in on Gründgens' side; Goebbels still places his hopes completely in Hitler's support: "He now wants to see the whole film again himself. Thinks that Gründgens has to be got rid of." (29.7.1937) On 4.8. he finally has to note: "Führer thinks *Capriolen* is very bad as well. But he also thinks that we shouldn't do anything at the moment." Apparently even the dictator himself was afraid of clashing with the Prussian Prime Minister Göring who was extremely powerful and self-confident at the time, and with whom there were anyway differences in other cultural spheres.[1026]

If one is to believe Goebbels' accounts, Hitler rejected even the most hesitant contradictions of official Nazi national community propaganda and disapproved of signs of this in social reality, but at the same time made the highest possible demands on political propaganda films, which he preferred to ban completely rather than letting them run in inadequately National Socialist versions. And yet one should not overestimate Hitler's activities as censor: after the war started he made only one personal decision about a controversial film screening, and that was in the case of *The Dismissal*.[1027]

Of course Goebbels had to take heed of interventions by his "Führer", but he consistently tried to resist any kind of interference from all sorts of forces within the regime.

For example, there was a clash of considerable proportions with Rudof Hess about the Heinz Rühmann film *Der Gasmann*. The première was on 15 February 1941, and Goebbels pronounced himself "very satisfied" with the film. (14.2.1941) A few days later he records "objections" to the comedy by Hess. Goebbels decided these were "quite unworthy of discussion" (20.1.1941), but apparently had to agree to changes ("We'll get there with *Der Gasmann* now as well", 22.1.1941) despite Göring's support. (21.1.1941) Hess had been displeased by a scene[1028] in which Heinz Rühmann is threatened with a "cousin in the Party" by a female national comrade, to which Rühmann responds by saying "Right then, Heil Hitler", which did in fact remain unique in Nazi film history as a "careful, ironic caricature of the Zeitgeist".[1029] While Goebbels now gives the impression that the objections had been dealt with ("*Gasmann* revised. It can be shown like this", 2.6.1941) and doesn't refer to the unpleasant clash again, documents from the Party Chancellery show that people there were not satisfied with Goebbels' cuts and made some additional critical points.[1030] *Der Gasmann* was not able to open again until August 1941 – the line of dialogue about the "cousin in the Party" was still in, but Rühmann's Nazi salute had been taken out. Goebbels, who set great store by his authority, did not forget the tug-of-war about censorship and the concessions to Hess and his successor Bormann for some time. He brought up resistance to *Der Gasmann* again later: Goebbels said that Fritz Sauckel, the Gauleiter of Thuringia, had now withdrawn his objection to *Der Gasmann*; Goebbels also complained about a lack of sense of humour in many Party offices. (28.9.1941)

Again it was Gustaf Gründgens who provided ambiguities and political allusions in *Zwei Welten* ("Two Worlds").[1031] Goebbels picked these up and clearly intended heavy cuts or even a ban. (30.12.1939) But these are not mentioned again after interventions by Gründgens (3.1.1940) and Göring. (4.1.1940) With apparent indifference, he confirms that the film has been passed and indeed that it has been commended: "A number of questions with Göring. ... Gründgens gets his good film grading."[1032] (11.1.1940)

Pressures from the Party bosses were not restricted to Hess or Göring: for example, Alfred Rosenberg, the Nazi's chief ideologue and Reich Minister for the occupied eastern territories and Goebbels' main rival in the field of culture and propaganda, tried to prevent the Bismarck film *The Dismissal* from being shown in September and October 1942; Goebbels was able to fend this off only by getting permission from Hitler personally. Hess's successor Bormann also interfered in film censorship and criticized the war film *Über alles in der Welt*. (23.3.1941) The Propaganda Minister did not have Hitler's support this time, and went down, in his own admission, against the "whole clique" – meaning Hitler's office, liaison officers and Party officials in Hitler's entourage –, even though he tried to present this as successfully fending off even more far-reaching demands: "Constant toing and froing about the Ritter film. The strongest men change their minds, but I will not give in. I finally get my way, and the film is released with minor changes."[1033] (23.3.1941) The Propaganda Minister seems to have realized that Bormann's intervention was highly dangerous for his power base in film censorship: "I write a very strong letter to Bormann about the Ritter film. There are some things that cannot be tolerated, even in wartime." (25.3.1941)

All sorts of National Socialist Party institutions below the regime bosses tried to influence censorship. There are cases of films being banned by unauthorized regional or local officials, Gauleiters, for example.[1034] Nazi functionaries other than Hess had objected to *Der Gasmann*. (28.9.1941) But the most active interference in film censorship came from employees of the NSDAP office under Hess and later under Bormann. Walter Tießler was responsible for this. He was the Party Chancellery's link man in the Propaganda Ministry and at the same time head of the Reichspropagandaleitung film department. Tießler regularly passed demands, complaints and reservations from all levels of the Party on to Goebbels, especially from the district propaganda departments and the Reichspropagandaleitung, and thus repeatedly attracted criticism from Goebbels. (25.5.1941)

A list drawn up by Tießler in June 1943[1035] shows how the Party Chancellery, representing a number of NSDAP groups, tried to remind film people to include "philosophical" and "educational" criteria in screenplays and films. Tießler mentions 30 completed films (features and documentaries), i.e. films that had already been shown from 1941 to 1943 or were about to open. He notes six cases in which Goebbels responded to the Party's reservations – in two cases by im-

47. *Punch Bowl* (1944): protests from teachers.

posing a complete ban[1036] – and only two films where Goebbels totally rejected suggested changes.[1037] Most of the criticism was about church scenes, the use of the Nazi salute, the portrayal of various professional groups, the use of foreign-looking actors and questions of national character.

A particular problem was posed for Goebbels here by the various professional organization attached to the Nazi Party who managed to influence censorship via the Party office and the Reichspropagandaleitung.[1038] Goebbels had recorded interference of this kind even in the thirties (8.6.1938) and constantly protested about them at later stages. (8.11.1941, 2.3.1942) Goebbels spoke against the attempts at influence and protests in public as well.[1039] Teachers, who were particularly well represented inside the Party turned out to be particularly stubborn. The Reichspropagandaleitung list shows the extent to which the various professional associations demanded the removal of scenes that displeased them: in two cases protests from pharmaceutical chemists are listed, and three from teachers alone. Thus we read in the context of *Hannerl und ihre Liebhaber* ("Hannerl and Her Lovers"): "withdrawn as a result of objections from the teachers' association".[1040] Goebbels saw to it that there were directives to protect the teaching profession when presented in public. In the particularly spectacular case of the school satire *Punch Bowl* – which has now amazingly achieved cult status again – where a great deal of fun was poked at the "beaks", he remained obdurate, however: "The new Rühmann film "Feuerzangenbowle" must be shown whatever happens. The Führer has insisted that I should not be intimidated by objections on the part of teachers or the Ministry of Education." (25.1.1944) But in fact the film had already passed the censors at the time of this obvious piece of window-dressing, and it opened three days later.

We have already seen from the clash over *Alarm in Peking* that foreign governments also attempted to stand in the way of films that the felt presented a threat to their image. They were quite often supported by the Foreign Office as well. The Foreign Office itself – not only from the point when Goebbels lost his foreign propaganda role to Ribbentrop – retained a right to share in decisions about the screening of German films abroad. Different criteria were applied from those for the Reich area, for which reason *The Dismissal*, for example, was banned for export because its presentation of blame for the 1914 war and the role of the Foreign Office in the fall of Bismarck were seen as excessively heavy National Socialist propaganda (in other words too critical of the Kaiser).[1041] Goebbels had to defend himself repeatedly against the Foreign Ministry's restrictive policies when trying to implement his plans for export and great power status for films.[1042] In any case there were special regulations for the German Occupied Poland and the protectorate of Bohemia and Moravia. Party offices had qualms about screening the Veit Harlan melodrama *Die goldene Stadt* in the protectorate because it might encourage "Czech chauvinism".[1043]

It was the armed forces who had the greatest scope for intervention in film censorship – even before September 1939. For Goebbels' Propaganda Ministry, military censorship was the only legitimate competition in the creation, suppression or alteration of films, pictures and propaganda material of all kinds. Goebbels' claim that only his ministry could be allowed the authority to decide in censorship questions (11.11.1936) could not be justified in peacetime or wartime. There were special links between the Propaganda Ministry and the OKH/OKW at an early stage, to bridge the "bipolarity between military and civilian propaganda".[1044] The liaison officers in the various military offices in the Propaganda Ministry hardly concerned themselves with post-censorship of feature and documentary films, however. What actually happened was that discussions took place at the preliminary stage, which also applied to the "war education films" before 1939.

Screenplays including military activity and films that were made with the involvement of military personnel were usually submitted to the army command. This tended to be associated, much to Goebbels' regret, with attempts, some of which were quite far-reaching, to influence the content of the film projects. "Ritter and Wieman are also complaining that the War Ministry now interferes with all film projects. I put a quick stop to this by invoking a very clear decree from the Führer."[1045] (24.8.1937) Here too even the most detailed interventions are dealt with at the highest level: "(Reich Defence Minister) Blomberg telephones. He wants a scene out of *Unternehmen Michael*. The navy's role in the war comes under heavy attack. I'll do him that favour." (4.9. 1937) After the start of the war there were sporadic differences between the Wehrmacht propaganda department in the OKW, whose liaison officers were involved in the preliminary stages of film projects, and the Propaganda Ministry about German officers' images in films.[1046] Subsequent objections, like the OKW protest about an "air-force office who spends a night with a famous singer" (23.5.1942) in Zarah Leander's *Die große Liebe*, which film historians love to quote from Goebbels' dairies, remained the exception.

The treatment of some OKW productions by the Propaganda Ministry also led to conflicts. Goebbels felt that the majority of productions by the Wehrmacht propaganda department's film office were ineffective as propaganda, and tried to prevent them from being passed.[1047] There was also a complex tissue of petty jealousies and rivalries between the individual Wehrmacht sections, caused for example by different film classifications allotted to feature and documentary films about the Luftwaffe (*Baptism of Fire* and *Kampfgeschwader Lützow*) and the army (*Sieg im Westen*). As none of the different sections of the armed forces wanted to come out worse than any of the others, corresponding pressure was exerted on the Propaganda Ministry. Goebbels found himself confronted with interventions of this kind even in the case of the Luftwaffe film *Baptism of Fire*, and again had to cite a decision by Hitler: "The Führer has now stated personally that, as I had suggested, the film *Baptism of fire* should be awarded the second and not the first film classification."[1048] (7.4.1940) When the army press officer in the OKW Wehrmacht propaganda department, Kurt Hesse, demanded "the highest film classification for *Sieg im Westen*, as had been awarded to *Kampfgeschader Lützow*",[1049] Goebbels also resisted. (1.3.1941) He benefited in the subsequent clash from animosity between the OKW chief, Keitel and von Brauchitsch, the supreme commander of the army, so that he even managed to have the army officer responsible for film matters dismissed.[1050]

"A cinematic epic of German heroism": Newsreel and documentary films as propaganda devices

Documentary films

Lack of interest?

There were many kinds of documentary film in the Nazi period. It would be extremely difficult to provide a precise definition of all the sub-genres[1051] that could be separated in terms of function, origin and content, from the scientific and technical documentaries to military educational films.

The National Socialists saw documentary films first and foremost as a "one-sided functional propaganda device",[1052] but left themselves the loophole of recourse to the "widespread erroneous belief in the factual nature of images identified as documentary".[1053] National Socialist innovations with respect to manipulative techniques and ostensible authenticity set standards in Germany for a long time. The basic pattern of successful manipulation techniques in documentary film production included: "falsifying facts by altering contexts; twisting causal relations by changing chronology; distorting visual truth by verbal corrections; adding 'what is missing from the force of the images' by means of (heroic) music" (Hilmar Hoffmann).[1054]

Goebbels felt that the documentary genre was best suited for direct, bold and simple propaganda, and not so could for the refined indoctrination that he favoured. Documentary films – unlike newsreels – were only to a limited extent able to provide subliminal propaganda blandishments that went beyond arousing emotions and appealing to instincts – unless it was in their most brilliant manifestation à la Riefenstahl. Aesthetic aspects were not alien to Goebbels, but documentary films were not allowed to prove themselves as a medium for formal experiments and exercises in artistic style. Form before content was not the rule here. There is no question that Goebbels developed a high level of understanding of non-fictional film forms: even before the "seizure of power" he enjoyed himself in the role of propaganda director of what were then still dilettante Party films.[1055] "If only we had greater technical resources" (5.4.1929) was a frequent cry in those years. But over and above a general admiration for Russian montage technique there are no signs of models for a Fascist film aesthetic nor vestiges of a theoretical programme. There is no surviving record of what Goebbels thought of innovative reportage and documentary work like Walther Ruttmann's *Symphonie einer Großstadt* (*Symphony of a Big City*, 1927) and agit-prop scripts like *Kuhle Wampe* (1932). He probably took as little notice of theories by anti-Nazi Walter Benjamin about the "aestheticization of politics" or his "biased art" interpretations as he did of Kracauer's remarks about film as a realistic art form. But he did not pay any particular attention to Ruttmann's work in the "Third Reich" either. And so the question of whether propaganda intentions were partially undermined by certain film forms[1056] in the case of Ruttmann or other documentary film people is never answered by Goebbels. His public attacks on aimless and purposeless "anaemic l'art pour l'art", "pale aestheticism" and everyday naturalism, as well as his rejection of Willy Zielke's semi-documentary film *Das Stahltier* show him to be a traditionalist who disapproved of visual experiments.

But Goebbels definitely saw himself as an expert. "I explained the basic concepts of documentary films to him." (19.4.1940) This applies to Hans Bertram, who started off as a pioneer airman and then turned himself into a knowledgeable and experienced documentary director, who had in fact just produced *Baptism of Fire*, an effectively assembled propaganda film about the Luftwaffe's involvement in the attack on Poland.

Something else that contributed to Goebbels' matter-of-fact view of documentary films was that even though he greatly admired Leni Riefenstahl's Party rally and Olympic films he was well aware that this "suggestive aestheticization of Fascism" (Hilmar Hoffmann) was an exceptional phenomenon that could not be simply copied and adopted as a specific National Socialist film aesthetic without appropriate talent. Another factor was that most of the non-fictional films produced, because of disappointing results from the SA and Hitler Youth feature films, fell into the domain of strictly ideological NSDAP film propaganda, of which Goebbels did not hold a very high opinion. Overall, the very fact that there is so little about documentary films in Goebbels' diary entries contradicts the view that he was much more interested in newsreels and documentaries than he was in feature films.[1057]

Goebbels also shows a great deal of linguistic confusion because there is not precise distinction between the "Kulturfilm" and the "Dokumentarfilm" in terms of film theory. His terminology in the diary is sometimes confused. "Propaganda film" usually describes a German or foreign documentary, "Tendenzfilm" properly applies to feature films, but is sometimes used for non-fictional forms as well. The "Kulturfilm" is usually scientific, academic and technical in content, but Goebbels uses the word for films glorifying the SS or other Party organizations. So the Propaganda Minister borrowed the language of contemporary film literature, but not its categories.[1058] In the context of both feature and documentary films, Goebbels' maxims tend to be at their clearest when he is describing concrete projects.

Champion of the "Kulturfilm"

From 1934 onwards, every cinema was obliged to include a short known as a "Kulturfilm" in the supporting programme, usually between the newsreel and the main film. Both the concept and the specific aesthetic are German inventions.[1059] Instructive films from "nature and science, art and national lore, craft and technology, military matters and politics"[1060] – a universal show, aimed at educating the people, and classless in its interest. There are many hundreds of the 15-minute one-acters, and they also provide a record of National Socialist modernization intentions and faith in technology,[1061] a "political and educational glossary of everyday life in Hitler's state".[1062] Images from the world of animals and nature provided a splendid illustration of the "social-Darwinist ideology of eating and being eaten".[1063] Numerous Party organizations, border guards, the Alpenkorps, paratroops and seamen were featured. The titles of the films, which were often used for experiments with visual and colour techniques, illustrate the range covered: *Röntgenstrahlen* ("X-rays", 1937), *Bunte Kriechtierwelt* ("The Colourful World of Reptiles", 1940), *Altgermanische Bauernkultur* ("Old Germanic Peasant Culture", 1939) or *Deutsche Panzer* ("German Tanks", 1941). The leading documentary directors of the Weimar period, like Carl Junghans, Svend Noldan, Arnold Fanck, Walther Ruttmann and Curt Oertel, were responsible for glorifying soldiers, the Olympic Games, work, Hitler's campaigns and Party organizations in the "Third Reich".[1064] Ruttmann's industrial film *Mannesmann* (1937) and Oertel's *Michelangelo* (1941) won international awards.

Goebbels was not able to examine all the many hundreds of qualitatively very uneven titles personally; we certainly cannot find out what criteria he adopted. His influence on production must have been limited in the early years. The railways, the big film studios, even industrial concerns had their own departments for making such films, and there were many small production firms specializing in this genre as well. This changed only slowly as the Propaganda Ministry built up its own Kulturfilm production section. It had its own Kulturfilm script editors, who were supposed to select and examine themes and subjects, in just the same way as feature films, but they were not able to intervene in individual projects to the same extent.

Goebbels simply consumed such films for his own entertainment at first ("very nice short film about the Deutsches Opernhaus", 22.3.1936), or treated them with a mixture of stylization and naïve response ("educational film *So lebt China*! / "How China Lives!" An absolutely nomadic, primitive people. Probably entirely unsuited to great historical forms", 6.2.1937). He does not seem to have acknowledged the importance of the Kulturfilm for propaganda purposes more positively until Ufa was nationalized: "Ufa Kulturfilme: an extensive organization. But more could be made of it. Bring it closer to the state." (20.2.1937) But clearly he had now started to intervene himself from time to time: he notes occasional corrections to finished films, for example to one made on the occasion of the 1938 Motor Show "about our racing victories", which was submitted to him by Adolf Hühnlein, director of the NSKK ("the NS motor vehicles organisation"): "Wonderfully made. Still suggested a few changes". (19.1.1938) Goebbels was less pleased by the popular, essentially scientific and educational expedition films. In *Sehnsucht nach Afrika* ("Yearning for Africa") the Swedish explorer Bengt Berg describes his voyage of discovery to the "dark continent", using documentary material and scenes using actors.[1065] Goebbels was displeased by this mixture of education and "semifiction": "Then we see a very boring Bengt Berg film *Afrika ruft*. Overpoweringly pushy". (18.1.1939) Goebbels must have seen a dozen similar colonial propaganda films since 1933, but he does not find them "pushy", as is confirmed a few days later when he described the full-length film *Deutsches Land in Afrika* ("German Territory in Africa")[1066] as a "fine film about our former colonies". (21.1.1939)

Kulturfilm production increased significantly in the year the war broke out because such films were increasingly popular with the public. The flood of films inevitably led to an uncoordinated accumulation of similar projects and thus to extravagant use of resources, which was intolerable

48. Curt Oertel filming *Michelangelo* (1941).

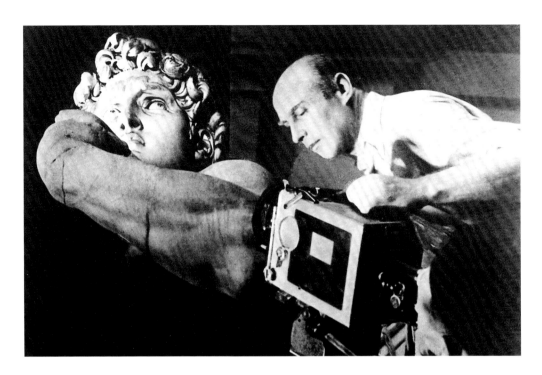

in wartime.[1067] An obligation to notify the Reichsfilmkammer introduced in March 1939 did nothing to alter this. Another guideline, laying down that films about 15 minutes long should not cost less than 30,000 Reichsmarks, was intended to encourage a more elaborate approach to content, technique and visual matters, and thus improve quality. Goebbels asked the cinemas to pay out three per cent of their net income to provide finance for Kulturfilme.[1068]

The Minister installed Carl Neumann, an experienced National Socialist film functionary and Kulturfilm script editor as head of the newly created department of Kulturfilm scripts in the Propaganda Ministry film department, with the brief of reorganizing Kulturfilm production.[1069] Neumann submitted several memos[1070] to Goebbels about building up a "production headquarters modelled on the newsreel headquarters". (28.3.1940) Goebbels intended to use this to put the Kulturfilm under rigid state control: "The Ministry regulates and leads. We must be successful here."[1071] (28.3.1940) The "Deutsche Kulturfilm-Zentrale" was founded with effect from 1 August 1940, with the brief of "directing the making of the German Kulturfilm more tightly in terms of politics, philosophy and organization, and relating production planning for all Kulturfilm makers more closely to the needs of our times".[1072] Following the model of the feature film (and complementing the appropriate pre-censorship decree of 18 November 1939), Kulturfilm projects (and also all other propaganda or supporting films) were now to be given four weeks before the start of shooting in which to submit the screenplay; they also had to draw up a general production plan for Kulturfilm material annually. Goebbels could count on Hitler's support for these activities: "He praises our Kulturfilm output very highly." (23.4.1940)

Goebbels continued to impose corrections on especially ambitious specimens of the Kulturfilm. One example of this is Curt Oertels' full-length German-Swiss documentary masterpiece *Michelangelo*, which won prizes after the war (including an Oscar in 1950). Goebbels wrote that his film did "only imperfect justice" to the painter's "genius": "The emotional accompanying text is particularly disturbing. It all needs to be said in a much more matter-of-fact and realistic way. The impression made by the work of art will be all the more profound then."[1073] (13.3.1940)

The Kulturfilm could be used in wartime both to boost morale and as part of the strategy for taking people's minds off the war.[1074] The Security Service reports showed that these films continued to be attractive, though people were asking for themes that "reflected their time more", and wanted to see the "Kulturfilme becoming increasingly topical",[1075] in addition to the films about animals, the countryside and science. For the Propaganda Minister, who also held annual "Reich German Kulturfilm weeks", German production in this medium was a big success story: "We lead the world in this field."[1076] (11.2.1941) In accordance with the "Leistungssteigerungsgesetz" ("performance improvement act") of February 1942, the Deutsche Kulturfilmzentrale was changed into a special Kulturfilm department under the Reichsfilmintendant; Heinrich Roellenbleg became director of this department in 1943. Goebbels stopped distinguishing between Kulturfilme, i.e. educational films and official, explicit Party propaganda films in about

1940/41. The name "Kulturfilm" was used from then on for almost all documentaries, but mainly for propaganda productions involving portraits of Party and state institutions.

Glorifying the Party, "race education" and war propaganda

National Socialist documentary film production was characterized by an almost impenetrable entanglement of state, semi-state and official Party, private and Wehrmacht productions. The competent authority for Party productions was the Reichspropagandaleitung's main film department, which accepted commissions for productions from Party sections and carried them out. Goebbels did try to impose order on the organizational chaos and to centralize production, but the diaries reveal how in the early days of National Socialist rule some NS documentary film projects failed because Party organizations and authorities had unduly large cinematic ambitions.

Carl Junghans' film about the Winter Olympics, *Jugend der Welt* ("Youth of the World", 1.6. 1936), distinguished by its "outstanding editing and montage techniques",[1077] is the only one of the major productions made under the influence of the Party up to 1938 to find favour with Goebbels. A film called *Der ewige Wald* ("The Eternal Forest") appeared in June 1936. It was commissioned by Alfred Rosenberg's National Socialist Kulturgemeinde, and its mystical babble about the "unity of people and forest" obviously appealed neither to Goebbels nor to Hitler.[1078] And as some other films initiated by Party organizations failed at their premières, something that Goebbels preferred to keep quiet about if it was a project he had approved, the Propaganda Minister sent out a circular letter on 28 August 1936 warning against extravagant use of public funds for "unartistic films" and required each and every manuscript to be submitted to him.[1079] Another NS-Kulturgemeinde film about the Reichsautobahnprogramm seems to have suffered a similar fate. Goebbels reports a ban by Hitler and can scarcely conceal his satisfaction about this: "Heavy blow. Now the second N.S. Kulturgemeinde film. They have now squandered 2 million on these dilettante jokes." (22.8.1937)

Goebbels' damning criticism of Party film productions continues throughout the diary entries. Goebbels feels that the colour film about the 1937 Nuremberg Rally, *Festliches Nürnberg* ("Festive Nuremberg"), is "something of a muddle. Typical Weidemann". (23.11.1937) He says something similar about a short film about Hitler's and Mussolini's rally on the Olympic site in September 1937. (30.9.1937)

The RPL film *Jahre der Entscheidung* ("Crucial Years") was intended to provide a universal retrospective of the history of the National Socialist movement from 1918.[1080] It was made by Carl Junghans and Hans Weidemann, and the process lasted for several years. It was censored in 1939, but was never shown. Goebbels criticized it sharply from the first draft onwards (14.8. 1937), and said that the second section of the planned two-part film was "a complete muddle": "Absolutely no clarity or overall view. Weidemann calls it dynamic ... film must be completely revised." (12.1.1938) Ostensibly, *Jahre der Entscheidung* also took so long to complete because the Propaganda Minister wanted it to do justice to all the recent events, from the Austrian "Anschluss" via the incorporation of the Sudeten to the "march on Prague".[1081] Another political Kulturfilm, *München – Hauptstadt der Bewegung* ("Munich, Headquarters of the Movement"), turned out to be "heartily inept" as far as Goebbels was concerned (27.5.1939), a judgement that Hitler shared and further underlined by banning the film.[1082]

In July 1937 the "Deutsche Filmherstellungs- und Verwertungsgesellschaft mbH" ("German film production and exploitation company Ltd."; DFG) was founded. This certainly meant that the major Party productions could now run under this less conspicuous imprint, rather than "RPL presents", which was sometimes counter-productive.[1083] But Goebbels reinforces his scepticism by laying down that the new production company should only "be taken up on a small scale" (10.6.1937) and make "above all 'Tendenzfilme'" (19.6.1937), with the aid of additional funds made available by NSDAP treasurer Schwarz. Although the original intention was to make only feature films following a strictly Nazi ideology,[1084] the DFG restricted itself to documentary films with a few exceptions.[1085] The feature films that it did propose were largely rejected by Goebbels.

Soon after this it became clear that the Propaganda Minister "did not particularly trust the newly created Party film production company either".[1086] He tried, with some success, to attract distinguished feature film directors for outstanding projects. Thus Gustav Ucicky made the 1938 election film *Wort und Tat* ("Words and Deeds") in 1938. (25.3.1938) In Goebbels' eyes the DFG failed to conceive effective war propaganda, particularly after the outbreak of war. "They come up with dreadful films", he wrote on 3.3.1940.[1087] Willy Krause was dismissed as head of the DFG shortly after this.[1088] Goebbels then looked for a "first-class artistic manager" (14.3. 1940), and finally appointed Fritz Kubach (17.4.1940) to be Krause's successor. A guideline that was to have major consequences showed that the Minister wanted the professional Kulturfilm producers to be able to make films about Party organizations as well, because Goebbels often found that the productions they made themselves were inept: "Talked to Neumann about Kulturfilm production. The D.F.G. is not to have a monopoly of films on Party work. Otherwise there will not be any competition and no good will come of it."[1089] (23.4.1940) On 4.8.1942 he states that films are better than say brochures for "education in social and racial questions", and that such films should represent "National Socialist thinking, rather then dwelling on National Socialist organization". The organizations would muck up the whole project with their interference.[1090] An appropriate analysis of Goebbels' decisions about prizes at the "Reich German Kulturfilm Week" in 1943 – he only gave prizes to films that were not about the Party[1091] – is to be found in the entry for 11.7.1943: "I am shown a sequence of Kulturfilme, one by the SS, one by the HJ (Hitler Youth). Neither is suitable for performance in the normal run of programmes, as they lay it on too thick in terms of propaganda. This is the cardinal error made by all films made by the Party or its sections. They think that propaganda has to be made with a sledgehammer. But this is never effective, as is well known." As a consequence of assessments like these, Goebbels started to dismantle the DFG in June 1943. He had been planning since December 1941 "to bring all the Kulturfilm and documentary projects together". (2.12.1941) The RPL's main film department did not make many Party films any more either. Instead of this, the "Ufa Sonderproduktion GmbH" ("special production company"), set up in 1943 under the Ufi umbrella, became the major commissioning producer for the Party and the Wehrmacht, and the provider for Kulturfilm projects.[1092] Goebbels still occasionally mentions the newsreel-like Hitler Youth film series *Junges Europa* ("Young Europe") until the end of the war; eight episodes of this were made from 1942 to 1945.[1093]

Goebbels tried to force the Party institutions out of film production less for aesthetic reasons than because he was concerned to make the maximum propaganda impact. However, there are some examples of titles from the thirties and forties that give some idea about his concrete thinking on documentaries, which always had to measure up to Hitler's views as well. Documentary films addressed the subject of "euthanasia", as the murder of mentally handicapped people was called later, even in the pre-war period. Three films were made about the "incurably sick" by the NSDAP "Rassenpolitisches Amt" ("Race policy office") in 1935/36. These were intended only for use within the Party, but in 1936/37 a series of pseudo-scientific "educational films on racial biology" were shown in cinemas. The most perfidious of these, the documentary film *Opfer der Vergangenheit* (*Victims of the Past*), which was made by the Rassenpolitisches Amt in co-operation with the RPL, was intended to prepare the ground for the systematic murder of the mentally ill, which began in 1939. It is said that Hitler hat seen the earlier film *Erbkrank* ("Congenitally Ill"), which was shown in 1936, and as a result proposed a more elaborate film suitable for the main programme.[1094]

Goebbels' comment on the film, which was completed in June 1936, was similar to one he made later about *The Eternal Jew*, characterized by annihilation phobia.[1095] But Hitler had reserved the right to make the final decision about using *Victims of the Past* in public for himself.[1096] Shortly after Goebbels enquired when Hitler could see and release this film, which lasted barely half an hour,[1097] the Minister noted on 11.2.1937: "Film *Victims of the Past*. Führer finds it very good. Must run in all German cinemas." Apparently Hitler even suggested that shots of Goebbels' three children should be edited in.[1098] After the première on 20 March 1937 in the Berlin Ufa-Palast am Zoo, the Reichsfilmkammer announced in April 1937: "The film *Victims of the Past* will shortly be shown in all 5.300 German cinemas."[1099] The cinema owners were compelled to show the film.[1100]

The dictator's commitment to *Victims of the Past* was not just a preliminary stage to his involvement in the making of *The Eternal Jew*. In many respects this documentary "euthanasia" film – Goebbels praised the "psychological and propaganda treatment of this material"[1101] particularly highly – was a model of the 1940 compilation film. Explicit images aiming to shock and a radical accompanying text[1102] illustrated Goebbels' recipe for documentary film. He emphasizes this again when plans for "scientific documentary films"[1103] about the mentally ill are taken up again in 1941/42 after *I Accuse*. At the same time, as tactics were handled extremely carefully in consideration of the popular mood and the war situation, Goebbels discussed with Phillip Bouhler how "it would be possible to present the horrifying images of illness that can be seen in the lunatic asylums in a documentary film". He said that the approach should not be too scientific, but that the audience should simply be shown the appropriate images, "to make it somewhat easier for us psychologically to liquidate these human beings who are no longer capable of survival". (5.9.1941) Goebbels relied on the effect of ostensible authenticity, following the recipe used for *The Eternal Jew* and *Victims of the Past*. The idea was not to encourage discussions about the rightness and morality of "euthanasia, but to use shockingly realistic "education" to arouse repugnance and openly "justify liquidation methods for the incurably mad": "I insist above all that no middle-of-the-road cases are to be shown, but only those that are absolutely convincing. On the other hand a section can be added to the film showing cases that are curable and that also should be cured. But in any case this film must not be treated from a medical and scientific point of view, which is what Bouhler's colleagues want. It must paint in black-and-white, otherwise it cannot convince the people."[1104] (30.1.1942)

Brutal images of this kind refute statements in film history that certain areas were "omitted in principle" from newsreels and documentary films in the National Socialist period: "The cinema screen does not show pogroms, books being burned, deportations, forced labour or concentrations camps, and films do not address the subjects of sterilization and euthanasia either" (Hilmar Hoffmann). "Anti-Semitic subversion was almost as taboo on the screen as concentration camps or sterilization, for example", writes Siegfried Kracauer. But the Oranienburg concentration camp was shown in an early newsreel and a short film, and books being burned, anti-Semitic pogroms and forced labour (purging the Jewish quarters in Riga and Wilna, acts of anti-Semitic violence, deportation) were deliberately addressed in newsreels and documentary shorts, along with "euthanasia" and sterilization in *Victims of the Past*.

In September 1939 Goebbels was working on the first manuscripts for war propaganda films. Documentary supporting films and shorts, working alongside the newsreels, had to fulfil the difficult task of compensating for the lack of recent propaganda in feature films. Here too the early stages were tough. The Ufa board stated "that 7 of the 10 manuscripts submitted to the Propaganda Ministry for propaganda films to be made in Kulturfilm form have been accepted",[1105] but Goebbels complains shortly afterwards: "Examined a few film manuscripts for war propaganda. Mostly unusable. Leading articles, but not films that must work from images, not from words." (3.10.1939)

This led to films like *Waffenschmiede Deutschland* ("Arms Foundry Germany"), *Luftschutz* ("Civil Air Defence"), *Aufbau im Osten* ("Build-up in the East") and *Helfende Hände* ("Helping Hands"), which Goebbels ended up by praising in their final versions. They were all in the cinemas in the early months of 1940.[1106] Goebbels felt that a lighter variant could be an important artistic device for educational films, as in an "Ufa propaganda film about air raid precautions, which tries a humorous approach, and very successful it is too". (2.11.1939) These films were intended, unlike the more ideological or instructive films, to familiarize people with the new measures and rules of behaviour during the war. After a few mistakes,[1107] which Goebbels blamed on inadequate examination of the manuscripts,[1108] he stressed at the Ministers' Conference on 3 November 1939 that "care (should) be taken that these films are not over-saturated philosophically; they should show cinemagoers the measures and difficult situations that are to be dealt with in a light and humorous form."[1109] He pursues the theme in the diary: "I criticize the most recent propaganda films: they are too didactic for my taste. The raised index finger is an evil." (4.11.1939) If undesirable behaviour is to be denounced, wrote Goebbels in February 1940, then the approach to follow is "making mistakes look ridiculous".[1110]

When dealing with "popular education", and especially in the case of actual ideological production, Goebbels relies on more concentration, simplicity, constant repetition and succinctness, following Hitler's propaganda maxims that have been valid since *Mein Kampf*: "Speak about propaganda films and their method. They are all too off-beat and too complicated. We assume too much of the people and so they simply don't understand us. I therefore insist that all our propaganda should be simpler." (11.11.1939) Goebbels also followed these guidelines while rapidly pushing forward his work on *The Eternal Jew* in those weeks, and on the documentary *Campaign in Poland*,[1111] which was put together from the first war newsreels. Goebbels' persisting discontent with propaganda films in the first few months of the war also led to the above-mentioned personnel changes at DFG.

Goebbels is particularly concerned with the commentary for the films: "Then the Minister criticized the propaganda film *Die Erde ruft* ("The Soil Is Calling"), which has good images but a poor text", runs a note in the minutes of the Ministers' Conference about a Hitler Youth film.[1112] As with *Michelangelo* and *Jahre der Entscheidung*, it was Goebbels' top priority that text and image should be consistent with each other. This was also behind a quarrel about the "anti-Bolshevik" training film *Wenn morgen Krieg wäre* ("If War Came Tomorrow"), which was assembled from Soviet feature films. The Propaganda Ministry film department passed the film, commissioned by Rosenberg's office in 1944, "only for restricted use at NSDAP training evenings".[1113] Goebbels provides us with a reason, not without a swipe at his opponent: "A propaganda film put together by Rosenberg's office from captured Soviet films shows me how some Party and state institutions still stand as far as Bolshevism is concerned. A dull speaker reads a theoretical text on the compilation of these film excerpts. But the images are so powerful and impressive that they are totally convincing for the viewer. Imagine what it would be like if dilettantes of this kind were in charge of German propaganda. It would very quickly unleash absolute chaos in terms of morale. I am unfortunately compelled to ban this film compilation." (29.10.1944)

Rosenberg did try to get the fifteen copies that had been made released at least for showing to a "limited circle of participants", but passed a message to Goebbels, showing unusual concord: "Reichsleiter Rosenberg entirely agrees with the Herr Minister that the powerful pictorial effect in the film cannot be neutralized by the speaker."[1114]

When anti-American propaganda started early in 1939 – Goebbels was thinking if banning American feature films at the same time – the Propaganda Minstry suggested to Ufa that a "film should be made from existing American newsreel material about the lack of culture in America".[1115] The Ufa board responded evasively at first by pointing out "existing contracts" with American newsreel firms and that Ufa held no rights over the material. As German policy before 1941 was aimed at not giving America any reason for entering the war there were smear campaigns in the press but no provocative films, which – if screened in America – might have been useful to Roosevelt's interventionist line (this slant was also largely omitted in feature films).[1116] Anti-American propaganda films were then made even before the US entered the war (*Rund um die Freiheitsstatue* / "Around the Statue of Liberty"), which presented a picture of America made up of social barbarity, bizarre amusements and brutal crime. Goebbels himself had a markedly anti-American attitude, even though he admired may Hollywood films. He regularly speaks of a "civilization desert" (27.5.1941) and remarks on 28.7.1941 about a "film on cultural life in the USA": "I have never seen such a lack of culture accumulated in one place."[1117] Incidentally he names Fritz Hippler as the author of the film. Hippler has not previously been known as a maker of anti-American Hetzfilme.

The newsreel virtuoso

The German weekly wartime newsreels, as documents of manipulated reality of historical importance were for a time the most effective propaganda device that the National Socialist had at their disposal. Their demagogic impact, the suggestive power of the authentic images, the carefully composed' post-dubbed soundtrack, effective musical effects and the revolutionary technique made these propaganda films in the guise of news films far superior to their Allied counterpart.

The battle reporting, experiencing the war from a cinema seat, particularly when it was not yet making itself much felt at home, made the newsreels more popular than may cinema films. The fiction of an ever-victorious Wehrmacht was made into a reality by the newsreels, and in fact was not really experienced until shown there.

The newsreel aesthetic made its mark on a whole generation of viewers and persisted into the sixties. Here we should not underestimate the potential for indoctrination, which lasted well into the post-war period, and the psychological (after-)effect of the racist "anti-Bolshevik" smears purveyed by the newsreels with their images of Asiatic "subhumans".

The newsreels were a educational device with a mass impact, serving as a vehicle for the whole range of shiny National Socialist ideology, together with humorously instructive films like *Tran und Helle*.

Neglect before the war?

Even the German weekly newsreels were not under the Nazis' control from the first day onwards. There were still many news films made on a non-centralized basis by various private film companies turning out uninhibited Nazi propaganda. But, like the first, favour-currying German nationalist films, this did not satisfy the propagandists around Goebbels.

It was not until May 1935 that an institution was created to bring German newsreels under state control. This was the "Deutsches Film-Nachrichtenbüro" ("German film news office"), under the direction of Hans Weidemann. At first all it did was pass on general subject requirements to the newsreel producers, and "co-ordinated the individual newsreel editions and supervised the arrangement of their contents and artistic design".[1118] A law passed to make film reporting easier on 30 April 1936 also fixed state deregulation of copyright and the privileged status of a uniformed group of "officially sanctioned film reporters". Weidemann and his colleagues only exercised post-censorship over the four different weekly newsreels, divided according to regions – Ufa-Tonwoche, Deulig-Tonwoche, Fox-Tönende Wochenschau and Bavaria, or Tobis-Woche from 1939 – without detailed interference into the creative process. But they did insist on a "tight thematic structure for the NS newsreel"[1119] in 1935/36, concentrating on parades, Party rallies, state visits and the national community's development achievements. State supervision of the newsreels was kept secret from the public at first.

As far as we can see from the material at present available, Goebbels first comment on a newsreel was in the entry for 13.7.1935.[1120] He mentions the news films indifferently and extremely rarely. This seems to confirm the assumption that the National Socialists tended to underestimate the newsreel in the first years after coming to power.[1121] Goebbels remains a passive consumer for longer than he did with films, and contents himself with expressing the highest praise: "Newsreels are the most captivating and dramatic things you can see today", he enthuses on 30.12.1935. Goebbels deliberately contrasts newsreels with light entertainment films, which he considers to be goods for the masses whose products are often only "utter nonsense": "in contrasts, the newsreels are real life". (8.1.1936) He picks out successful treatments of state propaganda events like the open of the winter relief fund in particular, his own PR campaigns ("delightful newsreel with my Christmas party", 31.1.1936), the Olympics (18.8.1936) or Party parades: "And then the newsreel of the 10th anniversary in Berlin. On a huge scale and delightful, The speeches come over wonderfully, especially the Führer's." (8.11.1936) Goebbels' comments are positive without exception in 1935/36, but it is only very rarely possible to link them with a particular studio because the individual editions are so uniform in content: "good newsreels, as ever", he announces on 2.9.1936.[1122]

Uninhibited striving for power and influence down to the last detail can be observed in the case of feature films by 1936 at the latest, but until mid 1938 Goebbels gives no sign of personal interest in using the newsreels for specific pieces of political agitation. The most striking example of this is that there are no "anti-Bolshevik" newsreel subjects from 1935 to June 1941.[1123] It seems as though the Propaganda Minister was satisfied with the above-mentioned pictorial reports about "positive development work" and the constant parades of National Socialist politicians. It would be going too far to accuse the newsreels of lacking in manipulative qualities up to 1938, but they were still not perceived as a propaganda device and there was also a lack of psychologically polished concepts. The decree of control of the newsreel practised by the Minister and also by Hitler remains hard to establish. The "Führer" seems merely to have carried out a kind of post-censorship of the Ufa-Tonwoche; he at least had a few subjects that he found distasteful removed: "Führer rings up: he has a few pieces cut out of the newsreel."[1124] (7.8.1937) It is clear that sporadic criticism came from Party organizations who did not feel that they had been put in the picture sufficiently.[1125]

Goebbels was caused a lot of problems by the newsreels' lack of topicality and range. By autumn 1938 only just under seven per cent of German viewers (discounting Austria and the Sudetenland) were able to see the latest edition. Also the number of copies in circulation was low – all four producers added up to about 400 copies per week.[1126] Even though very little material was "squandered on non-political themes",[1127] many edition spent weeks circulating round the cinemas, and their content was completely out of date, which restricted the possibilities of topical political reporting or the effectiveness of propaganda subjects (thus for example when images of the occupation of the Rhineland were not to be seen until weeks later). Goebbels was looking for ways out of this in late 1937,[1128] spurred on by reproofs from Hitler. He looked at "a number of newsreels" with him on 10.1.1938 in the Reich Chancellery: "Some of them are very clumsily presented. I shall give Weidemann a good talking to." The day after Goebbels again sums up by saying that the newsreels are "not political enough and too dull".

But then the newsreel shifted very firmly into Goebbels' and Hitler's field vision, just before the political and military crisis of summer 1938. The dictator examined numerous news film editions personally in this period,[1129] criticized them violently and issued new guidelines. He objected to the fact that "only shots of my person are taken at events" and insisted: "The detail of the events must be covered better." Hitler missed his favourite subjects like "new buildings going up" and – as a psychological preparation for military expansion – permanent glorification of the military: "The newsreels must be designed with more political acumen, thus for example show

shots of Czechoslovakia's nervous preparations now. Then at the end there must be a close-up of a German soldier. Not a week must go by without shots of the navy, the army and the Luftwaffe appearing."[1130]

As a consequence of this, Goebbels talked about a "plan for bringing our newsreels up to date politically" on 2.6.1938 and 15.6.1938. Shortly before this the Ufa board were still rejecting a "more instructive format for the newsreel"[1131] for fear of a diminishing effect on the public through too much politics. Goebbels himself presented the situation in a rather less dramatic light. He always agrees with Hitler's criticisms, but does not seem to have been dissatisfied with the newsreels. He had little reason to be, as he was a major presence on the screen. The Ufa and Deulig newsreels alone presented five different speeches by the Propaganda Minister in the period from 1 June to 6 July 1938, in other words in just under five weeks.

After repeated expressions of displeasure from Hitler ("The Führer has rightly found fault with out political newsreels", 3.8.1938)[1132] Goebbels did admit that perhaps he had been too lax in his control of news films: "I give orders that they are to be presented to me in advance on each occasion." But even now this regularly didn't happen.[1133] And on top of this, Goebbels changed the design of the editing and montage of the newsreels, though with not much success: "We see the newsreel in its new form. But the different images are too abrupt, and therefore no good at all."[1134] (20.8.1938) Then the militarization of the newsreel requested by Hitler started to appear with undue clarity in the editions from late September 1938 (e.g. DTW 352/1938/Z: 28.9.1938).

In late October 1938 Goebbels issued a few instructions making it compulsory for a newsreel to be shown at the beginning of every cinema programme; as well as this it became commercially more attractive for cinema-owners to present the most recent edition of the newsreel on each occasion.[1135] A fund fed by the film companies was set up to improve financial provision for newsreels, and the Propaganda Ministry issued a few guidelines, though admittedly they were very vague, aiming at more heroism and a more serious approach.[1136]

It was only renewed criticism from Hitler in December 1938[1137] – which was doubly threatening for Goebbels because he had been weakened by the Baarova affair – that seemed to trigger fundamental reforms in newsreel production: the "Deutsche Wochenschau-Zentrale" ("German newsreel headquarters") was founded at the Propaganda Ministry in January 1939. Fritz Hippler, who had been Weidemann's assistant until them, became director of the new institution on 1 February.[1138] The film companies' newsreel departments remained responsible for actually creating the newsreels, but the Ministry guidelines show increased possibilities for intervention: "(The Deutsche Wochenschau-Zentrale) plans, designs and distributes the individual subjects to be shot, in regular working meetings with the newsreel directors.."[1139] Goebbels was claiming the first successes even before the reorganization process was completed[1140]: "A good newsreel. The Führer is very satisfied with it now." (20.1.1939)

Surprising enough, Goebbels did not bother with the newsreel in 1939 until the summer, there is not even any sign of a regular "final edit".[1141] There are barely half a dozen relevant comments from February to July 1939, far fewer than one would expect, even allowing for Goebbels' extended absence from Berlin. Goebbels apparently did not see newsreels until the day they were censored in summer 1939 – and sometimes even later. They were still not always perfect: "a few good newsreels: unfortunately again too much America" (29.6.1939), is his reaction to the editions for late July 1939.[1142]

Organization and censorship procedures after the outbreak of war

Even though we cannot be clear about Goebbels' involvement, the year the war broke out saw the emergence of some highly effective propaganda messages, created with great technical refinement, including the famous newsreel for Hitler's 50th birthday.[1143] Then in the last six weeks before the outbreak of war Goebbels' careful work on the newsreels, which are quite unmistakably preparing for war, cannot be overlooked. This is shown quite unambiguously in his comments on the last two August editions, which are entirely dominated by the Wehrmacht making ready for invasion.[1144]

All the sound, pictures and other reportage for this were provided by the "Propagandakompanien" (PK groups), which had been formed as early as autumn 1938/39. Various agreements were made between the Propaganda Ministry and the Supreme Command of the Wehrmacht (OKW) in 1938/39, establishing far-reaching powers of intervention for the military,[1145] which Goebbels, hardly surprisingly, criticized sharply and regularly, similarly to his approach to Hitler's press officer Dietrich. As soldiers, the PK Groups were subject to the Wehrmacht. They often included over a hundred men, and were allotted to the individual services. The teams were made up of photographers, journalists, cameramen and radio announcers, and also laboratory technicians and film processors.[1146] There is constant criticism of these Wehrmacht's propaganda units from 1939 to 1943 – though in public Goebbels claimed some of the credit for the teams' admired propaganda work for himself.[1147] On 6.10.1939 he writes as follows about the "work of the prop. companies": "They are too militarily drilled, and this cannot develop any proper initiatives. … They are just soldiers, not propagandists." Whenever the newsreel's effectiveness diminished, Goebbels complained about the "failure of the PKs" (9.1.1940): sometimes he criticized their organization for being "too bureaucratic" (9.5.1941), and then again the constant "reorganizations" of the propaganda units are responsible for poor material from the fronts.[1148]

On several occasion he tried to gain more direct access to the PKs and their material for the Propaganda Ministry, without intervention from the OKW. But his repeated announcements that he was going to take the Wehrmacht propaganda department away from the OKW via Hitler[1149] remained ineffective. The OKW for their part disliked the newsreel makers' practice of staging a kind of personality cult involving individual generals who were notably faithful to the National Socialists, or Field Marshall Rommel, whom Goebbels particularly admired.[1150] Another major bone of contention between Goebbels and the OKW was the involvement of the military censorship authorities in releasing the PK groups material for the newsreel. On 18.2. 1941 the Minister complained, with his eye on "the O.K.H., who are taking the best people, cameramen and editors away from me": "The newsreel work is getting stuck everywhere, held up by censorship authorities, interference and similar things." The use of shots of the most recently developed weapons, like "railway gun", for example (17.8.1940) or the V1/V2 rockets, regularly met with objections from the censor.[1151] Goebbels also held the military censors responsible for the limited propaganda effect of the mass graves found in Katyn in the newsreels in May 1943.

After Hitler and Goebbels had got over their enthusiasm for the first wartime newsreels,[1152] the "Sitzkrieg" ("waiting war") in the west caused increasing technical difficulties, "lack of material" (7.11.1939) and first signs of being unsure how to handle non-military subjects. (21.11. 1939) This led to revision of the newsreels on the one hand (14.11.1939) and then made the dictator impatient as he was missing the heroic battle images. (28.11.1939. 10.12.1939) Finally Hitler called Goebbels' film propaganda sharply to account at his midday round table talk on 11.12. 1939, criticizing "the newsreels above all",[1153] as Goebbels admitted. Goebbels tried to make up for these embarrassing reproaches by complaining about the "bad French newsreels" (12.12. 1939) or the PK groups inability to organize their cameramen.[1154] (10./11.1.1940)

Immediately after the outbreak of war the four different newsreel editions were brought together to improve concentration and control. They retained opening credits that differed region by region at first for commercial reasons,[1155] but this also disappeared in June 1940 in favour of the uniform title Deutsche Wochenschau. Even before this, Goebbels had tried to find a way to get rid of the Fox Tönende Wochenschau, which was owned by the American film company Fox.[1156] The Ufa subsidiary Deutsche Wochenschau GmbH took over the powers of the Deutsche Wochenschau-Zentrale on 17 November 1940.[1157] This also underlined the newsreel's foreign ambitions to acquire a monopoly in Europe or in the neutral states with a specially compiled foreign edition.[1158] By now the PK groups had an army of over 14,000 members, and 1,000 copies went into occupied and neutral foreign countries, with versions in numerous European languages.

Hitler's discontent with the newsreels' approach and content made a considerable impact on almost all changes of organization and personnel. This was the case in December 1939/January 1940, and again in winter 1940/41. Goebbels was obviously not happy himself with the way in which the newsreels were performing. In January 1941 he once more had to announce that a newsreel edition had "not pleased the Führer". (14.1.1941) He therefore immediately announced an extensive reshuffle and "a series of organizational changes", "above all to meet the Führer's entirely justifiable requests": "The newsreel must have its own editor-in-chief …, clear statutes and a fixed working programme."[1159] (15.1.1941)

The number of copies available was raised immediately in September 1939, and then successively put up again until the war started in the west; in May a Ministry directive was suggesting at least 2,000 copies, with their circulation period halved from eight to four weeks.[1160] Information about the number of copies actually used fluctuate from 1700 to about 2,400 in 1943.[1161] The films also got longer, extending from about 300 to 1200 metres (approx. 40 minutes), which still represented only about four per cent of the material shot each week.

In May 1940, improved distribution and other organizational measures to strengthen the "propaganda weapon" were joined by the establishment of special newsreel cinemas, which screened the current edition for twelve hours a day, along with shorts and documentaries.[1162] Cinema attendances rose by almost 90 per cent from June 1939 to June 1940. This is not due solely to the popularity of the newsreel, but also to the general cinema boom,[1163] but this upturn did mean that the weekly propaganda slogans reached an enormous audience. In spring and summer 1940 many viewers went to the cinema just to see the newsreel, but others preferred – especially at times when little was happening – to wait in the foyer until the newsreel was over and then to go into the cinema just for the main film. Goebbels responded to this by ordering that the five minute break between the supporting programme and the feature film should be abolished and the box-office closed after the performance began, but this could obviously not be put into practice without some little difficulty.[1164]

From September 1939 to autumn 1944 at least Goebbels' diary, with next to no exceptions, comments on every newsreel edition. If the preliminary work or final examination were done without him, he mentions this specifically.[1165] The Propaganda Minister dedicated himself to detailed work on the newsreel editions twice a week as a rule, at first on Tuesday or Wednesday evening (later the rough-cut version was handed over as early as Sunday, without word or music), but it could be as many as four times a week. He spent an astonishing proportion of his time on newsreel work during the war. Fritz Hippler describes how the films were handled. This process usually took place in Goebbels' home in Schwanenwerder after the outbreak of war: "As a complete change from previous arrangements, I now had, with immediate effect, to appear in Goebbels' house every Saturday, Sunday, Monday and Tuesday evening, at the weekend to see the latest German feature films, then early in the week the silent rough cut of the newsreel, for which I read the text aloud, and then with the final cut, the music, which had now been added, and the revised text."[1166]

Goebbels lavished praise on the newsreels in his film speeches in February 1941 and February 1942, and then said of his own involvement "that I have myself sacrificed two evenings a week since the beginning of the war so that it is produced in a truly exemplary fashion".[1167] From early in 1941 permanent secretary Gutterer seems to have been more actively involved in the censorship process, along with Goebbels and Hippler.[1168] Heinrich Roellenbleg, until 1939 director of the newsreel department at Tobis/Bavaria, the newsreel boss at Ufa and from November 1940 managing director and editor-in-chief of the Deutsche Wochenschau GmbH, is scarcely mentioned in this context. The notes give no idea of the precise hierarchy within the censorship process, but on 28.6.1943 Goebbels writes as follows about mistaken assessments in the lower official channels at the preliminary examination stage: "I am very annoyed that these pictures were allowed through by the Staatssekretär." If Goebbels is to be believed, the propaganda impact of the newsreel suffered from the fact that as minister responsible for censorship he ranked behind Hitler and the OKW: "The military men in the Führer's headquartes have actually succeeded in getting the Katyn shots cut out of the newsreel again. Unfortunately the Führer does not have time to see them personally and may possible be prepared to release them for the next newsreel." (28.4.1943)

Goebbels' aesthetic and technical principles

Goebbels followed certain maxims in his meticulous work on the newsreels that were borrowed from the principles applied to making propaganda and documentary films: the overall effect was derived from perfectly composed use of commentary, music and montage; authenticity was added by the sound accompaniments and the use of tricks or map details. Logical scripting and an atmosphere aimed entirely at realism avoided artificially staged scenes, with a very few exceptions, so that "the visual and acoustic design fitted in completely with the prescribed content guidelines".[1169] This all relied on a perfectly functioning technical system for acquiring material, copying and distribution, and this was constantly improved in the course of the war. Shortly before the invasion of the Soviet Union the PK groups had mobile developing and copying apparatus at their disposal, which for Goebbels was a "technical miracle". (10.6.1941)

It was crucial for Goebbels as part of a coherent overall composition that a balanced relationship of commentary, images and music should be achieved. One component could be made stronger to compensate for weaknesses in the others. This applied mainly to the use of music, dynamic editing sequences and a spirited commentary. At critical times, when topicality was at a premium and only old shots were available, "it was mainly the commentary, supported by music and sound, that was allotted the task of interpreting the old images in such a way that they did justice to the contemporary events".[1170] A serious commentary, in keeping with the war situation, about the "severity of the fighting" could be used in association with images of military success to colour the statement subliminally and to give the viewer the desired impression: a feeling of objective information combined with fundamental confidence. Many newsreel commentaries came directly from Goebbels, right down to the smallest refinement in the formulation.

If there were no spectacular shots of battles, then Goebbels tried "to edit material, make the commentary more powerful and to make sure that the music used can try to add in its own right the power that is lacking in the images" (16.7.1941) or simply "to compensate for inadequacies by a particularly vivid musical accompaniment" (29.7.1941):[1171] "I now feel increasingly strongly that the newsreel should have a particularly effective musical accompaniment", he wrote on 4.8. 1941 about typical and varied pieces of music in DW no. 570, accompanying images of Russian prisoners and a visit to the front by Hitler. At the same Goebbels announced that the soundtracks are to be better archived, "so that in future the eternal search for effective musical accompaniments can be kept to a minimum".[1172] DW no. 558 was considered mediocre at first, "but it is good now that it has a lively musical accompaniment" (12.5.1941): the shots of the German advance into Egypt are disappointingly ordinary, but they are supported by a particularly high proportion of marches and soldiers' songs. Even in May 1944, when Goebbels was paying less attention to the newsreels, he specifically asked the producers to pay more attention to the music, sound effects and the re-appointment of the old speaker of the commentary whose thrilling voice of the master-race had been a key feature of the newsreel since 1940.[1173]

One thing that clearly did not increase the propaganda impact of the newsreels was that Hitler stubbornly refused – and this was anyway difficult to implement – to have his speeches shown in the newsreel with the original soundtrack. Goebbels was irritated by public criticism of the lack of the "Führer's" voice, and regularly tried to get him to change his mind, but to no avail.[1174] Thus the newsreel, with few exceptions (mainly to be seen in 1944) had to manage without the original soundtrack for clips from speeches by other leading National Socialist politicians as well, so that this could be passed off as a consistent creative concept. When Goebbels' "total war" speech in DW 651 surprisingly featured the original sound, the public apparently saw this break with tradition as suggesting that Hitler's speeches would soon be heard with the original soundtrack again. But then in DW 655 Hitler's words were again spoken by the commentator, which made the viewers very disappointed and increasingly discontented.[1175]

There was scarcely an alternative choice of film stock available. The black-and-white stock used for the newsreels is now said to have a particular suggestive force and aesthetic appeal, but Goebbels certainly does not seem to have preferred it over colour film, which was revolutionary at the time: "I had a number of colour newsreels of the eastern campaign shown in the evening. They have come out extraordinarily well. It is quite clear that a colour newsreel in far more effective than a black-and-white one. However, we don't have the technical facilities to copy them on a large scale. But we do want to make some colour newsreels for key locations in Europe, so that we can undermine enemy film propaganda by the technical miracle of a colour newsreel alone."[1176] (5.4.1943)

Goebbels' ideas in the first year of the war can be illustrated in concrete terms from UTW no. 507, the second newsreel edition after the beginning of the western campaign. His comment: "Enchanting in its structure, pace, music and text. It will strike like lightning. I shall just pep the music up a bit in the first part." (23.5.1940) He apparently felt that the shots of Rotterdam on fire and badly damaged by German air raids at the beginning of the western campaign were themselves so "fiercely and remorselessly realistic"[1177] (24.5.1940) that he passed them only when linked with a commentary that skilfully justified the invasion of Holland and glorified breaking through the Maginot line. He also felt it necessary to "have (the newsreel) justified in more detail in the press", to deal with any possible sympathy on the part of German viewers by underlining neutral Holland's alleged responsibility for the war. Several trick shots using maps structure the course of events and introduce the rapidly changing military theatres or advances, accompanied by march music. Captured French soldiers, mainly North Africans, are juxtaposed with German soldiers storming heroically onward or sleeping peacefully between the battles.

51. Emblem of the German war newsreels from 1940.

This stylistic device of constantly contrasting juxtaposition is to be found in a lot of newsreels: the German heroism of Aryan soldiers is contrasted with the cowardly enemy soldiers, usually North Africans on the French side and "Asiatics" on the Russian side, or blossoming German landscapes or set against wretched conditions in the conquered territories.[1178] Goebbels used this approach in the intelligence war as well: "I am building the enemy's lies about Charkov into the newsreel commentary. It has a positively devastating effect on the enemy propaganda in the context of the images shown there. For example, when we see the battlefield strewn with destroyed enemy weapons and the corpses of dead Bolsheviks, and the commentator says that Moscow has announced that they intend to start planting sugar beet here again, that is a contrast that could not be made more graphically and convincingly."[1179] (1.6.1942)

Goebbels used what he called "Auflockerung" – variety, relief – as a particular stylistic device for newsreels. This involved background images, which were intended, in the winter in particular, to cover up the temporary lack of effective military footage and at the same time to break up the rigid structure of the newsreel with its constant repetition of almost identical battle images. Sequences about "life behind the front" were introduced to provide the desired variety (providing and caring for soldiers, fun and leisure activities during lulls in the fighting), and then to an increasing extent "home subjects" as well, including sport, views of towns, cultural and entertainment events etc., images intended to underline the solidarity of the "home front" (women's community service work, armaments production). The first systematic use of this innovation dates from the start of crises in the Russian campaign in late summer 1941, when Goebbels was working on the newsreels more intensively than ever before, and increasingly realized how monotonous they were: "We are hearing some criticism of the newsreels: people say that it keeps repeating the same shots and that there is too little variety. I will have a much closer look at this problem."[1180] (25.8.1941)On the same day he wrote that DW no. 573 "has not come off very well, it presents the same images as the previous one and offers too little variety in its portrayal of background and people". Goebbels feared that showing the same battle pictures over and over again would lead to "emptiness and stagnation", and in 7.9.1941 he is intending to look for "new material and subjects". This was sometimes a difficult balancing act, as the "variety" and peaceful background footage could quickly raise false hopes for the watchful public: thus DW no. 575 (censored: 17.9.1941) came out "too peaceful and idyllic": "It certainly shows a huge amount of interesting material about supplies, about rest and convalescent horses and things like that; but we have not yet reached a stage in the east where we can do without battle pictures entirely. And so I restructure the front footage again during the night, and paste in a few real battle scenes. This means that the background material does not disappear, but that it is supported by the battle scenes. I think this is necessary for psychological reasons as well. If we start using the newsreel just to show background material in this situation the audience will conclude that we intend to direct public interest gradually towards ending the fighting in the east. This is not the case ... ."[1181] (15.9.1941)

But overall the more peaceful scenes and home images were a great success. The Security Service praised the fact that "these scenes were also of considerable value as propaganda as they show the soldiers' relatives that war is not all about battles and danger". Soldiers' wives and mothers allowed themselves to be consoled by the newsreel's idyll of the front for a time. But it has to be said that as the war continues, Goebbels often gives the impression that these background shots could always be used as a trump card in phases of military stagnation, and successfully every time. His frantic veering between more battles and then a preponderance of home subjects followed a popular mood that fluctuated just as much. He only rarely admits that the subjects providing variety and entertainment – from 1942 they also included popular sporting events of a definitely escapist nature[1182] – had their limitations, or that problems arose when presenting a light-hearted idyll at the front.

In the event, a change of subject was not in itself enough to maintain interest in the newsreels, so Goebbels also speculated on the public's thirst for sensation: all the available technical resources were regularly used to edit in particularly spectacular action shots of aerial battles and U-Boot engagements. These generally had the desired effect on the public.[1183] Cameras were attached to racing aircraft and diving U-Boots, and Goebbels was able to thrill to "images of the war in the air like there have never been before". (16.1.1944) As well as this he often puzzled for days over effective trick shots with maps. (26.10./1.11.1942) But each action-packed enhancement of the newsreels also increased the danger of disappointment and also the sinking feeling in the audience if there were no pictures of this kind.

The newsreels that were successful with the public certainly helped to boost the cinema boom in their most effective phase. Goebbels himself said in public that the newsreel was the "German cinema's great draw", and summed up on 20.2.1941: "The newsreel has prepared the way for the feature film, and at the end of the war film itself will undoubtedly be and remain one of the most important devices for leading and influencing the people."[1184] The newsreel also influenced the aesthetics and content of some feature films that appeared in the early stages, in 1940/41: they include *Request Concert*, *Stukas*, *Über alles in der Welt*. Goebbels was not overly enthusiastic about these "contemporary" or "real" films. They were so tightly linked with the heroic idea of victorious German troops that they were discontinued after the Blitzkrieg newsreels. But the state of tension between newsreels and feature films, which first became apparent in the French campaign, remained critical for only a short time.[1185] Goebbels publicly addressed this "apparently almost unbridgeable gulf ... between the realistic presentation of the war in the newsreel and in German films made in peacetime"[1186] during the offensives of 1939 and 1940, and made skilful play of the fact that a small number of cinemagoers had left the cinema after the newsreel and before mediocre feature films. However, it is not quite true that comedies and other lighter films were "almost ousted by the newsreels for months on end", and did not start to hold their own again until late 1940[1187]: the ban imposed on premières of "shallow" light entertainment films in May and June did not last for long, and large-scale deployment of political films in German cinemas began in late autumn 1940.

There was also a tension between newsreels and documentary films. Goebbels discusses this difficult line of demarcation in the context of DW no. 612, which was deliberately intended to be innovative and varied in terms of the rigid newsreel scheme. It was devoted exclusively to glorifying the achievements of German arms production and Goebbels announced it expectantly and portentously.[1188] When the public reacted less than positively,[1189] he looked for an explanation: "If the newsreel is forced into the straitjacket of documentary presentation, then it will undoubtedly lose a great deal of its immediate charm. This is demonstrated by the new and detailed presentation of our armaments industry in the last newsreel, which is by no means as appealing to the public as we had anticipated."

Overall supervision by the "Führer"

Adolf Hitler stepped down as the chief censor of feature films after the beginning of the war, but he continued to have the most recent edition of the newsreel shown to him. Hitler was not just intensely interested in German news films;[1190] his Minister's diaries even give the impression that in the years immediately before the war and in the early stages of the war the dictator constantly campaigned for the newsreels to be increasingly concerned with propaganda. If he had not been constantly breathing down Goebbels' neck, even if all he uttered were vague expressions of displeasure, the newsreels would perhaps nor have achieved their indisputable mass effectiveness. Despite all its vain posing and self-aggrandizement, Goebbels' diary does reveal a great deal about Hitler's creative demands, which are not recorded anywhere else.

Hitler and his headquarters had the last word, regardless of whether it was about correcting individual subjects, changing commentaries, "individual suggestions about musical and sound accompaniment" (30.6.1942) or the fundamental line adopted for news policy. Goebbels was often unsure what direction he should or could take, particularly when it came to informing the public via newsreels. For example, he found shots of German victories on the North African front in 1941 "impressive and in part unique". But he doubts "whether we can show these shots in such extended form at the moment. They speak for us very positively, but we never know how things in North Africa will develop. There there is no doubt that I need a decision from the Führer."[1191] Clear differences of opinion between the two propaganda merchants about the degree of news-policy realism the newsreel could allow itself began to make themselves felt as the war situation deteriorated after 1942. Unlike his Propaganda Minister, Hitler pursued a fairly strong line on the question of informing the public about the military situation. He wanted the newsreels to come up with shots of advancing troops and to "portray German heroism, whether there was any fighting going on or not".[1192] For instance, Goebbels was doubtful about the effectiveness of DW no. 631 in early October 1942: he felt that the shots at the front did not add anything new, were merely repetitive, and that "in the long run more home subjects" would have to be built into the newsreels. But he had to go into retreat on the very same day, after a meeting with Hitler: despite the standstill at the front, the dictator did not want "us to replace war subjects with domestic subjects". "The Führer still has operations in mind", says Goebbels, wriggling out of it, "and while that is the case we should still restrict ourselves mainly to material from the front." (4.10.1942) In subsequent weeks there were some reports from Berlin or Weimar, but they were few and far between compared with the military shots.

Hitler was certainly significantly involved in the consequent loss of credibility suffered by the newsreel. And there was now no secret made of the fact that, as Goebbels said in his speech to the film industry in February 1942, the newsreels were "examined by the Führer as well, almost at the last minute".

Hitler was particularly interested in images of large and decisive battles. He also liked highly racist and political sequences about Russian "atrocities" or newsreel editions in which he appeared himself. He still did this very frequently from 1939 to 1941. The DW no. 557 edition contains shots of Hitler making his Reichstag speech on 29 April and also of his visit to Austria: "The Führer thinks that this is technically the best one we have yet produced." (9.5.1941) Edition DW no. 514 was also praised (9.7.1940): almost 40 per cent of this consisted of shots of Hitler (with soldiers, visiting a cathedral). Hitler must also have been delighted with scenes dealing with revenge for the Treaty of Versailles, including for example the recovery from Compiègne of the train in which the German capitulation was signed in 1918 (including blowing up the monument there), or also a look back at the breaking of the Maginot Line.

There is sometimes a certain discrepancy between Hitler's opinion of the newsreel and Goebbels' own. Hitler did praise some editions that Goebbels found very weak: "The Führer is extraordinarily pleased with it despite its somewhat shaky character", noted Goebbels on 18.11.1941 about DW no. 585, even though this edition contained careful hints about the halting advance on Moscow (its original soundtrack: "Everything threatens to get stuck in this clay and filth"), but scarcely any succinct battle scenes.[1193] The explanation probably lay in shots of captured Russian soldiers, who are called a "special selection of Jews", and in sequences showing slums in the Soviet Union ("They were living worse than cattle").

Hitler was less bothered about the aesthetic or textual unity of the newsreels than about an uncompromising attitude to propaganda. The very first "anti-Bolshevik" newsreel after the beginning of the war consisted of skilfully compiled scenes, with an ingenious commentary, showing so-called atrocities involving Ukrainian civilian victims of the Red Army in Lemberg.[1194] Goebbels found this "a true work of cinematic and propaganda art" (10.7.1941), and Hitler was most enthusiastic about it.[1195] He promptly demanded more similarly cruel and brutal scenes for the next edition, while Goebbels obviously had certain reservations and preferred "to spare the relatives of the soldiers fighting in Russia the fear that these images would produce".[1196] The next newsreel did contain some anti-Semitic subjects, but Hitler's request about the Lemberg shots was not addressed until the next edition, probably so that audience reaction could be assessed first.[1197]

Hitler's corrections are even evident in places where Goebbels does not mention them. Alarmed by the catastrophe in Stalingrad, Goebbels thinks on 24.1.1943 that the planned newsreel focus on themes of "National Socialist achievements" as part of a detailed retrospective of ten years of National Socialist government should be cancelled: "But now, given the impression made by Stalingrad, these images are no longer effective. We cannot show shots of the parade down Wilhelmstraße or the cutting of the first turf for the Reich autobahns. All this fades into insignificance when confronted with heroic deaths at the front. I am therefore knocking the whole newsreel on the head, and intend not to refer to 30 January at all and showing more pictures from the front. We will have to content ourselves with just tackling 30 January retrospectively in the following week." But not only the next newsreel but one, as Goebbels intended, but the very next one, DW no. 647/27.1.1943, showed in detail the very subjects that the Propaganda Minster intended "not to refer" to: eliminating unemployment, housing construction, arts-related buildings, social aid schemes etc. – in other words Hitler's own pet themes: he obviously wanted to see proper attention paid to the auspicious date.[1198] DW no. 648/3.2.1943 contains a similar sequence of images about the celebration of the "seizure of power" in Berlin.

Hitler was euphoric about the likelihood of a German victory again[1199] in spring and summer 1942, and it seems that he felt the successful spring offensive on the southern front had not been presented heroically enough. Goebbels praises the first newsreel about the offensive, DW no. 611, which starts with the fighting on the Kerch peninsula, as "brilliantly successful and above all, it could not possibly be more up to date", on 18. and 19.5.1942. However, shortly afterwards he admits that there were problems with an incoherent and indecisive presentation of the fighting near Kharkov in DW no. 613: "We are having great difficulties with the newsreels again. The Führer is asking something rather more than we can deliver of the newsreels. Newsreels are not able to provide a perfectly finished documentary film every time. They can only use the material that is available to them at that time. Documenting a battle is a job for a documentary film, as the name suggests, at a later stage". (3.6.1942) Despite this, Goebbels proceeded particularly carefully with further treatment of the subject of Charkov, and in this case covered himself by close co-operation with the "officers of the general staff". Finally he is convinced "that we can now meet the Führer's wishes; he will be very pleased with this method of presentation".[1200] (8.6.1942) The entries for subsequent weeks seem to confirm that the "Führer" is pleased: "The newsreel is his favourite child in the film field. He thinks that the most recent newsreel in particular, featuring the fighting in and around Dieppe, is the best that we have produced so far." (21.8.1942)

The diaries do not provide us with seamless information about the editions Hitler actually saw during the rest of the war. Hitler's habitual interest in seeing the newsreels regularly and sometimes in the rough-cut version as well, seems to have waned after the end of the summer offensive in 1942. Instead of this, the "Führer's" headquarters took over the final review stage, although its responsibilities were not always clearly defined. From 1944/45 Hitler usually made decisions only about the release of images that were classified as secret.[1201] His last viewing of a German newsreel – to the best of our knowledge so far – is recorded on the diary entry for 23.1. 1945. This contained "shots of the V.2, which he found extraordinarily interesting". The last newsreel that Hitler and Goebbels saw together was, significantly, an American one. Both succumbed to enemy propaganda this time, drew far-reaching political conclusions from the images of rejoicing as General de Gaulle entered Paris and – just a curiosity – were amazed how like Goebbels' permanent secretary Hermann Esser de Gaulle seemed to be. (25.1.1945)

Guidelines on propaganda and content

The newsreels, as part of the mass media, were "tied into the National Socialist system of 'shaping' the information they chose to impart".[1202] They followed the official line on news policy,[1203] which in the war was on the one hand heavily dependent on the OKW and its information monopoly as far as military events were concerned, and also had to take Hitler's restrictive notions into account. Sometimes, as we can see from the difficulties the newsreel and other propaganda sources had in the sphere of "anti-Bolshevik" propaganda, this led to "a state of tension between programmatic aims and day-to-day political pragmatism":[1204] at first the newsreel producers hoped to be compensated for the contradictions that arose between various basic ideological convictions and national political necessities during the German-Russian non-aggression pact from 1939 to 1941. They intended to do this by using subtle cinematic devices (the Russian allies looked pale and subservient alongside the German soldiers),[1205] but this could not succeed in the long run.

Goebbels was definitely not in a position to fix the contents and priorities of the newsreels on his own. His scope was relatively heavily restricted by Hitler's interventions,, OKW censorship of military issues and the natural dominance exerted by the events of the war.

Co-ordination with the journalistic media was a key feature when choosing subjects for the war newsreels: aerial battles over England, "images of open hostilities between English and French prisoners and of the bestial meals eaten by black prisoners of war",[1206] the delicate matter of the evacuation of children from towns, mystical transfiguration of death through "links with Remembrance Day". (23.3.1943) The Security Service reports often made astonishingly precise comments even on the use of music and accompanying sound,[1207] and Goebbels tried to consider their suggestions and criticisms as far as possible.[1208]

Goebbels does not even mention many basic principles, like for example the fact, constantly repeated later, that the newsreels never showed dead German soldiers, but instead alluded to the mass deaths of Wehrmacht soldiers only indirectly, in scenes of "comrades'" funerals. He treats the problems associated with this only superficially: corpses of enemy soldiers, above all members of the Red Army, were shown in detail, which was registered as attentively and with no less concern by the public than they showed for silence about the German dead.[1209] Goebbels contents himself with the terse admission that the newsreel footage about the "Bolsheviks' bloody and deadly losses" would attract viewers' attention to the question of German losses as well.[1210] (1.3.1942)

Goebbels' comments also unintentionally draw attention to absolute flops and abortive developments in German propaganda, and show how difficult it was for the Minister to co-ordinate the approaches taken by the different media. The newsreels made during the western offensive from May to July 1940 provide a revealing example. At first Goebbels saw no confirmation of his secret fears that the newsreel footage of the war against France and the Benelux countries were more likely to arouse the public's sympathy than make them enthusiastic about the war because of the destruction they showed: "According to unanimous opinions from all over the country our newsreels and their realistic footage of the war are not filling people with horror, but with inward rage and satisfaction." (1.6.1940) Images picking out bloodthirsty coloured soldiers and maltreatment of Germans seems to have made the desired impact at first.[1211] But although German propaganda recognized even in early June 1940 that latent pity and "distress about the French tragedy" were being felt in the country, the press, radio and newsreel reports from occupied France after the capitulation often showed a sympathetic image of a destitute and blameless people, plunged into misery by the "criminal" Reynaud government. UTW no. 513/ censored: 3.7.1940 contains scenes showing ill-treated French women, children and refugees and pitiful old peasants. The fact that the situation in France is being normalized and refugees are being looked after by the Wehrmacht and the NSV is emphasized in the commentary,[1212] but the allocation of blame to Great Britain, without whose "treachery" France would not be in this position, is more likely to make people pity the French all the more.

Goebbels tried to take countermeasures,[1213] instructed the press "not to praise France too much. Otherwise we'll get real wave of Francophilia."[1214] (6.7.1940) And clearly this is exactly what happened: "Francophilia is rapidly increasing here. We are resisting this as hard as we can. … The polemic against Vichy is now being pushed even harder. The Security Service report also shares my concerns. But that will soon change." (11.7.1940) The SD report had confirmed the pro-French mood, but showed that the effect of the anti-French campaign being waged against it was limited because the general public did not understand it.[1215] Despite this and other information,[1216] Goebbels did not fully grasp the problem that many people saw France as a victim of British treachery and the German military machine. He impressed upon his departmental heads that "it is still essential to keep hatred of France alive and not to damp it down".[1217] Finally Hitler objected as well: "He is complaining that we are once more making people sentimental about France." Goebbels then even took the measure of taking up this unwelcome "sentimentality" about France in a newsreel with an humorous *Tran und Helle* supporting film[1218] (the longest so far)[1219] and to defuse pro-French arguments in the population through witty dialogue. This led to the paradoxical situation that the newsreel was now trying to curb a mood in the general public that it had previously helped to create.[1220]

Greatly to Goebbels' annoyance, unexpected obstacles cropped up to prevent the best possible selection of main propaganda motifs for the newsreels. Hitler's newsreel appearances were absolutely guaranteed to instil confidence.[1221] Before the war Hitler must have been seen in almost every third newsreel, on countless different occasions – from receptions and exhibition openings to state ceremonies, Party rituals and festivals.[1222] But as the war progressed, newsreels featuring the "Führer" became an increasing rarity, after the omnipresent visits to the front in the early stages. Hitler would usually allow the cameramen specially assigned to film him only a limited number of shot compositions and wide angle views. Goebbels repeatedly tried to persuade Hitler to allow more "personal" subject matter and private shots in the newsreels, but was usually unsuccessful: "Unfortunately he cannot make up his mind to include larger areas of his own activities in the newsreel, even though, as I always point out, the public absolutely longs to see the Führer's face in newsreels." (19.8.1941) Goebbels urgently needed scenes that were enormously popular with the public like the one showing Hitler playing with his Alsatian "Blondi" (in DW no. 611/20.5.1942).[1223] Once Goebbels realized "that the Führer is very reluctant to appear personally in newsreels", but that the public misses these pictures very much, he gave up for a time. (6.10.1942) Hitler had just had some shots of his Sportpalast speech to open the winter relief fund campaign on 30 September 1942. Two weeks later he even wrote: "The Führer has once more cut all the shots in which he features personally, which is very damaging to the newsreel. But the Führer is, as we know, extremely frugal in taking personal prominence. I am in something of a fix. The people want to see him; the Führer does not want to appear in newsreels. What am I to do?"

It is said that Hitler was afraid that his physical decay could become too obvious to the public in shots at state funerals or in the East Prussian Headquarters "Wolf's lair", but especially when he was making speeches.[1224] As it was, specially trained cameramen were trying to avoid showing any signs of Hitler's symptoms of illness.[1225] And even Goebbels quotes a Security Service report in early April 1943, saying that "the German people was profoundly distressed to see the Führer back in a newsreel again for the first time at the Remembrance Day ceremony in Berlin. His appearance had been so grief-stricken and careworn that they were terribly concerned about him."[1226](7.4.1943) Another unpleasant consequence was that the Security Service's opinion that "conclusions about his condition had (been) drawn from his features and his posture, and 'from there about the whole state of our cause'".[1227] The newsreel scenes showing Hitler shortly afterwards, on his 54th birthday, certainly seemed remarkably distanced.[1228]

From 1942 the credibility of the newsreels was lastingly shaken by Hitler's strict refusal to allow careful revelations about the true military situation. The dead silence about the disaster at Stalingrad from November 1942 to January 1943 contributed to this.[1229] Goebbels himself had been pleading for a considered and preventively "disillusioning" news policy and a "certain realism" since early 1942.[1230]

Goebbels is not prepared to take any responsibility for Hitler's and the OKW's information policy during the encirclement of Stalingrad: "We must now gradually accustom ourselves to the idea of instructing the German people about the situation there. This could actually have been done long ago, but so far the Führer has always been against it." (21.1.1943) At the same time he justifies his own indirectly admitted impotence, the fact that he has to hold back the realistic shots, and simply to wait and "wriggle through this dilemma for a few weeks" (10.1.1943), by saying that the propaganda company material on "the retreat from the Caucasus" was anyway "very depressing and in no way suitable for the public".[1231] (2.2.1943)

The shift from confidence to the will to hold out was tackled in the newsreels by using fear as a propaganda device. This is the light in which we should see one of the last high points for the shaping of content and propaganda in the newsreel, which Goebbels wanted to achieve with shots of the Polish victims of the Red Army found near Katyn in April 1943.[1232] This time it was Goebbels who wanted to feature the grim images, which had already been shown abroad, in home newsreels as well. He agreed that it was essential to "give some consideration to the relatives of German soldiers missing in the east", but not at the expense of "anti-Bolshevik" propaganda. (18.4.1943) So far Hitler had supported shock propaganda, but his trauma in 1918 now weighed more heavily, and he agreed with the military that the home front should not be unduly disturbed. Because the campaign had already been running for over two weeks in the other media, Goebbels was afraid that the OKW's delaying tactics would ultimately make "the images so old that they would no longer have topicality value".[1233] (28.4.1943)

Final remedies as the end draws near, 1942–1945

The newsreel was really already past its high point by the end of the Blitzkrieg in autumn and winter 1942.[1234] From late February to April 1942, before the Wehrmacht's spring offensive in the east, the reduced extent to which newsreel planning features in the diary is very clearly per-

ceptible, although Goebbels did assess the images positively again after the crisis-ridden weeks of November and December 1941.[1235] There was a renewed upswing from May to August 1942, in parallel with reviving hopes of a speedy victory, but then in September 1941 the public's increasing lack of interest in the newsreel led to the medium's first major crisis. Faced with editions that "unfortunately (lacked) any climaxes" (13.9.1942), Goebbels tried to find new ways of doing things. All the propaganda media, including the newsreel, were "all too set in stereotypes", with their "expressions and sayings that are as old as Methuselah", he writes on 27.9. 1942. This is followed by thoughts about giving the newsreels more of a plot: they must be given "a context again, and possibly even a kind of plot, at least for individual subjects". (13.10.1942)

But little stands of plot in the home front topics did not provide a fundamental solution for "newsreel fatigue". (7.3.1942) "The problem of the newsreel", wrote Goebbels on 25.5.1943, faced with transport difficulties and a lack of battle footage, "becomes increasingly difficult the longer the war lasts. It is very hard to know what to show." But Goebbels does not come up with an honest analysis. By giving the impression that response to the newsreel fluctuates according to subjects and quality, he avoids admitting the actual problem that the credibility of the monotonous films has been lastingly damaged. Sometimes he complains about the lack of battle shots, then again he wants to move over to home images and sporting events, because the said battle images are too repetitive. (11.9.1943) Even the home subjects, popular though they were, only made the newsreels more attractive for a short period in the run up to Christmas.[1236] Goebbels tried to get away from the inevitable monotony and to prevent the newsreel from completely losing its significance without changing the basic concept. There was no longer a coherent strategy. In late 1943 and 1944 his comments on the newsreels usually went little beyond "colourful and varied" or "very interesting".

In January 1944, after regularly saying that there would be "staff changes", as he had in the film sector,[1237] Goebbels appointed propaganda company lieutenant Fritz Dettmann to be head of the newsreel editorial team, which led to a final phase of gradual change and ultimately to satisfaction on the part of the Propaganda Minister: he said that Dettmann had "reformed every aspect of the newsreel from the bottom upwards. Seeing newsreels is pure pleasure again now." (16.4.1944) Goebbels was particularly taken with the newsreels that appeared from March to May 1944. Even Hitler had "long since noticed" the improvements under Dettmann, Goebbels was delighted to report on 27.4.1944.[1238] Dettmann summed up the way in which he had "reor-. dered and introduced variety into the domestic week", writing as "editor-in-chief of the German weekly newsreel" in a letter to Goebbels in April 1944. At the same time he asked for more resources and more authority: he reported that lines of communication from the propaganda committees to the newsreel editors, which used to be a laborious route via the OKW, had been shortened, the "introduction of original soundtracks in the military sector" had "made an (essential) contribution to the variety of the overall impression".[1239] As well as this, greater attention to civilian subjects within the newsreel, above all using shots of German cultural life (theatre, concerts. etc.)" had achieved their propaganda purpose, which was to "assure people standing on the sidelines that German cultural and intellectual life was moving forward, albeit under considerable difficulties". [1240]

But Goebbels does not seem to have accepted all the technical and aesthetic innovations. For example, this is his comment on the first newsreel with footage of the Allied invasion of Normandy:[1241] "But besides, Dettmann made the mistake of adding a series of old archive shots to this newsreel, making it unusable overall. It will have to be revised completely." (12.6.1944)

In summer 1944, when the processing laboratories and other Wochenschau–Zentrale premises had already been partially bombed out for months, Hinkel ordered economy measures in this sphere as well, including shortening the average length by a quarter to 400 metres.[1242] By then the technical facilities were so restricted that Goebbels often mentions long waiting times for topical material.[1243] In December 1944 he does identify some "outstanding war images" in the newsreel, but points out that they are going to have to wait about another week for reports on the Ardennes offensive – footage of this kind sometimes used to be in the cinemas by the next day. (17.12.1944) The newsreel then became "thin and unrewarding" because some images from the front never got through at all (14.1.1945), and if they did, then all they conveyed was "an impression of the enormous severity and power of the Soviet attack".[1244] (22.1.1945)

Town and cities that had been destroyed by air raids became a central dilemma for newsreel reporting in particular, which was psychologically more powerful than the radio and the press. The film people were aware that they could not avoid the subject entirely, but also that they could not show the full extent of the destruction. Hitler rejected a first attempt by Goebbels to deal with the air raids on Rostock in a newsreel, in April 1942.[1245] The approach taken by other pictorial reporting, involving stirring up hatred of the Allies by showing images of destruction, was also sharply rejected in mid 1942. From then onwards special permission had to be sought for material of this kind to be used.

But Goebbels was finding it increasingly difficult to find a compelling line here. He complained about the first version of DW no. 669/ censored: 30.6.1943, after a week of particularly heavy bombing of the Ruhr: "Unfortunately I have to make radical cuts here. Gutterer has passed images from the area involved in the war in the air that simply cannot be shown to the public. They would probably cause a certain amount of panic if they ran in German cinemas." He went on to say, as though he was not responsible for the propaganda line: "Up to a certain time

nothing was said about the war in the air, and now our propaganda merchants, who are too clever by half, want to get their teeth right into the consequences of the war in the air ... I am making some significant cuts in the newsreel. They will get rid of the extreme elements and yet give the German people an insight into the problems of the war in the air through the pictorial presentation as well." (28.6.1943) Goebbels also kept in the line of showing German cultural treasures that had been destroyed, but no victims, in the next edition: "We are showing footage of damage inside Cologne cathedral which is extraordinarily convincing: I will not allow images that go further than this to be published; they do not help in the present state of things." (4.7.1943) Even this published material seems to have been of only limited use, as the Security Service's informers reported that especially "in working class circles people can be heard saying that no one will be prepared to understand that the destruction of cultural items is pushed into the foreground while the fact that thousands of mothers and children have given their lives is scarcely mentioned".[1246]

After the severe air raids on Hamburg in August 1943, Goebbels comments on his intention to make propaganda abroad against the British by using "images of horrific scenes", and on the future line for propaganda in general: "All we can do now is make propaganda in reverse. So far we have made an impact with our victories, but we must now try to make an impact with our defeats." (8.8.1943) But he does not give an impression that he will have no difficulty in conveying this two-way propaganda and a break with the previously valid image of unshaken confidence and a will for victory to the public.[1247] He later went back on the approach of showing the terrible damage abroad: firstly, the Americans and British did not know "how much we are suffering from their terror air raids" (21.12.1944), and secondly, at this stage of the war, images of destruction were not going to make anyone sympathize with Germany any more.

At home this propaganda aimed at sympathy – which was never consistently realized – could not be sued anyway, and the newsreel had a great deal of momentous explaining to do because of the air raids: "Of course it is now very difficult to get hold of suitable images. Most home topics do not fit in wit the mood, an we can't use the ones that do, especially not those of the air raids." (8.8.1943) It became every more difficult to present a largely unscathed world at "home" despite the air raids and destruction: "We must not present images showing jovial, happy people in the newsreels wither; that would run too heavily counter to the facts." From late March 1943 Goebbels also had special responsibility for "air raid relief measures". He finally decided to make the many days of air raids on Berlin into a beacon for the clearance detachments that he had directed, and a "heroic song" for the Berlin people, but he obviously found that the material was not suitable for this purpose: "The newsreel just did not understand how to make anything at all out of the Berlin disaster ... The newsreel shots I have been shown of Berlin are being criticized by everyone. One sees nothing but hideous images of misery; there is nothing to be seen of the relief measures."[1248] (28.11.1943)

The newsreels remained well behind reality in their presentation of the air raids themselves, as well as in showing the extent of the damage.[1249] Here Goebbels picked out a "report on the daylight raids on Berlin" that was "colourfully and excitingly made": "There are shots here that are more dramatic than any we have seen before." (19.3.1944) The aerial battle scenes shot from on board German interceptor planes were spectacular and dynamically put together, if a little lame visually. But they remained a mere stylistic device: the commentator continues to speak of the "successful repulsion" of Allied bombers by German flak.

"The Führer doesn't like Gustaf Gründgens": star cult and persecution – Nazis and film artists in a new light

Like many politicians before and after him, Reichsminister Joseph Goebbels enjoyed being part of the art world. It gave Goebbels great satisfaction to deal as patron with the stars he had once idolized in the cinema.

But Goebbels was not prepared to put up with feigned respect from obsequious film stars. It was not enough for him – and this too he has in common with most of the more intelligent politicians – to be taken seriously just because of his power and authority. His ambitions went further.

For this reason the new Film Minister tried to gain the confidence of film people in 1933. He thus deliberately approached big names like Trenker and Riefenstahl, Werner Krauss ("politically quite harmless", 15.8.1933) and many others to propose film projects. Goebbels talks a great deal about the sparse flow of people from the art world back to Nazi Germany (for example Lilian Harvey from the USA), but rather less about the fact that the best talent was emigrating. He also regularly visited festivals in Venice, Bayreuth and Salzburg – and plunged into the world of art for days on end.

What can now be expected from Goebbels' writings about the relationship between Nazis and actors, between art and power? The subject is inexhaustible, of course, and has already been overworked in a number of treatises, often enough using the diaries. But unfortunately it is not enough to leaf through the index of names looking for plums that fit in well with existing legends.

Understandably there is nothing about Goebbels' absolutely legendary seduction skills, his sexual adventures and the young actresses he tormented. No, Goebbels is a model husband and father in the diary. However, there are certain code words Goebbels uses to identify some affairs – before and after his relationship with Lida Baarova. These were certainly greatly exaggerated after the war, but they did exist.

There are many points in the diaries containing recommendations from the Minister that Demandowsky, Hippler or the heads of production should "consider" young and unknown actresses (for example Jutta Freybe). But these do not always conceal a casting couch: often he is actually passing on his wife's wishes. Ultimately the historical interest is too slight to justify great research efforts in this field. Anyone interested in reading about lewd affairs and perpetuated legends will have to resort to appropriate scandal chronicles.[1250]

It is well known that Goebbels felt attracted to acting circles, both as a social climber and an intellectual. This is constantly confirmed in the diaries: "The artists are just a lot of children. But loveable". (18.3.1937) Goebbels admits that he "likes being with artists, They are so stimulating, and so capable of arousing enthusiasm" (29.3.1937), and then reproaches them gently for being "completely inept in practical matters". If things did not do his way for a time, the film people were even a "bunch of layabouts". (16.10.1937)

Goebbels devoted himself to actresses' problems with tax and marriage, with their job hunting and "many little worries", and even reports Hitler's "help" and involvement in completely unimportant matters like relationship problems or pregnancies. (8.3.1937)

We find out a great deal about the personal delight he took as the patron saint of these "childlike artists" who needed so much help, about the pleasure he took in finding out about the artists' private lives and problems and often in helping them as well. (15.11.1935) In these cases, reports about private audiences with the Minister go something like this: "Frau Tschechova tells me about her joys and sorrows." (9.10.1937) There were numerous outings or meetings in Goebbels' country house during the summer months from 1935 to 1937. For example, Luis Trenker and Carola Höhn accompanied him on a "boat trip on Lake Schwielow". (9.7.1936)

There is a great deal of this kind of patronage and considerateness in the diaries for 1937/38, when Goebbels was spending a lot of time with Lida Baarova. When this affair was over, the Minister came down to earth and developed a little more restraint. Perhaps he realized that his affair with Lida Baarova and his reputation as the "Babelsberg goat" had made him more part of the film world than he could readily accept. The start of the war was a good excuse for Goebbels to distance himself sharply from the art world and to start denouncing artists as unreliable idlers. He averred that these "lazy-bones" would live just as they did in peace-time, thanks to their privileges. (13.1.1943) Now even this kind of tone creeps in after an evening party: "I notice on this occasion how far one has distanced oneself from this purely artistic world as well." (26.9.1942)

Hitler, Goebbels, Göring and perhaps a few from the lower Nazi echelons like Baldur von Schirach, Hans Hinkel or Fritz Hippler, always imagined that they had a particular relationship

with art and with eminent artists. Goebbels, Göring, Martin Bormann (Manja Behrens), the Berlin Police Chief Helldorf (Else Elster) and Hans Hinkel had long-running or brief affairs with actresses.

A complex psychological network of contempt, envy, considerateness, arrogance, carrots and sticks emerged between top Nazis and actors. Goebbels himself certainly enjoyed humiliating and tormenting them, punishing and promoting. Fritz Hippler[1251] detects a "schizophrenic attitude, involving courting and reviling artists" in Hitler, Goebbels and other leading Nazis. The National Socialist politicians appeared as modern princes and patrons in a court of maintained artists. The artists were enticed by dream fees, propaganda commissions, theatre directorships, special tax-free payments, huge tax advantages, titles ranging from Staatsschauspieler to Professor, awards like the Goethe Medal or the Eagle Shield, their own "artists' receptions by state and Party luminaries from Göring to Hitler and Mussolini, and also by privileged living conditions and being excused from military service.[1252] Well-liked superstars could count on luxury and fame: "Aryanized" villas and cars, the status of a pampered darling of the people. After some initial difficulties, acclaim from the controlled press was guaranteed, and there was scarcely any public artistic criticism that could be taken seriously. Even the studio bosses could be outmanoeuvred by appealing directly to Goebbels.

Before the outbreak of war, they all met in the VIP boxes at the constant celebrations, receptions, parades and state visits. The leading National Socialist politicians used eminent artists as fashion accessories everywhere. "We enjoy ourselves too much", says Geobbels as early as 3.7. 1936: "The people are laughing at us." Shortly afterwards he threw an enormous party for almost 3,000 guests on the Pfaueninsel.

It was a special honour for some well-known actresses to be chosen as Hitler's partner at dinner. Lil Dagover, Anny Ondra, Luise Ullrich, Olga Tschechova and a few others were granted this pleasure.

Hitler too enjoyed large and small receptions in the usual entourage of aides-de-camp, Party luminaries and the light-hearted and pleasant atmosphere generated by a large group of eminent stage and film artists. As well as the individuals who have already been mentioned – with changing demand before and after the outbreak of war – frequent guests included Jenny Jugo, Leni Riefenstahl, Irene von Meyendorff, Willy Birgel, Viktor de Kowa, Carola Höhn, Johannes Riemann, Mathias Wieman, Heinrich George, Wolfgang Liebeneiner, Emil Jannings, Veit Harlan, Kristina Söderbaum and Hilde Krahl. Sitting around an open fire, Hitler revealed "the art behind his leadership of the people" to the stars, which made "a profound impression on the artists". (17.3.1937) The film evenings and artists' gatherings were not intended for the public eye: the press was forbidden to report on them.[1253]

However, a newsreel report on the Reichsfilmkammr's war conference in February 1941 did reveal which of the many stars the Nazi bosses saw as important advertisements: Riefenstahl, Wieman, George and Rühmann featured here as well.

As the important Nazi figures actually did not constitute a presentable "high society", the film stars functioned as a kind of substitute. Given that there was no publicly visible nobility or a court milieu, the public had to concentrate its need for sensation, identification and glamour on them. This too was part of the entertainment and distraction strategy: the "star cult as a propaganda device" was intended to enable "built-up identification figures to make their contribution to the nation".[1254] Goebbels wanted to use this to raise the social status of the film classes, which were popularly seen as dissolute. Lists of the enormous amounts of money taken at the box-office by films featuring Zarah Leander, for example, regularly passed across Goebbels' desk. They regularly showed him how valuable the screen stars were, and not just as advertisements, figures to identify with and idols of the public. With their help even average (political) material could be made into an enormous commercial success.

Actors' memoirs and recollections often suggest they felt the Nazi years were the period of their greatest professional success, and thus "the golden age of German films".[1255] A systematic examination of 59 biographies of film and theatre actors produces several recurring justifications: they were not politically inclined, and noticed nothing of much that was happening, whether the artists were working in film or theatre, this had been an isolated oasis, emigration impossible because there were no professional opportunities for foreigners as outsiders, and finally they had to help to protect others who were in danger. These "protestations of innocence in book form" (Georg Seeßlen) by the artists who wish to suppress things do not always agree with Goebbels' statements and the few remaining pieces of documentation.

Goebbels actually appears as an all-powerful demon in the memoirs of the former film élite, though a fairly toothless one from time to time. They almost all accuse themselves of having been very unpopular with Goebbels, whether it was for speaking out of turn, disrespectful behaviour or constant refusal to accede to the Minister's wishes, to join the Party, for example.[1256] "He always turns pale at the brave answers from the future writer of memoirs."[1257] At the same time, every female film star claims to have had sexual overtures from Goebbels, which were of course rejected despite the inevitable career blip, indeed Goebbels "must have been world 're-buff-fielding' champion".[1258]

There are no simple answers to the question about reasons for currying favour with the Nazi leaders, and certainly none that offer mere sweeping judgements of the actors. Certainly some middle-of-the-road talents sensed great opportunities after a few top stars had emigrated. Many people benefited from debarments from work through non-acceptance or exclusion from the Reichskulturkammer. In the field of comedy many must have welcomed the exodus of their more talented Jewish colleagues.

But the film people who really had artistic ambitions "succumbed less to the Fascist bacillus than to their own pipe-dreams and the illusion that the Propaganda Minister would fulfil them".[1259] For them, undreamed-of possibilities for realizing ideas, projects and screenplays that would probably not have stood a chance under a normal production system seemed to open up through the medium of Goebbels' dictatorial power. Goebbels even consulted them personally and paid court to them.

Quite a few films were made in this way, and quite a few of the top stars' dreams came true: for example, Emil Jannings was able to make *The Broken Jug* (1937), a project close to his heart. This encouraged a few creative spirits to suggest some entirely outlandish projects. In Emil Jannings' case alone Goebbels mentions numerous film plans, for example Fallada novels, "Fuhrmann Henschel", "Michael Kohlhaas" (25.10.1942), and a "Genghis Khan" project. The artists' hubris made them unable to see that the Propaganda Minister would never have given permission for films that ran counter to his policies for their sakes. For example, Goebbels dismisses Jannings' Genghis Khan idea: "It would scarcely be possible to think of a less timely subject" (2.7.1942). And he expresses himself just as clearly on the subject of Heinrich George's suggested film of Gerhart Hauptmann's "Schluck und Jau": "I will not allow this. There is scarcely any interest in these morbid, antisocial people today." (13.7.1940) It is not until the war is drawing to an end that ideas of suggesting fantasy projects just to show willingness to work are involved.

Winning Goebbels' favour brought a great deal of material advantage. Emil Jannings received many hundreds of thousands of marks from 1942 to 1945, even though he only made two films.

Zarah Leander's astronomical fees of 400,000 Reichsmarks per year are still lavish even by present (German) standards (a leading Ufa employee was paid 2,000 Reichsmarks per month, an official in the film department about 700 RM, and Reichsfilmintendant 1,500 RM).

Particularly "eminent" artists – an elastic and subjective definition made by Goebbels and various cultural functionaries – who earned good money were allowed to set 40 per cent of their income as a lump sum against tax as professional outlay. This was a perk available to most top film stars. However, the Propaganda Minister always owed a lot of tax, and so had himself put on the list.

During the war a "divinely gifted" list was added. It had over a thousand artists' names of it, some of whom were "irreplaceable", and was an effective disciplinary device as it defined the (film) artists' indispensability. Here too film and theatre artists were in the majority.[1260]

This overall placing of film performers in categories and hierarchies was taken a long way: several lists, often top secret, were drawn up defining the artists' significance, employment and merit. Creating high-handed lists of "artists particularly worthy of encouragement" was one of the Propaganda Minister's favourite occupations. He could hardly demonstrate his power over eminent artists more directly.

Apart from the top group of about a dozen artists who had to be permanently employed, including Rühmann and Leander, and the majority of the well-known performers on list 2, Goebbels took personal decisions about the use of many old hands and talents on each occasion. The final list contained the names of unwanted individuals who were not to be used again if possible.[1261]

The Propaganda Minister was not satisfied with the Reichsfilmkammer as a compulsory professional state bureaucratic organization. Goebbels' ideal notions of a tight studio system are derived from the heyday of the Hollywood moguls: controlled, disciplined ensembles of actors, rigidly attached to the individual companies, brought together in a "compulsory corporation as a household".[1262]

Permanent control and education were also devices for creating a new type of human being, the Nazi artist. Ultimately Goebbels wanted to stop "all artists (from being) politically characterless" (5.7.1935) by introducing new and better "human material" to films and the theatre. He paid a great deal of attention to the care of young artists' and actors' training, and forced his compliant theatre directors like Paul Hartmann to commit to this entirely. Unreliable, critical and excessively intellectual elements were to be replaced by strictly National Socialist newcomers, whom Goebbels intended to bring on with the aid of training plans he would develop himself and constant personal selection. But it was not as easy as he thought to get rid of the gifted stars of the present day. He admitted himself that the new pupils were bitterly disappointing: "The young film newcomers in the film industry are pretty mediocre. They seem too petit-bourgeois to me." (16.10.1941) Goebbels was looking for a universally marketable type, to fit in with his dreams of being a great film power: "If the German cinema is to conquer the world, then it must also put people into the limelight who can represent some sort of idea to the world." (16.10.1941)

This is linked with another question that is often raised by film historians: why was it not possible "to construct a positive homunculus for the 'new age', a prototype National Socialist being, from the still considerable number of well trained performers who are popular with the public".[1263] The 50-year-old great-super-fathers, kind authority figures and character actors Jannings and George could only partially meet the youthful ideal and the racial and facial demands; Paul Hartmann and Eugen Klöpfer did not meet it either. Hans Albers, who was actually the ideal type, was difficult to play on and already had a heroic but ambivalent profile, even before National Socialist ideas of building up a "Führer" figure could take hold. This left Willy Birgel, Gustav Fröhlich, Mathias Wieman etc. It is said that Goebbels and Hitler were dissatisfied with this range of sound characters.[1264] Goebbels criticized Wieman's officer performances (1.8.1937), and despite being absolutely faithful to the Party, Wieman did not get any more heroic parts. (20.10.1937) Goebbels said he was "still intolerable". (27.4.1938) Goebbels ignored Albers, who distanced himself from the regime. Fröhlich was his rival for Lida Baarova for a time, and was harassed for that reason. Hans Söhnker and Karl John made themselves unpopular with their affairs, and the two Nazi Party members Viktor de Kowa and Willy Fritsch (despite the latter's role in *Junge Adler*) were pigeonholed as light comedians. The only one whom Goebbels liked in private and on the screen was Birgel, a small-built German national type.

But was this search for a manly, Aryan "NS star", who could represent the cinema and the regime immaculately, ever pursued with any determination? Hitler's statements at no point suggest that he felt the lack of such a type. Hitler was much more inclined to be particularly interested in the women's roles in films – "noble sufferers" and "capable females"; he admired Greta Garbo and Pola Negri, and liked watching Jenny Jugo, Luise Ullrich, Brigitte Horney, Olga Tschechowa and Kristina Söderbaum. He thought that "if men were wrongly cast it often destroyed great women's performances". (25.1.1937) Nowhere is there any marked reference to "heroic" male figures, with the exception of Jannings and George. He liked films featuring Hans Albers and Gustav Fröhlich, but there was no acknowledgement of the lovers and lady-killers. Hitler liked comedians like Hans Moser, Attila Hörbiger, Heinz Rühmann and Weiß Ferdl. They offered him no competition in their roles as fools. Why should he share his people's admiration with a charismatic shining face from the silver screen, against which he would have paled superficially?

Perhaps despite all these hints Hitler did not worry about possible screen rivals, even though there was no lack of contemporary allusions.[1265] An intelligent analysis of possible competition between film star and "Führer" takes Albers as an example and shows that the two charismatic figures were not rivals for popular favour, but complementary figures whom the public never saw on the same plane.[1266]

Day-to-day dealings

Racial matters

Goebbels was fanatically anti-Semitic, and undertook a systematic "removal of Jews from the art world". But his opportunism and pragmatism come to the fore in his dealings with artists who were prepared to conform and in the give-and-take game.

Thus Goebbels issued numerous special licences for Jewish film people; these had to be confirmed by Hitler. In June 1939 there were 320 special licences of this kind for people in the Reichskulturkammer who were Jewish or "related to Jews by marriage".[1267] In the case of the film and theatre actress Trude Hesterberg the press had to be referred to Goebbels' special dispensation to stop attacks on the Jewish performer.[1268]

But in the diary Goebbels tends to parade his hard line against actors who intervene in favour of Jewish colleagues, or keeps completely quiet about such unreasonable requests. He does not want to give in to Pauly Wessely and Attila Hörbiger: "Attila is trying to rescue the Jew Reisch on behalf of his wife Paula Wessely. I am refusing to do this. We must remain firm about this now." (15.5.1936) This was about possible further work for the Viennese screenplay author Walter Reisch. Reisch then emigrated to Hollywood in the year of the Austrian "Anschluss" and worked with Ernst Lubitsch and Billy Wilder there. Immediately after the annexation of Austria Goebbels gave the Jewish actors living in Vienna a talking to. The Minister said that Paula Wessely had "too many Jewish friendships", and that Attila Hörbiger should put a stop to this. (1.4.1938)

Mixed marriages between Christians and Jews created a difficult problem, and most of the exceptional permissions applied to these. Even popular favourites like Hans Moser or Heinz Rühmann, or older stars admired by Hitler like Henny Porten were "related to Jews by marriage". Goebbels and his helpers, like the radical culture-functionary Hans Hinkel, naturally did all they could to have these marriages dissolved. Where the people involved were less famous, less effort tended to be made: "Georg Alexander isn't getting divorced from his Jewess after all. Let him stay with her, in God's name." (9.12.1937) Frank Wysbar, a very promising young director, did not divorce his Jewish wife under pressure from Goebbels until September 1938, then emigrated to the USA shortly afterwards.

Hans Albers' original refusal to separate from his Jewish partner Hansi Burg is said to have annoyed Goebbels particularly. But in the case of Albers, who was a living advertisement for the German cinema and the "physiological epitome of Germanness",[1269] Goebbels would not let go. Albers finally wrote to Goebbels in October 1935: "To fulfil my duty to the National Socialist state and in commitment to that state I have broken off my personal relationship with Frau Hansi Burg."[1270] Burg married a foreigner for the sake of appearances, but there was no real separation until 1939. The actress emigrated to England, but went back to Albers after the war.

Heinz Rühmann, a "nice, witty and charming chap" (18.12.1937) apparently had marital problems anyway, and complained, to Goebbels' delight, about his "marital misery with a Jewess". (6.11.1936) While Goebbels noted an assurance of help with film engagements and a trouble-free divorce, Rühmann denies that he was supported by the Propaganda Minister.[1271] Rühmann divorced his wife Maria Bernheim in November 1938 and married his actress colleague

Hertha Feiler. Rühmann got himself into trouble by failing to declare Maria Bernheim's fortune to the authorities after she had moved to neutral Sweden.

Goebbels diary entries also quite unambiguously contradict previous legends about a great thirties' film star, Renate Müller. Roles in numerous comedies like *Die Privatsekretärin* ("The Private Secretary", 1930) and *Viktor und Viktoria* (1933), but also in propaganda films like *Togger* (1937) made this blonde, flirtatious and tomboyish actress and singer very popular. Rumours flying around after the war speak of Goebbels' "persistent feud" against Renate Müller, and assert that he "hated" her uncontrollably.[1272] It is said that the reason for this was her relationship with a Jewish banker who went into exile in 1934, but the actress did not break off with him completely. Goebbels systematically demolished Renate Müller as a result of this, people went on to say. Another factor was her mysterious illness, possibly epilepsy, accompanied by addiction to tablets and alcohol. She died on 7 October 1937 in a Berlin sanatorium, rumours suggesting that she committed suicide. Goebbels' entries for 1933/34 are not yet available, but so far not a single negative word about Renate Müller has been found. Goebbels knew about her illness, as the actress sought him out personally just a few months before her death: "Renate Müller tells me her tale of woe. She is a sick woman." (3.4.1937) If there were questions about casting, Goebbels writes: "Renate Müller! I'm going to help her." (25.6.1937) After an investigation instigated by the Reichsfilmkammer, Goebbels even claims to have reprimanded the Berlin chief of police Helldorf "about Renate Müller, who was questioned in the most ignominious fashion". (6.4.1937) Goebbels only allows a hint at possible earlier conflicts in his comment on the news of her death: "I am in fact very sorry. At the age of 29. Terrible fate." (8.10.1937)

The status of a "privileged" marriage between an "Aryan" and a Jewish partner was introduced during the war, and did offer some security to the persecuted, but of course did not guarantee that they would escape arbitrariness altogether. The film and theatre actor Joachim Gottschalk was increasingly harassed by Goebbels and above all by Hans Hinkel because of his Jewish wife Meta from 1937 onwards. Gottschalk categorically refused to divorce her, and when the situation became intolerable to him and he was forbidden to work in May 1941, he committed suicide with his family on 5 November 1941.[1273] Goebbels commented cynically on this "somewhat painful piece of news" by averring that he wanted to be sure that "this humanly regrettable, objectively quite inevitable case is not used to foster alarming rumours". (7.11.1941) The director of the Volksbühne, Eugen Klöpfer, was also intended to help him with this. But the suicide did cause great consternation in the Berlin film and theatre world and well beyond. Goebbels forbade attendance at the funeral, but he was nevertheless compelled to see two of Hitler's favourite artists, Wolfgang Liebeneiner and Brigitte Horney, appearing up at the graveside.

It almost seems as though this incident influenced Hitler's and Goebbels' attitude to mixed Christian and Jewish marriages like Gottschalk's: only two weeks later Goebbels reports: "The Führer has recommended that I should act with some reserve over Jewish mixed marriages, as he feels that these marriages are gradually dying out anyway and that we should not worry about them unduly." (22.11.1941)

Hitler often asserted this opinion right up to the end of the war, if Goebbels is to be believed on this head. But there are also plenty of indications that Hitler did not entirely approve of Heydrich's persecution of "half-castes" and mixed marriages if too many members of German families were involved. Goebbels noted on 4.10.1942 that Hitler was against the introduction of the Star of David in mixed marriages: "This applies mainly to artists' marriages. Of course we must address this problem later as well, but first of all the Führer thinks we should get the pure Jews out of Berlin, who have nothing more to do with Aryan national comrades." Hitler's tolerant attitude to mixed marriages, which Goebbels constantly emphasizes, could also have influenced the incidents in Rosenstraße in Berlin in February/March 1943, when there were some successful protests about the deportation of Jewish partners from mixed marriages.[1274]

Could it be that Hitler was interested in individual cases here? Hitler was a great fan of Henny Porten, an actor who was the same age as the dictator. He had admired her silent film performances as well. "She once particularly impressed him when he was a soldier, and saw her for the first time in Lille, while on a short spell of leave from the front. The Führer never forgets impressions of this kind", Goebbels dictated on the subject of his boss's admiration for Henny Porten. Unfortunately Porten was married to a Jewish doctor, and she refused to divorce him. But this was not the (only) reason for her lack of film roles, as was later asserted.[1275] Henny Porten was protected by Göring and his wife, and even Hitler pronounced himself in favour of using her in new films. Henny Porten expressly thanked Hermann Göring as early as December 1937 for helping her to get a contract with Tobis.[1276] Goebbels also told Bavaria in 1941 that they could make a start on films with Henny Porten at any time, which means that there was no curb on her earning money. But the film companies maintained that they could not find any suitable roles for the ageing silent film star.[1277] Although Goebbels writes: "The Führer very much regrets that Henny Porten is not one of us because of her marriage to a Jew" (10.8.1943), she and her husband were left largely in peace, indeed according to Goebbels Hitler granted her "a monthly pension of a thousand marks". (25.1.1944) Henny Porten said after the war: "My greatest enemy was Dr. Joseph Goebbels, who took a true delight in tormenting me as a human being and in humiliating and humbling me as an artist."[1278]

Hitler was also very keen on the actor and director Wolfgang Liebeneiner. He expressly forebade Liebeneiner from being called up into the armed forces.[1279] The dictator and his Propaganda Minister even involved themselves in the marital problems of this creator of important propaganda material. While Goebbels was still discussing "a number of personal matters that are depressing him very much and that could potentially cause a personal crisis for him" with Liebeneiner and his partner Hilde Krahl (29.11.19420, Hitler had already cleared up "the matters": he agreed that after Liebeneiner's divorce from the Jewish actress Ruth Hellberg, her son from a previous marriage, who grew up as Andreas Liebeneiner, should not be sent to the extermination camp.[1280]

These individual cases seem strange, but it has long been known that Hitler also saved his mother's Jewish doctor from deportation. Anyway, cases like this meant that Goebbels still had "worries about artists in mixed Jewish marriages, especially in the film and theatre worlds" during the war, and that "one had to proceed with a degree of caution here". (24.1.1944)

Finally, there was a similar case that slipped through Goebbels' fingers. Harry Baur was one of the few gifted French actors who appeared in German films. Goebbels had not liked him at first, and no wonder, as Harry Baur was considered to be a Jew. (5.8.1937) But, allegedly at Goebbels' request, he was engaged for a German film, *Symphonie eines Lebens* ("Symphony of a Life"), by Hans Bertram.[1281] Goebbels saw this expensive film in September 1942 and was very positive about it. But Baur's allegedly Jewish origins then came up again. He had been arrested in Paris in May 1942, and the SS stated on 22 June that Baur was a "pure Jew". Now it seems that Goebbels didn't want to know anything more about it: "I would be very pleased if the film could be rescued, as Bauer's (sic!) Jewish descent is by no means certain. I don't believe it either. Our Paris offices have probably stuck too rigidly to the regulations here." (11.9.1942) In October Goebbels presented a Security Service report that tried to hide some mistakes behind typical anti-Semitic verbiage: Baur was not a Jew, but had tried to give the impression he was in France to further his career. Baur had also been released in the meantime, but died from the consequences in early April 1943, indeed was possibly murdered by the Gestapo.[1282] *Symphonie eines Lebens* opened in Germany a few days after his death.

Political matters

As well as persecuting people on racial grounds, Goebbels and his functionaries also tried to punish any political deviation in the film world. Even big names were not always spared repressive measures. The first film hero to fall into disgrace was the actor, director and film producer Luis Trenker, one of the best-known figures in German cinema. His sound and silent films set in the mountains were very popular with the public even before the beginning of the "Third Reich". Trenker was one of the stars whom Goebbels and Hitler admired even before the "seizure of power". A few days before 30 January 1933 the two men had a key experience (19.1.1933) on the way to the "German cinema's national breakthrough".[1283] with Trenker's resistance film *Der Rebell*. This "wild man" (20.5.1933) embodied courage, heroism and native love of home and fatherland in an ideal way. Trenker forbears to mention in his memoirs that he was a welcome guest of Goebbels during the period of many receptions in 1935/36. It must have been great fun at the 1936 Venice Film Festival, for example (30.8.1936), where Trenker won the Mussolini Cup for the best foreign film.

But Goebbels and Hitler started to feel displeased with *Condottieri* (1937): "Trenker is too Catholic: He is messing the whole thing up for us." (1.4.1937) Then the South Tyrol question meant the end for Trenker. The National Socialist government, after agreeing with Italy to give up South Tyrol, ordered all South Tyroleans of German origin to leave their homes and register in the Reich as Germans by 30.6.1940 ("opting") or they would lose all their political and cultural minority rights in South Tyrol. Early rumours started to circulate that Trenker would not toe

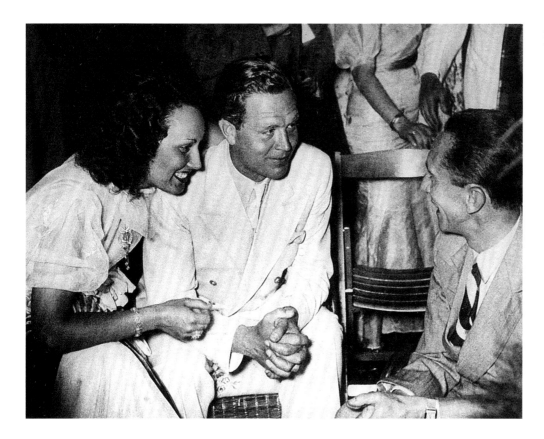

this line, even though he was quite naturally expected to be setting an example. Now Goebbels
tried to backtrack on his praise for Trenker: "Luis Trenker, that character vacuum, has opted for
Italy. We will give him a piece of our mind. The Führer has never thought much of him and I
have always warned people off him."[1284] (18.1.1940) In fact Trenker had not yet fully made his
mind up about this. He wrote to Hitler on 27.2.1940, contradicted all the rumours and asked:
"… I will do what you advise. Immediate emigration and break off all links with Italy and thus to
Mussolini's wishes or continue to work in a spirit of German-Italian cultural friendship here at
home and in the rest of the world."[1285] But Hitler was preparing the invasion in the west and was
not very interested in the business, and so Goebbels continued to deal with it (5.3.1940): "I see
Luis Trenker in the afternoon. He waffled on about his Germanness, which he is betraying today
with a cold smile. I remain cool and unmoved to the core of my being. A scoundrel, a bloke without a fatherland. Put him off and finish him one day."[1286] (7.3.1940) When his role during the
"Third Reich" was being discussed, Trenker liked to point to passages like this, after the publication of the Goebbels diaries in 1987. The fact is that he finally did opt for Germany on 28 March
1940 and was granted Reich German citizenship.[1287] Nevertheless, Goebbels made sure that
Trenker was not allowed to make any more films in Germany. All his new film projects were rejected.[1288] As an actor he was seen only in the colonial film *Germanin*, made in 1941. Because rumours persisted that he had campaigned in South Tyrol against the Berlin government's demands that all those of German descent should emigrate, Trenker even turned for help to
Reichsführer SS Heinrich Himmler, who also acted as "Reichskommissar für die Festigung des
deutschen Volkstums" ("Reich commissioner for the consolidation of German nationhood").
Ultimately Trenker, who called SS Brigade-Führer Hinkel an "old and benevolent friend", had
even praised the "Anschluss" of Austria and written in the most complimentary mode about the
"Führer". The SS consulted Goebbels, but he passed on the message that Trenker could no longer count on finding work in the German film industry.[1289] Trenker himself lived in Mussolini's
republic of Salo from 1943.[1290]

Just as the relationship between Goebbels and the artists cooled off after the war broke out,
a rougher political wind was now blowing as well. In April 1939 the actor Rudolf Platte, "who
has spoken disparagingly of our policies", got away with a warning (19.4.1939): "He also turns
out to be a true comedian in this situation, which is highly embarrassing for him." One of the
first to be affected was the bit-part actress Anneliese Spada-Kambeck. Goebbels summoned her
to the ministry and subsequently had her sent to a concentration camp in October 1939, for making statements critical of the regime.[1291] There was no further mention of this incident on 26 Sep-

tember 1932, when Spada-Kambeck married Hans Hinkel. His best man was none other than the Propaganda Minister. (27.9.1942)

Goebbels now attacks "rumours" and "defeatism" in artistic circles very vigorously in his diary. These constant threats intensified from 1941 onwards. One victim was the extremely popular performer Gustav Fröhlich, whom Goebbels had loathed since he began his affair with Lida Baarova. Even after their first meeting he described the heroic actor as "utterly stupid". (16.5.1937) Fröhlich made some derogatory remarks about Wehrmacht soldiers during the shooting of Veit Harlan's *The Great King*, and this seemed to be the opportunity that Goebbels had been waiting for. His staff collected incriminating material, to which Veit Harlan made a substantial contribution: Fröhlich was an undisciplined, "un-German, repulsive so-and-so", said Harlan, for the record. On the strength of this, Goebbels, acting on Hippler's suggestion, withdrew Fröhlich's indispensable status.[1292] Fröhlich joined the Wehrmach for at least 18 months in summer 1941, but expressly without service at the front. A confidential instruction to the production companies not to employ Fröhlich was not followed precisely. It seems that Fröhlich was so little needed by the Wehrmacht that his commanding officer wanted to send him home; alternatively, he was soon given leave for film and theatre appearances.[1293] In November 1943 Goebbels himself applied for Fröhlich to be reinstated as indispensable.[1294]

Goebbels was particularly severe in his punishment of some "stupid and silly rumours that are again being spread in film circles about political events. I will now knuckle down to it and call those responsible to account, as otherwise we will have no peace in this sector." (3.3.1942) The background to this was a curious episode during the shooting of the Bismarck film *The Dismissal*. It seems that actor Friedrich Maurer's convincing portrayal of August Bebel attracted attention. Apparently Maurer spoke the Social Democrat's anti-national slogans so credibly that they were understood on set as current political allusions. Jannings, said Goebbels, has "proved (to be) a little political slanderer. He asserted that an anti National Socialist demonstration had taken place in his studio, and when I go into the business a little more closely it turns out that he only said this because he was jealous of competition from a better actor." (3.3.1942) Fritz Hippler, who knew the diary entry from an earlier publication, said in his memoirs – which seem highly contrived at this point – that Goebbels himself was the victim of a rumour spread via Jannings, which quickly cleared itself up.[1295] Goebbels does not deviate from his version and continues to agitate against film people who "shrug off bad national or political behaviour by dismissing it as an artistic quirk". (16.4.1942) He also sounds off about "Jannings' inept rumour-mongering" in a group dining with Hitler. (27.4.1942) But: "Even the Führer agrees that most artists, above all actors, are quirky. That has to be taken duly into account. But of course artists must not be allowed to exploit the present war situation to their own advantage."[1296] (27.4.1942)

Mutual denunciations were incidentally no rarity among film artists: for example, Willy Fritsch complained that his director Viktor Tourjansky spoke too much Russian in the studio.[1297]

Shining examples, political praise and joy about expressions of loyalty are also found in Goebbels' writings. He expressly mentions Heinrich George, Brigitte Horney and Friedrich Kayßler as faithful supporters: "Kayßler enjoys the Führer's particular confidence." (27.4.1944) Goebbels also found things to be praised in Vienna. He was impressed by a meeting with Viennese film and theatre artists, including Paul Hörbiger: "The Viennese actors are relatively well aligned politically." (15.3.1942) The same thing could be said only of the younger generation of actors in Germany, which he had helped to bring up himself: they have understood that the nation is at war and that artists must fall in line, but we "have to keep making that clear to the old guard". (3.2.1942)

The first political victim of Goebbels' increasingly sharper approach during the war was Herbert Selpin, a very experienced and knowledgeable director who had also done propaganda work, in August 1942. Selpin was known to have a very short fuse. Terra had been reporting to the Reichsfilmkammer since 1935 about Selpin's violent outbursts of rage and cursing on location.[1298] A similar pattern seems to have been repeated during shooting for the film *Titanic* in 1943 – but this time it was aimed at the war and the Wehrmacht. Hinkel and Goebbels learned about these outbursts from Selpin's erstwhile friend, the screenplay author Walter Zerlett-Olfenius. At first Hinkel clearly wanted to sweep the case under the carpet. It was only when Selpin refused to recant that he was arrested for "utterances undermining military strength" – it is not clear whether this actually occurred in Goebbels' office after Selpin had been summoned there by the Minister,[1299] although a note made on 31.7.1942 suggests that this is possible: "I find myself obliged to arrest the film director Selpin and to hand him over to the "Volksgerichtshof" ("People's court"). He has been guilty of inept remarks about the Wehrmacht and the conduct of the war in general. He will probably have to be given a long custodial sentence." Selpin was found hanging in his cell on the morning of 1 August 1942. His colleagues were informed by notices posted in the studios that Selpin had "violated the ethics of war by despicable slander and insults to German soldiers and officers at the front." Rumour had it that Selpin had been murdered in prison by the Gestapo. Although this cannot be excluded, it would at least not have fitted in with Goebbels' intention to prove in the eyes of all that he was serious, that is to say that political misdemeanours could attract conviction, prison and even the death penalty. In fact Goebbels left no doubt about this, though he had first spoken about a "custodial sentence": he said that by committing suicide, Selpin had only "drawn the conclusions that would probably have been drawn by the state". (1.8.1942)

"As far as film actors are concerned, the Führer agrees with my approach of not dealing with political matters with undue severity; however, hostility to the state or the war cannot be tolerated anywhere. But on the other hand it is good if one is a little more magnanimous here. Artists cannot be taken seriously in the political field." Thus Goebbels once more justifies his line on 23.9.1943. Does this contradict permanent threats against artists? Only at a first glance, as hostility to the state can be quickly discerned if needed. Only grumbling about food rations, of the kind that cropped up in many intercepted letters, should be punished leniently.

"Cleaning up the film industry" is Goebbels' brutal phrase for using every means at his disposal to discipline film people. Anyone who had not been a friend of the regime from the earliest days lived in a climate of constant threat. The diaries also make it clear that the Propaganda Minister was looking for cases that would serve as deterrents, even if they were not particularly spectacular. Karl John was a dynamic blonde actor who usually played officers. His role as an immaculate sergeant on leave in *Zwei in einer großen Stadt* made him very well known and popular. Goebbels received him and other young actors in his ministerial apartment in January 1942. After that John worked mainly in the Deutsches Theater. He must have made himself unpopular at this time, as Goebbels mentions "some political unpleasantness" at the Deutsches Theater on 10.5.1943. He blames the director, Heinz Hilpert for this: he has always shown "a certain reserve vis-à-vis the Reich and National Socialist policies and the conduct of the war". The problem: "A new John case has cropped up here. The actor John came to my attention once before because of his detrimental remarks about the way the war is being conducted. I must grab him by the scruff of the neck." John had an accident on stage, which possibly saved him from the worst. His contract was not renewed, however, and he was released for military service. In January 1945 Hans Hinkel met John in a wretched state in a bunker at Bahnhof Zoo. Hinkel even wanted to give John money from his fund for artists in need, but Goebbels blocked the move.[1300]

John's actor colleague Rupert Dorsay was to suffer what John was spared because of his "detrimental remarks" a few months later. He was the first actor to be convicted of "hostility to the state" and executed. This case fitted in with the Minister's terror strategy. "There are a few unreliable characters in the film and theatre sector who are getting a little cheeky at the moment because they think they can see a chance. I am trying very hard to find a case to punish as an example. … I have always been completely aware that we cannot count on fanatical supporters in the German art world." Goebbels made this entry with his eye on Dorsay (14.8.1943), who was imprisoned in August 1943, by a special court of the Reich Supreme Military Court in the first place. Dorsay had told jokes about the "Führer" in the theatre canteen, and finally a letter from him was intercepted in which he also made fun of Hitler and the National Socialist Party. The case was heard again in the autumn, ending in a death penalty that had obviously been fixed in advance.[1301] Goebbels does present the case slightly differently from before, saying that Dorsay had made his first "defeatist" remarks "without my being able to nail him". But on the day of the execution he pronounced with brutal frankness that artists must at last "bow to national discipline", if not "they will lose their heads, like any other citizen". (29.10.1943) There is only one small reservation to mar the successful conclusion of the case: "I am very annoyed that Liebeneiner has spoken up for Dorsay as well; but that will not put me off." Goebbels announced the execution on posters as usual.

In 1944 alone 5,764 death sentences were carried out outside military jurisdiction, the vast majority for high treason and undermining military strength, in other words for grumbling or making jokes about the "Führer". Goebbels had two more people from the film world sentenced and executed for "utterances hostile to the state" by the Volksgerichtshof in the same year, the Terra and Ufa press officers, Erich Knauf and Richard Düwell.[1302] Interestingly, Goebbels refers to the fact that even the National Socialist Minister of Justice Thierack wanted to pardon Knauf, because, as Goebbels said cynically, Knauf "had written a few nice songs" in prison. But Goeb-

57. Actor Karl John: grab him by the scruff of the neck.

bels stood his ground: "The Führer is for going ahead and so am I ... He is guilty of such serious crimes against state security and military strength that he deserves to die. And the Führer will sign the death penalty for this reason as wel.l" (18.4.1944) Knauf, a former member of the SDP, was executed on 2 May 1944.

Although Ufa officially warned its employees against offences, and in particular against frivolous, derogatory remarks, their press officer Richard Düwell, a close friend of Wolfgang Liebeneiner, was also affected.[1303] Düwell was arrested in May, after months of surveillance for things he had said a long time ago, and executed, despite an intervention by Liebeneiner, on 28 August, when people were being dealt with more brutally than ever after the Stauffenberg assassination attempt on 20 July. In this case too the NS judiciary and the Gestapo were reticent as courts of appeal because some of the people who had denounced Düwell were very dubious, but Goebbels depended on sentence and execution. In December 1944 Goebbels felt that "a small Communist opposition has built up (in film circles), and I shall now destroy it root and branch". (5.12.1944) Whether by this Goebbels meant political assessments of Wolfgang Staudte, that he had in front of him at the time, or a Communist Party oriented resistance cell to which the film and stage actor Hans Meyer-Hanno belonged,[1304] can no longer be established with certainty.

A large number of film people address the extent to which they were threatened by the Nazis' arbitrary use of power in their post-war memoirs. Certainly some top stars could take greater risks than less well-known performers like Robert Dorsay. This also applies to Gustaf Gründgens, one of the most ambivalent figures in the film and theatre world of the "Third Reich", whose performance as Mephisto in Goethe's *Faust* had been a triumph in the Deutsches Theater as early as 1932. This intellectual actor and director was promoted by Hermann Göring in particular; Gründgens was under Göring's aegis Director General of the Prussian State Theatres from 1937. Even though the homophile stage star was an unparalleled irritant as far as Goebbels and Hitler were concerned, the Propaganda Minister had no direct access to Gründgens. It was said of Gründgens after the war that he was a "mortal enemy" to Goebbels as he "belonged to Göring's sphere of influence".[1305] On the other hand reproaches about alleged compliance with the wishes of the National Socialist regime are legion. At first Goebbels even seems to have admired this brilliant man of the theatre ("He has an interesting mind", 1.12.1935). He also defended him against the National Socialist cultural community of Party ideologue Alfred Rosenberg (14.5.1936), who repeatedly complained that Gründgens' theatre productions were "anti-Fascist",[1306] and also against "unjust" treatment by the "Reichsbühnendramaturg" ("Reich theatre script officer") Schlösser. (18.3.1937) Schlösser had denounced Gründgens' performance as Richard III as cultural Bolshevism.[1307] Gründgens felt so threatened for a time that he thought of going abroad for good,[1308] even though he had still appeared with Werner Krauß in the film version of Mussolini's Napoleon play *Cento Giorni* ("A Hundred Days").

But Goebbels' relatively positive image of Gründgens changed rapidly when Göring finally took on the role of patron saint. Goebbels repeatedly denounced Gründgens to Hitler, where his complaints about the homosexual "swamp in the state theatre" (27.7.1937) found a ready ear: "He feels that Gründgens has to go." (29.7.1937) Shortly after this, Göring made Gründgens a "Staatsrat" ("Prussian state councillor"), which meant that the actor could be arrested only with Göring's personal permission. This protection was a constant source of annoyance: "The Gründgens lot are all completely queer. I don't understand what Göring is up to there. I'm itching to do something about it." (21.1.1938) On the other hand, he called him a "smart and somehow sympathetic guy". (8.6.39)

Gründgens' films and his acting style did not very often appeal to Goebbels, but this not stop the two men from discussing new projects, nor Gründgens from bringing his "film and theatre worries" to Goebbels. (30.4.1938) Goebbels was obviously not disinclined to allow Gründgens to repeat his stage success of May 1940 in the play "Cavour" by Benito Mussolini and Giovacchino Forzano by making a film of the same name. As a alternative to this, he discussed the possibility of Gründgens staging the play "Cesare" by the same authors, based on a screenplay by Benito Mussolini. (3.8.1940)

Polemic against Gründgens intensified the more he came to the aid of beleaguered colleagues. Even so, there is no impression of deadly hostility to the Propaganda Minister, as Goebbels was still planning a major revue with Gründgens at the Metropol Theatre, although this was prevented by Hitler personally, who had again "expressed himself very sharply against Gründgens". (13.1.1943) Goebbels had to withdraw the project, which Gründgens had been pursuing energetically, and amazingly this happened "without Gründgens needing to be aware of the Führer's major misgivings about him". (13.1.1943) But Goebbels certainly was aware: "The Führer doesn't like Gustaf Gründgens. He is not masculine enough for him. He is of the opinion that homosexuality in public life is not to be tolerated under any circumstances.." (17.8.1941)

It is anyway extremely surprising to see how extensively Hitler occupied himself with the "stage intellectual" Gründgens, even during serious military crises. It is not just that he personally forbade a Gründgens production outside the state theatre at the height of the catastrophic developments in Stalingrad. Even shortly afterwards, when Gründgens volunteered for the armed forces[1309] – allegedly because he saw no other way out after the declaration of "total war" and would have been sent to a concentration camp – the Nazi bosses puzzled for weeks about the real reasons and motives: "I do not yet know the background to the whole business. In any case it is not true that the Führer has been dealing with this question. But he does not know what it is actually all about either. I will have to have enquiries made to Göring myself. In any case, things are not as clear and simple as Gründgens wants to make them look." (4.4.1943) While Gründgens maintains that he wanted to continue to direct the state theatre whatever happened, Goebbels reports that the Director General had practically forced the directorship on to Paul Hartmann, as Gründgens' successor. Goebbels of course suspects that there is an "something unpleasantly homosexual" (3.4.1943) behind Gründgens' joining Göring's Luftwaffe regiment. Had Gründgens found out about Hitler's increasingly aggressive attitude to him? Or is Goebbels exaggerating wildly here, and pushing Hitler forward to lend a little more weight to his own hatred? In any case, Goebbels dictated to his stenographer on 10.5.1943 that the "Führer" was still puzzled about Goebbels' motives, but "is of the opinion that Gründgens can do less harm in the Wehrmacht than in the theatre". (10.5.1943) In what was evidently his last meeting with Goebbels on 30.8.1944, Gründgens, who only spent six months in the Wehrmacht, intervened on behalf of his state theatres to try to prevent the closure of all German theatres, which was ordered on 1 September 1944.

It is amazing overall that Hitler's years of antipathy for the director of the state theatre had so few repercussions: Gründgens was left alone even after the more ruthless approach to all opposition after the Stauffenberg plot, even though Hitler regularly enquired about his behaviour. Goebbels liked supplying the answers: "The Führer is not at all surprised that Gründgens has refused to co-operate on a declaration of faith in the Führer. He has only contempt for him now." (5.12.1944) Possibly Göring's dwindling influence was still enough to protect Gründgens. But no one was absolutely safe: accounts were settled with a large number of old opponents, some of whom were already in custody, until the very last days of the war. At least one should not fundamentally dispute, despite all the inconsistencies, that Gründgens – as he asserts – could have been in danger of his life.

Jannings, who had been showered with every possible honour, came off just as badly as Gründgens from 1942 onwards. Even though Goebbels admired Jannings' genius and cinematic achievements he could not stand him personally. When they were working together very closely he regularly reviled him ("cowardly and unprincipled intriguer", 24.4.1938). Goebbels was also struck – and this was the worst conclusion of all for a Nazi – by a "striking similarity to Gregor Strasser", the Party "traitor" of 1932: "For that reason I am always somewhat sceptical." (25.2.1938)

Goebbels did not like Jannings' alleged rumour-mongering (see above), avarice and excessively ingenious contracts for his fees. And the Minister also repeatedly accused his former propaganda attraction of "cowardice". Like many other distinguished individuals – Goebbels mentions Ewald Balser, who nevertheless read the Clausewitz will on the radio for the new year 1942 as a special National Socialist ritual – Jannings avoided visiting the Reich capital too frequently, as it was constantly under the threat of air raids.[1310] This must have annoyed Goebbels all the more because he was in fact powerless against it. Jannings remained in his holiday home on the Wolfgangssee in Austria, where Goebbels used to spend extremely pleasant short stays with him. Now Hitler and his Minister were nursing thoughts of revenge: "In the evening we stayed chatting at the fireside for a few hours. I talk to the Führer about theatre, concert and film matters, which interest him considerably. He enquires in particular about the attitude of individual well-known artists to the stresses and strains of the war. Here Furtwängler is at the top and Jannings near the bottom. The Führer has nothing but contempt for the cowardice of the vacillators. But he also agrees with me that we should not forget. After the war the brave must be rewarded and the cowards punished." (14.3.1944)

Nevertheless, Jannings was accorded high honours by the Ufa bosses and the Nazi leadership on his 60th birthday on 23 July 1944. But the quarrel about the presence of notable artists in Berlin continued. Goebbels finally used the Jannings case as an excuse to refuse travelling expenses to film artists who were not prepared to live in their place of work.

Affairs and advantages

Fees and taxes

Goebbels presents the fight against rocketing actors' fees as an important element in his pre-war film policy. Insistently repeated complaints about excessively high fees (26.11.1937, 28.7.1938) show that Goebbels' announcements that he was going to take rigorous action against this trend were usually unsuccessful. And from 1935 onwards the Minister also complains regularly about a flood of begging letters and demands for money sent to him by notable artists. Every new fee structure immediately met with vociferous protests, which compelled Goebbels to proceed cautiously: "This is very difficult and has to be handled extraordinarily discreetly." (22.12.1937) Many of the stars were obviously very assertive about such matters: Goebbels was very cross about "shameless" demands for money by an artist like Jenny Jugo, for example. (3.5.1937)

Before the war it was very difficult to get a grip on explosive cost increases because of the fee element in film budgets. For instance, Hans Albers was on an annual fee of half a million marks as early as 1936. Ultimately Goebbels himself was not blameless as far as this development was concerned: his credo before the "Anschluss" of Austria was: "We must have all the great artists in Germany. And make financial sacrifices to this end." (8.12.1937) And of course artists knew how to make the most of recruitment campaigns of this kind.

Alongside fees, paying the least tax possible appears in Goebbels' writings as another thing film artists were interested in. There was scarcely one of them who did not discuss personal tax matters with Goebbels. "Tax-free extra fees", instigated or approved by Hitler himself, were no rarity. Emil Jannings, Fritz Hippler and Heinz Rühmann benefited just as much as Veit Harlan or Wolfgang Liebeneiner from donations of several tens of thousands of marks, which often came from Hitler's private "culture fund".[1311] Goebbels often agreed to generous help and benevolent tax inspections, even down to acquiring currency for foreign trips. Apparently Lilian Harvery made exaggerated demands, she "wants a whole heap of foreign currency". (5.4.1938) In fact currency smuggling was a vice that many film people indulged in. Heinz Rühmann was saddled with some tiresome proceedings on this head. Camilla Horn was even dismissed from the Reichsfilmkammer for trying to smuggle Reichsmarks over the border into Czechoslvakia in her shoe.[1312] (Then Goebbels granted her special payments again in 1942, because she was in financial difficulties.)

Fees were not raised as freely after 1940, and tax concessions were often cut completely. Hans Hinkel, the Reichskulturkammer manager, was personally appointed by Goebbels to be "special trustee for the work of culture-generating groups". He was assisted by a special official, Müller-Goerne,[1313] and his role was to stop fees from rising and examine contracts. But ultimately in many cases the level of fees, despite Goebbels' public enjoinder not to pester him with any more demands,[1314] remained linked to personal permission from the Minister. (25.2.1941)

Certainly Goebbels tried for a time to postpone the problem of reforming fee structures to the period after the war: "At the moment I do not want to address these problems, despite all the pressure", not least "to avoid triggering all the crises and possibilities for annoying people that they conceal." (3.2.1942) But the longer the war went on, the less this defensive attitude to the exorbitant fees commanded by some film stars fitted in with his renunciation propaganda, which was proclaimed everywhere. The annual contracts guaranteed large sums even when the film project concerned did not come about – now called "pay or play" – and were thus "contracts from the past, which are anything but National Socialist". (14.8.1942) Goebbels' attempt to make an example of Emil Jannings, "who has proved outrageously cunning in securing a contract for himself that wangles all the rights for him and all the obligations for Tobis" (14.8.1942), did not meet with the desired success.[1315] After *The Dismissal*, Jannings was seen in only one film before the end of the war (*Altes Herz wird wieder jung*). According to Goebbels he neglected all the other projects offered him, but continued to draw top wages. Another 225,000 marks had been set aside for the *Wo ist Herr Belling* ("Where is Mr. Belling?") project. A dispute with the Propaganda Ministry also led to Jannings' demand that his servant has to have a first class ticket with sleeping car paid for whenever he travelled to Berlin.

Towards the end of the war many artists had only two things in their heads: survival and money. To avoid being called up into the armed forces productions were kept going with all the resources available, which was just as Goebbels wished. The films shifted to exterior shots in the country because so many studios had been destroyed, and because of the constant air raids. This is why there are so many beautiful landscape shots in films made after 1943.

In 1944 there are requests and begging letters from almost all the film artists, varying in tone from flattering to demanding. Wolfgang Liebeneiner complained to Max Winkler several times from June 1944 to January 1945 that as Ufa production head ("a thankless task") he was now earning less than from his previous work as a director. He was unequivocally asking for more money, and also pointing out how much more Veit Harlan was drawing.[1316] Similar requests came from his wife Hilde Krahl. In June 1944, after resisting for some time, Goebbels finally granted her a lavish annual fee of 150,000 Reichsmarks.[1317]

In February 1944 – Hitler was involved this time as well –, Goebbels refused to pay Marika Rökk, the star of numerous revue films, a bridging fee between two film engagements because he had not liked her last appearance, in *Die Frau meiner Träume*.[1318] The actor and theatre director Eugen Klöpfer who joined the National Socialist Party in 1937, was paid an daily fee of 2,000 Reichsmarks even before the war. In May 1944 he asked for more, in the form of a lump sum of at least 50,000 Reichsmarks.[1319]

In January 1944, Goebbels wanted to cut Heinrich George's fee for his role in *Kolberg* from 150,000 to 120,000 Reichsmarks, but he met with such massive resistance that George finally kept his 150,000 Reichsmarks. A year later, Goebbels moved against high wages for Hans Albers, who was filming in Prague; Albers had already received over 400,000 marks for *Große Freiheit Nr. 7* (*Great Freedom No 7*). But Albers was paid what he asked for in 1945 as well. And so artists managed to get what they wanted from Goebbels despite very rigid economy measures.

Other film people were tormented with much more severe worries than just the danger of wage cuts. For example, Karl Ritter and Camilla Horn were up to their eyes in debt and turned to Goebbels with letters asking for special payments. As a propaganda specialist, Ritter was not in demand as a director after 1943, and he had already mortgaged his house in Griebnitz-see, Potsdam. Goebbels had already pronounced on 15.10.1940 that "Prof. Ritter was close to being bankrupt. I will bail him out." But this was unsuccessful, despite several extra sums of money, for which reason Hitler personally authorized to another tax-free payment of 100,000 Reichsmarks to pay off the former star director's debts.[1320] But Ritter was still not to make any more films.

Misdemeanours

Goebbels found himself permanently required to criticize the behaviour and life-style of eminent artists. This was done on the basis of his own sense of middle-class values, which were partly genuine and partly the product of holier-than-thou moralizing. Goebbels castigated the bohemian life, extravagance, élitist and arrogant attitudes and financial. Although adultery ("Worried about Werner Krauß. His Maria Bard is being unfaithful", 16.11.1937) and alcoholism were widely tolerated, Goebbels used these vices as a welcome target as well.

Goebbels went out of his way to draw up copious "indispensable lists" to prevent artists and employees of the film industry from having to go to the front after the war broke out, but he also regularly called them "shirkers", "idlers", "war profiteers" and "defeatists" for doing this. But the concrete reason for this was often little more than minor misdemeanours like breaks of several weeks between two films, black market deals, ignoring no smoking rules in studios or currency offences. Sated artists and certain Berlin "gourmet circles"[1321] are Goebbels' favourite examples when he wants to drum up a taste for "total war" with rabble-rousing rhetoric.

Goebbels was not pleased to notice that it was not enough to put in managements and heads of production when production chiefs, directors, script editors, screenplay writers and other employees were creating niches, private spaces and a life of their own at lower levels in the studios and production venues. Goebbels had only limited possibilities of access, as responsibility often lay with the head of production or of the company in the first place, and they were very often "incompetent". Goebbels detected circumstances of this kind above all at Tobis, which was under the direction of the "actual Nazi" von Demandowsky.[1322] (3.4.1942)

For example, at the Ufi directors' meeting on 3 June 1942 a decision was taken to "carry out merciless disciplinary measures against "representatives of the employees" who were guilty of misdemeanours.[1323] This seems to have done little good at first. On 30.7.1942 Goebbels again mentions a "series of corruption cases" in film circles "that are absolutely hair-raising": "I have now decided to move rigorously and drastically and not to make any more allowances."

In autumn 1942 Goebbels received reports of opposition movements, corruption and "protection rackets" in a "clique" around production head Karl Hartl at Wien-Film, Hartl, although the

Security Service had him down as a faithful National Socialist, was said even to have refused to use the Nazi salute at one time.[1324] Finally Goebbels removed indispensable status from some of Hartl's cronies, in order to "break up the clique".[1325]

Hans Bertram, the director of *Symphonie eines Lebens*, also incurred Goebbels' wrath: he was excluded from the Reichskulturkammer in October 1942 for alleged false statements and slander.[1326] A "Council of Honour for the German Cinema", a distinguished committee chaired by Reichsfilmintendant Hippler, was formed in 23 September 1942. Two days after Goebbels noted that the director could "hardly be saved now" (23.9.1942) it excluded Bertram from the Reichsfilmkammer at its very first meeting. Goebbels came up with the flimsy explanation that he wanted to keep himself out of staffing matters by putting the committee between him and such decisions: "I hope that it will give me a few advantages, above all that I am not directly drawn into every decision and can withdraw into the background rather more." In fact he always had the last word in decisions of this kind.

A group of extras who had misbehaved during location shooting in Gotenhafen for the film *Titanic* caused further annoyance. The meticulous investigation spoke of corruption, orgies and excessive alcohol consumption on board the Cap Arcona. The actress Sybille Schmitz – the model for Fassbinder's *Die Sehnsucht der Veronika Voss* (*Veronika Voss*) – was said to have been involved as well as the crew and Tobis employees.[1327] Once more Goebbels mentions "unpleasant events in the film sector". (11.12.1942) He thus reacted all the more severely a few weeks later to Hans Söhnker's breaks in shooting, which he felt were too long. He said it was about time to "involve lazy film and theatre artists who have indispensable status and sometimes have nothing to do for two or three months in entertaining the troops". (16.1.1943) He had a telegram sent to Söhnker during his spa treatment at Bad Aussee: "Ministry requires immediate action. Troop entertainment before next film role, as last film work ended October."[1328] And then the artists could not even do things right while entertaining the troops for Goebbels: he pointed out critically as early as 26.2.1942 that artist tended to operate as "war profiteers" on these occasions, as they "put on airs as the great intellectual troop entertainers at the front and get three four or five hundred marks an evening for reciting a poem."

Pets and favourites

After the war, film people like Emil Jannings, Werner Krauß, Paula Wessely or Leni Riefenstahl countered reproaches that they had collaborated with Goebbels by pointing out that when all was said and done they had not even been members of the National Socialist Party. But it was precisely these non-members who were much more important to Geobbels as propaganda actors and directors than Party-registered individuals like Viktor de Kowa and Willy Fritsch. The regime's calculations were dominated by "non-political to material preferences".[1329] It was often more concerned with eminence and the extent to which state-controlled art policies could benefit than formal Party loyalty.

Mere membership of the National Socialist Party was not necessarily an advantage to performers like Volker von Collande, Rudolf Fernau or Harry Piel. It only meant preferential treatment if the individuals concerned went on to proclaim their sympathy for the NS (as in the case of Johannes Riemann), by public statements, for example. Thus for example one of the most prominent film and theatre actresses, Elisabeth Flickenschildt, was listed as a member from 1 July 1932, thus joined before the seizure of power.[1330] But there are no indications of her being particularly faithful to the Party line. Goebbels does not seem to have been especially interested in her: he thought she was an outstanding theatre actress, but not good-looking enough for leading roles in films. (30.9.1938) Hilde Krahl joined the Party in 1936, but this did not lead to any visible privileges that could not have been acquired otherwise. Her star potential, rather than her Party membership card, must have been the main reason for Goebbels discussing film plans with her personally. ("She is extraordinarily clever", 20.9.1940)

This honour was granted only to a very few top stars like Leander and Jannings after the turning-point in the war in 1942/43, but surprising also to the Austrian actress Paula Wessely, with whom Goebbels exchanged "a few kind remarks" about film material as late as July 1943. The exotic Brigitte Horney, who had a few very patriotic roles to her credit, was received by Goebbels after a TB-related stay in a sanatorium in Davos. Here the Minister was pleased "that Brigitte Horney so much strengthened her National Socialist conviction during her stay in Davos. I saw few actors and actresses who display such clear opinions about the war as she does." (29.6.1944)

It helped film people more to be a personal friend or acquaintance of Goebbels, Hippler or Hinkel, involved beyond mere participation in the "inner circle", than to be a Party member. The director Hans H. Zerlett was friendly with Hans Hinkel. Käthe Haack, Hannelore Schroth's mother, was also well acquainted with Hinkel, possibly through her husband Heinrich, who like Hinkel was a member of the SS. She tried to wheedle her way into Hinkel's favour by addressing him as "dear little Hans". Contacts of this kind certainly helped to have her daughter excused from community service work, by means of a Goebbels-mediated decision by Hitler.[1331] And in Heinrich Himmler's diary there is a note of dinner with a "Fräulein Ilse Werner" on 6.9.1942, followed by some newsreel screenings.[1332]

The Berlin theatre actress Carola Höhn also maintained particularly close contact with Goebbels. She was even present at a few gatherings otherwise attended only by Goebbels' family and closest friends like the "Reich stage designer" Benno von Arent or Helldorf, the Berlin police chief. (17./18.4.1938, 5.6.1938) Such meetings led to: "Carola Höhn is worried" (3.4.1937), which Goebbels then took on: "I will get her a good part in the *Claudia* film (12.8.1937)[1333] or "I am checking the list of classified artists over again. I will rescue Carola Höhn's contract." (16.6.1937)

But being Goebbels' or Hitler's favourite did not last for ever. A number of people like Luise Ullrich and Jenny Jugo who were frequent guests of the NS leaders in the thirties soon found this out. When Veit Harlan left his wife Hilde Körber she went straight to Goebbels and Hitler to share her sorrows. "Hilde Körber tells me some sob-story" was Goebbels' cynical comment. (19.8.1938). But he did arrange a film contract with Tobis for the mother of three, who also wrote letters to the "Führer", but "as a social measure": Goebbels' personnel officer said in 1942 that Hilde Körber could "only be used in very limited contexts".[1334]

But people could go too far. Using a mixture of star quality and lack of concern, some top performers referred to alleged promises by Goebbels when they had problems with directors or production heads. Brigitte Horney rejected several cameramen when shooting *Geliebte Welt*, saying that Goebbels had agreed that all her wishes should be met. This led to laborious enquiries by the intimidated film people, until it became clear that "no discussion had ever taken place between the Minister and Fräulein Horney" on this subject.[1335]

Luise Ullrich was put down as an awkward customer when shooting as early as 1935. She had also lost credit with Goebbels because she allegedly intended to accept offers from Hollywood in 1938. After a long stay in South America she refused to play the film roles that Goebbels had

60. Leni Riefenstahl during shooting for the
Olympia film in 1936: hysteria or sabotage?
61. Reception for Leni for the première of the
Olympia film: "Leni is already very capable."

chosen for her. The Propaganda Minister issued a top secret instruction in April 1942 that she was not to be used in films for at least a year.[1336]

Jenny Jugo met Hitler and Goebbels in a small group on numerous occasions ("The Führer has sent her flowers", 11.10.1935), for which she thanked him in effusive "Heil mein Führer"-letters, but this was of increasingly little advantage to her during the war. Goebbels did give orders personally in May 1942 that her request for a fee of 80,000 Reichsmarks per film should be met. But in September 1944, when she was denounced by her own housekeeper for defeatist remarks, Goebbels brought in Hitler and instigated a simultaneous investigation into whether Jugo's husband Friedel Benfer had not been declared indispensable unjustifiably.[1337]

The behaviour of many of the Nazis' favourite film artists often produces a picture that is at best contradictory. Käthe Dorsch sent devoted telegrams to Hitler and tried to get better parts through her contacts with Nazi leaders, but also did what she could for Jews and distressed and needy colleagues. (14.12.1937, 19.1.1940, 12.2.1941) Wolfgang Liebeneiner interceded with Goebbels against the death penalty for Düwell, later lied about his involvement in the euthanasia film *I Accuse*, said after the war that that he had asked to be replaced as head of Ufa productions after Düwell's death, while Hans Hinkel, in letters to Goebbels, confirms that Liebeneiner was an assiduous worker. Henny Porten wrote nice letters to Hitler and Göring, but complained about the food situation in letters intercepted by the Gestapo and was cautioned about this by Goebbels. Despite all the indisputable currying of favour and conformity, very few artists had enough tactical skill to deal with the unpredictable Minister. They were not careful enough, arrogant and sometime actually apolitical.

Leni Riefenstahl, the "Third Reich's" only female film director, and also "the only star who understands us" (Goebbels), is probably the figure in National Socialist cinema who has been best described. Even the Goebbels diaries have been evaluated in detail on this subject, even though the most explosive material must be in the volumes for 1933–35, which have not yet been published.

Leni Riefenstahl came up with numerous untruths after the war. She has already been faced with the contradictions between her statements and Goebbels' notes with a camera rolling in Ray Müller's film documentary *Leni Riefenstahl – Die Macht der Bilder* (*Leni Riefenstahl – The Power of the Images*). This included in particular her constant social contacts with the National Socialist leaders, which began even before the "seizure of power". However, it certainly seems she has so internalized the version of innocence she has upheld over the years that she actually believes it today, without being aware that she is wrong.

62. Heinz Rühmann, Hermann Göring: frequent guest, makes "funny birthday film".

Leni Riefenstahl agreed to take part in a number of interviews relating to the debate about her exhibition of pictures in Hamburg in summer 1997. Among other things, she replied to questions about whether she had not noticed the exodus of Jewish actors and friends after January 1933 as follows: "I was not in Germany at all in the first few months after the takeover of power. I was shooting with an American team in Switzerland, on the Bernina pass. We lived in a mountain hut there, with no television and not even a radio. So I did not experience the takeover of power, and I had no idea about the book-burning. I did not come back to Germany until July 1933."[1338]

There must be other ways of proving that Leni Riefenstahl was in Germany at this time (Goebbels' diary as available so far does not start again until May 1933). But she appears in Goebbels' entries as early as 17 May 1933, bursting with energy: "p.m., Leni Riefenstahl: she tells me about her plans. I suggest a film about Hitler to her. She is enthusiastic about it." And a little later she is at an "unsuccessful picnic" with Goebbels and Hitler. (26.5.1933) Then in the weeks after that they worked on the film plans together. (12.6.1933)

Some legends, for example the suggestion that her *Olympia* film was financed without Reich funds or a telegram of thanks to Hitler that she disputes have long been cleared up in her disfavour. Her contacts with the *Stürmer* editor and Gauleiter of Nuremberg Julius Streicher, who wrote her glowing thank-you letters about "the hours that we spent in your house",[1339] remain dubious. Leni Riefenstahl claims to have seen Streicher only once in her memoirs, and to have attacked him immediately about his *Stürmer*. In fact, she visited him in his house in Nuremberg even during the war.[1340] A great deal about the relationship between Goebbels/Hitler and Riefenstahl will come to light when the diaries for 1933 to 1935 are fully accessible. Goebbels is said to have persecuted her continually with persistent hatred and intentions of sabotage; evidence of this will be particularly sought in the diaries.

As far as can so far be seen, Goebbels admired Leni Riefenstahls' work and also thought a great deal of her personally. But he must have been bothered by her direct line to Hitler and self-confident presentation of herself as a woman and brilliant film-maker, which he regularly marked down as "hysterical".

Leni Riefenstahl was still in very close touch with Goebbels in 1938, when they jointly planned marketing her Olympics film abroad and also her visit to America (Goebbels: "I'm sending her to Hollywood to study their techniques", 22.3.1938), but after that year she appears very little in his entries. Diary entries that are incriminating at first sight, in which Riefenstahl reports on "terror and boycott" by Jews in the USA (5.12.1939), are to be consumed with care. Riefenstahl certainly was annoyed about the rejection of her Olympics film in the USA. But the cheap anti-Semitic propaganda clichés are part of Goebbels' standard repertoire for presenting America. Riefenstahl's work on the film *Tiefland* (*Lowlands*), which was in part financed directly from the Reich budget, was dogged by ill luck. Goebbels thought the film was far too expensive (6.12. 1940),[1341] but did not want to intervene in its production. (30.3.1940) He comments on 16.12. 1942 that the film has made the director ill and that she is in urgent need of rest and relaxation. This is the last meeting noted by Goebbels.

Goebbels never has an unkind word for Marlene Dietrich, who emigrated to the USA before 1933. Passages about the screen legend's alleged willingness to come back remain mysterious. Goebbels despatched Heinz Hilpert, the director of the Deutsches Theater in Berlin, as an emissary to Paris to persuade the actress, who had become world-famous with *The Blue Angel*, to return to Germany. He notes on the basis of Hilpert's report: "Marlene Dietrich cannot appear in Berlin for a year. But she remains committed to Germany." (12.11.1937) But Marlene Dietrich herself said that she never intended coming to Berlin and didn't say anything about it either.[1342]

Heinz Rühmann was married to a Jewess, and is said to have been on the "hit list" for this reason, and his chances of working were at risk.[1343] He was on a list of people with special permission for a time, and moved on to the regular list only after he divorced Maria Bernheim in January 1939. A certain amount of pressure and isolated protests came from the lower echelons of the Party as well. But none of this came to much: although there were allegedly no offers, Rühmann made four films per year from 1936 to 1938. The Propaganda Minister is scarcely mentioned in Rühmann's memoirs, but the actor does feature frequently in Goebbels' diary. Rühmann was a "system-stabilizing comedian" (Karsten Witte), who symbolized conformist rebellion by the little man in the National Socialist state. He was esteemed very highly from the outset, and soon belonged to a relatively small circle around Goebbels. Rühmann could afford to be awkward to a certain extent. Goebbels once suspected him of knowing about "Jewish" involvement in the comedy *Der Mustergatte* ("The Model Husband", 10.10.1937). Later he even calls him "cheeky" and "a bit too shameless", indeed has him "cautioned". (7.4.1940) This was probably all about rumours fostered by Terra production head Peter Paul Brauer that Rühmann wanted to go abroad, though the matter was rapidly cleared up: "Rühmann has explained himself positively." (10.4.1940) Goebbels always notes his intention of helping the actor with both his private and professional difficulties ("Rühmann has worries about director Wisbar. I will relieve him of them", 18.12.1937).

The newsreel showed a request concert appearance by Heinz Rühmann in the war winter of 1940. Together with his friends Hans Brausewetter and Josef Sieber (from *Paradies der Jungesellen*/"Bachelors' Paradise") he sang an anti-Churchill version of a "sailor" hit: "That will distress the First Sea Lord, even if he lies like mad", in honour of Lieutenant-Commander Prien.

The gifted comedian surprised Goebbels on his 43rd birthday with a "funny birthday film" which "Heinz Rühmann had made with the children, made me laugh and cry, so beautiful". (30. 10.1940) A film fitting this description has survived,[1344] possibly there were several. Rühmann, who appeared in newsreels as an airman, also claims that he travelled to the "Führer's" headquarters with a copy of his school comedy *Punch Bowl*. He wanted to go behind Goebbels' back and appeal personally to Hitler and Göring not to ban the film.[1345] According to the diary that was not necessary: Goebbels himself who liked the film was instructed by Hitler to show the film despite protests. (25.1.1944)

Goebbels is said to have been a guest in Rühmann's house at no. 15 Am kleinen Wannsee on one occasion only.[1346] The occasion was the 65th birthday of Rühmann's regular director Carl Froelich, on 5 September 1940. But Rühmann must have visited Goebbels on several occasions; for example, he appeared there on 21 September 1940 in the most intimate circle of film propagandists, with Jannings, Karl Ritter and Gustav Ucicky, who had made NSDAP election films as early as 1938.

On 26 January 1941 a group met that included Rühmann, adjutant Hans-Leo Martin, the "Führer's" photographer Heinrich Hoffmann, Carl Froelich and the wife of "Reich set designer" Benno von Arent. There were still (semi-)private meetings with Goebbels during the war, for example when Rühmann and Hertha Feiler came to the Minister's apartment on 1 August 1942, with Hippler, Rolf Hansen, Jenny Jugo and her husband Friedel Benfer.

Veit Harlan, the director of lavish propaganda epics, also maintained very close contact with Goebbels. He was one of the exclusive circle of friends and film artists who also visited Goebbels at his country house on the Bogensee in Berlin. Goebbels noted after one such meeting: "Harlan is a clever chap. I shall keep him in mind." (24.4.1937) Shortly after this the Minister put the director in the supervisory board of Ufa, which had just been bought up. Goebbels saw Harlan as "a fanatic and fighter". (15.4.1938) Comparisons show that of all the directors and actors Harlan was Goebbels' most frequent guest on "spins", at "discussions" and film screenings, and indeed that Goebbels (and this is a great exception in his relationships with "film creators") for a time mentions more private than professional contacts with him. There is only a single invitation re-

63. Crowd puller Zarah Leander: "she likes being involved in things with us here."
64. Heinrich George: faithful warrior.

181

corded in Harlan's memoirs where the description differs substantially from Goebbels' diary entry.[1347] Harlan's name appears in the diary whenever Goebbels notes meetings with film people until well into the war. One sign of great favour is that Harlan and Söderbaum spent New Year's Eve with Goebbels, in 1940 and 1942 as well, in the most intimate circle of family and friends, in Goebbels' private apartment.

After the "divine" Greta Garbo, Marlene Dietrich and Ingrid Bergman had all declined to film in Germany, the Swedish actress Zarah Leander became the superstar, the "substitute Garbo" with the highest box-office returns. She was of inestimable value to the German cinema in the war. Zarah Leander was the embodiment of "that mysterious shimmer, that phlegmatic melancholy" (Klaus Kreimeier)[1348] and of the melodramatic cinema of stamina and holding out to which she brought enormous success with songs like "Es wird einmal ein Wunder geschehn" ("There will be a miracle one day").

Zarah Leander seems as apolitical in Goebbels' entries as she saw herself to be, but as the same time adaptable and tough in presenting her own interests. Remarkably enough, Goebbels did not notice Zarah Leander's charisma, box-office power and effect on the public in the early stages. In fact the Propaganda Minister resisted her engagement by Ufa at first. (8.2.2937) Apparently the driving force here was his collaborator Hans Weidemann. Goebbels calls her an "enemy of Germany" (15.1.1937), and says on the question of a permanent engagement in Germany: "I think that this woman is very much overestimated" (21.3.1937), but then allowed himself to be persuaded by the box-office returns: "She has been an enormous commercial success." (6.10.1937) Goebbels looked after and praised her from then on. (15.9.1938)

After the outbreak of war, Zarah Leander had to face the question of whether she should stay in Germany or return to Sweden. Goebbels tried to keep her with all the means at his disposal, offered her a new villa and undreamed-of privileges in a long discussion on 14 June 1939, and hoped that she would feel at home and like a German.[1349] Zarah Leander responded to a similar request by Ufa by writing to Ufa chairman Klitzsch in September 1939 in a somewhat roundabout way in view of the outbreak of war to say that "my feelings for Ufa and for my German friends have been further consolidated by recent events".[1350] She made herself available for more films in Germany and negotiated enormous fees for them, some of which had to be paid in Swedish kroners – an agreement that was soon very hard to honour because of the chronic lack of foreign currency in the war.

Goebbels regularly took care of his great star personally and frequently invited her to the Propaganda Ministry for short discussions. When the actress expressed concern "that Sweden could be drawn into the conflict", Goebbels notes: "Women are completely apolitical." (11.1.1940) Much more important: "She likes being involved in things with us here", he states on 7.12.1940. Visits to Goebbels in Schwanenwerder (8.10.1940) or for a "little chat with Frau Leander" in Lanke (4.9.1940) were no rarity. Goebbels even called on the diva after the première of *Die große Liebe* (*The Great Love*, 14.6.1942) – which, incidentally, the press was forbidden to report. Zarah Leander was just as little afraid to meet Goebbels and Hitler at countless social events as she was to appear at request concerts.

From autumn 1942 she spent very little time in Germany and made use of her permanent travel permit to Sweden, where she had an estate in Löno. Her contract with Ufa expired on 31 October 1942, and a further one for the melodrama *Damals* (*Back Then*)was intended to run to mid 1943. There was no breach with Ufa until after the première of this film. But Goebbels obviously tried to persuade Leander to make more films by suggesting material and titles. Her last "short conversation" (28.11.1942) had been harmonious: the actress reported to the Minister, as she had at similar meetings in the past, how well-disposed the Swedes at home were to Germany – at least Goebbels was all to pleased to think that this was what he heard. The diva is supposed to have finally moved back to Sweden in April 1943.[1351] Goebbels wanted to make her more offers in the same month; one feature was that she would receive 250,000 Reichsmarks for a single film, to be shot between April and June 1943. It is doubtful if there actually was talk about awarding her the title of "State Actress" at this time. In fact Goebbels had already failed to bring this about once. So he does write, on 21.11.1941: "I also bring up the case of Leander in this context. The Führer feels that of course Frau Leander must be made a State Actress, because firstly she is a great actress and secondly she has made a great contribution to world recognition of German cinema." But either Hitler changed his mind or Goebbels was somewhat precipitate. It was not until months later, after the première of *The Great Love*, that the incident crops up in the files: the Propaganda Ministry's film department was to find out Hitler's view of the matter.[1352] After sounding out the permanent secretary of the Presidential

Chancellery, Hans-Otto Meissner, the impression emerged that Hitler had reservations because of Zarah Leander's Swedish citizenship.[1353] Then in September 1942 came the express statement that Hitler was opposed to the appointment.[1354]

But setting aside honorary titles: Zarah Leander's departure did not take place as quickly as later described. She seems at least not to have rejected Goebbels' offers categorically. On the contrary, negotiations went on until September 1943, with Zarah Leander reacting very slowly to the material she was sent.[1355] All the same, she travelled to Paris for the dubbing of her last German film made in the war, *Damals*.[1356] The actress was also concerned to get her enormous assets and her valuables out of Berlin without any difficulty.

But did she, as is also regularly asserted,[1357] become a non-person after her departure from Germany, whose films and songs disappeared from the media? This may be true in the case of the press, but the film industry and the Propaganda Ministry present a very different picture. It was not until July 1944, when interviews with the actress that were allegedly "hostile to Germany" had appeared in the Stockholm press, that individual Party offices requested that all Leander films should be withdrawn. Hinkel submitted this question to Goebbels, with a note saying that ultimately these export hits were the "driving force behind all German production, whose sales would be called into question by this". The films could not be withdrawn at home or abroad for commercial reasons. Bans in individual districts would have to be lifted. And he continued: over 500 copies of the Leander films were in circulation, bringing in over three million Reichsmarks a year![1358] Shortly after this the Reichspropagandaleitung announced that *The Great Love* could still be shown.[1359] It was not until January 1945 that the Propaganda Ministry stated that no more Zarah Leander songs would be played on domestic radio.[1360]

Heinrich George's role under National Socialism is still a source of controversy. A new biographical defence has appeared recently.[1361] But minutes of George being questioned after his internment by the Soviet forces of occupation have also turned up, and here the actor comes over as extremely penitent. Did he have reason to be so?

The public at the time must have seen George as one of the most faithful Nazi supporters among the film people.[1362] His regular public oaths of allegiance, emotional tributes, his reading of nationalist texts on the radio, his propaganda roles in *Jud Süss* and *Kolberg* and his applause for Goebbels' "total war" speech that was seen in a newsreel did not allow any other conclusion. He was one of the first performers to be appointed "State Actor" and he was made Director-General of the Schillertheater on his 50th birthday in May 1943. Goebbels constantly praises this talented and passionate actor with a "full-blooded nature" – both artistically and politically – and reports that Hitler felt the same. The Minister was even annoyed that George was constantly played down in favour of Gründgens by what was left of Berlin's intellectual theatre criticism. (28.6.1944) In late 1944, Hans Albers and Gründgens refused to make a last public commitment to the "Führer", but George did so. "George is still the old valiant warrior for our cause, who will go along with us for good or ill", the Minister dictated in 1944.

Glossary and index of abbreviations

ARD	Arbeitsgemeinschaft der öffentlich-rechtlichen Rundfunkanstalten der Bundesrepublik Deutschland
BA/K	Bundesarchiv Koblenz
BA/P	Bundesarchiv Potsdam
BDC	Berlin Document Center
DAF	Deutsche Arbeitsfront
DFG	Deutsche Filmherstellungs- und Verwertungsgesellschaft mbH
DFV	Deutscher Film-Verleih
DNB	Deutsches Nachrichtenbüro
DTW	Deulig-Tonwoche
DW	Deutsche Wochenschau
FKB	Filmkreditbank
HA	Hauptamt
KddK	Kameradschaft der deutschen Künstler
KdF	Organisation Kraft durch Freude
NSBO	Nationalsozialistische Betriebszellenorganisation
NSDAP	Nationalsozialistische Deutsche Arbeiterpartei
NSKK	Nationalsozialistisches Kraftfahrkorps
NSV	Nationalsozialistische Volkswohlfahrt
PK	Propaganda-Kompanie
RAD	Reichsarbeitsdienst
RFD	Reichsfilmdramaturgie
RFI	Reichsfilmintendanz
RFK	Reichsfilmkammer
RFM	Reichsfinanzministerium
RKK	Reichskulturkammer
RMVP	Reichsministerium für Volksaufklärung und Propaganda
RPL	Reichspropagandaleitung der NSDAP
SA	Sturmabteilung der NSDAP
SD	Sicherheitsdienst der SS
SIPO	Sicherheitspolizei
SOPADE	Sozialdemokratische Partei Deutschlands (SPD in exile)
SS	Schutzstaffel der NSDAP
OKW	Oberkommando der Wehrmacht
OKH	Oberkommando des Heeres
UTW	Ufa-Tonwoche
ZDF	Zweites Deutsches Fernsehen

Notes

1 Elisabeth Bauschmidt, in: *Süddeutsche Zeitung*, 14. 1. 1997.

2 Speech on 25. 3. 1933 to radio managers and directors, in: Helmut Heiber (ed.), *Goebbels-Reden 1932–1939*, Düsseldorf 1971, p. 94. On earlier occasions Goebbels even used the word National Socialist rather than nationalist.

3 *Süddeutsche Zeitung*, 29. 3. 1995, p. 15.

4 Gerd Albrecht, *Nationalsozialistische Filmpolitik*, Stuttgart 1969 (Albrecht I), p. 56 f.

5 Rainer Rother, "Die Effekte der Unterhaltung", in: Wolfgang Jacobsen (ed.), *Babelsberg*, Berlin 1992, p. 213.

6 Arthur M. Rabenalt, *Joseph Goebbels und der "Großdeutsche" Film*, Munich 1985, p. 69.

7 Klaus Kreimeier, *Die Ufa-Story*, Munich 1992, p. 285.

8 Siegfried Zielinski, *Veit Harlan*, Frankfurt am Main 1981, pp. 10 f.

9 Hans-Michael Bock / Michael Töteberg (eds.), *Das Ufa-Buch*, Frankfurt am Main 1992; Wolfgang Jacobsen (ed.), *Babelsberg*, Berlin 1992; Klaus Kreimeier, *Die Ufa-Story*, Munich 1992.

10 Ulrich von Thüna, in: *Publizistik*, 34th year, 1989, p. 233.

11 Michaela Krützen, *Hans Albers. Eine deutsche Karriere*, Berlin 1995; Dodo Kresser / Michael Horvath, *Nur ein Komödiant? Hans Moser in den Jahren 1938–1945*, Vienna 1994; Maria Steiner, *Paula Wessely. Die verdrängten Jahre*, Vienna 1996.

12 Françis Courtade / Pierre Cadars, *Geschichte des Films im Dritten Reich*, Munich 1975; the French version, Françis Courtade / Pierre Cadars, *L'histoire du cinéma nazi*, Paris 1972, is preferable in places; Jerzy Toeplitz, *Geschichte des Films*, vol. 3: *1934–1939*, Berlin 1982, vol. 4: *1939 to 1945*, Berlin 1983; David Stewart Hull, *Film in the Third Reich*, Berkeley 1968.

13 Boguslaw Drewniak, *Der deutsche Film 1938 bis 1945*, Düsseldorf 1987.

14 Wolfgang Becker, *Film und Herrschaft*, Berlin 1973; Jürgen Spiker, *Film und Kapital*, Berlin 1975.

15 Albrecht I; same author (ed.), *Der Film im Dritten Reich. Eine Dokumentation*, Karlsruhe 1979 (Albrecht II).

16 Albrecht I, pp. 102 f.

17 Zielinski, pp. 101 f. There are also interesting contradictions between Albrecht's proposed assignments and Goebbels' own view of some productions on the borderline between politics and entertainment.

18 Klaus-Jürgen Maiwald, *Film-Zensur im NS-Staat*, Dortmund 1983; Kraft Wetzel / Peter Hagemann. *Zensur-verbotene deutsche Filme 1933 bis 1945*, Berlin 1978.

19 See note 7.

20 David Welch, *Propaganda and the German Cinema*, Oxford 1983; Erwin Leiser, *"Deutschland erwache". Propaganda im Film des Dritten Reiches*, Hamburg 1968. Hilmar Hoffmann, *"Und die Fahne führt uns in die Ewigkeit", Propaganda im NS-Film*, Frankfurt am Main 1988, deals with documentary propaganda films. Andrea Winkler-Mayerhöfer also complains about this dominance of the propaganda genre in: *Starkult als Propagandamittel im Dritten Reich*, Munich 1992, p. 61.

21 Dorothea Hollstein, *Antisemitische Filmpropaganda*, Munich / Berlin 1971; Zielinski; Peter Bucher, "Die Bedeutung des Films als historische Quelle: 'Der ewige Jude'" (1940), in: *Festschrift für Eberhard Kessel*, Munich 1982, pp. 301–327; Karl Ludwig Rost, *Sterilisation und Euthanasie im Film des "Dritten Reichs"*, med. diss. Berlin 1986; Udo Benzenhöfer / Wolfgang U. Eckart, "Medizin im Spielfilm des Nationalsozialismus", in: *Hannoversche Abhandlungen zur Geschichte der Medizin und der Naturwissenschaften*, no. 1, Tecklenburg 1990; Karl Heinz Roth, *Filmpropaganda für die Vernichtung der Geisteskranken und Behinderten im "Dritten Reich"*, med. diss. Hamburg 1986.

22 Klaus Kanzog, *"Staatspolitisch besonders wertvoll". Ein Handbuch zu 30 deutschen Spielfilmen der Jahre 1934 bis 1945*, Munich 1994; Wolf Donner, *Propaganda und Film im "Dritten Reich"*, Berlin 1995.

23 Karsten Witte, *Lachende Erben – Toller Tag*, Berlin 1995. The discussion was triggered by Arthur M. Rabenalt, *Film im Zwielicht*, Munich 1958. For the problems after two decades of "dispute on interpretation" see summary by Kreimeier, pp. 330 ff.

24 Witte, *Lachende Erben*, pp. 240, 259.

25 Hilmar Hoffmann, *100 Jahre Film. Von Lumière bis Spielberg 1894 bis 1994*, Düsseldorf 1994, p. 160.

26 Stephen Lowry, *Pathos und Politik*, Tübingen 1991, pp. 27 ff., also returns to Karsten Witte's concept of "aesthetic opposition" by directors like Wolfgang Staudte for his definition of nuances between "apolitical" and critical of the regime.

27 Witte, *Lachende Erben*, pp. 56 f.

28 Witte, *Filmkomödie*, p. 363 (1942, Paul Verhoeven, BA Film / B Film no. 06569).

29 Cf. e. g. BA/K R 1091/2139.

30 Dora Traudisch, *Mutterschaft mit Zucker. Frauenfeindliche Propaganda im NS Spielfim*, Pfaffenweiler 1991; Martin Loiperdinger / Klaus Schönekäs, "Die große Liebe – Propaganda im Unterhaltungsfilm", in: Rainer Rother (ed.), *Bilder schreiben Geschichte: Der Historiker im Kino*, Berlin 1991, pp. 143–153; Jens Thiele / Fred Ritzel, "Politische Botschaft und Unterhaltung – die Realität im NS-Film: Die große Liebe", in: Werner Faulstich / Helmut Korte (eds.), *Fischer Filmgeschichte*, Frankfurt am Main 1991, vol. 2, pp. 310–321; Andrea Huemer, *Die Frau im NS-Film*, Vienna 1985.

31 Hans C. Blumenberg, *Das Leben geht weiter. Der letzte Film des Dritten Reiches*, Berlin 1993.

32 Friedrich P. Kahlenberg, "'Die vom Niederrhein'– ein Spielfilm aus dem Jahre 1933", in: Karl Friedrich Reimers / Helmut Friedrich (eds.), *Zeitgeschichte in Film und Fernsehen*, Munich 1982, pp. 263 f. For this see also Peter Longerich, "Nationalsozialistische Propaganda", in: Karl Dietrich Bracher et al. (eds.), *Deutschland 1933–1945*, Düsseldorf 1992, p. 305.

33 Gero Gandert (ed.), *Der Film der Weimarer Republik: 1929*, Berlin 1993.

34 Peter Longerich, p. 305.

35 Ibid., p. 516.

36 Peter Bucher, "Film als Quelle", in: *Der Archivar*, 41st year, 1988, p. 523; Günther Moltmann / Karl Friedrich Reimers, *Zeitgeschichte in Bild- und Tondokumenten*, Göttingen 1970, p. 18.

37 Cf. also from a socio-historical point of view the introduction in Holger Schettler, *Arbeiter und Angestellte im Film*, Bielefeld 1932, pp. 22 to 30.

38 Hans-Jürgen Brandt, *NS-Filmtheorie und dokumentarische Praxis: Hippler, Noldan, Junghans*, Tübingen 1987. Various essays in: Manfred Hattendorf, *Perspektiven des Dokumentarfilms*, Munich 1995.

39 For this see the most recent analyses: Manfred Loiperdinger, *Der Parteitagsfilm "Triumph des Willens"*, Opladen 1987; Hilmar Hoffmann, *"Mythos Olympia"*, Berlin 1993; Klaus Kanzog, "Dokumentarfilm als politischer Katechismus: Triumph des Willens", in: Manfred Hattendorf, pp. 57–84.

40 Michael Marek, *Der Kulturfilm 1933–1945*, is about to be published.

41 Peter Bucher, "Goebbels und die deutsche Wochenschau", in: *Militärgeschichtliche Mitteilungen*, 40th year, 1986, pp. 53–69; Peter Bucher, "Der Kampf um Stalingrad in der deutschen Wochenschau", in: Friedrich P. Kahlenberg (ed.), *Aus der Arbeit der Archive. Festschrift für Hans Booms*, Boppard 1989, pp. 565–584; Bianca Pietrow-Ennker, "Die Sowjetunion in der Propaganda des Dritten Reiches. Das Beispiel der Wochenschau. Eine Dokumentation", in: *Militärgeschichtliche Mitteilungen*, 43rd year, 1989, pp. 79–120.

42 Cf. film editions by the Institut für den wissenschaftlichen Film, Göttingen; Gerd Albrecht, "Sozialwissenschaftliche Ziele und Methoden der systematischen Inhaltsanalyse von Filmen. Beispiel: UFA-Tonwoche 451/1939 – Hitlers 50. Geburtstag", in: Moltmann / Reimers, pp. 25–27, and Bucher, *Stalingrad*; Pietrow-Ennker.

43 Willi A. Boelcke (ed.), *Kriegspropaganda 1939 bis 1941. Geheime Konferenzen im Reichspropagandaministerium*, Stuttgart 1966; same author (ed.), *"Wollt ihr den totalen Krieg". Die geheimen Goebbels-Konferenzen 1939–1943*, Stuttgart 1967.

44 Albrecht I, pp. 439–500.

45 Gabriele Toepser-Ziegert (adap.), *NS-Presseanweisungen der Vorkriegszeit. Edition und Dokumentation*, 4 vols., Munich 1987 ff.

46 BA/K Zsg 102 (Sammlung Sänger), Zsg 101 (Brammer), Zsg 109 (Oberheitmann), and magazine service (ZD) and "Deutscher Wochendienst" 1939–1945 in BA/K R 55.

47 Heinz Boberach (ed.), *Meldungen aus dem Reich 1938–1945. Die geheimen Lageberichte des Sicherheitsdienstes der SS*, 16 vols., Herrsching 1984.

48 Boberach, p. 27, concludes from the frequent criticism by SD reporters of the propaganda devices that positive views of films "can be considered reliable".

49 Bucher, *Film als Quelle*, p. 524.

50 Cf. *Findbücher zu Beständen des Bundesarchivs*, vol 8, *Wochenchau und Dokumentarfilme 1895 bis 1950*, ed. by Peter Bucher, Koblenz 1984.

51 BA Filmarchiv Berlin (BA Film / B).

52 BA/K R 55, R 56 VI, R 109 II and III.

53 BA/P 50.01. As well as this there are some documents on Ufa's commercial policy in the Deutsche Bank's 80 BA 2 material.

54 Cf. e. g. BA/KR 1091/2139.

55 Material in the Reichskulturkammer / Reichsfilmkammer (BDC-RKK).

56 BA NS 18 and microfiche edition.

57 BA/K NS 10 (Adjutantur des Führers), R 43 (Reichskanzlei).

58 Peter Hartl (ed.), *Ursula von Kardorff. Berliner Aufzeichnungen 1942–1945*, Munich 1992; Heimannsberg/Laemmle/Schoeller (eds.), *Klaus Mann. Tagebücher 1936–1937*, Munich 1990; Jürgen Schebera (ed.), *William S. Shirer. Berliner Tagebuch. Aufzeichnungen 1934–1941*, Leipzig 1991, and *Aufzeichnungen 1944/45*, Leipzig 1994; Friedrich Freiherr Hiller von Gaertringen (ed.), *Die Hassel-Tagebücher 1938–1944. Ulrich von Hassell. Aufzeichnungen vom anderen Deutschland*, Berlin 1988; Inge Jens (ed.), *Thomas Mann: Tagebücher 1953–1955*, Frankfurt am Main 1995.

59 Bernd Sösemann (ed.), *Theodor Wolff. Tagebücher 1914–1919*, Boppard 1984, p. 1.

60 Gustav R. Hocke, *Europäische Tagebücher aus vier Jahrhunderten*, Munich 1978, p. 194.

61 The last entry to have appeared so far dates from 10.4.1945. The Moscow central archive provides references to 29.4.1945 as the day of the last entry: *Süddeutsche Zeitung* of 4/5.7.1992. See also *Der Spiegel*, no. 10, 3.3.1997, p. 18, on finds in the Führerbunker.

62 For example late December 1938 (Baarova affair) and 21/22.7.1944.

63 Cf. for the following sections: Bernd Sösemann, "Die Tagesaufzeichnungen des Joseph Goebbels und ihre unzulänglichen Veröffentlichungen", in: *Publizistik*, *no.* 2, 37th year, 1992, pp. 213–244; Elke Fröhlich (ed.), *Die Tagebücher von Joseph Goebbels. Sämtliche Fragmente. Teil I: 1924–1941*, 4 vols., Munich 1987 (Fröhlich I), here: vol. 1, VII to CIII; Ralf Georg Reuth (ed.), *Joseph Goebbels. Tagebücher 1924–1945*, 5 vols., Munich 1992, here vol. 1, pp. 3–19; Peter Stadelmayer (ed.), *Joseph Goebbels. Tagebücher 1945. Die letzten Aufzeichnungen*, Hamburg 1977, pp. 562–568.

64 *Süddeutsche Zeitung*, 4/5.7.1992 and 9.7.1992; *The Independent*, 3.7.1992. It is not known precisely when the reproduction work began. Goebbels mentions the photographic pioneer who was commissioned to do it, Joseph Goebel, and his filming system – but not in the context of the records – in an entry for 14.12.1944. For Goebbels' stenographer Richard Otte see "Nazism's witness. Goebbels' notetaker" in: *International Herald Tribune*, 18.7.1992, and *Die Welt*, 10.7.1992. For the technical process see Stadelmayer, pp. 564f.

65 "Eine Sensation auf gläsernen Platten", in: *Süddeutsche Zeitung*, 22.7.1992.

66 Cf. Fröhlich I, vol. 1, S.C, note 14. Also Sösemann, *Tagesaufzeichnungen*, p. 229.

67 As erroneously asserted in *Der Spiegel*, no. 29, 13.7.1992, p. 3.

68 Cf. Sösemann, *Inszenierungen*, p. 10.

69 Cf. "Nur drei Leute können die Schrift lesen", in: *Die Welt*, 10.7.1992.

70 For problems and textual evaluation of these possibly retrospectively prepared "side entries" see Sösemann, *Tagesaufzeichnungen*, pp. 232ff.

71 Sösemann, *Tagesaufzeichnungen*, p. 233. This refers to the gap from 18.12 to 29.12.1938. Goebbels does not begin the entry for 30.12.1938 with the usual "Yesterday:", but with "That was a dreadful fortnight. I was close to despair."

72 Cf. Fröhlich I, vol. 1, p. LXXXVI.

73 Sösemann, *Tagesaufzeichnungen*, p. 235.

74 For this see also the long entries for the first days of July 1941. In the following the dates of the diary entries will be given in Arabic numerals in the text, to distinguish them from all other dates not relating to the diary, which are written out.

75 In comparable situations, for example the first days of the invasion of Poland, the writing is similarly harassed and illegible (see entry for 9.9.1939).

76 Cf. Wilfried von Oven, *Wer war Goebbels?*, Munich 1987, p. 123.

77 Helmut Heiber, *Joseph Goebbels*, Munich 1965, p. 314. Also Fröhlich I, vol. 1, p. LXXXVIff.

78 Entry for 7.1.1943.

79 Entry for 25.12.1940.

80 Entry for 11.1.1938 on Hans Hinkel, the "Reich Culture Ruler".

81 For the falsifications in Eberhard Jäckel's collected writings of Hitler see Sösemann, *Tagesaufzeichnungen*, pp. 214f.; see also Josef Henke, "Die sogenannten Hitler-Tagebücher und der Nachweis ihrer Fälschung. Eine archivfachliche Nachbetrachtung", in: Friedrich P. Kahlenberg (ed.), *Aus der Arbeit der Archive. Festschrift für Hans Booms*, Boppard 1989, pp. 287–317.

82 Konrad Repgen, in: *Rheinischer Merkur*, 18.3.1988; Otto B. Roegele, in: *Rheinischer Merkur*, 21.1.1988; Albert M. Beer, *Die Tagebücher von Joseph Goebbels: Eine Fälschung?* Typed manuscript, Ellwangen 1988.

83 Fröhlich I, vol. 1, p. LXXIVf.; Hans-Günther Hockerts, "Die Goebbels-Tagebücher 1932–1941. Eine neue Hauptquelle zur Erforschung der nationalsozialistischen Kirchenpolitik", in: Dieter Albrecht et al. (eds.), *Politik und Konfession. Festschrift für Konrad Repgen*, Berlin 1981, p. 360. All the investigations are listed in *Der Spiegel*, no. 29, 13.7.1992, p. 109.

84 Cf. Siegfried Becker, "Ein Nachlaß im Streit", in: Kahlenberg, p. 276.

85 Cf. Karl-Heinz Janßen, in: *Die Zeit*, no. 10, 2.3.1990.

86 For example in the case of Helmut Heiber (ed.), *Goebbels-Reden 1932–1945*, 2 vols., Düsseldorf 1971/72, p. VIIf. For Genoud's influence see also Sösemann, *Tagesaufzeichnungen*, p. 277, note 79.

87 6.2.1938, vol. 3, p. 433.

88 Fröhlich I, vol. 1, p. LXXXIV.

89 Ralf Georg Reuth (ed.), *Joseph Goebbels. Tagebücher 1924–1935*, 5 vols., Munich 1992.

90 *Der Spiegel*, no. 32, 3.8.1992, p. 61.

91 This appeared in revised form in 1929 at the party-owned Eher-Verlag as *Michael. Ein deutsches Schicksal in Tagebuchblättern*.

92 BA/K NL Goebbels 118/126.

93 The period in between is so far not available.

94 Entry for 30.3.1941: "I am moving my diaries, 20 thick volumes, into the underground vaults of the Reichsbank. They are far too valuable to be exposed to the risk of falling victim to an air-raid. They portray my whole life and our era. If my fate allows me a few years to do so, I intend to revise them for future generations. They will probably arouse some little interest out there." A few days before Goebbels had mentioned the plan to attack the Soviet Union for the first time.

95 Heiber, *Joseph Goebbels*, p. 264.

96 Bernd Sösemann, "Ein tieferer geschichtlicher Sinn aus dem Wahnsinn. Die Goebbels-Tagebuchaufzeichnungen als Quelle für das Verständnis des nationalsozialistischen Herrschaftssystems und seiner Propaganda", in: Thomas Nipperdey et al. (eds.), *Weltbürgerkrieg der Ideologien. Antworten an Ernst Nolte*. Festschrift zum 70. Geburtstag, Frankfurt am Main/Berlin 1993, p. 148.

97 See below p. 52.

98 Ibid., p. 151.

99 Fröhlich II, p. 7.

100 Bella Fromm, *Als Hitler mir die Hand küßte*, Berlin 1992, among others her entry for 24.10.1936.

101 *Der Spiegel*, no. 31 of 27.7.1992, p. 110 (28.2.1933): "Then call from Hanfstaengl: the Reichstag is on fire; incredible imagination. But it is true. Rushed straight down with Hitler, the whole building is in flames … Started by the Commies. Göring beside himself, Hitler in a rage … This was all we needed. Now we are completely over it. Culprit caught: a 24-year-old Dutch Communist."

102 Cf. *Frankfurter Allgemeine Zeitung*, 12.8.1992; *Die Weltwoche*, 23.7.1992.

103 Hans Mommsen, "Van der Lubbes Weg in den Reichstag – der Ablauf der Ereignisse", in: Uwe Backes et al., *Reichstagsbrand. Aufklärung einer historischen Legende*, Munich 1986, pp. 53f.

104 *Der Spiegel*, no. 31, 27.7.1992, pp. 110f.

105 Cf. also entry for 17.11.1939: "The background to the Munich assassination attempt is now fairly clear: the actual assassin is a creature of Otto Strasser, who was in Switzerland on the day in question. After the attempt he sloped off to England, in other words to his paymasters and employers. The work of the secret service. We are still keeping everything secret, so as not to make the men behind the scenes suspicious." It is more than questionable whether Goebbels actually had information of this kind in front of him. There is nothing about it in the internal investigations and questioning records for Georg Elser, the would-be assassin. But it is well known that Hitler could not be persuaded, despite a complete lack of proof, that the British secret service was not behind the attempt: Anton Hoch, "Das Attentat auf Hitler im Münchner Bürgerbräu-Keller", in: *Vierteljahreshefte für Zeitgeschichte*, 17th year, 1969, pp. 383–413.

106 Entry for 12.8.1941: "I do not want to go through the Jewish question being resolved by the mob again, as happened in 1938."

107 Entry for 10.11.1938: "I present the matter to the Führer. He decides: let the demonstrations continue. Withdraw police. The Jews should get a sense of the people's anger for once. That is correct. I give appropriate instructions to police and Party straight away … The Führer has ordered that 20–30000 Jews should be arrested immediately." 11.11.1938: "I report to the Führer in the Osteria. He agrees with everything. His views are very radical and aggressive … The Führer wants to move towards very severe measures against the Jews."

108 Cf. chapter III, pp. 192–194.

109 Even *Der Spiegel*, no. 30, 20.7.1992, corrects Goebbels' over-hasty assertion that General Fromm headed the conspiracy. Only a few details

on the events of the day might provide indications that would bear examination.

[110] Entry for 7.6.1944: "If we repel the invasion, then of course the whole picture of the war will be completely changed. The Führer is certainly counting on this. He is scarcely worried that it might not succeed. I am a little more reticent on this head."

[111] Entry for 18.5.1940: "Our propaganda is working in masterly fashion. This is recognized throughout the country and probably also throughout the world."

[112] Bernd Sösemann/Jürgen Michael Schulz/Annette Weinke, in: *Aviso-Informationsdienst der DGPuK*, no. 4, December 1991.

[113] Entry for 13.12.1940: "The most offensive propagandist on the other side is Rauschnigg (sic!). His book 'Gespräche mit Hitler' is extraordinarily skilfully written and is enormously dangerous as far as we are concerned."

[114] Entry for 21.12.1943. For this cf. SD report of 22.2.1943. in: Heinz Boberach (ed.), *Meldungen aus dem Reich 1938–1945. Die geheimen Lageberichte des Sicherheitsdienstes der SS*, 16 vols., Herrsching 1984, p. 4831. The circulation of the reports was restricted as a result of pressure from Goebbels and later stopped completely: Manfred Wirl, *Die öffentliche Meinung unter dem NS-Regime*, diss., Mainz 1990, pp. 12 ff.; Boberach, pp. 27 and 36, and entries for 27.4.1943, 12.5.1943 and 18.5.1944.

[115] Cf. entries for 15.3.1936, 29.3.1938, numerous entries for July 1939 and for 13.3.1942.

[116] Fröhlich I, vol. 1, p. XLV; Reuth, *Goebbels*, pp. 420 ff., and the TV programme *Joseph Goebbels, gesehen von Lida Baarova*; ARD 7.4.1991, 10.30 p.m. The relevant quotations from the diary are used here, and Lida Baarova talks in public for the first time about her affair with Goebbels.

[117] Sösemann, *Ein tieferer Sinn*, p. 147, sees the private subjects as "artificial" and "stuck on later".

[118] Sösemann, *Ein tieferer Sinn*, p. 157.

[119] Hitler's mistaken assessment of France's and England's readiness to go to war is expressed only indirectly: "The Führer also does not believe that England will intervene" (1.9.1939).

[120] Entry for 28.10.1944: "Ribbentrop is not a German foreign minister, but a pest threatening our war policy, who must be removed as quickly as possible" and countless other passages.

[121] Entry for 2.2.1943.

[122] Entry for 22.3.1941.

[123] Entry for 27.1.1943.

[124] Entry for 2.3.1943.

[125] Entries mainly in the pre-war period, e.g. 14.11.1937.

[126] Cf. also entry for 11.7.1944.

[127] Entries for 30.11.1937, 25.7.1938.

[128] Entries for 11.6.1938, 22.6.1938. For this see Reuth, pp. 383 ff.

[129] Cf. also entries for 5/6.12.1939 and 20.7.1940.

[130] This quotation, which quickly became familiar through Lochner, is evaluated in research literature as proof that the Nazi leadership were very quickly informed: Gerald Fleming, *Hitler und die Endlösung*, Berlin 1987, p. 125; Dieter Pohl, *Von der "Judenpolitik" zum Judenmord*, Frankfurt am Main 1993, p. 125; Pohl assumes that a mere ten days after the events in Lublin Goebbels could only have been informed directly by Himmler or Hitler. But Czeslaw Madajczyk, "Hitler's direct influence on decisions affecting jews during World War II", in: *Yad Vashem Studies*, 20th year, 1990, p. 59, sees Goebbels' acquaintance Ernst Zoerner, the governor of Lublin, as the informer.

[131] Entries for 24.1.1942, 2.6.1942, 13.5.1943, 25.5.1943, 23.2.1944, 13.3.1944, 26.4.1944. For Goebbels' response to the Holocaust in Hungary see Fröhlich, *Krisenjahr*, pp. 210 f.

[132] Entry for 2.3.1943. For this cf. Gernot Jochheim, *Frauenprotest in der Rosenstraße*, Berlin 1992, p. 133, and Nathan Stotzfus, *Resistance of the Heart. Intermarriage and the Rosenstraße Protest in Nazi Germany*, Boston 1996.

[133] This "prophecy" is also to be found in the entries for 20.6.1941 and 11.8.1941. See also Siegfried Maruhn in: *Die Zeit*, 26.5.1995, p. 52.

[134] Cf. *Frankfurter Allgemeine Zeitung*, 6.12.1997, p. 33.

[135] "He has been working on it since July last year, and now the moment has come." This refers to Hitler's instruction "to finish" the Soviet Union in a war of aggression in spring 1941, see Franz Halder, *Kriegstagebuch. Tägliche Aufzeichnungen des Chefs des Generalstabes des Heeres 1939–1942*, ed. Hans Adolf Jacobsen, 3 vols., Stuttgart 1962 ff., here: vol. 2, p. 49 (31.7.1940).

[136] Wegner, p. 120, interprets this as proof that Hitler's *Lebensraum* programme is still in existence. Cf. also entry for 9.11.1939.

[137] Cf. entry for 1.10.1939: "Ribbentrop talks about Moscow at midday. I believe that he is seeing things too optimistically. As though Bolshevism were just a kind of National Socialism. I speak against it." For the genesis of the pact from Goebbels' point of view see also entries for 11.6.1939 ("He [Hitler] does not know what Moscow wants"), 24.8.1939 and 30.9.1939: "Tête-à-tête conference with the Führer … He is convinced of Russia's loyalty. Stalin is certainly gaining a great deal."

[138] Entry for 29.4.1941: "But at the moment we have no reason to fear it (Russia)." Cf. also entry for 4.12.1940: "But it will never move against us – through fear."

[139] Entry for 16.6.1941: "But Russia would attack us if we become weak, and then we would have war on two fronts, which we are avoiding by this preventive action."

[140] Entries for 20.4.1941 and 6.6.1941.

[141] Cf. entry for 18.6.1941. For this see Boberach's introduction, p. 25, and the SD report of 12.6.1941: Boberach, p. 2394, and the SD report of 16.6.1941: Boberach, p. 2408. Goebbels' description of 16.6.1941 falls back behind this: "The Führer asks me what the people thinks. It believes we were in agreement with Russia, but it will be bold if we challenge it."

[142] The present investigation is based on about 90 per cent of the surviving material from Goebbels' diaries that are now available in archives and editions.

[143] Hanns Zischler, *Kafka geht ins Kino*, Reinbek 1996.

[144] Victor Klemperer, *Ich will Zeugnis ablegen bis zum letzten. Tagebücher 1933–1945*, 2 vols., Berlin 1995; same author, *Leben sammeln, nicht fragen wozu und warum. Tagebücher 1918–1932*, 2 vols., Berlin 1996. For this see also Heinrich August Winkler in *Die Zeit,* no. 41, 4.10.1996, p. 27.

[145] Cf. entry for 10.3.1929: "*Der Patriot* ("The Patriot") with Emil Jannings. A fabulous performer. The drama is entirely heroic. One man gives his life for the people. That is almost the biggest thing that one can see", on 23.9.1928 (*Der letzte Befehl/*"The Last Command") and on 19.3.1930 on *Die letzte Kompagnie/The Last Company*: "Full of heroic conviction, but free of sentimental kitsch. Moving and powerful. Also lucid in its conception. Conrad Veidt in great form." For the stamina drama *The Last Command* on the Prussian Wars of Liberation against Napoleon see Christa Bandmann/Joe Hembus, *Klassiker des deutschen Tonfilms*, Munich 1980, p. 222; Françis Courtade/Pierre Cadars, *Geschichte des Films im Dritten Reich*, Munich 1974, p. 39.

[146] Cf. also entry for 3.12.1928: "… Saw 'Hollywood' film. What horrible lack of strength in this Hollywood. No style, and immature. These so-called flickering film-stars shown in a vain reflection of themselves. Simply horrific. Jewish kitsch. One saw practically nothing but Hebrews."

[147] Speech on 9.2.1934 to the Reichsfachschaft Film in the *Völkischer Beobachter* (Berlin edition), 11.12.1934, and speech on 25.3.1933 to radio administrators, printed in: Helmut Heiber (ed.), *Goebbels-Reden 1932–1929*, Düsseldorf 1971, p. 94.

[148] Cf. entry for 28.10.1928.

[149] Cf. Felix Moeller, "I Gusti del Führer", in: *Il cinema dei dittatori*, Bologna 1992, p. 261. Hitler officially defined the *Battleship Potemkin* as "High State of bestiality": *Völkischer Beobachter* (Munich edition), 26.5.1926.

[150] Thomas Hanna-Dauod, *Die NSDAP und der Film vor der Machtergreifung*, Cologne 1996.

[151] Cf. Peter Reichel, *Der schöne Schein des Dritten Reiches*, Munich/Vienna 1991, p. 95.

[152] Cf. Peter Jarchow/Ralf Stabel, *Palucca,* Berlin 1997, p. 44 f.

[153] Thomas Mathieu, *Kunstauffassungen und Kulturpolitik im Nationalsozialismus*, Saarbrücken 1997, pp. 82–91.

[154] Helmut Heiber, *Joseph Goebbels*, Munich 1965, p. 197.

[155] Ibid.

[156] Courtade/Cadars, p. 8.

[157] Klaus Kreimeier, *Die Ufa-Story*, Munich 1992, p. 246.

[158] Arthur M. Rabenalt, *Joseph Goebbels und der "Großdeutsche" Film*, Munich 1985, p. 68; Curt Ries, *Joseph Goebbels*, Baden-Baden 1950, p. 205; Richard Manvell/Heinrich Fraenkel, *Goebbels. Der Ver-führer*, Cologne 1960, pp. 215 ff.; Courtade/Cadars, p. 8; Leiser, pp. 16 ff.

[159] Karsten Witte, *Lachende Erben – Toller Tag*, Berlin 1995, however, derives a compelling film theory for Goebbels from remarks like this: p. 123.

[160] Rabenalt, p. 68.

[161] Only a single reference indicates that Goebbels might have known Kracauer's writings, for example. During the planning stages of the Frederick II film *The Great King*, he notes on 26.4.1940: "But I now want the Frederick after Kunersdorf, not actor Otto Gebühr's garden-arbour Friedrich." "Gartenlaube-Friedrich" was a coinage by Kra-

cauer for the figure of the Prussian king, always drawn as reactionary in numerous films from the late 20s onwards.

162 Speech on 5.3.1937, printed in: Gerd Albrecht, *Nationalsozialistische Filmpolitik*, Stuttgart 1969, p. 447.

163 Speech on 5.3.1937, printed in: Albrecht I, p. 461.

164 "Goebbels' Filmthesen", printed in: William Bredow, *Film und Gesellschaft in Deutschland*, Hamburg 1975, p. 178.

165 Speech on 5.3.1937, printed in: Albrecht I, p. 457.

166 According to Rabenalt, p. 61, Goebbels wanted to write a treatise like this himself. Cf. also speech on 5.3.1937, printed in Albrecht I, p. 451.

167 Ibid., p. 455. Goebbels also repeated his polemic against "seasonal business" in later film speeches.

168 Speech on 14.2.1941, printed in: Albrecht I, pp. 472 f.

169 Speech on 28.3.1933, printed in: Albrecht I, p. 439.

170 Speech on 5.3.1937, printed in: Albrecht I, p. 449.

171 This evaluation was by no means unshakeable; remarks violently rejecting later films by Greta Garbo and Luis Trenker were made; cf. entry for 21.4.1934 on *Queen Christina*.

172 Cf. some typical examples in the entries for 7.12.1936 ("Films in the evening: Albers-Ucicky *Unter heißem Himmel*, overloaded, somewhat grubby milieu, plot too broad and incomprehensible, not a hit. Albers also seems too mannered (!). *Port Artur*, with Karin Hardt and Wohlbrück. A direct hit, heroic and seen on a large scale in the plot, good direction, credible, very tragic conflict. Wonderful performances from the actors.") and 21.1.1937 ("… *Ball im Metropol*/"Metropol Ball" filmed by Wysbar with Hilde Weißner and George: idea good, actors good too, but weak, excessively insistent direction. No pace.") and for 11.4.1937, 18.5.1939, 24.3.1939.

173 For the film see Bandmann/Hembus, pp. 33 ff.; Ulrich Gregor/Enno Patalas, *Geschichte des deutschen Films*, Gütersloh 1962, p. 146.

174 Heiber, *Goebbels*, p. 169.

175 The film was one of the first to be banned after the Nazis came to power.

176 One of the most successful films of 1933, directed by Kurt Gerron, who first emigrated and was then murdered in Auschwitz in 1944.

177 For Schünzel's *Land der Liebe* (1937), cf. also entry for 28.4.1937 ("a typical Jewish sham. Quite intolerable") and Kreimeier, p. 333.

178 Kreimeier, p. 279.

179 Witte, p. 110.

180 Cf. also entry for 12.6.1936 on the film operetta *Boccaccio*: "Burlesque and a lot of racket. Do not like this endless singing."

181 Courtade/Cadars, p. 243.

182 Witte, p. 177.

183 Cf. entry for 23.7.1940 and speech on 15.2.1941, printed in Albrecht I, p. 470.

184 Entry for 18.5.1938: "An enchantingly made film. This way of presenting people, the drawing of a circus milieu, of tragic conflicts, all this is masterly, superb. … I am quite carried away. The material itself is somewhat distasteful. But here I do not see the content as much as the method, the presentation." Cf. also entry for 3.1.1936 on Feyder's German-French co-production *La Kermesse héroique/Die klugen Frauen* (1936): "Superior direction. Really skilful, with witty dialogue."

185 Cf. Jerzy Toeplitz, *Geschichte des Films*, Berlin 1982 ff., vol. 3, p. 171. This makes Rabenalt's assertion, p. 71, that Goebbels only liked *Romance in a Minor Key* because it was filmed in the internationally successful French film style of the 1930s seem more than dubious.

186 The print went into the Reich Film Archive. BA/B Film archive film no. 11049. Cf. also entry on 13.12.1940 about *De Lénin à Hitler*.

187 Cf. also entry for 17.5.1937.

188 Cf. Hans Dieter Schäfer, *Das gespaltene Bewußtsein. Über deutsche Kultur und Lebenswirklichkeit 1933–1945*, Frankfurt am Main 1981, pp. 165 to 171, esp. 169.

189 Cf. also entry for 3.11.1940 and ministerial conference on 21.11.1940: Willi A. Boelcke (ed.), *Kriegspropaganda 1939–1941. Geheime Konferenzen im Reichspropagandaministerium*, Stuttgart 1966, p. 570.

190 For the first openly anti-Nazi American film *Confessions of a Nazi Spy* and Martin Kosleck's wonderful performance as Goebbels, see Bernard F. Dick, *The Star Spangled Screen. The American World War II Film*, Lexington 1985, pp. 59 ff. Manvell/Fraenkel, p. 220, spread the rumour that Goebbels was annoyed that his ministerial office was presented as a sanctuary filled with ostentatious Nazi splendour.

191 Goebbels did not see the film until one and a half years after its world première.

192 Cf. entry for 14.2.1942 and 27.5.1941: "Hippler shows me a film of American cultural life: horrific! That is not a country, that is a desert in terms of civilization. And they want to teach us culture."

193 Cf. Ullrich Höver, *Joseph Goebbels – ein nationaler Sozialist*, Bonn 1992, pp. 203 ff.

194 Cf. also entry for 5.8.1940.

195 Cf. for this film: David Welch, *Propaganda and the German Cinema*, Oxford 1983, p. 250; Jerzy Toeplitz, vol. 4, p. 34 f.

196 Goebbels associated similar propaganda with the documentary *Leningrad im Kampf* (16.1.1943). A statement was made on this subject at the ministerial conference on 16 January 1943: "He (Goebbels) gave instructions that those responsible for German propaganda watch this film because it shows the enormous difference between German and Russian investment of strength, and how slightly the German civilian population is involved in comparison with Russian civilians." Ministerial conference on 16.1.1943: Willi A. Boelcke (ed.), *Wollt ihr den totalen Krieg? Die geheimen Goebbels-Konferenzen 1939–1943*, Stuttgart 1967, pp. 320 f.

197 Goebbels was concerned to bring all the copies of these Soviet propaganda films, which were distributed throughout every possible Reich and Party office, into his own safe-keeping: BA/K R 43 II/389, no. 191, letter from Goebbels to Lammers on 26.3.1943.

198 Toeplitz, vol. 4, p. 261.

199 Cf. for example entry for 7.2.1942.

200 Heiber, *Goebbels*, p. 259.

201 For Goebbels' reaction to the scenes filmed in the Warsaw ghetto see Veit Harlan, *Im Schatten meiner Filme*, Gütersloh 1966, p. 122.

202 For this film, directed by Michal Wazynski in 1937, see Toeplitz, vol. 3, pp. 384 f.

203 Cf. Wolfgang Becker, *Film und Herrschaft*, Berlin 1973, p. 31.

204 Cf. Manfred Behn, "Gleichschritt in die 'neue Zeit'. Filmpolitik zwischen SPIO und NS", in: Hans Michael Bock/Michael Töteberg (eds.), *Das Ufa-Buch*, Frankfurt am Main 1992, p. 341.

205 Stephen Lowry, *Pathos und Politik*, Tübingen 1991, p. 12.

206 Jürgen Spiker, *Film und Kapital*, Berlin 1975, p. 143.

207 Ibid., p. 158.

208 Ibid., p. 157.

209 Michael Töteberg, "Die graue Eminenz: Bürgermeister Max Winkler", in: Bock/Töteberg, p. 391.

210 For Winkler as an individual see Becker, p. 55, note 358.

211 Spiker, pp. 152 f.

212 Goebbels usually writes "Klitsch" rather than the correct form, Klitzsch. For the setting up of the Film Bank cf. also entry for 14.12. and 27.5.1933, and for 8.6.1933.

213 Spiker, p. 168.

214 Letter from RMVP Staatssekretär Walther Funk to the Finance Ministry, dated 14.12.1936, printed in: Albrecht I, p. 524.

215 See p. 112.

216 Spiker, p. 158.

217 Klaus Kreimeier, *Die Ufa-Story*, Munich 1992, p. 304.

218 Entry for 10.3.1937: "Ufa film *Menschen ohne Vaterland* gets wonderful reviews. That's the way to make your mark. The press has worked well. Klitsch and Ufa are already quite worn down."

219 BA/K R 109/1032 a, no. 79, minute no. 1218 for 11.3.1937.

220 Töteberg, *Treuer Diener*, p. 202.

221 Cf. Becker, p. 159.

222 Cf. Spiker, p. 175.

223 Spiker, p. 174; cf. also Manfred Behn, "Diskrete Transaktionen. Bürgermeister Winkler und die Cautio", in: Bock/Töteberg, p. 390.

224 BA/K NL Hugenberg 98, no. 97 ff. Explanation by Klitzsch dating from 17.6.1949.

225 This is also supported by the entries: "He (Klitzsch) could have had that more cheaply," or: "This letter will cost them at least 3 million marks".

226 Kreimeier, p. 305, incomprehensibly ignores Goebbels' writings when describing the takeover.

227 Ralf Georg Reuth does try to do this, *Goebbels*, Munich 1991, p. 365.

228 Cf. Becker, p. 163, and entry for 26.6.1937.

229 For this cf. entry for 14.1.1938.

230 Spiker, p. 185.

231 Cf. Becker, p. 194.

232 Cf. entry for 26.4.1940: "Row with a small film company. They are simply disregarding our orders."

233 Cf. Marcus S. Phillips, *The German Film Industry and the Third Reich*, diss., East Anglia 1974, p. 270, and entries for 1.6., 31.7. and 8.8.1941.

234 Correctly: Graf Schwerin von Krosigk.

235 Spiker, p. 199.

236 Becker, pp. 180 f.

237 Phillips, pp. 246 ff. Cf. also entry for 7. 12. 1940.

238 Entry for 9. 1. 1942: "Winkler complains to me about increasing production costs for a normal film. They are indeed enormous, and energetic steps must be taken to reduce them."

239 Spiker, p. 206.

240 There are no earlier concrete references, but the remarks in December 1940 suggest that Winkler was picking up his failed plan from 1939.

241 Phillips, p. 350, is still puzzling over how the timing of the preparations went in the second half of 1941. Cf. also entries for 20. 11.: "We are about to release the art film companies completely from their financial entanglements, and to bring all German cinema's financial interests together in a large holding company, I.G. Film", and for 21. 11. 1941: "I discuss the foundation of the new Film I.G. with Hippler again. I will tackle the details next week. This is a major project, which needs mature reflection."

242 BA/K R 109/4792, dated 19. 12. 1941 Winkler to RFM. Goebbels originally wanted to use the name "I.G. Film" – which was also introduced in the diaries. Cf. also speech on 28. 2. 1942, printed in: Albrecht I, p. 493.

243 Speech, dated 28. 2. 1942, printed in: Albrecht I, pp. 529 f. The following section deals with the internal organizational structure and personnel and hierarchy in film production.

244 Spiker, p. 209.

245 Kreimeier, p. 402; Spiker, p. 235. It is just as impermissible to confuse films that had been passed for showing and films that had been produced as it is to confuse periods of time: according to the third implementation order to the Leistungssteigerungs-erlaß of 27. 4. 1942 a financial and production year ran from 1 June to 30 May, but performances are calculated from January to December: Phillips, pp. 370 f.

246 Cf. BA/K R 109III/10, Ufi companies' and production managers' meeting. The figure 1120 is also mentioned there.

247 By 20. 7. 1943 Goebbels is talking of only a hundred films.

248 Cf. entry for 20. 7. 1943: "If we are not in a position to produce a hundred German films in German studios using German resources, then we should look for alternative facilities in Paris. Continental is still run by (Alfred) Greven, but they should now make mainly German films rather than French ones. Greven will be commissioned to produce about ten to fifteen German films, while making French films on the side. … Greven will resist this tooth and nail, but nevertheless it must happen." But this is precisely what did not happen: Continental produced only French films until late 1944: Georges Sturm, "UFrAnce 1940–1944. Collaboration and film production in France", in: Bock / Töteberg, pp. 408–415.

249 Especially as a great deal was being creamed off for private purposes. Goebbels received financial contribution in millions for his villas in Schwanenwerder and on Bogensee: Reuth, p. 462. Hitler received 5 million marks from the same source for his "Culture Fund", according to the entry for 1. 4. 1941.

250 Entry for 1. 4. 1942: "The Finance Ministry want to hit us with new taxes, so that it scarcely seems possible to accumulate capital to use after the war. But Winkler is a shrewd financial operator who understands a great deal more about these things than the bureaucrats in the Finance Ministry, and he has already found a way out that it extraordinarily intelligent and unusual, and that will doubtless achieve the desired aim", and for 21. 5. 1942: "He (Winkler) has again reached a number of particularly advantageous agreements with the Finance Ministry, which allow us to continue to keep the whole film business on a sound basis." These concessions (tax reductions against interest payments, higher write-offs, remission of land transfer tax), made by the Finance Ministry on the same day, are confirmed in the minutes of the Ufi board meeting: BA/K R 55/774, no. 115, minutes for 21. 5. 1942.

251 Kreimeier, p. 402.

252 Cf. Spiker, pp. 233 ff., and entry for 10. 5. 1943.

253 For this cf. also entry for 13. 7. 1941. Goebbels felt that this point also applied to cinemas.

254 Thus Goebbels refutes the view expressed by Becker, pp. 228 f., that the Minister considered reprivatization.

255 Goebbels continues: "Winkler fought against it tooth and nail, but I can no longer support him. Private individuals are allowed to own cinemas, and so the public should be allowed to do so as well. Winkler takes rather too narrow a view of this." For this question see also Boguslaw Drewniak, Der deutsche Film 1938–1945, Düsseldorf 1987, pp. 616 f.

256 Cf. for example entry for 26. 1. 1937.

257 BA/K R 109I/1029a, no. 279, minute no. 890, dated 3. 2. 1933: "Herr Klitzsch reserves the right to deal with the government himself."

258 Cf. Michael Töteberg, "Personen minderen Rechts – Die 'Entjudung' der Ufa", in: Bock / Töteberg, pp. 344–347.

259 Kreimeier, p. 251.

260 Cf. entry for 15. 5. 1936.

261 Entry for 8. 9. 1936: "Lenich has in fact now acquired responsibility for film fee agreements. And he does it as stupidly as possible. They only act commercially, as though films had nothing to do with art. I will have to keep my eyes open. They would most like to treat me like Father Christmas."

262 After the war, Winkler had this to say about Goebbels' interventions: "He read every film manuscript that was submitted, decided whether they should be accepted or rejected, gave orders for further revision or the preparation of a screenplay, or changed the content and meaning of the film idea himself. Goebbels then read the screenplays himself and shaped them as he wished, chose the director and settled the major casting questions, negotiated directly with actors and also intervened whenever he wished while the film was being made." Institut für Zeitgeschichte (IfZ), Mc 31 Spruchgerichtsakte Hippler: Eidesstattliche Erklärung Max Winkler.

263 BA/K R 109I/1032a, no. 64, minute no. 1221, dated 23. 3. 1937.

264 Kreimeier, p. 275.

265 BA/K R 109I/1033a, no. 214, minute no. 1284, dated 1. 2. 1938.

266 BA/K R 1091c, no. 217, minute no. 1375, dated 30. 6. 1939.

267 List by Reichsmeister BA/K R 109 I/2129, no. 1–2 undated, and Hippler list, no. 30. Cf. other examples in: Klaus-Jürgen Maiwald, Filmzensur im NS-Staat, Dortmund 1983, p. 169, notes 400–403.

268 Schneider-Edenkoben made only one more film before 1945 (Sylvesternacht am Alexanderplatz, 1939), but Zerlett continued to be one of the busiest directors, despite Goebbels' announcement.

269 For example, directors threatened with being forbidden to work carried on making films; foreign actors that were approached never filmed in Germany; and fees continued to rise.

270 For the film Mein Sohn der Herr Minister, in which Paul Dahlke did appear, but Wolfgang Liebeneiner did not.

271 Cf, entry for 15. 1. / 21. 3. / 6. 10. 1937 and BA/K R 1091/1031b, minute no. 1192, dated 27. 10. 1936.

272 BA/K R 43 II/489, no. 31, RMVP to Reichskanzlei, dated 19. 4. 1937. Cf. also entry for 12. 5. 1937: "To the Führer with Frau Imperio Argentina. We talk about film matters. He is quite enchanted with her", for 31. 7., 20. 8. ("She is not learning German"), 26. 10. 1937 ("One should not court these ladies too much. Otherwise they are prone to megalomania") and 6. 11. 1937 and BA/K R 1091/1032b, no. 118, minute no. 1253, dated 24. 8. 1937: "Ministry wants engagement despite language deficiency."

273 Cf. Drewniak, p. 130.

274 For this see entry for 13. 8. 1942.

275 BA/K R 55/665, no. 147, Ministeramt to Hinkel, dated 26. 7. 1944.

276 Cf. also entry for 12. 5. 1937: "I commission Funk and Winkler to undertake a systematic elimination of Jews in the Tobis and Ufa foreign subsidiaries. We shall soon succeed here." This applied to the branches in the USA, France, Holland, Czechoslovakia, Switzerland, Hungary and Austria. Cf. the material on Tobis-Sascha, BA/K 56 I/30 on "representatives of non-Aryan interests abroad".

277 Cf. Maraun's reports to Goebbels on recruiting, with hand-written corrections by the Minister, in BA/K R 55/657 and 658.

278 Cf. Becker, p. 268, note 540.

279 BA/K R 55/657, no. 92, Ministeramt to Maraun on 16. 7. 1942.

280 BA/K R 55/657, no. 94, Ministeramt to Maraun on 16. 7. 1942.

281 BA/K R 55/658, no. 2, Maraun's report on 7. 1. 1943.

282 Cf. entry for 16. 10. 1941: "The guidelines that I have laid down are now being ruthlessly implemented within the production companies."

283 For this cf. entries for 13. 5. 1942, 26. 2. 1943, 12/23. 5. 1944.

284 BA/K R 55/658, no. 99, note on document by Maraun in 17. 6. 1943.

285 Joseph Wulf, Film und Theater im Dritten Reich, Frankfurt am Main 1966, p. 283; Phillips, pp. 74 ff.

286 Willi A. Boelcke (ed.), Kriegspropaganda 1939–1941. Geheime Konferenzen im Reichspropagandaministerium, Stuttgart 1966, p. 168.

287 Georg Wilhelm Müller, Das Reichsministerium für Volksaufklärung und Propaganda, Berlin 1940, p. 23. For the film department see also Becker, pp. 101 f., and Phillips, pp. 193 f.

288 Becker, p. 101.

289 Reichslichtspielgesetz of 19.2.1934, printed in: Maiwald, pp. 95–99.

290 Becker, p. 78.

291 Kraft Wetzel / Peter A. Hagemann, *Zensur. Verbotene deutsche Filme 1933–1945*, Berlin 1978, p. 12.

292 BA/P 80 BA 2/19078, Klitzsch to von Stauss on 31.10.1934.

293 Phillips, p. 325.

294 Order from the President of the Reichsfilmkammer on 24.11.1935 in: *Völkischer Beobachter*, 1.12.1935. Cf. also Maiwald, p. 150.

295 Cf. Maiwald, pp. 148 ff.

296 Ibid., p. 144.

297 Decree, main 18.11.1939, printed in: Albrecht I, p. 526. Cf. also entry for 14.11.1939: "… manuscripts to be submitted a month before shooting starts. In other words a kind of pre-censorship. That is better than post-censorship", and ministers' conference on 3.11.1939: Boelcke, p. 219.

298 Cf. Alfred Bauer, *Die diktatorische Bevormundung des deutschen Filmschaffens durch das Nazi-Regime*. Typescript in: BA/K R 109I/1726, p. 6. Bauer worked for the Reichfilmintendanz until 1945.

299 Cf. entry for 30.3.1940 and Phillips, p. 326, and examples in BA/K R 109I/2139.

300 Wien Film board meeting on 3.11.1939, quoted from Phillips, p. 324.

301 For this cf. entry for 18.12.1936.

302 Maiwald, p. 153, and entry for 19.5.1936: "Nierentz takes the opportunity of telling me about his plans as Reichsfilmdramaturg. He is not allowed to make any films of his own. Has to provide inspiration. Be everywhere at once. And always be on top of things."

303 For this cf. also entries for 17.9.1938 and 5.10.1938.

304 Cf. also entry for 17.5.1940: "Introduced 4 new film script editors to their work. Showed them how to view and examine in a way that is appropriate to the purpose. We will probably be able to expect better films soon as well."

305 Cf. entry for 1.11.1940: "Our Reichsfilmdramaturgie does not work reliably enough. Makes too many wrong decisions. Intervention essential", and for 10.12.1940: "Reichsfilmdramaturgie question in the ministry. Stricter supervision needed. The gentlemen are not sufficiently in touch with me. Some of the recent films were very bad. But we must produce films, otherwise there will be a general shortage."

306 BA/K R 109 I/2139, no. 115, document note by Schweikart on 27.12.1940. Another striking note by Schweikart, pronounced confidential, recorded the informal approach to approving material: "Herr von Reichsmeister rang me up at home yesterday and told me that he was not in a position to approve the screenplay for *Alarmstufe* ("High Alert Level") that has been submitted to him. He said he could not imagine that this dull, conventional script could produce a film worthy of being made by a state company. … I told Herr v. R. that we were anyway revising the screenplay with the director of the film (probably Lippl). He asked for a resubmission with, as he put it, 'total' revisions and intended to give me an interim decision."

307 Speech on 15.12.1941, printed in: Albrecht I, p. 475.

308 BA/K R109 I/2139a, no. 62, Hippler to Schweikart on 17.5.1941; BA/K R 109 I/2139a, no. 30, Hippler's list of orders, no date: "Every production project must be submitted to the Reichsfilmdramaturg without exception."

309 Implementation regulations for the Leistungssteigerungserlaß of 28.2.1942, printed in: Albrecht I, p. 529.

310 Winkler suggested in autumn 1941 that the film department's constant interference was responsible for the high production costs: Phillips. p. 327.

311 For this cf. also entries for 29.7. and 14.8.1943.

312 Cf. Michael Töteberg, "Affären, Intrigen, Politik. Hugo Correll's personal file", in: Bock / Töteberg, pp. 330 f., using the relevant passages from the records.

313 Kreimeier, p. 301.

314 BA/K R 1091/2420, minutes of the meeting of the board's working committee on 14.12.1936.

315 Cf. entry for 10.11.1936: "A lot of trouble with films. The Führer is also very unhappy about some things."

316 Cf. entries for 6.2.1937 and 20.2.1937: "Long discussion with Klitsch and Corell: I want to get a few artists on to the Ufa board. Klitsch is resisting this tooth and nail. But it won't get him anywhere. He cannot resist my logical arguments. He wants to think it over again."

317 Speech on 5.3.1937, printed in: Albrecht I, p. 454.

318 Cf. DNB announcement on 1.5.1937, quoted in: Phillips, p. 168. For detail on the art committees see also Friedrich P. Kahlenberg, "Starke Herzen. Quellennotizen über die Produktion eines Ufa-Films im Jahre 1937", in: Wetzel/Hagemann, pp. 119 f.

319 Cf. the listing of the committee's powers vis-à-vis the board and the production chief: BA/K R 1091/2420, Ufa board minutes for 4.5.1937.

320 Cf. Maiwald, pp. 161 f.

321 For this cf. entry for 10.12.1936 and BA/K R 1091/1032b, no. 114, minute no. 1254, dated 27.8.1937: draft of a letter from Klitzsch to Froelich. Goebbels usually spells the director incorrectly: "Fröhlich" or "Frölich".

322 Cf. also entry for 3.11.1937: "I forbid the notion of 'overall artistic control', which the well-known actors have been trying to adopt for themselves. The director is responsible, and is thus in charge."

323 Film-Finanz GmbH committee meeting on 3.2.1939, quoted from Phillips, p. 172, note 106.

324 Cf. also entries for 20.11.1937 and 1.12.1937.

325 Cf. entry for 8.10.1937: "Studied minutes of Ufa art committee meeting. All hell let loose. Quarrels about authority between Klitsch and Prof. Frölich."

326 Cf. also entry for 11.1.1938: "Ufa art committee minutes. Frölich and Corell understand each other now."

327 GmbH committee meeting on 3.2.1939.

328 Speech on 15.2.1941, printed in: Albrecht I, p. 475.

329 Cf. also entry for 28.1.1938: "I should like to put an experienced financial expert who can really understand art at the top of every film company. But I cannot find these people."

330 Seeger banned the Remarque film *All Quiet on the Western Front* on the grounds that it was a "threat to German esteem": BA/K R 43I/2500, no. 163, justification by the censorship board.

331 Cf. Phillips, p. 189.

332 Becker, p. 107 and p. 55: "The reasons for this lay in the transfer of new powers to the field of film and not in a compulsory departure due to a fall from favour." The BDC–RKK personal files do not give any information on this head. But there are still accusations of corruption against Raether in the RPL files in 1941: BA/K NS 18/362b, Reichsmeister to Fischer on 10.9.1941.

333 Cf. Phillips, p. 195, and entry for 19.1.1936 ("Now intend to fix him up in industry") and for 2/17.4.1937.

334 Not to be confused with the director Alfred Weidenmann.

335 BA/K R 109 I/2828, Ufa script department to Correll on 3.10.1936; Ritter to Correll on 1.10.1936. Klitzsch wrote to Staatssekretär Funk: "It would be disastrous in the highest degree, for Herr Weidemann as well, if he were to claim the success of the film *Verräter* as proof of his activity and derive ambitions from this", quoted from Correll's personal file from Rainer Rother, "Die Effekte der Unterhaltung", in: Wolfgang Jacobsen (ed.), *Babelsberg*, Berlin 1992, p. 189.

336 Phillips, p. 167.

337 It is possible that even at this time Hanke wanted to install his protégé Ernst von Leichtenstern, who was then brought into the ministry in January 1938.

338 BDC-RKK Hans Weidemann: Danzmann (pers. dept.) to Goebbels on 25.6.1937.

339 Becker, pp. 99 f.

340 BA/K R109I/1034b, no. 2, minute no. 1480 for 15.1.1942. See also chap. 4, p. 286, and Phillips, p. 198 (Hippler's questioning). After that the records say that Weidemann moved to Ufa in May 1939 because of a clash with Goebbels over the documentary film *Jahre der Entscheidung*.

341 Entries on 10./22.10., 17.11 and 3.7.12.1937. The unsuccessful search is also suggested by the fact that Seeger's name is mentioned at least 14 times after his death.

342 Becker asserts this, p. 100.

343 *Der Kinematograph,* 3.2.1934.

344 Cf. Krause's film and outline reports in BA/P 80 2/19078.

345 Cf. Wulf, p. 296.

346 Correll mentions the possible disadvantages for the company of rejecting Krause in a confidential note to Klitzsch: BA/K 109I/2828, Correll to Klitzsch on 11.11.1936. At first the Ufa board tried to fob Krause off by buying the rights to his radio plays: BA/K R 109I/1023a, no. 140, minute no. 1209 for 22.1.1937.

347 Entries for 4.2.1938: "How can someone in whom one has invested so much hope fail like this." After frequently repeated announcements ("Willi Krause is not to make any more films", 7.12.1937), Goebbels apparently did not manage to stop Krause making films until 1940 ("I am eliminating Krause", 3.3.1940).

348 Becker, p. 85.

349 Wulf. p. 296.

350 Cf. Becker, p. 55; Wulf, p. 324.

351 Entry for 25. 7. 1935: "Raether and Erckmann Filmkammer. Complaints about Scheuermann. He must go. Decision taken", and entry for 29. 7. 1935: "I am dismissing Scheuermann."

352 Entry for 19. 10. 1935: "Raether is not being straight. But Scheuermann has got to go." According to Becker, p. 55, he was "removed from all offices and honorary posts within Goebbels' departmental sphere of influence", but later exonerated from all blame and rehabilitated. But this dismissal did not seem to relate to the chairmanship of the Filmkreditbank board at first. Cf. entry for 11. 1. 1936 and for 23. 1. 1936: "Scheuermann must go. A corruption merchant."

353 Goebbels also spells Lehnich incorrectly all the time ("Lenich"). Otto B. Roegele misinterpreted this peculiar spelling on Goebbels' part as an incorrect transcription: *Rheinischer Merkur / Christ und Welt*, 4. 3. 1988.

354 For anti-Semitic statements by Lehnich see Michele Sakkara, *Die große Zeit des deutschen Films*, Leoni 1980, p. 10. Lehnich was one of the first German professors to join the NSDAP and the SS as a supporting member: Wulf, p. 313.

355 Entry for 4. 12. 1936: "He just goes on and on about finance. He understands nothing of films as art."

356 Becker, p. 108, mentions "anti-Nazi accusations" involving the Filmkammer president and "quarrels" with Goebbels.

357 The rest of the sentence is missing on the microfilm section no. 3/2 BA/P, Nachlaß Goebbels. Cf. also entry for 16. 12. 1936: "I am putting the screws on Prof. Lenich, giving him strict guidelines, complaining about the bureaucracy, which is taking over, our people should manage, but not make films themselves, they must get to work now, otherwise I shall abolish the jobs."

358 Entries for 2. 10. 1940: "Hippler is warned to proceed somewhat more calmly and not quite so brashly. He lays too much stress on the point of view of authority", 3. 10. 1940: ("It is necessary above all to bring Hippler down a peg or two.") and 28. 4. 1941: "He is a clever chap, just a bit too arrogant." For Hippler cf. also Boelcke, pp. 83 ff.

359 Fritz Hippler, *Betrachtungen zum Filmschaffen*, Berlin 1942; for this essay cf. Kreimeier, p. 311, and Leif Furhammer / Folke Isaksson, *Politics and film*, London 1971, pp. 119 f.

360 Cf. Fritz Hippler, *Die Verstrickung*, Düsseldorf no date (1982), p. 220.

361 Cf. entry for 9. 10. 1941. Hippler, *Verstrickung*, p. 253, mentions angina and a stomach ulcer he had suffered from during the war. According to Goebbels Hippler was seriously ill for three weeks as early as February 1940, and was about to be replaced: entry for 27. 2. 1940.

362 Speech on 28. 2. 1942, printed in: Albrecht I, p. 495.

363 From point 2 of the Leistungssteigerungserlaß of 28. 2. 1942, printed in: Albrecht I, p. 529.

364 Cf. entries for 13. 5. 1941, 3. 8. 1942 and 15. 9. 1942: "He has made some mistakes again, which are caused by the faulty structure of his department. He also does not know how to make the

connections necessary for establishing himself effectively on all sides. ... I will try again to sort things out with him amicably. If that does not work, then I shall have to make a staff change in the film department."

365 Entry for 17. 4. 1943: "Winkler lectured me in this context about a whole series of failures that Hippler has been guilty of."

366 Cf. documents from May to October 1942: BA / Dokz. ZM 1305 A. 14.

367 Hippler, pp. 253 f. Set against this are entries for 28. 2. 1943 (alcoholism), 23. 5. 1943 (possible director of the ministry's foreign department), 4. 4. 1943 (possible production chief for Terra), 7. 3. 1943 (Hippler in a sanatorium), 20. 3. 1943 (search for a successor), 17. 4. 1943, 23. 5. 1943 (search for replacement positions), 12. 5. 1943 ("has again proved guilty of things that will finally finish him off", suspension, "It would do him good to be in the armed forces for once, but unfortunately he is unfit for war service"), 12. 6. 1943 (taking up post in new department), 31. 10. 1943 (working in new position). But there can be no doubt that he did late serve at the front, as this was also conveyed to the press: BA/K R 109II/26, Reichsfilmintendant to DNB on 17. 11. 1944.

368 BA/P 50.01/26, no. 33, Kulturinformation no. 10, dated 1. 7. 1943.

369 *Völkischer Beobachter*, 7. 6. 1940. There is a good character sketch of Frowein in: Hans C. Blumenberg, *Das Leben geht weiter. Der letzte Film des Dritten Reichs*, Berlin 1993, pp. 33 f. Carl-Dieter von Reichsmeister, previously editor of the *Deutsche Allgemeine Zeitung* and adviser to the Reich government press officer, was Reichsfilmdramaturg from 1939 to 1943.

370 Cf. entries for 16/20. 3. 1943 and 11. 4. 1943.

371 Entry for 27. 5. 1943: "So far the removal of Hippler has had only positive consequences."

372 Cf. entry for 17. 4. 1943 on "family material".

373 Cf. Becker, p. 222.

374 BA/K R 109I/1484, Frowein to Winkler on 16. 2. 1944 and Pfennig to Kaelber on 6. 1. 1944.

375 This can be seen very vividly in the case of the film *Philharmoniker* ("Members of the Philharmonie"): the project started in 1943, and many entries indicate repeated changes in 1943/44, so that the première could not be until 4. 12. 1944.

376 BA/K R 109I/1483, minutes of the management meeting on 13. 3. 1944. The "generous assent" refers to Goebbels' remarks on preliminary censorship given above.

377 Becker, p. 235, note 66.

378 For Hinkel see Boelcke, pp. 84 f., and materials from BA/Dokz. ZM 1358 A.2.

379 Cf. also entry for 6. 4. 1944: "I discuss the status of the Reichsfilmintendant with Hinkel and Parbel. Hinkel is to be granted sweeping powers and will be director of the film department as well as Reichsfilmintendant. Parbel has agreed to act as his deputy in the film department; he will also be his deputy as Reichsfilmintendant. Frowein is to be on a par with Parbel. I hope that Hinkel's energy and prudence will soon create order in the film sector."

380 Cf. BDC-RKK Leopold Gutterer: Naumann to Winkler on 5. 7. 1944 and Hinkel to Goebbels on 30. 8. 1944. Cf. also entry for 31. 8. 1944. Gutterer

was dismissed on 1. 11. 1944, not just in the film sphere by Goebbels, but also officially from all his Party offices by Hitler, and called up into the armed forces: BDC-RKK Leopold Gutterer: personnel card.

381 BDC-RKK Max Winkler: Hinkel's listing on 29. 7. 1944 based on decisions by Goebbels on 28. 7. 1944.

382 BDC-RKK Max Winkler: Hinkel to Winkler on 9. 8. 1944.

383 BDC-RKK Hans H. Zerlett: Hinkel to Zerlett on 12. 8. 1944.

384 BDC-RKK Max Winkler: Winkler to Goebbels on 11. 9. 1944 and BA/K R 109 III/3 Winkler to Goebbels on 13. 9. 1944. Cf. also Becker, p. 225.

385 "Organization plan for the German film business", dated 13. 11. 1944, printed in: Albrecht I, pp. 531–532.

386 Becker, p. 226.

387 BDC-RKK Max Winkler: Goebbels' instruction of 1. 10. 1944.

388 Goebbels also regularly used these slogans about film as an industrial and "seasonal business" in his film speeches: speech on 5. 3. 1937, printed in: Albrecht I, p. 455, and on 15. 2. 1941, printed in: Albrecht I, p. 473.

389 Cf. also entry for 16. 4. 1942: "I will appoint a new head of personnel for the whole film area in the next few days, who will have the job of handling personalities in film as soundly and correctly as happens in any large department or industrial establishment. It is absolutely typical that no one has had such an idea in the film sphere. I hope to use this measure to dismantle another remnant of the lack of soundness of the Weimar era." Goebbels did not appoint the personnel officer for the Reichsfilmintendant, Hilleke, as the head of a separate office for personnel matters affecting everyone working in the film industry until the end of the year. For this cf. entry for 1. 1. 1943 and Hippler, *Verstrickung*, p. 231.

390 Dietrich Kuhlbrodt, "Der Kult des Unpolitischen. Produktionschef Wolfgang Liebeneiner", in: Bock / Töteberg, p. 449. It is possible that there was mutual inspiration, as Goebbels and Liebeneiner conducted some debates of this kind.

391 Cf. Kreimeier, p. 306.

392 Cf. documents in BA/K R 109/2139.

393 Entry for 29. 6. 1937:"I inform Winkler about his renewed contract with Correll. He has fallen up the stairs for half a million. But I get (crafty) on that point. I demand that the contract be rescinded immediately, and Winkler meekly gives in. I will smash this German-national clique." For this cf. Töteberg, *Affären*, p. 331.

394 Entry for 6. 10. 1937: "Zerlett is not getting by with the commercial people at Tobis."

395 Cf. Becker, p. 291.

396 Becker, p. 292.

397 There is some very revealing information about Greven and the cover firm Continental Films directed by him in Paris in the entries up to 1943 (for example 20. 11. 1941 and 21. 5. 1942). For this cf. also Roy Armes, "Kino der Widersprüche. Französische Filmarbeit unter der Besatzung", in: Gerhard Hirschfeld / Patrick Marsh (eds.), *Kollaboration in Frankreich*, Frankfurt am Main 1991, pp. 161–177.

398 Leichtenstern moved into local politics in 1941, first as mayor of Görlitz, from March 1944 of Breslau: BDC-RKK Ernst von Leichtenstern: staff card.

399 BA/K R 1091/1034b, no. 136, minute no. 1430, dated 16.10.1940.

400 BA/K R 1091/2193b Schweikart to Winkler, dated 20.7.1939.

401 Cf. entry for 8.5.1942: "Bavaria is certainly making progress under Schreiber's new leadership. Schweikart was too literary to manage a large film company responsibly. He will have to be entrusted with directing films and not weighed down with administrative work"; 30.5.1942: "The Führer completely agrees with the decision that Schreiber should replace Schweikart, whom he values extraordinarily highly as a poet and director, as production chief at Bavaria."

402 Goebbels usually spells the name "Demandowski".

403 But in spring 1942 Tobis came out in a poor position in the middle of the range in meeting its quota: BA/K R 109II/6, minute of the production and company chiefs' meeting on 26.5.1942. BA/K R 55/774, no. 174, appendix 4, to the minutes of the Ufi supervisory board meeting on 9.2.1943: "Tobis is way out at the top with 108 per cent (of the quota to be met). 4 of the 5 most commercially successful films produced are by them … ."

404 BDC-RKK Ewald von Demandowsky: Fritzsche to Demandowsky on 28.6.1944; von Demandowsky to Fritzsche on 29.6.1944; Fritzsche to Winkler on 29.6.1944. For this cf. also Phillips, p. 370.

405 Hildegard Knef, Der geschenkte Gaul, Munich 1982, p. 66.

406 For this cf. BA/K R109I/9, minute of the production and company chiefs' meeting on 12.5.1942. Also on 12.6.1942: according to this, after four months Ufa had met only 18 per cent of the annual production quota set in February 1942.

407 BA/K R109II/6, minute of the production and company chiefs' meeting on 26.5.1942.

408 Entry for 21.5.1942: "The production chiefs are causing a lot of worry at the moment. Some of them are just not up to their jobs."

409 BA/K NL Hugenberg: Klitzsch an Hugenberg on 4.11.1943.

410 For example as member of the Reichstheaterkammer committee; director of the RFK Filmfachschaft ("film department"); member of the "Council of Honour for German Film".

411 BDC-RKK Herbert Maisch: ministerial memo, dated 13.1.1943.

412 Cf. entry for 8.2.1944 and also for 18.3.1944 and Siker, p. 292. Emo took up his post in March 1944.

413 To be on the safe side the Propaganda Ministry applied to the Gestapo in September 1943 for information about the political reliability of the company and production chiefs, although he did not receive a reply until April 1944. The was no "politically disadvantageous" information about any of the production chiefs, and some of them were even Party members – though they had joined rather late: BA/K R55/174, nos. 163–167 and 172–175, RSHA to RMVP on 23.4.1944.

414 Cf. entry for 25.8.1943: "I speak to the German film company production chiefs. I explain my new measures and lighter controls on film management. But I also make things clear about the political and military situation and make the production chiefs responsible for the film-makers' political approach."

415 Cf. entries for 8.2.1944 and 2.6.1944: "I speak to the German film production chiefs at midday. I announce the most recent staff changes, with comments, draw the production chiefs' attention to good and bad films and also deal with a large number of critical and also delicate questions pertaining to the current state of film production. I think that this talk made quite an impression." But Goebbels did not restrict himself to speeches in this context, he also expresses notes talks to the lower-level directors and production managers (14.7.1943).

416 Entry for 1.2.1944: "A report by Frowein on Liebeneiner's work at Ufa shows me that Liebeneiner has so far achieved more at Ufa than I had previously realized. His projects are still only at the production stage and cannot be ready yet. The films that Ufa is showing now still date from the Jahn era and cannot be blamed on Liebeneiner."

417 Versprich mir nichts ("Promise Me Nothing") is the title of a 1937 film by Liebeneiner.

418 Cf. entry for 27.5.1943: "The Führer has some extraordinarily positive things to say about Liebeneiner", and entry for 10.5.1943.

419 The question of Jonen's dismissal was apparently used by Frowein and Hinkel in the dispute with Winkler and the Ufi management; Frowein and Hinkel wanted to replace Jonen as deputy production chief, but keep him as head of the company: BA/K R 109I/1483, minutes of the Ufa board meetings on 31.5.1944 and 12.6.1944.

420 BA/K R 55/662, no. 7, Hinkel to Goebbels on 31.8.1944.

421 Spiker, p. 217.

422 Ibid., p. 228.

423 Ibid., p. 229.

424 Cf. Peter Reichel, Der schöne Schein des Dritten Reiches, Munich 1991, pp. 84ff.

425 Speech on 28.3.1933, printed in: Albrecht I, p. 440.

426 Ibid., p. 439

427 Ibid., p. 441. This sentence contradicts Jerzy Toeplitz, Geschichte des Films, vol. 3, Berlin 1982, p. 252, where he says that Goebbels' speech in March 1933 contained "not a single clearly anti-Semitic note".

428 Albrecht I, p. 445.

429 Ibid., p. 442.

430 Ibid., p. 443.

431 Albrecht I, p. 446.

432 Licht-Bild-Bühne, no. 35, 10.2.1934. Goebbels was no more specific in an address billed as a "major speech" to the NSBO group in the Babelsberg Studios on 26.4.1933: Joseph Wulf, Theater und Film im Dritten Reich, Frankfurt am Main 1966, p. 292.

433 Toeplitz, vol. 3, p. 254.

434 Martin Loiperdinger (ed.), Märtyrerlegenden im NS-Film, Opladen 1991, p. 29.

435 Klaus Kreimeier, Die Ufa-Story, Munich 1992, pp. 254f.

436 According to the Berlin première theatres: Arthur M. Rabenalt, Joseph Goebbels und der "Großdeutsche" Film, Munich 1985, pp. 40f.

437 Cf. Rainer Rother (ed.), "Ufa-Magazin Nr. 10 zur Ausstellung Die Ufa 1917–1945", in: Das deutsche Bildimperium, Berlin 1992, p. 1.

438 Toeplitz, vol. 3, pp. 255f. Fugitives won the State Prize in the film category on 1.4.1934.

439 Other films from the early years that should be included here: Um das Menschenrecht ("For the Rights of Man"), an "anti-Bolshevik" film dating from 1934; Das alte Recht ("The Old Right"), a somewhat simplified justification of the farming inheritance laws; Rider of the White Horse (1934), Stoßtrupp 1917 (1934) and Die Reiter von Deutsch-Ostafrika, an anglophile film dating from 1934. When the chairman of the Deutsche Bank and Hugenberg's deputy on the Ufa supervisory board, Emil Georg von Stauss, said to Ufa director general Klitzsch that he felt that to few Ufa films were taking the "philosophy of the new state" into account, Ufa justified itself by sending von Stauss an extensive list of ten films made in the 1933/34 production period that they defined as National Socialist themselves and thus calculated that 59% of their films adopted a "national political approach" – for example the Prussian film Des jungen Dessauers große Liebe ("The Great Love of the Young Dessauer") because of the "French court cliques" and the prince's devotion to his people as "father of the country and leader". The very broad interpretation is unmistakable on closer examination, but it is interesting evidence of the film company's opportunism: BA/P 80 BA 2/19078, Ufa board members Meydam and Lehmann to von Stauss on 14.5.1934.

440 Cf. David Welch, Propaganda and the German cinema, Oxford 1983, p. 258; it should be noted that these are not yet films commissioned by the state.

441 A clear chronology and summary of these clashes caused by Ufa can be found in BA/P 80 BA 2/19080.

442 Cf. Hans Barkhausen, "Die NSDAP als Filmproduzentin", in: Günther Moltmann/Karl Friedrich Reimers, Zeitgeschichte in Bild- und Tondokumenten, Göttingen 1970, pp. 145–196; Kreimeier, p. 255.

443 BA/K R 109 I/1029a, no. 232ff., Ufa board minutes no. 900 for 10.3.1933. They wanted even this programme to have the blessing of the Ministry: BA/K R 109 I/1029a, no. 218, minute no. 905 for 29.3.1933.

444 Karsten Witte, Lachende Erben – Toller Tag, Berlin 1995, p. 50.

445 Cf. entry for 5.10.1932 about the election propaganda film Hitler über Deutschland (1932).

446 Cf. Barkhausen, p. 148. Thomas Hanna-Daoud, Die NSDAP und der Film vor der Machtergreifung, Cologne 1996.

447 All Party film matters were put under Goebbels in October 1931: Wolfgang Becker, Film und Herrschaft, Berlin 1973, p. 25.

448 Francis Courtade/Pierre Cadars, Geschichte des Films im Dritten Reich, Munich 1975, p. 111.

449 See also Goebbels' amendment in the "Kaiserhof" text under 18.1.1933.

450 Wolfgang Paul, *Bewegte Bilder – Die NS-Propaganda vor 1933,* Bonn 1990, p. 188.

451 Goebbels reconfirms this judgement on 7.1. 1940, when the film – with some changes – was released again after the beginning of the war: "There is too much patriotic talk." Goebbels specifically identifies the line of dialogue that has always been picked out since in film literature as evidence of the glorification of death in Nazi films: "We Germans may not understand life, but we are fabulous at dying." Cf. Erwin Leiser, *"Deutschland erwache". Propaganda im Film des Dritten Reiches"*, Hamburg 1968, p. 25.

452 Toeplitz, vol. 3, p. 255.

453 Loiperdinger, *Märtyerlegenden*, p. 33.

454 *Der Angriff*, 16.6.1933; Welch, *German Cinema*, p. 52.

455 Rabenalt, pp. 40f., reports that the film played for only 14 days in Berlin première theatres.

456 Toeplitz, vol. 3, p. 255.

457 For production history see Friedrich P. Kahlenberg, "Hitlerjunge Quex", in: Bundesarchiv/Kulturamt der Stadt Koblenz (ed.), catalogue for the film series for the "Jugend im NS-Staat" exhibition, Koblenz 1978.

458 Cf. *Der Angriff*, 25.9.1933.

459 Loiperdinger, *Märtyrerlegenden*, p. 39.

460 Cf. Dorothea Hollstein, *Antisemitische Filmpropaganda*, Munich 1971, p. 36.

461 The ban was justified by Goebbels in *Der Kinematograph*, 11.10.1933; *Der Angriff*, 10.10. 1933.

462 Loiperdinger, *Märtyrerlegenden*, p. 35.

463 *Der Kinematograph*, 11.10.1933.

464 Cf. Hartmut Bitomski, *Die Ufa*, television programme, ARD, 10.9.1992, 11 p.m.

465 Cf. Leni Riefenstahl, *Memoiren 1902–1905*, Frankfurt am Main 1990, pp. 202 ff. But there is no doubt that Goebbels' entries make Riefenstahl's version sound extremely implausible. Leni Riefenstahl is confronted with the Goebbels' quotations for the first time in Ray Müller's film documentary *Leni Riefenstahl – The Power of the Images.*

466 Toeplitz, vol. 3, p. 270.

467 Cf. Kreimeier, p. 251.

468 Cf. Fred Gehler/Ullrich Kasten, *Fritz Lang. Die Stimme von Metropolis*, Berlin 1990, pp. 156f., and Patrick McGilligan, *Fritz Lang. The Nature of the Beast*, New York 1997, pp. 174–181. Lang's passport with visas for June and July 1933 with currency exchange stamp can be seen in the Stiftung Deutsche Kinemathek, i.e. Lang was still visiting Germany months after the conversation with Goebbels. McGilligan and *Der Spiegel* both cite the diaries as a source for the fact that Lang's version of events is a legend. But the "Kaiserhof" version is still the only one available for the appropriate period. The fact that the offer to Lang is not to be found there does not prove anything at all.

469 But the decision to do this must have been made earlier: Kraft Wetzel/Peter A. Hagemann, *Zensur – Verbotene deutsche Filme 1933–1945*, Berlin 1978, pp. 161 f.

470 Karsten Witte, "Die Filmkomödie im Dritten Reich", in: Horst Denkler/Karl Prüm, *Die deutsche Literatur im Dritten Reich*, Stuttgart 1976, p. 348.

471 Kreimeier, pp. 278ff.

472 Kreimeier, p. 279. The intention was definitely to make elaborate political films: BA/K 109 I/1030a, no. 179, minute no. 1059, dated 12.2.1935.

473 They include *Der rote Reiter* ("The Red Horseman"), *Mein Leben für Maria Isabel* ("My Life for Maria Isabel"), *Hundert Tage,* (German-Italian co-production), *Lockspitzel Asew* ("Stool Pigeon Asew"), *Soldaten-Kameraden* ("Soldiers and Comrades") and in 1934 *Das alte Recht, Stoßtrupp 1917* or *Grenzfeuer.*

474 Courtade/Cadars, p. 255.

475 Courtade/Cadars give an account of the film, p. 256.

476 Including also Heinz Hilpert's *Lady Windermere's Fan,* based on the play by Oscar Wilde (28.10.1935) or Hans H. Zerlett's *Moral,* based on Ludwig Thoma (21.8.1936).

477 Kreimeier, p. 278.

478 Kreimeier, p. 278.

479 For Goebbels' diary entries on Schünzel see also Jörg Schöning, *Reinhold Schünzel – Schauspieler und Regisseur*, Munich 1989, p. 60.

480 The title was forbidden at first in 1934.

481 For example with the star tenor Jan Kiepura ([27.]2.1936), Jenny Jugo, Luis Trenker (27.5. 1936), Luise Ullrich (8.8.1936).

482 Cf. entries for 27.9./3.10./17.10.1935; 13.8./21./8//2.9./4.9./5.9.1936.

483 Cf. also entry for 15.11.1936: "Führer has seen *Friesennot* and *Mazurka*. He is most enthusiastic about them. A great joy for me, as I was behind the projects once more." The film is described in Welch, *German Cinema*, pp. 242–246.

484 Cf. contrary view from Luis Trenker, "Alles gut gegangen", Munich 1965, pp. 344 ff.

485 Speech on 1.5.1935, in: "*Film-Kurier,* dated 2.5.1935.

486 Cf. Kreimeier, p. 324.

487 There is disagreement about the extent to which the Propaganda Ministry could influence joint productions: Albrecht I, p. 98, sees this influence as minimal or very difficult to assess, and thus does not include such co-productions in his list of films, while Kahlenberg takes the example of *Andalusische Nächte* ("Andalusian Nights") to show creative possibilities on the German side: Friedrich P. Kahlenberg, "Spielfilm als historische Quelle? Das example of *Andalusische Nächte*", in: Heinz Boberach (ed.), *Aus der Arbeit des Bundesarchivs,* Boppard 1978, pp. 518ff.

488 Cf. Boguslaw Drewniak, *Der deutsche Film 1938–1945*, Düsseldorf 1987, p. 330 f.

489 Welch, *German Cinema*, p. 259.

490 Leiser, p. 89.

491 *Der höhere Befehl* is a "patriotic rebel" film that plays in the Prussian Wars of Liberation. Courtade/ Cadars, p. 113, are dubious about its quality, saying that the lighter scenes are a mixture of "village comedy" and the Lubitsch style. *Henker, Frauen und Soldaten* is a patriotic anti-French, anti-Soviet production without any markedly new qualities, playing in and after the First World War against the often-deployed background of the falling Tsarist empire, with Hans Albers in the role of an officer in the volunteer corps.

492 Entry for 18.8.1936: "… a god war film from the Tyrol, very masculine and heroic, with good characters and a straightforward approach. The Italians will not be very pleased, but we should not make too many concessions to them."

493 Entry for 9.12.1936: "Now totally acceptable. … Correct tendency." See also chap. 5, p. 134. The revision was clearly directed mainly at the conclusion which – just noticeably – was re-shot and contained anti-Communist slogans that sounded entirely up to date.

494 Courtade/Cadars, p. 174.

495 Cf. also entry for 15.11.1936: "After dinner I had a detailed discussion with the Führer. He is very happy with the situation. Rearmament continues. We are investing fabulous sums. We will be ready in 1938. We shall soon be settling the issue with Bolshevism. … We are as good as certain to dominate Europe. Führer determined about everything."

496 Reichel, p. 98.

497 Cf. entry of 10.11.1936.

498 For example: "Talked director Ritter's new film plans over with him. Ufa seems to want to improve himself" (5.11.1936); "We will involve ourselves more from now on. The Party above all. Weidemann should look for some material first of all" (14.11.1936).

499 Friedrich P. Kahlenberg, "Starke Herzen". Source notes about the production of a Ufa film in 1937, in: Wetzel/Hagemann, p. 113.

500 *Starke Herzen* is first mentioned by the Ufa board on 2 September 1936: BA/K R 1091/1031 b no. 112, minute no. 1180, 2.9.1936. *Menschen ohne Vaterland* was already in Ufa's Babelsberg studio by October: Jörg Schöning, "Filmografie der Ufa", in: Wolfgang Jacobsen, *Babelsberg*, Berlin 1992, p. 349.

501 BA/K R 109 I/1032a, no. 206, minute no. 1202, 9.12.1936.

502 Speech in *Völkischer Beobachter* (Berlin edition), 28.11.1936.

503 *Starke Herzen* did not come into being because of Goebbels' "anti-Bolshevik" demands of November 1936, as Kreimeier suggests, p. 328.

504 With the exception of *Starke Herzen*, which was banned, here entitled *Bela Kunin*. Welch, *German Cinema*, p. 247, draws the final conclusion that Goebbels deliberately chose not to place greater emphasis on "anti-Bolshevism" in feature films. But he fails to take the failed *Starke Herzen* into consideration.

505 Welch, *German Cinema*, p. 247.

506 See chapter 5, pp. 323 f.

507 Cf. discussion on the bad notices for *Menschen ohne Vaterland* by the Ufa board: BA/K R 109 1032a, no. 79, minute no. 1218 on 11.3.1937.

508 Cf. the cases of *Land der Liebe* and *Menschen ohne Vaterland.*

509 See chap. 5, p. 128f.

510 Cf. Courtade/Cadars, pp. 135f., who did not think the film was a success, but "politically important and cinematically interesting".

511 For the prize award see entry for 10.4.1937.

512 Cf. Courtade/Cadars, p. 136.

513 BA Film/K film no. 10274.

514 Cf. Karsten Witte, "Film im Nationalsozialismus", in: Wolfgang Jacobsen et al. (ed.), *Geschichte des deutschen Films*, Stuttgart 1993, pp. 134f.

515 Cf. *Deutschland-Berichte der Sozialdemokratischen Partei Deutschlands* (SOPADE) *1934–40*, 4th

year, 1937, reprint Salzhausen/Frankfurt am Main, pp. 912 f. and entry for 10.4.1937: "Führer can only see the funny side of protests from the commercial world about this film."

[516] "The mood in the country, above all among the labour force, started to become a little shaky. We must intervene again."

[517] It is doubtful that this speech really was so "socialist". Hitler had said this among other things about the structure of the German motor-car industry: "And there can be no doubt about this: either so-called free enterprise is able to solve these problems or it is not able to continue to exist as free enterprise! ... Employers and employees are both adversaries within the German commercial process, and no one is entitled to damage the interests of the people as a whole through the way in which he sees his own interests." Speech by Hitler at the opening of the International Motor and Motor-bike show on 20.2.1937, printed in: Max Domarus (ed.), *Hitler. Reden und Proklamationen*, vol. 1, Würzburg 1962, p. 680.

[518] Veit Harlan, *Im Schatten meiner Filme*, Gütersloh 1966, p. 38.

[519] CF. in the same period entries about a "film on German suffering" (30.1.1937).

[520] BA/K R 56 VI/7, no. 90, Köhn to Seeger on 30.10.1936.

[521] See chap. 5., p. 134.

[522] BA/K R 109 I/1032a, no. 157, minute no. 1206 on 12.1.1937. Goebbels usually incorrectly rites "Wiemann" rather than Wieman.

[523] BA/K R 109 I/1032a, no. 61, minute no. 1222 on 31.3.1937.

[524] Speech printed in: Albrecht I, p. 459.

[525] Ibid., p. 450.

[526] Ibid., p. 457.

[527] Ibid., p. 450.

[528] Ibid., p. 455.

[529] Ibid., p. 456.

[530] Ibid., p. 456.

[531] Ibid., p. 458. There is also a persuasive analysis of the speech in Witte, *Lachende Erben*, pp. 122 f.

[532] Première: 6.7.1937. Cf. also Courtade / Cadars, pp. 175 f.

[533] Entry for 22.12.1937 on a conversation with Hitler: "He wants a bit of peace from the Church question at the moment. ... He is waiting for the right moment to get the Holy Joes on trial again." The "noisy agitation" (Hockerts) was tamped down as it, like the "Holy Joe" trials did not have the desired effect in the Christian context. Hans Günther Hockerts, "Die Goebbels-Tagebücher 1932–1941. Eine neue Hauptquelle zur Erforschung der nationalsozialistischen Kirchenpolitik", in: Dieter Albrecht et. al (ed.), *Politik und Konfession. Festschrift für Konrad Repgen*, Berlin 1983, p. 379.

[534] Entry for 10.6.1937: "Well made. From the time of the Lawrence rebellion. A grandiose background."

[535] Cf. also entry for 6.11.1937: "Colonial question in press and propaganda held back a bit for the time being. ... Otherwise people will end up by thinking that we have reached that position. But this is by no means the case. We must not shoot off our propaganda powder too soon."

[536] The entries on *Der Katzensteg*, a national film from the period of Prussian resistance against Napoleon's troops in 1806, remain mysterious in this context. Despite unusually euphoric comments on 12.11.1937, he writes two weeks later: "Demandowski is reworking *Katzensteg*. But there is probably not much to be done about it." (24.11.1937)

[537] Courtade/Cadars, p. 138.

[538] BA Film/K film no. 10616.

[539] Rainer Rother, "Die Effekte der Unterhaltung", in: Jacobsen, p. 195.

[540] For Ritter's artistic and political career see Rainer Rother, "Hier erhielt der Gedanke eine feste Form – Karl Ritters Regie-Karriere", in: Hans-Michael Bock/Michael Töteberg, *Das Ufa-Buch*, Frankfurt am Main 1992, pp. 422–427; same author, *Effekte*, pp. 191–195, and Kreimeier, p. 327.

[541] Cf. entry for 19.12.1937.

[542] 109I/1032b no. 246, minute no. 1232 on 25.5.1937.

[543] Cf. Courtade/Cadars, pp. 125 ff.; Leiser, p. 34.

[544] Kreimeier, pp. 324 f.

[545] SOPADE, 4th year, 1937, pp. 913 f.

[546] This was the film *Der Maulkorb* (première: 10.12.1938): entry for 30.1.1938.

[547] Roger Manvell/Heinrich Fraenkel, *Goebbels*, Cologne 1960, p. 206. According to this, Jannings wanted to use the film to "get even with" Goebbels, who was surprised and mocked by the audience. In fact Goebbels had seen the film before the première, and so could not have been surprised by the alleged scenes of parody. For the film see Hans-Gerd Happel, *Der historische Spielfilm im Nationalsozialismus*, Frankfurt am Main 1984, p. 28.

[548] Cf. entries for 11./20.10.1937 ("received with markedly little enthusiasm" and 5.11.1937 (Jannings "depressed" because of Goebbels' reaction). Goebbels registers Hitler's high esteem for the film with express amazement (21.10.1937).

[549] In the entry for 15.7.1937 Goebbels announces the dismissal of the directors of three bad films. And indeed the directors of *Austernlilli* (E.W. Emo), *Karussell* (Alwin Elling) and *The Irresistible Man* (Geza von Bolvary) made no more films for the state concerns after this, but just for small private firms. It was not until 1943 that Bolvary, for example, worked for one of the big companies again: information from Alfred Bauer, *Deutscher Spielfilm-Almanach*, Munich 1976.

[550] Christa Bandmann/Joe Hembus, *Klassiker des deutschen Tonfilms*, Munich 1980, p. 108.

[551] More highly critical and pessimistic remarks about the quality of popular production are to be found on 21./27.10.,5.17.11. and 29.11.1937.

[552] Goebbels was obviously impressed by Harlan's directorial skills from the outset (19.1.1937 on *Kreutzersonate* "The Kreutzer Sonata"), 31.12.1937 on *Jugend*).

[553] Wilhelm Deist et al., *Ursachen und Voraussetzungen des Zweiten Weltkriegs*, Frankfurt am Main 1989, p. 150.

[554] Ibid., p. 168; Ian Kershaw, "How effective was Nazi propaganda", in: David Welch (ed.), *Nazi Propaganda. The power and the limitations,* London 1983, pp. 200 f., Ian Kershaw, *Der Hitler-Mythos. Volksstimmung und Propaganda im Dritten Reich*, Stuttgart 1980, p. 120 ff.

[555] Deist, p. 150.

[556] Toeplitz, vol. 4, p. 214. According to this, German cinematography was "systematically" prepared for war. Rother, *Effekte*, p. 200, also asserts that the film industry had "long been prepared for the 'real thing'".

[557] The remarks that follow are based on Deist, pp. 150–169, and also Wolfram Wette, "Zur psychologischen Mobilmachung der deutschen Bevölkerung 1933–1939", in: Wolfgang Michalka (ed.), *Der Zweite Weltkrieg*, Munich 1989, pp. 205–223; Jutta Sywottek, *Mobilmachung für den totalen Krieg. Die propagandistische Vorbereitung der deutschen Bevölkerung auf den Zweiten Weltkrieg*, Opladen 1976; Simone Walther, "Faschistische Pressepropaganda bei der Entfesselung des Zweiten Weltkriegs im September 1939", in: *Bulletin Arbeitskreis Zweiter Weltkrieg*, H.1/2, 1987, pp. 60–80; Hellmuth Auerbach, "Volksstimmung und veröffentlichte Meinung in Deutschland zwischen März und Dezember 1938", in: Franz Knipping/Klaus Jürgen Müller (ed.), *Machtbewußtsein in Deutschland am Vorabend des Zweiten Weltkriegs*, Paderborn 1984, pp. 273–293. Helmut Michels, *Ideologie und Propaganda. Die Rolle von Joseph Goebbels in der nationalsozialistischen Außenpolitik bis 1939*, Frankfurt am Main 1992, pp. 382–394, describes the Ministry's instructions to the press vividly and in detail.

[558] Cf. Wilhelm Treue, "Rede Hitlers (10.11.1938) vor der deutschen Presse", in: *Vierteljahreshefte für Zeitgeschichte 6*, vol. 6, 1958, pp. 175 ff., and Wolfram Wette, *Mobilmachung*, pp. 216 f. Hitler had already perceived the Sudeten crisis as the start of this change, and part and parcel of it. He indicated that the propaganda line had been different for months, by which he could have meant press, radio and newsreels, but not film, as there was scarcely a propaganda film running in German cinemas in summer 1938.

[559] Bernd-Jürgen Wendt, *Großdeutschland. Außenpolitk und Kreigsvorbereitung des Hitler-Regimes*, Munich 1987, p. 155.

[560] Wette, *Mobilmachung*, p. 217.

[561] Ibid., p. 218.

[562] Cf. also entries for 27./28.1.1938.

[563] Goebbels himself mentions the *Essener Nationalzeitung* of 10.11.1937, for example. The SS newspaper *Das schwarze Korps* was also constantly criticizing the film programmes.

[564] Printed in: Albrecht I, p. 504.

[565] *Der deutsche Film* H., no. 1/1938. Cf. also Welch, *German Cinema*, p. 43.

[566] Toeplitz, vol. 3, p. 278.

[567] They include *Die kleine und die große Liebe* ("The Great and the Little Love", première: 29.4.1938), *Wie einst im Mai* ("As Once in May", première: 11.2.1938), *Heiratsschwindler* ("The Marriage Impostor", première: 15.2.1938), *Zwischen den Eltern* ("Between the Parents", première: 15.2.1938).

[568] The positive judgement of *Du und ich* emerged only after a long-drawn-out revision period (cf. for example comment on 17.9.1938).

[569] For this tendency see Goebbels' speech to the workers on 28.10.1938 in: *Völkischer Beobachter* (Berlin edition), 29.10.1938, and speech on 19.11.1938, printed in: Helmut Heiber (ed.), *Goebbels-Reden 1932–1939*, Düsseldorf 1971, p. 327, as

a skilful combination of social themes, military and confidence propaganda.

570 Karlheinz Wendtland, *Geliebter Kintopp* 1937 and 1938 vol., Berlin no date, p. 154.

571 Welch, *German Cinema,* p. 43, although his way of counting seems to raise similar problems to Albrecht's.

572 1937: nine films in this "military" category (military conflict, military terminology and protagonists): *Weiße Sklaven, Ritt in die Freiheit, Fridericus, Menschen ohne Vaterland, Alarm in Peking, Die Warschauer Zitadelle, Unternehmen Michael, Patrioten, Signal in der Nacht;* 1938: seven films: *Katzensteg, Kameraden auf See, Furlough on Word of Honor, Mit versiegelter Order, Ziel in den Wolken, Dreizehn Mann und eine Kanone, Pour le Mérite* (four of these appeared in the months of January and December, which were furthest away from the political and military crisis); 1939 (January to August): four films: *Tumult in Damaskus, Drei Unteroffiziere, Grenzfeuer, Flucht ins Dunkel,* of which only one from June to September.

573 There is nothing by Goebbels on two of the titles.

574 Kreimeier, p. 332.

575 BA/K R 109I/1033c, no. 140, minute no. 1385 for 13.9.1939.

576 Kreimeier p. 332.

577 Witte, *Film im Nationalsozialismus*, p. 131.

578 Martin Broszat (ed.), "Der Zweite Weltkrieg: Ein Krieg der 'alten' Eliten, der Nationalsozialisten oder der Krieg Hitlers?", in: same author/Klaus Schwabe, *Die deutschen Eliten und der Weg in den Zweiten Weltkrieg*, pp. 27–71, esp. pp. 48–61.

579 Cf. entries for 3./12./18./24. 8. 1938.

580 Cf. Friedrich Freiherr von Gaertringen (ed.), *Die Hassell-Tagebücher*, Berlin 1988, p. 54 (17.9.1938); Leonidas E. Hill (ed.), *Die Weizsäcker-Papiere 1933–1950*, Frankfurt am Main 1974, pp. 145 and 171, also Michels, p. 392.

581 "The opinion is spreading in the country that war is inevitable. I will try to damp that down a little. Otherwise there will be panic in the long run" (16.7.1938); "Our campaign against Prague is wearying the public a little. It is not possible to keep a crisis going for months. So a little more restraint, and don't use all our ammo at once. Besides there is an increasing sense of panic about war in the country. People believe that war has become inevitable. No one feels comfortable with this. Such fatalism is the most dangerous thing of all" (17.7.1938).

582 Cf. also an entry as early as 24.11.1937: "Talked things out at length with Ribbentrop … The view of foreign policy that he is presenting is highly inadequate and unclear. He feels a profound hatred for England and sees her as our arch-enemy. I do not think that is quite right."

583 The Zarah Leander films *La Habanera* and *Zu neuen Ufern* ("To New Shores"), both 1937, certainly did show a clear tendency directed against Great Britain's colonial imperialism, greasy South Americans and also against colonialism in general: Kreimeier, p. 352.

584 The same applies to Hitler: BA/K NS 10/44, no. 11, aide-de-camp's office to Leichtenstern on *Capriccio* on 20.9.1938.

585 Toepliz, vol. 3, p. 277.

586 *Völkischer Beobachter* (Berlin edition) on 11.3.1939.

587 *Völkischer Beobachter* (Berlin edition) on 2.2.1939.

588 Film review in the *Völkischer Beobachter* (Berlin edition) on 23.2.1939.

589 The last entry about this so far known is on 6.11.1939.

590 Drewniak, p. 269.

591 BA/Film/K no. 10408.

592 BA?K R 109I/1033b, no. 33, minute no. 1355 on 14.2.1939: according to this the Propaganda Ministry wanted more shots of the autobahns, which affected the closing scenes in particular.

593 BA/K R 109 I/1033c, no. 81, minute no. 1368 on 23.5.1939.

594 BA Film/K Film no. 144131.

595 He was away from Berlin from 27.3. to 16.4.1939.

596 Jürgen Spiker, *Film und Kapital*, Berlin 1974, p. 292.

597 BA/K R 109I/1033c, no. 295, minute no. 1366 for 9.5.1939.

598 It is not possible to see any change of plan between May and June as a result of new instructions from Goebbels, because the planned films, about 35 in all, are not listed in either month.

599 BA/K R 109I/1033c, no. 295, minute no. 1366 on 9.5.1939 and no. 375 f., minute no. 1370 on 8.6.1939.

600 BA/K R 109I/1033c, no. 257, minute no. 1370 on 8.6.1939.

601 Ibid.

602 BA/K 55/1319, no. 29 ff., Winkler to Goebbels on 27.10.1939.

603 In a list appended to the minutes on 27 June that obviously includes all the projects, *Offiziersehe* and *Attacke* are already missing; *Der Stammbaum des Dr. Pistorius* and *Kennwort Machalin* can be identified as additional political projects, of which the latter was also not made: BA/K R 109I/1033c, appendix 1 to minute no. 1374 on 27.6.1939.

604 Drewniak, p. 415. See also Goebbels' essentially negative comment in the entry for 30.7.1939.

605 "Plan 21" in minute no. 1370 on 8.6.1939, no. 258; "no. 19" in the appendix to the meeting on 27.6.1939.

606 *Völkischer Beobachter* (Berlin edition) on 28.7.1939.

607 Michels, p. 407 and 410, using numerous passages from the daily entries

608 Cf. for example the entry for 18.8.1939: "Discussed Gründgens' new film *Zwei Welten* with him. If it is skilfully made, it is potentially very interesting." Goebbels, who at this point urgently needed political films, is disappointed with the result: "A contemporary film about help with the harvest – at least that it what it is supposed to be. But it hasn't come off. Too intellectual, and almost exclusively brain-work" (27.12.1939).

609 Michels, p. 403

610 Courtade/Cadars, p. 224. Witte provides an exemplary analysis of the film, *Filmkomödie*, pp. 356 f.

611 *Völkischer Beobachter* (Berlin edition) for 6.10.1939.

612 BA/K 55/1319 no. 29ff., Winkler to Goebbels on 27.10.1939 (here no. 32).

613 This was probably forthcoming in March or early April, as the Ufa board took it off on 21.3.1939. Kreimeier, p. 336, puts the significance in terms of war preparation into perspective: he says that the essentially contradictory film contained "subversive protests" against the military.

614 BA/K NS 10/48, SS-Obersturmbannführer Bahls to Leichtenstern on 16.6.1939.

615 BA/K NS 10/48, no. 14, Bahls to RMVP on 24.4.1939.

616 BA/K NS 10/48, no. 14, Bahls to RMVP on 24.4.1939. The two propaganda merchants' different view of *Der Gouverneur* seems interesting. Hitler, who preferred a direct approach to indirect allusions and always wanted the enemy to be named probably rejected the film because it was set in an imaginary, anarchic parliamentary system rather than definitely in the Weimar Republic.

617 BA/K NS 10/48, no. 11, Bahls to Leichtenstern on 13.6.1939.

618 Ibid.

619 BA/K NS 10/48, no. 14, Bahls to RMVP on 24.4.1939.

620 Kreimeier, p. 356 – contradicting himself – names 29.8.1939, the date of Klitzsch's letter, as the latest possible moment.

621 BA/K R 109I/1033c, no. 156, Klitzsch to Winkler on 29.8.1939, appendix 2 to minute no. 1383.

622 Rother, *Effekte*, p. 200. Goebbels says that *Alarm auf Station III* is just a "quite nice popular film" on 29.10.1939.

623 Kreimeier, p. 357. The Security Service report of 23.10.1939 shows that the ban was not followed in all arts of the Reich: Heinz Boberach (ed.), *Meldungen aus dem Reich 1938–1945. Die geheimen Lageberichte des Sicherheitsdienstes der SS*, Herrsching 1984, p. 384, where the following appears about a spy film directed against the Red Army: "Given the political relationship with Russia a number of our countrymen could not understand why the film was being shown. – Similarly, reports have come in from Reichenberg that the people do not understand why anti-Bolshevik films like *Henker, Frauen und Soldaten* or *Fugitives* continue to be shown." For the titles of the banned films see Winkler's list, no. 36/37.

624 Drewniak, p. 348, presents this inevitable measure as co-ordination of foreign policy and film production.

625 Cf. Jürgen Hagemann, *Die Presselenkung im Dritten Reich*, Bonn 1970, pp. 160 f.

626 BA/K R 109I/1033c, no. 164, minute no. 1382 on 23.8.1939.

627 This suggests that the reasons were not the start of the war and material costs, as stated by Bauer, p. 470.

628 BA/K R 55/1319, no. 29 ff., Winkler to Goebbels on 27.10.1939.

629 BA/K R 109I/1033c no. 145 minute no. 1384 on 6.9.1939.

630 Kreimeier, p. 364.

631 For the most important propaganda productions a large-scale launch happened after a few weeks. Thus *The Great King* opened in all major cities four weeks after its première in Berlin and Potsdam on 3.2.1942.

632 Michael Maaß, "Aspekte von Kultur und Freizeit in Nürnberg", in: *Archiv für Sozialgeschichte*, 33rd year, pp. 334 f., provides concrete evidence of this for *Triumph des Willens* and other films in Nuremberg.

633 Cf. *Jahrbuch der Reichsfilmkammer 1939*, speech by Hugo Fischer on "Film als Propagandawaffe der Partei", pp. 66–75. Curt Belling mentions that there were already 300 film vans by 1936 in *Filmkurier,* no. 52 on 31.12.1936. Cf. also Curt Belling, *Der Film in Staat und Partei*, Berlin 1936, p. 118, and *Völkischer Beobachter* (Berlin edition) on 11.3.1939, where 600 film vans are mentioned, and also Barkhausen, pp. 147, 163. In 1941 about two thirds of the population must have had access to conventional cinemas: Spiker, p. 196. Cf. also the Security Service annual report for 1938: Boberach p. 116: "The Gau film offices were very active, and able to provide very large sections of the German population with good (usually older) films." Distribution throughout the country of *documentary* propaganda films by the Landesbildstelle was constantly improved up to 1943: Hilmar Hoffmann, *Und die Fahne führt uns in die Ewigkeit*, *Propaganda im NS-Film*, Frankfurt am Main 1988, p. 111.

634 Toeplitz, vol. 3, p. 265.

635 *Völkischer Beobachter* (Berlin edition) on 9./10.4.1939.

636 Andrea Naica-Loebell, "Das totale Kino. Die Arbeit der Gaufilmstellen der NSDAP und die Jugendfilmstunde, konkretisiert am Beispiel München-Oberbayern", in: Michael Staudig (ed.), *Positionen deutscher Filmgeschichte*, Munich 1996, p. 188.

637 Cf. ministerial conference on 8.1.1940: Willi A. Boelcke (ed.), *Kriegspropaganda 1939–1941*, *Geheime Konferenzen im Reichspropagandaministerium*, Stuttgart 1966, (Boelcke I), p. 259.

638 The Security Service reports constantly point out how strongly the rural population could be impressed and influenced by the film performances (cf. Security Service report for 8.11.1939: Boberach, pp. 432 f.); obviously much more permanently than by the radio or the press. But the urban population was directly affected by the war (air raids and food shortages), and so provided a better measure for the public mood and attitudes. The rural population certainly rose as the war proceeded, as a result of evacuation from the conurbations (by 15 million in March 1944), but by this stage the film performances could scarcely be provided for technical reasons: Spiker, p. 238.

639 Cf. Hoffmann, pp. 102 ff. Passages in the minutes of the ministerial conferences also record the value of "film education" for young people as provided by the "film ceremonies", and so suitable films were chosen, and scenes that might put "young people at risk" were cut: ministerial conference on 29.11.1939: Boelcke I, p. 230.

640 This film was often used in revival programmes after the outbreak of war as well. The Security Service report says that it met with objections "because on the one hand it deals only with the horror, death and ruin caused by war, without any deeper meaning, and allocates light and darkness entirely evenly, indeed almost to the advantage of the enemy side. German soldiers appeared in it as old, bearded, emaciated and exhausted figures": report, dated 14.2.1940: Boberach, p. 760.

641 Drewniak, p. 645, though he mentions no specific places.

642 Toeplitz, vol. 3, p. 281.

643 Cf. also Maaß, p. 338, with the same observation for Nuremberg.

644 Kreimeier, p. 323.

645 Drewniak, pp. 348 ff.

646 See chapter 4, pp. 245 ff.

647 Filmfinanz GmbH minutes for 3.2.1939, quoted from Marcus S. Philips, *The German Film Industry and the Third Reich*, diss., East Anglia 1972, p. 161.

648 Ibid., p. 243.

649 Albrecht I, p. 218 (table p. 417).

650 Phillips, p. 161, asserts that cinema attendance in Berlin rose by twelve per cent as a result of *Pour le mérite* alone in January 1939. But a glance at the cinema programmes for this month shows that the film was very little in evidence.

651 Karl Ludwig Rost shows this in *Sterilisation und Euthanasie im Film des "Dritten Reichs",* med. diss., Berlin 1986, p. 305, with reference to *I Accuse.*

652 Cf. also Kreimeier, pp. 327 ff.

653 BA/K R 109I/1033c, no. 149, minute no. 1383, dating from 28.8.1939.

654 BA/K R 109I/1033c, no. 133, minute no. 1386, dating from 20.9.1939.

655 Ibid., no. 136.

656 The leading role was actually filled not by Emil Jannings. who had already played Bismarck on stage in 1936/37, but by the "Staatsschauspieler" and theatre manager Paul Hartmann. The film also shows Bismarck not only at the outbreak of war in 1866, but includes the years 1862 to 1871.

657 William S. Shirer, *Berliner Tagebuch. Aufzeichnungen 1934–41*, ed. by Jürgen Schebera, Leipzig 1991, pp. 198 f. (10.11.9.1939).

658 Cf. also entries for 1./23.10., 10.11., 12./14./15./22.12.1939.

659 Cf. also entry for 31.10.1939 on Heinz Rühmann's comedy promoting the joys of parenthood *Hurra! I'm a Papa!*: "Not a particularly good Rühmann film. But it can be used for the war."

660 The entry for 6.11.1939 gives only an indirectly positive assessment of *D III 88*, an unambiguously military Luftwaffe film.

661 Cf. Ulrike Reim, "Der "Robert-Koch"-Film (1939) von Hans Steinhoff. Kunst oder Propaganda?", in: Udo Benzenhöfer/Wolfgang U. Eckart, *Medizin im Spielfilm des Nationalsozialismus*, Tecklenburg 1990, pp. 22–23.

662 Entry for 9.8.1939, further entry for 29.7.1939 ("fabulous work of art", "wonderful cultural painting"). The *Völkischer Beobachter* (Berlin edition) announced 5.8 million viewers for *Robert Koch* in 45 days at 180 cinemas in the Reich as early as 16.11.1939.

663 Security Service report on 11.10.1939: Boberach, p. 342; Security Service report on 4.12.1939: Boberach, p. 527.

664 Security Service report on 4.12.1939: Boberach, p. 527.

665 U(fa) T(on) W(oche) 487/1940/Z: 4.1.1940. Cf. also ministerial conference on 29.12.1939: Boelcke I, p. 254, and the Security Service report on 14.2.1940, which is contradictory though Party-oriented and thus one-sided: Boberach, pp. 759 f.

666 Hans Günter Seraphim (ed.), *Das politische Tagebuch Alfred Rosenbergs 1934/35 und 1939/40*,

Göttingen 1946, p. 91 (11.12.1939), author's additions.

667 Goebbels had only anticipated the moment of reckoning about the newsreel in several entries about editorial demands from Hitler.

668 *Das Reich,* no. 8 for 14.7.1940; cf. also Hollstein, p. 64.

669 Speech on 15.2.1941, printed in Albrecht I, p. 470.

670 For this cf. the Security Service report for 22.12.1939: Boberach, p. 595: "The people's involvement in political and military events has lessened generally because of preparations for Christmas.

671 BA/K R 109 I/1033c, no. 39, minute no. 1402, dated 1.2.1940.

672 Cf. also Minister's conference on 22.4.1940: Willi A. Boelcke (ed.), *Kriegspropaganda 1939–1941. Geheime Konferenzen im Reichspropagandaministerium*, Stuttgart 1966 (Boelcke I), p. 326: "Herr Hippler is to make sure that films stop showing nonsense about marital problems and marital conflicts."

673 Security Service report, dated 19.4.1940: Heinz Boberach (ed.), *Meldungen aus dem Reich 1938 to 1945. Die geheimen Lageberichte des Sicherheitsdienstes der SS,* Herrsching 1984, pp. 1024 f. Otherwise the report is completely positive. Criticism of *The Desert Song* and *Wir tanzen um die Welt* apparently came only from the rural population.

674 Hand-written notes by someone present at the meeting, dated 23.4.1940, printed in: Albrecht I, p. 143

675 The 50:50 ratio actually was achieved. The Tobis annual report, dated 30.6.1940 for the production year 1940/41 shows eight openly political films and eight films in other categories: BA/K R 109 I/4809, no. 168, Tobis-Filmkunst company report, dated 30.6.1942.

676 BA/K R 109 I/1034a, no. 252, minute no. 1411, dated 8.5.1940.

677 Possibly the *Stukas* project was the only result of the demand.

678 BA/K R 109 I/2139a, no. 181, note by Schreiber, dated 13.6.1940.

679 Cf. also entry for 4.6.1940: "Our dear production chiefs are working in too much of a vacuum."

680 *Der deutsche Film*, issue 1, July 1940.

681 Security Service report, dated 3.4.1941: Boberach, pp. 2176 f.

682 Speech on 15.2.1941, printed in: Albrecht I, p. 468.

683 Cf. Security Service reports, dated 19.4.1940: Boberach, p. 1024, about *Die Reise nach Tilsit* ("Trip to Tisit") ("Women in particular feel that the film's clear emphasis on the concept of honour and Elske's deeply human behaviour as a mother are estimable") and 22.7.1940: Boberach, p. 1404 on *Aus erster Ehe* ("People say that it was particularly welcome to see really estimable people and their view of life in this film. They feel that it is 'true to life'") and 27.1.1941: Boberach, p. 1944, on *Feinde.*

684 BA/K R 109 I/2139a, no. 1, Reichsmeister's general orders, dated 5.4.1941.

685 Entry for 17.2.1940.

686 Cf. Dorothea Hollstein, *Antisemitische Filmpropaganda*, Munich 1971, p. 64, about Goebbels' speech on 10.4.1940. Cf. also RE 5.12.1940.

687 Speech on 15.2.1941, printed in: Albrecht I, p. 470.

688 Ibid., p. 468.

689 Ibid.

690 Cf. Minister's conference on 10.1.1940: Boelcke I, p. 263.

691 This also casts a different light on the view of himself presented by someone like the district film screenings officer, Hugo Fischer, for example, especially in terms of the autumn and winter. Minister's conference on 8.1.1940: Boelcke I, p. 259.

692 BA/K R 109 I/1033c, no. 20, minute no. 1406, dated 28.2.1940.

693 Security Service report, dated 4.12.1939: Boberach, p. 527. Ufa had the ban lifted in the spring.

694 Cf. Minister's conference on 2.6.1940: Boelcke I, p. 375; Peter Bucher, "Goebbels und die deutsche Wochenschau", in: Militärgeschichtliche Mitteilungen, 40th vol., 1986, p. 54.

695 Cf. also entry for 22.5.1940: "Our people are in a magnificent mood." It is in fact doubtful whether the people were so positively in favour of the regime's actions at the beginning of the western offensive as they were after the victory over France. William L. Shirer, Berliner Tagebuch. Aufzeichnungen 1934–41, ed. by Jürgen Schebera, Leipzig 1991, p. 329 (19.5.1940): "I had thought that the night bombing of west Germany, whose deadly effects the BBC had been boasting about since the beginning of the western offensive would have had a deleterious effect on the morale of the population. But during our journey through the Ruhr we saw people – particularly women – standing on the bridges over the main roads and cheering on the troops moving through in the direction of Belgium and France."

696 Security Service report, dated 14.2.1940: Boberach, p. 759.

697 Security Service report, dated 6.3.1940: Boberach, p. 846. For this see also entry for 10.3.1940.

698 Security Service report, dated 14.5.1940: Boberach, p. 1131. Shirer noticed a similar reaction, p. 313 (8.5.1940); cf. also Hilmar Hoffmann, "Und die Fahne führt uns in die Ewigkeit." Propaganda im NS-Film, Frankfurt am Main 1988, pp. 171 f.; David Welch, Propaganda and the German Cinema, Oxford 1983, pp. 204 ff.

699 Minister's conference on 1.2.1941: Boelcke I, p. 610.

700 Minister's conference on 27.6.1940: Boelcke I, p. 409. Cf. also entry for 28.6.1940: "I am introducing some variety into music and light entertainment for radio and film."

701 Security Service report, dated 22.7.1940: Boberach, p. 1405.

702 For the only exception (Der Fuchs von Glenavron) see below p. 252.

703 Hollstein, p. 64.

704 Speech on 15.2.1941, printed in: Albrecht I, p. 470.

705 Klaus Kreimeier, Die Ufa-Story, Munich 1992, p. 364.

706 Security Service report, dated 22.7.1940: Boberach, pp. 1404 f.

707 The film's mixed reception after its première in November 1940 proved Goebbels right: Security Service report, dated 27.1.1941: Boberach, p. 1944.

708 Security Service report, dated 10.10.1940: Boberach, p. 1655.

709 Ibid., p. 1656.

710 He arrived at this view after censoring The Lady from Barnhelm and Ein Leben lang.

711 No comments are available on the other political productions.

712 Minister's conference on 4.4.1941: Boelcke I, pp. 656 f.

713 Text of the court judgement, printed in: Filmpress, dated 22.7.1950.

714 Cf. Peter Bucher, "Die Bedeutung des Films als historische Quelle: 'Der ewige Jude'"(1940), in: Heinz Duchhardt/Manfred Schlenke (ed.), Festschrift für Eberhard Kessel, Munich 1982, pp. 302 and 319. According to this, Goebbels had been working "on a major anti-Semitic film programme since October/November 1938".

715 Cf. Boguslaw Drewniak, Der deutsche Film 1938–1945, Düsseldorf 1987, pp. 307 f.

716 Hollstein, p. 62.

717 Ibid., p. 39.

718 Cf. Ralf Georg Reuth, Goebbels, Munich 1991, pp. 383 ff.; Helmut Michels, Ideologie und Propaganda. Die Rolle von Joseph Goebbels in der nationalsozialistischen Außenpolitik bis 1939, Frankfurt am Main 1992, p. 339. Cf. also entries for 23./24.6.1938.

719 Andrea Naica-Lobell, "Das totale Kino", in: Michael Schaudig (ed.), Positionen deutscher Filmgeschichte, Munich 1996, p. 187.

720 Goebbels reports a "Jewish demonstration against an anti-Semitic film" (15.7.1935). But according to newspaper reports there was no "demonstration" on the Kurfürstendamm, but just whistling directed at Peterson und Bendel; but it is possible that there were acts of anti-Semitic violence: Neue Zürcher Zeitung on 16.7.1935. Cf. also Michels, p. 337.

721 See diary entry for 23.5.1939: "Examined film Robert und Bertram: A weak piece of work by Zerlett. ... The Jewish problem is touched upon very superficially, without any real sense of empathy." Hans Günter Seraphim (ed.), Das politische Tagebuch Alfred Rosenbergs 1934/35 und 1939/40, Göttingen 1956, pp. 110 f. (11.12.1939). According to this, Hitler said: "The new Robert u. Bertram does down the German".

722 Hollstein, p. 53.

723 BA/K R 109 I/1033c, no. 133, minute no. 1386, dated 20.9.1939: "He also agreed with some Rothschild material that had been conveyed to him".

724 Fritz Hippler, "Der ewige Jude", in: Deutsche Annalen, 1991, pp. 210 f. Cf. also Fritz Hippler, Die Verstrickung, Düsseldorf 1982, p. 187, and Yizak Ahren/Stig Hornshöj-Möller/Christoph B. Melchers, Wie Goebbels hetzte, Aachen 1990, pp. 15 ff. Bucher and Hornshöj/Melchers, using other quotations from Goebbels' diaries – though the 5.10 passage was not known to them –, have described the history of the production vividly.

725 Cf. Bucher, Der ewige Jude, pp. 304 ff. There is no doubt that it is difficult to ascribe the shape of certain scenes in the film to direct interventions by Hitler, even though attempts have been made to do this: Peter Cohen, Architektur des Untergangs, Bayerischer Rundfunk, 30.1.1993, 9.20 p.m.

726 This quotation may refer to Goebbels' assessment of the toned down young people's and matinee version. However, the film was completed in the first week in September 1940 at the earliest.

727 According to Bucher, Der ewige Jude, p. 305, Goebbels did not want to risk endangering the success of Jud Süss by satiating the public with the brutal film Der ewige Jude. But Bucher certainly overlooks the fact that according to the entry for 11.10.1940 Der ewige Jude was not completed until after the première of Jud Süss on 24 September. Jerzy Toeplitz, Geschichte des Films, vol. 4, Berlin 1983, p. 218, is also mistaken, wrongly explaining the failure of Der ewige Jude by suggesting that the film appeared "too early", i.e. two months before Jud Süss. Cf. also Siegfried Zielinski, Veit Harlan, Frankfurt am Main 1981, p. 26.

728 Security Service report, dated 20.1.1941: Boberach, pp. 1917 f. The film was withdrawn from the first cinemas after running for about half the week.

729 During the first days after Hitlers release Goebbels was in Norway.

730 Also according to the Harlan judgement text Goebbels is said to have asked Terra production chief Brauer how Jud Süss was coming along in February 1939. This contradicts the later first entry on the manuscript of the film on 9.11.1939 (see below).

731 Veit Harlan, Im Schatten meiner Filme, Gütersloh 1966, p. 100. Cf. also Leni Riefenstahl's version, Memoiren, Frankfurt am Main/Berlin 1987, pp. 358 f.

732 This also shows that Goebbels apparently did not see Eberhard Wolfgang Möller's screenplay until late autumn, while in Harlan's trial in 1950 the summer was mentioned – before the war, in other words: judgement, dated 15.7.1950.

733 Entry for 5.12.1939. According to Hollstein, p. 80, the direction was not handed over to Harlan, to Harlan's surprise, until January 1940.

734 For example on 5./18.1.1940, 15.2.1940, 26.4.1940, 18./19.8.1940, 6./7./10.9.1940.

735 The film had taken 5,3 mill. RM at the box office after five months: Hollstein, p. 229.

736 Friedrich Knilli in: tip-magazin, 19/1997, p. 74. Security Service report, dated 28.11.1940: Boberach, pp. 1811 f: he says that rarely had oppinions of a film been "as unanimous" as they were for Jud Süss. Stephen Lowry, Pathos und Politik, Tübingen 1991, p. 29, also refers to the "effective mixture of anti-Semitic propaganda with elements of the conventional light entertainment film". See also Witte's analysis of the film in: Jacobsen et al. (ed.), Geschichte des deutschen Films, Stuttgart 1993, pp. 152 ff.

737 Goebbels passed the report on to Hitler. In fact it mentions uproar in the Budapest cinemas, but not street demonstrations: BA/K R 43 II/1389, no. 158 f. Min.amt RMVP to Lammers on 31.3.1941. Cf. also speech on 28.2.1942, printed in: Albrecht I, p. 499: "... even the actor, if he had to think during every scene how many people would see this later, would probably start to feel bemused. ... For example Herr (Ferdinand) Marian, did not know when he played Jud Süss that major demonstrations and pogroms against Jews would take place in Dutch towns as a result of this film, and that afterwards half a dozen Jews would have to be hanged be-

cause they had attempted to kill Germans." It is possible that Goebbels shifted the location of the pogroms from Hungary to Holland because of alliance policies or because of Hungarian Jewish policies.

738 Cf. entries for 7./17./19./23.7., 10.8., 1.9. and 10.9.1940. Cf. also Fritz Hippler, *Betrachtungen zum Filmschaffen*, Berlin 1943, p. 100. Hippler indirectly mentions the drawing of figures and characters in *Die Rothschilds* as a negative example.

739 BA/K R 109 I/1034b, no. 155 minute, no. 1427, dated 25.9.1940. Here a retreat in favour of Jud Süss seems to make more sense; cf. Hollstein, p. 75. It was not re-released until July 1941 and ran in some Berlin cinemas again from August: BA/K R 109 I/1034b, no. 140, minute no. 1461, dated 2.7.1941.

740 Cf. Karl Ludwig Rost, *Sterilisation und Euthanasie im Film des "Dritten Reichs"*, med. diss., Berlin 1986; Karl Heinz Roth, *Filmpropaganda für die Vernichtung der Geisteskranken und Behinderten im "Dritten Reich"*, med. diss., Hamburg 1986.

741 Of which two are of minor importance: Goebbels reports how badly the film was received at the Venice Film Festival (15.9.1941), and also a dispute about it with Carlotta Bonomi, the wife of the Italian ambassador in Berlin (6.12.1941).

742 BA Film/B Film-no. 12560. Ernst Klee, *"Euthanasie" im NS-Staat*, Frankfurt am Main 1983, pp. 242 f.

743 Hans-Walter Schmuhl, "Philipp Bouhler – Vorreiter des Massenmords", in: Ronald Smelser et al. (ed.), *Die braune Elite II*, Darmstadt 1993, p. 46.

744 Cf. entry for 1.5.1940: "Bouhler reports on the liquidation of lunatics, which is so necessary and is now being carried out. Still secret. It is proving most difficult."

745 Rost, p. 168: Wolfgang Liebeneiner had probably been working on the screenplay at least since September 1940.

746 Ibid., p. 299, note 964: letter from Liebeneiner to Rost, dated 13.2.1983.

747 Ibid., p. 168.

748 Ibid., p. 153.

749 The annihilations had become known in many parts of the Reich through rumours and a pastoral letter by the two churches, dated 6.7.1941. However, on 28 September 1941 von Galen justified the Russian campaign as a struggle against "Moscow's Jewish-Bolshevik despotism": Stefan Rahner et al., *"Treu deutsch sind wir – wir sind auch treu katholisch". Kardinal zu Galen und das Dritte Reich*, Münster 1987, p. 43.

750 Roth, p. 126.

751 BA/K Zsg 102/63, dated 21.8.1941.

752 Klee, p. 339 f.

753 Ian Kershaw, "How effective was Nazi Propaganda", in: David Welch (ed.), *Nazi Propaganda – the Power and the Limitations*, London 1983, p. 194, sees the film as a failure. Cf. also Welch, *German Cinema*, pp. 130 ff. Roth, pp. 136 f., comes to the conclusion that it caused "resistance to 'euthanasia' to lose some breadth without a doubt, but it seems that the rebellious core groups were not decisively weakened. ... But *I Accuse* was absolutely not able to achieve open affirmation of the practice of annihilation that was in train ...".

754 Rost, p. 204.

755 Cf. copious collections and correspondence in BA/K NS 18/348.

756 BA/K NS 18/348, Gauleitung Hannover an Parteikanzlei, dated 10.1.1942.

757 The Security Service report about reactions to *I Accuse* is the longest of all on an individual film: Security Service report, dated 15.1.1942: Boberach, pp. 3175 ff.; Roth, p. 137; Rost, p. 207.

758 See chap. 6, p. 360.

759 Statement on 11.8.1947 in facsimile, printed in: Hippler, *Verstrickung*, p. 297.

760 Cf. also entries for 10.2.1940 and 5.3.1941.

761 Cf. entry for 5.4.1941: "Opinions divided on *Ohm Krüger*. Some find it too cruel. But it has to be if it is to be effective with the people. And that is what it is for."

762 Security Service report, dated 12.5.1941: Boberach, p. 2295.

763 Ibid.

764 For this cf. Welch, *German Cinema*, pp. 277 f.

765 BA/K R 55/1320, no. 115ff: results from 1.7.1940 to 31.5.1941 with comparative titles. Cf. also entry for 22.5.1941.

766 With the exception of *Der ewige Jude*, no film is mentioned more frequently, even in the hand-written diary to 1941.

767 24.6.1940. Cf. Minister's conference on 23.6.1940: Boelcke I, pp. 401 f.

768 26.7.1940. Cf. also Ulrich Höver, *Joseph Goebbels – ein nationaler Sozialist*, Bonn 1992, pp. 438 ff., who has examined the daily entry quotations for these weeks in detail.

769 Erwin Leiser, *Deutschland erwache. Propaganda im Film des Dritten Reiches*, Hamburg 1968, p. 90, is also repeated and reinforced by Drewniak, p. 330.

770 Alfred Rosenberg's diary (9.5.1940): Seraphim, p. 115. According to this Rosenberg also saw *The Desert Song* as pro-English.

771 Security Service report, dated 20.5.1940: Boberach, p. 1155. Cf. also Minister's conference on 22.4.1940: Boelcke I, p. 327. Failure was also reported from Lorraine: Security Service report, dated 18.11.1940: Boberach, p. 1779. *Maria Ilona* was reproached with "pro-Hungarian tendencies" in the Ostmark: Minister's conference on 1.2.40: Boelcke I, p. 278 and Security Service report, dated 29.1.1940: Boberach, p. 702.

772 Cf. also the somewhat more positive comment, dated 2.2.1941, after revision (première: 17.2.1941).

773 Except for *Stukas* (entry for 18.9.1940).

774 For the essential features of the genre see Françis Courtade/Pierre Cadars, *Geschichte des Films im Dritten Reich*, Munich 1975, pp. 198–205.

775 Cf. also the film storyboard in BA/P 90 RI g, Nachlaß Karl Ritter.

776 Bucher, *Goebbels*, p. 55, also confirms the Propaganda Minister's essentially negative assessment of the "realistic" military films based on a newsreel-style approach.

777 Cf. also entries for 14./18.2.1941.

778 Toeplitz, vol. 4, p. 231.

779 BA/K R 55/1320, no. 113 ff.

780 According to the tables drawn up by Gerd Albrecht, who distinguished between estimated and actual results: Albrecht I, p. 410. The advance assessments are in fact quite frequently problemati-

cal: even box-office hits and extremely effective films like *Die grosse Liebe* seem not to meet expectations; they also do not take the different numbers of copies into consideration.

781 Cf. Drewniak, p. 394.

782 Cf. the announcement of these films in *Film-Welt*, no. 37/1941.

783 For its significance and sobering effect on the German leadership and the behaviour of their Japanese allies see Andreas Hillgruber, *Die Zerstörung Europas*, Frankfurt am Main/Berlin 1988, pp. 296–312.

784 Cf. Helmut Heiber, *Joseph Goebbels*, Munich 1965, p. 274. For Hitler's confidence in victory see also Martin Vogt, "Selbstbespiegelung in Erwartung des Sieges", in: Wolfgang Michalka (ed.), *Der zweite Weltkrieg*, Munich 1989, pp. 641–656. Hitler had

declared in the Berlin Sportpalast on 3 October 1941 that Russia would "never rise again".

785 This information was passed on by the Reich press conference and this supposed "end of the eastern campaign" also appears in the following newsreel: Willi A. Boelcke (ed.), *"Wollt ihr den totalen Krieg". Die geheimen Goebbels-Konferenzen 1939–1943*, Stuttgart 1967 (Boelcke II), p. 189; Deutsche Wochenschau, no. 579//1941/Z: 16.10.1941.

786 For Goebbels' "early, quite sober assessment of the situation" cf. Reuth, p. 492. Security Service report, dated 3.11.1941: Boberach, p. 2938.

787 Here Goebbels is essentially reporting the Security Service bulletins for this period, or the Reichspropagandaämter activities reports and the reports from the administrative district heads.

788 Speech "Der Dank der Heimat an die Front", printed in: Joseph Goebbels, *Das eherne Herz*, Munich 1943, pp. 131–137.

789 Heiber, *Joseph Goebbels*, p. 268.

790 Goebbels set the direction for anti-Soviet propaganda in subsequent months with his essay "Der Schleier fällt" (The veil falls) on 6.7.1941 in the *Völkischer Beobachter* (Berlin edition).

791 Cf. entry for 15.7.1941; Welch, *German Cinema*, p. 249 and entry for 18.8.1941: "He (Karl Ritter) explains a new subject to me called 'GPU', a strong, anti-Bolshevik plot which I very much approve of."

792 See chap. 6, pp. 380 f.., and Bucher, *Goebbels*, p. 57.

793 Goebbels apparently had some trouble with this: "The ongoing adjustment to our radio programme to place more stress on entertainment is making a lot of work for me" (20.9.1941). Other passages on radio programme adjustments in autumn 1941 are to be found on 9./15.10.1941 and 14.11.1941.

794 Première: 10.10.1941.

795 Entry for 20.8.1941.

796 Speech on 15.2.1941, printed in: Albrecht I, p. 480.

797 Ibid., p. 482.

798 Ibid., p. 483.

799 Cf. also entry for 9.1.1942 on theatre.

800 Entries for 27.2.1942 and 2.5.1942.

801 BA/K R 55/1321, no. 64, dated 6.2.1942.

802 Ibid., no. 59. None of the "politically significant films" was realized.

803 "It (the production programme) is to be designed in such a way that some films with political, military or other specially estimable themes will be made, but that otherwise the wartime programme will consist predominantly of entertaining films": "Leistungssteigerungserlaß", dated 28.2.1942, printed in: Albrecht I, pp. 529 ff.

804 Speech on 28.2.1942, printed in: Albrecht I, p. 486.

805 Ibid., p. 489.

806 Ibid., pp. 490 f.

807 Ibid., p. 495.

808 Ibid., pp. 495 f.: "I am of the opinion that if people have worked 10, 14 and 20 hours a day then they need to relax"; "So I don't need to be so didactic in films; I must make sure that art provides relaxation at times with such high tension levels."

809 Toeplitz, vol. 4, p. 234.

810 Goebbels also praised this film, which was very successful with the public, though he did not mention the title, in his film speech on 28.2.1942; printed in: Albrecht I, p.492.

811 Martin Loiperdinger/Klaus Schönekäs, "Die große Liebe – Propaganda im Unterhaltungsfilm", in: Rainer Rother (ed.), Bilder schreiben Geschichte: Der Historiker im Kino, Berlin 1991, pp. 143–153; Jens Thiele/Fred Ritzel, "Politische Botschaft und Unterhaltung – die Realität im NS-Film: Die große Liebe", in: Werner Faulstich/Helmut Korte (eds.), Fischer Filmgeschichte, vol. 2, pp. 310–321; Rainer Rother (ed.), Ufa-Magazin no. 18 zur Ausstellung: Die Ufa 1917–1945 – Das deutsche Bildimperium, Berlin 1992.

812 Loiperdinger/Schönekäs, p. 144.

813 Ibid., p. 153.

814 BA/P 50.01/729, no. 2–16 box offices returns, dated 13.11.1944.

815 For the allegedly subliminally effective ideological message ("disturbed power relationships"), "for raising the working morale of women doing war service in 1942", cf. Karsten Witte, "Die Filmkomödie im Dritten Reich", in: Horst Denkler/Karl Prümm (eds.), Die deutsche Literatur im Dritten Reich, Stuttgart 1976, p. 360.

816 Herbert Holba, Reclams deutsches Filmlexikon, Stuttgart 1984, p. 99.

817 For Christa Bandmann/Joe Hembus, Klassiker des deutschen Tonfilms, Munich 1980, p. 220, Kleine Residenz is a comedy full of ambiguities and a "gentle satire on the love conflict popular in Nazi films, complete with the noble ideology of renunciation". They say that even the first scene is a parody of Der grosse König (première: March 1942) and Goebbels' "Do you want total war?" (February 1943). But both of these things were introduced only after the film had been made by director Hans H. Zerlett.

818 For this film see Lowry, pp. 57 ff.

819 Peter Reichel, Der schöne Schein des Dritten Reiches, Munich / Vienna 1991, p.189.

820 Ibid., p. 195.

821 Courtade/Cadars, p. 96.

822 Reichel, p. 195.

823 But shortly before he had given permission for another "Rembrandt film" (11.7.1941, 26.6.1941). Only the Ufa project Therese Modrell was banned outright on 24.7.1941: BA/K R 109I/2139, no.89, note in file by Schweikart, dated 24.7.1941. Toe-

plitz's version reduced this development ad absurdum, vol. 4, p. 32: "In the years before 1939 there seemed to be a Führer in almost every propaganda film, but from 1940 to 1942 the accent was placed much more on a group working together in unity and harmony."

824 BA/K R 109 II/10, Ufa production suggestion, no date (1942/43).

825 The Clara Schumann material was modified and shown in 1944 as Träumerei.

826 BA/K R 55/1321, no. 63 f. Productions report, dated 6.2.1942.

827 Wien 1910 was almost complete. Permission for Paracelsus had also been given in July 1941: Albrecht I, p. 78.

828 Cf. entry for 15.3.1943 on the rural drama Der Flachsacker.

829 Cf. also entry for 31.1.1943 on similar problems relating to radio.

830 Kreimeier, p. 400

831 For this see the numerous complaints in BA/K NS 18/ 357.

832 BA/K NS 18/357, submission by Tießler to Party Office on 7.11.1942.

833 BA/K R 109 I/9, note by Berlin Film, dated 10.7.1942 about the production chiefs' meeting on 3.7.1942.

834 BA/K R 109 I/9, note by Berlin Film, dated 1.2.1943, on the last company and production chiefs' meeting.

835 Entry for 13.1.1943: "It's right to say that it is essentially a comedy, a light entertainment film, but with a modern approach."

836 From the entry for 28.5.1943: "It is not true that our films only deal with artists or doctors."

837 Referring to the film Man rede mir nicht von Liebe ("Don't Talk About Love").

838 BA/K R 109 I/1076, meeting on 28.8.1942; BA/K R 109 I/9, note by Berlin Film, dated 1.2.1943 about the last company and production chiefs' meeting.

839 Entry for 7.7.1943. All further entries on this project (including 16./17.7.1943), which Goebbels gave to Emil Jannings, anticipate failure: "One of the things we talk about is a new family film project, which I had already discussed with Jannings. Unfortunately he had completely failed to produce an appropriate manuscript" (28.3.1944). The same also applied to a "folk-song film" (3.5.1942), unless the Hans Albers Film Grosse Freiheit no. 7 is seen as a result of the Propaganda Ministry's demands, which Courtade/Cadars suggest on p.224.

840 Arthur M. Rabenalt, Joseph Goebbels und der "Großdeutsche" Film, Munich 1985, pp. 200 f.

841 Phillips argues similarly, p. 369.

842 BA/K NS 18/282, head of film to Tießler on 27.3.1942.

843 BA/K R 55/774, no. 185, annexed minute of Ufa-Film GmbH supervisory board meeting on 9.2.1943, no. 185.

844 BA/K R 109 II/15. Deutscher Kulturdienst, which was published by the Propaganda Ministry, and the internal Kulturinformation also report on foreign premières and the films' reception: BA/P 50.01/26, no. 34 ff; BA/P 50.01/640; BA/P 50.01/729, no. 13 f.

845 Der weisse Traum (première: 10.9.1943) was extraordinarily successful abroad, but it was also

the most successful black-and-white production of the Nazi period, earning over 10 million RM at the box-office. By September 1944 it had been seen by about 24 million people in a record time of one year: BA/P 50.01/729, no. 2–16, box-office returns dated 13.11.1944. Zirkus Renz is in 8th place in the list for November 1944.

846 Cf. also entry for 21.5.1944: "Our film production is very inconsistent in its achievements. Extraordinarily dilettant work alternates with real masterpieces."

847 8.12.1944 on Am Abend nach der Oper ("After the Opera").

848 Entry for 12.12.1944. Reichsfilmdramaturg Frowein reports similarly on Goebbels' attitude to a banned chamber music film: "The Herr Minister rejected the material, as he saw it above all as a plan of the type that he had always warned against most strongly: a film about artists that is also set in a past that is over for us, emotionally and actually." He said that it merely "evoked the apparent reality of a world that has ceased to exist and is remembered only with difficulty even by today's older generation": BDC-RKK Hans H. Zerlett: Frowein to Hinkel 17.8.1944.

849 Harlan has always asserted that Goebbels changed nothing else: Kristina Söderbaum, Nichts bleibt wie es ist, Munich 1992, pp. 174 ff.

850 Leiser, p. 63, describes the scene that deals with "settling in the east" in detail. Cf. also Leiser's 1968 documentary Deutschland, erwache!.

851 Cf. also Kraft Wetzel/Peter A. Hagemann, Zensur – Verbotene deutsche Filme 1933–1945, Berlin 1978, pp. 61 f., and entry for 29.3.1943: "The film deals with the fate of the crew of a long-range reconnaissance aircraft, and is very appealing in both tone and plot. However, it would have been better suited to the second year of the war rather than the fourth. Therefore I am somewhat sceptical about the new Ritter production's chances of success."

852 BA/K 109 II/10, Ufa production suggestion, no date.

853 BA/K R 109 II/10, Ufa production suggestion, no date (1943). This first permission date is contained in it.

854 BA/K R 109 II/15, Frowein to Goebbels on 8.1.1945.

855 BA/K R II/10, Ufa production suggestion, no date (1943).

856 Cf. Hollstein, pp. 165 f. Wien 1910 had been planned since 1940 and was already complete in 1942. Cf. also entries for 8.8.1941, 15.3.1942 and 14.6.1942: "The relationship between Lueger and Schönerer is extraordinarily well done, and above all historically correct."

857 Cf. Brigitte Hamann, Hitlers Wien, Munich 1996, pp. 393 ff.

858 BA/K R 109 I/2139, note by Schweikart, dated 27.8.1941.

859 BA/K R 109 II/14, film assessment by Frowein (1944).

860 Cf. Karlheinz Wendtland, Geliebter Kintopp. Sämtliche deutsche Spielfilme, 1943 to 1945 vol., p. 130.

861 BA/P 50.01/955, Frowein to Goebbels on 31.8.1944.

862 Alfred Bauer, Deutscher Film-Almanach, Munich 1976, p. 653.

[863] BA/K R 55/664, no. 194 Ministeramt to Frowein on 5.8.1944 and other correspondence.

[864] Cf. for example BA/K NS 18/362b "Party film planning for 1943", dated 4.2.1943. This mentions a "full-length nationalist film (anti-Bolshevik feature film)".

[865] Cf. Rainer Rother, "Grauen, Panik, Untergang. Karl Ritters Propagandafilm 'GPU'", in: Hans-Michael Bock/ Michael Töteberg, *Das Ufa-Buch*, Frankfurt am Main 1992, pp. 430–433. Toeplitz, vol. 4, p. 222, identifies *GPU* as one of the poorest of all the wartime propaganda films.

[866] Hollstein, p. 156; BA Film/B Film-no. 05287.

[867] BA/K R 109 I/2786, note by Bacmeister on 17.12.1943. Cf. also entry for 23.3.1943: "Professor Ritter, the director, tells me about an idea for a film, of no particular significance."

[868] Cf. Hollstein, p. 160, and Security Service reports, dated 17.8.1942: Boberach, pp. 4084ff., and 15.4.1943: Boberach, pp. 5128–5136. Here it says that the people were "still convinced by the state media that the war against the Soviet regime is necessary", but that increasingly they were "inclined to the view that people from the Soviet Union were better than, or at least not as bad as they had thought, and that this led to … certain inconsistencies with the image so far presented by German propaganda. … Where anti-Bolshevik propaganda continued to work with old and familiar arguments, it no longer met with the same interest and belief as had been the case before the beginning and in the early stages of the German-Soviet war."

[869] BA Film/B Film-no.08679, entry for 14.8.1942. The film was entirely successful with the public, however, and took about 6 million RM at the box-office, at least as much as the massively promoted *Der grosse König*: BA/P 50.01/729, Bacmeister to Goebbels on 6.12.1944.

[870] The film is still sold on video.

[871] With the exception of the Großfilme ("major films") introduced in the next section.

[872] Cf. Bernard F. Dick, *The Star-Spangled Screen. The American World War II Film*, Lexington 1985, pp. 182f; Leiser, p. 21, wrongly identifies *Mrs. Miniver* as an English film, but states correctly that a similarly skilful everyday film would have been inconceivable under National Socialism. For *Mrs. Miniver* as a propaganda model see also Hans C. Blumenberg, *Das Leben geht weiter*, Berlin 1993, pp. 118ff.

[873] Toeplitz, vol. 4, p. 240, corrects this incorrect assertion on the very next page and states that such a genre had not continued to be effective.

[874] BA/K R 109/48, communication from Hinkel, dated 6.9.1944.

[875] Cf. BDC-RKK Hilde Krahl: note from Ministeramt on 5.6.1944: "The Herr Minister is particularly interested in this material and would like to be informed about planning at a stage that will allow him to make any changes he may require without causing difficult situations or annoyance."

[875] Cf. film surveillance reports in R 109I/1729a no. 205 1944/45, Blumenberg and same author, "Hier spricht der deutsche Mensch. Das Leben geht weiter" – Der letzte Durchhaltefilm der Ufa 1944/45", in: *Der Spiegel*, no. 48, dated 23.11.1992, pp. 156–169, and no. 49, dated 30.11.1992, pp. 161

to 182, and also material in the F. W. Murnau-Stiftung, Wiesbaden. Blumenberg, who missed the passage on 30.3.1944, asserts that Goebbels wrote the screenplay himself.

[877] Entries for 29.6.1943 and 5.8.1943.

[878] Cf. also Toeplitz, vol. 4, p. 242.

[879] The correspondence between Frowein and the Party Office, about Helmut Käutners *Romance in a Minor Key*, for example, in BA/K NS 18/357, Frowein to Tiessler 17.1.1944 and his "Filmbeurteilungen", for example BA/K R 55/664 134f., underline this. Even though he was responsible for examining film manuscripts, his influence remained slight because the production chiefs were so powerful.

[880] Cf. also entries for 2. and 26.6.1944.

[881] Cf. film plans in BA/K R 109 II/2.

[882] BDC-RKK Hans H. Zerlett: Frowein to Hinkel on 22.1.1945.

[883] BA/K Zsg 115/15, no. 72, Kulturpolitische Information no. 39/1944, dated 27.10.1944.

[884] BA/K R 55/663, no. 149, Hinkel to Goebbels on 15.11.1944.

[885] BA/K R 55/663, no. 152–155, Hinkel to Goebbels on 24.11.1944. Goebbels had *Der Katzensteg* blocked immediately – as he had in 1940.

[886] BA/K R 109 I/1716a, no. 33, minute no. 1577, dated 16.11.1944; Kreimeier, p. 419.

[887] BA/K R 55/663, no. 127, head of film to Goebbels on 26.4.1944 and no. 265, head of film to Goebbels on 20.11.1944.

[888] Cf. Drewniak, p. 626.

[889] Cf. tables in: Welch, *German Cinema*, p. 35.

[890] Phillips, p. 244; Kreimeier, p. 418 for Ufa.

[891] BA/K R 55/663, no. 256, head of film to Goebbels on 19.9.1944.

[892] Kreimeier, p. 416.

[893] Cf. Phillips, p. 248.

[894] BA/K R 55/663, no. 126, head of film to Goebbels on 31.3.1944.

[895] Cf. Klaus Kanzog, "*Staatspolitisch besonders wertvoll*". *Ein Handbuch zu 30 deutschen Spielfilmen der Jahre 1934 bis 1945*, Munich 1994. Kanzog too used some passages from Goebbels' diaries for the production dates of the films. In the case of *Kolberg* he was unfortunately misinformed by Elke Fröhlich and the IfZ and thus missed the point of important passages in the diaries.

[896] "Gartenlaube-Friedrich" could go back to a twenties characterization by Kracauer.

[897] BDC-RKK Paul Hartmann: Demandowsky to Hartmann on 5.9.1941.

[898] "Talked to Jannings about his Bismarck project. The Kaiser must not appear in it. He is gradually starting to understand this now."

[899] Entry for 14.11.1941: "It will even be difficult to get away with a second Bismarck film. If there were a third, the public would start asking if Bismarck was the only figure in German history."

[900] "I hereby commission you to make a major film, 'Kolberg'. The purpose of this film will be to use the town that gives its name to the film to show that a people united at home and at the front can overcome any enemy. I empower you to ask all Wehrmacht, state and Party offices to help you where necessary, and in doing this to refer to the fact that the film I herein commissioned is at the

service of our intellectual conduct of the war.": printed in Leiser, pp. 110f.

[901] For the dramatic developments in terms of public morale in spring/summer 1943 see Manfred Wirl, *Die öffentliche Meinung unter dem NS-Regime*, doctoral thesis, Mainz 1990, pp. 160ff.

[902] Cf. entry for 8.7.1943 and page 257. The passage ends: "It will be difficult to explain that to him; but nevertheless there is no alternative to revising the screenplay again." This means that we cannot know for certain whether Goebbels actually did rewrite the screenplay personally several times: Kreimeier, p. 411.

[903] This may also explain the reference to a street in the working-class Berlin district of Wedding.

[904] Kanzog, p. 306.

[905] Bandmann/Hembus, p. 143.

[906] Ibid.

[907] See chap. 5, page 337.

[908] Minister's conference on 2.3.1943: Boelcke II, p. 220.

[909] But he then took up this "parallel with the present" theme – in places using almost the same words as in the diary entries – in his speech for Hitler's birthday on 19.4.1942, where he went into detail about the film and Frederick the Great: Helmut Heiber (ed.), *Goebbels-Reden 1939–1945*, Düsseldorf 1972, pp. 112ff. Goebbels used Frederick the Great as a symbol and the "spirit of Fridericus" in his propaganda right up to the end of the war. When the American president Roosevelt died in April 1945, both Goebbels und Hitler are alleged to have believed in a second "miracle of the House of Brandenburg": Heiber, *Joseph Goebbels*, pp. 328f; Reuth, pp. 592f.

[910] Ibid., p. 114, note 4. The historical inaccuracies also led to protest by National Socialist groups in Austria, cf. correspondence in BA/K NS 18/342.

[911] Cf. Courtade/Cadars, pp. 75f.

[912] Press release, dated 2.3.1942, printed in: Boelke II, p. 220.

[913] BA/P 50.01/729, list, dated 13.11.1944, no. 2–3.

[914] BA/P 50.01 729, no. 9, listing, dated 3.6.1942. Cf. also Security Service report, dated 28.5.1942: Boberach, p. 3759, for the reception of the film in Austria.

[915] But the press release mentioned that the film was a great success in Venice: BA/K Zsg. 102/63, dated 4.9.1942.

[916] All quotations from the Security Service report, dated 28.5.1942: Boberach , pp. 3759f.

[917] Hollstein, p. 165.

[918] BA/K NS/18 283, five-page presentation, dated 27.7.1942 with questionnaire results.

[919] BA/K NS/18 283, summary by Tießler, dated 5.8.1942.

[920] Cf. Minister's conference on 21.8.1942: Boelcke II, p. 273; BA/K Zsg 109/37 12.9.1942 and Zsg 102/63 28.8.1942. Cf. also Albrecht I, p. 71.

[921] BA/K NS 18/283, Rosenberg to Bormann 25.9.1942. Rosenberg repeated criticism of "Kaiser Wilhelm's unfortunate policy" and declared the film to be "intolerable in terms of foreign policy, even expressly damaging, and by no means necessary in terms of home policy".

[922] Printed in extracts in: Boelcke II, p. 274.

[923] It does not appear in the box-office returns for November 1944.

924 BA/K R 55/655 RFI production survey, dated 14.1.1944.

925 BA/K R 55/774, no. 167, minutes of meeting at RFM, dated 10.7.1943.

926 Rainer Rother (ed.), *Ufa-Magazin, no. 20 zur Ausstellung Die Ufa 1917–1945 – Das deutsche Bilderimperium*, Berlin 1992, p. 3.

927 Cf. also BA/K R 109I/957 with documents on the screening for 150 leading NS officers on 6.12. 1944.

928 Goebbels' requests for changes and Harlan's readiness to meet them emerge from BA/K R55/664, no. 6ff., Hinkel to Goebbels, dated 6.12. 1944; cf. also Rother, *Ufa-Magazin,* no. 20, p. 3.

929 Harlan, pp. 192ff. Kanzog also sums up the suggestions for change, p. 361, note 182.

930 BA/K R55/664, no. 6, Hinkel to Goebbels on 6.12.1944.

931 BA/K R 109 II/13, Frowein to Naumann on 18.10.1944.

932 Klaus-Jürgen Maiwald, *Filmzensur im NS-Staat,* Dortmund 1983, p. 194.

933 Ibid.

934 Speech on 28.2.1942, printed in: Albrecht I, p. 475.

935 Ibid., p. 79.

936 Text of the act printed in: Albrecht I, pp. 515 to 523. The act became law on 1.3.1934.

937 Endangering essential state interests; infringement of religious sensibilities; infringement of German esteem; endangering Germany's relations with foreign states.

938 Maiwald, p. 133.

939 *Der Kinematograph,* dated 30.11.1934. Both films were later passed again.

940 Second amendment to the Cinema Act of 28.6. 1935, printed in: Albrecht I, p. 523.

941 Maiwald, p. 157.

942 Maiwald , p. 158.For the re-authorization of films made before 1933 cf. press release, dated 14.1.1937: BA/K Zsg 102/62.

943 Given the missing material this is not a final, but a representative figure. Screening rough-cuts of films (e.g. 24.10.1935) remained the exception: cf. also entry on Luis Trenker's *The Emperor of California*: "We still must change the end a little" (17.6.1936).

944 From 1937 it is no longer the date of the première but the gap between comments on the film and the official censorship day that is the key to whether revision was probable.

945 The gaps between screenings for Goebbels and the official censorship date fluctuate a great deal in the following – they extend from a few days to several months – without there being any recognizable rules or priorities. It is essentially true that political films were examined before "harmless" entertainment films, and that the individual production firms had a regular screening cycle. It is questionable to draw far-reaching conclusions from this, as Albrecht I does, pp. 74ff.

946 Cf. entry for 2.2.1943.

947 Entry for 12.11.1938: "From now on bans may only be imposed by me personally in all the Ministry's spheres of activity. Otherwise things get messed up too much."

948 Entry for 17.12.1937: "*Pension Nottebohm* ("Boarding-house Nottebohm"), a crime film that was to have been banned. I don't know why. I am going to pass it."

949 Other false conclusions are drawn in Albrecht I, pp. 74ff., for instance that Goebbels does not mention revisions and thus was not particularly interested in feature films. In some cases, when there had been negative comments about films or Goebbels was not sure what effect they would have, test performances were arranged in middle-sized towns, with only the local press allowed to review them. For this see the cases of *The Dismissal,* chap. 4, p. 307, and *Mutter* ("Mother"): after devastating criticism from Goebbels' (10.7.1941) the film was screened in Göttingen at first, on 25.7. 1941.

950 A few references to requests for change by the Propaganda Ministry are to be found only in the film companies' records; laborious reconstructions are possible on this basis.

951 Cf. entries for 6.12.1936 (*Im Weissen Rössl,* première: 6.12.1936) or 14.12.1936 (*Der lustige Witwenball*/"The Merry Widow's Ball", première: 21.12.1936). Cf. also entries for 6.9.1936 and 15.3. 1937 on the singing films *Ein Lied klagt an* und *Sänger ihrer Hoheit* and for 18.11.1940 on *Herz geht vor Anker*/"A Heart drops Anchor") and entry for 12.8.1941 *(Krach im Vorderhaus*/"Trouble in the Front Building", censored: 18.8.1941, première: 19.8.1941) and for 29.1.1941 ("A shoddy effort that we can scarcely show") on *Kopf hoch, Johannes* (censored: 5.2.1941, première: 11.3.1941).

952 Cf. entries for 28.–30. 4. and 6./7.5.1937. For film and director see Jörg Schöning, *Reinhold Schünzel – Schauspieler und Regisseur*, Munich 1989, pp. 60f. The entries for 18./19.3.1937 on *Condottieri*, directed by Luis Trenker, offer a vivid example of criticism and pronouncements about revision.

953 Cf. Gabriele Lange, *Das Kino als moralische Anstalt*, Frankfurt am Main 1994 pp. 120ff.

954 Cf. entry for 30.1.1939 on conversation with Hitler.

955 Cf. entry for 11.9.1937: "I am having the last remaining films from the past in which Jews still feature banned wholesale."

956 Subject and plot (complex political situation, protagonists of a wide variety of nationalities) offered a number of possibilities for blurring images of the enemy and the National Socialist view of history.

957 Cf. François Courtade / Pierre Cadars, *Geschichte des Films im Dritten Reich*, Munich 1975, p. 252; Christa Bandmann/Joe Hembus, *Klassiker des deutschen Tonfilms*, Munich 1980, p. 126.

958 The censorship date (7.2.1939) speaks against cuts.

959 Cf. Bandmann/Hembus, p. 118. But Albrecht I, p. 268, favours the view that the public did not notice the undertones at the time. The screenplay authors Steinhoff (directed *Hitler Youth Quex* et al.), Hans Rehberg and Willi Krause (Reichsfilmdramaturg until 1936, here under his pseudonym "Peter Hagen") were all convinced National Socialists and were probably aiming for a satirically packaged anti-French slant.

960 Kraft Wetzel/Peter A. Hagemann, *Zensur – Verbotene deutsche Filme 1933–1945*, Berlin 1978, pp. 49–145.

961 Ibid, pp. 15–20.

962 Survey in Patrick McGilligan, *Fritz Lang. The Nature of the Beast*, New York 1997, pp. 174ff.

963 Wetzel/Hagemann, p. 20.

964 Ibid., p. 22: statement by director Willy Zielke.

965 Goebbels' "long debate" remark could also be understood to this effect.

966 Leni Riefenstahl, *Memoiren*, Frankfurt am Main / Berlin 1987, pp. 242f.

967 Friedrich P. Kahlenberg, "Starke Herzen. Quellennotizen über die Produktion eines Ufa-Films im Jahre 1937", in: Wetzel/Hagemann, pp. 110 to 125.

968 Ibid., p. 115.

969 Ibid., p. 117.

970 Kahlenberg assumes this, p. 118, in an over-interpretation as grounds for a ban.

971 Ibid., p. 118.

972 Ibid.

973 Wetzel/Hagemann, pp. 30 and 58. BA/K R 109 I/1033b, no. 19, minute no. 1358, dated 4.3. 1939.

974 Ban date from Alfred Bauer, *Deutscher Spielfilm-Almanach*, Munich 1976, p. 558.

975 Ibid.; Wetzel/Hagemann, p. 70; BDC-RKK Fritz Kirchhoff: Magistrat Berlin, dept. of Education to Creative Artists' committee on 8.4.1946.

976 Boguslaw Drewniak, *Der deutsche Film 1938 bis 1945*, Düsseldorf 1987, p. 395.

977 Wetzel/Hagemann, pp. 55ff., cite passages from Fritz Hippler's 1943 essay *Betrachtungen über das Filmschaffen*.

978 Kraft Wetzel /Peter A. Hagemann, *Zensur – Verbotene deutsche Filme 1933–1945*, Berlin 1978, pp. 61–63.

979 Wetzel/Hagemann, p. 75.

980 Wetzel/Hagemann, pp. 40f.

981 BA/K R 109II/10, Ufa to RFI, 20.9.1944.

982 According to Wetzel/Hagemann, pp. 59f., in December 1943.

983 Cf. BA/K NS 18/355, Tießler to Waldmann on 17.6.1943 and NS 18/357, ministerial draft, dated 22.10.1942. This discusses negative effects by fashionable, city-based films on rural communities and rejection of a realistic depiction of city life by the urban public.

984 Cf. Klaus Kreimeier, *Die Ufa-Story*, Munich 1992, p. 407.

985 Wetzel/Hagemann, p. 143f.

986 BA/K R 109 II/10, Ufa production suggestion.

987 The Propaganda Minister drafted some of the changes himself: BDC-RKK Wolfgang Liebeneiner: Liebeneiner to Hinkel on 19.7.1944.

988 Goebbels sheds no light on the most frequently mentioned bans, *Grosse Freiheit no. 7* and *Titanic*. There is just one passage on the anti-English *Titanic* film: this suggests that the "stuck on" ending with the trial was due directly to Goebbels (17.12.1942). For this cf. Courtade/Cadars, p. 265.

989 Speech on 28.3.1933, printed in Albrecht I, p. 442.

990 Joachim C. Fest, *Hitler*, Frankfurt am Main 1973, p. 721.

991 Entry for 12.11.1936.

992 BA NS 10/44, no. 3: *Andalusische Nächte*, NS 10/45, no. 2: *Tanz auf dem Vulkan*.

993 BA NS 10/44, no. 138.

994 BA NS 10/45, no. 2.

995 Entry for 22.12.1937; BA NS 10/48, no. 50. Cf. also Carsten Laqua, *Wie Micky unter die Nazis fiel*, Hamburg 1992, pp. 84 ff.

996 BA NS 10/44, no. 152.

997 Cf. Henry Picker, *Hitlers Tischgespräche*, Stuttgart 1963, p. 121.

998 Cf. Henry Picker, *Hitlers Tischgespräche im Führerhauptquartier 1941–42*, Frankfurt am Main 1989. Notes taken on 29.5.1942, p. 337. It appears that one and the same remark by Hitler is the basis of both these records.

999 "The Führer intends to have a new *The Nibelungs* sound film made. It is to be quite monumental. Teaching material for schools. A standard work. Possibly even in colour. He saw the old silent film recently and was profoundly impressed."(31.12.1936). Similarly on 12.9.1940 and 22.11.1940.

1000 Cf. Jochmann, p. 265.

1001 For Hitler's role as film censor see also Maiwald, pp. 632 ff.

1002 Maiwald, p. 157.

1003 Wetzel/Hagemann , pp. 50 f., quote the example of the American film *Tip-off-Girls*, which was allegedly not passed for showing in Germany after Hitler showed disapproval. But the date when Hitler saw it (19. June 1938) is later than the date given for the ban (16. June 1938).

1004 Cf. Henry Picker, *Hitlers Tischgespräche im Führerhauptquartier*, Frankfurt am Main 1989, p. 45. Goebbels confirms on 23.9.1943, that Hitler "did not see a single feature film during the war", and again on 25.1.1944.

1005 Cf. Heinrich Hoffmann, *Hitler was my friend*, London 1955, p. 191, and entry for 12.6.1943: "The film *Germanin* did not meet with a very warm response in the Führer's headquarters. The criticism I expressed of it was also confirmed in the Führer's headquarters", and for 24.6.1943: "I am having some trouble with a number of film classifications that the Führer grumbled about on the Obersalzberg." The Berghof entourage had apparently tried to influence Hitler's taste in films in previous years, as an entry for 18.3.1937 illustrates: "Führer rings up again late. He has seen *Condottieri* and is just as disappointed with it as I am. And so once again I have been proved right, rather than (Hitler's office head Philipp) Bouhler and (Hitlers house photographer Heinrich) Hoffmann."

1006 Cf. various documents in BA/K NS 10/ 44–48.

1007 Report by Arnold Bacmeister, a member of the censorship department, quoted in Maiwald, p. 190. After *The Eternal Mask* was banned Goebbels said: "A medical film *Weiße Maske* with Wiemann cannot be shown as it is too depressing" (9.10.1935). The press was forbidden to mention the original ban in their reviews of *The Eternal Mask*: press release, dated 15.10.1935, printed in: Gabriele Toepser-Ziegert (rev.), *NS-Presseanweisungen der Vorkriegszeit*, vol. 3, Munich 1988, p. 674. Production companies or distributors also often approached Hitler's office directly in the case of foreign productions, of which as a number were banned by the quota office: BA/K NS 10/48, no. 11, Paramount Film AG to Hitler's office on 4.10.1937.

1008 Wetzel/Hagemann, pp. 58 and 90.

1009 BA/K R 109 I/1033b, no. 94, minute no. 1348, dated 3.1.1939.

1010 The Propaganda Ministry and the Reichskanzlei could receive final versions simultaneously in the case of political and other outstanding productions.

1011 Entry for 15.10.1936: "Against a ban that comes from the Obersalzberg. 'On the Führer's' orders is now the most popular excuse. I shall appeal to higher authority. I hope I will get it lifted." Cf. also entries for 14. and 16./17.10.1936.

1012 BA-Film/B Film-no. 01982.

1013 Possibly this film is identical with *Spanien in Flammen* ("Spain is Burning"), shown in 1937, in which case it was not banned or passed later after all: Helmut Regel, "Han pasado – Sie sind durchgekommen. Der Spanische Bürgerkrieg im NS-Kino", in: Rainer Rother (ed.), *Bilder schreiben Geschichte: Der Historiker im Kino*, Berlin 1991, p. 129.

1014 For the film cf. also BA/K R 55/1321, no. 3 ff., minutes of Bavaria supervisory board meeting on 14.12.1939.

1015 BA/K NS 10/46, no. 179, Leichtenstern to Hitler's office on 18.2.1939.

1016 Cf. Regel, p. 139.

1017 Entry for 15.7.1941: "Certainly the Führer will also refuse to allow all the denominational and ecclesiastical scenes to be shown in Germany. The Duce has expressly asked me to be lenient here, but unfortunately we cannot oblige him in this case." The crucial scene is missing in the version shown at the time (première: 21.9. 1941, BA Film/B Film-no. 02100). Cf. also Regel, p. 139.

1018 Hans-Günther Hockerts, "Die Goebbels Tagebücher 1932–1941. Eine neue Hauptquelle zur Erforschung der nationalsozialistischen Kirchenpolitik", in: Dieter Albrecht et al. (ed.), *Politik und Konfession. Festschrift für Konrad Repgen*, Berlin 1983, pp. 387 ff. Cf. also entry for 11.7.1941 on the "denominational question" and entries for 18./19. and 22./29.8.1941.

1019 Entries for 1.7.1937 and 11.7.1937: "Now the Chinese are threatening to demonstrate against the film *Alarm in Peking*."

1020 No more data on this incident has survived. The première was not until 20.8.1937. The censorship date of 6.7.1937 makes it well-nigh impossible that this film was cut.

1021 Cf. for example the account by Friedrich P. Kahlenberg, "Preußen als Filmsujet in der Propagandasprache der NS-Zeit", in: Axel Marquardt/Heinz Rathsack (ed.), *Preußen im Film*, Hamburg 1981, p. 158, and in Albrecht I, pp. 81 f., and Drewniak, p. 192.

1022 Entry for 2.3.1942: "The film *The Great King* is shown at headquarters once again. Some of the general staff have objected to the fact that at the crucial moment Frederick the Great is left in the lurch by his generals as well. ... I arrange for the film *The Great King* to be shown to the entire OKW and OKH general staff in the afternoon. Field-Marshal Keitel supports the film vigorously and the rest of the general staff accept it under pressure from him."

1023 As far as can be seen, the scenes concerned were retained in the film uncut.

1024 Cf. entries for 27.7. and 29.7.1937.

1025 Hitler had probably seen only parts of the film on 17.7. or relied on statements from his entourage

and had it shown to him once more: BA/K NS 10/48, no. 49, Seeger to Hitler's office on 30.7.1937. Here *Capriolen* is identified as the "film already seen on 17.7.1937".

1026 Cf. entry for 4.8.1937 on the "purge" of the Prussian museums. *Capriolen* was premièred on 10.8.1937.

1027 See chapter 4, page 305 f.

1028 BA/K NS 18/347, draft by Tießler, no date (February 1941).

1029 Gregor Ball/Eberhard Spiess, *Heinz Rühmann und seine Filme*, Munich 1982, p. 102.

1030 BA/K NS 18/347, draft by Tießler/Party office, dated 2.7.1941.

1031 Entry for 27.12.1939: "A current film about harvest aid, at least that's what it's supposed to be. But it has not come off. Too intellectual and almost entirely brainwork".

1032 Bandmann/Hembus, p. 249, accept that the film "undermined NS propaganda through irony".

1033 As the film had already had its première in the Berlin Ufa-Palast am Zoo on 17.3., the cuts mentioned probably relate to the première version, before the film went on to other cinemas.

1034 Cf. Maiwald, p. 198.

1035 BA/K NS 18/357, no date. The last date on the list relates to film evaluation on 16.6.1943. This suggests that a date around June 1943 is probable.

1036 This referred to films including *Mit den Augen einer Frau* ("A Woman's View"). After complaints from the Party ("impossible kitsch in NS Germany") Goebbels had the film taken off the day after the première on 30.10.1942: BA/K NS 18/282, draft Tießler/Goebbels, dated 31.10.1942.

1037 The remainder refers to criticism from the districts that was rejected by the Party office itself, and films and screenplays to which no objections had been made.

1038 Lange, pp. 75 ff.

1039 Speech on 19.5.1933, printed in: Albrecht I, p. 444. Fritz Hippler also criticized the activities of various professional bodies in *Der deutsche Film* in 1942. He said the press should work towards preventing "professions or regions or pressure groups from continuing to make constant complaints and objections that may well be justifiable as such but should not be permitted a hearing in the field of artistic activity": printed in Gerd Albrecht (ed.), *Der Film im Dritten Reich. Eine Dokumentation*, Karlsruhe 1979 (Albrecht II), p. 150. Cf. also Fritz Hippler, *Betrachtungen über das Filmschaffen*, Berlin 1943, pp. 103 ff.

1040 BA/K NS 18/357, no date p. 4. For the "broad negative effect" of "caricatures of teachers in films" see also Security Service report, dated 19.1.1942: Heinz Boberach (ed.), *Meldungen aus dem Reich 1938–1945. Die geheimen Lageberichte des Sicherheitsdienstes der SS*, Herrsching 1984, pp. 3180 f.

1041 Willi A. Boelcke (ed.), *"Wollt ihr den totalen Krieg". Die geheimen Goebbels-Konferenzen 1939–1943*, Stuttgart 1967 (Boelcke II), p. 274.

1042 Cf. Minister's conference on 14.2.1941: Willi A. Boelcke (ed.), *Kriegspropaganda 1939–1942. Geheime Konferenzen im Reichspropagandaministerium*, Stuttgart 1966 (Boelcke I), p. 619.

1043 BA/K NS 18/449, note by Tießler for Hippler, dated 4.2.1943.

[1044] Boelcke I, p. 103.

[1045] There is room for doubt whether this "putting a stop" was successful. Karl Ritter and Mathias Wieman were responsible for "war education films" on the Ufa art committee.

[1046] Cf. entry for 12.10.1941 and entry for 11.5. 1942 :"I speak to the Reichsmarschall on the telephone again. He is complaining about the OKW, who are protesting about the new Leander film. This film features an air force officer who spends a night with a famous singer. The OKW are taking moral exception to this because they do not think an airman would behave like this ... . Göring is very amused by the OKW's prissiness, which suits me down to the ground, as the OKW are making my film work in general very difficult."

[1047] Cf. entry for 22.2.1940: "'Feind hört mit'. A stupid O.K.W. spy information film" and Minister's conference on 22.2.1940: Boelcke I, p. 291. Goebbels kept an eye on the OKW's attempts to set up its own film department and make its own films.
In June 1942 he issued a warning to "the supreme Reich administrative authorities that film projects from all sections of the state, the Party and the armed forces must be submitted to me, as the Reich Minister and Reichsleiter responsible for film policy as a whole. ... Films made contrary to this instruction can no longer count of being passed for public performance in future." BA/K R 43II/ 389, no. 171 RMVP to supreme Reich administrative authorities on 30.6.1942.

[1048] In fact Baptism of Fire was not awarded the highest political classification "staatspolitisch besonders wertvoll"(highly estimable), but just "staatspolitisch wertvoll" (estimable).

[1049] Cf. BA/K NS 18/348, Hesse to Hippler on 28.2.1941. Hesse criticized the "boring plot" of the Luftwaffe film Kampfgeschwader Lützow and demanded, "that the film Sieg im Westen should be assessed in the same way as the Tobis film on the two heads on which Kampfgeschwader Lützow had been judged better, e.g. politically and artistically, and should thus be rated 'staatspolitisch besonders wertvoll' and 'künstlerisch besonders wertvoll'." For this see also entry for 4.3. 1941.

[1050] Cf. entries for 4. to 9.3.1941 and Boelcke I, p. 636: Minister's conference on 7.3.1941, here also further references to the incident, including material from Franz Halder's war diary.

[1051] An attempt to identify groups and types appears in: Christian Delage, La vision Nazie de L'Histoire à travers le cinéma documentaire du Troisième Reich, Lausanne 1989, pp. 17–30.

[1052] Hilmar Hoffmann, "Und die Fahne führt uns in die Ewigkeit". Propaganda im NS-Film, Frankfurt am Main 1988, p. 126.

[1053] Ibid., p. 137.

[1054] Ibid., p. 134.

[1055] Goebbels was not involved in the making of the 1927 and 1929 Party Rally films; the Munich Party managers were responsible for these. Thus cf. entry for 28.9.1929 on the 1929 Party Rally film: "Munich Kitsch".

[1056] Martin Loiperdinger, "Neue Sachlichkeit", in: Manfred Hattendorf (ed.), Perspektiven des Dokumentarfilms, Munich 1995, p. 56.

[1057] Gerd Albrecht, Nationalsozialistische Filmpolitik, Stuttgart 1969 (Albrecht I), p. 88.

[1058] This lack of clear distinctions is also found in the official definitions and listing in the Reich Film Archive. For this see BA/P 50.01/648.

[1059] Hoffmann, p. 113.

[1060] Boguslaw Drewniak, Der deutsche Film 1938 to 1945, Düsseldorf 1987, p. 50.

[1061] Klaus Kreimeier, Die Ufa-Story, Munich 1992, p. 318.

[1062] A monograph on the "Kulturfilm" is to appear shortly: Michael Marek, Der Kulturfilm 1933 to 1945.

[1063] Hoffmann, p. 123.

[1064] Cf. Hans Jürgen Brandt, NS-Filmtheorie und dokumentarische Praxis: Hippler, Noldan, Junghans, Tübingen 1987.

[1065] Drewniak, p. 295. Première: 13.1.1939.

[1066] Hans Barkhausen, "Die NSDAP als Filmproduzentin", in: Günther Moltmann/Friedrich Karl Reimers, Zeitgeschichte in Film- und Tondokumenten, Göttingen 1970, p. 173 (quotation: 29.3. 1939). For the increased deployment of this film, and its apparently considerable effect after the war started cf. Security Service report, dated 9.2. 1940: Heinz Boberach (ed.), Meldungen aus dem Reich 1938–1945. Die geheimen Lageberichte des Sicherheitsdienstes der SS, Herrsching 1984, p. 740.

[1067] Cf. Drewniak, pp. 51 f.

[1068] Cf. entry for 6.3.1940. Drewniak, p. 52, mentions 1–2 %. For this see BA/K R 55/180, no. 10 to 17, Neumann to Goebbels on 23.3.1940 on "Kulturfilmabgabe".

[1069] Cf. entry for 9.3.1940: "Neumann is taking over Kulturfilm production in the Ministry. He is to sort it out. I shall give him guidelines."

[1070] Cf. Michael Töteberg, "Im Auftrag der Partei: Deutsche Kulturfilm-Zentrale und Ufa-Sonderproduktion", in: Hans-Michael Bock/Michael Töteberg (ed.), Das Ufa-Buch, Frankfurt am Main 1992, pp. 438–443.

[1071] Cf. also entry for 7.4.1940.

[1072] BA/K R 55, no. 30, draft decree by Hippler on 6.4.1940.

[1073] Cf. also entry for 17.4.1940. For the film see. Drewniak, pp. 211 f.

[1074] Hoffmann, p. 129

[1075] Security Service report, dated 16.4.1940: Boberach, pp. 1578 f.

[1076] Formulaic praise of this kind is to be found regularly until 1944, in almost the same words.

[1077] Barkhausen, p. 162,

[1078] Cf. entries for 17.7.1936 and 27.8.1936. It is still not clear whether Hitler blocked release after censorship on 20.8.1936: correspondence in BA/K R 43 II/390a and Barkhausen, pp. 159ff.

[1079] Cf. Marcus S. Phillips, The German Film Industry and the Third Reich, doctoral thesis, East Anglia, 1974, p. 218; Barkhausen, p. 160.

[1080] BA Film/K Film-no. 1238.

[1081] According to Barkhausen, p. 163, the film was "put on ice" after the war began. For this see Goebbels' contradictory instructions at the Minister's conference on 8.11.1939: Willi A. Boelcke (ed.), Kriegspropaganda 1939–1941. Geheime Konferenzen im Reichspropagandaministerium, Stuttgart 1966 (Boelcke I), p. 221 ("The Minister agrees that the film Jahre der Entscheidung will now be used") and on 10.11.1939: Boelcke I, p. 223 ("The film Jahre der Entscheidung is to be revised. A coherent, comprehensible text is to be written for this outstanding pictorial material").

[1082] BA/K NS 10/47, no. 11, Hitler's office to Leichtenstern on 13.6.1939: "very bad (banned)".

[1083] Barkhausen, p. 165.

[1084] The idea of founding the DFG dates from about December 1936. Months of negotiation between Goebbels and the NSDAP Reichsschatzmeister followed: Phillips, p. 218.

[1085] Later Goebbels even banned the DFG from making films or fobbed it off with vague agreements about "special commissions", whereupon the RPL protested strongly: BA/K NS 18/362b, Raether (RPL HA Film) to Hinkel on 6.10.1941. Cf. also entry for 7.6.1941: "With Hippler and (the head of film production in the RPL film department Hugo) Fischer on Party film production. This should restrict itself to propaganda, cultural and documentary films. Fischer wants to make feature films as well, but his people aren't capable of that." The DFG did make the Hitler Youth feature Hände hoch (1942), for example, but it was shown almost exclusively at special young people's screenings. When Heinz Tackmanns became the new head of the RPL HA Film, Goebbels reaffirmed the line that the department should confine itself "exclusively to documentary and propaganda films"; feature films could be made only by Ufa-Film GmbH's production companies (28.4. 1944). For this see BA/K R 55/760, no. 35, Aktenvermerk Büro Staatssekretär, dated 20.5.1944.

[1086] Barkhausen, p. 165.

[1087] For this see also his negative comment on 27./28.2.1940 about Willi Krause and a "Propagandafilm by the R. Prop. Leitung", probably Kampf und Befreiung des Sudetenlands ("Struggle and Liberation of the Sudetenland").

[1088] On 9.3.1940 he writes about a film apparently made by Krause: Propaganda film Kamerad Frau. Absolute rubbish, by Krause again. But that's enough of that."

[1089] Cf. Phillips, p. 80.

[1090] Cf. also BA/K NS 18/360, draft by Tießler on 16.6.1942. According to this Goebbels had instructed that short films of this kind "should be used quite specifically for dealing with philosophical questions, whether these are in the biological, racial-political, social, hygienic or other fields. But he was concerned that there should be as little contact as possible with official organization when making such films. ... This special instruction was given because Dr. Hippler had remarked that when trying to make a philosophical documentary about racial and biological questions the responsible organizations, and he mentioned the Reich Chief Medical Officer in particular, had put such obstacles in the way of the film that it finally did not happen at all." Goebbels was reacting to Security Service reports about the continuing major impact of shorts and "Kulturfilme": Security Service report, dated 1.6.1942: Boberach, pp. 3811 ff.

[1091] Hoffmann, p. 129.

[1092] BA/K R 55/760 RMVP, note, dated 12.10.1943. Cf. here too Winkler's contract with the NSDAP (Reichsschatzmeister), dated 18.8.1943 on carrying out some HA Film projects under the auspices of Ufa Film GmbH.

[1093] For the series cf. David Welch, *Propaganda and the German Cinema*, Oxford 1983, pp. 80 ff.

[1094] Cf. Karl Ludwig Rost, *Sterilisation und Euthanasie im Film des "Dritten Reichs"*, med. diss., Berlin 1986, p. 63.

[1095] Entry for 4. 12. 1936: "Then a film of lunatic asylums to justify the Sterilization Act. Horrible material. Some wonderful shots. Your blood runs cold merely at the sight of it. Here sterilization can only be a blessing". Cf. also entry for 10. 12. 1936.

[1096] Rost, p. 66.

[1097] BA/K NS 10/48, no. 121 RMVP to Hitler's office, dated 8. 2. 1937.

[1098] Entries for 11. and 23. 3. 1937. On 22. 2. 1937 the Propaganda Ministry sent Hitler's Office a "a spool of film containing pictures of the Herr Minister's children, with a request that it should be shown to the Führer": BA/K NS 10/48, no. 114, RMVP to Adjutantur on 22. 2. 1937. On 23. 2. 1937 Goebbels also notes on this topic: "Film *Victims of the Past* with our children at the end. They all three come over very charmingly." Three children actually can be seen playing at the end of the film, but the very end consists of images of Hitler at a mass meeting: BA Film/B Film-no. 04702.

[1099] Joseph Wulf, *Theater und Film im Dritten Reich*, Frankfurt am Main 1966, p. 424. For the success of the film see Karl-Heinz Roth, *Filmpropaganda für die Vernichtung von Geisteskranken und Behinderten im Dritten Reich*, med. diss., Hamburg 1986, p. 19.

[1100] Rost, p. 67.

[1101] BA/K NS 10/64, no. 123, Racial Policy Office to Adjutantur on 23. 3. 1937.

[1102] Film minute, printed in Rost, pp. 234–237.

[1103] Roth, pp. 165–167.

[1104] The scripts for documentary films, which started to be planned again after a long break, fitted in with these ideas Goebbels has of "absolutely convincing" cases: Rost, pp. 130 ff.; Roth, pp. 165–173.

[1105] BA/K R109I/1033c, no. 130, minute no. 1387, dated 27. 9. 1939.

[1106] Cf. list "Kulturfilme der Ufa 1939–1941", in: Bock/Töteberg, p. 433.

[1107] Entry for 13. 10. 1939: "Tobis propaganda film *Üb immer Treu und Redlichkeit*, a primitive sham without sense or understanding".

[1108] For this see entry for 3. 11. 1939 ("Examined propaganda films in the evening. Some not good. I need to keep a more careful eye on this now.") and Minister's conference on 3. 11. 1939: Boelcke I, p. 219: "In future all propaganda films are to be examined by the film department in co-operation with the Propaganda Department and Herr Fischer (R.P.L.). No film can be started if the manuscript has not been examined and the film must be presented in rough-cut form before it is finally completed".

[1109] Minister's conference on 3. 11. 1939: Boelcke I, p. 219.

[1110] Minister's conference on 1. 2. 1940: Boelcke I, p. 279.

[1111] For *Campaign in Poland* cf. entries for 3./28. 10., 2. 11. and 16. 11. 1939: "'Polenfeldzug' has turned out very well, fluent with very effective compelling tricks … ." But Hitler still had objec-

tions, especially to the trick shots, so Goebbels states on 13. 12. 1939: "The Polish film has to be revised at the Führer's request as well": BA/K NS 10/49, no. 67, Adjutantur to Hippler on 14. 12. 1939.

[1112] Minister's conference on 12. 12. 1939: Boelcke I, p. 241. For this see also entries for 6./13. 12. 1939.

[1113] BA/K R 55/663, no. 46, head of film to Goebbels on 20. 10. 1944.

[1114] BA/K R 55/663, no. 55 ff., head of film to Goebbels on 16. 12. 1944.

[1115] BA/K R 109 I/1033b, no. 55, minute no. 1352, dated 24. 1. 1939.

[1116] Apart from anti-American films like the 1939 courtroom film *Sensationsprozess Casilla* ("The Sensational Casilla Trial") about US press practices, screened again in early 1942 as part of the anti-American propaganda campaign: BA/K Zsg. 102/63, dated 13. 2. 1942. For the line taken by National Socialist propaganda on the USA see Peter M.R. Stirk, "Anti-Americanism in National Socialist propaganda during the Second World War", in: same author./M.L. Smith (ed.), *Making the New Europe*, London 1990, pp. 66–86.

[1117] It is not absolutely clear whether this is the film *Rund um die Freiheitsstatue – Ein Spaziergang durch die USA* (BA Film/K Film-no. 49), censored on 20. 12. 1941, or a film that was never shown. According to Goebbels, Hitler ordered that "this film should be shown to as many of the German public as possible" (10. 2. 1942), as it "had met with a certain approval" (15. 2. 1942).

[1118] Peter Bucher, "Wochenschau und Staat 1895 bis 1945", in: *Geschichte in Wissenschaft und Unterricht*, 35th year, 1984, p. 751.

[1119] Hoffmann, p. 187. For distribution of responsibilities and creative and control procedures for the pre-war newsreel, see Albrecht I, p. 65.

[1120] Bucher, *Wochenschau und Staat*, p. 756, note 34, thinks that this is about U(fa)T(on)W(oche) 253/1936/Z: 10. 7. 1935.

[1121] Ibid., p. 750.

[1122] Cf. also similar exclusively positive entries for 9./21./27. 9. 1935, 5. 11. 1935, 29. 1. 1936, 12. 6. 1936, 4./11. 11. 1936 and 14. 12. 1936.

[1123] Bianka Pietrow-Enker, "Das Feindbild im Wandel: Die Sowjetunion in den nationalsozialistischen Wochenschauen 1935–1941", in: *Geschichte in Wissenschaft und Unterricht*, 41st year, 1990, p. 341. Two reports appeared, in summer 1935 only.

[1124] It is not possible to establish whether Hitler saw the edition concerned before it appeared.

[1125] Cf. entry for 9. 9. 1937.

[1126] Phillips, pp. 200 f.

[1127] Hoffmann, p. 187.

[1128] Entry for 16. 12. 1937: "Weidemann tells me about plans for bringing the newsreels up to date. I approve them. But it will cost a lot of money."

[1129] Though admittedly this examination usually took place after films had been passed for performance: BA/K NS 10/45, no. 134, Adjutantur to Leichtenstern on 23. 6. 1938 (UTW 406/1938/Z: 15. 6. 1938): "Shots of Dr. Goebbels very bad"; NS 10/45, no. 31 Adjutantur to Leichtenstern on 16. 7. 1938 (UTW 409/1938/Z: 6. 7. 1938); NS 10/45, no. 2 Adjutantur to Leichtenstern on 22. 11. 1938 (Tobis-Wochenschau); NS 10/45, no. 19, Adjutantur to Leichtenstern on 22. 7. 1938 (Bavaria Wochenschau).

[1130] BA/K NS 10/44 no. 72 draft of a letter from Adjutantur to the Propaganda Ministry on 1. 6. 1938. Directives of this kind applied to all the media, which Hitler praised and criticized alternately in just the same way: Engelbert Schwarzenbeck, *Nationalsozialistische Pressepolitik und die Sudetenkrise*, Munich 1979, p. 369

[1131] BA/K R 109I/1033a, no. 67, minute no. 1311, dated 20. 5. 1938.

[1132] This does not show precisely which editions displeased Hitler. It is possible that he was put out by the lavish coverage of the English King's visit to Paris or the French national holiday in UTW 411/1938/Z: 20. 7. 1938 or D(eulig) T(on) W(oche) 343/1938/Z: 27. 7. 1938.

[1133] Bucher, *Wochenschau und Staat*, p. 752. Cf. also Albrecht I, pp. 65 f.

[1134] A faster rhythm in the editing can be seen sporadically in subsequent months, ostensibly due to Weidemann; Hitler is said to have stopped this personally in summer 1939: interview with Hippler in 1970, quoted in Phillips, p. 198.

[1135] Hoffmann, p. 194; Phillips, p. 201.

[1136] BA/K R 109I/1033b, no. 73, minute no. 1340, dated 8. 11. 1938.

[1137] Entry for 17. 12. 1938: "The Führer has complained about the newsreels. I must put new people at the helm there. Weidemann is too much of a starry-eyed idealist and can't be bothered with them either."

[1138] It is no longer possible to piece together precisely if this is the exact moment when Weidemann left newsreel work, as asserted by Bucher, *Wochenschau und Staat*, p. 752. Cf. also BA/K R 109I/1033b, no. 93, ancillary minute to no. 1349, dated 10. 1. 1939. Fritz Hippler, *Die Verstrickung*, Düsseldorf (1982), p. 165, dates the handover as early as 1938.

[1139] BA/K R 55/175, no. 82, ministerial draft, dated 1. 2. 1939

[1140] Cf. entries for 27./28. 1. 1939 and 1. 2. 1939.

[1141] Bucher suggests that Goebbels did this. According to Phillips, p. 198, Weidemann and Hippler were responsible for editing the newsreels in spring 1939; they were finally approved by Goebbels' Staatssekretär Hanke.

[1142] DTW 391/1939/Z: 28. 6. 1939; UTW 459/1939/Z: 21. 6. 1939; UTW 460/1939/Z: 28. 6. 1939. There is some coverage of events in the USA in these fragments.

[1143] Gerd Albrecht, "Sozialwissenschaftliche Ziele und Methoden der systematischen Inhaltsanalyse von Filmen. Beispiel: UFA-Tonwoche 451/1939 – Hitlers 50. Geburtstag", in: Reimers/Moltmann, pp. 25–27; Hoffmann, pp. 195–199.

[1144] Cf. for example entries for 23. 8. 1939 and 30. 8. 1939.

[1145] Cf. Barkhausen, pp. 211 ff.

[1146] For the Propaganda Companies see Doris Kohlmann-Viand, *NS-Pressepolitik im Zweiten Weltkrieg*, Munich 1991, pp. 46 ff.

[1147] Cf. "Goebbels' essay 'PK'" in: *Das Reich*, no. 20 on 18. 5. 1941 and in: Joseph Goebbels, *Zeit ohne Beispiel*, Munich 1941, pp. 481–485.

[1148] Cf. entry for 17. 5. 1943 and for criticisms of the Propaganda Companies also the entry for 22. 2. 1944. In fact the PK's were reorganized several times from 1942/43; they became an "independent arm of the Wehrmacht as a whole" in 1943: cf. Hasso von Wedel, *Die Propagandatruppen der deutschen Wehrmacht*, Neckargemünd 1962, pp. 58–69.

[1149] Cf. entry for 29.8.1943: "Newsreel in the evening. It is a bit thin in places; a lack of combat images in particular. The PK's in the East are being reorganized again. The OKW prop. dept. is unusually inept when it comes to organization. It is high time I asked the Führer to put me in personal charge of this department".

[1150] Phillips, p. 295.

[1151] Cf. entries for 24.4.1943 and 11.7.1943. For procedure and who represented the OKW for newsreel censorship see also BA/K R 43/389, no. 206 ff., Keitel to Lammers on 29.9.1943.

[1152] Cf. entries for 12.9.1939 and 3.10.1939.

[1153] See also chap. 3, pp. 224 f.

[1154] Cf. also Hippler, p. 189, and entry for 10.1.1940: "Speech to Prop. Company bosses, who have come to Berlin from the front. I complain about all the faults that have occurred in the severest possible terms. I'm looking for a synthesis between creative initiative and military discipline."

[1155] Bucher, *Wochenschau und Staat*, p. 752.

[1156] Entry for 15.3.1940: "Fox Wochenschau could be shut down completely. The Americans are too impudent and shameless."

[1157] BA/K 773, no. 58 ff. about the establishment of the Deutsche Wochenschau GmbH.

[1158] Cf. Boelcke I, p. 170.

[1159] After a few more improvements to a new "Newsreel Working Statute" (17./28.1.1941) Goebbels announced that the measures had been successful as early as 17.2.. Cf. also the organization plan in BA/K 773, no. 58 f. about the establishment of the Deutsche Wochenschau GmbH, dated 31.1.1941.

[1160] BA/K R 109I/1034b, no. 237, minute no. 1414, dated 29.5.1940; Hippler, p. 185.

[1161] Cf. Hoffmann, p. 202.

[1162] Peter Bucher, "Goebbels und die deutsche Wochenschau", in: *Militärgeschichtliche Mitteilungen*, 40. vol., 1986, p. 54. Cf. also entry for 16./17.5.1940.

[1163] Cf. Wilhelm van Kampen, "Die Entwicklung der Kriegswochenschauen", in: Rainer Rother (ed.), *Ufa-Magazin no. 18*, Berlin 1992, p. 11. The Tobis figures for monthly film attendance from June 1940 to July 1941 show that it was not the content of the newsreel but the light entertainment films showing – none at all in June 1940 – that was responsible for fluctuating cinema attendance figures: Phillips, p. 243.

[1164] Cf. Security Service report, dated 27.3.1941: Boberach, pp. 2152 f.; Minister's conference on 2.6.1940: Boelcke I, p. 375; Minister's conference on 9.4.1941: Boelcke I, p. 672. Minister's conference on 31.3.1941; Boelcke I, p. 652.

[1165] Cf. for example entries for 22.1.1942 and 19.3.1942.

[1166] Hippler, pp. 185 f.

[1167] Speech on 28.2.1942, printed in: Albrecht I, p. 494.

[1168] Cf. entry for 21.1.1941.

[1169] Bucher, Goebbels, p. 56.

[1170] Cf. Peter Bucher, "Der Kampf um Stalingrad in der deutschen Wochenschau", in: Friedrich P. Kahlenberg (ed.), *Aus der Arbeit der Archive. Festschrift für Hans Booms*, Boppard 1989, p. 582.

[1171] Cf. also entry for 12.5.1941.

[1172] Apparently this intention could not be fully realized because of the large amount of time required: "We try out a lot of music and find a solution that I think is excellent" ([1].7.1942). Even at the beginning of the war Goebbels had asked for "good soldiers' choirs to be used" to accompany the newsreels: Minister's conference on 27.1.1940: Boelcke I, p. 274.

[1173] BA/K R 109 II/67, note by Hinkel on 20.5.1944.

[1174] Minister's conference on 4.11.1940: Boelcke I, p. 565; Minister's conference on 28.3.1941: Boelcke I, p. 630.

[1175] Security Service report, dated 1.4.1943: Boberach, pp. 5038 f.

[1176] This Goebbels project could not be realized; cf. Barkhausen, pp. 238 f. Several thousand metres of colour footage shot by specially commissioned camera crews of the southern Russian front have survived in BA Film/K. For the colour foreign journal *Panorama* initiated by Goebbels see Stamm.

[1177] UTW 507/1940/Z: 23.5.1940.

[1178] Cf. entry for 4.8.1941: "And the main thing is that we have now received some extraordinarily effective shots of social conditions in the Soviet Union. They are being edited into this newsreel to great effect and will certainly give the German people a very clear picture of conditions in the so-called 'workers' and peasants' paradise'." These images of misery were used in numerous newsreels until the Security Service noticed that credibility was being strained: Bianka Pietrow-Ennker, "Die Sowjetunion in der Propaganda des Dritten Reiches: Das Beispiel der Wochenschau", in: *Militärgeschichtliche Mitteilungen*, 43. vol., 1989, p. 95; Cf. for example Security Service report, dated 4.12.1941: Boberach, p. 3063.

[1179] Re. DW 614/1942/Z: 11.6.1942.

[1180] Goebbels was obviously aware of the first reports about the observations that were then recorded in the Security Service report, dated 28.8.1941: Boberach, pp. 2703 f., according to which "the recent newsreels have been very similar to each other and presented 'scarcely anything new'". A week later the Security Service reporters made similar observations about the "uniformity of the combat scenes". At the same time Goebbels found out how popular the first attempts at background scenes were: how "gratefully new pictorial motifs conveying the most varied impressions possible of soldiers' life in the east are received" is shown by "the great approval with which the shots of breaks with bathing in the river, animals and similar scenes are met": Security Service report, dated 4.9.1941: Boberach, p. 2727.

[1181] Security Service report, dated 16.10.1941, Boberach, p. 2873: "Introducing variety into the newsreel with images of the troops' life in camp met with great approval." "Introducing variety into the newsreel with shots of the RAD in action and above all the shots of the troops taking breaks was generally received very positively and in many cases with great enthusiasm": Security Service report, dated 25.9.1941, Boberach, p. 2799. For these themes cf. also the entries for 18.9.1941 and 4./17./18.11.1941: "... now we have more opportunity in the newsreels to show life behind the front. I am setting up special crews to get hold of suitable material for this."

[1182] Cf. van Kampen, p. 11.

[1183] Cf. entries for 2.2.1943 and for 23.2.1942 about a German U-boat outside New York in DW 599/1942/Z: 25.2.1942 (Security Service report, dated 5.3.1942: Boberach, p. 3412), 16.2.1942 and entry for 11.12.1942 about coverage of Eastern Asia in DW 640/1942/Z: 9.12.1942 (Security Service report, dated 17.12.1942: Boberach, p. 4578).

[1184] Speech on 14.2.1941, printed in: Albrecht I, p. 472 .Cf. entry for 20.2.1942, similar speech on 28.2.1942, printed in: Albrecht I, p. 494.

[1185] Cf. entry for 4.6.1940: "Comedy films are gradually being withdrawn. They conflict with the newsreel to much."

[1186] Speech on 14.2.1941, printed in: Albrecht I, p. 472.

[1187] Bucher, *Goebbels*, p. 56.

[1188] Entry for 23.5.1942: "Images of overwhelming force are shown here, though the majority of them are secret. I will be there in person when they are shown to the Führer and will see that I get as many of them released as possible. What is shown is sure to be reassuring at home and is bound to be reassuring abroad. This newsreel will have enormous propaganda value."

[1189] Security Service report, dated 4.6.1942: Boberach, pp. 3791 f.

[1190] Henry Picker, *Hitlers Tischgespräche im Führerhauptquartier*, reprint Frankfurt am Main 1989, p. 45, days on the subject of Hitler's newsreel censorship: "The second canteen dining-room was set up for this purpose once a week. Hitler had the individual films shown once or twice, made criticisms and suggestions or dictated new commentaries."

[1191] The decision went this way at least for DW 587 (censored: 3.12.1941). Cf. also entry for 2.12.1941.

[1192] Bucher, *Goebbels*, p. 59.

[1193] For the effect cf. the entry for 23.11.1941 and Security Service report, dated 27.11.1941: Boberach, pp. 3035 f.

[1194] DW 566/1941/Z: 10.7.1941. For this see Pietrow-Ennker, *Sowjetunion*, p. 94.

[1195] Entry for 8.7.1941: "With shattering scenes of the Bolshevik atrocities in Lemberg. A furioso! The Führer telephones: he says this is the best newsreel we have ever made."

[1196] BA/K NS 18/282, Tiessler to Bormann on 14.7.1941. Goebbels does not mention this difference with Hitler about "putting back the publication of the images for a time" in the diary; it emerges only from the above-mentioned document. Cf. also Pietrow-Ennker, *Sowjetunion*, p. 94.

[1197] Cf. Security Service report, dated 17.7.1941: Boberach, p. 2535: According to this the shots went "beyond the bounds of the tolerable only in the opinion of a very small number of women", but they had "far exceeded the effect of previous press and radio reports on Bolshevik atrocities in their horrific realism".

[1198] Footage on this was available; Goebbels had already examined a "proposal for the 10th anniversary of our revolution on 30 January" in the previous week. "This compilation needs fundamental changes, but it does clearly show all we have achieved in these ten short years" (17.1.1943).

[1199] Cf. Joachim C. Fest, *Hitler*, Berlin 1973, pp. 901 f.

[1200] For this see entry for 10.6.1942: "He tells me that the recent depiction of the battle of Kharkov in the new newsreel was positively exemplary."

[1201] BA/K R 55/663, no. 74, head of film to Staatssekretär on 4.7.1944 about the Führer's decision on releasing shots of the V1 and textual changes; no. 75, head of film to Staatssekretär on 6.7.1944 about postponing censorship because Hitler wanted to examine the added footage again. Censorship practice in the Führer's headquarters emerges from an extremely revealing letter from Hinkel to Goebbels in December 1944: BA/K R 55/663, no. 92, dated 7.12.1944. For the letter see also Maiwald, pp. 189 f.

[1202] Bucher, *Stalingrad*, p. 580.

[1203] It seems to have been exceptional for newsreels to contain images or themes that were actually banned by instructions to the press and the other media: Kohlmann-Viand, pp. 83 f.

[1204] Bianka Pietrow-Ennker, "Das Feindbild im Wandel: Die Sowjetunion in den nationalsozialistischen Wochenschauen 1935–1941", in: *Geschichte in Wissenschaft und Unterricht*, 41st year, 1990, p. 341.

[1205] Ibid., pp. 343 f.

[1206] Minister's conference on 4.7.1940: Boelcke I, p. 413.

[1207] Cf. for example Security Service report, dated 18.9.1941: Boberach, p. 2776 (musical accompaniment); Security Service report, dated 30.10.1941: Boberach, p. 2934 (sketch maps too short); Security Service report, dated 6.11.1941: Boberach, 2954 (final sequences); Security Service report, dated 20.11.1941: Boberach, p. 3013 (original noises).

[1208] Minister's conference on 29.5.1941: Boelcke I, p. 755; Minister's conference on 28.3.1941: Boelcke I, p. 630; Minister's conference on 16.2.1940: Boelcke I, p. 287.

[1209] Cf. Security Service report, dated 26.2.1942: Boberach, p. 3371; Security Service report, dated 5.3.1942: Boberach, p. 3412.

[1210] Probably refers to DW 599 or 598; DW 600 also contains shots of this kind.

[1211] Security Service report, dated 3.6.1940: Boberach, p. 1207.

[1212] For this see Paul Maine, "L'image de Paris et de la France occupée dans les actualités allemandes (Deutsche Wochenschau) de mai 1940 à novembre 1942", in: Deutsches Historisches Institut Paris/Institut d'Histoire des conflits contemporaires, *La France et l'Allemagne en guerre*. Septembre 1939–novembre 1942, Paris 1990, pp. 392 f.

[1213] Entry for 27.6.1940 and Minister's conference on 27.6.1940: Boelcke I, p. 409.

[1214] Similar remarks are to be found on 7./8.7.1940; Minister's conference on 19.7.1940: Boelcke I, pp. 430 f.

[1215] Security Service report, dated 11.7.1940: Boberach, pp. 1363 f.

[1216] Entries for 13./14.7.1940.

[1217] Cf. entry for 27.7.1940 ("The press is getting very sentimental about France again") and Minister's conference on 26.7.1940: Boelcke I, pp. 439 f.: "The Minister is making the departmental heads in press, propaganda, radio and film respon-

sible for making sure that there is no sentimentality in reports about France in future."

[1218] Cf. Hans-Jürgen Singer, "'Tran und Helle'. Aspekte unterhaltender Aufklärung im Dritten Reich", in: *Publizistik*, 3/4, 1986, pp. 347–356. Some of these short films were quite successful in articulating prejudices and discontent in the population as a whole in humorous form and refuting them by means of propaganda.

[1219] UTW 517/1940/Z: 1.8.1940.

[1220] Lack of popular positive response to these campaigns and concentration on anti-English propaganda finally brought the process to a close: Minister's conference on 5.8.1940: Boelcke I, p. 447: "There are to be no attacks on France at the moment."

[1221] Cf. entry for 18.9.1941 on Security Service report, dated 25.9.1941: Boberach, p. 2799: "Shots showing the Führer are particularly popular with the public ... The more secure and self-confident the Führer seems in the newsreel, the more positive is the effect made by these films."

[1222] Stefan Dolezel/Martin Loiperdinger, "Hitler in Parteitagsfilm und Wochenschau", in: Loiperdinger et al. (ed.), *Führerbilder*, Munich 1995, pp. 92 ff.

[1223] Security Service report, dated 28.4.1942, p. 3758.

[1224] Cf. Welch, *German Cinema*, p. 200.

[1225] Loiperdinger/Dolezel, pp. 98 f.

[1226] This refers to the extremely revealing Security Service report, dated 1.4.1943: Boberach, pp. 5038 f. DW 655/1943/Z: 24.3.1943.

[1227] Ibid., p. 5038.

[1228] DW 660/1943/Z: 28.4.1943.

[1229] Cf. Bucher, *Stalingrad*, p. 584.

[1230] Cf. entry for 27.1.1942.

[1231] Anyhow the line of consistently keeping quiet and introducing scenes providing variety and distraction was highly acceptable to the majority of viewers even according to Security Service reports. Women in particular would "welcome the introduction of more variety into the newsreels by showing shots of quieter phases of the conflict, given that the emotional strain is otherwise very great, and would find the newsreel's sequences of images a relief from intense pressure." These circles wanted "to gain reassurance and confidence when seeing newsreels": Security Service report, dated 28.1.1943: Boberach, p. 4722.

[1232] For this see John P. Fox, "Der Fall Katyn und die Propaganda des NS-Regimes", in: *Vierteljahresschrift für Zeitgeschichte*, 30. year., 1982, pp. 462 to 499.

[1233] For Goebbels' instructions on the use of "images of atrocities" in 1944 newsreels cf. BA/K R 55/663, no. 85, head of film to Goebbels on 30.10.1944.

[1234] Bucher, *Goebbels*, pp. 58 ff.; "David Welch, Goebbels, Götterdämmerung, and the Deutsche Wochenschauen", in: K.M. Short (ed.), *Newsreel witness*, London 1986, pp. 84 ff.

[1235] Entries for 17.2.1942 and 23.2.1942.

[1236] Cf. entry for 14.9.1942: " We shall soon have to find our way to showing images from home to make the newsreels more varied", and for 13.12.1942: "... showing more home coverage as we are gradually running out of footage from the front and at Christmas-time in particular the public pre-

fer things that are not to do with the war" (refers to DW 641/1942/Z: 16.12.1942). Although the newsreel did not have much success with this at first, as Goebbels admits on 19.12.1942 (the public obviously felt that the shift to home and entertainment material like the boxing match in DW 641 was evasive: Bucher, *Goebbels*, p. 61), this approach was obviously to be stepped up in subsequent editions: "We must try for more home coverage, particularly in the winter" (19.12.1942). So all the Christmas "magic was not to get the upper hand" in the press and on the radio, but the newsreels were to have a "very Christmassy feel" (18.12.1942). The Christmas newsreel DW 642/1942/Z: 21.12.1942 did indeed elicit a better response from the public: Security Service report, dated 7.1.1943: Boberach, p. 4633.

[1237] Cf. entry for 28.11.1943: "I want to give Roellenbleg a head of scripts with great propaganda talents to help to create the newsreel."

[1238] For Goebbels' praise of Dettmann cf. also entries for 5./19.3.1944 and for 7./21.5.1944.

[1239] This original sound was used for other coverage from mid 1943: Bucher, *Goebbels*; p. 62. For this see entries for 28.6.1943 and for 15.8.1943.

[1240] BA/K R 109II/67, Dettmann to Goebbels, no date (April 1944).

[1241] DW 719/1944/Z: 14.6.1944.

[1242] BA/K R 55/663, no. 81, Hinkel to Goebbels on 3.8.1944.

[1243] Cf. Bucher, *Goebbels*, pp. 63 f.

[1244] DW 750/25.1.1945.

[1245] Cf. Bucher, *Goebbels*, p. 59.

[1246] For the dubious emphasis on Cologne cathedral and the lack of "appropriate appreciation of the dead victims of the terror raid on Cologne" among the people: Security Service report on home questions, dated 8.7.1943, Boberach, pp. 5449 f.: "There have also been various expressions of surprise that despite National Socialism's negative attitude to the Catholic church damage to a cathedral is now being so heavily emphasized."

[1247] "Here we have to take feelings at home very much into consideration and it is extraordinarily difficult at the moment to balance the interests of home and foreign policy" (9.7.1943).

[1248] Refers to DW 691/1943/Z: 1.12.1943. The air raids on Berlin did not feature until the next newsreel.

[1249] For the subject of the war in the air in newsreels cf. Welch, *Götterdämmerung*, p. 89.

[1250] Paul Werner, *Skandalchronik des deutschen Films von 1910 bis 1945*, Frankfurt am Main 1990, who throws the entries together to suit his purposes. Friedemann Beyer, *Die Ufa-Stars im Dritten Reich*, Munich 1991; Arthur M. Rabenalt, *Joseph Goebbels und der "Großdeutsche" Film*, Munich 1985.

[1251] Fritz Hippler, *Die Verstrickung*, Düsseldorf (1982), p. 239.

[1252] Cf. Wolfgang Becker, *Film und Herrschaft*, Berlin 1973, p. 175.

[1253] Cf. press release for 16.5.1935, in: Gabriele Töpser-Ziegert, *NS-Presseanweisungen der Vorkriegszeit*, Munich 1987, p. 295.

[1254] Andrea Winkler-Mayerhöfer, *Starkult als Propagandamittel*, Munich 1992, p. 147.

[1255] Helmar Harald Fischer, "'Was gestrichen ist, kann nicht durchfallen.' Wie sich Schauspieler an ihre Arbeit im Dritten Reich erinnern" in: *Theater heute*, no 9, 1989, pp. 1–19. An outline of the actors' self-justifications is also offered in Michaela Krützen, *Hans Albers. Eine deutsche Karierre*, Weinheim / Berlin 1995, pp. 243 ff.

[1256] Micaela Jary, *Ich weiß, es wird einmal ein Wunder geschehen*, Berlin 1993, p. 222.

[1257] Fischer, p. 13.

[1258] Georg Seeßlen, *Tanz den Adolf Hitler*, Berlin 1994, p. 47.

[1259] Klaus Kreimeier, *Die Ufa-Story*, Munich 1992, p. 347.

[1260] Oliver Rathkolb, *Führertreu und gottbegnadet*, Vienna 1991, pp. 174ff.

[1261] Gerd Albrecht, *Nationalsozialistische Filmpolitik*, Stuttgart 1969, pp. 214–217.

[1262] Witte, *Lachende Erben – Toller Tag*, Berlin 1995, p. 124.

[1263] Kreimeier, p. 345.

[1264] Beyer, p. 30.

[1265] Hans C. Blumenberg, *In meinem Herzen, Schatz ...*, Frankfurt am Main 1991, p. 65.

[1266] Krützen, p. 352.

[1267] Oliver Rathkolb, *Führertreu und gottbegnadet*, Vienna 1991, p. 33. See also Albrecht I, p. 208.

[1268] BA/K Sammlung Sänger Zsg 102/60, dated 30.8.1935.

[1269] Kreimeier, p. 342.

[1270] BDC-RKK Hans Albers: typewritten copy of a letter from Albers to Goebbels, dated 15.10.1935.

[1271] Gregor Ball, *Heinz Rühmann*, Munich 1981, p. 82.; Heinz Rühmann, *Das war's*, Frankfurt am Main / Berlin 1982, p. 132.

[1272] Werner, pp. 244–250.

[1273] Cf. Ulrich Liebe, *Verehrt, verfolgt, vergessen. Schauspieler als Naziopfer*, Berlin 1992, pp. 90 ff.

[1274] Nathan Stoltzfus, *Resistance of the heart. Intermarriage and the Rosenstrasse protest in Nazi Germany*, London 1996.

[1275] Cinzia Romani, *Die Filmdivas des Dritten Reichs*, Munich 1982, pp. 45 f.

[1276] BDC-RKK Henny Porten: Porten to Göring on 21.12.1937. Cf. also Boguslaw Drewniak, *Das Theater im NS-Staat*, Düsseldorf 1983, p. 166.

[1277] BDC-RKK Henny Porten: Hinkel to Demandowsky on 12.2.1938.

[1278] Letter to Fritz Hippler, dated 13.6.1947, in Hippler II, p. 165.

[1279] Entries for 10./27.5.1943.

[1280] BDC-RKK Wolfgang Liebeneiner: hand-written note by Gutterer on 27.11.1942 about Hitler's agreement as conveyed by Bormann.

[1281] Boguslaw Drewniak, *Der Deutsche Film 1938–1945*, Düsseldorf 1987, p. 434. But the press was instructed not to report that Baur had been engaged: BA Sammlung Sänger, Zsg 102/63 of 26.6.1942.

[1282] BDC-RKK Harry Baur: report from Hilleke to Goebbels on 17.10.1942 and staff card. The file also contains the announcement of death in the *Filmkurier*, dated 15.4.1943, according to which Baur had "died after a short illness in a Parisian clinic".

[1283] Joseph Wulf, *Theater und Film im Dritten Reich*, Frankfurt am Main 1966, p. 370.

[1284] Goebbels is reporting correctly according his own knowledge: at this time he had seen SS Security Service reports stating that Trenker had not "opted" for Germany as the National Socialists had wished.

[1285] BDC-RFK: Trenker files: Trenker to Hitler on 27.2.1940.

[1286] Cf. Trenker, p. 386, but he is wrong about the time of the meeting with Goebbels.

[1287] BDC-RFK: Trenker files: staff card. Trenker does not mention this in his memoirs: pp. 385 f.

[1288] BDC-RFK: Trenker files: film department to "Luis Trenker Filmproduktion" on 7.1.1941 BDC-RFK Trenker Akten: Himmler staff to SS-HStführer Wolf on 2.9.1942.

[1289] BDC-RFK Luis Trenker: Trenker to Himmler on 4.11.1941; Hippler to Himmler staff on 21.9.1942.

[1290] Cf. Drewniak, *Film*, p. 77.

[1291] BDC-RS Hans Hinkel. Chef Sipo and SD to Himmler on 14.11.1942 and entries for 16./17.10.1939 and 19/20.10.1939.

[1292] BDC-RKK Gustav Fröhlich. Hippler to Goebbels on 17.4.1941; written record, dated 10.4.1941 on Harlan's statement to Hippler and Bacmeister.

[1293] Cf. Gustav Fröhlich, *Waren das Zeiten*, Berlin 1989, pp. 185 ff.

[1294] BA R55/412, film department to RV department on 2.12.1944.

[1295] Cf. Hippler, pp. 235 f. It cannot be ruled out that Hippler put this version about to replace an exonerating explanation by Jannings on 11.3.1947.

[1296] For Hitler's attitude cf. also Henry Picker, *Hitlers Tischgespräche im Führerhauptquartier*, Frankfurt am Main 1989, p. 246 (26.4.1942).

[1297] BDC-RKK Viktor v. Tourjansky. Note by Hilleke, dated 12.2.1941.

[1298] BDC-RKK Herbert Selpin: Terra production management to RFK on 14.4.1936.

[1299] Kreimeier, p. 385; Wulf, p. 329.

[1300] BDC-RKK Karl John: Hinkel to Goebbels on 12.1.1945.

[1301] Liebe, pp. 22–27.

[1302] For this see BDC-RKK Erich Knauf: staff card. Cf. also Kreimeier, p. 420.

[1303] Michael Töteberg, "Der Pressechef und die Gestapo", in: Hans Michael Bock/Michael Töteberg, *Das Ufa Buch*, Frankfurt am Main, 1992, pp. 450–451; Maiwald, p. 200. For this incident see also BDC-RKK Wolfgang Liebeneiner: Hinkel to Goebbels on 31.8.1944.

[1304] Liebe, p. 238.

[1305] Heinrich Goertz, *Gustaf Gründgens*, Hamburg 1982, p. 43.

[1306] Gustaf Gründgens, *Briefe Aufsätze Reden*, Hamburg 1967, p. 17.

[1307] Goertz, p. 67.

[1308] Gründgens, pp. 18 f.

[1309] Gründgens, p. 73. Although Goebbels records a peaciful joint session looking at songs for the film *Grosstadtmelodie* with Gründgens and his wife Marianne Hoppe on 10.1.1943.

[1310] Drewniak, *Film*, p. 179.

[1311] Drewniak, *Theater*, p. 164.

[1312] BDC-RKK Camilla Horn: RFK to Camilla Horn on 2.8.1935. The exclusion was later lifted by Goebbels as a "pardon".

[1313] For this see Marcus S. Phillips, *The German Film Industry and the Third Reich*, diss., East Anglia 1974, p. 238.

[1314] Speech on 15.2.1941 in Albrecht I, p. 477.

[1315] Cf. BDC-RKK Emil Jannings: Contract Jannings/Tobis-Filmkunst, dated 1.4.1941. Goebbels successfully had a new contract negotiated by threatening to stop payments to Jannings. However, this did not mean any substantial deterioration in Jannings' income and rights: cf. copious correspondence on this in BDC-RKK, Emil Jannings esp. Tobis Filmkunst to Jannings on 26.9.1942.

[1316] BDC-RKK Wolfgang Liebeneiner. Liebeneiner to Winkler on 30.1.1945. BA 109 III/note by Winkler, dated 12.6.1944.

[1317] BDC-RKK Hilde Krahl. Note on the ministerial draft of 4.6.1944.

[1318] BA R 109I/2786 Jonen to Winkler on 29.2.1944. See also entry for 16.1.1944.

[1319] BDC-RKK Eugen Klöpfer. Note by Müller-Goerne for Hinkel on 12.5.1944.

[1320] BA R 109I/2786, Goebbels to Winkler on 23.5.1944.

[1321] Cf. entry for 7.2.1943 on the closure of Horcher, the Berlin luxury restaurant, and entries for 19.5/21.5. and 20.6.1943 on VIP involvement in ration card manipulation.

[1322] Von Demandowsky was fined 12,000 RM in July 1942 for "offences against the Leistungssteigerungserlaß": BDC-RKK von Demandowsky: head of film to production chiefs on 29.7.1942.

[1323] BA/K R109I/1483, minutes of Ufi management meeting on 3.6.1942.

[1324] BA/K R 55/164, political information on the production chiefs.

[1325] BA/K R 109II/63, Hilleke to president of the RFK on 16.11.1942 and BA/K R 109II/63, Hilleke to Goebbels on 1.10.1942.

[1326] Drewniak, *Film*, p. 90.

[1327] Correspondence in BDC-RKK Sybille Schmitz and BA R 109/45.

[1328] BDC-RKK Söhnker: telegram from Hilleke to Söhnker on 20.1.1942; Hilleke to Goebbels on 14.1.1943 and head of film to Goebbels on 18.1.1943.

[1329] Rathkolb, p. 169.

[1330] BDC-RKK Elisabeth Flickenschildt: staff card.

[1331] BDC-RKK Hannelore Schroth. President of the RKK to president of the RFK on 24.11.1941. According to this, all female singers and dancers would benefit from the decision.

[1332] Zentrum für die Aufbewahrung Historisch-Dokumentarischer Sammlungen Moskau, R–1372-5-23.

[1333] Nothing became of this role: Jutta Freybe, another of the Minister's acquaintances, was given the leading part in *Gewitterflug zu Claudia* ("Stormy Flight to Claudia").

[1334] BDC-RKK Hilde Körber-Harlan: Müller-Goerne to Hilleke on 3.8.1942.

[1335] BDC-RKK Brigitte Horney: Müller-Goerne to Hilleke on 22.8.1942.

[1336] BDC-RKK Luise Ullrich: head of film to Reichsmeister on 27.4.1942.

[1337] BDC-RKK Jenny Jugo: Hinkel to Goebbels on 28.9.1944; Ministeramt to Hinkel on 6.10.1944.

[1338] Interview in *Zeit-Magazin*, no. 36/1997, p. 13.

[1339] BDC-RKK Leni Riefenstahl: power of attorney on 11.12.1933 to Julius Streicher and "copy of a hand-written letter from the Gauleiter to Leni Riefenstahl", printed in Rathkolb, pp. 227 f.

[1340] Leni Riefenstahl, *Memoiren*, Munich 1987, p. 207; IfZ Gestapoleitstelle Nürnberg to RSHA on 1.11.43.

[1341] For this see documents in BA/R 43 II/810b.

[1342] For this episode see Steven Bach, *Marlene Dietrich, Leben und Legende*, Düsseldorf 1993, pp. 323ff.

[1343] Ball, p. 80.

[1344] BA-Film, no. 1843.

[1345] Rühmann, pp. 152 ff. Cf. entry for 25.1.1944.

[1346] Ball, p. 97.

[1347] Harlan, *Im Schatten meiner Filme*, Gütersloh 1966, pp. 56 f.

[1348] Kreimeier, p. 352.

[1349] BA R 109I/ 2874, note for Klitzsch on 15.6.1939.

[1350] BA R 109I/2, Leander to Klitzsch on 14.9.1939.

[1351] Kreimeier, pp. 354 f.

[1352] BA R 55/118, no. 5, Ministeramt to film dept. on 24.5.1942.

[1353] BA R 55/118, no. 3, statement by personnel dept. on 19.6.1942.

[1354] BA R 55/118, no. 9, note by personnel dept., on 9.9.1942.

[1355] Cf. Paul Seiler, *Zarah Leander. Ich bin eine Stimme*, Berlin 1997, pp. 64 f.

[1356] See documents on personnel file BA R 109I /2874.

[1357] Cornelia Zumkeller, *Zarah Leander*, Munich 1988, p. 133, is repeated by Kreimeier, p. 355.

[1358] BDC-RKK Zarah Leander. Ministerial draft, dated 18.7.1944.

[1358] BDC-RKK Zarah Leander. Head of RPL to RPA Bayreuth on 21.7.1944.

[1360] BDC-RKK Zarah Leander. Reichsmeister to Hinkel on 8.1.1945.

[1361] Werner Maser, *Heinrich George. Mensch, aus Erde gemacht*, Berlin 1998.

[1362] See also interview with George in the *Völkischer Beobachter*, 28.4.1938, p. 5.

Bibliography

1. Archive material (selection)

Bundesarchiv Koblenz (BA/K)

R 2	Reichsfinanzministerium
R 43	Reichskanzlei
R 55	Reichsministerium für Volksaufklärung und Propaganda
R 56 I	Reichskulturkammer
R 56 VI	Reichsfilmkammer
R 109 I	Universum Film AG
R 109 II	Reichsfilmintendanz
R 109 III	Reichsbeauftragter für die deutsche Filmwirtschaft
NS 10	Adjutantur des Führers
NS 18	Reichspropagandaleitung der NSDAP
NL 118	Joseph Goebbels
NL 98	Alfred Hugenberg
Zsg. 102	Sammlung Sänger
Zsg. 101	Sammlung Brammer
Zsg. 109	Sammlung Oberheitmann

Bundesarchiv Abt. Potsdam (BA/P)

50.01	Reichsministerium für Volksaufklärung und Propaganda
80 BA 2	Deutsche Bank
90 GO	Nachlaß Joseph Goebbels
90 RI	Nachlaß Karl Ritter

Bundesarchiv-Filmarchiv Koblenz (BA-Film/K) and Berlin (BA-Film/B)

Over 150 feature films 1933 to 1945 and newsreel editions 1935 to 1945

Bundesarchiv Dokumentationszentrum (BA/Dokz.)

Unsorted, mixed material, personnel and general files from the Reichsministerium für Volksaufklärung und Propaganda

Berlin Document Center (BDC)

Film personnel files from the Reichskulturkammer

Institut für Zeitgeschichte, Munich (IfZ)

Nachlaß Goebbels ED 83, ED 172, MA 137O, F12, Nr. 1–34.
MC 31 Spruchgerichtsakte Hippler

2. Published files, records, editions, diaries (selection)

Akten der Parteikanzlei der NSDAP. Rekonstruktion eines verlorenenen Bestandes, Part I, ed. by Helmut Heiber: 4 vols., (2 index vols.), Munich et al. 1983; part II: ed. by Peter Longerich. 4 vols., (2 index vols.), Munich et al. 1992.

Albrecht, Gerd, *Der Film im Dritten Reich. Eine Dokumentation*, Karlsruhe 1979.

Boberach, Heinz (ed.), *Meldungen aus dem Reich 1938–1945. Die geheimen Lageberichte des Sicherheitsdienstes der SS*, 16 vols., Herrsching 1984.

Boelcke, Willi A. (ed.), *Kriegspropaganda 1939 bis 1941. Geheime Konferenzen im Reichspropagandaministerium*, Stuttgart 1966.

Boelcke, Willi A. (ed.), *"Wollt ihr den totalen Krieg?". Die geheimen Goebbels-Konferenzen 1939–1943*, Stuttgart 1967.

Deutschland-Berichte der Sozialdemokratischen Partei Deutschlands (SOPADE) 1934–1940, 7 vols., reprint Salzhausen / Frankfurt am Main 1980.

Domarus, Max (ed.), *Hitler. Reden und Proklamationen 1932–1945*, 2 vols., Würzburg 1962/1963.

Fröhlich, Elke (ed.), *Die Tagebücher von Joseph Goebbels. Sämtliche Fragmente. Teil I, 1924 bis 1941*, 4 vols., Munich et al. 1987.

Fröhlich, Elke (ed.), *Die Tagebücher von Joseph Goebbels. Teil II. Die Diktate 1941–1945*, 15 vols., Munich et al. 1993 ff.

Halder, Franz, *Kriegstagebuch. Tägliche Aufzeichnungen des Chefs des Generalstabes des Heeres 1939–1942*, ed. by Hans-Adolf Jacobsen, 3 vols., Stuttgart 1962 ff.

Heiber, Helmut (ed.), *Das Tagebuch des Joseph Goebbels 1925/26*, Stuttgart 1960.

Heiber, Helmut (ed.), *Goebbels-Reden 1932–1945*, 2 vols., Düsseldorf 1971/72 (reprint Bindlach 1991).

Hill, Leonidas E. (ed.), *Die Weizsäcker-Papiere 1933–1950*, Frankfurt am Main et al. 1974.

Jochmann, Werner (ed.), *Adolf Hitler. Monologe im Führerhauptquartier 1941–1944. Die Aufzeichnungen Heinrich Heims*, Hamburg 1980.

Kardorff, Ursula von, *Berliner Aufzeichnungen 1941 bis 1945*, ed. by Peter Hartl, Munich 1992.

Klemperer, Victor, *Ich will Zeugnis ablegen bis zum letzten, Tagebücher 1933–1945*, 2 vols., Berlin 1995; id., *Leben sammeln, nicht fragen wozu und warum. Tagebücher 1918–1932*, 2 vols., Berlin 1996.

Lochner, Louis P. (ed.), *The Goebbels diaries 1942–1943*, New York 1948.

Lochner, Louis P. (ed.), *Goebbels-Tagebücher aus den Jahren 1942–1943*, Zurich 1948.

Picker, Henry, *Hitlers Tischgespräche im Führerhauptquartier*, Stuttgart 1951 (reprint Frankfurt am Main / Berlin 1989).

Reuth, Ralf Georg (ed.), *Joseph Goebbels. Tagebücher 1924–1945*, 5 vols., Munich 1992.

Schebera, Jürgen (ed.), *William L. Shirer. Berliner Tagebuch. Aufzeichnungen 1934–1941*, Leipzig 1991.

Seraphim, Hans Günter (ed.), *Das politische Tagebuch Alfred Rosenbergs 1934/35 und 1939/40*, Göttingen 1956.

Stadelmayer, Peter (ed.), *Joseph Goebbels. Tagebücher 1945. Die letzten Aufzeichnungen*, Hamburg 1977.

Sösemann, Bernd (ed.), *Theodor Wolff. Tagebücher 1914–1919*, Boppard 1984.

Toepser-Ziegert, Gabriele (ed.), *NS-Presseanweisungen der Vorkriegszeit. Edition und Dokumentation 1933–1936*, 4 vols., Munich 1987 ff.

Ulrich von Hassell, *Die Hassell-Tagebücher 1938–1944. Aufzeichnungen vom anderen Deutschland*, ed. by Friedrich Freiherr Hiller von Gaertringen, Berlin 1988.

Wulf, Joseph, *Film und Theater im Dritten Reich*, Frankfurt am Main 1966.

3. Memoirs, published personal testimonies (selection)

Badenhausen, Rolf (ed.), *Gustaf Gründgens. "Laß mich ausschlafen"*, Munich / Vienna 1982 (reprint Frankfurt am Main / Berlin 1987).

Badenhausen, Rolf (ed.), *Gustaf Gründgens. Briefe, Aufsätze, Reden*, Hamburg 1967.

Below, Nicolas, *Als Hitlers Adjutant. 1937–1945*, Mainz 1980.

Dietrich, Marlene, *Nehmt nur mein Leben*, Munich 1979.

Goebbels, Joseph, *Vom Kaiserhof zur Reichskanzlei*, Berlin 1934.

Hanfstaengl, Ernst, *Zwischen Weißem und Braunem Haus. Memoiren eines politischen Außenseiters*, Munich 1970.

Harlan, Veit, *Im Schatten meiner Filme*, Gütersloh 1966.

Hippler, Fritz, *Die Verstrickung*, Düsseldorf, no date (1982).

Hoffmann, Heinrich, *Hitler was my friend*, London 1955.

Fröhlich, Gustav, *Waren das Zeiten. Mein Film-Heldenleben*, Munich / Berlin 1983 (reprint Frankfurt am Main / Berlin 1989).

Knef, Hildegard, *Der geschenkte Gaul*, Munich 1982.

Krämer, Willi, *Vom Stab Heß zu Dr. Goebbels*, Vlotho 1979.

Martin, Hans Leo, *Unser Mann bei Goebbels*, Neckargemünd 1973.

Riefenstahl, Leni, *Memoiren*, Munich 1987.

Rühmann, Heinz, *Das war's*, Frankfurt am Main / Berlin 1982.

Trenker, Luis, *Alles gut gegangen. Geschichten aus meinem Leben*, Munich et al. 1965 (reprint 1974).

Wiedemann, Fritz, *Der Mann, der Feldherr werden wollte*, Velbert and Kettwig 1964.

4. Journals and magazines (selection)

Der Angriff
Der deutsche Film
Essener Nationalzeitung
Filmkurier
Frankfurter Zeitung
Der Kinematograph
Licht-Bild-Bühne
Neue Zürcher Zeitung
Das Reich
Völkischer Beobachter

5. Contemporary literature (selection)

Belling, Curt, *Der Film in Staat und Partei*, Berlin 1936.

Goebbels, Joseph, *Michael. Ein deutsches Schicksal in Tagebuchblättern*, Munich 1929.

Goebbels, Joseph, *Zeit ohne Beispiel*, Munich 1941.

Goebbels, Joseph, *Das eherne Herz*, Munich 1943.

Hippler, Fritz, *Betrachtungen über das Filmschaffen*, Berlin 1943.

Jahrbuch der Reichsfilmkammer 1937.

Kriegk, Otto, *Der deutsche Film im Spiegel der Ufa*, Berlin 1943.

Müller, Georg Wilhelm, *Das Reichsministerium für Volksaufklärung und Propaganda*, Berlin 1940.

Traub, Hans, *Die Ufa. Ein Beitrag zur Entwicklungsgeschichte des deutschen Filmschaffens*, Berlin 1943.

6. Studies (selection)

Abel, Karl-Dietrich, *Presselenkung im NS-Staat. Eine Studie zur Geschichte der Publizistik in der nationalsozialistischen Zeit*, Berlin 1968.

Albrecht, Gerd, *Nationalsozialistische Filmpolitik*, Stuttgart 1969.

Auerbach, Hellmuth, "Volksstimmung und veröffentlichte Meinung in Deutschland zwischen März und November 1938", in: Knipping, Franz / Müller, Klaus Jürgen (eds.), *Machtbewußtsein in Deutschland am Vorabend des Zweiten Weltkrieges*, Paderborn 1984, pp. 273–293.

August, Wolf-Eberhard, *Die Stellung der Schauspieler im Dritten Reich*, diss. phil., Munich, 1973.

Bärsch, Claus-E., *Erlösung und Vernichtung. Dr. phil. Joseph Goebbels 1923–1927*, Munich 1987.

Balfour, Michael, *Propaganda in War 1939–45. Organisations, Policies and Publics in Britain and Germany*, London 1979.

Bandmann, Christa/Hembus, Joe, *Klassiker des deutschen Tonfilms*, Munich 1980.

Bauer, Alfred, *Deutscher Spielfilm-Almanach 1929–1950*, Berlin 1950 (revised edition Munich 1976).

Barkhausen, Hans, *Filmpropaganda für Deutschland im Ersten und Zweiten Weltkrieg*, Hildesheim et al. 1982.

Becker, Wolfgang, *Film und Herrschaft*, Berlin 1973.

Behrens, Tobias, *Die Entstehung der Massenmedien in Deutschland*, Frankfurt am Main 1986.

Belach, Helga, *Wir tanzen um die Welt. Deutsche Revuefilme 1933–1945*, Munich 1979.

Benzenhöfer, Udo/Eckart, Wolfgang U. (eds.), *Medizin im Spielfilm des Nationalsozialismus*, Tecklenburg 1990.

Bering, Dietz, *Kampf um Namen: Joseph Goebbels contra Bernhard Weiss*, Stuttgart 1991.

Blumenberg, Hans C., *In meinem Herzen, Schatz …*, Frankfurt am Main 1991.

Blumenberg, Hans C., *Das Leben geht weiter. Der letzte Film des Dritten Reiches*, Berlin 1993.

Bock, Hans-Michael/Töteberg, Michael (eds.), *Das Ufa-Buch*, Frankfurt am Main 1992.

Bohse, Jörg, *Inszenierte Kriegsbegeisterung und ohnmächtiger Friedenswille. Meinungslenkung und Propaganda im Nationalsozialismus*, Stuttgart 1988.

Borgelt, Hans, *Die Ufa – Ein Traum*, Berlin 1993.

Broszat, Martin / Schwabe, Klaus (eds.), *Die deutschen Eliten und der Weg in den Zweiten Weltkrieg*, Munich 1989.

Browning, Christopher R., *The path to genocide*, Cambridge 1992.

Bracher, Karl Dietrich et al. (ed.), *Nationalsozialistische Diktatur. Eine Bilanz*, Bonn 1986.

Bramsted, Ernest K., *Goebbels and National Socialist Propaganda 1925–1945*, Michigan 1965.

Brandt, Hans-Jürgen, *NS-Filmtheorie und dokumentarische Praxis: Hippler, Noldan, Junghans*, Tübingen 1987.

Bredow, Wilfried von/Zurek, Rolf, *Film und Gesellschaft in Deutschland*, Hamburg 1975.

Broszat, Martin, "Zur Edition der Goebbels-Tagebücher", in: *Vierteljahreshefte für Zeitgeschichte*, vol. 37, 1989, pp. 156–162.

Bucher, Peter, "Die Bedeutung des Films als historische Quelle: 'Der ewige Jude'(1940)", in: Duchhardt, Heinz / Schlenke, Manfred (eds.), *Festschrift für Eberhard Kessel*, Munich 1982, pp. 300–329.

Bucher, Peter, "Goebbels und die deutsche Wochenschau", in: *Militärgeschichtliche Mitteilungen*, vol. 40, 1986, pp. 53–69.

Bucher, Peter, "Film als Quelle", in: *Der Archivar*, vol. 41, 1988, pp. 498–524.

Bucher, Peter, "Die Tagebücher von Joseph Goebbels", in: *1999. Zeitschrift für Sozialgeschichte des 20./21. Jhdts*, vol. 2, 1988, pp. 89–95.

Courtade, Françis / Cadars, Pierre, *L'histoire du cinema nazi*, Paris 1972.

Courtade, Françis / Cadars, Pierre, *Geschichte des Films im Dritten Reich*, Munich 1975.

Dahm, Volker, "Anfänge und Ideologie der Reichskulturkammer", in: *Vierteljahreshefte für Zeitgeschichte*, vol. 34, 1986, pp. 53–84.

Deist, Wilhelm et al., *Ursachen und Voraussetzungen der deutschen Kriegspolitik*, Frankfurt am Main 1989 (= *Das Deutsche Reich und der Zweite Weltkrieg*, vol. 1, Stuttgart 1979).

Delage, Christian, *La vision Nazie de L'Histoire à travers le cinéma documentaire du Troisième Reich*, Lausanne 1989.

Dick, Bernard F., *The Star Spangled Screen. The American World War II Film*, Lexington 1985.

Diller, Ansgar, *Rundfunkpolitik im Dritten Reich*, Munich 1980.

Donner, Wolf, *Propaganda und Film im "Dritten Reich"*, Berlin 1995.

Döscher, Hans Jürgen, *»Reichskristallnacht«*, Frankfurt am Main / Berlin 1988.

Drewniak, Boguslaw, *Das Theater im NS-Staat*, Düsseldorf 1983.

Drewniak, Boguslaw, *Der deutsche Film 1938 bis 1945*, Düsseldorf 1987.

Faulstich, Werner/Korte, Helmut (eds.), *Fischer Filmgeschichte, Bd. 2, 1925–1944*, Frankfurt am Main 1991.

Fest, Joachim C., *Hitler*, Berlin 1973.

Fleming, Gerald, *Hitler und die Endlösung*, Berlin 1987.

Förster, Jürgen (ed.), *Stalingrad. Ereignis. Symbol. Wirkung*, Munich 1992.

Fox, John P., "Der Fall Katyn und die Propaganda des NS-Regimes", in: *Vierteljahreshefte für Zeitgeschichte*, vol. 30, 1982, pp. 462–499.

Furhammar, Leif/Isaksson, Folke, *Politics and film*, London 1971.

Gandert, Gero (ed.), *Der Film der Weimarer Republik: 1929*, Berlin 1993.

Gellermann, Günther W., *…und lauschten für Hitler. Geheime Reichssache. Die Abhörzentralen des Dritten Reichs*, Bonn 1991.

Goerner, Rüdiger, *Das Tagebuch*, Munich and Zurich 1986.

Goertz, Heinrich, *Gustaf Gründgens*, Hamburg 1982.

Gregor, Ulrich/Patalas, Enno, *Geschichte des deutschen Films*, Gütersloh 1962.

Hagemann, Jürgen, *Presselenkung im Dritten Reich*, Bonn 1970.

Hamann, Brigitte, *Hitlers Wien*, Munich 1996.

Hanna-Dauod, Thomas, *Die NSDAP und der Film vor der Machtergreifung*, Cologne 1996.

Happel, Hans-Gerd, *Der historische Spielfilm im Nationalsozialismus*, Frankfurt am Main 1974.

Hattendorf, Manfred (ed.), *Perspektiven des Dokumentarfilms*, Munich 1996.

Hehl, Ullrich von, "Die Kontroverse um den Reichstagsbrand", in: *Vierteljahreshefte für Zeitgeschichte*, vol. 36, 1988, pp. 259–280.

Heiber, Helmut, *Joseph Goebbels*, Munich[3] 1988.

Herzstein, Robert E., *The war that Hitler won*, London 1979.

Hilberg, Raoul, *Die Vernichtung der europäischen Juden. Die Gesamtgeschichte des Holocaust*, Berlin 1982.

Hillgruber, Andreas, *Hitlers Strategie, Politik und Kriegsführung 1940–1941*, Munich[2] 1982.

Hillgruber, Andreas, *Die Zerstörung Europas*, Frankfurt am Main / Berlin 1988.

Hocke, Gustav René, *Europäische Tagebücher aus vier Jahrhunderten*, Munich 1978.

Höver, Ulrich, *Joseph Goebbels – ein nationaler Sozialist*, Bonn 1992.

Hoffmann, Hilmar, *"Und die Fahne führt uns in die Ewigkeit". Propaganda im NS-Film*, Frankfurt am Main 1988.

Hoffmann, Hilmar, *Mythos Olympia*, Berlin 1993.

Hoffmann, Hilmar, *100 Jahre Film. Von Lumière bis Spielberg 1894 bis 1994*, Düsseldorf 1994.

Hollstein, Dorothea, *Antisemitische Filmpropaganda*, Munich / Berlin 1971.

Hollstein, Dorothea, *"Jud Süß" und die Deutschen*, Frankfurt am Main et al., 1983.

Huemer, Andrea, *Die Frau im NS-Film*, Vienna 1985.

Hull, David Stewart, *Film in the Third Reich*, Berkeley 1968.

Irving, David, *Hitler, 2.*, rev. edition, London 1989.

Jacobsen, Wolfgang (ed.), *Babelsberg*, Berlin 1992.

Jäckel, Eberhard / Rohwer, Jürgen (eds.), *Der Mord an den Juden im Zweiten Weltkrieg. Entschlußbildung und Verwirklichung*, Stuttgart 1985.

Jäckel, Eberhard/Rohwer, Jürgen (eds.), *Kriegswende 1941*, Koblenz 1984.

Janßen, Karl Heinz/Tobias, Fritz, *Der Sturz der Generäle. Hitler und die Blomberg-Fritsch-Krise 1938*, Munich 1994.

Jochheim, Gernot, *Frauenprotest in der Rosenstraße*, Berlin 1992.

Kahlenberg, Friedrich P., "*Starke Herzen*. Quellen-Notizen über die Produktion eines Ufa-Films im Jahre 1937", in: Wetzel, Kraft/Hagemann, Peter A., *Zensur – Verbotene deutsche Filme 1933–1945*, Berlin 1978, pp. 110–125.

Kahlenberg, Friedrich P. (ed.), *Aus der Arbeit der Archive. Festschrift für Hans Booms*, Boppard 1989.

Kanzog, Klaus, *»Staatspolitisch besonders wertvoll«. Ein Handbuch zu 30 deutschen Spielfilmen der Jahre 1934 bis 1945*, Munich 1994

Kershaw, Ian, "How effective was Nazi Propaganda", in: Welch, David (ed.), *Nazi Propaganda – the Power and the Limitations*, London 1983, pp. 180–205.

Kershaw, Ian, *The Hitler Myth*, Oxford[2] 1987.

Kershaw, Ian, *Hitlers Macht,* Munich 1992.

Kershaw, Ian, *Der NS-Staat. 2.*, extended and rev. edition, Hamburg 1994.

Kessemeier, Carin, *Der Leitartikler Goebbels in den NS-Organen "Der Angriff" und "Das Reich",* Münster 1967.

Klee, Ernst, *"Euthanasie" im NS-Staat. Die "Vernichtung unwerten Lebens"*, Frankfurt am Main 1983.

Klingler, Walther, *NS-Rundfunkpolitik 1942–1945*, Mannheim 1983.

Knilli, Friedrich et al., *"Jud Süß"*, Berlin 1983.

Koch, Peter-Ferdinand (ed.), *Die Tagebücher des Doktor Joseph Goebbels*, Hamburg 1988.

Kracauer, Siegfried, *Von Caligari bis Hitler*, Frankfurt/M. 1979.

Kreimeier, Klaus, *Die Ufa-Story*, Munich 1992.

Kresser, Dodo/Horvath, Michael, *Nur ein Komödiant? Hans Moser in den Jahren 1938–1945*, Vienna 1994.

Krützen, Michaela, *Hans Albers. Eine deutsche Karierre*, Berlin 1995.

Leiser, Erwin, *"Deutschland erwache". Propaganda im Film des Dritten Reiches*, 2. rev. edition, Hamburg 1989.

Liebe, Ulrich, *Verehrt, verfolgt, vergessen. Schauspieler als Naziopfer*, Berlin 1992.

Lizzani, Carlo, *Il cinema italiano*, Rome 1982.

Loiperdinger, Manfred, *Der Parteitagsfilm "Triumph des Willens"*, Opladen 1987.

Loiperdinger, Martin/Schönekäs, Klaus, "Die große Liebe – Propaganda im Unterhaltungsfilm", in: Rother, Rainer (ed.), *Bilder schreiben Geschichte: Der Historiker im Kino*, Berlin 1991, pp. 143–153.

Loiperdinger, Martin et al. (ed.), *Führerbilder*, Munich 1995.

Longerich, Peter, *Propagandisten im Krieg. Die Presseabteilung des Auswärtigen Amtes unter Ribbentrop*, Munich 1987.

Longerich, Peter (ed.), *Die Ermordung der europäischen Juden. Eine umfassende Dokumentation des Holocaust 1941–1945*, Munich 1989.

Longerich, Peter, "Nationalsozialistische Propaganda", in: Bracher, Karl Dietrich et al. (ed.), *Deutschland 1933–1945*, Düsseldorf 1992, pp. 291–314.

Lowry, Stephen, *Pathos und Politik*, Tübingen 1991.

Maaß, Michael, "Aspekte von Kultur und Freizeit in Nürnberg", *Archiv für Sozialgeschichte*, vol. 33, 1993, pp. 329–356.

Maibohm, Ludwig, *Fritz Lang*, Munich 1981.

Maiwald, Klaus Jürgen, *Filmzensur im NS-Staat*, Dortmund 1983.

Manvell, Richard/Fraenkel, Heinrich, *Goebbels. Der Verführer*, Cologne 1960 (reprint Munich 1989).

Martens, Stefan, *Hermann Göring. "Erster Paladin des Führers" und "Zweiter Mann im Reich"*, Paderborn 1985.

Mathieu, Thomas, *Kunstauffassungen und Kulturpolitik im Nationalsozialismus*, Saarbrücken 1997.

McGilligan, Patrick, *Fritz Lang. The Nature of the Beast*, New York 1997.

Michalka, Wolfgang (ed.), *Der Zweite Weltkrieg*, Munich 1989.

Michels, Helmut, *Ideologie und Propaganda. Die Rolle von Joseph Goebbels in der nationalsozialistischen Außenpolitik bis 1939*, Frankfurt/M 1992.

Moeller, Felix, "I Gusti del Führer", in: *Il cinema dei dittatori*, Bologna 1992, pp. 261–268.

Moeller, Felix, "Blitzkrieg und Filmpropaganda: Aus den Tagebüchern von Joseph Goebbels 1939–1941", in: Siemann, Wolfgang/Daniel, Ute (eds.), *Propaganda*, Frankfurt am Main 1994.

Moltmann, Günther, "Goebbels' Rede zum totalen Krieg am 18. Februar 1943", in: *Vierteljahreshefte für Zeitgeschichte*, vol. 12, 1964, pp. 13–43.

Moltmann, Günther/Reimers, Karl Friedrich, *Zeitgeschichte in Bild- und Tondokumenten*, Göttingen 1970.

Müller, Hans-Dieter, *Der junge Goebbels. Zur ideologischen Entwicklung eines politischen Propagandisten*, diss. phil., Mannheim 1974.

Nill, Ulrich, *Die »geniale Vereinfachung«. Anti-Intellektualismus in Ideologie und Sprachgebrauch bei Joseph Goebbels*, Frankfurt am Main 1991.

Nordemann, Wilhelm, "Die 'Tagebücher' des Joseph Goebbels im Spannungsfeld von Besatzungs-, Persönlichkeits-, und Urheberrecht", in: Westermann, Harm Peter/Rosner, Wolfgang (eds.), *Festschrift für Karlheinz Quack zum 65. Geburtstag*, Berlin 1991, pp. 73–88.

Obst, Dieter, *"Reichskristallnacht": Ursachen und Verlauf des antisemitischen Pogroms vom November 1938*, Frankfurt am Main 1991.

Ogan, Bernd/Weiss, Werner (eds.), *Faszination und Gewalt. Zur politischen Ästhetik des Nationalsozialismus*, Nürnberg 1992.

Osterkamp, Marold, *Die populäre Kultur im Dritten Reich – Bestandsaufnahme und Wertung unter besonderer Berücksichtigung des Unterhaltungsfilms*, diss. phil., Berlin 1986.

Oven, Wilfried von, *Wer war Goebbels?*, Munich 1987.

Panse, Barbara, "Diese Künstler sind wie Kinder", in: *Theater heute*, Nr. 9/1989, pp. 4–21.

Paul, Gerhard, *Aufstand der Bilder. Die NS-Propaganda vor 1933*, Bonn 1990.

Phillips, Marcus S., *The German Film Industry and the Third Reich*, diss., East Anglia 1974.

Pietrow-Ennker, Bianka, "Die Sowjetunion in der Propaganda des Dritten Reiches. Das Beispiel der Wochenschau. Eine Dokumentation", in: *Militärgeschichtliche Mitteilungen*, vol. 46, 1989, pp. 79–120.

Pohl, Dieter, *Von der "Judenpolitik" zum Judenmord*, Frankfurt am Main 1993.

Rabenalt, Arthur M., *Film im Zwielicht*, Munich 1958.

Rabenalt, Arthur M., *Joseph Goebbels und der "Großdeutsche" Film*, Munich 1985.

Rathkolb, Oliver, *Führertreu und gottbegnadet*, Vienna 1991.

Rebentisch, Dieter, *Führerstaat und Verwaltung im Zweiten Weltkrieg. Verfassungsentwicklung und Verwaltungspolitik 1939–1945*, Stuttgart 1989.

Recker, Marie-Luise, *Die Außenpolitik des Dritten Reiches*, Munich 1990.

Reichel, Peter, *Der schöne Schein des Dritten Reiches*, Munich/Vienna 1991.

Reimann, Viktor, *Dr. Joseph Goebbels*, Vienna et al. 1971.

Reimers, Karl Friedrich/Friedrich, Helmut (eds.), *Zeitgeschichte in Film und Fernsehen*, Munich 1982.

Rentschler, Eric, *The Ministry of Illusion*, Cambridge 1996.

Reuth, Ralf Georg, *Goebbels*, Munich 1991.

Riess, Curt, *Die große Zeit des deutschen Films*, 4 vols., Vienna/Munich 1977.

Riess, Curt, *Das gab's nur einmal*, 3 vols., Frankfurt/M. et al. 1985.

Rost, Karl Ludwig, *Sterilisation und Euthanasie im Film des "Dritten Reichs"*, diss. med., Berlin 1986.

Roth, Karl Heinz, *Filmpropaganda für die Vernichtung der Geisteskranken und Behinderten im "Dritten Reich"*, diss. med., Hamburg 1986.

Sänger, Fritz, *Politik der Täuschungen. Mißbrauch der Presse im Dritten Reich. Weisungen, Informationen, Notizen 1933–1939*, Vienna 1975.

Sakkara, Michele, *Die große Zeit des deutschen Films*, Leoni 1980.

Schäfer, Hans Dieter, *Das gespaltene Bewußtsein. Über deutsche Kultur und Lebenswirklichkeit 1933–1945*, Frankfurt am Main 1981.

Schaudig, Michael (ed.), *Positionen deutscher Filmgeschichte*, Munich 1996.

Schettler, Holger, *Arbeiter und Angestellte im Film*, Bielefeld 1992.

Schreiber, Gerhard, *Hitler. Interpretationen 1923–1983. Ergebnisse, Methoden und Probleme der Forschung*, 2. rev. edition, Darmstadt 1988.

Schulz, Jürgen Michael, "Die Identität des Täters. Joseph Goebbels als Tagebuch-Autor", in: Lange, Ulrich Thomas (ed.), *Identität, Integration und Verantwortung. Vorträge und Referate der ersten Görlitzer Wissenschaftstagung*, Berlin 1994, pp. 194–204.

Seiler, Paul, *Zarah Leander. Ich bin eine Stimme*, Berlin 1997.

Singer, Hans-Jürgen, "'Tran und Helle'". Aspekte unterhaltender Aufklärung im Dritten Reich", in: *Publizistik*, no. 3/4, vol. 31, 1986, pp. 347 to 356.

Smelser, Roland/Zitelmann, Rainer, *Die braune Elite*, Darmstadt 1989.

Spiker, Jürgen, *Film und Kapital*, Berlin 1975.

Sösemann, Bernd, "Voraussetzungen und Wirkungen publizistischer Opposition im Dritten Reich", in: *Publizistik,* no. 2/3, vol. 30, 1985, pp. 195–215.

Sösemann, Bernd, "Die Tagesaufzeichnungen des Joseph Goebbels und ihre unzulänglichen Veröffentlichungen", in: *Publizistik,* no. 2, vol. 7, 1992, pp. 213–244.

Sösemann, Bernd, "Inszenierungen für die Nachwelt. Editionswissenschaftliche und textkritische Untersuchungen zu Joseph Goebbels' Erinnerungen, diaristischen Notizen und täglichen Diktaten", in: *Historische Zeitschrift*, special issue, 16, 1992, pp. 1–45.

Sösemann, Bernd, "'Ein tieferer geschichtlicher Sinn aus dem Wahnsinn'. Die Goebbels-Tagebuchaufzeichnungen als Quelle für das Verständnis des nationalsozialistischen Herrschaftssystems und seiner Propaganda", in: Nipperdey, Thomas et al. (ed.), *Weltbürgerkrieg der Ideologien. Antworten an Ernst Nolte. Festschrift zum 70. Geburtstag*, Berlin 1993, pp. 136–174.

Steiner, Maria, *Paula Wessely. Die verdrängten Jahre*, Vienna 1996

Steinweis, Allan E., "Hans Hinkel and German Jewry 1933–1941", in: *Leo Baeck Institute Year Book 1993*, pp. 209–219.

Stephan, Werner, *Joseph Goebbels. Dämon einer Diktatur,* Stuttgart 1949.

Stirk, Peter M. R., "Anti-Americanism in National Socialist Propaganda during the Second World War", in: same author/Smith, M. L. (eds.), *Making the New Europe*, London 1990, pp. 66–86.

Stoltzfus, Nathan, *Social Limitations on the Nazi Dictatorship: The Rosenstraße Protest and the Case of German-Jewish Intermarriage*, Boston 1996.

Sywottek, Jutta, *Mobilmachung für den totalen Krieg. Die propagandistische Vorbereitung der deutschen Bevölkerung auf den Zweiten Weltkrieg*, Opladen 1976.

Terveen, Fritz, "Die Rede des Reichsministers Dr. Goebbels vor den Filmschaffenden in Berlin am 28. Februar 1942", in: *Publizistik*, vol. 4, 1959, pp. 29–48.

Toeplitz, Jerzy, *Geschichte des Films, 1934–1939,* vol. 3, Berlin 1982.

Toeplitz, Jerzy, *Geschichte des Films, 1939–1945* vol. 4, Berlin 1983.

Traudisch, Dora, *Mutterschaft mit Zucker. Frauenfeindliche Propaganda im NS-Spielfilm*, Pfaffenweiler 1991.

Wedel, Hasso von, *Die Propagandatruppen der deutschen Wehrmacht,* Neckargemünd 1962.

Wegner, Bernd (ed.), *Zwei Wege nach Moskau. Vom Hitler-Stalin-Pakt zum "Unternehmen Barbarossa"*, Munich 1991.

Weinberg, David, "Approaches to the Study of Film in the Third Reich: A Critical Appraisal", in: *Journal of Contemporary History*, vol. 19, 1984, pp. 105–126.

Welch, David, *Propaganda and the German Cinema*, Oxford 1983.

Welch, David, "Goebbels, Götterdämmerung, and the Deutsche Wochenschauen", in: Short, K. M. (ed.), *Newsreel witness*, London 1986, pp. 80–99.

Wendtland, Karlheinz, *Geliebter Kintopp. Sämtliche deutsche Spielfilme von 1929–1945*, 7 vols., Berlin, no date.

Wetzel, Kraft/Hagemann, Peter A., *Liebe, Tod und Technik. Kino des Phantastischen 1933–1945*, Berlin 1977.

Wetzel, Kraft/Hagemann, Peter A., *Zensur – Verbotene deutsche Filme 1933–1945*, Berlin 1978.

Winkler, Klaus, *Fernsehen unterm Hakenkreuz. Organisation. Programm. Personal*, Cologne et al. 1994.

Winkler-Mayerhöfer, Andrea, *Starkult als Propagandamittel im Dritten Reich*, Munich 1992.

Wirl, Manfred, *Die öffentliche Meinung unter dem NS-Regime*, diss. phil., Mainz 1990.

Witte, Karsten, "Die Filmkomödie im Dritten Reich", in: Denkler, Horst/Prümm, Karl, *Die deutsche Literatur im Dritten Reich*, Stuttgart 1976, pp. 347–365.

Witte, Karsten, *Filmkomödie im Faschismus*, diss. phil., Frankfurt am Main 1986.

Witte, Karsten, "Film im Nationalsozialismus. Blendung und Überblendung", in: Jacobsen, Wolfgang et al. (ed.), *Geschichte des deutschen Films*, Stuttgart 1993, pp. 119–170.

Witte, Karsten, *Lachende Erben – Toller Tag*, Berlin 1995.

Wykes, Alan, *Joseph Goebbels. Der Reichspropagandaminister*, Rastatt 1986.

Zielinski, Siegfried, *Veit Harlan*, Frankfurt am Main 1981.

Zumkeller, Cornelia, *Zarah Leander*, Munich 1988.

Index of names